POLITICS IN THE AMERICAN STATES

Politics in the American States

A COMPARATIVE ANALYSIS

SIXTH EDITION

Editors

VIRGINIA GRAY, *University of Minnesota*

HERBERT JACOB, *Northwestern University*

CQ PRESS
A Division of Congressional Quarterly Inc.
Washington, D.C.

Copyright © 1996 Congressional Quarterly Inc.
1414 22nd Street, N.W., Washington, D.C. 20037

Cover and book design: Kachergis Book Design, Pittsboro, North Carolina

LIBRARY OF CONGRESS CATALOGING-IN-PUBLICATION DATA
Politics in the American States : a comparative approach / editors,
Virginia Gray, Herbert Jacob.—6th ed.
        p. cm.
    includes bibliographical references and index.
    ISBN 1-56802-035-X (alk. paper)
    1. State governments—United States.   I. Gray, Virginia.
  II. Jacob, Herbert.
    JK2408.P64   1995
    320.973—dc20
                                                                        95-33573
                                                                        CIP

Contents

Tables

Figures

Preface

Once relegated to the scrap heap of history, state governments in the United States continue to thrive and play a vital role in American politics. Although it is difficult to believe that many citizens feel deep attachments to their state roots—given the fact that Americans are so mobile—state-level government nevertheless appears closer to their lives than the distant but raucous voice of the federal government in Washington, D.C. Moreover, from the perspective of federal politicians, the states are an attractive dumping ground for programs they believe the nation needs but which they do not want the nation as a whole to fund. Thus since 1969, the first year of the administration of Richard M. Nixon, there have been successive efforts by the federal government to shift programs to the states while downsizing the federal government. These efforts have placed enormous burdens on the states and have made state politics increasingly central to our understanding of government and politics in the United States.

The study of state politics by American political scientists, however, has not kept pace with its growing importance. Although no longer quite a stepchild, the subject has not yet been fully adopted as a primary part of political science. Like bank robbers, political scientists go where the money is. Although, as has been demonstrated in this book for more than thirty years, the rich data of state politics provide many quasi-experimental situations and an opportunity to analyze political data over a long period of time, political scientists still find the study of politics in Washington, D.C., more attractive. To be the leading scholar of presidents or of Congress still garners more prestige than to be the leading scholar of governors or of state legislatures. That is to the detriment of American political science, for there is more to be learned about governing from state governors and legislatures, which exhibit a rich variety of traits, than from attention to singular national institutions.

We feel fortunate to present to our readers the work of some of the finest scholars of state politics. As always, this has been a collaborative effort. As editors, we have made suggestions and provided occasional guidance, but all our authors have approached their subject matter in their own way. We are also responsible for the choice of subject matter, and as has each new edition, the sixth includes substantial changes. We have added a new chapter on the politics of family policy by Susan Welch, Sue Thomas, and Margery M. Ambrosius. Four other chapters have been written by new authors. The chapter on transportation has been dropped. The remaining chapters have each been extensively revised to represent new scholarship and changed events. For instance, the chapter on legislatures reflects some of the many changes that resulted from the November 1994 elections, as do the chapters on parties and governors. A book, however, is not the morning newspaper; our authors can only write about events that have already occurred and about which data are available. Thus, in this era of swift political and social change, instructors will continue to be challenged to provide up-to-date information to their students. We feel confident, however, that the analytic paradigms and tools our authors present will provide the means for their doing so.

Our goal in *Politics in the American States* continues to be both the instruction of students and the advancement of knowledge about state politics. Our authors not only convey statistical information but also provide the anecdotal settings of state politics, for we wish to promote not only a rigorous analysis but also a nuanced understanding of state politics. Thus our readers can make systematic comparisons between states and also become sensitive to the many subtleties of political life at the state level. As the careful reader will notice, however, many gaps remain in our understanding. We hope that this edition, like previous ones, will stimulate future scholars to fill them.

Over the years, we have worked with wonderful colleagues. We are particularly grateful to the late Kenneth N. Vines, whose foresight stimulated the original edition of this book. We appreciate Stacey Hecht's help in securing the permissions, Joanne Ainsworth's superb copyediting, and Ann O'Malley's careful attention to production details. We are also thankful for the vision of Brenda Carter of Congressional Quarterly, Inc., who rescued this book from the turmoil of corporate mergers and acquisitions and brought it to its new publication home.

Virginia Gray
Herbert Jacob

Contributors

MARGERY M. AMBROSIUS, who received her Ph.D. from the University of Nebraska, is associate professor of political science at Kansas State University. She has published widely in the area of state public policy and administration, with particular emphasis on the relationship between state policy and economic development.

THAD BEYLE is Thomas C. Pearsall professor of political science at the University of North Carolina at Chapel Hill and was board chairman of the North Carolina Center for Public Policy Research for ten years. He is editor of *Governors and Hard Times* (1992) and since 1985 has edited annual editions of *State Government: CQ's Guide to Current Issues and Activities.*

JOHN F. BIBBY is professor of political science at the University of Wisconsin, Milwaukee. He is the author of *Politics, Parties, and Elections in America* (3d ed., 1996) and *Governing by Consent* (2d ed., 1995) and is coauthor of *Party Organizations in American Politics* (1989). In addition to writing articles and chapters on political parties, he has held leadership positions in national and state party organizations.

SUSAN E. CLARKE is associate professor of political science and director of the Center for Public Policy Research at the University of Colorado at Boulder. Her articles on state and local economic development policies have appeared in American and international journals. In addition to her academic background, she served as a visiting scholar at the U.S. Department of Housing and Urban Development.

RICHARD C. ELLING is professor of political science at Wayne State University in Detroit. Most of his published research has focused on issues of state management and bureaucratic politics and includes his book *Public Management in the States: A Comparative Study of Administrative Performance and Politics* (1992). He is presently conducting a multistate study of patterns and determinants of state employee turnover and the implications of such turnover for the performances of state bureaucracies.

VIRGINIA GRAY is professor of political science at the University of Minnesota. She has published widely on numerous topics in state politics and public policy, including interest groups, economic development, and policy innovation. She also served as faculty lobbyist in the Minnesota legislature for four years. Her most recent book is *American States and Cities* (1991), written with Peter Eisinger.

RUSSELL L. HANSON is professor of political science at Indiana University, Bloomington. He has published articles on state political culture, economic development, and welfare policy. He has just completed a major study of the implementation of the Social Security Act of 1935 and is joining William Berry in a comprehensive study of the political economy of Aid to Families with Dependent Children programs in the states. He is the author of *The Democratic Imagination in America* (1985) and *Reconsidering the Democratic Public* (1993).

THOMAS M. HOLBROOK is currently an associate professor of political science at the University of Wisconsin, Milwaukee. His research interests include electoral politics and state politics. He has published articles in several of the leading political science journals (*American Political Science Review, American Journal of Political Science, Journal of Politics,* and others) and is currently writing a book on the electoral effect of presidential campaigns.

RONALD J. HREBENAR is professor of political science at the University of Utah. His research and teaching focuses on interest groups, political parties, public policy, and Japanese politics. He has published several books and articles, including *Interest Group Politics in America* (2d ed., 1990). He was a Fulbright-Hays Scholar in 1982–1983.

HERBERT JACOB is professor of political science at Northwestern University. He is past president of the Law and Society Association and has taught at Tulane University, the University of Wisconsin, and Johns Hopkins University. He has published widely on courts and the political process. His most recent publications include *Law and Politics in the United States* (2d ed., 1995) and, as editor and contributor, *Courts, Law, and Politics in a Comparative Perspective* (1996). He is currently doing research on the ways in which trial judges are induced to collaborate with one another in large urban courts.

DAN A. LEWIS is a professor of education and social policy at Northwestern University, where he has served on the faculty since 1980. Professor Lewis is also on the research faculty at the Center for Urban Affairs and Policy Research at the same university. He received his doctorate from the University of California at

Santa Cruz in 1980. He has served as an associate dean and director of under-graduate education at the School of Education and Social Policy and as associate director of the Center for Urban Affairs. He was also chair of the graduate program in human development and social policy. His latest book is *Race and Educational Reform* (1995).

SHADD MARUNA is a graduate student in human development and social policy at Northwestern University. He graduated from Illinois State University with a bachelor's degree in philosophy and is currently working on research involving the relationship of education to criminal rehabilitation and crime prevention.

SAMUEL C. PATTERSON is professor of political science at Ohio State University. He served as managing editor of the *American Political Science Review* from 1985 to 1991. He is the author of many research articles on state legislatures and the U.S. Congress. He is an author or editor of *The Legislative Process in the United States* (4th ed., 1986), *Representatives and Represented* (1975), *Comparing Legislatures* (1979), the *Handbook of Legislative Research* (1985), and *Parliaments in the Modern World* (1994).

MARK ROM is an assistant professor of government and public policy at Georgetown University, where he is also the director of the District of Columbia Family Policy Seminar. Before moving to Georgetown he was a senior evaluator at the U.S. General Accounting Office and a research fellow at the Brookings Institution. He is currently working on a book about AIDS policy.

MARTIN R. SAIZ is assistant professor of political science at the University of Notre Dame. He was a neighborhood activist in Denver, Colorado, where he served two terms on the Planning Commission. He is the author of several articles on urban politics, public policy, and Latino politics. He is currently completing a book on the politics of economic development policy among the American states.

WESLEY G. SKOGAN is professor of political science and urban affairs at Northwestern University. His research focuses on the police, crime prevention and crime policy, services for victims, and program evaluation. He is the author of several reports published by the British government on policing in that country. He has recently been conducting research on the Chicago Police Department.

CLIVE S. THOMAS is professor of political science at the University of Alaska, Juneau. His publications include works on interest groups, the legislative process, and state politics. He is director of the University of Alaska Statewide Legislative Internship Program, has been a volunteer lobbyist, and teaches seminars on lobby organizations and tactics.

SUE THOMAS, who received her Ph.D. from the University of Nebraska, is associate professor of government at Georgetown University. Her research specialty is legislative behavior, with primary emphasis on women officeholders. She recently authored *How Women Legislate* (1994) and coedited *The Year of the Woman: Myths and Realities* (1994).

SUSAN WELCH, who received her Ph.D. from the University of Illinois, is a professor of political science and dean of the College of Liberal Arts at Pennsylvania State University. She has published widely in the areas of women's politics, black politics, and American public policy. Her most recent book is *Black Americans' Views of Racial Inequality* (1991), coauthored with Lee Sigelman.

BRUCE A. WILLIAMS teaches at the University of Illinois at Urbana-Champaign, where he is associate professor of urban and regional planning and research associate professor of communications. In his most recent book, *Democracy, Dialogue, and Social Regulation: The Contested Languages of Environmental Disputes* (1995), written with Albert R. Matheny, he examines the dynamics of environmental disputes and the competing languages used by citizens, policy makers, experts, and interest groups as they struggle over public policy. He is currently working on a new project in which he examines the ways the mass media, especially television, influences how ordinary citizens talk about a variety of political issues—environmental protection, crime, and race.

RICHARD F. WINTERS is professor of government at Dartmouth College. He has published several articles on the making of taxing and spending policies in the American states. He is also coauthor, with Denis G. Sullivan and Robert T. Nakamura, of *How America Is Ruled* (1980). He is currently conducting a study of the conditions under which general taxes get adopted and changed in the states, the conditions under which taxes to pursue specific and particular ends are adopted, and how political leaders reduce the electoral consequences of these new tax burdens.

CHAPTER 1

The Socioeconomic and Political Context of States

VIRGINIA GRAY

State governments deal with many of the pressing issues of our time: economic revitalization, disposal of hazardous wastes, resettlement of refugees, and AIDS. They operate large public enterprises, such as prisons, hospitals, and universities; they build new highways and bridges; they regulate the cost of electricity and insurance. They are important partners in the federal system, implementing many federal programs and inventing new programs that are later adopted by Congress. State government is the place where many national politicians get their start; thus, the caliber of people attracted to state service has an impact on the quality of our national leadership.

This is a particularly exciting time to learn about state politics and government. Many states experienced a resurgence in the 1980s. In part, the renaissance was a result of President Ronald Reagan's attempts to reduce the scope of the national government. While the federal government was engaged in making budgetary cuts, state governments were forced to bear the financial burden of some of the threatened programs. This shift created new stresses on fiscally strapped states, but it also generated new programs and problem-solving activity. The Republican takeover of Congress in 1995 may provide yet another opportunity for states to respond to the devolution of federal authority and to fiscal constraints.

The 1980s modernization of state governmental institutions is another reason for the states' resurgence. A "new breed" of governors promoted significant reforms in education and championed economic development. State legislatures

1

were better equipped to deal with the challenges of rising health care costs and increasing welfare populations. Consequently, state leaders are more active today on a broader range of issues, and state government is where the action is.

The authors of this volume study and compare the fifty states by analyzing policy differences and then explaining these differences by using the methods of political science. We find these political differences both fascinating and intriguing to analyze. The social and economic differences among states are also significant. This chapter will make you aware of some of the differences among states in population, natural resources, and wealth.

Political and economic differences, in turn, relate to another way in which states differ. States offer different levels of services and benefits to their citizens and allocate costs for those benefits differently. In this book we explore these policy differences and some of the political reasons for them. Expect to learn how state government operates in general, that is, the similarities among the fifty states, and expect to learn how the politics of various states differ. As the authors develop these points, you will also see that state governments and their politics are different from the national government and its politics. States, for example, are subject to many competitive pressures from other states. These pressures constrain state actions on taxation and rachet up spending on economic development.

IMPORTANT STATE FUNCTIONS AND HOW THEY DIFFER

Education

The provision of education, the largest item in most states' budgets, illustrates the magnitude of policy differences among the fifty states. It is also an area in which state leaders in the 1980s and the first half of the 1990s initiated dramatic reforms.

The state of Mississippi has traditionally been near the bottom of rankings for educational support. In 1992, for example, it was fiftieth in expenditure per pupil, allocating only $3,344 per student (U.S. Bureau of the Census 1993, 164). It was forty-ninth in teachers' salaries, paying an annual average of $24,400 per teacher (U.S. Bureau of the Census 1993, 161). Although expenditures and teachers' salaries do not totally determine the quality of education, they are certainly important elements in its assessment. Several indicators of quality are distressing: one-third of Mississippi's adults cannot read, and more than half who began higher education in the late 1980s dropped out (Barone and Ujifusa 1993, 708).

The state of New Jersey provides a very different level of support. In 1992, New Jersey ranked first in per pupil expenditure at $10,219, three times Mississippi's expenditure (U.S. Bureau of the Census 1993, 164). The salaries of New Jersey teachers averaged $41,000 per year; only five other states paid their teachers more than $40,000 in 1992 (U.S. Bureau of the Census 1993, 161). Thus, the level of public support for education is considerably higher in New Jersey than in Mississippi. Even so, in the 1990s the equalization of the New Jersey school aid formula has been a controversial subject, contributing to a governor's defeat.

Why are New Jersey students on average better off than Mississippi students? There are particular economic and political reasons for it. Mississippi is very poor, ranking last among the states in personal income. Its citizens averaged $14,088 in income in 1992 (U.S. Bureau of the Census 1993, 451). Its poverty rate is the nation's highest: in 1991 nearly one-quarter of its population was poor according to the U.S. government's definition (U.S. Bureau of the Census 1992). New Jersey, in contrast, is among the more economically advantaged states. In 1992 it ranked second in per capita income at $26,457 (U.S. Bureau of the Census 1992, 451). The difference is that New Jersey simply has more resources to finance its public education.

But there are also political reasons for the difference between Mississippi and New Jersey's educational support. Mississippi's political system has been labeled antiquated, conservative, and corrupt ("Playing Catch-Up" 1988). Its government is saddled with an outmoded state constitution and cumbersome executive agencies that make it difficult to control problems like illiteracy. Two moderate governors of the 1980s, however—William Winter and Ray Mabus—have viewed progress in the state's educational system as the wellspring of economic progress. They were partially successful in pushing major educational reforms through the legislature: kindergarten was made mandatory, and the legal dropout age was raised to fourteen. But in 1991 Mabus was defeated by a gubernatorial candidate who did not emphasize spending on education.

Welfare

In many areas the federal government has become the dominant financial partner of states, often at the prodding of state and local governments. Welfare is an example of this type of partnership. The federal government pays about one-half of the expenses, the state pays most of the other half and administers the program, and the county or local government delivers the service. Still, even with the substantial federal share, welfare constitutes the second largest item in a state's budget. Because each state determines the benefits received by its welfare recipients, those benefits vary among states.

To make a sample comparison of welfare benefits between states, let's choose two states that are relatively similar. By choosing similar instead of diverse states, we minimize the number of explanatory variables. Illinois and Wisconsin are neighboring midwestern states with average or above average income levels. Illinois ranked seventh in per capita personal income in 1992 and Wisconsin twenty-fifth (U.S. Bureau of the Census 1993, 451). Yet, Illinois—the richer state—provides lower welfare benefits. The Illinois Aid to Families with Dependent Children (AFDC) program, for example, gave eligible families only $346 per month in 1991, while Wisconsin gave them $466 per month. Welfare recipients in both states also receive food stamps. Therefore, the average Illinois family had $346 to pay for all expenses beyond food, such as housing, clothes, and energy costs, whereas the average Wisconsin welfare family had $466 per month.

Why do neighboring states have such different welfare programs? In this case the answer is not economic, as it was in our comparison between New Jersey and Mississippi, because the richer state, Illinois, provides lower benefits. Perhaps the answer is political. On the surface the states appear similar: both are two-party competitive states, yet beneath the surface, key political differences exist. John Fenton (1966) observed many years ago that political competition in Illinois (like that in Ohio and Indiana) revolved around patronage for politicians, while the competition in Wisconsin (like that in Minnesota and Michigan) revolved around important issues such as welfare. He argued that more generous welfare programs are found where the political competition is oriented toward issues. Later research by Thomas Dye (1984) demonstrates that the two states continue to differ in the nature of their political competition. Thus, differences in political attitudes and the nature of political competition can produce different attitudes toward a state's responsibility to the poor.

This brief comparison of the welfare system in two adjoining states illustrates that an individual state government can make a big difference in the level of service, even where the policy is substantially subsidized by the federal government. Considerable interstate policy differences exist that are important to citizens who might eventually be on welfare. In fact, these differences have fueled an intense political debate in Wisconsin. Some Wisconsin state leaders fear their generosity makes them a "welfare magnet," attracting the poor, especially the minority poor, from Chicago and other urban centers of Illinois (Peterson and Rom 1990, 25). Gov. Tommy G. Thompson, following his election in 1986, set out to "demagnetize" his state's welfare system. He froze welfare benefits and introduced several experimental programs limiting benefits in certain circumstances (for example, when children fail to attend school). These have met with success: Wisconsin welfare caseloads have dropped 23 percent since he took office in 1987 ("Leader of the Pack" 1994, A13). In an effort to embarrass the Republican governor, the Democratic legislature voted in 1993 to end AFDC in 1999, although no alternative program has yet been enacted. Regardless of these experiments, their passage in Wisconsin signals some new political and economic realities among state governments. There is mounting pressure on generous states to bring their welfare benefits into line with less generous states.

Health Care Reform

Barely noticed in the 1994 national debate over health care reform is the fact that states have proceeded on their own without waiting for national action. In 1992–1993, Florida, Minnesota, and Washington enacted comprehensive programs incorporating elements of managed competition and cost control regulation, although these elements took different forms in each state. Massachusetts and Oregon had already enacted (but not implemented) major reforms based on the "play or pay" philosophy in which employers either provide health insurance to their employees or pay a tax for governmentally provided insurance; in addition, Oregon's plan included "rationing" Medicaid. Montana and Vermont adopted comprehensive reform frameworks, leaving the details to be worked out later. And Hawaii led the way in 1974 with its employer mandate, although it does not regulate costs.

These actions illustrate the principle that the states function as "the laboratories of democracy." They are places where new ideas can be tried out; one state can learn from another; the federal government can learn what works and what doesn't from state experiments. New ideas can spread horizontally (from one state to another) or vertically (from a state to the government in Washington).

Although it is too soon for scholars to have analyzed why these states were the first to act on health care, a considerable body of literature exists on the general question of why some states are more innovative than others. One explanation is the internal determinants model: the idea that each state has characteristics that determine whether it will act on new ideas or delay. Earlier investigators (for example, Gray 1973; Walker 1969) found that larger, wealthier states adopted new ideas first. But later investigations (for example, Berry and Berry 1990) found that states adopt new ideas during fiscal crises, following the adage "Necessity is the mother of invention." In addition to these economic factors, political and social factors predispose states to innovate.

A second explanation is the external determinants model: the notion that factors outside the state motivate innovation. Regional diffusion models are the most popular, in which a state's actions are assumed to be influenced by its neighbors' actions. Other external factors include federal incentives and the role of professional associations in disseminating new ideas. In trying to apply these explanations to the health care reforms of the 1990s, we immediately run up against analytic difficulties. Consider the factor of population size: among the innovators, only Florida is among the top ten in population. Or consider wealth: only Massachusetts is among the top ten in personal income per capita. Perception of a fiscal crisis, however, does seem to be a factor cited in many reports from these states. Regional ties do not seem to operate as one of the external determinants, because the adopting states are widely scattered geographically. Nor do federal incentives exist in this situation. One determinant seems to be that health care has abundant professional associations through which reform ideas may have been spread.

Scholars will be trying to explain why these states (and by now probably other states) are health care innovators. If the standard explanations of horizontal diffusion do not apply (as now seems likely), then they will have to come up with new theories of diffusion to explain this situation and then test them in other policy arenas. There are lots of unsolved puzzles like this in state politics.

EXPLAINING POLICY DIFFERENCES

The preceding comparisons provide an idea of how state governments differ and how their policies may change our lives. The second half of this book focuses on a state government's many activities. These outputs of a government's activities are called *public policies,* and a public policy is usually defined as "a means to governmental ends." The public policies reviewed in this book deal with taxes, criminal justice, health and welfare, education, regulation, economic development, and family.

Scholars have spent years trying to understand the differences among states' public policies. The intellectual task is to explain interstate patterns; that is, what conditions or characteristics of states lead to generous educational expenditure, low welfare expenditure, or innovation in health policy? Generally, these investigations focus on two broad sets of variables: political characteristics and socioeconomic factors. Among a state's political variables, researchers have found the following to be important: political party control and interparty competition, interest group strength, gubernatorial power, the political background of judges, professionalism of the legislature, public and elite opinion, and political culture. Subsequent chapters in this book examine the major governmental institutions, both in their own right and as policy makers. Other chapters focus on key political actors such as interest groups and political parties.

In this chapter, I examine the set of socioeconomic factors that may affect patterns of state policy. Included in these factors are the following: population size and composition, migration and urbanization, physical characteristics and natural resources, types of economic activities stemming from a state's physical endowments, wealth, and regional economic forces. These factors structure a state government's problems and affect a state government's ability to deal with them. I also explore the broader political context that affects state governments, such as political culture, public opinion, and national political forces. An understanding of the broader context will aid in the understanding of the role of political players and of each state's governmental institutions.

THE PEOPLE

The first state resource that I examine is the human resource. What kinds of people live where? How does the movement of people back and forth affect states? Why are trends in population growth and economic competition important for a state's future?

Population Size

A fundamental fact influencing a state's policies is its population size. In Table 1-1, I list each state's population in 1992. The largest state, California, has more than 30 million residents. California can be considered more the size of a nation than of a state. In fact, California's population is larger than that of Canada's, and

Table 1-1 Population Size of States, 1992, and Percentage of Population Living in Metropolitan Areas, 1990

State	Rank	Population	Rank	% in metropolitan areas*
California	1	30,867,000	2	96.8
New York	2	18,119,000	8	91.8
Texas	3	17,656,000	13	83.4
Florida	4	13,488,000	6	92.9
Pennsylvania	5	12,009,000	9	84.9
Illinois	6	11,631,000	12	83.8
Ohio	7	11,016,000	18	81.4
Michigan	8	9,437,000	16	82.8
New Jersey	9	7,789,000	1	100.0
North Carolina	10	6,843,000	32	65.2
Georgia	11	6,751,000	30	66.9
Virginia	12	6,377,000	20	77.1
Massachusetts	13	5,998,000	3	96.2
Indiana	14	5,662,000	23	71.5
Missouri	15	5,193,000	27	68.2
Washington	16	5,136,000	15	82.9
Tennessee	17	5,024,000	31	65.5
Wisconsin	18	5,007,000	28	68.1
Maryland	19	4,908,000	7	92.8
Minnesota	20	4,480,000	26	68.8
Louisiana	21	4,278,000	22	73.5
Alabama	22	4,136,000	29	67.1
Arizona	23	3,832,000	10	84.7
Kentucky	24	3,755,000	38	47.6
South Carolina	25	3,603,000	25	69.5
Colorado	26	3,470,000	17	81.5
Connecticut	27	3,281,000	4	95.7
Oklahoma	28	3,212,000	33	59.4
Oregon	29	2,977,000	24	69.8
Iowa	30	2,812,000	40	43.2
Mississippi	31	2,614,000	46	30.1
Kansas	32	2,523,000	36	53.8
Arkansas	33	2,399,000	39	44.2
Utah	34	1,813,000	19	77.5
West Virginia	35	1,812,000	41	41.7
Nebraska	36	1,606,000	37	49.9
New Mexico	37	1,581,000	35	55.6
Nevada	38	1,327,000	11	84.4
Maine	39	1,235,000	44	36.1
Hawaii	40	1,160,000	21	75.5
New Hampshire	41	1,111,000	34	59.4
Idaho	42	1,067,000	48	29.4
Rhode Island	43	1,005,000	5	93.5
Montana	44	824,000	50	23.9
South Dakota	45	711,000	45	31.7
Delaware	46	689,000	14	83.0
North Dakota	47	636,000	43	40.3
Alaska	48	587,000	42	41.1
Vermont	49	570,000	49	26.9
Wyoming	50	466,000	47	29.6

SOURCE: U.S. Bureau of the Census, 1993, 28–29, xiii.
*Greater metropolitan areas of at least 50,000 people.

California's provision for education, highways, hospitals, and housing is on the same scale as many nations. California's massive size is illustrated in other ways too. For example, its state legislative districts are the size of congressional districts in other states.

Some less populous states are also the size of foreign countries. New York, for instance, ranks second in U.S. population and is about the size of Malaysia. Minnesota is a medium-size state by U.S. standards, ranking twentieth in population; yet it is the same size as Norway. We must appreciate the fact that American state governments are large enterprises.

There are also some small states; and again, size has its consequences. Alaska and Wyoming are among the sparsest populated states, but they are huge in the number of square miles. Thus, the unit cost of building highways and providing other services is high. Alaska and Wyoming cannot achieve economies of scale. Smaller democracies have difficulties and opportunities not found in California and New York.

Population Growth

Once a state achieves a certain population size, its leaders develop ways to cope with that size. More difficult to control in the short run are changes in population. States experiencing sudden population growth have difficulties providing schools, roads, bridges, and housing needed for an expanding population. States experiencing population decline, on the other hand, have a different set of concerns. As people leave the state and businesses die, the tax base erodes; if a state government adjusts by raising taxes, more people may leave and accentuate a vicious cycle. Obviously, states would rather be growing than shrinking.

Changes in population between 1980 and 1990 are shown in Figure 1-1. During this period when the national increase was 9.8 percent, the Sunbelt (from California to Florida) and the Mountain West states (Alaska, Arizona, Colorado, Idaho, Montana, Nevada, New Mexico, Utah, and Wyoming) experienced high growth. Nevada doubled in population; Arizona, Alaska, and Florida grew by a third. Population shifts among states are a result of different fertility rates and different rates of net migration. Net migration is the difference in the number of people moving into a state and the number moving out of that state. Migration patterns, in turn, are a function of economic opportunities: people usually move to find better jobs and a better quality of life. State leaders, therefore, focus on economic growth and full employment as a means to retain old citizens and to attract new ones. Quality of life, in contrast, is in the eye of the beholder: retirees have one set of preferences and young people another, although perhaps both may agree on the virtues of a warm or moderate climate.

Florida's problems are illustrative of high-growth states. "Every day, Florida needs about two miles of new highways, two new classrooms, two new teachers, two more police officers, two more state prison beds, and one more local jail cell"

Figure 1-1 Increase in State Population, 1980–1990

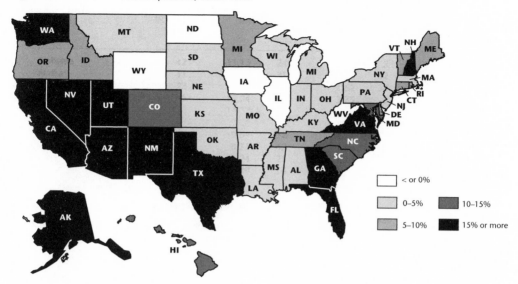

SOURCE: U.S. Bureau of the Census 1993, 29.

("As Florida Booms" 1987, 88). It was estimated that Florida needs a staggering $53 billion in new revenues to pay for its growth in the next decade ("As Florida Booms" 1987, 88). The way to finance this growth became a political controversy as Florida adopted and then later rescinded a controversial sales tax on services.

Florida's population explosion was caused by immigration, first of northern whites and later of Latin Americans, especially Cubans. The influx of northern whites has changed the southern political culture. By 1980, Florida was the only southern state in which northern-born whites constituted a majority of the white population (Black and Black 1987, 16). Yankees, and not the native whites, are, therefore, in the dominant social and political position. This creates political tensions that are now compounded by the influx of Central Americans and Cubans into southern Florida. As its own governor says, Florida is "more of a crowd than a community" (Barone and Ujifusa 1993, 272).

The populations of Iowa, North Dakota, West Virginia, and Wyoming decreased during the ten-year period, while that of Illinois neither increased nor decreased (Figure 1-1). In the declining states a major problem is the necessity for school consolidation in sparsely populated rural areas. A school is often the focal point of a community, so its loss is a blow to community pride and identity. The loss of the sports teams associated with the schools is a further blow to a small town's esteem. For instance, in the last decade North Dakota lost 9.2 percent of its public school population outside its few large cities. Some now refer to the state football championship as the "Hyphen Bowl" in which one consolidated school plays another.

These descriptions point out the differences among states because of the pace of population growth. Florida is illustrative of those states struggling to keep up with an expanding population and struggling to cope with the political values of new residents. North Dakota, in contrast, is a state dealing with the psychological and economic impact of population decline. Most states are in the middle of the two extremes, growing at a moderate rate. Even in cases of moderate population growth, state governments need to plan ahead to meet the needs of a growing population, but the needs are rarely as critical as those found in states like Florida. Moderate-growth states certainly have their share of economic problems, but they are not as severe as those found in North Dakota.

Population Density

States also vary in the extent to which citizens live in densely populated urban areas or in more sparsely populated rural areas. As the U.S. population has grown, it has become more urbanized and less rural. In Table 1-1 a metropolitan area is defined as a city of at least 50,000 inhabitants, including its nearby urbanized areas. Approximately three-quarters of our population now live in these metropolitan statistical areas.

As is demonstrated in the last two columns of the table, the most populous states tend to be among the most urbanized, although there are interesting exceptions: Rhode Island ranks forty-third in population but fifth in population density; North Carolina is tenth in population size but thirty-second in population density. There is a regional pattern as well. States on the East or West coast—California and New Jersey, for example—tend to be densely populated, while states in the South and Mountain West are clearly the least metropolitan. Even so, the growth of the metropolitan sector in the South has led to profound changes in the southern electorate.

The different interests of rural and urbanized areas often furnish the basis for sharp intrastate conflict. Illinois is a state with well-known metropolitan-downstate splits; 64 percent of its population lives in the Chicago metropolitan area. As governed by the late Mayor Richard J. Daley from 1955 to 1976, Chicago was the classic Democratic city machine. Its fiscal interests were often at odds with those in the rest of the state. In fact, the columnist Mike Royko once suggested that the city secede from the state in order to free itself from the control of "downstate hayseeds and polyester-leisure suit suburbanites" (Peirce and Hagstrom 1984, 225).[1] The inhabitants of the ring or "collar" of suburban counties around Chicago outnumber Chicago residents and usually vote Republican; their needs are different from the needs of those in the inner city. The rest of Illi-

---

1. Evidently, this idea did not achieve widespread support. In a survey conducted in the late 1980s, only 11 percent of respondents in the state favored secession, ranging from 16.9 percent in the downstate area to 9.8 percent in Chicago to 6.2 percent in the suburban "collar" counties that surround Chicago (Nardulli and Krassa 1989, 268–269).

nois, termed *downstate,* is somewhat more mixed politically. Still, because the economic base of downstate Illinois is farming, its concerns are quite different from either big city or suburb.

Many other states manifest urban-rural splits or other sectional divisions. In heavily urbanized Florida, for example, there is a split between northern Florida and southern Florida. In the northern part of the state the traditional "southern" flavor pervades, whereas in southern Florida northern migrants furnish a "Yankee" flavor and Latino immigrants provide their own flavor. In California, from San Francisco north, more liberal political values are prevalent, whereas in Southern California, near Los Angeles, right-wing politics are prevalent. Such intrastate sectional differences influence and structure voting patterns and electoral outcomes.

Population Composition

States also differ in the composition of their population, that is, in the types of demographic groups that are typical. States vary in the proportion of old people to young people, in the number of poor people, in the number of foreign-born people, and in the number of minorities. The increasingly diverse mix of people presents challenges to government and often provides a basis for political conflict.

Poverty. Altogether 35 million people in the United States fall below the U.S. government's poverty line, but poverty is not equally distributed among the states. About 24 percent of Mississippi's population is poor, whereas only 7.3 percent of New Hampshire's population is poor. In Table 1-2 the states are ranked according to the percentage of residents with incomes below what is defined by the government as providing a minimal standard of living. Clearly, the rate of poverty is highest in the South.

The size of the population in poverty presents a direct challenge and burden to state governments. States, even with aid from the federal government, struggle to provide cash benefits, medical care, and housing to the poor within their borders. The states like Mississippi that can least afford it are the states with the largest number of potential recipients. The states that can more easily afford to support the poor may exercise restraint because they fear greater benefits will attract poor people from out of state. The "welfare magnet" concept has been a popularly accepted one, although it receives only mixed support in scholarly literature. The perception by policy makers, however, that high welfare benefits act as a magnet can constrain the level of benefits (Peterson and Rom 1990).

Poverty is associated with a syndrome of other social problems. People are often poor because they lack a good education and job skills; thus, the need for education and training is greater in a state with significant portions of its population in poverty. Poverty is also often correlated with crime, especially in urban

Table 1-2 Percentage of the Population in Poverty, 1991

State	% in Poverty	Rank	State	% in poverty	Rank
Mississippi	23.7	1	Illinois	13.5	26
New Mexico	22.4	2	Oregon	13.5	26
Louisiana	19.0	3	Ohio	13.4	28
Alabama	18.8	4	Minnesota	12.9	29
Kentucky	18.8	4	Utah	12.9	29
West Virginia	17.9	6	Vermont	12.6	31
Texas	17.5	7	Kansas	12.3	32
Arkansas	17.3	8	Alaska	11.8	33
Georgia	17.2	9	Nevada	11.4	34
Oklahoma	17.0	10	Massachusetts	11.0	35
South Carolina	16.4	11	Pennsylvania	11.0	35
California	15.7	12	Colorado	10.4	37
Indiana	15.7	12	Rhode Island	10.4	37
Tennessee	15.5	14	Virginia	9.9	39
Florida	15.4	15	Wisconsin	9.9	39
Montana	15.4	15	Wyoming	9.9	39
New York	15.3	17	New Jersey	9.7	42
Arizona	14.8	18	Iowa	9.6	43
Missouri	14.8	18	Nebraska	9.5	44
North Carolina	14.5	20	Washington	9.5	44
North Dakota	14.5	20	Maryland	9.1	46
Maine	14.1	22	Connecticut	8.6	47
Michigan	14.1	22	Hawaii	7.7	48
South Dakota	14.0	24	Delaware	7.5	49
Idaho	13.9	25	New Hampshire	7.3	50

SOURCE: U.S. Bureau of the Census 1992.

areas. The criminal justice system is, therefore, often more burdened in poorer states (see Chapter 10).

Education and Skills. Another important characteristic of a state's population is the level of education attained by its citizens. Education is crucial for many reasons, but mostly because it is related to income, social class, and many other aspects of socioeconomic status. Thus, it is an avenue of upward mobility for economically disadvantaged persons. A good educational system is increasingly being recognized as a critical factor to a state's economic development. As American industry becomes more complex, the required job skills increase. Businesses are reluctant to locate in states where the labor force is inadequately trained. Finally, the level of educational attainment is related to policy choices the states make. An educated citizenry typically demands a higher level of public service than does an uneducated citizenry. Without educated citizens, the opportunities of democracy cannot be realized.

In Chapter 12 you will learn more about the politics of education. Here I concentrate on the differences among states in educational attainment. As one would expect, a ranking on educational achievement would correlate inversely with the poverty ranking in Table 1-2: states with many poor people have fewer high school graduates. On average, about one-quarter of the U.S. population has not completed high school, but in Alabama, Arkansas, Kentucky, Mississippi, and

West Virginia the figure is one-third. The western states have a high concentration of high school graduates. This means that businesses have more trained workers from which to choose than in states with fewer high school graduates. The presence of an educated work force has helped to attract new businesses to the West.

Immigrants. The United States is a nation formed by immigrants. Much of our nation's history can be told by reviewing the arrival of the different waves of immigrants—the Italians, the Irish, the Scandinavians, and so forth. Indeed, the process of assimilating these ethnic groups into the political system formed the basis of many political cleavages. In the 1980s two new waves of immigrants reached America's borders—Latin Americans and Southeast Asians. In the long run the country will reap substantial benefits from the arrival of these immigrants, just as it did from earlier immigrants. But in the short run the states in which refugees, regular immigrants, and illegal aliens locate experience difficulties in absorbing them. About three-quarters of the immigrants in the last decade settled in just six states: California, Florida, Illinois, New Jersey, New York, and Texas. And the wave continues: throughout the 1990s approximately a million newcomers will arrive each year (800,000 legal immigrants and refugees and 300,000 illegals) (Kirschten 1994, 1418).

Many Southeast Asians sought refugee status (a status for those escaping persecution) in the United States because the Vietnam War made it impossible for them to return to their homelands in Cambodia, Laos, Thailand, and Vietnam. More than a quarter of a million Asian refugees came in the first half of the 1980s; today, Asians are more likely to be regular immigrants who come for economic and family reasons and who come from a variety of countries, such as China, Korea, and the Philippines.

By 1990 the Latin American (including Mexico) immigration stream was larger than the Asian. The Latin American migration includes political refugees from Haiti and Cuba (for example, the Mariel "boatlift" in 1980, when 125,000 Cuban refugees suddenly arrived in Miami after being expelled by Fidel Castro), people fleeing from political and economic instability in Nicaragua and neighboring countries, and the continuing exodus from Mexico. Miami, Florida, has absorbed several hundred thousand Cubans, Haitians, and Nicaraguans since 1980. The magnitude of the influx and the resulting strain on health and social services and on the local economy have increased tensions between Miami's black community and its Hispanics. At times racial animosity has erupted into violence and rioting, as it did in January 1989 during the Super Bowl. Thus, when a flood of Cubans sought refuge in Florida in 1994, the welcome mat was not out; thousands were picked up at sea by the U.S. Coast Guard and detained at the U.S. naval station at Guantánamo Bay.

The new arrivals need bilingual education, English-language instruction, job training, and financial and medical assistance. The impact on the public school systems is great, especially in communities that experience a sudden influx of immigrants. Almost one-third of the residents of Los Angeles are foreign-born; in Lowell, Massachusetts, Cambodian refugees constitute one-quarter of the population (Gurwitt 1992). Twenty percent or more of the residents of several states—Arizona, California, Hawaii, New Mexico, New York, and Texas—do not speak English at home (U.S. Bureau of the Census 1993, 52). States such as these have a greater task in helping people of other cultures adapt to this one. Hawaii has been successful in doing so for a long time and may provide a race relations model for other states.

Federal, state, and local governments divide the labor imposed by immigration: the federal government sets the terms under which people enter, and states, localities, and private agencies help them settle here. Federal financial assistance is available, depending on a person's immigration status, but the amount of federal aid has been declining, leading to increased bitterness among state officials toward the federal government. In 1993–1994 the governors of Arizona, California, Florida, and Texas sued the federal government to recover some of the costs incurred by providing criminal justice and social services to illegal immigrants. They argued that the nation has lost control of its borders, and therefore, the nation, not the states, should pay for the consequences. Other governors voiced similar complaints. Newcomers' need for assistance is short-lived, however; after ten years in this country, legal immigrants and refugees have average household incomes that surpass those of natives (Kirschten 1994, 1420).

In November 1994 the sentiment against illegal immigrants in California was starkly expressed in the passage of Proposition 187. This ballot initiative cuts off all benefits, including schooling and nonemergency health care, to undocumented immigrants. It requires teachers, doctors, and social workers to report any persons without proper documents. The constitutionality of this law was immediately questioned, and the fate of the immigrants lies with the courts.

Minorities. States also vary in the ethnic and racial composition of their populations. Ethnic and racial characteristics form the basis for significant political conflict in many states. Perhaps nowhere is this more true than in the South. Historically, the politics of individual southern states have varied according to the proportion of blacks. The Deep South states—Alabama, Georgia, Louisiana, Mississippi, and South Carolina—with the highest concentration of blacks were much more conservative than the peripheral South. Political behavior varied because where there were more blacks, whites were more likely to unite behind racial conservatism (Black and Black 1987, 15; 1992, 169–175). Such whites were called *black-belt whites* by V. O. Key, Jr. (1949), the leading scholar of southern politics.

Racial differences also show up in the contemporary South. In that region, 77 percent of blacks identified with the Democratic party in 1984, whereas only 45 percent of the native whites and 35 percent of immigrant whites were Democratic identifiers (Black and Black 1987, 241). The voting record of blacks for Democratic presidential candidates also exceeds that of southern whites. The impact of blacks' voting is reduced, however, because white registered voters out-number them five to one in the South (Black and Black 1987, 294). Thus, African-Americans have gained political clout compared with what they had in the past, but they are not yet fully equal in voting power.

Since blacks tend to be more liberal ideologically than southern whites, their influence dilutes the overwhelmingly conservative advantage. Black southerners favor passage of the Equal Rights Amendment, more government services, and the use of quotas in hiring and college admissions. They also believe government is responsible for the economic well-being of citizens (Black and Black 1992, 235). The black vote, therefore, moves state government marginally toward assuming a wider scope of governmental responsibility.

Another large and rapidly growing minority group is the Hispanic ethnic community. Like blacks, Hispanics (Latinos) are a disadvantaged minority; they have low incomes and low levels of education and they suffer from discrimination. Unlike blacks many Hispanics lack fluency in English, which further handicaps them in obtaining jobs (Reimers 1984). The population of Hispanic origin is growing much faster than either the black or Anglo-white populations. Between 1990 and 2010 it is expected to increase by 75 percent, from 22.5 million to 39.3 million (middle estimate of U.S. Bureau of the Census 1993, 8, 9). In contrast, the black population is predicted to rise by 30 percent and the Anglo-white population by only 7 percent. Already, Hispanics constitute more than 25 percent of the population in California, New Mexico, and Texas.

The social and political implications of this change are enormous. One area of conflict—between African-Americans and Latinos over jobs—has already been mentioned. Another conflict is over language and national identity. By 1989, seventeen states had passed laws making English their official language ("Say It in English" 1989). Aimed at Hispanics and to a lesser extent at Asians, the passage of such laws indicates an increase in the degree of ethnic and racial tension and an uneasiness over the assimilation of diverse groups into American society.

Politically speaking, Latinos (other than Cubans) tend to vote Democratic. Their voting cohesion and their turnout is not as great as blacks, however, and they are less liberal (Cain and Kiewiet 1984; see also de la Garza et al. 1992). Still, they have achieved the governorship more often than blacks. Both Florida and New Mexico in the 1980s and Arizona in the 1970s elected Hispanic governors. Not until 1989, when Douglas Wilder was elected governor of Virginia, did an African-American attain this office.

THE PLACE

States also differ in terms of their physical characteristics. Some of these attributes are fixed and cannot be changed: the land area, the location, and the climate. State leaders can try to overcome the effects of a remote location, a cold or unpleasant climate, or small size, but for the most part they are constrained by nature. Similarly, states are constrained by their natural resource endowments:

some states have rich soil; others can't grow much. Some states have plenty of water, forests, minerals, oil, or coal. Others have to get their water from other states and must rely on imported oil and coal. The net effect of the maldistribution of natural resources is that states vary in the types of economic activities performed. The overall wealth of states, in turn, depends on the vigor of the economy. These natural economic advantages and disadvantages affect state government a great deal.

Land

States vary enormously in their land area. We all know that Alaska is the largest state, followed by Texas. What is less well known, however, is how big Alaska is in relation to other states. It is more than twice the size of Texas. In fact, the twenty-two smallest states could be combined before an area as large as Alaska is reached.

What difference to a state does its geographic size make? First, there are distinct differences in a state's political style. In larger states, legislative districts are by necessity quite large. In some instances they are as large as the congressional districts in some other states. In wide-ranging districts it is hard for legislators to keep in touch with constituents; airplanes are frequently used for campaigning in Alaska, for instance.

In Texas, rural districts are vast. In one House district the distance from one corner to the opposite corner is more than 300 miles (Jewell 1982). Moreover, legislators must travel hundreds of miles away from their homes and jobs to Austin, the state capital. The travel burden affects the type of people who can afford to serve in the legislature. In smaller states, like New Hampshire and Vermont, districts are small and compact. Legislators can run very personal, almost one-on-one campaigns. Once in office, they can commute to the capital on a daily basis, continuing in their regular occupations. The result is more of an amateur, small-town flavor in politics.

Second, geographic size has policy implications. In the provision of highways, for instance, geographic area and population density determine expense. Alaska, Montana, and Wyoming are large and sparsely populated states; their per capita highway expenditures are among the highest in the nation. Rhode Island is a small state with a compact population; its expenditure is among the lowest. The state's size affects the delivery of services in many other policy areas as well.

Third, land can be the basis of political conflict. Among the most divisive issues in the western states is that the federal government owns much of the land. Eighty-two percent of Nevada is owned by the federal government; more than 60 percent of Alaska, California, Idaho, and Utah is federal domain. This means that vast areas of the West are not under state jurisdiction; this land can be put only to the uses allowed by the federal government. Federal ownership, therefore, constrains urban growth and economic development in many western cities. Federal lands are often rich in mineral and other natural resources, assets lost to state governments. The federal government does, however, pay state royalties for the lost tax revenues. Occasionally, unrest over federal landholding rises, and outbreaks occur, such as the Sagebrush Rebellion in 1979. This symbolic revolution began when Nevada passed a law requiring the U.S. government to turn much of its land over to the state; several other states passed similar laws. Naturally, the federal government ignored these laws, and the rebellion gradually died out.

Location and Climate

In addition to the extent of a state's land, another physical characteristic is crucial: a state's location. A state's location might be an asset because it is located on an ocean or on another waterway, or it might be an asset because of a favorable climate or because of its proximity to profitable markets. Unfortunately, other states have to deal with less desirable and more remote locations, where the costs of transportation to markets are higher.

States located near major markets have a natural economic advantage over states in more distant locations. Traditionally, access to markets and to transportation has been among the more important factors in making decisions about where to locate an industry. For example, Tennessee was victorious over thirty-seven other competitors in attracting the General Motors' Saturn plant (see Chapter 14 for more on the "car wars"). A key factor in General Motors' decision was Tennessee's central location close to suppliers and markets. Other states, in fact, offered the company better financial incentives. Similarly, Japanese investment in a Tennessee Nissan plant was secured when the governor showed the visitors satellite photographs of the United States taken at night, illustrating how many Americans live within a day's drive of Tennessee. Location was a feature that other states could not overcome with money.

Climate accompanies a state's location, and it is an important feature. Climate determines the length of the growing season and thus the type of agricultural crops that can be grown. For instance, oranges are an important crop in Florida and California, but not in the Dakotas. The climatic conditions in the Plains states—Iowa, Kansas, Minnesota, Missouri, Nebraska, North Dakota, Oklahoma, South Dakota, Texas—favor wheat instead. A state's climate is also a factor in where people choose to live. More people express a preference to move to a warmer area than to a colder one. Some of this preference relates to the greater economic opportunities in the Sunbelt than in the Frostbelt. The names *frost* and *sun*, however, reinforce the climatic aspect of the economic conflict among regions.

Natural Resources

Natural resources such as soil, water, minerals, and energy resources are attached to the land. The distribution of natural resources has great economic consequences: it allows states blessed with abundant water and rich topsoil to concentrate on crop production. Other, less fortunate states must import their water and some of their food. Some states receive income from the coal, oil, and minerals extracted from the land. Not only do these states have access to these nonrenewable resources, they can also derive tax revenue from their usage. In essence, resource-rich states can tax the citizens of other states for consuming their oil, coal, and natural gas, thereby reducing their own tax burden.

To begin, first consider the rich topsoil that makes some states substantial agricultural producers. California is the top farm producer, as measured by gross state product (GSP), followed by Texas, Iowa, Minnesota, Illinois, Wisconsin, and Nebraska.[2] Most of the other midwestern states rank fairly high, and the New England states rank low. Their state economies produce little agriculture. In no state, however, is agriculture the dominant sector of the state's GSP (see Table 1-3 for major sector data). But agriculture looms large in other ways. For example, more than 10 percent of the acreage in Iowa, Kansas, Nebraska, North Dakota, and South Dakota is farmland. In the rural states, there is a sense of pride and identification with the land. Iowa, for example, has on its billboards the slogan: "Iowa, a Place to Grow," suggesting simultaneously the growth of crops and the growth of sturdy young children. The floods that occurred in the summer of 1993 were devastating to the farm economy and to the rural lifestyle in Iowa and surrounding states.

In addition to fertile topsoil, agriculture requires the availability of water. The Midwest is blessed with sufficient water, while the West is not. Nowhere is water a more important issue than in the Southwest. On the wall of the Colorado state capitol, an inscription reads, "Here is the land where life is written in water." The same statement applies to Arizona, New Mexico, and Utah, where water is equally precious. Historically, in these four states 90 percent of the water has been consumed by agriculture. But economic development, the rapidly increasing population, and some energy projects all require water. The allocation of water to agriculture rather than to other competing economic interests is a fierce and constant battle.

Since few untapped sources of water exist, developers must purchase water rights from previous users, such as farmers. Indeed, agriculture's share of water consumption decreased in the 1980s. Naturally, the price of water rights is escalating rapidly. As they say in the Southwest, "Water flows uphill to money" (Brown and Ingram 1987, 1). Federal funds had previously subsidized expensive solutions to the problem of water scarcity, but cutbacks during the Reagan administration diminished much of this support. Residents of other regions have also become much less sympathetic about helping westerners solve this problem. Access to water, therefore, is a problem that western states will have to solve

2. GSP is the gross market value of the goods and services attributable to labor and property located in a state. It is the state equivalent of the gross national product.

themselves. The conflicts involving water between old and new residents and between rural and urban interests will probably increase in the future.

Finally, nonrenewable natural resources are unevenly distributed across the
states. Minerals, coal, and petroleum are found only in some locations. Coal is
found in large quantities in Kentucky, Pennsylvania, West Virginia, and the surrounding states, and in the West, particularly in New Mexico and Wyoming. Oil
is located in the South and Southwest, primarily Louisiana, Oklahoma, and
Texas, and in Alaska. The unequal distribution of natural resources has at least
two major consequences for state governments. One favorable consequence for a
state that has such resources is that they can be taxed. This tax is called a severance tax, and it is levied on the oil consumer located in other states. Oil-produc-
ing states can derive substantial revenues from the severance tax, thereby avoiding taxing their own citizens as heavily. The states where the severance tax
constitutes over 10 percent of the state budget are Alaska (71.1 percent in 1991),
Louisiana, Montana, New Mexico, North Dakota, Oklahoma, and Wyoming
(U.S. Bureau of the Census 1993, 307). Some of these states do not have an income tax (for example, Alaska and Wyoming), while the rest tax incomes only
slightly. For years Alaska even gave its citizens a rebate—$915.84 in 1992.

Reliance on the severance tax to the exclusion of other taxes, however, has an
undesirable consequence. When the price of the nonrenewable resource drops,
tax revenue plummets. Louisiana, in particular, experienced severe budget crises
in the last decade when oil prices fell; energy produced 41 percent of state government revenues in 1982 but only 13 percent in 1992 (Barone and Ujifusa 1993,
528). A similar fate befell Alaska in 1994; oil revenues fell so much that budget
cuts were implemented, and the imposition of an income tax was even contem-
plated. Thus, the severance tax introduces an element of unpredictability into
state budgeting.

THE ECONOMIC CONTEXT

States' economic performance depends on their natural resources, on national
and international economic trends, and on the spending patterns of the federal
government.

State Economic Activities

The land and its natural resources initially determine the type of economic
activities that will prosper in different regions of the country. As Jackson et al.
(1982, 3) state:

> It is thus no historical accident that the nation's steel and auto industries are con-
> centrated in the East North Central region; its grain farming in the West North
> Central region; its produce farming in California and the South Atlantic; its finan-
> cial and insurance institutions in the Northeast; and its energy producers in the
> West South Central, Mountain, and Pacific regions.

Table 1-3 Value of Gross State Product (in millions) and Size of Dominant Economic Sector, 1990

Rank	State	GSP	Dominant sector	% of GSP
1	California	744,729	Services	21
2	New York	466,828	Finance, insurance, real estate	24
3	Texas	371,988	Manufacturing	18
4	Illinois	272,197	Services	20
5	Pennsylvania	244,634	Services	21
6	Florida	244,624	Services	23
7	Ohio	222,126	Manufacturing	27
8	New Jersey	208,422	Services	21
9	Michigan	188,041	Manufacturing	27
10	Massachusetts	153,928	Services	24
11	Virginia	141,650	Services	18
12	North Carolina	141,149	Manufacturing	31
13	Georgia	136,875	Manufacturing	19
14	Indiana	111,851	Manufacturing	30
15	Washington	109,362	Manufacturing	19
16	Maryland	108,570	Services	22
17	Missouri	103,674	Manufacturing	21
18	Wisconsin	100,617	Manufacturing	28
19	Minnesota	100,005	Manufacturing	22
20	Tennessee	95,447	Manufacturing	23
21	Connecticut	93,910	Finance, insurance, real estate	23
22	Louisiana	90,882	Manufacturing	19
23	Colorado	71,470	Services	20
24	Alabama	70,346	Manufacturing	23
25	Kentucky	67,492	Manufacturing	25
26	Arizona	67,265	Services	20
27	South Carolina	63,756	Manufacturing	25
28	Iowa	56,099	Manufacturing	23
29	Oklahoma	56,019	Manufacturing	16
30	Oregon	55,426	Manufacturing	20
31	Kansas	51,112	Manufacturing	19
32	Mississippi	39,821	Manufacturing	24
33	Arkansas	38,737	Manufacturing	25
34	Nebraska	33,375	Finance, insurance, real estate	16
35	Nevada	30,749	Services	34
36	Utah	30,603	Services	18
37	Hawaii	28,649	Services	23
38	West Virginia	28,312	Manufacturing	17
39	New Mexico	26,687	Services	19
40	Alaska	26,270	Mining	36
41	New Hampshire	23,885	Manufacturing	22
42	Maine	23,267	Manufacturing	19
43	Rhode Island	20,978	Finance, insurance, real estate	21
44	Delaware	19,628	Finance, insurance, real estate	30
45	Idaho	18,555	Finance, insurance, real estate	19
46	Montana	13,331	Services	17
47	South Dakota	13,078	Finance, insurance, real estate	21
48	Wyoming	12,594	Manufacturing	30
49	North Dakota	12,087	Finance, insurance, real estate	17
50	Vermont	11,228	Manufacturing	20

SOURCE: Beemiller and Dunbar 1993. Percentages computed by the author.

The regions' different resource bases mean that they concentrate on different economic activities, and they enjoy different levels of prosperity. Table 1-3 relates some of these differences. As you see, California has by far the largest economy, followed by New York, Texas, Illinois, Pennsylvania, and Florida.

Historically, the largest single sector of the national economy has been the manufacturing sector. As can be seen in the table, however, in twenty-four states manufacturing is now surpassed in value by some other economic sector. For example, the service sector is the single largest sector in fifteen states, including the former industrial states of Illinois, Massachusetts, and Pennsylvania as well as California, Florida, Hawaii, Nevada, Virginia, and much of the Mountain West. Primarily, this sector is composed of business services, but in California the motion picture industry is important. In Florida and Hawaii, tourism is important, and in Nevada, gambling. In other states the financial sector is the most important: New York, the established financial capital, has been joined in financial circles by eight other states, like Idaho, Nebraska, North Dakota, and South Dakota. Some of the latter states offer especially favorable regulatory conditions to the banking and insurance industries, so banks locate their subsidiary operations there. Finally, only one state—Alaska—relies on the mining of natural resources as the dominant economic sector.

In nearly all states, the manufacturing sector is very important, even when it is no longer the single dominant economic activity. Each state's natural resources heavily determine the type of manufacturing base. Midwestern states like Illinois, Michigan, and Wisconsin focus on the production of machinery. In parts of the South—Georgia, North Carolina, and South Carolina—the manufacturing base rests on the textile industry. Food and food processing is the major manufacturing activity in other parts of the South—Arkansas, Florida, Kentucky— and in the Midwest—Nebraska, North Dakota, and South Dakota. The chemical industry is crucial to the economies of Alabama, Delaware, Louisiana, New Jersey, Tennessee, and West Virginia.

In summary, the states' economies vary in size, in which economic sector is most important (manufacturing, services, finance, mining, and so on), and in the major goods produced. Many of the variations result from the natural resources of each state, that is, its minerals, timber, soil, and access to waterways. These physical advantages give each state's economy its unique cast.

States, however, cannot rest on their natural resource advantages. Over time the sectors of the economy based on natural resources have declined in dollar value and in employment relative to the rest of the economy. The proportion of the population engaged in farming has decreased, as well as the proportion of the population engaged in manufacturing. These two occupations are heavily tied to the land. The proportion of the population engaged in services, in trade, in finance, and in government work has increased. These tend to be more mobile occupations, such as trading, servicing of business, and finance. Government work, of course, goes on everywhere. These occupations do not necessarily depend on particular natural resources, although they do depend on business activity in general. Thus the resource advantages and disadvantages of the states, although important, do not determine economic vitality as much as they once did.

These changes in economic circumstances were caused by changes in the national and international economies. We are now part of a world economy. The "globalization of capitalism" means that states increasingly feel the effects of surges and declines in prices, labor markets, and exchange rates thousands of miles away (Sawers and Tabb 1984). Some of the effects on traditional sectors are quite dramatic. Manufacturing's share of employment shrank from 31 percent in 1975 to 16.8 percent in 1992 (U.S. Bureau of the Census 1993, 418). This is referred to as the "deindustrialization of America." Manufacturing jobs have disappeared from New England, the Middle Atlantic states, and the Midwest. Some of the less-skilled jobs have moved overseas.

At the same time, the service sector's share of employment has increased from 13.0 percent to 26.7 percent. These service jobs, however, are often in the growing regions, not in the stagnating regions. The shift in the U.S. economy from industrialization to postindustrialization has affected states unevenly and profoundly. Leaders in states whose economies were heavily industrialized have had to work especially hard to attract new types of economic activities. Some of their attempts are described in Chapter 14.

Spending by the federal government also vitally affects the economies of the states. The federal government can "prime the pump" of state economies through transfer payments (a government payment to an individual, such as social security) and defense spending. Other chapters in this book describe various federal transfer programs that provide aid to citizens. Often overlooked is the stimulative effect of federal defense spending on states. In fiscal 1987 the defense establishment spent $282 billion on personnel, manufacturing, bases, procurement, ships, weapons, and so forth. Each $1 billion in defense spending adds about 35,000 jobs to the local economy ("After the Boom" 1987, 3197). Thus, how much Congress decides to spend and where it decides to spend it significantly affects state economies. In the 1990s, defense spending has declined precipitously; the Clinton administration's budget request for 1995 is one-third less than spending at the peak of the Reagan defense buildup. Defense spending is concentrated: about half of all defense-related jobs are in just eight states—California, Florida, Massachusetts, New York, Ohio, Pennsylvania, Texas, and Virginia (Sylvester 1992, 64). So these states' economies have been especially hurt by the cuts in defense spending, although the cuts have been offset a bit by federal assistance in conversion of plants to peacetime uses.

State Personal Income

The net effect of states' natural resources, national and international economic trends, and the flow of federal funds is reflected in state wealth, usually mea-

Table 1-4   Per Capita Personal Income by State, 1992 (in current dollars)

State	Rank	PCPI	State	Rank	PCPI
Connecticut	1	26,979	Ohio	26	18,624
New Jersey	2	26,457	Iowa	27	18,287
Massachusetts	3	24,059	Maine	28	18,226
New York	4	23,534	Oregon	29	18,202
Maryland	5	22,974	Georgia	30	18,130
New Hampshire	6	22,934	Indiana	31	18,043
Illinois	7	21,608	Texas	32	17,892
Alaska	8	21,603	North Carolina	33	17,667
Delaware	9	21,451	Wyoming	34	17,423
California	10	21,278	Tennessee	35	17,341
Hawaii	11	21,218	Arizona	36	17,119
Virginia	12	20,629	North Dakota	37	16,854
Washington	13	20,398	South Dakota	38	16,558
Rhode Island	14	20,299	Kentucky	39	16,534
Nevada	15	20,266	Alabama	40	16,220
Pennsylvania	16	20,253	Oklahoma	41	16,198
Colorado	17	20,124	Idaho	42	16,067
Minnesota	18	20,049	Montana	43	16,062
Michigan	19	19,508	South Carolina	44	15,989
Florida	20	19,397	Louisiana	45	15,712
Kansas	21	19,376	Arkansas	46	15,439
Nebraska	22	19,084	New Mexico	47	15,353
Missouri	23	18,835	Utah	48	15,325
Vermont	24	18,834	West Virginia	49	15,065
Wisconsin	25	18,727	Mississippi	50	14,088

SOURCE: U.S. Bureau of the Census, 1993, 451.

sured by per capita personal income. This figure includes the income of individuals from all sources; a state's growth in personal income over time is a good index of how well its economy is doing. In Table 1-4 I list the average personal income per person in 1992 for each state. It is clear that there are significant disparities in income between states and between regions. In general, the southern states cluster at the bottom; the New England and Middle Atlantic states toward the top. The disparity, however, has lessened over the years, so the South does not lag as far behind the rest of the country as it once did.

Paul Brace (1993) has investigated change in per capita income from 1968 to 1989, specifically asking how much of the change can be attributed to national economic forces and how much to state economic performance. Using statistical techniques to apportion the variance over time into either national or state trends, he produced the classification of growing and declining states seen in Table 1-5. For the most part, state income is strongly tied to the nation's economic performance. Yet, there are interesting variations in state patterns. Some states are growing because of their dependence on the national economy (upper right cell in the table)—for example, Michigan, whose automobile sales are tied to national economic health. Others are growing independently of national trends (upper left cell). New York's growth is much more a product of its own resources. Similarly, among the declining states, some (lower right cell) are closely bound to

Table 1-5 Classification of State Personal Income according to Responsiveness to National and State-Level Economic Trends

State-level trend	Responsiveness to national economic fluctuations	
	Independent	Dependent
Growth	California, Connecticut, Georgia, Maine, Maryland, Massachusetts, New Jersey, New York, Pennsylvania, Rhode Island, Vermont, Wisconsin	Delaware, Illinois, Indiana, Michigan, Minnesota, Missouri, Nevada, New Hampshire, Oregon, Virginia, Washington
Decline	Colorado, Iowa, Kansas, Louisiana, New Mexico, North Dakota, Oklahoma, South Dakota, Texas, Utah, West Virginia, Wyoming	Alabama, Arizona, Arkansas, Florida, Idaho, Kentucky, Mississippi, Montana, Nebraska, North Carolina, Ohio, South Carolina, Tennessee

SOURCE: Adapted from Brace 1993, 72.

the national economy. Arizona, for example, is adversely affected by national trends, while others (lower left cell) decline independently. Texas, for instance, is a victim of its own circumstances, including declining oil revenues.

Personal income is an important constraint on state programs because wealth determines what a state can afford to do on its own. States like Mississippi do not have a lot of taxable income. States toward the top of the income ranking, such as Connecticut, have a larger tax base and can afford to offer more generous benefits to their citizens. The irony is, of course, that Mississippi's needs are greater than Connecticut's. Federal aid can reduce these interstate disparities to some extent. How states make their decisions in regard to taxing and spending is described in Chapter 9.

State leaders do not, however, simply "convert" economic wealth into expenditures for public programs. There are too many anomalies in state wealth and expenditure rankings for simple conversion to be a convincing explanation. Moreover, as we have seen, states change their economic performance over time. Some develop new fiscal capacities that might be tapped by government; the fiscal capacity of others shrinks, leaving them with overdeveloped public sectors. Politics shape how economic resources will be translated into public policies. In the next section, I introduce some of the political dimensions that structure how states use their economic resources.

THE POLITICAL CONTEXT

Historical Differences

Many of the political differences in states today—differences in voter turnout and party competition, for example—are long-standing ones. The South in particular has had a different political history from the rest of the country. Some of the South's differences from other regions of the country are rooted in distinct economic interests. But another important historical difference is the South's political culture. It shapes the habits, perspectives, and attitudes that influence present-day political life.

Daniel Elazar (1984) has written extensively on how state political cultures have shaped the operations of state political systems. He believes that the United States shares a general political culture that is, in turn, a synthesis of three major subcultures. The values of each subculture were brought to this country by the early settlers and spread unevenly across the country as various ethnic and religious groups moved westward. These migration streams have deposited their political values much like the Ice Age left permanent geological traces on the earth. Today's differences, Elazar says, can be traced to the political values and perspectives of the earliest settlers.

Elazar identifies the three major subcultures as individualistic, moralistic, and traditionalistic. The individualistic subculture emphasizes the marketplace. Government has a limited role, primarily to keep the marketplace working properly. Politicians run for office out of material motivations in order to advance themselves professionally. Bureaucracy is viewed negatively as a deterrent to the spoils system. Corruption in office is tolerated because politics are conceived of as a dirty business. Political competition tends to be partisan and oriented toward gaining office rather than toward dealing with issues.

The individualistic view of politics, Elazar maintains, originated with English and German groups who settled the Middle Atlantic colonies. They were seeking individual economic opportunities and thus wanted a government that would advance, not inhibit, their materialistic interests. As their descendants moved westward into New York and Pennsylvania, the lower Midwest, Missouri, and the western states, they brought along the belief that government's role should be sharply limited.

In distinct contrast is the moralistic subculture that emphasizes the commonwealth. Government's role is to advance the public interest or the good of the commonwealth. Thus, government is a positive force in the lives of citizens. Politics revolve around issues, and politicians run for office on the basis of issues. Corruption is not tolerated because government service is seen as public service, not a business. The bureaucracy is viewed favorably and as a means to achieving the public good. Politics are a matter of concern to all citizens; thus, it is a citizen's duty to participate in elections.

The moralistic view was brought to the New World by the Puritans, who settled New England in a series of religious communities. Their Yankee descendants transported these values as they moved westward across the upper Great Lakes into the Midwest and across the Northwest; later waves of Scandinavian and northern European groups with similar values reinforced their moralism. Politics in states settled by these groups tend to be participatory and oriented toward advancing the common good, Elazar observes.

The third subculture, the traditionalistic, is rooted in an ambivalent attitude toward the marketplace and the commonwealth. The purpose of government is to maintain the existing social and economic hierarchy. Politicians come from society's elite, who have almost a familial obligation to govern. Ordinary citizens are not expected to participate in political affairs, or even to vote. Political competition tends to occur between rival factions within the elite rather than between class-based political parties. Bureaucracy is regarded as suspect because it interferes with personal relationships.

The traditionalistic values were brought to this country by the people who originally settled the southern colonies. They were seeking economic opportunity through a plantation-centered agricultural system. Their descendants moved westward throughout the southern and Border tier of states into the Southwest. In states settled by these groups fewer people participate in politics, and government's role is limited to maintenance of the existing social order, according to Elazar's theory.

Elazar classified the dominant political subcultures of each state, using the settlement patterns completed by the early twentieth century (Figure 1-2). Few states are pure examples of one subculture, but usually there is a dominant culture that gives the state its particular political style. In general, the states of the South are dominated by the traditionalistic subculture. The individualistic states stretch across the country's middle section in a southwesterly direction. The states of the far North, Northwest, and Pacific Coast are dominated by the moralistic culture. Sometimes two subcultures coexist in a single state, leading to political conflict between cultural groups.

Figure 1-2 Dominant Political Culture by State

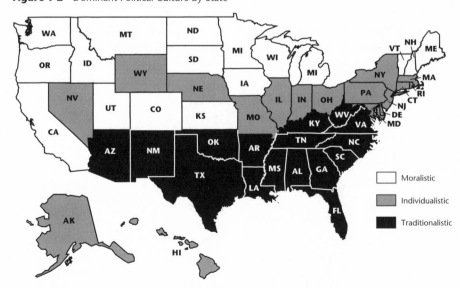

SOURCE: Elazar 1984, 137.

Contemporary migration patterns between regions may either reinforce or override the cultural base laid by the first settlers. For example, if people leave individualistic states like Pennsylvania and Ohio to seek better jobs in Texas, they will reinforce the individualism within the Texas political culture and move it away from traditionalism. Or if the population influx is quite large, as in Florida, the cultural base may be eroded. States with stable populations, like Michigan, Minnesota, North Dakota, and Wisconsin, remain relatively pure examples of moralism.

Elazar's cultural theory has a great deal of intuitive appeal to many scholars of state politics. It is consistent with general impressions about state differences in political values, style, and tone. It also provides a historical explanation for many differences. Many researchers, therefore, have subjected his thesis to empirical investigation; that is, they have tested his predictions about political and policy differences between the three subcultures and found some support for them. An investigation by Fitzpatrick and Hero (1988), for example, confirmed many of Elazar's hypotheses at the system level (but see Nardulli 1990 for disconfirmation at the individual level). They found that the competition between parties was stronger in moralistic states than in other types of states and that it had greater relevance to policy. Moralistic states made greater use of merit systems than did other states. They demonstrated greater policy innovation and greater economic equality.

One interesting question is what happens to people who move from one political culture to another. Russell Hanson (1992) found that migrants' adjustment to different norms depended on their culture of origin. Persons raised as moralists were dutiful wherever they lived; traditionalists and individualists conformed to their new surroundings, becoming either more or less dutiful, depending on the new culture.

Further evidence that political attitudes are conditioned by local political culture or context is provided by Erikson, Wright, and McIver (1993). Since their *Statehouse Democracy* is a significant study that we refer to throughout the book, it is worthwhile explaining their methods. To get around the usual objection that there are no public opinion polls that are comparable across all states, they pooled 122 CBS News/*New York Times* telephone surveys from 1976 to 1988 to obtain measures of ideology and party identification by state.

They are able to show that state political context has a dramatic effect on individual attitudes. They control for the obvious demographic variables that explain individuals' attitudes (education, income, age, race, religion, gender, and size of place) and still find that the state of residence has a significant effect, approximately equal to the demographic effects. For example, the difference in party identification produced by living in Democratic Arkansas as opposed to living in Republican New Hampshire approaches the magnitude of the partisan differences produced by being Jewish instead of Protestant or being black instead of white. While the authors cannot account for the source of these state effects (cultural or otherwise), they conclude that "the political attitudes of American citizens vary in important ways on the basis of where in the United States they live" (Erikson, Wright, and McIver 1993, 72). Thus, they demonstrate that something about a state's background affects its citizens' views; in further analyses they find strong support for Elazar's particular categorization of culture. State boundaries do make a difference.

Contemporary Differences

In addition to the historical differences among states, there are many contemporary differences in their political makeup, especially public opinion. Public opinion constitutes the attitudes of individual citizens toward public issues: should their state spend more on welfare? should their state allow abortions? should a state lottery be established? The cultural thesis outlined above suggests that public opinion on these and other issues should vary by state, and indeed it does. An even more important question, given our policy focus, is whether state policy differences are related to (or caused by) differences in public opinion.

Erikson, Wright, and McIver (1993) provide a persuasive demonstration that public opinion does matter. They combined a set of eight policy measures into a single index of policy liberalism; a high score on this measure indicates that a state spends more or intervenes more in a liberal direction than do other states. Their measure of public opinion was the standard ideology question: "How would you describe your views on most political matters? Generally, do you think of yourself as liberal, moderate, or conservative?" Since in every state conservatives outnumber liberals, their ideological scale (the percentage of liberals minus the percentage of conservatives) is always a negative number. They found that state opinion liberalism was highly correlated ($r = +.82$) with state policy liberalism.

Their results are displayed in Figure 1-3. Clearly, the most liberal states— mostly the northeastern ones—tend to enact the most liberal policies, whereas the more conservative states—chiefly southern and Mountain states—adopt the most conservative policies. The authors also introduced the usual set of socioeconomic variables and found that the linkage between public opinion and public policy still held. Thus, their work confirms our notion that politics structure how states translate economic factors into policies.

In addition to public opinion, states' political organizations are crucial in policy making. In this book we examine in detail two types of organizations: the political party, treated in Chapter 3, and interest groups, discussed in Chapter 4. The authors describe how parties and groups function and how they differ from state to state. In this chapter, I consider only the question of whether these political organizations affect public policy. Many scholars have examined this question, particularly the extent to which the party-policy relationship exists independently of economic causes.

Figure 1-3   State Policy and Public Opinion

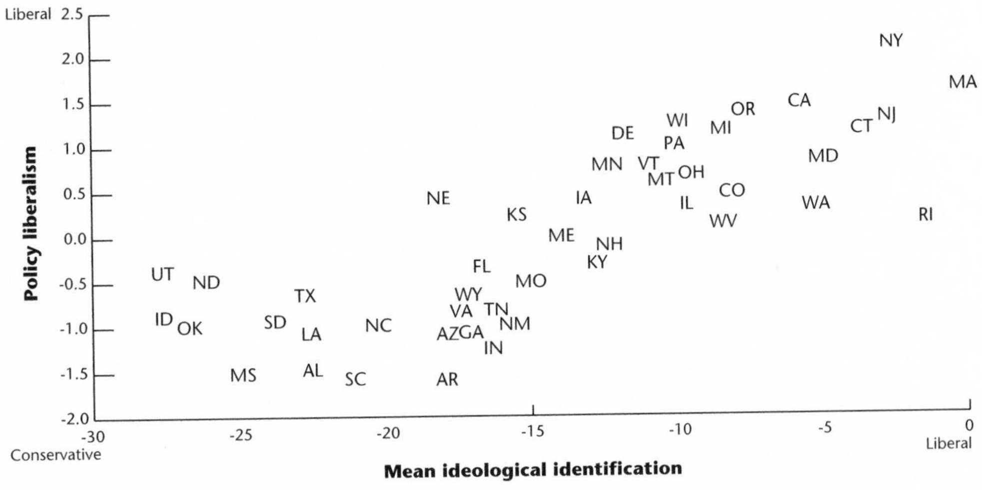

SOURCE: Erikson, Wright, and McIver 1993, 79. Reprinted with permission.

One of the best examinations is that of Thomas Dye (1984), who related party competition to welfare policy. He was interested in the conditions under which the party in control has relevance for public policy, that is, whether policies change when parties change. He found that the party in power makes a difference where there is a high degree of competition between the parties and where each party is cohesive and focused on the issues.

Interest groups also have a major influence on public policy. They put issues on the policy agenda; they block the issues of the opposition; they shape legislation throughout its passage and its implementation. Gray and Lowery (1994) have shown that states with more interest groups pass fewer bills; in other words, interest groups lead to government gridlock. As shown in Chapter 13, groups are particularly powerful in the arena of regulatory policy. Although convinced of their importance, political scientists have not been able to analyze systematically the effect of groups on policy because they lacked comparable data from the fifty states. In Chapter 4, new data on group influence are presented, which may allow for such rigorous comparisons in the future.

National Forces

The states' political context is also conditioned by national political trends. These external forces do have an effect on the linkages between politics and policy within states. An article by John Chubb (1988; see also Stein 1990) captures the statistical impact of external political and economic forces on state legislative and gubernatorial elections. Chubb found that presidential and senatorial coattails, turnout surges and declines, and national economic conditions have all affected the outcomes of state legislative races since 1940. Gubernatorial electoral outcomes were also significantly affected by the same set of external forces but to a lesser extent than were the outcomes of legislative races. Thus, national political and economic trends may indirectly affect state government through their impact on state elections.

Besides the electoral forces Chubb analyzed, other national political factors may affect the states. One such factor is the hierarchy of national offices that exists in the United States. As Schlesinger (1966, 1991) and Sabato (1983) have documented, there is a regular career progression from state legislative and other entry-level offices to the governorship to Washington-based positions such as senator, vice president, and president. Most people who achieve high office in Washington have "worked their way up" through this office hierarchy. Governors Jimmy Carter, Ronald Reagan, and Bill Clinton are three examples of this phenomenon. Since many politicians are ambitious people who want to top off their careers with service in Washington, they behave in response to their office goals, according to Schlesinger (1966). In other words, they take stands on issues with an eye on the next rung of their career ladder. The records of ambitious governors are scrutinized carefully by the voters; controversial decisions can come back to haunt them, as the Massachusetts governor Michael Dukakis found out in the presidential election of 1988. His prison furlough program seemed to attract more attention from the nation's voters than did his balancing of the state's budget. His rejection by the national electorate may lead other ambitious governors to avoid making tough decisions, even though making tough decisions is a daily requirement for governors.

Another nationalizing force is the power of the national Democratic and Republican parties. The two national parties have become more powerful relative to the one hundred state parties, as is shown in Chapter 3. They have adopted rule changes limiting the autonomy of state parties and forced them to comply. This change is particularly apparent in the selection of delegates to the national nominating conventions. In the past, state party leaders handpicked the delegates and functioned as power brokers at the national conventions. With the increased reliance on state primaries to select delegates, state party leaders no longer control the state's delegation. Because the presidential nomination is a natural focal point, its nationalization inevitably reduces the influence of state leaders. They no longer have political plums to distribute (that is, a trip to the national convention), and they can no longer collect a reward from the president whose nomination they delivered.

These are but a few of the ways in which national political trends may affect state politics. Together with the historical and contemporary political differences among states, they structure how states handle their problems. Fiscal resources offer only the opportunity to solve problems; political means must still be used to confront the problems. In the final section of this chapter, I examine these problems and discuss the capacity of states to face them.

STATES' ABILITY TO GOVERN

Today the fifty states face a number of serious concerns. One is the issue of growth and decline. Some states, primarily in the Sunbelt, struggle with the problems accompanying rapid population growth. Some states can't implement programs fast enough to cope with the influx of new residents. Other states are faced with the problem of decline in the economy and in the population, and they must adjust to a lower tax base and reduced public services. Both growth and decline require action from state government.

Another issue the states face is distribution and redistribution. All states have to distribute goods and services to their citizens. The mechanisms for doing this may differ in small, densely populated states from the arrangements used in large, sparsely populated states. The economies of scale are quite different in the two instances. All states also face the problem of redistribution; that is, they have to redirect resources from the rich to the poor. As discussed earlier, some states have demographic groups that require extra resources—the poor, minorities, and immigrants. Yet, the well-off in some states—moralistic ones, for example—seem more willing to support redistributive programs than the rich in other states. Too great an emphasis on redistribution may lead affluent citizens to relocate to states where the tax burden is lower. Thus, the balance between distribution and redistribution is tenuous in the face of interstate competitive pressures.

A third issue confronting the states is the growing diversity of the population. The United States has experienced a demographic revolution since the 1960s. The shift from European to primarily Asian and Latin American immigration, as well as different birth rates between whites and minorities, alters the composition of the population into the next century. The work force will be much more diverse, and the school-age population will be more heterogeneous. Meeting the needs of minorities will continue to challenge the school system and the welfare system, both of which are state responsibilities. Assimilating immigrants into communities and minimizing social conflicts will also be the province of state governments.

These broad issues, in turn, affect how states cope with their traditional responsibilities—education, welfare, hospitals, highways, corrections, and a myriad of smaller spending programs. As shown in Chapters 10 to 15, these responsibilities are the major objects of state expenditure. Population growth and decline certainly affect the cost of public services. The presence of refugees and other immigrants affects the provision of many services. The issues of distribution and redistribution come up in each policy area but loom especially large in welfare and regulation. Therefore, all traditional areas of state responsibility will undergo scrutiny as the economy and society change.

Fortunately, states seem to be ready to take on these challenges. They entered the decade of the 1990s in far better shape than in any previous decade. As documented in Chapters 5 to 8, the states have vastly improved their capacity for dealing with problems. In the legislative arena, increased staffing, longer sessions, better pay for members, new committee structures, and other changes allow a greater capacity for effective decision making than in the past. Similarly, state executive branches have undergone many dramatic changes during the past decade or two. Much of this reform has been directed toward enhancing the governor's authority and centralizing the executive functions within fewer agencies. The improvement in the capacity of executive and legislative branches to solve problems has been accompanied by an improvement in the caliber of people willing to serve in these institutions. Most observers agree that there is a "new breed" of legislators and governors. In addition, state judicial systems have been modernized and improved in the same time period. Thus, state governments now have the institutional capacity to address the challenges of the 1990s and beyond.

Improvement in the governance capability of states is good news, given the general concern about the "ungovernability" of advanced industrial societies. Much has been written in the past two decades about the impotence of national governments in the face of strong interests and under the pressure of fiscal crises. By taking a close look at smaller political systems like the American states, ones that have undeniably improved their institutional capacities, we may be able to find cause for optimism about governance in general.

REFERENCES

"After the Boom." 1987. *National Journal,* December 19, 3193–3198.
"As Florida Booms, Its Problems Explode." 1987. *Business Week,* April 20.
Barone, Michael, and Grant Ujifusa. 1993. *The Almanac of American Politics, 1994.* Washington, D.C.: National Journal.
Beemiller, Richard M., and Ann E. Dunbar. 1993. "Gross State Product 1977–1990." *Survey of Current Business* 73, no. 12:28–49.
Berry, Frances Stokes, and William D. Berry. 1990. "State Lottery Adoptions as Policy Innovations: An Event History Analysis." *American Political Science Review* 84:395–416.
Black, Earl, and Merle Black. 1987. *Politics and Society in the South.* Cambridge: Harvard University Press.
———. 1992. *The Vital South: How Presidents Are Elected.* Cambridge: Harvard University Press.
Brace, Paul. 1993. *State Government and Economic Performance.* Baltimore, Md.: Johns Hopkins University Press.
Brown, F. Lee, and Helen M. Ingram. 1987. *Water and Poverty in the Southwest.* Tucson: University of Arizona Press.
Cain, Bruce, and D. Roderick Kiewiet. 1984. "Ethnicity and Electoral Choice: Mexican American Voting Behavior in the California 30th Congressional District." *Social Science Quarterly* 65:315–332.
Chubb, John. 1988. "Institutions, the Economy, and the Dynamics of State Elections." *American Political Science Review* 82:133–154.
de la Garza, Rodolfo O., Louis DeSipio, F. Chris Garcia, John Garcia, and Angelo Falcon. 1992. *Latino Voices: Mexican, Puerto Rican, and Cuban Perspectives on American Politics.* Boulder, Colo.: Westview Press.
Dye, Thomas R. 1984. "Party and Policy in the States." *Journal of Politics* 46:1097–1116.
Elazar, Daniel J. 1984. *American Federalism: A View from the States.* 3d ed. New York: Harper and Row.

Erikson, Robert S., Gerald C. Wright, and John P. McIver. 1993. *Statehouse Democracy: Public Opinion and Policy in the American States.* Cambridge: Cambridge University Press.

Fenton, John H. 1966. *Midwest Politics.* New York: Holt, Rinehart and Winston.

Fitzpatrick, Jody L., and Rodney E. Hero. 1988. "Political Culture and Political Characteristics of the American States: A Consideration of Some Old and New Questions." *Western Political Quarterly* 41:145–153.

Gray, Virginia. 1973. "Innovation in the States: A Diffusion Study." *American Political Science Review* 67:1174–1193.

Gray, Virginia, and David Lowery. 1994. "Interest Representation and Democratic Gridlock." Paper presented at the annual meeting of the American Political Science Association, New York, September 1–4.

Gurwitt, Rob. 1992. "Back to the Melting Pot." *Governing,* June, 31–35.

Hanson, Russell L. 1992. "The Political Acculturation of Migrants in the American States." *Western Political Quarterly* 45:355–384.

Jackson, Gregory, George Masnick, Roger Bolton, Susan Bartlett, and John Pitkin. 1982. *Regional Diversity.* Boston: Auburn House.

Jewell, Malcolm. 1982. *Representation in State Legislatures.* Lexington: University Press of Kentucky.

Key, V. O., Jr. 1949. *Southern Politics in State and Nation.* New York: Random House.

Kirschten, Dick. 1994. "Immigration, and Rancor, Are Soaring." *National Journal,* June 18, 1416–1420.

"The Leader of the Pack on a Hot-Button Issue." 1994. *New York Times,* October 20, sec. A.

Nardulli, Peter F. 1990. "Political Subcultures in the American States." *American Politics Quarterly* 18:287–315.

Nardulli, Peter F., and Michael Krassa. 1989. "Regional Animosities in Illinois: Perceptual Dimensions." In *Diversity, Conflict, and State Politics,* edited by Peter F. Nardulli. Urbana: University of Illinois Press.

Peirce, Neal R., and Jerry Hagstrom. 1984. *The Book of America.* New York: Warner Books.

Peterson, Paul E., and Mark C. Rom. 1990. *Welfare Magnets.* Washington, D.C.: Brookings Institution.

"Playing Catch-Up." 1988. *National Journal,* March 19, 740–743.

Reimers, Cordelia. 1984. "The Wage Structure of Hispanic Men: Implications for Policy." *Social Science Quarterly* 65:401–416.

Sabato, Larry. 1983. *Goodbye to Good-time Charlie.* 2d ed. Washington, D.C.: CQ Press.

Sawers, Larry, and William K. Tabb, eds. 1984. *Sunbelt/Snowbelt.* New York: Oxford University Press.

"Say It in English." 1989. *Newsweek,* February 20, 22–23.

Schlesinger, Joseph A. 1966. *Ambition and Politics.* Chicago: Rand McNally.

———. 1991. *Political Parties and the Winning of Office.* Ann Arbor: University of Michigan Press.

Sylvester, Kathleen. 1992. "Retooling for Peace." *Governing,* July, 63–67.

Stein, Robert M. 1990. "Economic Voting for Governor and U.S. Senator: The Electoral Consequences of Federalism." *Journal of Politics* 52:29–53.

U.S. Bureau of the Census. 1992. *Poverty in the United States, 1991.* Washington, D.C.: U.S. Government Printing Office.

———. 1993. *Statistical Abstract of the United States, 1993.* Washington, D.C.: U.S. Government Printing Office.

Walker, Jack L., Jr. 1969. "The Diffusion of Innovations in the American States." *American Political Science Review* 63:880–899.

SUGGESTED READINGS

Blair, Diane D. *Arkansas Politics and Government.* Lincoln: University of Nebraska Press, 1988. One of the best in a distinguished series on the fifty states.

Brace, Paul. *State Government and Economic Performance.* Baltimore, Md.: Johns Hopkins University Press, 1993. Treats the economic fortunes of the states in historical and comparative perspective.

Elazar, Daniel J. *American Federalism: A View from the States.* 3d ed. New York: Harper and Row,

1984. An analysis of nation-state relations in the United States, stressing the political role of the states in our federal system. Describes and applies Elazar's theory of political culture.

Erikson, Robert S., Gerald C. Wright, and John P. McIver. *Statehouse Democracy: Public Opinion and Policy in the American States.* Cambridge: Cambridge University Press, 1993. A sophisticated study of public opinion in the states and its effect on public policy.

U.S. Bureau of the Census. *Statistical Abstract of the United States, 1993.* Washington, D.C.: U.S. Government Printing Office, 1994. The official source of statistics on many aspects of state demography, economy, and policy.

CHAPTER 2

Intergovernmental Relations

RUSSELL L. HANSON

Many American political scientists view national, state, and local politics as distinct fields of inquiry. They proceed as if government at one level can be studied in virtual isolation from other levels of American government. Thus scholars write books and teach courses on national *or* state *or* local government without dwelling on relations between the different levels. Such specialization may be a sign of intellectual development in other disciplines, but in political science it ignores an important fact: American governments are thoroughly interdependent and they are becoming more so with the passage of time. Already a vast array of public goods and services is made available by national, state, and local governments working as partners. Undoubtedly the same method will be used in future domestic undertakings, including health insurance reform (which failed to pass Congress in 1994 in part because the administration of President Bill Clinton pursued an alternative mode of organization—health alliances—that was unfamiliar and, as it turned out, highly unpopular).

American governments are well aware of their interdependence. Most state governments have special agencies for managing relations with other levels of government. Cities, too, employ people who are responsible for coordinating action with state and national officials. At the national level, various subcommittees in Congress focus on intergovernmental relations, and the U.S. Advisory Commission on Intergovernmental Relations, formed in 1959, monitors the "galloping intergovernmentalization" of American politics and the problems it presents (Reeves 1981).

The prevalence of intergovernmental relations is important, but so is their evolving form. In the past two decades relations between levels of government have been transformed dramatically. The national government is no longer the senior member of the partnership, as it was during the 1960s and early 1970s, when Congress led the way in domestic policy making. Now Congress is more conservative, and if the Republican "Contract with America" is enacted, even if not in full, the domestic activities of the national government will be curtailed sharply. Initiative will then shift to the states in such important policy areas as environmental regulation, economic development, welfare, and the provision of affordable health care.

Reinforcing this tendency is the increasing dependence of local governments on their respective state governments. Local governments are suffering the effects of massive economic dislocation caused by the decline of manufacturing and the rise of service industries. In some cities the loss of jobs and people makes it impossible to raise sufficient local revenue to provide goods and services to the residents who are left behind, particularly since they often form a needy population. The new boom towns face difficult problems, too; the demand for new schools, streets, and expanded public services overwhelms the resources of local governments. Since the national government is less susceptible to pleas for urban assistance, local governments are turning to the states for help, and finding it.

Thus, higher and lower levels of government are looking to the states for solutions to important problems. Long-established patterns of political responsibility and accountability are being altered, and if these trends continue we will witness a new chapter in American political history, one in which the states assume the leading role in domestic policy making. This resurgence of the states, as Bowman and Kearney (1986) describe it, is the leitmotif of this chapter, in which I examine the development of American intergovernmental relations. A brief outline of the overall structure of intergovernmental relations in the United States will highlight the expanding role of state governments in our political system.

THE VARIETY OF INTERGOVERNMENTAL RELATIONS

The U.S. Constitution and the fifty state constitutions define our system of intergovernmental relations. The U.S. Constitution specifies a general relationship between the national and state governments, provides the basic guidelines within which interstate relations occur, and establishes the fundamental liberties of all American citizens. State constitutions determine the relationship between state and local units of government and identify the rights, privileges, and obligations of people who live under their jurisdiction. Together, these basic arrangements *constitute* the role of governments in our political system and define the field of intergovernmental relations.

Federalism is only one, albeit a very important, sector of intergovernmental relations in the United States. *Federalism* refers to the division of power between the national government—that is, the federal government in Washington, D.C.—and the governments of the fifty states. In a federal system, both national and state governments have substantial or in some cases complete authority to make important policy decisions. In certain areas—for example, foreign policy—the national government predominates. In other areas—for example, education—state governments have more power (except when civil rights are at risk). But in the vast majority of cases involving domestic policy, both governments have the constitutional authority to act, and they vie with one another to control policy. Thus, intergovernmental relations in the federal sector may be seen as a competition between governments seeking to expand their domains of influence, in a context where neither is likely to prevail completely or in all areas of policy.

Relations between states are not federal. They are confederal, to use an older terminology that is still useful in conveying the importance of sovereignty in this sector of interactions. As sovereign entities, states are on equal footing; none has constitutional powers larger than those of any other state in the Union. There are differences in political power and influence, to be sure, but the symmetry of constitutional authority means that state governments must negotiate their differences, just as sovereign nations do. Therefore, intergovernmental relations in this sector proceed diplomatically, with the important difference that military options are not available to any of the parties. Also, some disputes between state governments may be decided by agencies of the national government, a situation that differs from world affairs, where no supreme authority exists (although the United Nations or World Court tries to fill this role with varying degrees of success).

Relations between state governments and their local units of government are unitary. Localities do not enjoy sovereignty; they are creations of state government. This sector of intergovernmental relations is one in which the asymmetry of power is incontestable, although it is seldom displayed openly. Rather, it forms the background for political relations that are not one-sided and that therefore dampen the effects of unitary rule. The states vary tremendously in their treatment of local units of government, and so this sector of intergovernmental relations is further characterized by great diversity.

In each of these three sectors, state governments play an important role, although their role differs from sector to sector. States also mediate the relation between national and local governments, carrying the goals and concerns of one to the other, while adding the preferences and resources of state governments to the mix. Similarly, states regulate interactions between local governments, arbitrating conflicts and creating regional agencies for coordinating the actions of neighboring localities. Thus, state governments are at the center of an elaborate web of intergovernmental relations; they transmit disturbances from one sector of the web to others, sometimes magnifying shocks, and sometimes dampening them, in a manner that will become more apparent as each of the different sectors of intergovernmental relations is discussed in more detail.

CONFEDERALISM

It is appropriate to begin with an examination of relations between states, since federalism in the United States was itself a product of dissatisfaction with the Articles of Confederation (1781–1788). Under the articles each of the thirteen former colonies of Great Britain retained full sovereignty. The confederal Congress was an assembly of states that formed an alliance to address problems of mutual concern (chiefly their common defense). Yet the states were unwilling to cede power to this Congress to address these problems. Congress could neither levy taxes nor conscript citizens directly; it could only request assistance from state governments—and then only if an extraordinary or super majority of states agreed that such a request should be made. Individual states could and did refuse with impunity to honor these requests, just as nations in our time withhold money or troops from peace-keeping ventures of a modern confederacy, the United Nations.

Dissatisfaction with the Articles of Confederation led the Federalists to propose the establishment of a more energetic central government. Their Constitution, which was ratified in 1788, created a national government with powers of its own—powers that once belonged exclusively to state governments. The proud sovereignty of the states was thereby undermined; the residual "states' rights" bore little resemblance to the full autonomy enjoyed by states under the Articles of Confederation.

The loss of autonomy was probably greatest in the area of economic regulation, which had been left to the states in the Confederation. However, Article I, section 10, of the Constitution enjoins states from passing laws that interfere with contractual obligations. Equally important is the ban on taxing imports and exports as a way of raising revenues for use by state governments. States may not coin money or issue credit; these powers belong only to the national government. Nor may states establish religion, limit expression, or otherwise infringe on liberties protected under the Bill of Rights.

States are also forbidden from entering into treaties, alliances, or confederations with other nations, although international agreements occasionally allow for the involvement of officials in states most affected by them. For example, in 1909 the United States and Canada established the International Joint Commission for managing the Great Lakes and resolving questions about water levels, quality, and use as well as boundary disputes. The members of the commission are appointed by the two national governments, but the commission is served by several boards and councils, which advise it on specific policy matters. One of these is the Great Lakes Water Quality Board, which typically includes environmental policy makers from the affected states. Thus, states influence the conduct of organizations established by treaties, even though they are not parties to the original agreement.

Treaty-making powers belong to the national government, but state actions may nullify or weaken them. For example, states and localities have passed a significant amount of protectionist legislation to stem the flow of imported goods and services, and this has caused problems for a national government seeking fair trade on an international scale. Thus, in the Uruguay Round of talks on the General Agreement on Tariffs and Trade the European Community pressed the United States government to eliminate "buy American" requirements in forty states and to lower other trade barriers erected in 2,700 states and municipalities (Weiler 1994). No doubt the North American Free Trade Agreement will bring similar requests from Mexico and Canada, over the objection of state and local officials. These officials have influence in Congress, which must approve such agreements and legislation needed to implement them.

States act like sovereigns in other ways, too. With the emergence of a well-integrated global economy, every state now devotes considerable attention to foreign trade. Most state governments have offices in Japan, and states on both coasts cultivate relations with their principal overseas trading partners. Team Washington, for instance, was created by the state of Washington in 1985 to promote export industries and stimulate investment by Asian businesses. The organization promotes exports from the states by exploring overseas markets, providing information and technical assistance to exporting firms, and even financing their activities. Foreign investors are wooed by trade missions from many states, the prospect of joint ventures with domestic firms, and investment assistance and incentives (Clarke 1986). Thirty states conduct similar activities in Europe, building ties to the European Union and its members (Levine 1994).

Just as states interact extensively with foreign countries, they develop relations with other state governments. Some of these interactions are expressed in formal compacts, wherein states agree to joint action on common problems. Other, less formal, transactions have become frequent and thoroughly routine—a distinct departure from earlier times, when encounters were more sporadic. Finally, a growing network of professional associations now links state officials together in a web of information exchange, policy promulgation, and political lobbying. As a result, the structure of intergovernmental relations in the United States has developed a horizontal dimension, in addition to its traditional vertical, or hierarchical, dimension.

The legal framework within which these transactions occur is established in the Constitution. While Article IV ostensibly refers to interstate relations, its specific provisions deal with the relationship between a citizen of one state and the government of another: "Full Faith and Credit shall be given in each state to the public Acts, Records, and judicial Proceedings of every other State." Therefore, birth certificates, marriage licenses, divorce settlements, and the like are legal in all states, regardless of where they were originally executed. Citizens of each state are also entitled to the "Privileges and Immunities" of all citizens of the nation, a guarantee strengthened by the Fourteenth Amendment.

The most important provisions governing relations between the states themselves are found in Article III, which stipulates that legal controversies between states shall be resolved by the Supreme Court. An interesting case of this nature was settled in 1985, when the Supreme Court resolved a dispute between Kentucky and Indiana over the location of their boundary. The Court placed the boundary near the northern shore of the Ohio River in *Kentucky v. Indiana* (474 U.S. 1). That decision is the basis of Kentucky's current efforts to prevent riverboat gambling, which the Indiana General Assembly authorized in 1993. The new legislation permits gambling on the Ohio River, but not when floating casinos are moored; the vessels must be under way for gambling to be legal. Large riverboats, however, cannot get under way without crossing into Kentucky, and the attorney general from the Bluegrass State has said he will enforce Kentucky laws against casino gambling, which threatens his state's lucrative horse-racing industry and the betting that surrounds it. The Supreme Court may be asked to resolve this difference between the two states.

Increasingly, states are resorting to political means of settling persistent disagreements, such as interstate compacts. The power to form compacts is implied in Article I, section 10, which requires that such treaties between states must be approved by Congress. Before 1920, only three dozen compacts were signed by states. Since then, more than 150 compacts have been established—100 of them since World War II. These compacts cover boundaries, conservation, navigation on interstate waterways, law enforcement, metropolitan development across state lines, pollution, transportation, energy, and natural resources. They may be concluded between two, several, or all fifty states, depending on the problem or policy area involved (CSG 1977). Bilateral compacts are the most common, of course, but regional and national compacts have become increasingly important as states begin to cooperate on problems of mutual concern, such as economic development.

The significance of compacts lies in their provision of formal mechanisms for problem solving among the states without a substantial amount of involvement on the part of the national government. To be sure, some compacts incorporate agencies of the national government as parties to the agreement. Still, the interstate compact has become an important way of preempting (or at least limiting) national intervention in state affairs. For that reason such compacts represent what Elazar (1984) calls "federalism without Washington." The Delaware River Compact and the Colorado River Compact are two instances in which states make regional allocations of water without resorting to Congress. In fact, the upper-basin states in the Colorado River agreement have their own compact within a compact to allocate water from the Colorado River among themselves (Lord and Kenney 1993).

Interstate compacts allow states to oppose the national government, not simply preempt its involvement in activities traditionally left to state and local discretion. For example, at the suggestion of Congress, four areas of the country entered into compacts governing the disposal of hazardous waste and radioactive materials (Feigenbaum 1988). In so doing they took the lead in setting policy in this area, to the point of enforcing their standards on the national government. The governors of Colorado and New Mexico threatened to follow the example of Cecil D. Andrus, the former governor of Idaho, who in 1988 stopped accepting radioactive materials generated by plants that manufactured nuclear weapons for the national government. The governors wanted the national government to meet their conditions for disposing of waste in a safe, environmentally sound manner, and the Department of Energy agreed to accommodate their demands (Wald 1988).

Compacts are not the only means of ensuring interstate cooperation. Many states have reciprocal ties with neighboring states. Within the area of higher education, for example, neighbors may offer the equivalent of in-state tuition to residents of adjacent states in exchange for similar treatment of their own citizens. These and other ad hoc routines make up an important part of interstate relations, although they lack the formality of compacts.

Then there are the national associations of governors, lieutenant governors, attorneys general, and other state officials, which exchange information and policy recommendations on matters relevant to state government (Freeman 1985). These associations, as well as professional organizations that link administrators and policy specialists, provide a well-developed communications network among the states, alerting them to emerging problems and, above all, to alterations in the ties that bind state agencies to bureaus at the national level.

Organizations of subnational officials act as interest groups at the national level, trying to influence the legislature and administration on behalf of state and local interests (Haider 1974). Public interest groups—for example, the National Governors' Association, National Conference of State Legislatures, National League of Cities, U.S. Conference of Mayors, and National Association of Counties—now make up a formidable lobby in national politics. The success of this lobby contributed heavily to the growth of social welfare spending in the United States, which now taxes the revenue-raising capacity of the national government, as one prominent scholar noted in the late 1970s (Beer 1978). This outcome was anticipated by James Madison, who wrote in *The Federalist Papers* (No. 46) that the sentiments or "prepossessions, which the members [of Congress] themselves will carry into the federal government will generally be favorable to the States" (Madison, Hamilton, and Jay 1987).

Indeed, Madison feared that members of Congress would be too attached to local interests, causing them to sacrifice national interests to parochial concerns. Hence the Federalists' desire to insulate the central government from states, so that public-spirited leaders would have the freedom to pursue policies in the national interest (Hanson 1988). Their constitutional design was successful; the sovereignty of states declined as the strength of the national government increased over time. A very different federal relation emerged, one that seems to confirm the original suspicions of Antifederalists about the consolidating, or centralizing, tendency of the Constitution. This is the subject of the next section, in which I discuss the undeniable political strength of states in Congress matched against their diminished constitutional status in the courts, in a contemporary version of the Federalist-Antifederalist debate over the vitality of federalism.

FEDERALISM

Federalism is a form of government in which a national government and one or more subnational levels of government enjoy substantial policy-making powers, often in the same areas. In the United States, the formal allocation of power between state and national governments may be summarized as follows. In the first place, the Constitution defines powers that are denied to one or both levels of government. Powers denied to state governments have already been mentioned, but certain powers are also specifically denied to the national government; it may not, for example, alter state boundaries or governments. Neither government may grant titles of nobility, pass bills of attainder, establish religion, abridge free expression, violate due process, or infringe on other liberties protected in the Constitution and the Bill of Rights. These represent the limits on what may be done by government in our society; they are why we have a "limited government."

The Constitution not only limits power; it also distributes powers granted by the people to various levels of government. Some of these powers—for example, the power to conduct foreign relations or the power to provide for the common defense—are given exclusively to the national government. Others—for example, the power to conduct elections—are given to the states, which must respect the nationally recognized rights of citizens when exercising this authority. Still other, unspecified powers are reserved to the states and the people under the Tenth Amendment; they may include the power to create and destroy local governments (although Supreme Court interpretations between 1985 and 1994 cast doubt on the meaning of the amendment). Then there are powers concurrently exercised by national and state governments, including the authority to tax and borrow money, make and enforce laws, and so forth. Within this group of concurrent powers there are some—for example, the power of amendment—that must be exercised jointly for action to occur.

A schematic representation of this distribution of authority at the time of ratification is shown on the left-hand side of Figure 2-1. The largest circle represents the power of the people, some of which was delegated to the national and state governments under a federal arrangement. As shown here, a broad area of power was reserved to the people, reflecting the founders' restrictive view of the limits on government proper to their day and age. The overlap between the national and state circles of power symbolizes the range of concurrent powers just mentioned. State powers were large under this schema, again manifesting the founders' belief in an expansive role for state governments in a federal arrangement. This role included complete constitutional authority over local govern-

Figure 2-1   The Distribution of Constitutional Authority in the United States

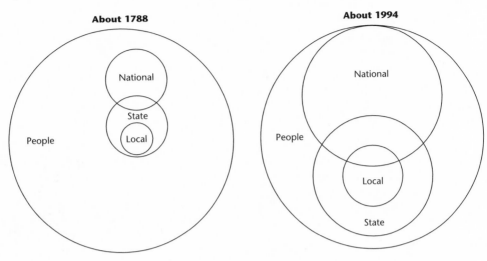

ments, which stand in a unitary, rather than federal, relationship to their state governments.

Federalism is not static. It is dynamic, and the boundaries on national and state powers shift as the different governments, driven by the factional energies of the compound republic, strive to expand their influence. As Alexander Hamilton observed in *Federalist* No. 28:

> Power being almost always the rival of power, the general government will at all times stand ready to check the usurpations of the state governments, and these will have the same disposition towards the general government. The people, by throwing themselves into either scale, will infallibly make it preponderate. If their rights are invaded by either, they can make use of the other as the instrument of redress. How wise will it be in them by cherishing the union to preserve to themselves an advantage which can never be too highly prized! (Madison, Hamilton, and Jay 1987)

Hamilton assumed that the overall balance of power between national and state governments would be fairly stable. But most contemporary observers probably would agree that the fears of the Antifederalists have been realized; over the long run the powers of the national government have increased, as is suggested in the right-hand side of Figure 2-1. To a significant extent this is the cumulative result of Supreme Court interpretations of the Constitution. As the umpire of the federal system, the Court has claimed the power of judicial review over state actions; increased the power of Congress to regulate interstate transactions, particularly those related to commerce; and enlarged executive powers it deemed necessary to the fulfillment of the Constitution. It has even allowed some degree of national control over local affairs, especially in matters pertaining to civil rights, but also in regard to public employment. At the same time the Court has been quite reluctant to interpret other clauses of the Constitution, including the reserved powers clause of the Tenth Amendment, in ways that could augment the constitutional position of states in relation to the national government.

Federal power developed over a long period of time, and the Supreme Court has not been the only agent of change. Congress, too, played a role in this process, by enacting legislation that gave rise to judicial challenges to national authority in the first place. The executive, or rather certain executives, tested the limits of federalism, pushing them back from time to time. Finally, the people themselves bestowed new authority on the national government by enacting amendments to the Constitution, including the power to tax income (which has made it possible for the national government to fund a broad array of new activities, including entitlement programs).

It would be incorrect to see this shift simply as an invasion of the prerogatives of the states, for three reasons. In the first place, these "intrusions" represent actions by the national government in response to political pressures generated by the people, who live in the states themselves, and who have sometimes been frustrated by the inability or unwillingness of state governments to satisfy their demands. In a democracy, governments act at the behest of or with the acquiescence of the people, or at least a majority of them. Although government agencies can be remarkably self-sustaining or even expansionary, they must first be set in motion by a legislature responding to popular demands. Hence national intrusions are at some level popularly inspired.

Moreover, these intrusions often assume the form of national incentives for particular state actions or forbearances, rather than a simple coercion of state governments by national authorities. The national government mandates compliance with some of its objectives, but more often it relies on inducements to action. These inducements or incentives generally take the form of financial assistance that is made available to governments willing to pursue national goals. These programs are voluntary, but in virtually all cases the amount of assistance is attractive enough to bring about state and local participation—under the supervision of national agencies, and subject to national guidelines, of course. Yet this way of proceeding is manifestly less authoritarian than is acknowledged by superficial arguments about the decline of states' rights in the United States.

Finally, the use of incentives to bring about compliance by states with national objectives has generated a concomitant expansion of state powers, so that the real intrusions (if that is what they are) have been against powers previously reserved to the people. All levels of government have become more active in the twentieth century, not just the national government. State and local governments together employ more than 80 percent of all civilian government workers. That share increased steadily during the 1970s, 1980s, and 1990s, when national employment hovered around 3 million civilians. By 1991, state employment had risen to about 4.5 million, and local employment to 11 million workers. State and

Figure 2-2   Velocity of Federal, State, and Local Governments, 1927–1992

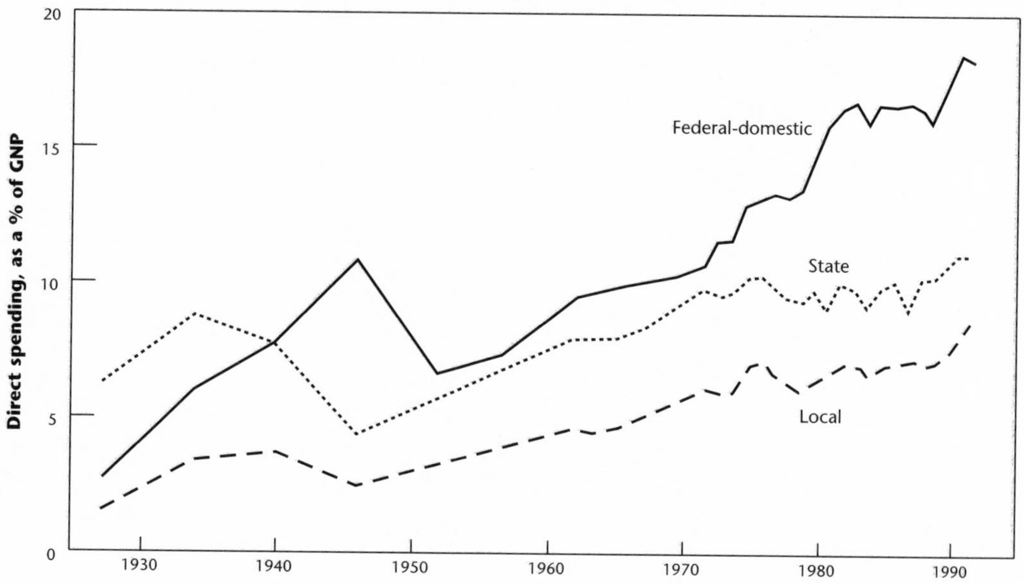

SOURCE: Calculated from U.S. Advisory Commission 1993a, tables A and 20; U.S. Bureau of the Census 1994b.

local governments are therefore part of the "big government" we now have; in fact they are the largest part of that government.

This phenomenal growth of domestic government in the United States has not been smooth. It has occurred in bursts of expansion, followed by more conservative eras of policy making. This cycle tends to reflect the rising and falling influence of liberal political forces over national institutions (Nathan, Doolittle, and Associates 1987). Different phases of federalism may therefore be discerned, each characterized by distinctive relations between state and national governments, as shown in the following discussion.

Phases of Federalism

The increasing activity, or velocity, of the national government—its expansion of power—is partially reflected in patterns of government spending. By examining the expenditure of different levels of government, we can compare the changes in the relative velocity of each and the combined velocity of all. In Figure 2-2, I show how spending by national, state, and local governments has changed in selected years since 1927. (To facilitate comparisons with state and local spending, only spending on domestic programs by the national government is shown; it is calculated by subtracting outlays for defense from total national expenditure.)

The velocity of national government has increased substantially in this century. Just before the Great Depression, direct spending by local governments was about 2 percent of the gross national product (GNP). This was only a little less than the national government spent on domestic matters. States played a much larger role, spending twice as much as the national government and three times as much as local governments. Clearly, domestic policy making was dominated by states before the New Deal.

The minuscule involvement of the national government in domestic affairs reflected more than a century of *dual federalism* (Corwin 1934). According to this doctrine federalism entailed a sharp division of responsibilities, some of which were assigned to the national government and some of which were reserved to the states. For the most part, national responsibilities centered on defense and foreign policy, regulation of currency, and, to a much lesser extent, interstate trade. Property laws, civil rights, and the provision of basic services were under the purview of state governments, and through them, local communities. The two spheres of responsibility were considered more or less distinct, and conflicts between governments over the right to make policy in specific cases were generally decided in favor of one or the other by the Supreme Court. Seldom did the Court recognize joint responsibilities; it preferred a system of constitutionally segregated responsibilities, which scholars have likened to a layer cake.

Not surprisingly, the doctrine of dual federalism retarded the activity of the national government in domestic affairs, with several notable exceptions—for example, the Civil War, the disposition of western lands, and the trustbusting of the Progressive era. During the Great Depression, however, the velocity of national government accelerated rapidly; as a proportion of the GNP, direct national spending on the home front tripled by the onset of World War II. This was a period in which the foundations of the American welfare state were laid. Social security, unemployment insurance, and public assistance were all established at this time. Massive public works projects were also undertaken at the behest of President Franklin D. Roosevelt and the New Dealers. The national government subsidized the construction of roads, dams, public buildings, and other such projects undertaken by state and local governments, and it initiated wholly national programs, for example, the Works Progress Administration. The subsequent mixing of powers and resources in programs for maintaining incomes and stimulating growth has been described as "marble cake federalism," to distinguish it from its layer-cake predecessor (Grodzins 1966).

The federal partnership continued after World War II as veterans' benefits were added to income security programs and new public works, such as the interstate highway system, were constructed. The expansion of activities funded by the national government accelerated in the 1960s during the War on Poverty, a period of "Creative Federalism." The velocity of all governments rose steadily in this period, as is evident in Figure 2-2. Beginning in 1975, though, the national government began to outpace state and local governments. Even the presidency of Ronald Reagan brought a burst of speed unmatched by any corresponding increase in the velocity of state and local governments. This was followed by still another sharp upturn in 1990, when the so-called peace dividend swelled the domestic side of the national budget and financed new programs in health, education, and the conversion of defense industries. While the economy stagnated, federal spending increased significantly, leaving a sizable gap between the level of its activity and that of state and local governments.

How has the increased velocity of national government affected the velocity of state and local governments? Has it come at their expense, as some argue? Or has it stimulated them to become more active themselves, leading to an even larger public sector?

It can be seen in Figure 2-2 that the velocity of state government increased during the 1930s, as states joined the efforts of the national government to combat the Depression. State activities also expanded during the War on Poverty in the 1960s. By the mid-1970s state spending as a proportion of the GNP stabilized at about 8 or 9 percent. In the early 1990s it grew to about 11 percent. During the same period, local spending grew slowly and now represents about 8 percent of the GNP. Altogether, national domestic, state, and local spending consumed about 35 percent of the GNP in 1992, a considerably smaller portion than most countries in western Europe spend on domestic affairs.

If spending is a measure of energy, the national government has overtaken and surpassed state and local governments. In fact, the true velocity of national government is understated in Figure 2-2, insofar as it does not take intergovernmental transfers or grants-in-aid into account (Bahl 1984; Break 1980). In fiscal year 1993 the direct domestic expenditure of the national government amounted to $1.5 trillion; in addition, the national government gave more than $200 billion in financial assistance to state and local governments (a sum equal to two-thirds of the national government's deficit in that year). State governments passed a good portion of the funds to local governments and added an even larger sum of their own monies to this subsidy. Without this twin subsidy, direct spending by local governments would have been much less, and the difference in the velocities of national and local governments would have been greater than is indicated in Figure 2-2.

Because a sizable portion of national domestic spending is actually a transfer to state and local governments, increases in the velocity of national government tend to bring about increases in the velocity of subnational political units. The author of one study (Chubb 1985) concluded that federal aid has been a leading cause of the growth of state bureaucracy. Similarly, state aid, some of which consists of national monies being passed on, has stimulated increases in employment by local governments. In short, the increasing activity of the national government has made subnational governments more energetic, stimulating them to expand their own efforts, albeit under national supervision. As Gov. Richard A. Snelling of Vermont bitterly complained, "things have changed enormously in the last 20 years. Now, four out of ten state and local employees are actually federal employees in disguise, marching like a secret army to the guidelines and regulations of Washington" (Snelling 1980, 168).

Even this remark suggests that the growth of the national government has not occurred entirely at the expense of state and local governments. By Governor Snelling's own count, six of ten state and local workers remain loyal to the states and local communities that employ them, and many of them are new workers! In several policy areas, the power and authority of state and local government have been enhanced by national funds that enable them to meet the increasing demands of citizens for public goods and services. In demanding more from government, citizens have been willing to cede the authority needed to satisfy their desires—or so Alexander Hamilton and James Madison argued two hundred years ago in defending the creation of an energetic central government where none previously existed. If any powers have been diminished in this process, they are powers once reserved to the people, not the states, which had generally avoided action in civil rights, comprehensive income security, and the like.

Not everyone believes that an expanded authority to make domestic policy ought to be exercised primarily by the national government, however. Certainly, there are areas of public policy in which subnational governments have been displaced by national policy makers, civil rights being a prime example. This displacement has fueled popular resentment of the intrusiveness of "big government," expressed so well by Ronald Reagan, who in 1980 launched his successful presidential campaign in Philadelphia, Mississippi, with a speech that celebrated states' rights. According to Reagan, the imposition of mandates by the national government is often an unwarranted intrusion in state and local affairs. Worse, it is an encroachment on powers protected by the Tenth Amendment, which stipulates that "[t]he powers not delegated to the United States by the Constitution, nor prohibited by it to the States, are reserved to the States respectively, or to the people."

Of course, it is often difficult to know when mandates derive from powers usurped by Congress or the executive, or when they rest on firm constitutional ground. The Supreme Court decides these matters; during the twentieth century, at least, it has allowed the national government great leeway in levying mandates. Successively broader interpretations of the commerce clause of the Constitution have permitted Congress to regulate economic affairs quite generally, even when tangentially related to interstate commerce.

In 1976, however, the Court seemed to retreat from its permissive interpretation of the commerce clause. Prior to 1974, most employees of state and local governments were not protected by minimum wage and overtime provisions of the National Fair Labor Standards Act. During that year Congress amended the act to include these employees, a move that was resisted by state and local governments, which had to pay the costs associated with this mandate. The new legislation was subsequently challenged on the grounds that it infringed on powers reserved under the Tenth Amendment. In *National League of Cities v. Usery* (426 U.S. 833 [1976]) the Supreme Court ruled in favor of this challenge, holding that Congress did not have the authority to impose this requirement on state and local governments whose employees were carrying out "traditional governmental functions," such as fire and police protection, sanitation, public health administration, and the administration of parks and recreation.

The issue was not settled, though. In later decisions the Court decided that "traditional government functions" included licensing automobile drivers, operating a highway authority, and operating a municipal airport—but not the regulation of traffic on public roads or the regulation of air transportation. The difficulty of establishing a reasonable constitutional test for deciding which activities were traditional, and which were not, eventually led Justice Harry Blackmun to a change of heart. Blackmun, who had voted with the majority on *National League of Cities,* joined four others in overturning that decision in 1985. In *Garcia v. San Antonio Metropolitan Transit Authority* (105 S.Ct. 1005, 1011 [1985]) the Court held that Joe Garcia, an employee of the transit authority, was entitled to overtime pay under the National Fair Labor Standards Act, and it rejected as unsound in principle and unworkable in practice a rule protecting "traditional governmental functions" from congressional regulation.

This decision was reaffirmed and broadened in 1988, when the Court decided in *South Carolina v. Baker* (485 U.S. 505 [1988]) that Congress was entitled to tax the interest on bonds sold by state and local governments. As in *Garcia* the justices in the majority refused to offer judicial protection for state and local activities over which Congress sought influence. As Justice Brennan observed in *Baker* (485 U.S. 512 [1988]), "The states must find their protection from congressional regulation through the national political process, not through judicially defined spheres of unregulable state activity." Only by exerting power and influence over representatives in Congress could state and local officials legitimately limit the imposition of mandates.

For some, the Court's position spelled the end of federalism. According to Hawkins (1988, 74), "No activity of state and local governments is now beyond the scope of congressional regulation, and indeed, takeover—not criminal justice, not corporation chartering, not taxing authority, not banking and insurance regulation, not even political subdivision." This was in fact the greatest fear of the Antifederalists in 1787–1788, when they opposed ratification of the Constitution because they suspected its "consolidating" tendencies would ultimately diminish or even destroy the authority of state governments (Hanson 1988).

The Supreme Court's position is evolving, though. In *U.S. v. Lopez* (63 L.W. 4343 [1995]) a deeply divided Court invalidated a federal statute prohibiting the possession of firearms in school zones. Siding with the majority, Justices Anthony M. Kennedy and Sandra Day O'Connor wrote: "The Statute now before us forecloses the States from experimenting and exercising their own judgment in an area to which States lay claim by right of history and expertise, and it does so by regulating an activity beyond the realm of commerce in the ordinary and usual sense of that term" (63 L.W. 4353).

Four justices dissented strongly, accusing their conservative brethren of ignoring precedent and disturbing a settled area of constitutional law. Outside observers wonder if the *Lopez* decision signals the Court's desire to restrict Congress by narrowly interpreting the commerce clause and reviving the Tenth Amendment. Chief Justice Rehnquist, writing for the majority, conceded that Congress's authority under the commerce clause was broad, although it "does not include the authority to regulate each and every aspect of local schools" (63 L.W. 4348). In other words, the power of Congress is limited, but the limits may not be terribly confining, since the power is still "broad."

It may not matter where the Court decides to draw the line on congressional power. Republicans in control of Congress want to reduce the role of national government in domestic affairs. They are not inclined to use the commerce clause as aggressively as Democratically controlled Congresses did. Ironically, this shows that state and local governments can protect themselves by political means. Some who doubt their ability to mount such a defense over the long run have suggested amendments to the Constitution as a way of guarding against national encroachments on state power (Hunter and Oakerson 1986). Others argue that the states are now much stronger than they have been in the past years (U.S. Advisory Commission 1987). They point to the transformation of fiscal federalism during the last fifteen years as confirmation of the capacity of states and localities to win redress for their grievances through the political process itself. An extended discussion of these changes in intergovernmental relations is therefore in order, to illuminate the ability of states to defend their interests in Congress, if not before the Supreme Court.

Fiscal Federalism

Although officials of state and local government do not welcome mandates from the national government, they are not reluctant to accept grants-in-aid, even when such grants come with strings attached. These grants allow officials to do more for their constituents without raising state and local taxes, or at least without raising taxes in proportion to spending increases. The political advantages of this financing arrangement undoubtedly explain the enthusiasm with which subnational policy makers have lobbied for the creation of new grants-in-aid and the expansion of programs already in existence.

Consequently, financial grants-in-aid are the chief incentives by which national policy makers induce state governments to enact programs and policies intended to serve national objectives. An extraordinary amount of money has been used to subsidize these activities, and a large number of scholars have attempted to analyze "the politics of federal grants" (Brown 1984; Hale and Palley

1981). The political origins of grants, the different forms they assume, and the bureaucratic linkages they bring into existence are best described by Anton (1989), who views grants as the product of "vertical coalitions."

These coalitions consist of widely dispersed individuals and groups who are unable to influence policy makers at the local or state level. Individually, they are too weak to challenge the power of the horizontal coalitions, which dominate politics in their community and state. By forming alliances with other, similarly situated, groups across the country, however, they may be strong enough to gain a favorable hearing at the national level. To national policy makers, weak local coalitions seem powerful because they are acting in unison. Moreover, by attending to the needs of such vertical coalitions, national policy makers gain important political advantages:

> Legislators can appear to be responsive to societal needs and at the same time take credit for new program dollars that flow into their districts. Administrators can also appear to be responsive while simultaneously expanding budget and staff to deliver the new benefits. Lower-level officials who receive the benefits have new resources to be devoted in various ways to the problem or problems that originally motivated their search for assistance. When vertical coalitions are successful, in short, everyone benefits. (Anton 1988, 85)

Grant programs are particularly well suited to the demands of vertical coalitions. Serious political differences can be sublimated under general, unobjectionable statements about policy goals, while many of the important details of program design and implementation are left to the discretion of state and local policy makers. This placates members of horizontal coalitions who initially resisted action on problems of interest to weak actors on the local level. Grants are also highly resistant to attack; clients who receive services, government employees who provide them, administrators who oversee them, and politicians who claim credit for these programs regularly and effectively lobby to continue grants. Even in the face of rising deficits, created in part by the successes of many vertical coalitions, Congress and the president have been reluctant to eliminate grant programs.

More often, Congress has been persuaded to reduce the requirements that must be met in order for states and localities to qualify for grants-in-aid. Aid programs typically originate as categorical project grants closely controlled by the national government. *Categorical grants* may be used only for narrow purposes approved by Congress. *Project grants* are awarded on a more or less competitive basis to governmental units that have submitted proposals for review and funding to an agency of the national government. A categorical project grant, then, allows the national government to determine which governments will receive money, and for which purposes; that is, it enables it to control the aid.

Categorical grants also stimulate the development of bureaucratic alliances that span levels of government. An administrative subsystem forms around each grant program, as program specialists and professionals from different levels of government develop routines and forms of interaction that may be exceedingly difficult to comprehend or influence, even for politicians who created the programs in the first place. This produces considerable fragmentation of policy at the national level, since programs are both isolated and insulated from each other by the existence of distinct bureaucratic subsystems (Sundquist 1969). At state and local levels, it causes great consternation among elected officials, who desire control over local administrators. These political officeholders often discover that personnel in local agencies are strongly oriented toward patron agencies at the national level and either cannot or will not respond adequately to the preferences of subnational policy makers (Howitt 1984).

This development has been called *picket fence federalism* because of the narrow ties that run between higher and lower levels of government, the verticle pieces in the fence (Wright 1988). State and local officials and their allies have long advocated reforms that would eliminate the bureaucratic maze of picket fence federalism and simultaneously reduce national control over the disposition of grant monies. These reforms have been accomplished in two ways. Categorical grants have been combined or consolidated into block grants, which permit recipients to determine, within broad limits, the uses to which aid will be put. Another way of reducing national control involves the distribution of aid according to some formula, rather than by project. Under formula grants, eligibility for assistance is automatic, so national agencies no longer determine which governments will receive aid. When block grants are awarded according to a congressionally approved formula, national influence is minimized, and state and local discretion is correspondingly enhanced.

This was the rationale behind the New Federalism of Richard Nixon's administration, which combined some categorical grants with block-formula grants (Conlan 1988). The latter were called special revenue-sharing grants, to distinguish them from general revenue-sharing grants, which awarded money to state and local governments on the basis of population, per capita income, levels of taxation, and several other factors. Subnational governments were virtually free to decide how funds would be used, and the amounts of money were not trivial: tens of billions of dollars were distributed between 1972 and 1986, when general revenue-sharing ceased. Not coincidentally, the shift toward block-formula grants and general revenue sharing bestowed greater assistance on fast-growing cities in the Sunbelt, as well as suburbs, small cities, and rural areas—all integral to the emerging Republican presidential coalition (Brown 1984).

The same coalition elected Ronald Reagan in 1980, who characteristically took New Federalism one step further. Reagan proposed swapping national and state responsibilities in Aid to Families with Dependent Children (AFDC) and Medicaid; the states would assume full responsibility for AFDC (and food stamps), while the national government would assume complete financial responsibility for the increasingly expensive Medicaid program. In addition, a $28 billion "super revenue sharing" fund would be used to replace forty national grant programs in education, health, social services, community development, and transportation. When these funds were exhausted, state and local governments would assume complete responsibility for any programs they chose to continue. This would maximize state and local discretion by allowing them to decide which programs to support with their own tax dollars (Conlan and Walker 1983). In a single move, Reagan hoped to bring about at least a partial return to a system of dual federalism.

Although the Omnibus Reconciliation Act of 1981 did consolidate some categorical grants, the most ambitious parts of Reagan's New Federalism were never adopted. State and local policy makers viewed the proposals with suspicion; substantial alterations in the grant system were simply not welcome, even if they involved reducing funds to help balance the national budget. Moreover, the timing of the proposals was unlucky; as the economic recession deepened and states' ability to raise revenue declined, many state leaders feared the loss of national grant monies (Benton 1986). Opposition also came from city policy makers, their employees and clients, all of whom had become dependent on national funds that might not be replaced by state legislatures (Fossett 1984).

Until Republicans gained control in 1995, categorical grants remained very popular with Congress. In fiscal year 1993, almost 600 grants-in-aid were in operation. The grants were worth $200 billion, but less than $20 million of that amount was provided through block grants. The rest was channeled into categorical grants, 419 of them awarded on a project basis. Clearly, categorical project grants are the runaway favorite of representatives and senators seeking benefits for their districts and states. Such grants allow politicians to dictate the use of funds and claim credit for arranging help for their constituents. (While some consider this political pork, that is not how grants are understood by their authors, at least not when *their* projects are at stake!)

The existence of so many grants, and the availability of so much grant money, has made subnational governments dependent on federal aid. The extent of this fiscal dependency on higher levels of government is shown in Figure 2-3, for selected years from 1955 to 1992. The graphs in Figure 2-3 compare the size of intergovernmental subsidies with all general revenues raised by state and local governments. When intergovernmental revenues constitute a high proportion of total revenues, subnational governments are fiscally dependent—a condition of subjection into which local governments had fallen in the late 1970s, and from which they have never recovered fully.

As seen in the right-hand side of Figure 2-3, the dependence of local governments has abated somewhat since 1979, mostly because the flow of funds from the national government slowed during the administrations of Jimmy Carter and Reagan. The real value of grants declined in 1979, 1980, 1981, and 1982, when inflation outstripped spending increases. Nominal grant outlays actually fell in

Figure 2-3   Intergovernmental Revenue Flows, 1955–1992

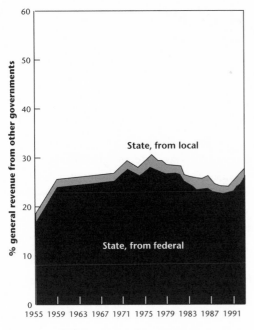
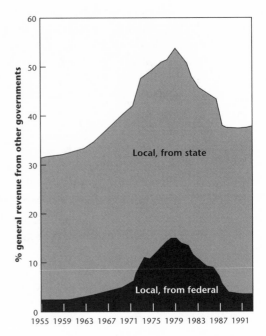

SOURCE: Calculated from U.S. Bureau of the Census, various years.

1982, the year after states lost access to general revenue sharing, and again in 1987, when the program ended and localities lost general revenue-sharing funds. The demise of the Comprehensive Employment and Training Act, which heavily subsidized public work forces in many cities, also precipitated retrenchment of services in some areas (Fossett 1984).

Thus, budget shortfalls at the national level trickled down to the local level and forced officials to make difficult decisions about taxing and spending priorities. Not surprisingly, local governments took little consolation from the fact that they became less dependent on national funds and less vulnerable to future shifts in national orientation. Of course, they remain exposed to the actions of states, which still provide local governments with more than a third of their total revenue. The dependency is even more pronounced in large, industrialized cities of the Northeast and the Great Lakes area, where state aid sometimes amounts to well over half of all revenues.

State aid to local governments has increased, but not enough to offset the declining value of federal grants. When the period of Creative Federalism began in the early 1960s, states supplied about 33 percent of the general revenue of local governments; now they provide almost 36 percent. Over the same period, though, federal grants increased from 3 percent of local general revenues to almost 15 percent, fell back to about 5 percent, and have begun to rise again. The precipitous decline in federal aid after 1978 was not offset by a comparable increase in state aid, and local governments have had to exploit their own revenue sources more intensively. Because revenue from their own sources has increased at a faster rate than state aid, the fiscal dependency of local government has decreased a little, but remains high.

State governments themselves are less dependent on national grants, as shown in the left-hand side of Figure 2-3. Overall, less than 25 percent of all state revenues comes from Washington. Of course, the percentage is much higher in some states and much lower in others; the grant system is not geographically neutral, nor is it intended to be. One of its principal functions is to achieve some degree of equalization by redistributing resources to states and localities with great needs but few resources of their own. That is why a substantial portion of national grant monies is directed to deprived areas, as measured by legislative formulas that incorporate various indicators of need and financial ability. To the extent that these formulas succeed in targeting aid, some states reap especially large shares of financial assistance from the national government, while other states receive smaller shares (Stein 1981).

The amount of redistribution can be approximated by estimating the amount of taxes paid by residents in each state to finance the national grant system (Tax Foundation 1993). This can be compared with the value of grants-in-aid received by governments in each state. Whenever residents of a state pay less than their governments receive in aid, they benefit from a redistributive grant system. Citizens who give more than they get are financing a disproportionate share of the system. In either case, the extent of redistribution is measured by the ratio of grants received to taxes paid for the purpose of maintaining a national grant system.

State ratios for fiscal year 1992 are depicted in Figure 2-4. A majority of states have ratios less than one, meaning they receive more grant dollars than their citizens pay in taxes for grants. Some of these states are big winners indeed; small, rural states (for example, Louisiana, Mississippi, West Virginia, and Wyoming) have grant tax burdens only one-half the size of grants-in-aid they receive. Roughly speaking, they pay less than $0.50 for every $1.00 they receive in grants from the national government. In contrast, populous states (for example, Florida, Illinois, and New Jersey) have tax burdens half again as large as the value of grants received by their governments. Their citizens pay about $1.50 for each $1.00 in grants received by state and local governments. Residents in these states are effectively subsidizing the operations of government in small, rural states.

Through grant formulas and administrative decisions about the distribution of grant funds, resources are redistributed on a rather large scale. Not surprisingly, losing states complain about this treatment; what counts as equalization for some is a form of discrimination for others. This gives rise to computer politics in Congress, that is, pitched battles over the composition of formulas for distributing aid (Stanfield 1978). Representatives from states with divergent interests,

Figure 2-4 Ratio of Grant Tax Burden to Grants, 1992

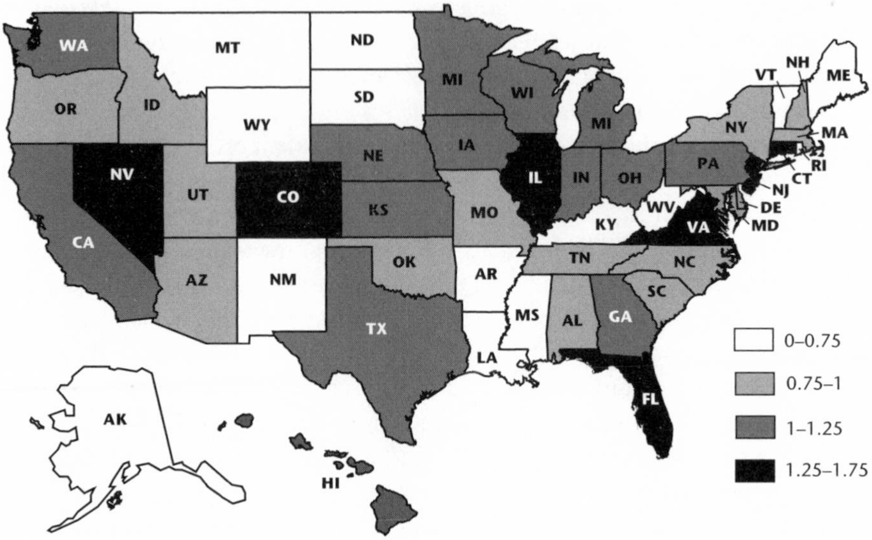

☐	0–0.75
▨	0.75–1
▩	1–1.25
■	1.25–1.75

SOURCES: Calculated from U.S. Bureau of the Census 1994a, table 11; Tax Foundation 1993, table C56.

each supplied with statistical analyses of the estimated impact of alternative formulas, must then resolve their differences. Thus, in 1976, members of Congress from the Northeast and Midwest formed a coalition to reduce their states' "losses" under a redistributive grant system. They succeeded in altering the Community Development Program, which made block grants to correct urban blight. The grants were originally distributed according to a formula based on population, poverty, and overcrowded housing, which favored Sunbelt cities because of their rapid growth and serious housing shortages. The coalition succeeded in revising the formula in 1977 to emphasize the percentage of housing built before 1940, which shifted funds to Frostbelt cities (Dilger 1982).

Small regional biases are evident in Figure 2-4. Southern states are typically winners, perhaps because they tend to be poorer than other states, and many grants are based partly on need. Mountain states, with the exception of Colorado, also benefit from redistribution under the grant system. Yet these biases, if that is what they are, are small and seem to be diminishing over time. At no time during the 1960s, 1970s, and 1980s have there been significant differences between northern and southern states (Bahl 1984). Western states did substantially better than northern states until 1975; they also did better than southern states until 1978. After that, significant regional differences vanished. Regions became more alike in their needs and tax bases, and redistributive effects became smaller, although wealthier states still subsidize poorer states (inside and outside of their own regions).

The budgetary impact of grants-in-aid is significant. Most grants require matching funds from states, and depending on the stringency of these requirements, states may have to commit a substantial portion of their own revenues to purposes served by the grants. States may also exceed matching fund requirements in some policy areas, if they are stimulated to enlarge on national policy objectives. As a result, grants have leverage beyond their size, giving them broad influence over state and local spending patterns (Stonecash 1979, 1988).

In part, this is what Congress generally intends, but grant programs skew the priorities of state policy makers who concentrate on obtaining grants with low matching fund requirements. These programs give a bigger "bang for the buck" than programs in which matching fund requirements are high, or where national funds are not available at all. Budget-conscious policy makers may therefore neglect important state and local concerns, if those concerns are not sufficiently general to warrant attention by the national government. Clever state officials, however, may discover methods that allow them to substitute national dollars for their own or those of their counterparts at the local level. This permits officials to divert state and local revenues to popular causes, or alternatively, to avoid tax increases. Congress has therefore begun to perfect other means of ensuring compliance with its objectives. One consequence has been the proliferation of congressional mandates.

According to the U.S. Advisory Commission on Intergovernmental Relations (1984), four different kinds of mandate have been employed by Congress (and the executive). A *direct order,* in the form of a law or regulation, may be issued in policy areas where national power has been well established under the supremacy clause of the Constitution. Thus, subnational governments must abide by the Equal Employment Opportunity Act, the Fair Labor Standards Act, and the Occupational Safety and Health Act, and they risk civil and criminal sanctions if they do not respond to orders of compliance.

Crosscutting regulations are across-the-board requirements that affect all or most federal assistance programs. They involve provisions that prohibit the use of funds from any national source in programs that discriminate on the basis of race, ethnicity, sex, or religious belief, for example. Another familiar crosscutting regulation requires the preparation of an environmental impact statement for any construction project involving national funds. State and local governments must provide evidence of compliance with these regulations, and they incur administrative costs for preparing the necessary scientific and technical reports.

National officials may terminate or reduce funding or aid in a specified program if state and local officials do not comply with the requirements of another grant-in-aid program. This is a *crossover sanction.* National highway funds are often used in this way to force states to adopt policies preferred by Congress (Sevin 1989). Thus, states that did not raise their minimum drinking age to twenty-one by 1986 would lose 5 percent of their national highway funds, under a law passed in 1984. The penalty was supposed to increase by 10 percent for each subsequent

year in which the states failed to act. All states eventually complied with this demand, although in 1988 the Wyoming legislature considered lowering the drinking age and risk losing funds as a show of independence.

The fourth type of regulation is *partial preemption* and often rests on the
commerce clause of the Constitution. By engaging in this type of regulation the
national government essentially sets national minimum standards by issuing appropriate regulations for, say, air or water quality, if a state refuses to do so.
Should a state refuse to enforce standards issued by an agency of the national
government, then the agency will assume jurisdiction for enforcement. States are
entitled to adopt and implement more stringent standards, but weak or nonexistent standards are preemptively denied by Congress and its delegates (Zimmerman 1988).

Whatever the form, state (and local) government officials strongly resent
mandates. "Feeling less like partners, and more like 'the field hands of federalism,'" they have begun to rebel (Calmes 1988, 21). In a few, notable cases they
have gained satisfaction through the national political process, as the Court has
said they must: Congress eventually agreed to rescind the fifty-five-mile-per-
hour speed limit on rural interstate highways constructed with national funds,
for instance. (Congress maintained its insistence on a legal drinking age of twenty-one as a condition for highway aid, however.)

In other cases, states and localities have not been successful lobbyists. Faced
with demands to reduce the national deficit, Congress eliminated general revenue-sharing funds, first for state governments and then for local governments,
too, despite sustained lobbying by officials from the affected governments. Similarly, state and local officials have been unable to persuade their representatives
in Congress to compensate them for the expense of complying with national
mandates (Calmes 1988). If anything, the huge deficit now inclines members of
Congress to shift more—not less—of the costs of compliance to lower levels of
government, while retaining ultimate responsibility for establishing the goals of
policy.

Indeed, the political viability of Congress now rests heavily on its ability to
meet the demands of interest groups by unfunded mandates (Kincaid 1994).
Ironically, the expanding capacity of state governments now invites Congress to
conscript them for its own use. As Derthick (1986, 36) puts it, Congress is giving
orders to states "as if they were administrative agents of the national government, while expecting state officials and electorates to bear whatever costs ensue." While there was some sentiment in Congress for mandate relief, no such
legislation was enacted until 1995.

Nor has Congress's willingness to conscript the states been slowed by a movement toward deregulation begun by President Reagan and continued by President George Bush. According to a study published in 1992, at least thirty-six significant mandates were in force as of 1980; another twenty-seven were added by
1990, and more than a dozen others were passed by the 102d Congress before it

adjourned in 1992. Few of them were accompanied by grants-in-aid, although the cumulative cost of mandates adopted between 1983 and 1990 alone was between $8.9 billion and $12.7 billion, according to one of the lower estimates of the burden on state and local governments (Conlan and Beam 1992). The projected cost of mandates will be much higher at the end of the decade. That, plus the national intrusion into traditional areas of state responsibility, explains why subnational officials believe that "mandates are putting a stranglehold on state budgets" (Conlan and Beam 1992, 1). It also explains why many subnational governments celebrate National Unfunded Mandates Week as a way of calling attention to their plight.

The message has been received. After the Republican landslide of 1994, the 104th Congress quickly adopted the second plank of the Contract with America. With the support of many Democrats, including President Clinton, the Republicans enacted legislation requiring the Congressional Budget Office to estimate the cost of all mandates proposed in Congress. Bills that impose new mandates in excess of $50 million on state and local governments must be approved by a majority of each chamber in a separate vote. Meanwhile, the Advisory Commission on Intergovernmental Relations will prepare recommendations for reducing or eliminating previously enacted mandates ("GOP Attains Top 'Contract' Goal" 1995).

Of course, what seems to be a case of Congress imposing its will on state and local officials may on closer inspection turn out to be an instance of policy makers of one persuasion or region seeking to impose their will on those of another by way of national legislation or regulation (Bensel 1984). Such efforts are not necessarily wrong; few now dispute the desirability of establishing a national guarantee of civil rights over the objections of the South (although there is much debate over whether that guarantee entails affirmative action in hiring, set asides for minority contractors, and other such policies). Regionalism is also apparent when states suffering from the effects of acid rain seek the enactment of national environmental policies that would penalize states that burn coal that has a high sulfur content (indirectly hurting states that produce such coal). So far, these efforts have been unsuccessful. A national majority in favor of restrictive laws has not yet formed in Congress.

Mandates also reflect ideological battles. The Family Medical Leave Act of 1993 requires businesses with fifty or more employees to grant workers up to twelve weeks of unpaid leave for the birth or adoption of a child or if there is serious illness in the immediate family. The legislation was popular among workers and their families but was opposed by business organizations. The National Voter Registration Act of 1993 compels states to provide voter registration in conjunction with applications for driver's licenses, welfare benefits, or other public services. Democrats favored this legislation, but most Republicans did not. Clearly, the merits of such legislation are debatable; what is indisputable is the profoundly political nature of these decisions and their uneven geographical impact. In acknowledging this the Supreme Court has ensured that the sentiments of the majority, as expressed in Congress, will determine the limits of national power in regard to subnational units of government.

RELATIONS BETWEEN STATE AND LOCAL GOVERNMENTS

Another major sector of intergovernmental relations consists of interactions between state and local governments. The character of these interactions is strongly influenced by the legal status of local governments, which are mere conveniences of the state, constitutionally speaking. Local governments are created by state government, their institutional structures are defined by state government, their responsibilities are delimited by state government, and their powers of taxation are derived from state government. As such, local governments do not enjoy sovereignty, and the relationship between states and localities is unitary rather than federal.

The distribution of power among state and local governments is quite different in principle from the allocation of power among national and state governments. Whereas the national government generally relies on a more or less cooperative approach in the exercise of its power, state governments use their constitutional authority to exact "cooperation" from local governments. States can coerce their local governments into compliance with state policy objectives, and they do. This is perhaps most evident in states' long-standing propensity to mandate policy responsibilities to local governments, often without providing the funds or taxing authority needed by local governments to carry out these newly assigned responsibilities.

The AFDC program nicely illustrates the differences between these two strategies for obtaining compliance. Aid to dependent children was initiated under Title IV-A of the Social Security Act and made federal matching funds available to states willing to participate in a nationally inspired effort to ease the plight of indigent children. Participation by states is voluntary, but the fiscal incentives for participation have induced all fifty states to establish the program. (See Chapter 11 for more details.)

However, when states implement AFDC programs they may require local governments to administer the program and even help pay for it. Localities have no choice in this matter; the states may simply insist that they manage the program on a day-to-day basis, determining eligibility, making payments, hearing appeals from those denied assistance, and so forth. In 1993, thirty-two states delegated responsibility for AFDC to county and city offices, and ten states (including California and New York, the states with the largest programs) imposed part of the costs of rendering assistance on local governments. This contributes significantly to the fiscal distress of local governments, particularly if state governments also limit their ability to raise revenues via taxation.

The AFDC program is typical of intergovernmental relations in action:

whereas the national government typically induces cooperation on the part of state governments, the latter regularly impose their policy objectives on their political subdivisions. Because they are sovereign, state governments have the capacity to resist national policy makers, who in most cases depend deeply on substantial cooperation by state officials for implementing policy (Derthick 1986). But local governments are administrative conveniences of the state, and they find it harder to resist state officials determined to have their way. As a result, local governments labor under hundreds or even thousands of mandates from their state governments (Zimmerman and Clark 1994).

Local opposition to state mandating has spread, and some states now restrict the practice (perhaps because their own experience with congressional mandating has made state officials more sympathetic to local complaints). Half the states now have constitutional limits or statutory restrictions on mandating; the latter have become especially popular in the past ten years. Typical measures require approval of mandates by local governments or prohibit mandating unless the state legislature provides funding for the activity in question, reimburses local governments for the cost of mandates, or provides them with a new source of funding to cover those costs (Zimmerman 1994). Of course, the very existence of restrictions on state mandating is evidence of state legislatures' propensity to mandate, particularly when demands on state government far exceed available resources.

Political Considerations

Local governments' terms of existence are spelled out in charters of incorporation or special acts of the state legislature, which establish units of local government. According to Dillon's Rule, a doctrine adopted by federal and state courts alike, local governments may exercise only those powers expressly granted in the charter or act of incorporation, powers necessarily implied therein, or powers that are indispensable (not merely convenient) for carrying out the assigned responsibilities of local government. In contrast, state governments may, at their discretion, alter the functions, powers, and structures of local government as they see fit.

Thus, states may create special purpose districts, stripping existing governments of previously held authority to make policy in certain policy areas—for example, mass transit, fire protection, water and sewer services—and providing for libraries, hospitals, and parks. This has been a common practice in the states; according to the Bureau of the Census, 33,131 special districts existed in 1992, about two and one-half times as many as were in existence forty years earlier (Bureau of the Census 1994c). Most of these districts perform a single function; consequently, the proliferation of districts has fragmented local policy making along narrow functional lines. In so doing it has multiplied the number of opportunities for political participation by creating a host of governing boards, but it has also made it virtually impossible for all but the most informed citizens to know which officials to hold responsible for policy failures.

When special districts improve services and reduce costs, citizens and local officials welcome their establishment, even though it reduces their control. Other reductions in local control are conceded only grudgingly. This is particularly true in the case of independent school districts. Immediately after World War II, many state governments consolidated local school districts by abolishing small, rural districts and transferring their students to urban districts so that education could be provided more efficiently and inexpensively. Local objections were overridden by state policy makers, who controlled state aid for transportation and schooling. Thus, the power to create—and destroy—local governments was effectively used to bring about consolidation, and the number of school districts nationwide fell from 67,346 in 1952 to 14,556 in 1992. (In the same period, two new states were added to the Union and the number of children enrolled in public elementary and secondary schools climbed 40 percent, accentuating the trend toward larger school districts.)

Nevertheless, the constitutional vulnerability of local governments is mitigated by other considerations. A commitment to local determination is central to Americans' political heritage. In the Northeast, state constitutions were not adopted until after the Declaration of Independence, more than a hundred years after the first local governments were formed under the authority of the Crown or other proprietors. Other areas of the country, too, were settled, and towns established, well before territories became states. As a result, strong traditions of localism exist, particularly in northern states (Elazar 1984). In these states, communities may be legally powerless to prevent states from limiting their autonomy, but in practice they enjoy substantial independence because tradition favors delegation of authority. Once delegated, this authority may be difficult to recover; and, indeed, some state courts have begun to protect local prerogatives in such areas as land use and school financing (Briffault 1987).

Furthermore, the same forces that make Congress (and to a far lesser extent, the executive) responsive to states also make states responsive to local government. Representation in the legislature is by locality, if not local government, and elected representatives often have prior experience in local affairs. They are sensitive to the desire of local policy makers for autonomy, and they quickly learn of resentment over state mandating and other practices that infringe on local determination. Indeed, representatives are usually forewarned of opposition to pending legislation by lobbying associations of local governments and mayors, law enforcement officers, school superintendents, and the like. Members of the state legislature are therefore not inclined to enact measures that localities find too objectionable.

The major political consideration is not whether states will be responsive to local governments but rather to which set of local governments they will be most responsive. Historically, the malapportionment of state legislatures gave rural interests a disproportionate voice in state policy making. Reapportionment has strengthened the representation of urban and suburban areas in state legislatures, but in many states rural areas still elect a substantial number of members, many of whom occupy positions of leadership by virtue of their seniority. Consequently, the interests of urban areas are not always well served, or at least are not as well served as their local governments might like.

It was precisely this situation that led Mike Royko, a Chicago columnist, to suggest facetiously that Chicago ought to secede from the state of Illinois because the city was not faring well at the hands of downstate Republican legislators in the General Assembly. A more serious case of secessionist sentiment is found in northern California, the source of water for much of the southern part of the state. Tired of seeing water diverted by state government canals, and wary of uncontrolled development, some northern residents want to become the nation's fifty-first state. In June 1993 an advisory referendum on secession was held in thirty-one of California's fifty-eight counties; secession was the preference in twenty-seven counties. The result vividly illustrates the tension between state governments and powerful local constituencies (north and south, in this case).

The political influence of certain locales may be enough to win favored treatment from state government. For example, big central cities, particularly those in otherwise rural states, commonly enjoy home rule charters, designed to promote local autonomy. The amount of autonomy under home rule varies from state to state and even across cities within the same state, and of course home rule charters may be withdrawn (as may other charters). Nevertheless, the existence of home rule charters is evidence of the political leverage that may be brought to bear on sovereign state governments by important local governments.

The most systematic examination of local autonomy in the American states shows that local governments enjoy different kinds of discretion (U.S. Advisory Commission 1981; 1993b). When the residents of a locale petition for the establishment of a local government, they may in some states be able to draft their own charter of incorporation. In other states, they may be able to choose from a variety of alternative forms of government, depending on the size of the local population and type of government desired. Local powers to amend charters may also be broad, and local units may be given limited or broad powers of annexation, further affecting control over the structure of local government.

A second area of discretion involves the range of functions local units may undertake. The greatest discretion exists in states that devolve authority to local governments, that is, in states in which local governments (or at least some of them) enjoy powers that are not specifically denied to them by the legislature or the constitution. At the other extreme are Dillon's Rule states, which insist on enumerating the powers and functions of local governments; powers not explicitly given are denied, although the legal understanding of granted powers may be fairly liberal. More subtle ways of affecting the level and kind of services provided by local governments include the restriction of revenues, or earmarking, to certain uses, and the establishment of performance standards.

Although services may be provided through contractual arrangements with private concerns, they are most often supplied by public employees, and the conditions of employment by local government are stipulated in detail by state governments. The most important requirements concern the extent to which merit considerations inform hiring, promoting, and firing decisions. But states may also establish training, licensing, and certification standards for employees; define procedures for determining wage and salary levels (for example, collective bargaining and compulsory arbitration rules); set actual salary and wage levels for certain categories of employees; control hours of employment and working conditions; regulate disability benefits; and mandate retirement programs (MacManus 1983).

The exercise of local discretion in all three areas (structure, function, and personnel matters) is often limited by the absence of discretion in fiscal affairs. Although cities in Arizona, Illinois, Maine, and Texas have substantial latitude in fiscal matters, local units in other states do not. In most states the constitution or legislature determines which taxes may be levied by local units and what sort of exemptions must be granted. Additionally, the magnitude of tax increases is often restricted by constitutional amendments enacted during the tax revolts of the late 1970s and early 1980s. Local borrowing is also tightly regulated in most states; overall debt loads are limited, and the type of debts that may be incurred, as well as the interest rates that may be paid on bonds, are typically defined by the legislature. Similar restrictions may affect spending practices, and in New Mexico, cities and counties must submit their entire budgets to an agency of the state government for approval.

Local autonomy is a function of discretion in all four of these areas. It is generally greatest for municipal governments; counties, towns, and other local units typically enjoy less autonomy. Of course, there is enormous variation across states in the degree of autonomy granted to local governments, as shown in Table 2-1.

Table 2-1 is a summary of the autonomy of city and county governments in the fifty states as of 1990. In most states, cities have considerable freedom to choose structures of governance, although there are exceptions in every region of the country, particularly in the South. Counties are less likely to enjoy structural home rule, however. In New England and the Southwest, counties must accept structural forms imposed by state governments, and they enjoy relatively little autonomy.

The incidence of functional home rule varies, too. States may allow a lot of freedom to operate—or they may grant little or none at all. Cities in New England, the Great Lakes region, and the Far West have functional powers that are quite restricted compared with those of cities in the upper midwestern states or the Southeast. Relatively few counties have broad operating authority, except for

Table 2-1 Degree of Local Autonomy, by State, 1990

	Region and state	Cities			Counties		
		Structural home rule	Broad functional home rule	Limited functional home rule	Structural home rule	Broad functional home rule	Limited functional home rule
New England	Connecticut	•		•	na	na	na
	Maine	•		•	•		
	Massachusetts	•		•			
	New Hampshire	•		•			•
	Rhode Island	•		•	na	na	na
	Vermont						
Middle Atlantic	Delaware	•	•				
	Maryland	•	•			•	
	New Jersey	•	•		•	•	
	New York	•	•		•	•	
	Pennsylvania	•		•	•		•
Great Lakes	Ohio	•	•		•		•
	Wisconsin	•	•		•	•	
	Illinois	•		•	•		•
	Michigan	•		•	•		•
	Indiana			•			•
Midwest	Iowa	•	•			•	
	Kansas	•	•				•
	Minnesota	•	•		•		•
	Missouri	•	•		•	•	
	North Dakota	•	•		•	•	
	South Dakota	•	•		•		
	Nebraska						
South	Florida	•	•		•	•	
	Kentucky	•	•			•	
	Louisiana	•	•		•	•	
	Mississippi	•	•				
	Tennessee	•	•		•		
	West Virginia	•	•				
	Arkansas	•		•	•	•	•
	South Carolina	•		•	•		
	Georgia		•		•	•	
	Virginia			•			
	Alabama						
	North Carolina						
Southwest	Arizona	•	•				•
	New Mexico	•	•		•	•	
	Texas	•	•				
	Oklahoma	•					
Mountain	Colorado	•	•		•	•	
	Montana	•	•		•	•	
	Utah	•	•				•
	Wyoming	•	•				
	Idaho		•			•	
Pacific	California	•	•		•	•	
	Hawaii	•		•	•		•
	Oregon	•		•			•
	Washington	•		•	•	•	
	Alaska			•			
	Nevada			•			•

SOURCE: Adapted from U.S. Advisory Commission 1993b, table A.
NOTE: na = not applicable.

those in states along the mid-Atlantic coast. This is because counties were created by states to administer justice and other state programs; the same is true of special districts. Cities have a life of their own, however; most came into existence as socioeconomic entities before they obtained legal recognition by the state, and even before statehood, in some cases. Hence they have generally been given more freedom of action.

Variations among the states in the autonomy of local governments are the result of many factors. The political culture of a state plays a role because traditional beliefs about the most appropriate relation between state and local government clearly influence specific actions bearing on local discretion. The length of legislative sessions and the number of local governments in a state have an effect, too. Legislatures cannot closely supervise a large number of local units, especially if they meet infrequently and for short periods of time. Under these circumstances legislatures are more inclined to grant higher degrees of local autonomy, especially since the existence of a large number of governments is associated with strong associations of local officials capable of influencing legislators. (It is also associated with large public employee unions, which may persuade legislatures to mandate actions on their behalf, over the objections of local policy makers.)

Finally, the complexity of a state's constitution and the ease of amending it can influence the amount of discretion permitted local governments. The constitution of a state may make it extremely difficult for legislatures to exercise authority over local governments in a timely fashion, particularly if incorporation of the governments is by constitutional amendment; in that case, further amendments must be adopted for the legislature to have its way. Of course, this in itself testifies to the ability of local governments to improve their constitutional position, and more generally about the strength of political traditions that favor localism over centralism. But even in states where constitutions are not an impediment to legislative control, trends since the mid-1970s favor the expansion of local discretion and home rule (Zimmerman 1981; Zimmerman and Clark 1994).

Fiscal Relations between State and Local Governments

Although the discretionary powers of local governments have increased in many states, the capacity to exercise discretion has not grown apace. The convergence of several factors explains this curious phenomenon. First, and perhaps most important, as they are now constituted local governments often lack the resources needed to address problems on their own. Economic instability, weak infrastructure, environmental degradation, and inadequate school systems pose great challenges to local policy makers, not just in older, central cities, but in many boom towns, suburbs, and rural areas as well. At the same time, local governments cannot raise sufficient revenue to cope with these problems; tax bases have eroded, voters have imposed restrictions on taxing and spending powers, and the national government has decreased its support for grant programs

aimed at local governments. Unable fully to discharge the responsibilities assigned them by state government or demanded by constituents, local policy
makers have turned to state leaders for assistance.

State governments are willing to provide leadership, and as a result policy
making is becoming more centralized. Of course, centralization has not increased by the same amount in all states, nor is it the same across different policy
areas within the same state. For example, states are most likely to take the lead in
constructing highways, providing welfare, maintaining correctional institutions
and mental health hospitals, and regulating natural resources. Municipal governments tend to provide public safety, sanitation, and sewage disposal, and school
districts manage educational services. Yet even these locally provided services are
heavily influenced by state actions, insofar as many state governments provide
huge sums of money to the responsible local units.

In fact, financial dominance can be an indicator of policy centralization. State
aid to localities has grown rapidly since the early 1980s. From 1980 to 1991, total
state spending for local governments increased from $82.8 billion to $182.6 billion—an increase of 125 percent. (Inflation increased by 65 percent during the
same period.) This produced a higher degree of fiscal centralization, meaning
that states became the principal financiers of many public services, even those
provided by local governments. New legal requirements and general policy
guidelines were imposed as state officials began to demand greater accountability
from local governments seeking assistance. Thus, state governments now control
or influence many areas of policy making long dominated by local governments—a development that, as Wright (1988, 319) observes, may also make it increasingly difficult for the national government to channel funds to local governments for purposes that are inconsistent with state policies.

Increased state aid is only one path to fiscal centralization, however. As
Stonecash (1985) argues, states can achieve the same result by providing goods
and services directly, without involving local governments. This requires substantial outlays by state governments, since local governments contribute nothing under this arrangement, but it does permit greater control over the formulation and implementation of public policy. Under this method, no intermediaries
are needed—or rather, the intermediaries are agencies and employees of state
government, whose actions are presumably easier to regulate than those of local
government officials.

Thus, greater fiscal centralization can be achieved indirectly, by increasing
state aid, or directly, via state provision of goods and services. Although the general trend has been toward fiscal centralization, states differ in the extent to
which they rely on direct or indirect methods of accomplishing this. These differences are apparent in Figure 2-5.

States are listed by region in Figure 2-5 according to their overall or combined
level of fiscal centralization, which is indicated by the combined length of the
dark and light bars for each state. The western states are at the bottom; above

Figure 2-5 Centralization of State and Local Finances, 1992

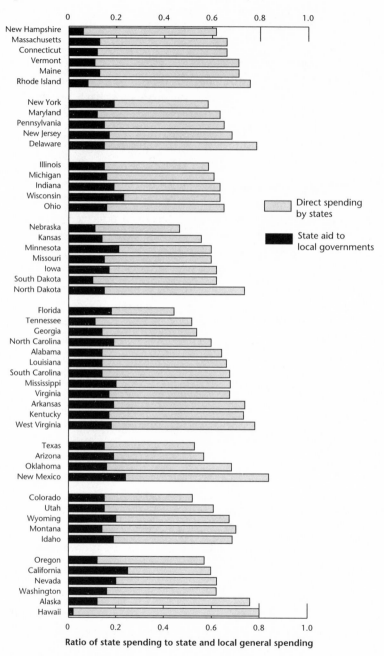

Ratio of state spending to state and local general spending

SOURCE: Calculated from U.S. Bureau of the Census 1994b, table 23.

them are the mountain, southwestern, southern, midwestern, Great Lakes, Middle Atlantic, and New England states. The least centralized states are at the top of each region's listing, while the most centralized states are toward the bottom. Generally speaking, small, rural states tend to be most centralized: state governments in North Dakota and New Mexico, for instance, directly and indirectly account for three-quarters of all state and local spending there. Near the other extreme are several large, diverse states, for example, Florida and Texas, where direct and indirect state expenditure amounts to half of all state and local outlays.

Among the more highly centralized states there are clear differences on the two dimensions of centralization. Hawaii and New Mexico are almost equally centralized, but they arrive at this end by quite different routes. Hawaii provides almost no state aid at all; instead, it funds services out of the state treasury (see Figure 2-5). When the share of direct state spending is high, state governments rely less on local governments, and more on themselves, to provide basic goods and services to citizens. As it happens, Hawaii is the only state in the Union that funds public education entirely from state funds, and since education is the most expensive service provided by state and local governments, the state ranks high in terms of fiscal centralization.

New Mexico, by contrast, augments direct spending with a significant amount of state aid, mostly for local school systems (see Figure 2-5). The use to which the money is put may be the same as in Hawaii, but the method of financing is indirect. In New Mexico, the importance of state aid in funding education allows the state government substantial control over this vital service.

State aid and direct spending by states are not perfect substitutes. This is evident in the tendency of states to become more centralized on both dimensions over time (Stonecash 1985, 1995). States that were initially centralized on both dimensions have remained so, while those that emphasized state aid have begun to stress direct spending more. States with traditions of heavy direct spending have maintained them, but they have also shown more interest in indirect financing of services. Finally, states not originally centralized on either dimension have become more centralized on both—even in Nebraska, state spending now accounts for more than 40 percent of all state and local outlays, when state aid and direct spending is combined.

The continuing importance of state aid in this process of fiscal centralization, especially in California, New York, Florida, and the Great Lakes states is quite significant. In simple terms, it represents a political determination of these state governments to work with, rather than without, local governments in fulfilling basic functions. In part this reflects political realities: in these and similar states, local governments are powerful enough to be able to persuade legislatures to assist them financially. Many of them are also capable policy makers, with long histories of service provision and relatively high levels of citizen satisfaction with local government. The idea of a partnership between state and local government is particularly strong in such states. Even though state governments have assumed primary responsibility for financing the activities of government, local governments still occupy an important position in this division of labor.

One reflection of the prominence of local governments under this form of fiscal centralization is the form in which state aid is given. The lion's share of state aid goes to categorical grants for education and public welfare. But state revenue sharing is next in importance; some states return a portion of sales and income taxes to the jurisdiction in which they were collected. Others reimburse local governments for property tax exemptions granted by the state, or replace tax revenues lost because of general limitations on increases in property tax rates. State revenue-sharing funds are also distributed in some states on a per capita basis, although states are turning toward more complex formulas based on differences in need and ability to raise revenue (Peliserro 1985; Stein 1988).

State revenue-sharing funds are relatively unrestricted; local governments that receive them are free to decide how these funds will be used. The monies therefore preserve local discretion and serve local priorities. State policy makers do not control or strongly influence the use of revenue-sharing funds, as they often do where categorical grants are involved, and as they most certainly do when funds are spent directly by agencies of the state. To the extent that fiscal centralization occurs when state aid is increased, and to the extent that this aid is unconditionally awarded, policy making may remain decentralized, even if financing does not.

INTERGOVERNMENTAL RELATIONS IN THE 1990S

Fundamental changes in American intergovernmental relations have occurred in the past two decades, and further alterations are likely as new circumstances dictate new political arrangements. Not surprisingly, economic factors play a leading role in this process. Their impact on intergovernmental finances has already been great; although a wide river of money still flows into the grant system from the national treasury, the real value of national grants crested in 1978. Since then the national deficit has grown and Congress has begun the politically painful process of retrenchment. That process has proceeded timidly, and it is quite unlikely that the deficit will shrink quickly. Pressure to restrict spending will therefore continue, and further reductions in grants are possible, particularly if a balanced budget amendment is adopted (Caraley and Schlussel, 1986). Ironically, action by the states to force consideration of this amendment might produce cuts in grant programs that would make it extremely difficult for state and local policy makers to balance their own budgets without substantial tax increases or reductions in service. Recognizing this, in 1995, Republican governors cautioned their party leaders in Congress against balancing the national budget at the expense of states. The Senate responded by killing a balanced budget amendment in the spring of 1995, although the issue is bound to resurface.

Local governments have been most affected by austerity measures, largely because many of them were deeply dependent on intergovernmental revenues. As the national government pulled back, local governments turned to state governments for fiscal relief, either in the form of state aid or by the dispensation of new taxing authority. This has deepened the dependency of local governments on state governments, and after two decades of attending closely to national policies, local governments are reorienting themselves from the national government to state governments.

In turn, the dependency of local governments increases the fiscal dominance of states in the intergovernmental system. State aid and direct state spending for services have perhaps never been so important as they are today. National and local governments have simultaneously begun to shift some of their financial burdens to state governments, and to an impressive extent states have accepted these burdens. The states differ greatly from one another on this score, but overall it is apparent that the size of the states' current fiscal role is unprecedented.

A second development reinforces the tendency of states to bear a larger share of the fiscal burden. Congress has grown reluctant to undertake new domestic policy initiatives, especially expensive ones. In part this reflects budgetary considerations, and in part it reflects deep divisions among the members of Congress, or between Congress and the executive. The paralysis of the national policy-making process has left important needs unmet. By default, state governments have become policy leaders in many key areas, including industrial policy, child care, educational reform, hazardous waste disposal, and health insurance for those with low incomes, to name but a few. In the process, state governments have resumed their role as innovators in the federal system, reflecting an improved capacity for action and changed public expectations about the function of state governments.

For many observers, this decentralization of power to the state level is cause for great hope, while others fear its consequences (Chubb 1986). Proponents of decentralization anticipate that it will bring greater efficiency in the delivery of goods and services by better matching demand with supply. They also expect that decentralization will make policy makers more responsive to citizens by bringing them into closer contact with the needs of specific regions and locales. In turn, this expectation is linked to the wish to preserve a pluralistic society in which policy differences are respected, not undermined, by governing structures that are truly federal in nature.

The hopes of those preferring decentralization were raised by the ascendance of Ronald Reagan to the presidency in 1981. Reagan personified conservatives' opposition to big government and their celebration of the virtues of private decision making. His eight years in office were marked by a singular determination to reduce the presence of government in American life by deregulating industry, curtailing welfare, reducing taxation, and promoting volunteerism and privatism. At the same time, Reagan also attempted to shift much of the remaining responsibility of government to the state and local levels, primarily (although not exclusively) by his New Federalism proposals.

Conlan (1988) shows that these two aims—reducing the overall size of government and moving its center of gravity to the subnational level—were in fact intimately connected during the Reagan administration. The instigators of the so-called Reagan Revolution were convinced that a genuine devolution of authority to state and local governments would lead them to abandon objectionable or ineffective programs. New Federalism would thereby reduce government activity and not simply transfer responsibility from national to subnational governments. In that sense, Reagan's version of New Federalism was quite different from the New Federalism of another Republican president, Richard Nixon, who assumed that states and localities would have greater discretion over the administration of policies and programs but not over their very existence.

Reagan's ambitious plan was never fully realized. Even at the national level, his administration fell short of its announced goal of substantially deactivating government, as Nathan, Doolittle, and Associates (1987) observe. Still, he accomplished far more than many observers expected, and the deficit created by his tax reductions will undoubtedly limit for the foreseeable future any growth of domestic spending by the national government. Similarly, although Reagan's New Federalism failed for lack of support, his administration succeeded in establishing what some have called a de facto New Federalism by limiting the flow of intergovernmental revenue and diverting it toward grants that permit greater discretion for state and local governments.

Ironically, this did not produce retrenchment of governmental activity at the subnational level. As Nathan, Doolittle, and Associates (1987) and the contributors to Palmer and Sawhill (1984) demonstrate, state governments have shown a surprising willingness to continue and even improve programs that have been curtailed at the national level. To be sure, the response has varied from state to state and across policy areas, but the evidence suggests that Reagan's stamp on domestic policy "appears to have been canceled—not fully, but partially—by state government policies and actions" (Nathan, Doolittle, and Associates 1987, 362). In short, the presumption that decentralization would eventually lead to abandonment or retrenchment of social policy has been contradicted.

For their part, liberals, who opposed Reagan's policies, have gained a fuller appreciation of decentralization. Traditionally, liberals have been suspicious of state governments, desiring, instead, an energetic national government of the sort so vehemently disliked by Reagan. Reagan's partial success at the national level has deprived liberals of realizing this desire; it seems quite unlikely that Congress will soon act again as it did during the War on Poverty or even under the New Federalism of Richard Nixon. Still, the reaction of some state governments to the challenges presented by the Reagan legacy implies that liberals may hope to be victorious at the state and local level, if not in Washington. Decentralization may therefore have certain political advantages for liberals, at least during periods in which a conservative orientation dominates the national government (Nathan, Doolittle, and Associates 1987).

Yet decentralization raises serious questions about equity. Will state governments be as willing as the national government to protect the rights and interests of racial, ethnic, and religious minorities, or those of women and the poor? Even if they are willing (and many have not been in the past), will state governments have the resources to ensure equitable treatment, particularly if their economies falter? And how should the members of a democratic society view the inevitable differences in treatment that will arise, as some states act vigorously, while others do not?

These questions may be answered as the decentralization proceeds in the 1990s. If Republicans maintain control of Congress and pursue their Contract with America, the Reagan Revolution may finally be completed. The Contract promises to shrink the size of the national government and increase the discretion of state governments in social welfare policy and environmental regulation. The House of Representatives moved quickly in this direction during the 103d Congress; the Senate's pace was more deliberate. Some elements of the Contract will be rejected, and others will be modified in order to win congressional approval and avoid presidential vetoes. The end result will be less than conservatives hope, and more than liberals want, on specific legislation.

More important, the terms of political discussion have shifted. Some issues, for example, health care reform and environmental protection, have dropped off the national agenda, at least temporarily. They have been replaced by issues like the reform of Aid to Families with Dependent Children, a federal welfare program. An expanded role for state governments is virtually certain to emerge from this debate; the only question is how much additional authority states will obtain from Congress. A new era of federalism is in the offing.

Nonfederal sectors of intergovernmental relations will become more complex and variegated in the years to come. Interstate relations will become more significant as states seek solutions to problems without resorting to the national government, or as a way of preempting national actions. Relations between state and local governments, too, will become much more important as the national government retreats from fiscal responsibilities and the local governments correspondingly reorient themselves to their state houses. In short, intergovernmental relations among subnational actors are likely to dominate our domestic political system during the 1990s, just as federal relations once did during the period of Creative Federalism.

If such a change does occur, an intricate web of relations will form as each of the fifty states becomes a nodal point for new policy ventures and new connections with local government. Fiscal considerations aside, states now seem more inclined to relinquish authority to local units of government (although, again, interstate differences are significant). The decentralization of policy making to the state level and its subsequent devolution to the local level portend a system of intergovernmental relations as differentiated as the preferences of local settlements themselves. Movements to privatize public services, already well under way in some areas of the country and in some services, would further extend this differentiation.

The greatest uncertainty in this scenario is the long-term impact of *Garcia v. San Antonio Metropolitan Transit Authority,* and the door it opens to activism by a national government inclined to act vigorously in domestic affairs. Because of *Garcia,* Congress's willingness to mandate policy is difficult to challenge on constitutional grounds, although the Supreme Court, bolstered by Reagan and Bush appointees, has signaled its willingness to return to Tenth Amendment issues. In *New York v. United States* (112 S.Ct. 2408 1992 at p. 2428) the Court held that Congress "crossed the line distinguishing encouragement from coercion" in forcing states to join regional compacts for hazardous waste disposal or else assume full responsibility for all such waste generated within their boundaries, whether by public or private entities. However, the ruling was narrowly based, and many state and local officials believe their best remedy is President Bill Clinton, who led the National Governors' Association in its efforts to obtain relief from mandates and regulations.

President Clinton has pledged support for deregulation of subnational governments and a retrenchment of federal mandates. In fact, the National Performance Review, which was issued by Vice President Albert Gore in the fall of 1993, made several recommendations for restoring balance to our system of intergovernmental relations. As Kincaid (1994) explains, the review urged Clinton to issue executive orders authorizing cabinet secretaries to grant selective relief from regulations or costly mandates in programs under their supervision. The review also urged the creation of a simpler system of monitoring state and local governments' compliance with the terms of grants-in-aid and suggested using the Advisory Commission on Intergovernmental Relations to develop ways of improving the national-state-local partnership (monitoring progress in that direction).

Shortly after the National Performance Review was released, President Clinton began acting on its recommendations for "reinventing federalism." He authorized the establishment of community boards for coordinating national, state, and local efforts to promote economic development in specially designated enterprise zones. Clinton also insisted that the Office of Management and Budget begin regular consultations with state, local, and tribal officials for the purpose of eliminating unnecessary regulations. Perhaps most important, the president ordered executive agencies to reduce the number of unfunded mandates arising from administrative action and to provide subnational governments an opportunity to influence rules for implementing new mandates and regulations authorized by Congress. (Legislation enacted in 1995 does not ban mandates, it only requires that Congress approve expensive mandates in a separate vote.)

As a result of President Clinton's actions, states are enjoying more flexibility in administering costly grant-in-aid programs—for example, Medicaid—and more freedom to experiment with reform measures. The devolution of authority may well permit subnational relations to flourish, particularly in health care reform, now that Congress has decided against a national insurance program (Hanson 1993). Once established, these relations may prove quite durable. In the end, that may prove a powerful bulwark against national majorities seeking to extend the domestic reach of Congress.

REFERENCES

Anton, Thomas J. 1989. *American Federalism and Public Policy: How the System Works.* New York: Random House.

Bahl, Roy. 1984. *Financing State and Local Government in the 1980s.* New York: Oxford University Press.

Beer, Samuel H. 1978. "Federalism, Nationalism, and Democracy in America." *American Political Science Review* 72:9–21.

Bensel, Richard F. 1984. *Sectionalism and American Political Development, 1880–1980.* Madison: University of Wisconsin Press.

Benton, J. Edwin. 1986. "Economic Considerations and Reagan's New Federalism Swap Proposals." *Publius* 16, no. 2:17–32.

Bowman, Ann O'M., and Richard Kearney. 1986. *The Resurgence of the States.* Englewood Cliffs, N.J.: Prentice-Hall.

Break, George F. 1980. *Financing Government in a Federal System.* Washington, D.C.: Brookings Institution.

Briffault, Richard. 1987. "State-Local Relations and Constitutional Law." *Intergovernmental Perspective* 13, no. 3/4:10–14.

Brown, Lawrence D. 1984. "The Politics of Devolution in Nixon's New Federalism." In *The Changing Politics of Federal Grants,* edited by Lawrence D. Brown, James W. Fossett, and Kenneth T. Palmer. Washington, D.C.: Brookings Institution.

Calmes, Jacqueline. 1988. "Bricks without Straw: The Complaints Go on but Congress Keeps Mandating." *Governing,* September, 21–26.

Caraley, Demetrius, and Yvette R. Schlussel. 1986. "Congress and Reagan's New Federalism." *Publius* 16, no. 1:49–79.

Chubb, John E. 1985. "Federalism and the Bias for Centralization." In *The New Direction in American Politics,* edited by John E. Chubb and Paul E. Peterson. Washington, D.C.: Brookings Institution.

———. 1986. "Hope, Fears, and Federalism." Working Paper on the Constitution as a Working Document. Ellis L. Phillips Foundation, Dartmouth College.

Clarke, Marianne K. 1986. *Revitalizing State Economies: A Review of State Economic Development Policies and Programs.* Washington D.C.: Center for Policy Research and Analysis, National Governors' Association.

Conlan, Timothy J. 1988. *New Federalism: Intergovernmental Reform from Nixon to Reagan.* Washington, D.C.: Brookings Institution.

Conlan, Timothy J., and David R. Beam. 1992. "Federal Mandates: The Record of Reform and Future Prospects." *Intergovernmental Perspective* 18, no. 4: 7–11.

Conlan, Timothy J., and David B. Walker. 1983. "Reagan's New Federalism: Design, Debate, and Discord." *Intergovernmental Perspective* 8, no. 4:6–22.

Corwin, Edwin S. 1934. *The Twilight of the Supreme Court.* New Haven: Yale University Press.

CSG (Council of State Governments). 1977. *Interstate Compacts: 1783–1977.* Rev. ed., Lexington, Ky.: Council of State Governments.

Derthick, Martha. 1986. "Preserving Federalism: Congress, the States, and the Supreme Court." *Brookings Review* 4, no. 2:32–37.

Dilger, Robert Jay. 1982. *The Sunbelt/Snowbelt Controversy: The War over Federal Funds.* New York: New York University Press.

Elazar, Daniel J. 1984. *American Federalism: A View from the States.* 3d ed. New York: Harper and Row.

Feigenbaum, Edward D. 1988. "Interstate Compacts and Agreements." In *The Book of the States, 1988–89.* Lexington, Ky.: Council of State Governments.

Fossett, James W. 1984. "The Politics of Dependence: Federal Aid to Big Cities." In *The Changing*

Politics of Federal Grants, edited by Lawrence D. Brown, James W. Fossett, and Kenneth T. Palmer. Washington, D.C.: Brookings Institution.

Freeman, Patricia K. 1985. "Interstate Communication among State Legislators regarding Energy Policy Innovations." *Publius* 15, no. 4:99–111.

"GOP Attains Top 'Contract' Goal as Mandates Bill Clears." 1995. *Congressional Quarterly Weekly Report,* March 18, 805–806.

Grodzins, Morton. 1966. *The American Political System.* Chicago: Rand McNally.

Haider, Donald. 1974. *When Governments Come to Washington.* New York: Free Press.

Hale, George E., and Marian Lief Palley. 1981. *The Politics of Federal Grants.* Washington D.C.: Congressional Quarterly Inc.

Hanson, Russell L. 1988. "'Commons' and 'Commonwealth' at the American Founding." In *Conceptual Change and the Constitution,* edited by J. G. A. Pocock and Terence Ball. Lawrence: University Press of Kansas.

———. 1993. "Defining a Role for States in a Federal Health Care System." *American Behavioral Scientist* 36:760–781.

Hawkins, Robert B., Jr. 1988. "An Ode to the 10th Amendment (May Federalism Rest in Peace)." *Governing,* July, 74.

Howitt, Arnold M. 1984. *Managing Federalism: Studies in Intergovernmental Relations.* Washington, D.C.: CQ Press.

Hunter, Lawrence A., and Ronald J. Oakerson. 1986. "An Intellectual Crisis in American Federalism: The Meaning of *Garcia.*" *Publius* 16, no. 3:33–50.

Kincaid, John. 1994. "Developments in Federal-State Relations, 1992–93." In *The Book of the States, 1994–95.* Lexington, Ky.: Council of State Governments.

Levine, Jerry. 1994. "American State Offices in Europe: Activities and Connections." *Intergovernmental Perspective* 20, no. 1:44–46.

Lord, William B., and Douglas S. Kenney. 1993. "Resolving Interstate Water Conflicts: The Compact Approach." *Intergovernmental Perspective* 19, no. 1: 19–23.

MacManus, Susan A. 1983. "State Government: The Overseer of Municipal Finance." In *The Municipal Money Chase: The Politics of Local Government Finance,* edited by Alberta M. Sbragia. Boulder, Colo.: Westview Press.

Madison, James, Alexander Hamilton, and John Jay. [1788] 1987. *The Federalist Papers.* Reprint. Edited by Isaac Kramnick. Harmondsworth, England: Penguin Books.

Nathan, Richard P., Fred Doolittle, and Associates. 1987. *Reagan and the States.* Princeton, N.J.: Princeton University Press.

Palmer, John L., and Isabel V. Sawhill, eds. 1984. *The Reagan Record.* Cambridge, Mass.: Ballinger Publishing.

Peliserro, John P. 1985. "State Revenue Sharing with Large Cities: A Policy Analysis over Time." *Policy Studies Journal* 13:643–652.

Reeves, Mavis Mann. 1981. "Galloping Intergovernmentalization as a Factor in State Management." *State Government* 54:102–108.

Sevin, Ali F. 1989. "Highway Sanctions: Circumventing the Constitution." *State Legislatures* 15, no. 2:25–29.

Snelling, Richard A. 1980. "American Federalism in the Eighties." *State Government* 53:168–170.

Stanfield, Rochelle L. 1978. "Playing Computer Politics with Local Aid Formulas." *National Journal,* December 9, 1977–1981.

Stein, Robert M. 1981. "The Allocation of Federal Aid Monies: The Synthesis of Demand-Side and Supply-Side Explanations." *American Political Science Review* 75:334–343.

———. 1988. "Explaining the Incidence of State Aid Transfers." Paper presented at the annual meeting of the American Political Science Association, Washington, D.C.: September 1–4.

Stonecash, Jeffery M. 1979. "Intergovernmental Aid and Local Response Patterns: A Refocusing of Aid Impact Studies." *Publius* 9, no. 3:101–117.

———. 1985. "Paths of Fiscal Centralization in the American States." *Policy Studies Journal* 13:653–661.

———. 1988. "Fiscal Centralization in the American States: Findings from Another Perspective." *Public Budgeting and Finance* 8, no. 4: 81–89.

———. 1995. *American State and Local Politics.* New York: Harcourt Brace.

Sundquist, James L. 1969. *Making Federalism Work.* Washington, D.C.: Brookings Institution.

Tax Foundation. 1993. *Facts and Figures on Government Finance.* Washington, D.C.: Tax Foundation.

U.S. Advisory Commission on Intergovernmental Relations. 1981. *Measuring Local Discretionary Authority.* Washington, D.C.: U.S. Government Printing Office.

————. 1984. *Regulatory Federalism: Policy, Process, Impact, and Reform.* Washington, D.C.: U.S. Government Printing Office.

————. 1987. "Resolving Federal-State Issues through the Political Process," by Paul E. Peterson. In *Is Constitutional Reform Necessary to Reinvigorate Federalism? A Roundtable Discussion.* Washington, D.C.: U.S. Government Printing Office.

————. 1993a. *Significant Features of Fiscal Federalism, 1993.* Washington, D.C.: U.S. Government Printing Office.

————. 1993b. *State Laws Governing Local Government Structure and Administration.* ACIR M-186. Washington, D.C.: U.S. Government Printing Office.

U.S. Bureau of the Census. 1994a. *Federal Expenditures by State for Fiscal Year 1993.* Washington, D.C.: U.S. Government Printing Office.

————. 1994b. *Government Finances: 1991–92.* Preliminary Report. Washington, D.C.: U.S. Government Printing Office.

————. 1994c. *1992 Census of Governments: Government Organizations.* Washington, D.C.: U.S. Government Printing Office.

————. Various years. *Government Finances.* Washington, D.C.: U.S. Government Printing OYce.

Wald, Matthew L. 1988. "3 States Ask Waste Cleanup as Price of Atomic Operation." *New York Times,* December 17, sec. A.

Weiler, Conrad. 1993–1994. "GATT, NAFTA, and State and Local Powers." *Intergovernmental Perspective* 20, no. 1:38–41.

Wright, Deil S. 1988. *Understanding Intergovernmental Relations.* 3d ed. Pacific Grove, Calif.: Brooks/Cole.

Zimmerman, Joseph F. 1981. *The Discretionary Authority of Local Governments, Urban Data Service Reports.* Vol. 13, no. 11. Washington, D.C.: International City Management Association.

————. 1988. "The Silent Revolution: Federal Preemption." Paper presented at the annual meeting of the American Political Science Association, Washington, D.C., September 1–4.

————. 1994. "State Mandate Relief: A Quick Look." *Intergovernmental Perspective* 20, no. 2:28–30.

Zimmerman, Joseph F., and Julie M. Clark. 1994. "The Political Dynamics of State-Local Relations, 1991–93." In *The Book of the States, 1994–95.* Lexington, Ky: Council of State Governments.

SUGGESTED READINGS

The Book of the States. An annual publication of the Council of State Governments in Lexington, Ky. The bible of research on state politics, it contains a wealth of comparative data and information, along with reviews of trends in all aspects of state politics and policy.

Intergovernmental Perspective. A quarterly publication of the U.S. Advisory Commission on Intergovernmental Relations (ACIR). Many issues focus on a common problem or theme in intergovernmental relations, and all provide brief descriptions of published and ongoing studies of the ACIR and other governing bodies.

Publius: The Journal of Federalism. A scholarly journal devoted primarily to research on American federalism, although comparative studies are occasionally included. It is published quarterly, and one issue each year centers on the state of American federalism in that year.

U.S. Advisory Commission on Intergovernmental Relations. *Significant Features of Fiscal Federalism [year].* Washington, D.C.: U.S. Government Printing Office. An indispensable reference on all aspects of government taxation and spending, across all levels of government. It is an annual publication and contains numerous measures of fiscal capacity and dependency, financial breakdowns by functional category, changes in national and state tax laws, and so forth.

Wright, Deil S. *Understanding Intergovernmental Relations.* 3d ed. Pacific Grove, Calif.: Brooks/Cole, 1988. Provides the definitive review of intergovernmental relations in the United States, as well as a comprehensive survey of relevant research from a variety of disciplines.

CHAPTER 3

Parties and Elections

JOHN F. BIBBY AND
THOMAS M. HOLBROOK

The development of political parties in Western democracies has been closely linked to the extension of suffrage and the spread of the belief that governments derive their authority from the consent of the governed. Political scientists have for decades exhibited a strong commitment to political parties as the principal intermediaries between the people and their governments. The parties have, indeed, played a strong role in aggregating and mobilizing the interests of vast numbers of citizens, increasing the ability of voters to hold public officials accountable for their stewardship in office, nominating candidates, contesting elections, acting as agents of political socialization, and organizing the decision-making institutions of government. For example, Schattschneider (1942, 1) opened his classic study of American parties by asserting that "political parties created democracy and modern democracy is unthinkable save in terms of parties."

While political scientists' commitment to parties has remained relatively constant (Epstein 1986, 9–39), the status of American parties has undergone a succession of changes. In this century they have been buffeted by a series of potentially threatening challenges: the loss of the patronage traditionally used to sustain their organizations; the loss of control over nominations as states adopted the direct primary and presidential primary; an apparent loss of public support; and competition from political action committees (PACs), candidate organizations, and campaign consultants. These party-weakening challenges have caused American politics to become less party-centered and increasingly candidate-centered (Wattenberg 1991). Yet despite the challenges they have had to face, parties at the national, state, and local levels have demonstrated amazing adaptability and durability.

Political parties permeate every aspect of state government. It is still Republicans and Democrats who "make the major decisions regarding who pays and who receives in the states" (Morehouse 1981, 29). Since 1950, only 4 persons have been elected to a governorship as independents; and after the 1994 elections only 4 state legislators (0.0005 percent) out of a total of 7,375 were not Republicans or Democrats (excluding the nonpartisan legislature of Nebraska). In addition, state legislatures are typically organized on the basis of partisanship, with powerful chamber and committee leadership posts going to members of the majority party. Governors also tend to appoint fellow party members to their administrations. Clearly, partisans are the movers and shakers of statehouse decision making, and understanding state politics requires attention to the role and status of state party organizations as well as the nature of the electoral process.

Because the role and strength of state party organizations are directly affected by government policies toward them, we begin by considering their legal status and state regulatory practices. We then focus on the changing nature of state party organizations, the role of parties in campaigns and elections, nominating practices and their impact on state organizations, the extent of interparty competition within the states, participation in state elections, the increasingly candidate-centered nature of elections, and the pattern of election outcomes within the states. Of special concern throughout the chapter are the patterns of change occurring in state electoral politics and within American parties as they seek to adapt to changing conditions.

STATE PUBLIC POLICY TOWARD PARTIES

In most Western democracies political parties are considered to be private associations not unlike the Elks, the Knights of Columbus, or the Urban League. They are therefore permitted to transact business in private, largely unregulated by government. American political parties, by contrast, are heavily regulated by state laws. They function in a manner similar to that of public utilities in that they provide essential public services (for example, nominating candidates, contesting elections, organizing the government) that affect the public sufficiently to justify government regulation (Epstein 1986, 157).

State regulation of parties was encouraged by the introduction in the 1890s of the Australian ballot: a secret general election ballot provided by the government with candidates designated by party labels. By granting official recognition to political parties on government-provided ballots, the states acquired a legal justification for regulating the parties (Epstein 1986, 152–167). The most significant state regulatory device has been the requirement that parties nominate their candidates via the direct primary (discussed later in this chapter). State regulation of parties, however, extends well beyond nominating procedures.

Ballot Access

State laws define what constitutes an officially recognized political party that is eligible for a line on the general election ballot. The requirements for parties gaining ballot access ordinarily involve winning a specified percentage of the vote for governor in the previous election (the percentage ranges from 20 percent in Georgia to a low of 1 percent in Wisconsin). New parties or independent candidates who seek ballot access must secure signatures from a designated percentage of the voters. Whatever the specific form statutes governing ballot access may take, their general effect is to protect the dominant status of the two major parties and serve as barriers to independent candidacies and the emergence of third-party movements.

Party Membership

In all but a handful of states, statutes provide a description of the requirements for party membership—that is, who is eligible to vote in partisan primary elections. Usually, requirements include minimum age, state or local residence, citizenship, and, depending on the type of primary election system employed in the state, party affiliation. By limiting participation in primaries to registered Democrats or Republicans, as is done in *closed* primary states, the law is, in effect, defining party membership. Party bylaws sometimes define membership in the party organization by making more substantial demands on voters and party activists. The Republican party of Hawaii, for example, has required a signed affirmation of support for party principles before issuing a membership card; and the Democratic party of West Virginia requires people who wish to participate in the activities of the party organization to register as Democrats. In contrast, there are also numerous state party organizations that automatically issue legally meaningless "sustaining membership" cards to anyone who contributes to the party's treasury.

Organizational Structure

State regulations frequently extend to matters of internal party organization, such as procedures for selecting officers, composition of party committees, dates and locations of meetings, and powers of party units. Only five states (Alaska, Delaware, Hawaii, Kentucky, and North Carolina) do not specify in state law some aspect of party internal organizational structure (U.S. Advisory Commission 1986, 128). Both of the two major parties have a state central committee and a state chair (Republicans use the term *chairman*). In most states, the state committee is composed of members elected by county committees, state and congressional district conventions, or party primaries. State committees range in size from about twenty in Iowa to more than a thousand in California. The state committee's duties vary from state to state but normally include calling the state convention, adopting party policies, fund-raising, assisting with campaigns, aiding local party units, and serving as a party public relations agency. Most state party organizations have vested an executive committee with the same powers as the parent state central committee and authorize it to act for the party between the infrequent meetings of the central body.

More than three-quarters (77 percent) of the chairs of state party organizations are elected for two-year terms, whereas 23 percent have four-year terms. Turnover, however, is high, and tenure averages less than three years for chairs in both parties. State chairs or the party executive directors act as the operational heads of the state party organization and are responsible for fund-raising, candidate recruitment, campaign activities, party publicity, and liaison with local and national party organizations and elected officials. Both Republican and Democratic state chairs serve on their parties' national committees.

State chairs are frequently handpicked by their party's governor and, therefore, expected to advance and protect gubernatorial interests within the party. For the party out of power—lacking control of the governor's office—the state chair may be the real party leader and its principal spokesperson.

Congressional district, legislative district, county, city, ward, and precinct organizations constitute the remainder of the formal party structure. Each level of party organization is controlled by a committee headed by an elected leader. In reality the state party organization is much more encompassing than the above description would suggest. The party can be viewed as a network of individuals and organizations with an array of resources upon which the party can draw. Included in this network are allied interest groups (unions and teachers for the Democrats; business groups for the Republicans), PACs, the campaign organizations of individual candidates, political consultants, and the state legislative campaign committees that are controlled by legislative leaders (Schwartz 1990).

Campaign Finance

States have long set at least some minimal limits on campaign spending and activities. Most ban Election Day expenditures; all prohibit bribery and vote buying; and most impose some form of public disclosure and reporting of campaign receipts and expenditures. Since the Watergate scandals of the 1970s, campaign finance legislation has been the most rapidly growing body of election law. As of 1992, thirty-two states had imposed some limits on individual contributions, and forty-four states had set restrictions or limits on contributions by corporations, unions, regulated industries, or parties (Council of State Governments 1994, 304–316). Nevada, alone among the states, imposes no limitations on individual or organizational contributions. Despite the growing body of state regulations, the effectiveness of state regulatory activity has in general not matched that of the federal government.

Almost half of the states (twenty-three) have enacted programs to provide some form of state financing of elections. In thirteen states, public funds go to the political parties; in eight, state funds go directly to the candidates; and two states provide funding to both parties and candidates. State funding, however, tends to be inadequate. Indeed, in Wisconsin it has been found that public funding has failed to encourage challengers to take on state legislative incumbents and has also been ineffective in holding down campaign costs (Mayer and Wood 1995).

The Changing Legal Status of State Party Organizations

As state statutes have provided legal standing and special benefits to parties (for example, ballot access and public funding) and have stipulated the functions the parties will perform as well as regulated how those functions will be carried out, the parties have become quasi-public agencies. As adjuncts of state government, their existence has been practically mandated by state law and their continued existence virtually assured.

The legal status of parties is, however, in the process of modification as a result of a series of Supreme Court decisions. These decisions have extended First and Fourteenth Amendment freedom-of-association rights to political parties and have struck down a series of state-imposed restrictions on parties.

In *Tashjian v. Connecticut* (479 U.S. 20 [1986]), the Court held that Connecticut could not prevent voters registered as independents from voting in a Republican primary, if the state GOP wanted to permit independents to vote in its primaries. This case has potentially long-term implications for state regulatory policy, but its immediate consequences appear limited. While the *Tashjian* decision gives state party organizations greater control over the nominating process, only a few parties have actually used this court-granted power to modify the primary election procedures mandated by state law. The parties in several states have opened their primaries to independents, but the Alaska Republicans have imposed restrictions on participation in the state's "blanket" primary law that permits people to vote in the primaries of both parties as long as they vote for only one candidate per office. GOP rules in Alaska permit only registered Republicans and persons unaffiliated with any other party to vote in their primary (McBeath 1994). There is, however, no likelihood that the Republican or Democratic parties will use the power granted to them by *Tashjian* to abolish state-mandated direct primaries. The direct primary is just too popular and well ingrained in the American political culture (Epstein 1989, 260–274).

Citing the parties' rights of free association under the Constitution, the Supreme Court in 1989 further limited state regulatory authority over parties. In *Eu v. San Francisco County Democratic Central Committee* (49 U.S. 214 [1989]), it threw out a California law that banned party organizations from endorsing candidates in primaries, limited the length of state party organization chairs' terms to two years, and required rotating the state chairs' position between northern and southern California every two years.

In these cases, the Supreme Court has stated clearly that there are limits on the extent of regulation that states may impose on political parties. However, even though the Court has indicated a willingness to relieve the state party organizations of burdensome regulations, recent cases have not unleashed a movement to privatize them. The Republican and Democratic parties long ago adapted themselves to state regulation and have not, therefore, moved in significant ways to challenge the existing regulations. Also working against privatization of the parties has been the willingness of lower federal courts to adopt the view that states have a legitimate interest in regulating parties. For example, the U.S. Court of Appeals in the Seventh Circuit has upheld a Wisconsin law that bans candidates from cross-filing—seeking the nomination of more than one party (*Swamp v. Kennedy*, 950 F.2d 383 [7th Cir. 1991]). In this case, the court rejected the Labor-Farm party's contention that its right of free association permitted it to nominate a candidate whose name also appeared on the Democratic primary ballot. The three-judge panel ruled that Wisconsin's law served a compelling state interest in avoiding voter confusion, preserving the integrity of the electoral process, and ensuring that the winner of an election was the choice of at least a plurality of the voters. Although the Wisconsin case shows that there are limits to a party's right of free association, it does demonstrate that the doctrine of party First Amendment rights is likely to be a source of continuing litigation concerning the legal status of parties.

STATE PARTY ORGANIZATIONS: INSTITUTIONALIZED SERVICE AGENCIES

In the title of his book *The Party's Over*, the senior political reporter for the *Washington Post*, David Broder, aptly captured a widely accepted assessment of state party organizational strength during the 1960s and 1970s (Broder 1971). The party organizations were viewed as being in a state of steady decline (Key 1956, 271, 287). Predictions of their demise, however, were premature. The state party organizations of the 1990s have become more professional and stronger in the sense that most can provide campaign services to their candidates and assistance to their local affiliates. The once largely autonomous state party organizations are also now closely integrated with the national party organizations, which use them in their presidential, senatorial, and congressional campaign operations.

The institutionalization of state parties as campaign service organizations parallels the resurgence of party organizations at the national level, where a massive fund-raising capacity has transformed the once weak Republican and Democratic national committees (Cotter and Hennessy 1964) into major service agencies to candidates and state and local party organizations. There are also parallels between the major campaign roles played at the national level by the senatorial and congressional campaign committees and state legislative campaign committees, which have emerged as the principal party campaign resource for legislative candidates. The emergence of state central committees and legislative campaign committees as major providers of campaign services to candidates reflects the increasingly candidate-centered rather than party-centered nature of state politics.

The Passing of the Traditional State Party Organization

Although state party organizations went through a resurgence in the late 1970s and 1980s, they bear scant resemblance to the traditional party organizations that dominated state politics, particularly in the Mid-Atlantic, New England, and lower Great Lakes states, at the turn of the century (Mayhew 1986). These patronage-based organizations, which controlled nominations and ran their candidates' campaigns, had largely passed from the scene by the mid-1980s (Reichley 1992, 383–384). Unlike their predecessors, the revitalized state organizations of the 1990s neither control nominations nor run campaigns. They are, instead, service agencies for candidates and local parties as well as the vehicles through which national party organizations carry out their campaign strategies. Patronage as a basis for party organizations was severely weakened by civil service laws, strengthened public employee unions, and a critical public. In the 1970s the might of the Supreme Court began to supplement these antipatronage forces. In a series of cases, the Court hit at the heart of the large-scale patronage operations run by both Democrats and Republicans in Illinois. It ruled that the Cook County Democratic organization could no longer fire people on the basis of their party affiliation (*Elrod v. Burns*, 427 U.S. 347 [1976]), and it followed this decision with one declaring that the state GOP could not use "party affiliation and support" as the basis for filling state jobs unless party affiliation was an "appropriate requirement" for the position (*Rutan v. Republican Party*, 488 U.S. 1872, [1990]).

In once patronage-rich Illinois, the Democratic state chair observed that "the party no longer functions as an employment agency. More and more, we must rely on the spirit of volunteerism that moves so many other organizations" (Reichley 1992, 385). And Governor Robert Casey of Pennsylvania (1987–1995) lamented that "the unions and civil service have just about put an end to patronage. We still have a personnel office that checks with county chairmen to fill what jobs we have. But the jobs just aren't there anymore" (Reichley 1992, 385). Even in Indiana, a state not noted for a sensitivity to political favoritism, the system of giving the franchise to sell driver's and auto licenses to county leaders of the governor's party was abolished in 1986. Under this arrangement, the loyal party franchise holder passed on to the party organization a percentage of the profits from the sale of licenses (Freedman 1994, 76–77). Some elected officials in the state, however, continue to operate a system in which state party contributions are automatically deducted from their employees' paychecks (Gurwitt 1989).

Even though patronage jobs no longer provide the basis for party workers and funds, other forms of patronage remain important. Gubernatorial appointments to state boards and commissions that control professional licensing, gambling, higher education, hospitals, state investments, environmental and recreation policy, and cultural activities are assignments that are much sought after by persons seeking policy influence, recognition, and material gain. Partisan considerations often affect state decisions regarding state contracts, bank deposits, economic development, and the purchase of legal and consulting services. James Reichley, after surveying state politics, noted that these types of preferments are used primarily for party and candidate fund-raising. But they do not provide campaign workers, as patronage-based organizations once did (Reichley 1992, 385).

The Service-Oriented State Party Organization

Among the indicators of the capacity of most state party organizations to provide meaningful services to candidates and local party units are permanent headquarters; professional leadership and staffing; and adequate budgets and programs to maintain the organization, support candidates and officeholders, and assist local units (Cotter et al. 1984, 386–391).

Permanent Headquarters. As late as the early 1970s, state party organizations were frequently run out of the offices or homes of the state chair. This ad hoc type of operation has now largely ceased to exist as the parties have established permanent headquarters in the state capital. These headquarters are increasingly housed in modern office buildings stocked with high-tech equipment for data processing, fund-raising, communications, and printing.

Professional Staffing. In the 1960s most state party headquarters operated with a minimal staff, often only a secretary, executive director, and a few volunteers. Today virtually all of the state party organizations have full-time professional leadership. Over 30 percent of the state chairs work full time at the job and nearly every state party organization has a full-time chair or executive director (Cotter et al. 1984, 416–419; Reichley 1992, 389). State headquarters staffs have also grown in size, and there is increased specialization among the personnel. Turnover, however, is high at headquarters. State chairs usually serve only two to three years, and their professional operatives tend to be transients who move about the country from job to job with party organizations, candidates, and campaign consultants (Reichley 1992, 391–392).

Finances. Operating a professional headquarters requires an ability to raise significant amounts of money on a continuing basis. The data in Table 3-1 demonstrate that state party organizations have for the most part developed substantial financial resources. In the 1991–1992 election cycle, only 22 percent of all state party organizations reported to the Federal Election Commission that they raised less than $500,000—whereas 96 percent of all PACs operating in the same period raised less than $500,000 (Biersack 1994). Although the Republican orga-

Table 3-1   State Party Receipts Reported to the Federal Election Commission, 1991–1992 Election Cycle

Party receipts	Democratic state party organizations		Republican state party organizations		Total state party organizations	
	N	%	N	%	N	%
Under $500,000	10	20	12	24	22	22
$500,000–999,000	11	22	10	20	21	21
$1,000,000–1,999,999	15	30	9	18	24	24
$2,000,000–2,999,999	5	10	11	22	16	16
$3,000,000–4,999,999	7	14	4	8	11	11
$5,000,000+	2	4	4	8	6	6
Total	50	100	50	100	100	100

SOURCE: Calculated from Federal Election Commission data reported in Biersack 1994, 118–119.

NOTE: Total reported receipts of Democratic state party organizations were $93,551,960; total reported receipts of Republican state party organizations were $92,952,545. All receipts include those allocatable to the bulk of overhead and generic party-building activity as well as all other revenues allocatable to federal elections. Data do not reflect funding from programs or activities directed exclusively toward state and local campaigns.

nizations in the past have generally had more substantial budgets than their Democratic counterparts, the 1991–1992 data show that the two parties have remarkably equal access to financial resources. There are, however, differences between the parties in the sources of funding. The Republican state party organizations depend more on contributions from individuals (57 percent for GOP; 38 percent for Democrats) and less on national party organizations or other organizations (for example, unions and PACs) than Democratic state units.

Party Activities: Organizational Building and Maintenance. Since the 1960s state party organizations have expanded their programs aimed at building and maintaining the organizations. More now have multifaceted fund-raising operations, run voter identification and mobilization operations, publish newsletters, engage in public opinion polling and issue development, and assist local party units (Cotter et al. 1984, 19–26).

Party Activities: Candidate Support. The active role played by state party organizations in assisting candidates is revealed in Table 3-2, which contains the results of a survey conducted by the U.S. Advisory Commission on Intergovernmental Relations. In these candidate support activities, Republican state organizations tend to be more active than the Democratic ones (see also Reichley 1992, 390). Although state party organizations can now provide an array of campaign services, their role is clearly supplementary to that of the candidates' own organizations.

Most state party organizations are either unable or unwilling to become heavily involved in primary elections. Thus Reichley reports that only 16 out of 92 party chairs he contacted said that their organizations regularly supported candidates before the primaries—a form of involvement that old line party machines would have regarded as normal and essential for maintaining effectiveness. Some state chairs do attempt to avoid primary fights by seeking to persuade aspiring

Table 3-2   Campaign Assistance to Candidates Provided by State
Parties (in percent)

Type of assistance provided to candidates	Republican state parties	Democratic state parties
Financial contributions		
To gubernatorial candidates	81	54
To congressional candidates	71	55
To state legislative candidates	95	52
To local candidates	39	23
Fund-raising assistance		
To state candidates	96	63
To congressional candidates	63	30
Voter registration drives	73	81
Public opinion polling	78	50
Media consulting	75	46
Campaign seminars and training	100	76
Coordinating PAC contributions	52	31

SOURCES: U.S. Advisory Commission 1986, 115; Reichley 1992, 390.

candidates not to run, but many chairs abstain from even this type of intervention (Reichley 1992, 390). As a result, candidates are forced to build their own personal organizations to contest the primaries.

And with state party organizations able to provide only selected professional services to candidates, and not in a position to manage their nominees' general election campaigns, it is small wonder that candidates rely on their own organizations in the general election. Thus, while the role of the state party organization in campaigns is often significant, especially in such areas as candidate training, voter identification, and get-out-the-vote drives (for example, the Florida GOP operates a program to contact more than a million potential absentee voters), the party role in campaigns is restricted and supplementary in character. The state organizations have adopted a role consistent with the candidate-centered nature of 1990s politics.

Party Differences

Studies of state central committees have generally shown the Republicans to be organizationally stronger than their Democratic counterparts (Cotter et al. 1984; Reichley 1992, 387–391; U.S. Advisory Commission 1986). This reflects a key difference between the parties: Republican state organizations tend to be a more important source of campaign support than do Democratic organizations. This does not mean that Democratic candidates are necessarily lacking or unequal in resources, but it does mean that Democrats derive support from somewhat different sources. Democratic state organizations and their candidates rely more heavily than do Republicans for campaign assistance from allied nonparty organizations such as organized labor, especially teachers' unions. These organizations provide services—get-out-the-vote drives, financial assistance, technical services—that for Republican candidates and organizations might be provided by the party.

The Electoral Impact of Party Organizations

Although in this era of candidate-centered politics in which the party organization is rarely involved in direct campaign management, the level of party organizational strength within a state can affect election outcomes. Thus analyses of gubernatorial elections show that the state party with an organizational strength advantage gains increments of voters over the opposition party (Cotter et al. 1984, 100–101). However, because a state party organization develops itself into a more sophisticated campaign service organization does not necessarily mean that it will automatically and simultaneously become more successful in winning elections. The relationship between organizational strength and party electoral success in the states is complex, and the organization's impact is often indirect in character. In some instances, strong party organizations (for example, Illinois and New York Democratic lower house campaign committees; and the Michigan Democratic, Ohio Republican, and Indiana Republican state committees) have clearly contributed to the victories of their candidates, and electoral success has been an incentive to maintain the organizations. But in other states, where a party has long been dominant, there may be little incentive to develop strong party organizations. The Democrats in the South, for example, have lagged behind other Democratic parties in developing strong state committees and legislative campaign organizations. Similarly, the electorally dominant Massachusetts Democrats have had little incentive to build a strong party organization.

By contrast, in some states where a party was electorally weak, the party developed a strong state organization as a first step toward achieving electoral success. This has certainly been the case for the southern Republicans. After a period of organization building, which began in the 1960s, they have made significant electoral gains since the 1970s. Of course, other factors (for example, the disaffection of many southern whites with the national Democratic party) have also contributed to the GOP gains in the South. It appears, therefore, that the importance of party organizational strength may not be just its impact in any given year. Rather, the real significance of such strength may be its role in providing the infrastructure for candidates and activists to continue to compete in the face of short-term defeats and even long-term minority status. Republican successes in southern gubernatorial elections during the 1980s and early 1990s provide evidence that a minority party that is organizationally strong can take advantage of favorable circumstances (for example, divisiveness within the dominant party or the retirement of an incumbent).

The indirect effect of party organization strength on electoral fortunes is also demonstrated by local party organizations, which, far from withering away, have continued to function and provide limited levels of support to candidates (Cotter et al. 1984; Frendreis et al. 1994; Gibson, Frendreis, and Vertz 1989). Studies of well-structured and active local organizations, especially minority party organizations, suggest that their major electoral impact is one of running full slates of candidates. These local candidates can have a "trickle up" effect of adding increments of voters to the party's total vote for offices higher up on the ballot (Frendreis, Gibson, and Vertz 1990).

The Emergence of Legislative Campaign Committees and Leadership PACs

As is the case at the national level, the state party organizational structure is multifaceted and decentralized, with a variety of organizations focusing on different activities. Thus, while the Republican and Democratic national committees concentrate primarily on presidential politics and working with their constituent state organizations, the congressional and senatorial campaign committees are the principal party support agencies for House and Senate candidates, to whom they provide money (including assistance with PAC financing), polling, media advertising, and other technical assistance (Herrnson 1988, 1994). Similarly, at the state level, while the state central committees concentrate on statewide races and working with their local affiliates, the state legislative campaign committees have emerged as the primary sources of party assistance to legislative candidates.

Reasons for the Development of Legislative Campaign Committees. Legislative campaign committees are composed of incumbent legislators in both the upper and lower chambers and are most often led by the party leaders in each chamber. These committees emerged as the principal party support mechanisms for legislative candidates in response to intensifying partisan competition for control of legislative chambers, the rising costs of campaigns, increased uncertainty about election outcomes, and the inability of many state party organizations during the 1970s to provide meaningful assistance to legislative candidates (Gierzynski 1992, 11–14; Rosenthal 1993, 5). Thus the most active legislative campaign committees are found in states with substantial levels of interparty competition, high campaign costs, and weak state central committees. In the South, where the Democrats continue to dominate the legislative elections, legislative campaign committees are less well developed than in states with longer traditions of competitive two-party politics, such as Illinois, New Jersey, New York, Ohio, and Wisconsin. And where the Democratic state central committees are weak—as in Indiana, Maine, Minnesota, and Wisconsin—the legislative campaign committees are particularly well developed.

In addition, the development of strong legislative campaign committees is also linked to increased legislative professionalism—full-time legislators who are paid a reasonable salary and backed up by ample staff. Thus, as legislative service increases in value and margins of legislative majorities narrow, legislative leaders have created campaign committees to protect their own interests as well as the stakes of the party and individual members. At the same time, a legislatively based campaign organization requires an institutional capacity to operate—virtually full-time legislative leaders, a legislative caucus staff with proximity to the process, and computer and media resources (Rosenthal 1993, 4–5). In New York, legislative staffs are particularly active in supporting candidates (Stonecash 1988, 484).

Unlike state central committees, in which the GOP tends to be organizationally stronger, Democratic legislative campaign committees do not generally labor at a disadvantage. This can be explained by the Democrats' having controlled in recent decades significantly more legislative chambers than the Republicans. With the power that accompanies incumbency and chamber control, Democratic legislative campaign committees have been able to raise large warchests to support their candidates with cash and services. In many states, alliances with activist teachers' unions have increased the effectiveness of Democratic campaign committees (Gierzynski 1992, 56).

The legislative campaign committee's active involvement in candidate recruitment is particularly crucial. These recruitment activities have a significant influence on the quality of candidates, which in turn affects the ability of individual candidates to raise money, recruit campaign workers, and make a competitive run for the legislative seat. As the state politics expert Alan Ehrenhalt noted:

> Every other year, Democrats and Republicans battle for legislative control . . . in what is advertised as a debate about which party best reflects the views of the electorate. Within the corridors of the state capitol, however, the biennial legislative elections are recognized for what they really are: a competition to attract candidates who have the skills and energy to win and the desire and resourcefulness to stay in office. (1989, 29–30)

Full-Service Campaign Agencies. Legislative campaign committees began as mechanisms to raise and distribute funds to candidates. Increasingly, however, they have developed into what the chief of staff of the Ohio Senate Republican Caucus described as a "full service operation for individual campaigns" ("Guru in Ohio" 1989, 2977). Thus the former Speaker of the Wisconsin Assembly, Tom Loftus, described the range of services his Democratic Assembly Campaign Committee provided as follows:

> We raised [money] to help Democrats running in marginal seats. In most cases we recruited the candidate. We provide training through campaign schools. We provide personnel and logistical support, issue papers, press releases, speakers for fund raisers, fund raisers themselves, and phone banks; we pay for the recount if it's a close race; we pay for the lawyer if it goes to court; if they have kids we pay for the baby-sitter. . . . We do everything a political party is supposed to do. (1985, 100)

The scope of legislative campaign committee spending and services is extensive. In Ohio, the Republican Senate Caucus provides candidates with a "highly structured package of in-house polling, campaign managers, phone banks, media planning, issues research, and other campaign services," which costs more than $3.5 million in each election cycle ("Guru in Ohio" 1989). And in Illinois during 1992, the House Democratic Majority Committee in conjunction with the Democratic Speaker's personal PAC spent more than $2.5 million on legislative elections (58 percent of the total spending in targeted races), while the House Republican Campaign Committee and minority leader's PAC spent $1.9 million (Redfield 1993, 22–24).

Leadership PACs. As the Illinois example above indicates, the emergence of leadership PACs has further increased the role of the legislative party in campaigns. Leadership PACs are controlled by legislative leaders who by virtue of their positions are able to raise substantially more money than they need for their own reelection. Legislative leaders are therefore able to dispense funds to targeted races in a manner that furthers their party's (and their own) interests. Leadership PACs specialize in transferring excess campaign funds to needy candidates, whereas legislative campaign committees specialize in assisting candidates through services. Party and leadership interests are not necessarily identical, and there have been instances in which leadership PAC money went to further the leaders' own careers in the legislature rather than to advance party interests (Gierzynski 1992, 68, 101).

Electoral Strategies. Legislative campaign committees concentrate their resources on close or competitive races—either to maintain or gain control of a legislative chamber. Minority parties are thus more likely to provide support for nonincumbents than are majority parties, which are seeking to maintain their dominant status. Thus, in New York Assembly races, the majority Democrats, who are concerned primarily with preservation, devote most of their resources to incumbents, while the minority Republicans put their money on challengers in close races (Stonecash 1990, 259). Campaign strategy is also affected by special features of a state's politics. For example, the majority Republicans in the New York State Senate have put heavier emphasis on challengers than incumbents because they recognized that their incumbents were older and that the party needed to find new, younger members (Stonecash 1990, 259). Legislative campaign committees also respond to conditions at the local or district level—for example, heavy spending against an incumbent, or a favorable, or unfavorable, trend toward the party in a particular district (Gierzynski 1992, 110–111).

Shared goals, party loyalty, and personal connections do encourage an element of cooperation and coordinated activity between legislative campaign committees and state committees. Thus, periodically, a legislative leader will simultaneously serve as chair of the state central committee. However, because legislative campaign committees are led and dominated by legislative leaders, the committees tend to operate independently of state central committees. The campaign finance expert Frank Sorauf (1992, 120) observed that legislative campaign committees are party organizations built and maintained by incumbents that serve primarily the agendas and priorities of legislative partisans and "insulate them from the pressures of other parts of their party. Collective action has helped to bring legislative parties freedom from the agendas of presidential or gubernatorial parties" (Sorauf 1992, 120).

GOVERNORS AND THE STATE PARTY ORGANIZATION

It is an unusual governor who actively seeks to direct the affairs of the state central committee. In a nationwide study, less than 50 percent of the chairs of state party organizations reported that they believed it necessary to have the governor's approval before taking action. Most considered the governor's role in the party affairs to be advisory rather than controlling (Cotter et al. 1984, 112). And just as governors do not exert day-to-day control over their state party organizations, state party organizations play only a supportive or supplementary role in gubernatorial campaigns. In this era of candidate-centered politics, governors rely primarily on their own personal campaign organizations. Even governors like Tommy Thompson (R-Wis.), who have been particularly supportive of their parties, carefully cultivate a personal following that transcends partisanship and engage in the extensive fund-raising required to maintain a sophisticated personal campaign apparatus.

Governors do frequently seek to influence the selection of the chair of a state party organization, lest the apparatus of the organization fall into unfriendly hands. In 1988, for example, Gov. James Martin of North Carolina successfully fended off an attempt by his intraparty rival, Sen. Jesse Helms, to control selection of the state GOP chairman.

Since the interests of the governor and the state party organization are seldom identical, conflicts are not uncommon. Thus, in 1991, Gov. William Schaefer (D-Md.), sought to have his party's state chair removed when they disagreed over legislative redistricting. And in Virginia in 1992, Gov. Douglas Wilder's appointee as state chair was forced to share power with the steering committee of the state Democratic party when he was accused of placing the governor's national political ambitions ahead of the electoral interests of the state party organization (Baker 1992, B4).

The actual pattern of relations between the governor and the state party organization varies from those in which the organization is dominated by the governor and closely tied to his or her political fortunes to those exhibiting the type of outright hostility described above. In an interview, a New England Democratic chair described a tightly linked relationship between the governor and the state party organization as follows: "I'm the governor's agent. My job is to work with him. If I look good, he looks good, because I'm his man. I don't bother him with messy stuff. He expects me to handle it my way. I meet with the [local] leaders on his behalf. I'm liaison to city and town leaders." Some governors also rely on their state party chairs to assist them in influencing state legislators in support of the governor's legislative agenda.

More common, however, is a relationship of coordinate responsibility: the governor and state chair consult with one another on appointments, candidate recruitment, fund-raising, and other major party activities. And the governor assists the party with fund-raising and candidate recruitment, but neither the governor nor his or her staff runs the state central committee and headquarters. Likewise, the state party chair does not seek to manage the governor's campaign organization or determine gubernatorial policy. In an interview, a Republican chair in a midwestern state that has had a long tradition of professional party leadership summarized his relationship with a governor of his party as follows: "I don't go to his office and he doesn't come over here. . . . A lot of people think he isn't interested in the party. But that's just not true. He cares and he helps me. His attitude is 'What can I do to help?'" The governor corroborated these comments in an interview by saying that his state party chair "doesn't want to be governor and I don't want to be party chairman."

PACS AND PARTIES

PACs are commonly viewed as a threat to political parties. Yet during the same period in which PACs have become an increasingly important source of campaign funds, both state central committees and legislative campaign committees have strengthened their capacity to provide services to candidates. As has been the case at the national level, state party organizations have learned to adapt to a political environment in which PACs are major participants—providing in excess of 50 percent of legislative campaign funds in some states.

State central committees and particularly legislative leaders and their legislative campaign committees have become adept at soliciting funds directly from PACs. In 1992, for example, over 75 percent of the $7.1 million raised by legislative leaders in Illinois came from interest groups and corporations (Redfield, Shinn, and Van Der Slik 1993).

Party organizations also work closely with PACs to channel PAC money to candidates. In these efforts, the parties have been aided by the fact that many state-level PACs are run by persons who are not specialists in electoral politics or by lobbyists who have expertise in legislative politics but not in statewide electoral strategies. Parties are, therefore, in a position to provide PAC leaders with political intelligence. In addition, legislative campaign committees can assist candidates by giving them a mark of legitimacy, which is bestowed when the party identifies them as candidates who constitute good investments for PACs (Gierzynski 1992, 117). Thus the executive assistant to the Speaker of the Indiana House of Representatives observed that "for every one dollar we [the legislative campaign committee] raise, we direct two dollars of interest group money"; and the president of the Maine Senate said that his committee performs a "matchmaking service" by "identifying a candidate's philosophy with PACs and connecting them" (quoted by Gierzynski 1992, 55).

By channeling PAC money to candidates as well as by soliciting PAC funds di-

rectly, the parties have infused campaigns with new funds that "carried the im-
primatur of the party at no direct expense to party coffers" (Jones 1984, 197).
State party organizations and allied PACs have also coordinated their efforts to
provide in-kind services to candidates.

THE IMPACT OF NATIONAL PARTY ORGANIZATIONS AND THE NATIONAL-STATE PARTY INTEGRATION

Until the late 1970s, political scientists emphasized the decentralized and confederate nature of American party organizations (Key 1964, 334). The Republican
and Democratic national committees were considered so lacking in power and
influence that a landmark study even characterized them as "politics without
power" (Cotter and Hennessy 1964). Informed political observers would not describe them in that manner today. The two national committees have been transformed into well-heeled, professional institutions capable of providing significant assistance to state party organizations and to candidates. In the process, they
have acquired a capacity to exert substantial influence over their state affiliates.
This increased influence of national party organizations has been accompanied
by heightened integration and interdependence between national and state party
structures.

Enforcing the Rules of National Party Organizations

Since 1968 the national Democratic party organization has intensified efforts
begun in 1948 to use its rule-making authority to ensure the loyalty of state party
organizations to the national ticket. Starting with the McGovern-Fraser Commission in the late 1960s and a series of successor commissions, the national
Democratic party has developed elaborate national convention delegate selection
procedures that the state party organizations are required to follow. These procedures have been vigorously enforced by the Democratic National Committee
(DNC). For example, when Wisconsin Democrats failed in 1984 to comply with
national party rules that prohibited use of the state's traditional open presidential primary to select national convention delegates, the DNC forced the state
party to select their delegates by a caucus system. In addition, the National Democratic Charter, adopted in 1974, contains stipulations concerning the organization and operation of state party affiliates. The DNC's power to require compliance with its rules has been upheld in a series of Supreme Court decisions (for
example, *Cousins v. Wigoda*, 419 U.S. 450 [1975]; *Democratic Party of the U.S. v. ex
rel La Follette*, 450 U.S. 107 [1981]).

Unlike the Democrats, the national GOP has not sought to gain influence
over its state affiliates through tough rule enforcement. Instead, it has maintained the confederate legal structure of the party, and the Republican National
Committee (RNC) has assumed a relatively passive role in delegate section procedures and internal party organization. Nevertheless, party centralization and

integration has moved forward dramatically in the GOP. The national party has gained power through providing assistance to state organizations and their candidates (Bibby 1981).

Providing Assistance to State Party Organizations and the
Nationalization of Campaigns

The RNC's efforts to assist state party organizations and candidates began in a modest way in 1965 under the leadership of the national chairman, Ray C. Bliss (1965–1969), and was expanded to unprecedented levels during the tenure of Bill Brock (1977–1981). Brock's successors have continued his initiatives with multi-million-dollar programs benefiting state party organizations, selected county organizations, and candidates. These programs have included cash grants, professional staff, data processing, consulting services for organizational development, fund-raising, campaigning, media relations, and redistricting. There have also been large-scale investments of money and personnel to assist state party organizations in the development of voter lists and efforts to get out the vote.

The advantages held by the RNC in fund-raising enabled it to initiate and expand its programs of direct aid to state party affiliates well before the DNC began consciously to copy the RNC's programs after the 1984 elections. Thus, since the RNC initiated unprecedented national party involvement in state legislative elections in 1978 (Bibby 1979), the Democrats have followed the GOP example. With both parties anxious to do well in legislative elections because of congressional redistricting that would occur in 1991–1992, both national parties conducted major state legislative campaign support operations in 1990.

Under the leadership of Paul Kirk, the national chairman from 1985 to 1989, the DNC broadened its services to state party organizations and in 1986 created and funded an "Election Force" of trained professionals in sixteen key states. In these states, the DNC paid for a full-time political operative and a fund-raiser. In exchange for an infusion of $1.2 million in resources, the recipient state party organizations were required to sign commitments that pledged them to continue DNC-sponsored party-building programs and to cooperate with the DNC in presidential nomination procedures and national campaigns (Broder 1986, A23).

After the 1988 elections, Ron Brown, the DNC chair, sought to expand national party support programs by subsidizing the creation of "Coordinated Campaign" structures in thirty-six states to serve a broad range of candidates in the 1990 elections (Longley 1992, 8–9). The Coordinated Campaign organization was geared to provide basic campaign services—voter registration, voter-list development, get-out-the-vote drives, polling, targeting, press relations, media purchases, and scheduling—to Democratic candidates within a state. These coordinated state campaign operations were funded jointly by the DNC, state party organizations, candidates, in some instances legislative campaign committees, and allied groups like organized labor. The Democrats used the Coordinated Campaign again, in expanded form, in 1992.

Instituting a coordinated campaign structure within a state involves extensive negotiation among the cooperating state party units, candidates, allied interest groups, and the DNC. In 1992, DNC support was always contingent on its approval of a negotiated campaign plan. The level of national party involvement in the actual implementation of a coordinated campaign depended heavily on the strength of the state party organization. In those states in which the state party organization was deemed to be strong enough, it was allowed to run the coordinated campaign (for example, Wisconsin in 1992). But in those states in which the organization was thought incapable of running an effective coordinated campaign, the DNC sent in its own personnel to run the operation on a temporary basis.

The Republicans in recent elections have operated programs similar to the Democrats' Coordinated Campaign. Thus the GOP's "Victory '92" organizations ran state-level voter identification and get-out-the-vote programs. These programs operated under the legal aegis of state organizations, received funding from the RNC, the Bush-Quayle organization, the national-level senatorial and congressional campaign committees, the candidates, and other state sources. In some states the RNC placed carefully selected campaign operatives in state organizations. As a prominent GOP state chair put it in an interview in 1993, RNC "parachuted people into state headquarters over a year in advance of the election to be sure that the operation was ready to go."

Programs of financial and in-kind assistance sponsored by the national party organization and operations such as the Democrats' Coordinated Campaign and the GOP's Victory '92 have in many instances strengthened the state organizations by providing them with major campaign assets—such as computer capabilities and voter lists used for get-out-the-vote drives. In addition, intraparty cohesion among party units, candidates, and allied interest groups has been furthered in some states through coordinated campaign activities.

It is also apparent, however, that assistance from the national party organization tends to flow to those state organizations that are considered crucial to achieving national party objectives in a given election cycle. As a result, not all state party organizations benefit equally, and continuity of support from election cycle to election cycle is by no means assured. A state party organization can thus be the favored beneficiary of largess from the national organization in one election and be virtually ignored in the next.

For state parties, especially those lacking in organizational strength, being the beneficiary of national party involvement holds other risks as well. Weak state organizations can be quite literally taken over by national party operatives in presidential election years as staff are brought in to run the campaign effort. These personnel and their backup resources are usually pulled out just as soon as the election is over, leaving the state organization in about the same condition as before the campaign. State party organizations also run the risk of becoming overly dependent on the national party organizations, which periodically go through dry spells in fund-raising and have shifting priorities.

Money Transfers from National to State Party Organizations

As the campaign efforts described above demonstrate, state party organizations became an integral component of national campaign strategies during the 1980s and 1990s. A crucial aspect of this process of integrating the state organizations into national campaign efforts has been the massive transfers of funds from national to state and local party organizations. These transfers are encouraged by the Federal Election Campaign Act (FECA), which imposes strict limits on the amounts of money that national party organizations can contribute or expend on behalf of federal candidates. The act, however, permits state and local party organizations to spend without limit on "party building" activities: voter registration, phone banks, get-out-the-vote drives, and facilities. As a result of this FECA provision and the fact that the Republican and Democratic national organizations can raise more money than they can legally spend on federal elections, both national parties have embarked on large-scale programs to collect and transfer money to state and local organizations to support party-building activities that benefit their presidential, senatorial, and congressional candidates. In addition, the national party operatives have directed contributions from large givers to party organizations in states considered critical to winning these elections.

In 1988 an estimated $55 million was solicited for state party organizations to support the Democratic and Republican presidential campaigns. As shown in Table 3-3, a torrent of funds again flowed from the national to state organizations

Table 3-3   National Party Organization Disbursements from Nonfederal Accounts, 1991–1992

Party	Transfers to state party organizations	Contributions to state and local candidates	Share of joint activity*
Republican			
National Committee	$5,371,110	$1,247,000	$17,853,015
National Senatorial Committee	1,674,603	0	4,055,306
National Congressional Committee	1,732,150	n/a	600,602
Total	8,777,863	1,247,000	22,508,923
Democratic			
National Committee	9,458,112	212,091	16,318,348
Senatorial Campaign Committee	0	0	0
Congressional Campaign Committee	34,550	565,781	1,641,614
Total	9,492,662	777,872	17,959,962

SOURCE: Federal Election Commission 1992.
  * Joint activity includes party-building activities such as voter registration, voter list development, and get-out-the-vote drives.

in 1991–1992. These funds included direct transfers of dollars and contributions to state and local candidates, and, most important, support for joint activities (assisting both federal and state candidates) being run under the legal aegis of the state parties (the Republicans' Victory '92 and the Democrats' Coordinated Campaign). The money that the national parties use for these purposes is referred to as *soft money*—money raised outside the restrictions of federal law but nonetheless intended to influence federal elections (Sorauf 1992, 147). Soft money is held in nonfederal accounts, which are separate from the *hard money* held in federal accounts for direct contributions or expenditures on behalf of federal candidates.

Heightened Party Integration

Because FECA has encouraged national party organizations to channel funds into their state affiliates in an effort to influence federal elections, the state organizations have now been integrated into the national campaign structure to play a significant role in presidential, senatorial, and House elections. As a consequence, the traditional distinctions between national and state party organizations and between party organizations and candidates' personal organizations have become rather hazy at the state level. The national organizations' multimillion dollar programs to strengthen state affiliates and their use of these affiliates to achieve their own goals in federal elections have brought in their wake a significant change in the relative power positions of national and state parties. Prior to the 1970s, the flow of intraparty funds was from state party organizations to the national committees. Today, however, the direction of flow is the opposite. This shift of direction has been accompanied by a change in the direction of intraparty influence. Instead of being dependent on their state organizations, the RNC and DNC have gained substantial autonomy as well as increased leverage over state and local affiliates because of their superior financial and technical resources. The political parties scholar Leon Epstein (1986, 223) has characterized this process of nationalizing the parties' campaign efforts as being analogous to the federal government's grant-in-aid system. Like the federal government's categorical grants that require state and local governments to follow federal guidelines, the RNC and DNC also attach conditions (frequently rather permissive and flexible ones) to the assistance they give to state party organizations and candidates.

Transfers of funds and technical assistance from national to state organizations and joint campaign activities have resulted in an unprecedented level of national-state party integration. This constitutes a major change in the American party system and renders out of date such traditional descriptions of American parties as that found in the classic text of V. O. Key, Jr., which asserted that "no national party organization exists. . . . Rather, each party consists of a working coalition of state and local parties" (Key 1964, 315). The national party organizations are now major players in federal and state elections, and thanks to their programs of assistance state organizations have become stronger. However, the state affiliates have also become more dependent on the national party organizations and have lost much of their traditional autonomy.

PARTY NOMINATIONS

The nomination process is crucial for parties because selecting the "right" candidate can determine whether a party wins or loses an election. In addition, control of the party is at stake. Influence over the selection of candidates goes a long way toward determining which party factions will gain ascendancy, who receives the rewards that elected officials bestow on their supporters, and the party's policy orientation. The critical importance of nominations was aptly summarized by Schattschneider (1942, 64) when he observed in his classic work that "[t]he nature of the nomination procedure determines the nature of the party; he who can make nominations is the owner of the party."

In most Western democracies, party candidates are selected by party organization leaders. Operating largely without government regulation, these party leaders designate the party's candidates and there is no appeal of their decisions to the voters. Rank and file voters participate only in the general election—a contest between parties—not in the intraparty contest to select nominees. By contrast, the widespread use of the direct primary election in the American states involves not only party activists but voters in the nomination process. Because it gives rank and file voters a deciding voice in nominations, the direct primary has weakened the capacity of party hierarchies to control candidate selection. Among Western democracies, the American direct primary is unique, not only for the amount of popular participation it permits, but also for the wide variety and extensive state-level statutory regulation that accompanies it.

Early in the twentieth century the direct primary gradually replaced nominations by party conventions and caucuses as part of the Progressive Era reform movement, whose leaders decried bossism and corrupt party machines and believed that ordinary voters should have a direct say in who the party candidates would be. The absence of real two-party competition in much of the country also furthered the spread of the direct primary. In one-party areas, nomination by party leaders was tantamount to election. As a result, instituting primary elections to nominate candidates constituted a means of assuring meaningful popular participation in elections. As V. O. Key, Jr. (1956, 81) concluded, the direct primary was "an escape from one-partyism."

Types of Direct Primaries

The constitutional principal of federalism permits the states wide latitude in regulating the nominating process. They can specify the circumstances under which a primary must be used and the type of primary to be used in order for a

Table 3-4 Types of Direct Primaries

Closed (Party registration required)	Semi-closed (Voters may register or change registration on Election Day)	Semi-open (Voters required to request party ballot publicly)	Open (Voter may vote in any party primary)	Blanket	Nonpartisan
Arizona	Colorado*	Alabama	Hawaii	Alaska§	Louisiana
California	Iowa†	Arkansas	Idaho	Washington	
Connecticut	Kansas*	Georgia	Michigan		
Delaware	Maine*	Illinois	Minnesota		
Florida	Massachusetts‡	Indiana	Montana		
Kentucky	New Hampshire‡	Mississippi	North Dakota		
Maryland	New Jersey*	Missouri	Utah		
Nebraska	Ohio†	South Carolina	Vermont		
Nevada	Rhode Island*	Tennessee	Wisconsin		
New Mexico	Wyoming†	Texas			
New York		Virginia			
North Carolina					
Oklahoma					
Oregon					
Pennsylvania					
South Dakota					
West Virginia					

SOURCE: Updated and adapted from Jewell and Olson 1988, 90–92.
* Persons not previously voting in a party primary may register with a party on Election Day.
† Party registration may be changed on Election Day.
‡ Independents are permitted to change registration on Election Day.
§ State law specifies a blanket primary, but Republican party rules restrict participation in the Republican primary to registered Republicans and voters without a partisan affiliation.

party's candidates to secure a slot on the general election ballot. Thus state laws regulating party nominating procedures vary significantly in terms of the degree of public disclosure of party preference required of voters, and whether voters are allowed to participate in the primary of more than one party (see Table 3-4).

Open Primary Systems. Twelve states have an *open* primary system, in which a public affirmation of partisan preference is not required in order to vote in primaries. In nine of those states voters receive a ballot containing the names of both parties' candidates and then decide in the secrecy of the voting booth in which party's primary they will vote. An even more open system is the *blanket* primary used in the state of Washington, which permits the voter to take part in more than one party's primary, switching back and forth between parties from office to office. Although Alaska statutes also provide for a blanket primary, the rules of the state Republican party organization restrict participation in the GOP primary to registered Republicans and voters without a partisan affiliation (McBeath 1994).

Louisiana has a *nonpartisan* primary, in which all the candidates for each office are placed on the ballot with no listing of their party affiliation. If a candidate receives a majority of the votes cast in the primary, he or she is elected and no general election is held for that office (as happened, for example, in the gubernatorial primaries of 1983 and 1987). But if no candidate receives a majority of the votes in the primary, the two candidates with the highest number of votes, irrespective of party, must face each other in the general election. Louisiana's system appears to have worked as its sponsors intended; that is, it has aided incumbent legislators in gaining reelection and discouraged legislative candidacies among the minority Republicans (Kazee 1983).

Closed Primaries. Seventeen states operate *closed* primary systems, in which voters must be registered as Democrats or Republicans in order to vote in partisan primaries. They are permitted to vote in the primary of the party in which they are registered. New York and Kentucky are particularly restrictive. Persons wishing to change party registration and vote in primaries are required to make the switch ten to eleven months prior to the primary election (Carr and Scott 1984, 472).

A *semi-closed* system is used in ten states. In these states, voters are permitted to change their party registration on Election Day. Eleven states operate *semi-open* primary systems, under which voters are required to request publicly a party ballot, but no record is kept of the party primary in which they voted. In states that use either semi-closed or semi-open systems, the voters achieve freedom of selection that approximates that of an open primary except that a public statement of party preference has been exacted from them.

The Effect of Open and Closed Primaries. Open primary systems encourage crossover voting—partisans of one party voting in the primary of the other party—whereas closed primary systems largely preclude this type of behavior. Crossover voting tends to occur in the party's primary in which there is a meaningful nomination contest, and those voters who cross over typically are engaging in *sincere* rather than *strategic* crossover voting. That is, they vote for their most preferred candidate rather than for their preferred candidate's weakest opponent. Because this pattern of voter behavior can affect primary outcomes, the candidates with policy positions closest to the median voter's views are more likely to be selected in open primary systems than in closed primaries (Gerber and Morton 1994).

Run-off Primaries. Usually, the candidate who receives the most votes (a plurality) in the primary gains the nomination, even if that individual receives less than a majority of the total vote cast. In nine southern and Border states, a majority of the vote in the primary is required for nomination (40 percent in North Carolina). If no candidate receives a majority, then a second, or run-off, primary is held between the top two finishers in the first primary. This system was instituted in the South when the Democratic party was so dominant that winning the party's primary was equivalent to being elected. To ensure that the person nominated in the Democratic primary and therefore "elected" had the support of a majority of Democrats, the run-off primary was instituted. Research on the impact of the direct primary demonstrates that (a) run-offs are required in about 10 percent of the races; (b) the leader in the first primary goes on to win the run-off 70 percent of the time, although the success rate falls to 50 percent for African-

American candidates; and (c) women are not at a disadvantage in the run-off system (Bullock and Johnson 1992).

Nominating Conventions and Preprimary Endorsements

Although the direct primary is the predominant method of nominating candidates, thirteen states either permit or require conventions for nominations. Thus four southern states (Alabama, Georgia, South Carolina, and Virginia) permit the parties to nominate either by party convention or primary. There are also states that use *preprimary conventions*. In Connecticut, Delaware, New Mexico, New York, and Utah, primaries are not mandatory and are held if two or more candidates whose names are placed before the state party convention receive a specified share of the delegate vote (25 percent in New York, 20 percent in Connecticut and New Mexico, and 35 percent in Delaware). In Utah, the convention designates for each office two candidates whose names are placed on the primary ballot, although if one receives 70 percent of the convention vote that person is automatically declared the nominee. In Colorado, the convention winner is listed first on the ballot, and others receiving 30 percent of the convention vote are also placed on the ballot. However, candidates can avoid a primary by winning 50 percent of the convention delegates. In some of the states that use preprimary conventions (for example, Delaware, New York, and Rhode Island), candidates may also get on the primary ballot by securing a requisite number of signatures on a petition.

Some state party organizations also engage in *preprimary endorsements* through nonstatutory or extralegal procedures. For example, both parties in Massachusetts and Minnesota regularly endorse candidates at state party conventions. Although there have been instances when endorsed candidates failed to win their party's primary, winners of the convention endorsement usually go on to win the primary. Thus, the principal effect of convention systems is that they permit greater party organizational influence on the nominating process, reduce competition in the primaries, and inhibit self-starter candidates who have limited political experience and party involvement.

Consequences of the Direct Primary

Just as the Progressive reformers had hoped, the direct primary has undercut the influence and control that parties can exert over the nominations. With nominations ultimately in the hands of the voters, party organizations cannot unilaterally designate party nominees. Primaries therefore encourage a candidate-centered style of politics, because without parties capable of controlling nominations, candidates have an incentive to set up personal campaign organizations. Preprimary endorsement procedures do not eliminate the need for these personal organizations because it is still possible to win a primary election after having been denied the party's convention endorsement. For example, in his first race for governor of New York (1982), Mario Cuomo won the Democratic primary after being denied convention endorsement; and in 1994 two nonendorsed candidates, Governor Arne Carlson (R-Minn.) and State Comptroller William Curry (D-Conn.) won gubernatorial primaries.

Although the introduction of the direct primary has severely weakened the control over nominations wielded by party organizations, it has not made party support irrelevant, especially in states with preprimary endorsements. It has been demonstrated that the party backing that a candidate receives as a result of a preprimary endorsement significantly diminishes the effect that campaign spending has on primary outcomes (Morehouse 1987, 1994).

Direct primaries, however, have never fulfilled the expectations of the Progressive reformers who sponsored their enactment. Voter turnout is typically much lower than in general elections. Thus between 1962 and 1994 in states holding primaries, the average turnout in the midterm elections, when most of the nation's governors are elected, was 23.9 percent of the voting-age population (Center for the Study of the American Electorate 1994). In addition, the extent of vigorous competition in primaries has been limited. Incumbents not only usually win renomination but are frequently either unopposed or face only token opposition. Over 90 percent of incumbent governors and U.S. House members win renomination. Contests occur most often within the party that has the greatest opportunity of winning the general election and when there is no incumbent seeking renomination.

POLITICAL COMPETITION

Since V. O. Key's seminal work on southern state politics (1949), scholars have recognized the importance political competition can have on the nature of politics in the states. First, it is generally recognized that competition is related to the types of policies a state produces. States with highly competitive environments tend to spend more on social welfare public policies, while noncompetitive states generally spend less on programs for what Key referred to as the "have nots." Second, it is widely recognized that states with competitive environments generally have higher levels of voter turnout in their elections.

An analysis of political competition in the states requires an examination of two different aspects of competition: interparty competition for control of government (the governorship and the state legislature) and electoral competition (the percentage of votes won in state elections).

Competition for Control of Government

A measure of interparty competition developed by Austin Ranney (1976, 59–60) constitutes a widely used and long-standing indicator of competition for control of government. The Ranney index has several different components.

Proportion of Success: the percentage of votes won by the parties in gubernatorial elections and the percentage of seats won by the parties in each house of the legislature

Duration of Success: the length of time the parties controlled the governorship and the length of time the parties controlled the legislature

Frequency of Divided Control: the proportion of time the governorship and the legislature has been divided between the two parties

Ranney used these three dimensions to calculate his index of interparty competition, which we have updated for 1989–1994.[1] The index is actually a measure of control of government, with a score of 0 indicating complete Republican control and a score of 1 indicating absolute Democratic control. At its midpoint (.5000), control of government is evenly split between the two parties, indicating a highly competitive environment. Ranney used this index to classify states by party control, using the following categories and definitions:

.8500 or higher: one-party Democratic
.6500 to .8499: modified one-party Democratic
.3500 to .6499: two-party
.1500 to .3499: modified one-party Republican
.0000 to .1499: one-party Republican

The values of the Ranney party control index calculated for the period 1989 to 1994 are presented in Table 3-5, where several patterns emerge. First, no state qualifies as a one-party state. This is a major change from previous years, when usually several states could be considered one-party Democratic states. Second, although the majority of states can be classified as two-party states, the Democrats still hold a distinct advantage over the Republicans in state government. There are thirteen modified one-party Democratic states and only six modified Republican states. Finally, party control of states exhibits a distinct regional pattern. The Democratic party is strongest in the South, whereas the Republican party is strongest in many Mountain West states (Arizona, Colorado, Idaho, Montana, Utah, and Wyoming) and Plains states (Kansas, North Dakota, and South Dakota).

The Ranney index can be recalculated to indicate the level of competition between the parties for control of government, rather than the degree of Democratic or Republican control.[2] Consider the most competitive states in Table 3-5,

1. Specifically, we calculated the average percentage of the popular vote won by Democratic gubernatorial candidates; the average percentage of seats held by Democrats in the state senate, in all legislative sessions; the average percentage of seats held by Democrats in the state house of representatives, in all sessions; and the percentage of all gubernatorial, senate, and house terms that were controlled by the Democrats. For each state we averaged these four percentages together to create an index value representing the degree of interparty competition. Because Nebraska has a nonpartisan legislature, its interparty competition estimate is based only on control of the governorship and on party support in gubernatorial elections.

2. In the professional literature, this is called the folded Ranney index.

Table 3-5 States Classified according to Degree of Interparty Competition for Control of Government, 1989–1994

State	Ranney party control index	Ranney competition index	State	Ranney party control index	Ranney competition index
Modified one-party: Democratic					
Arkansas	.831	.669	Georgia	.739	.761
Louisiana	.828	.672	Mississippi	.709	.791
Hawaii	.814	.686	Alabama	.666	.834
West Virginia	.798	.702	Nebraska	.660	.840
Rhode Island	.776	.724	Oklahoma	.659	.841
Maryland	.776	.724	Massachusetts	.658	.842
Kentucky	.741	.759			
Two-party competition					
Tennessee	.649	.851	Delaware	.519	.981
New Mexico	.645	.855	Indiana	.518	.982
North Carolina	.636	.864	Connecticut	.518	.982
Missouri	.633	.867	Wisconsin	.496	.996
Texas	.618	.882	Pennsylvania	.496	.996
Virginia	.617	.883	Iowa	.481	.981
Minnesota	.608	.892	Alaska	.467	.967
Florida	.594	.906	Illinois	.462	.962
Washington	.568	.932	Montana	.453	.953
Vermont	.568	.932	Colorado	.438	.938
South Carolina	.550	.950	Michigan	.421	.921
Nevada	.548	.952	New Jersey	.410	.910
California	.537	.963	North Dakota	.394	.894
Oregon	.534	.966	Ohio	.384	.884
New York	.530	.970	Kansas	.359	.859
Maine	.528	.972			
Modified one-party: Republican					
Idaho	.338	.838	Wyoming	.313	.813
South Dakota	.322	.822	New Hampshire	.259	.759
Arizona	.316	.816	Utah	.232	.732

SOURCE: Calculated by authors.

Wisconsin and Pennsylvania, which have a Ranney party control index value of .496. As you move away from Wisconsin and Pennsylvania, in both directions, the states are less and less competitive. For instance, even though Kentucky and New Hampshire are in different partisan camps, their party control values (.741 and .259, respectively) make them equally noncompetitive: both states are .241 units away from the point of perfect competition, .500. The Ranney competition index is derived from the original Ranney index and represents how close the states are to perfect competition between the parties for control of government.[3] The Ranney competition index ranges from .500 (no competition) to 1.000 (perfect competition). The data in Table 3-5 indicate that the least competitive states are located in the South and, to some degree, in the Mountain West re-

3. The formula for the folded Ranney index is $1 - |(.5 - \text{Ranney})|$. The folded index measures how close a state's level of interparty competition is to "perfect" competition on the Ranney index.

gion. The most competitive states tend to be found in the Midwest and the Northeast.

Although the classifications in Table 3-5 are useful, it is important to realize the limitations of such an index. First, the Ranney index is based exclusively on state offices and does not reflect the strength of the parties at other levels. For instance, until the 1992 election, the Democratic presidential ticket had not won more than a single southern state (Georgia, 1980) since 1976, when a southerner, Jimmy Carter, headed the ticket. This is exactly the opposite of what would be expected, based on the degree of Democratic party strength as measured by the Ranney index. Also, the significant gains made by Republicans in U.S. House and Senate elections in the South in recent years are not reflected in the Ranney index.

Second, the Ranney index gives more weight to some state offices than to others. The way the index is constructed, the state legislature is given much more weight than the governorship. This may also result in underestimating the strength of the Republican party in southern states, since many of the party's gains have been made in the governorships. It is also worth noting that the Ranney index does not include other statewide offices, such as lieutenant governor (where separately elected), attorney general, state auditor, and state treasurer. Not all states elect these offices, but most of them do.

Third, this measure of interparty competition is "a snapshot of an object moving in time and hence does not always capture change that may be occurring when the measurement is taken" (Ranney 1976, 60–61). Although interparty competition is a long-term phenomenon and, as such, should be relatively stable, significant change in the nature of competition for control of government has taken place. The changes in the mean level of Democratic control, as measured in Table 3-5, and the mean level of interparty competition, based on the Ranney competition index, which ranges from .50 (no competition) to 1.00 (perfect competition), from 1948 to 1994 are presented in Table 3-6. In these two measures there are signs of both stability and change. First, the mean score of Democratic control in the Ranney index has always leaned to the Democratic side, indicating a long-standing Democratic dominance of state government. Second, the Democratic party grew in strength from 1948 to 1980 and lost strength from 1981 to

Table 3-6 Changes in the Ranney Index of Interparty Competition, 1948–1994

	1948–60	1962–73	1974–80	1981–88	1989–94
Mean level of Democratic control (Range: 0–1)	.56	.58	.64	.60	.55
Mean level of interparty competition (Range: .5–1)	.78	.83	.81	.84	.87

SOURCES: Compiled from data in Patterson and Caldeira 1984; Bibby et al. 1990, table 3.5.

1994. The Democrats are currently about as strong in state government as they were in the 1960s. Much of the decline in Democratic strength in the 1980s has occurred in southern states, where Republicans have been making inroads. Finally, in the level of competition for control of government, the least competitive period was from 1948 to 1960, and the most competitive period was from 1989 to 1994. In large part, Republican gains in southern states account for the increase in competition in recent years.

Electoral Competition

One of the limitations of the Ranney index is that, since it is based on control of government, it is not an ideal measure of electoral competition. This is especially disconcerting because many of the hypotheses concerning the effect of competition on state politics are about how electoral competition affects state politics and policy making. To measure electoral competition in the states more accurately, an index based on district-level state legislative election outcomes from 1982 to 1986 has been developed (Holbrook and Van Dunk 1993).[4] In the Holbrook–Van Dunk index, a value for each state is derived from several different indicators: the average margin of victory, the average percentage of the vote going to the winning candidate, the percentage of seats uncontested, and the percentage of seats considered "safe" (won by five percentage points or more).[5] The crucial difference between this index and the Ranney index is that the Holbrook–Van Dunk index is based entirely on election outcomes, while the Ranney index is based primarily on partisan control of state government. Another important difference is that this index is based solely on state legislative elections, whereas the Ranney index is based on control of both the state legislature and the governorship.

The values on the Holbrook–Van Dunk index, presented in Table 3-7, are easily interpreted: low values on this index indicate low levels of electoral competition; high values indicate high levels of electoral competition. While there is wide variation in the level of electoral competition in the states, there is, to some extent, a familiar regional pattern; the ten least competitive states are all southern states or Border states. At the other end of the scale, however, there is no clear regional pattern among the most competitive states. The observant reader will note some overlap between the Holbrook–Van Dunk index and the Ranney competition index. Indeed, although the two are conceptually distinct, the relationship between the Ranney competition index and the Holbrook–Van Dunk index is moderately strong ($r = .68$).

4. The data used to construct this index are available only from 1968 through 1986.

5. The formula for the index is:

Competition $= 1 - $ [(average margin of victory + average winning percentage + percentage uncontested + percentage safe seats)/4].

The index is based on district-level state legislative election outcomes from 1982 to 1988 and does not include multimember free-for-all districts. Because data were missing, the index could not be calculated for Louisiana. See Holbrook and Van Dunk 1993 for more details.

Table 3-7   District-Level Electoral Competition in the States, 1982–1986

State	Competition	Rank	State	Competition	Rank
North Dakota	56.58	1	Delaware	39.66	26
Oregon	54.25	2	Rhode Island	39.49	27
Nebraska	54.06	3	South Dakota	39.19	28
Washington	53.94	4	New Mexico	37.10	29
Alaska	53.46	5	Kansas	35.81	30
Connecticut	52.81	6	Idaho	35.60	31
Minnesota	52.44	7	Arizona	33.90	32
New Jersey	51.81	8	North Carolina	33.42	33
Ohio	49.61	9	Hawaii	33.40	34
Nevada	49.60	10	Florida	31.13	35
Michigan	49.58	11	Maryland	31.00	36
Vermont	49.16	12	Wyoming	30.46	37
Wisconsin	49.13	13	Massachusetts	30.39	38
Iowa	48.55	14	New Hampshire	29.01	39
New York	47.68	15	South Carolina	28.32	40
California	47.29	16	Kentucky	27.81	41
Maine	45.90	17	Alabama	27.27	42
Utah	45.29	18	Missouri	27.12	43
West Virginia	44.97	19	Tennessee	26.72	44
Indiana	44.59	20	Oklahoma	25.49	45
Montana	43.34	21	Texas	21.96	46
Illinois	41.61	22	Mississippi	16.48	47
Virginia	40.71	23	Georgia	16.19	48
Pennsylvania	40.19	24	Arkansas	9.26	49
Colorado	40.18	25	Louisiana	—	—

SOURCE: Holbrook and Van Dunk 1993.
NOTE: Dashes = not available.

Many of the limitations of the Ranney index also apply to the Holbrook–Van Dunk index. First, the Holbrook–Van Dunk index is based only on state legislative elections and does not necessarily say anything about competition at other levels of office. Second, this index is also only a snapshot in time of a phenomenon that could be in a state of flux. Indeed, although the state values of the Holbrook–Van Dunk index are highly correlated over time (the correlation between values from 1972 to 1976 and 1982 to 1986 is .89), there have been changes in the index. Although the analysis of the Ranney index in Table 3-6 indicated an increase in competition for control of government, there has been a decrease in the level of electoral competition. The average score on the Holbrook–Van Dunk index from 1972 to 1976 was 42.92; the average score from 1982 to 1986 was 39.04. This reflects a trend found in other elections, where the advantages of incumbency and the increasing costs of campaigns are leading to less competitive elections. Another possibility, however, is that relatively small changes such as these might only reflect random fluctuations in the data.

Correlates of Competition
   Consequences of Competition. As mentioned earlier, it is widely expected that competition has an influence on public policy and voter turnout. Specifically, it

is expected that competitive states will produce more liberal public policies and have higher rates of voter turnout than noncompetitive states. To a large extent, the data bear out these propositions, especially for the Holbrook–Van Dunk index. The Ranney competition index is moderately related to policy outcomes and voter turnout, but the relationship is inconsistent and, in many cases, disappears when the effects of other important variables, such as state wealth, political ideology, and partisanship, are taken into account (Holbrook and Van Dunk 1993). The results are much stronger for the Holbrook–Van Dunk index, however. Holbrook and Van Dunk examined a broad range of policies and found that electoral competition has a strong influence on policy outcomes, even when there is a control for other important influences. The same results are found when the effect of electoral competition on voter turnout is examined (Holbrook and Van Dunk 1993).

Determinants of Competition. As we pointed out earlier, competition follows a regional pattern; on both measures of competition, southern states are distinctly less competitive than the rest of the country. To a large extent, this strates the long-lasting effect of the Civil War and Reconstruction on southern politics.

Beyond the effects of region, several other variables help explain state differences in competition. First, states with diverse populations have more competitive political systems than do states with homogeneous populations (Barrilleaux 1986; Patterson and Caldeira 1984). Second, some states have lower levels of competition because they have higher levels of partisan bias in the electorate. If a state's electorate is overwhelmingly Democratic, then it makes sense that the Democrats would face little competition at the polls and would be able to establish control of state government (Barrilleaux 1986; Holbrook, Mangum, and Garand 1994). Finally, incumbency has been found to suppress electoral competition, and highly populous legislative districts have been found to enhance electoral competition (Holbrook, Mangum, and Garand 1994). Note that both incumbency and district size can be manipulated in order to increase competition. Term limits, of course, could minimize the effect of incumbency, and reducing the size of the legislative body would result in larger electoral districts.

POLITICAL PARTICIPATION

Political participation in the United States takes many different forms: contributing to campaigns; attending rallies or protest events; writing letters to elected representatives; working for a campaign or community cause; attending town meetings or school board meetings; and, of course, voting in elections. Although voting is the most commonly practiced form of political participation, the degree to which citizens across the states take advantage of their right to vote varies widely.

Table 3-8 Average Rates of Voter Turnout in the States, by Office, 1989–1994

State	Total	President	Governor	U.S. Senate	U.S. House
Montana	63.9	70.1	69.6	55.7	60.1
North Dakota	62.0	67.3	66.6	58.5	55.4
Maine	60.7	72.0	55.1	55.6	60.3
South Dakota	60.2	67.0	55.6	59.3	58.8
Minnesota	59.7	71.6	53.8	54.4	58.9
Utah	58.5	65.1	66.8	54.0	48.1
Vermont	57.2	67.5	48.5	58.0	54.9
Wyoming	56.7	62.3	54.2	54.2	56.0
Oregon	55.8	65.7	46.6	56.6	54.4
Missouri	55.8	62.0	60.8	53.3	47.2
Alaska	55.4	65.4	47.7	55.2	53.1
Idaho	55.2	65.2	48.3	54.7	52.5
Nebraska	53.9	63.2	49.3	50.1	53.3
Iowa	53.9	65.3	47.0	55.0	48.2
Washington	53.8	59.9	59.5	50.3	45.5
Wisconsin	52.3	69.0	39.8	54.2	46.2
Kansas	51.9	63.0	43.2	52.3	49.2
Connecticut	51.9	63.8	45.4	51.3	46.8
Massachusetts	51.5	60.2	48.7	48.8	48.1
Colorado	50.5	62.7	41.2	51.9	46.3
Ohio	49.6	60.6	41.6	50.1	46.1
Rhode Island	49.3	58.4	45.8	46.1	47.0
Indiana	48.1	55.2	53.4	41.8	42.0
New Hampshire	47.7	63.1	36.0	47.8	43.8
Oklahoma	47.1	59.7	39.7	45.0	44.2
Michigan	47.0	61.7	40.8	40.5	44.9
Illinois	46.6	58.9	36.8	48.0	42.5
Delaware	46.3	55.2	52.8	36.1	41.1
Louisiana	46.2	59.8	57.8	37.4	29.7
North Carolina	46.1	50.1	49.7	45.2	39.3
Alabama	45.2	55.2	39.3	45.6	40.6
Arkansas	44.1	53.8	39.8	40.3	42.5
Arizona	44.0	54.1	36.1	44.3	41.6
Pennsylvania	43.2	54.3	36.3	42.6	39.4
New Mexico	42.5	51.6	38.6	38.8	41.1
Maryland	42.0	53.4	33.4	43.0	38.2
New Jersey	41.9	56.3	39.7	33.5	38.2
Nevada	41.3	50.0	34.3	42.2	38.9
Hawaii	41.1	41.9	40.7	41.7	40.1
California	41.0	49.1	34.3	42.2	38.4
West Virginia	40.6	50.6	48.7	30.1	32.9
Florida	40.3	50.2	36.6	42.3	32.0
New York	40.1	50.9	33.4	41.3	34.7
Virginia	40.0	52.8	37.9	32.2	37.3
Kentucky	39.9	53.7	30.5	40.7	34.8
Mississippi	37.5	52.8	38.8	23.4	34.8
Texas	37.0	49.1	32.6	31.9	34.3
South Carolina	36.6	45.0	31.7	36.6	33.1
Tennessee	36.3	52.4	29.6	29.3	33.8
Georgia	36.2	46.9	30.1	33.5	34.3

SOURCE: Calculated from data in various sources.

Table 3-9   Mean Percentage of Voter Turnout in the States, by Year and Office, 1989–1994

Year	President	Governor	U.S. Senate	U.S. House
1990	—	40.9	38.6	37.8
1992	58.3	59.2	55.2	54.3
1994	—	41.9	41.8	40.2
1990–94	58.3	44.5	45.5	44.1
Presidential Year Increase		17.8	15.0	15.3

SOURCE: Calculated from data in Table 3-8.
NOTE: The turnout rates for the 1989 and 1991 gubernatorial elections are included in the 1990 figure, and the turnout rate for the 1993 gubernatorial elections is included in the 1994 figure.

Patterns of Turnout across the States

For a variety of reasons some people decide not to take advantage of their right to vote in elections. Although individual attributes have a lot to do with whether or not a person votes, turnout rates can also be affected by the type of election being held and by certain aspects of the state political environment. The traditional way of measuring turnout is to take the total number of votes cast as a percentage of the voting-age population in the state. In Table 3-8 this method is used to calculate the level of turnout in all states for presidential, gubernatorial, and congressional elections, from 1989 to 1994. The first column in Table 3-8 presents the average rate of turnout across all four types of elections for each state. Once again, we see the emergence of a regional pattern: nine out of the ten lowest turnout states are southern or Border states. At the other end of the scale we do not find a clear regional pattern, but most of the highest turnout states are small, sparsely populated states.

Besides differences across the states, it is clear in Table 3-9 that there are substantial differences in turnout in different types of elections. From 1989 to 1994, turnout was the highest in presidential elections, then in congressional elections, and lowest in gubernatorial elections. One of the reasons gubernatorial turnout is lower overall is that most gubernatorial elections are held in nonpresidential election years. Within each year, however, turnout is actually higher for gubernatorial elections than for the other types of elections. This helps illustrate an important point: turnout is always higher in presidential election years. Turnout was roughly 15 to 18 percentage points higher for all offices in 1992 than in the midterm election years of 1990 and 1994. This is because presidential elections are high visibility events that generate a lot of interest and bring out a lot of voters who do not turn out to vote in elections for lower offices.

The turnout data in Tables 3-8 and 3-9 need to be interpreted with some caution. Because turnout is expressed as a percentage of the voting-age population, the numbers are probably slightly different from what they would have been if turnout had been expressed as a percentage of the eligible voting-age electorate.

The voting-age population of a state includes significant numbers of people who are not eligible to vote because they are not citizens or are institutionalized in correctional or mental health facilities. Nevertheless, there is every reason to believe that the patterns of turnout found in Tables 3-8 and 3-9 would not be substantially different if all ineligible voters were excluded.

What Determines Turnout?

Many factors help explain differences in voter turnout across states and individuals. For the individual voter, a variety of important demographic and attitudinal variables are related to turnout (Rosenstone and Hansen 1993; Wolfinger and Rosenstone 1980). For example, middle-aged people with high levels of income and education have a high probability of voting. People with a strong sense of political efficacy and strong ties to political parties are also very likely to vote. Many of these variables also help explain the pattern of turnout in the states. Socioeconomic differences across the states, for instance, are strongly related to differences in voter turnout; wealthy states and states with well-educated citizens generally have the highest rates of voter turnout (Kim, Petrocik, and Enokson 1975).

But state politics also have an effect on voter turnout. First, turnout is higher in states with high levels of electoral competition. In noncompetitive environments the elections are less likely to generate much interest and voters are less likely to vote. The relatively strong correlation between electoral competition and overall voter turnout ($r = .50$) demonstrates the strength of this relationship. Turnout can also be influenced by the level of campaign spending in particular races (Patterson and Caldeira, 1983). As more money is spent in a campaign, voters are provided with more information about the candidates, which increases the likelihood that they will vote.

Another important determinant of turnout is the stringency of state voter registration laws (Wolfinger and Rosenstone 1980). In states where it is difficult for voters to register or to stay registered, fewer people will register and voter turnout will be lower than it would be if registration laws made it easier to register. One example of such a law is the closing date for registration, or the number of days before the election that one must register in order to vote. In many states the closing date ranges from zero (Election Day registration or, in North Dakota, no voter registration) to fifty days before the election. The difference in turnout between states with a closing date of ten or fewer days before the election and states with a closing date of thirty or more days before the election illustrates the effect registration laws can have: the average overall rate of turnout in the former is 53 percent, and the average turnout in the latter is 45 percent.

DIRECT DEMOCRACY

In addition to choosing between candidates in elections, voters in some states are given the opportunity to vote directly on matters of public policy. This process is sometimes referred to as direct democracy because it allows the people to legislate directly, through the ballot box, rather than indirectly, through elected representatives. Several different forms of direct democracy are available to the voters, depending on where they live. In many cases the ballot propositions do not originate with the people but are submitted by the legislature for the approval of the people. Forty-nine states (Delaware is the exception) require voter approval of constitutional amendments through *constitutional referendums;* nineteen states require that certain types of legislation, usually bond issues and debt authorizations, be approved by the voters in a *constitutionally mandated referendum;* twenty-four states authorize the legislature to submit measures to the people for their approval in a *legislative referendum;* twenty-three states permit the people, after gathering a required number of signatures, to use a *petition referendum* to force an issue passed by the legislature onto the ballot, where it must gain a majority approval before taking effect.

Other forms of direct democracy are much more direct, with the proposition originating from the people. Twenty-three states permit the *legislative initiative,* which takes two forms: direct and indirect. The direct initiative forces a proposed statute onto the ballot on the petition of a specified number of voters. In three of these states, however, the *indirect initiative* is used, which requires that all such measures be submitted to the legislature first, allowing it an opportunity to approve the measure. In such cases, if the legislature does not approve the measure, it can then be submitted to the voters for their approval. Five states allow the use of both the direct and indirect legislative initiatives. Seventeen states use the *constitutional initiative,* which provides for direct placement of constitutional amendments on the ballot after a petition has been signed by a specified number of voters (Council of State Governments 1994; Magleby 1988, 601).

Every election year there are several instances in which voters use the machinery of direct democracy to make important public policy decisions. Many of the issues addressed through direct democracy have far-reaching policy consequences. One example of this is Proposition 13, which was a constitutional initiative placed on the ballot in California in 1978. Proposition 13, which rolled back property taxes, was approved by the voters and is frequently cited as the impetus for antitax movements in several other states. Another important issue that has recently been addressed through the initiative process is term limits for elected officials. In 1992, fourteen states had measures on the ballot for limiting the number of terms that members of Congress could serve; term limits were approved in all fourteen states by an average margin of 2 to 1 (Galvin 1992). Other issues that are routinely addressed through the initiative process are limits on taxing and spending, the rights of the accused, the regulation of industries, and certain public morality issues, such as abortion, gay rights, and gambling. Of course, many issues like term limits still have to withstand constitutional challenges in a court of law.

The use of direct democracy was popular in the early part this century, but from 1940 through the 1970s it waned in the public favor. Since then, it seems to have experienced a resurgence in popularity. From 1981 to 1986, there were 144 initiatives placed on the ballot. From 1987 to 1992, there were 202 items on the ballot, representing a 40 percent increase in use over the early 1980s (Kehler and Stern 1994). During the 1980s, more initiatives appeared on the ballot than at any time since the 1930s (Magleby 1988).

One criticism of direct democracy is that it may not, in fact, be democratic because of the low levels of turnout in referendum elections. Turnout in referendum elections is usually measured by how much the level of voting drops off from that in candidate elections occurring at the same time (that is, presidential, congressional, gubernatorial). For a variety of reasons, turnout in referendum elections tends to be much lower than turnout in other types of elections. As a result the active electorate for ballot propositions is severely biased because the poor and uneducated, who have low turnout rates anyway, are even less likely to vote on ballot propositions than in other types of elections (Magleby 1984). Several factors can, however, influence the rate of drop-off in referendum elections. First, drop-off is lower when the ballot measure comes directly from the people, through the initiative process, than when it is referred by the legislature. Second, drop-off is higher in constitutional referendums than in statutory referendums. Finally, drop-off is lower when more money is spent on the referendum campaigns (Bowler, Donovan, and Happ 1992).

ELECTION OUTCOMES

Although presidential elections generate a great deal of attention every four years, other important elections are being contested in the states in almost every year. Of course, the most visible of these elections are gubernatorial and state legislative elections. But there are also elections for other important statewide officials, such as the lieutenant governor, attorney general, state treasurer, secretary of state, and state auditor. These officials are appointed in some states, but a majority of the states elect at least some of them. In addition, in twenty-five states, judges are elected directly by the people.

Determinants of Election Outcomes

What determines these election outcomes? No single variable determines who wins these elections. Instead, state election outcomes are the result of many different variables.

Partisanship. One of the most important variables in determining voting behavior in American elections has been party identification. People tend to identify with a political party and vote for that party's candidates in elections. While partisanship still plays an important role in elections, it has lost much of its impact. Some have argued that state elections are becoming more and more like presidential and congressional elections, where the influence of party has been diminished by increasingly candidate-oriented campaigns (Salmore and Salmore 1993). Indeed, the evidence is undeniable that party is no longer as strong a voting cue in state elections as it once was. One indicator of the decline of party can be found in the increasing willingness of individuals to split their ticket and vote for candidates of different parties for different offices. In the late 1940s more than 70 percent of all state governments were unified along party lines, indicating that people tended to vote for the same party in both the gubernatorial and state legislative races. By the late 1980s, however, less than 45 percent of all state governments were unified along party lines (Fiorina 1992). This percentage has held fairly constant: following the 1994 elections, only twenty-three states had one-party control of the governorship and state legislature.

Despite growing evidence that the influence of partisanship in elections is declining, there are still ample indications that it has not disappeared. Studies of state legislative, gubernatorial, and other statewide elections continue to find that party strength in the electorate is an important determinant of election outcomes (Gierzynski and Breaux 1991; Holbrook 1993; Squire 1992).

Incumbency. One variable that may be supplanting partisanship as an influence on election outcomes is incumbency. It is now widely known that incumbent members of Congress are almost certain to get reelected if they choose to run. Members of the U.S. House, for instance, have long had an incumbent reelection rate of more than 90 percent (Jacobson 1992). As the data in Table 3-10 illustrate, the same type of electoral advantage accrues to elected officials in the states. Among state officials, governors face the greatest chance of losing their reelection bids, although roughly three-quarters of those who run do win. State legislators and statewide constitutional officers (attorneys general, lieutenant governors, secretaries of state, treasurers, and auditors) have an incumbency advantage that approaches that of members of the U.S. House. With more than 85 percent of all incumbent state legislators and statewide officers winning reelection, potential challengers can find little cause for optimism. Even in gubernatorial elections, where the incumbent is most vulnerable, the odds are against a challenger's winning.

Table 3-10 Incumbent Success Rate of Those Who Sought Reelection in State Elections, 1968–1994 (in percent)

Years	Governors	State representative	State senator	Statewide officers*
1968–78	74	89	85	88
1979–89	81	91	87	93
1990–94	76	—†	—†	85
Average	77	90	86	89

SOURCES: Stanley and Niemi 1994; *State Legislative Election Returns in the United States,* 1968–1986 (ICPSR no. 8907); Monardi 1994; Monardi, personal communication, December 1994; *Congressional Quarterly Weekly Report,* November 12, 1994, 3301–3308.
*Statewide officers include lieutenant governors (where separately elected), attorneys general, secretaries of state, state auditors, and state treasurers. Data were available only through 1993.
†Dashes = not available.

Incumbents have an advantage over challengers for several reasons. First, because incumbents are much more visible than challengers, voters are more likely to recognize the incumbent's name and therefore more likely to vote for the incumbent. Second, incumbents have already been elected once, so they have a base in the electorate. Finally, and perhaps most important, incumbents have an easier time raising money (Moncrief 1992), which becomes more important as campaigning becomes more expensive.

Campaign Spending. Campaign spending is an extremely important determinant of state election outcomes. Money buys resources, organization, and exposure. Money can also scare off potential challengers. If an incumbent governor, for instance, raises a campaign war chest of two million dollars during the first couple of years of his or her term, the governor is likely to scare off potential challengers who do not want, or are unable, to raise that kind of money.

Although it is difficult to get accurate information on all state races, the costs of campaigning have clearly gone up. Gierzynski and Breaux (1991) examined campaign spending in state legislative races in five states and found that from 1978 to 1986 campaign spending increased, on average, more than 200 percent. Moncrief (1992) controlled for inflation in his study of spending patterns in nine states from 1980 to 1988 and found that the average increase in spending, in constant dollars, was 78 percent, still a substantial increase.

Beyle (1994) has documented the increase in the cost of gubernatorial campaigns (see Chapter 6). Although spending increases in gubernatorial races leveled off in the 1990s, they increased substantially during the 1980s. From the late 1970s (1977–1980) to the early 1990s (1990–1993), the costs of gubernatorial campaigns, in constant dollars, went up 48 percent. Some recent races stand out as particularly expensive. A total of $25 million dollars was spent on the 1990 gubernatorial race in California, and more than $11 million were spent in the 1990 races in Texas and Illinois.

While campaign spending has been shown to be an important influence in both state legislative (Gierzynski and Breaux 1991) and gubernatorial races (Svoboda 1995), the effects of spending are different for challengers and incumbents. The amount of money spent by challengers is much more important to the overall outcome than the amount spent by incumbents. Generally, challengers get many more votes per dollar spent than do incumbents. Unfortunately for the challengers, they are usually unable to raise enough money to overcome the advantage of incumbency. This is not to say that challengers would always be able to beat incumbents if they were able to spend more money than the incumbents. Incumbency carries more electoral advantages than just being able to raise more money.

Candidate Quality. The candidates, of course, have something to do with election outcomes. A challenger with little political experience usually poses little threat to a sitting governor. In contrast, a challenger with political experience, especially elected office experience, poses a much more serious threat, because he or she may have greater visibility and will probably have an easier time raising money than most other challengers. One reason why governors have a somewhat lower reelection rate than other state officials is probably because of the experience level of the challengers they face. Whereas members of the U.S. House of Representatives face candidates with elected office experience about 25 percent of the time (Jacobson 1992), governors face experienced challengers about 75 percent of the time (Holbrook 1991; Squire 1992). Many of these challengers are the electorally secure members of the state legislature or other statewide elected constitutional officers.

National Politics. In addition to the factors associated with the state or the candidates, national politics also influence state elections. Studies of gubernatorial and state legislative elections have revealed that the state of the national economy and the popularity of the sitting president can have an effect on how his party does in state elections (Campbell 1986; Chubb 1988; Holbrook 1987). Salmore and Salmore (1993) suggest, however, that this relationship may be becoming weaker as fewer and fewer states hold their gubernatorial elections in presidential election years. One need look no further than the 1994 elections, however, to see that national politics can influence state elections, even in midterm election years.

Referendum Election Outcomes

Besides voting for candidates, voters in many states also have the opportunity to vote in statutory or constitutional referendums. Many of these ballot proposals originate from the direct initiative, but some of them are also referred to the voters by the legislature. Generally, the odds are against most referendums getting voter approval. Between 1981 and 1992 only 44 percent of initiatives on the ballot won voter approval (Kehler and Stern 1994). Part of the reason for the difficulty in getting ballot propositions passed is that they almost always threaten the status quo, so there is a natural tendency to oppose them. Certain factors can, however, influence the odds that a measure will be passed (Bowler, Donovan, Happ 1992; Magleby 1984). First, spending is important; proponents can increase the probability of winning by outspending opponents. Spending levels in initiative campaigns can be quite high. In 1988, a total of $129 million was spent on initiative campaigns in California alone (Kehler and Stern 1994). Second, ballot location can also affect the likelihood that an initiative will pass. Items at the top of the ballot are more likely to pass than those found farther down on the ballot. Finally, measures submitted to the voters by the legislature are more likely to be approved than those that originate in the direct initiative process.

PARTY ADAPTABILITY AND DURABILITY IN AN ERA OF CANDIDATE-CENTERED POLITICS

The theme of change runs consistently through this survey of state political parties and elections. Since the 1960s and 1970s, state party organizations have developed into increasingly professional service agencies assisting candidates and local parties. Autonomous state legislative campaign committees have emerged as the primary party support agency for state legislative candidates. PACs have grown in numbers and in their importance for campaign funding. Campaign costs have escalated as candidates have sought to take advantage of the latest techniques and technologies. State regulation of campaign finance has been tightened, and an increasing number of states provide some form of public financing of elections. Candidates now rely primarily on their own personal campaign organizations rather than party machinery. State electoral politics thus focus more and more on the candidate rather than the party.

Parties, however, remain a major force in state electoral politics. Interparty competition has intensified since the 1970s, and partisanship continues to be a major determinant of voter choice on Election Day. Even in the face of an increasingly candidate-centered style of politics, both state central committees and legislative campaign committees have become more sophisticated and capable of providing an array of services to their clienteles. These committees have also shown an ability to solicit and channel PAC money. At the same time, the massive flow of national party resources into state party organizations has produced an unprecedented level of intraparty integration that has undermined the traditional autonomy of state party organizations. The history of state political organizations since World War II is thus one of adaptability and durability in a changing political environment. Although American state party organizations of the 1990s neither control nominations nor actively manage their candidates' campaigns, they nevertheless remain the principal agencies for making nominations, contesting elections, recruiting leaders, and providing a link between citizens and their government.

REFERENCES

Baker, Donald P. 1992. "Va. Democratic Chief Survives Bid to Oust Him." *Washington Post,* June 10.

Barrilleaux, Charles. 1986. "A Dynamic Model of Partisan Competition in the American States." *American Journal of Political Science* 30:822–840.

Beyle, Thad L. 1994. "The Governors, 1992–1993." In *The Book of the States, 1992–93.* Lexington, Ky.: Council of State Governments.

Bibby, John F. 1979. "Political Parties and Federalism: The National Republican Committee Involvement in Gubernatorial and Legislative Elections." *Publius* 9:229–236.

———. 1981. "Party Renewal in the National Republican Party." In *Party Renewal in America: Theory and Practice,* edited by Gerald M. Pomper. New York: Praeger.

Bibby, John F., Cornelius P. Cotter, James L. Gibson, and Robert J. Huckshorn. 1990. "Parties in State Politics." In *Politics in the American States,* 5th ed., edited by Virginia Gray, Herbert Jacob, and Robert B. Albritton. Glenview, Ill.: Scott, Foresman.

Biersack, Robert. 1994. "Hard Facts and Soft Money: State Party Finance in the 1992 Federal Elections." In *The State of the Parties: The Changing Role of Contemporary Parties,* edited by Daniel M. Shea and John C. Green. Lanham, Md.: Rowman and Littlefield.

Bowler, Shaun, Todd Donovan, and Trudi Happ. 1992. "Ballot Propositions and Information Costs: Direct Democracy and the Fatigued Voter." *Western Political Quarterly* 45:559–568.

Broder, David S. 1971. *The Party's Over: The Failure of American Politics.* New York: Harper and Row.

———. 1986. "The Force." *Washington Post*, April 2.

Bullock, Charles S., III, and Loch K. Johnson. 1992. *Runoff Elections in the United States*. Chapel Hill: University of North Carolina Press.

Campbell, James. 1986. "Presidential Coattails and Midterm Losses in State Legislative Elections." *American Political Science Review* 80:45–65.

Carr, Craig L., and Gary L. Scott. 1984. "The Logic of State Primary Classification Schemes." *American Politics Quarterly* 12:465–479.

Center for the Study of the American Electorate. 1994. *Primary Turnout Low*. Washington, D.C.: Center for the Study of the American Electorate.

Chubb, John. 1988. "Institutions, the Economy, and the Dynamics of State Elections." *American Political Science Review* 82:133–154.

Cotter, Cornelius P., and Bernard Hennessy. 1964. *Politics without Power: National Party Committees*. New York: Atherton.

Cotter, Cornelius P., James L. Gibson, John F. Bibby, and Robert J. Huckshorn. 1984. *Party Organizations in American Politics*. New York: Praeger.

Council of State Governments. 1994. *The Book of the States, 1992–93*. Lexington, Ky.: Council of State Governments.

Epstein, Leon D. 1986. *Parties in the American Mold*. Madison: University of Wisconsin Press.

———. 1989. "Will American Political Parties Be Privatized?" *Journal of Law and Politics* 5:239–274.

Ehrenhalt, Alan. 1989. "How a Party of Enthusiasts Keeps Its Hammerlock on a State Legislature." *Governing*, June, 28–33.

Federal Election Commission. 1992. "Democratic Party Closed Fundraising Gap with Republicans." Press release. December 12.

Fiorina, Morris. 1992. *Divided Government*. New York: Macmillan.

Freedman, Anne. 1994. *Patronage: An American Tradition*. Chicago: Nelson-Hall.

Frendreis, John P., James L. Gibson, and Laura L. Vertz. 1990. "The Electoral Relevance of Local Party Organizations." *American Political Science Review* 86:226–235.

Frendreis, John P., Alan R. Gitelson, Gregory Flemming, and Anne Layzell. 1994. "Local Parties and Legislative Races in 1992." In *The State of the Parties: The Changing Role of Contemporary American Parties*, edited by Daniel M. Shea and John C. Green. Lanham, Md.: Rowland and Littlefield.

Galvin, Thomas. 1992. "Limits Score a Perfect 14-for-14, but Court Challenges Loom." *Congressional Quarterly Weekly Report*, November 7, 3593–3594.

Gerber, Elizabeth, and Rebecca B. Morton. 1994. "Primary Election Laws and the Nomination of Congressional Candidates." Paper presented at the annual meeting of the American Political Science Association, New York, September 1–4.

Gibson, James L., John P. Frendreis, and Laura L. Vertz. 1989. "Party Dynamics in the 1980s: Changes in County Party Organizational Strength, 1980–1984." *American Journal of Political Science* 33:67–90.

Gierzynski, Anthony. 1992. *Legislative Party Campaign Committees in the American States*. Lexington: University Press of Kentucky.

Gierzynski, Anthony, and David Breaux. 1991. "Money and Votes in State Legislative Elections." Paper presented at the annual meeting of the American Political Science Association, Chicago, August 29–September 1.

"Guru in Ohio." 1989. *Congressional Quarterly Weekly Report*, November 4, 2977.

Gurwitt, Rob. 1989. "Indiana Curbs Party Payroll Deductions." *Governing*, August, 16.

Herrnson, Paul S. 1988. *Party Campaigning in the 1980s*. Cambridge: Harvard University Press.

———. 1994. "The Revitalization of National Party Organizations." In *The Parties Respond: Changes in the American Party System*, 2d ed., edited by L. Sandy Maisel. Boulder, Colo.: Westview Press.

Holbrook, Thomas M. 1987. "National Factors in Gubernatorial Elections." *American Politics Quarterly* 15:471–483.

———. 1991. "Candidates, Economics, and Gubernatorial Elections." Paper presented at the annual meeting of the American Political Science Association, Chicago, August 29–September 1.

Holbrook, Thomas M., Maurice Mangum, and James Garand. 1994. "Sources of Electoral Competition in the American States." Paper presented at the annual meeting of the American Political Science Association, New York, September 1–4.

Holbrook, Thomas M., and Emily Van Dunk. 1993. "Electoral Competition in the American States." *American Political Science Review* 87:955–962.

Jacobson, Gary C. 1992. *The Politics of Congressional Elections.* 3d ed. New York: HarperCollins.

Jewell, Malcolm E., and David M. Olson. 1988. *Political Parties and Elections in American States.* 3d ed. Chicago: Dorsey Press.

Jones, Ruth S. 1984. "Financing State Elections." In *Money and Politics in the United States,* edited by Michael J. Malbin. Washington, D.C.: American Enterprise Institute.

Kazee, Thomas H. 1983. "The Impact of Electoral Reform: 'Open Elections' and the Louisiana Party System." *Publius* 13:135–138.

Kehler, David, and Robert Stern. 1994. "Initiatives in the 1980s and 1990s." In *The Book of the States, 1992–93.* Lexington, Ky.: Council of State Governments.

Key, V. O., Jr. 1949. *Southern Politics in State and Nation.* New York: Alfred A. Knopf.

———. 1956. *American State Politics: An Introduction.* New York: Alfred A. Knopf.

———. 1964. *Politics, Parties, and Pressure Groups.* 5th ed. New York: Thomas Y. Crowell.

Kim, Jae-On, John R. Petrocik, and Stephen E. Enokson. 1975. "Voter Turnout among the American States: Systemic and Individual Components." *American Political Science Review* 69:107–123.

Loftus, Thomas. 1985. "The 'New Politics' Parties in State Legislatures." *State Government* 58:108–109.

Longley, Lawrence. 1992. "The Gradual Institutionalization of the National Democratic Party in the 1980s and 1990s." *Vox Pop: Newsletter of Political Organizations and Parties* 2:4.

McBeath, Gerald A. 1994. "Transformation of the Alaska Blanket Primary System." *Comparative State Politics* 15 (August): 25–41.

Magleby, David. 1984. *Direct Legislation.* Baltimore: Johns Hopkins University Press.

———. 1988. "Taking the Initiative: Direct Legislation and Direct Democracy in the 1980s." *PS* 11:600–611.

Mayer, Kenneth R., and John M. Wood. 1995. "The Impact of Public Financing on Electoral Competitiveness: Evidence from Wisconsin, 1964–1990." *Legislative Studies Quarterly* 20:69–88.

Mayhew, David R. 1986. *Placing Parties in American Politics.* Princeton, N.J.: Princeton University Press.

Monardi, Fred M. 1994. "Election Outcomes at the Sub-Gubernatorial Level." Paper presented at the annual meeting of the Midwest Political Science Association, Chicago, April 14–16.

Moncrief, Garry. 1992. "The Increase in State Legislative Campaign Expenditures: A Comparison of Four Northeastern States." *Western Political Quarterly* 45:549–689.

Morehouse, Sarah McCally. 1981. *State Politics, Parties, and Policy.* New York: Holt, Rinehart and Winston.

———. 1987. "Money versus Party Effort: Nominating for Governor." Paper presented at the annual meeting of the American Political Science Association, Chicago. September 3–6.

———. 1994. "Party Organization and Party Nominations." Paper presented at the annual meeting of the American Political Science Association, New York, September 1–4.

Patterson, Samuel, and Gregory Caldeira. 1983. "Getting Out the Vote: Participation in Gubernatorial Elections." *American Political Science Review* 77:675–689.

———. 1984. "Etiology of Partisan Competition." *American Political Science Review* 78:691–707.

Ranney, Austin. 1976. "Parties in State Politics." In *Politics in the American States: A Comparative Analysis,* 3d ed., edited by Herbert Jacob and Kenneth Vines. Boston: Little, Brown.

Redfield, Kent D. 1993. "Candidates, Campaigns, and Cash." *Comparative State Politics* 14:17–25.

Redfield, Kent D., Doh C. Shinn, and Jack R. Van Der Slik. 1993. "Campaign Finance in Illinois: Public Opinion Constraints Collide with Expanding Campaign Expenditures." Paper presented at the annual meeting of the Midwest Political Science Association, Chicago, April 15–17.

Reichley, A. James. 1992. *The Life of the Parties: A History of American Political Parties.* New York: Free Press.

Rosenstone, Steven J., and John Mark Hanson. 1993. *Mobilization, Participation, and Democracy in America.* New York: Macmillan.

Rosenthal, Cindy Simon. 1993. "Partners or Solo Players: Legislative Campaign Committees and State Parties." Paper presented at the Ray C. Bliss Institute of Applied Politics, Akron, Ohio, September 23–24.

Salmore, Stephen, and Barbara Salmore. 1993. "The Transformation of State Electoral Politics." In *State of the States*, 2d ed., edited by Carl Van Horn. Washington, D.C.: CQ Press.

Schattschneider, E. E. 1942. *Party Government*. New York: Rinehart.

Schwartz, Mildred A. 1990. *The Party Network: The Robust Organization of Illinois Republicans*. Madison: University of Wisconsin Press.

Sorauf, Frank J. 1992. *Inside Campaign Finance: Myths and Realities*. New Haven: Yale University Press.

Squire, Peverill. 1992. "Challenger Profile and Gubernatorial Elections." *Western Political Quarterly* 45:125–142.

Stanley, Harold, and Richard Niemi. 1994. *Vital Statistics on American Politics*. 4th ed. Washington, D.C.: CQ Press.

Stonecash, Jeffrey M. 1990. "Campaign Finance in New York Senate Elections." *Legislative Studies Quarterly* 15:247–262.

———. 1988. "Working at the Margins: Campaign Finance and Strategy in New York Assembly Elections." *Legislative Studies Quarterly* 13:477–494.

Svoboda, Craig. 1995. "Measuring Indirect Effects in Gubernatorial Elections." Paper presented at the annual meeting of the Midwest Political Science Association, Chicago, April 6–8.

U.S. Advisory Commission on Intergovernmental Relations. 1986. *The Transformation in American Politics: Implications for Federalism*. Washington, D.C.: U.S. Government Printing Office.

Wattenberg, Martin P. 1991. *The Rise of Candidate-Centered Politics: Presidential Elections of the 1980s*. Cambridge: Harvard University Press.

Wolfinger, Raymond E., and Steven J. Rosenstone. 1980. *Who Votes?* New Haven: Yale University Press.

SUGGESTED READINGS

Cotter, Cornelius P., James L. Gibson, John F. Bibby, and Robert J. Huckshorn. *Party Organizations in American Politics*. New York: Praeger, 1984. An analysis of the status, activities, and impact of state and local party organizations, based on a nationwide survey.

Epstein, Leon D. *Political Parties in the American Mold*. Madison: University of Wisconsin Press, 1986. A comprehensive treatise on American parties, with significant insights concerning state parties in Chapters 5 and 6.

Mayhew, David R. *Placing Parties in American Politics*. Princeton, N.J.: Princeton University Press, 1986. An exhaustive survey of party organizations in each of the fifty states, with an analysis of the factors influencing organizational development.

Schwartz, Mildred S. *The Party Network: The Robust Organization of Illinois Republicans*. Madison: University of Wisconsin Press, 1990. A detailed account and analysis of a state party that uses the organization theory of sociology.

Shea, Daniel M. *Transforming Democracy: Legislative Campaign Committees and Political Parties*. Albany, N.Y.: State University Press of New York, 1995. An analysis of legislative campaign committees that illustrates their autonomy from the regular party organization.

CHAPTER 4

 Interest Groups in the States

CLIVE S. THOMAS AND
RONALD J. HREBENAR

If you walk around the streets near the legislature and state offices in any of the fifty state capitals, from Augusta, Maine, to Sacramento, California, you will find the headquarters and branch offices of a host of groups and organizations plus the offices of several lobbyists and some lobbying firms. Whether they have an office in the capital, hire a lobbyist, or do both, an increasing number of interest groups, from bankers to chiropractors to animal rights advocates, are establishing a presence close to the nerve center of state government for one important reason—to promote and protect their interests in the never-ending process of public policy making.

Historically, all states have gone through eras in which one or a handful of interests dominated state politics to the extent that they could determine what state government did and, often of equal or more importance, what it did not do. During the late nineteenth and early twentieth centuries, railroad interests dominated politics in all the forty-eight contiguous states. In California it was the Southern Pacific; in Kentucky, the Louisville and Nashville Railroad; and in Maryland, the Baltimore and Ohio. As late as the 1950s, Texas politics were dominated by the Big Four—oil, chemicals, the Texas Manufacturers Association, and, again, the railroads. The oil industry was dominant in Louisiana and Oklahoma; the Farm Bureau, county court houses, and utilities, in many southern states; the coal companies, in West Virginia; salmon canneries, mining, forestry, and shipping interests, in Alaska. And the list goes on.

In all but a few states the power of the railroads has long since waned, and many of the old manufacturing, agricultural, mining, and forestry interests have seen their political power eroded. While some states still have a prominent interest (gaming in Nevada, the Du Pont Company in Delaware, the automakers and autoworkers in Michigan, for example), the days of states being dominated by one or a few interests are likely gone forever. In addition, there have been many other changes in the interest group and lobbying scene in state capitals since the 1960s. Yet, these changes do not mean that the importance and impact of interest groups on state politics have declined. In all states, interest groups are still major forces shaping state politics and determining what government does or does not do. In fact, in some ways interest groups in the states are more important now than they have ever been.

The contemporary interest group scene in the states can best be understood by exploring (a) why interest groups exist, what they do, and how they relate to other state political institutions; (b) what accounts for the interest group system—its makeup, operational techniques, and extent of group power—in any particular state; (c) how interest group systems can be compared across states; and (d) how different state interest group activity is today than it was thirty years or so ago. First we explain the basic aspects of group activity in the states, then we present a conceptual framework to provide assistance in understanding the often complex world of state interest group politics.[1]

WHAT IS AN INTEREST GROUP?

Broadly defined, an *interest group* is an association of individuals or organizations, usually formally organized, that attempts to influence public policy. Many researchers define the term *interest group* more narrowly than this. Most often they use the legal definition, confining their focus to those groups required to register under state laws and excluding those not required to do so. Yet many groups and organizations engage in lobbying but are not required to register. The most important of these are those representing government itself and particularly state government agencies. Most states do not require public officials at any level of government to register as lobbyists.

Our findings indicate, however, that on any one day anywhere between a quarter and a half of those trying to influence state elected or appointed officials are themselves from state, federal, or local government agencies. In fact, all government agencies and jurisdictions engage in lobbying for their own interests

1. The data in this chapter come mainly from the Hrebenar-Thomas study of interest groups in all fifty states conducted between 1983 and 1988 and from research for an update of that study done in 1994. The results of the original project, which involved eighty political scientists, can be found in Hrebenar and Thomas 1987, 1990, 1992, 1993a, and 1993b, and a synthesis can be found in Gray, Jacob, and Albritton 1990, chap. 4. Research for the update of that project focused on changes in interest group power and the range of groups in all fifty states. Those contributing data to this update are listed at the end of the text of this chapter.

and are no less "special interests" than many private groups. In addition to government agencies, there are other groups and interests that are not required to register as lobbying entities. In most cases this is because they do not spend enough time or money on lobbying to meet the minimum legal definition for registration set down in state law. Many community and social issue groups fall into this category. But so do potentially more powerful interests, such as a loose-knit association of business people or a prominent family that is focused and organized enough to exert influence on public policy. Groups and organizations active in state politics but not required to register are often referred to as "hidden lobbies."

To ignore this army of nonregistered groups and interests distorts the picture of both interest group activity and the lobbying community in state capitals. For this reason it is unsatisfactory to use only official registration lists in making comparisons between states. By our definition, therefore, not only are the Delaware Bankers Association and the Missouri Bus and Truck Association examples of interest groups, but so are the City of Detroit, the State University of New York, and an informal group of leading citizens in Kentucky working to improve their state's quality of public education.

In essence, the activities of interest groups in relation to public policy making involve a two-stage process: first, groups must gain access to public policy makers (legislators, bureaucrats, and so forth); second, they must influence the decisions of those policy makers in their group's favor. Interest groups operate in the state public policy–making process mainly by using one or more lobbyists. A *lobbyist* is a person who represents an interest group in order to influence governmental decisions in that group's favor. The decisions most often targeted by lobbyists are those concerning public policies; but they also include decisions about who gets elected and appointed to make those policies. Lobbyists include not only those required to register by law but also those representing hidden, or nonregistered, groups and organizations, particularly government. The various types of lobbyists with their different backgrounds and different power bases are discussed in a later section.

The terms *interest, lobby,* and *sector* are used in a variety of ways. Most often in interest group studies they are used synonymously and interchangeably as generic terms for the collection of individuals, groups, and organizations within a particular part of society, such as business, senior citizens, minorities (the business lobby, the business interest, the business sector, and so forth). The term *lobby* always has political connotations; but *interest* and *sector* may or may not. They may simply refer to a part (a sector) of society with similar concerns or a common identity that may or may not engage in political activity. It is from these similar concerns and common identities of interests and sectors, however, that interest groups and lobbies are formed. Furthermore, the distinction between an interest and a lobby on the one hand and an organized interest group on the other is sometimes difficult to make in practice. This is partly because organized groups such as the National Rifle Association, a state chamber of commerce, or a local group representing African Americans often act and are perceived as representing a broader political interest than their official membership.

INTEREST GROUPS ACTIVE IN THE STATES TODAY AND YESTERDAY

As of the mid-1990s there were more groups and a wider variety of them trying to influence public policy in the states than ever before. Research even reveals an expansion in both numbers and variety of groups since the late 1980s. As recently as the 1960s and early 1970s there were far fewer groups active in state capitals and a much narrower range of interests operating. During those years and probably for several decades before, the so-called traditional interests—business, labor, education, farmers, and local government groups—were the major interests active in the states (Zeigler 1983, 99). Why, then, has there been a sudden and continuing expansion?

This marked expansion in the number and variety of groups is due to many factors, but four are particularly important. First, as state governments became more and more involved in the economic and social life of their states from the 1960s onward in areas such as business regulation, environmental protection, and health, more and more interests were affected. They became politically active either to protect their interest from government or to take advantage of some new state program or benefit. Second, the expanding range and complexity of issues dealt with by government meant that the old general interest organizations, such as trade associations, were not able to deal with many of the specific needs of their members. The result has been a fragmentation of certain traditional interests. Fragmentation has been particularly evident within the business and local government lobbies. Individual corporations and businesses and individual cities and special districts (especially school districts) have increasingly lobbied on their own. While they usually remain part of an umbrella organization, they see their specific interests as best served by a separate lobbying operation. Third, a combination of factors—heightened political awareness (resulting from such events as the Vietnam War and the civil rights movement), an increase in the size of the middle class, the transition of America into a postindustrial society—has propelled the rise of many social issue and public interest groups, from environmentalists to gay rights groups to abortion groups. And fourth, although there is less hard evidence for this, the decline of political parties, especially their increasing inability to deliver satisfactory results on specific issues, has apparently led many people to join an interest group in an attempt to achieve their specific goals.

Besides the greater number and variety of groups operating in state capitals, there is a third dimension to this expansion in group activity since the 1960s. Groups are lobbying more intensively than was the case in the mid-1970s or even in the mid-1980s. They have more regular contact with public officials and use more sophisticated techniques, as will be shown later in this chapter.

Most informed observers agree that an expansion in group activity has occurred during the last twenty years or so; but they disagree about the extent of these changes (Gray 1984). These disagreements stem largely from differences in methods of investigation and of defining interest groups. The methodology and definitions that we used place us in the camp that believes that this expansion has been extensive, particularly in regard to the range of groups that are active. Our listing of those interests currently active in state capitals will be easier to appreciate if we first briefly explain the method we used in compiling the list.

We explained earlier that our definition of *interest group* enabled us to identify the so-called hidden lobbies and that we focused on interest activity in state government as a whole—on the entire state capital, not just the capitol building. It has been well documented that as state government expands and becomes more complex, more and more lobbying is directed toward the bureaucracy (Morehouse 1981, 135–137; Zeigler 1983, 119–127) and, to an increasing extent, to the courts. Yet most studies of group and lobbying activity focus almost entirely on state legislatures.

Another way in which our methodology differs from many previous studies is in its time span. To get an accurate picture of the range of groups operating in a state it is necessary to study not just one but several legislative sessions. Because some sessions do not involve issues that affect certain groups, to study only one or two years of activity can produce misleading results. Using this approach we identified several interests that alternate between being continually active and intermittently active but nevertheless appear consistently across the states. For example, doctors and lawyers have been well organized for several decades but have previously gone unnoticed by many researchers.

A further difference in our method relates to categorization of interests or lobbies. Many previous analyses have used too broad a categorization of interests. Most problematic of all is the category of business. While we all know instinctively what business is, it is far too broad a category to be of any real value for analytical purposes. To say that 50 percent of groups lobbying in state capitals are business groups tells us little. There is often bitter competition between business interests—railroads and truckers, for example; so to categorize all business groups together as the business lobby gives an impression of much greater political cohesion than exists in practice. The categorization of the other four traditional interests—labor, education, agriculture, and local government—suffers from the same problems. What is more helpful is to identify specific types of interests as opposed to broad categories.

In our listing in Table 4-1, therefore, we have abandoned the general categories in favor of specific types of interests. These are listed on the basis of two criteria. The first is the extent of their presence in the fifty states. The second criteria is whether an interest is active continually or only intermittently in the states where

Table 4-1 Types of Interests and Their Frequency of Presence in the Fifty States

Present in more than 45 states	Present in 25–45 states	Present in fewer than 25 states
Continually active		
Individual business corporations*	Manufacturing companies	Foreign businesses
Local government units (cities, districts, etc.)	Tourism groups	(especially from Japan)
State departments, boards, and commissions	Manufacturers' associations	Native American groups
Business and trade associations†	Railroads	
Utility companies and associations (public and private)	Agribusiness corporations	
Banks and financial institutions and associations	Sportsmen's groups (especially	
Insurance companies and associations	hunting and fishing)	
Public employee unions and associations	Commercial fishermen	
(state and local)	Health care corporations	
Universities and colleges (public and private)	Mining companies	
School teachers unions and associations	Gaming (race tracks / casinos / lotteries)	
Local government associations	Latino groups	
Farmers' organizations and commodity associations		
Traditional labor unions		
Labor associations (mainly AFL-CIO)		
Environmentalists		
Oil and gas companies and associations		
Hospital associations		
Contractors, builders, developers		
Senior citizens		
Intermittently active		
Physicians	Pro-development and land use	Children's rights groups
Trial lawyers and state bar associations	groups	Animal rights groups
Liquor, wine, beer interests	Groups for the physically and	"Think tanks" (public
Retailers' associations	mentally handicapped	and private)
Real estate interests	Student groups	Political consultants
Police and Firemen's associations	Nurses	
Communication interests (telecommunications,	Chiropractors	
cable TV, and the like)	Taxpayer groups	
Nursing home operators	Gay rights groups	
Truckers	Parent-teacher associations	
Women's groups	Media associations	
Groups for the arts	Consumer groups	
Pro-choice and anti-abortion groups	Veterans' groups	
Mothers Against Drunk Driving	Term limit and government	
Church organizations	reform groups	
African American groups	Moral Majority/Christian Right	
Pro- and anti-smoking interests	Community groups	
Social service groups and coalitions	Pro- and anti-gun control groups	
Good government groups (League of Women Voters,	Victims' rights groups	
Common Cause)		
American Civil Liberties Union		
Various professional groups (accountants, engineers,		
architects, and the like)		
Federal agencies		

SOURCE: Compiled and updated from data in Hrebenar and Thomas, 1987, 1992, 1993a and 1993b. See Gray, Jacob, and Albritton 1990, 576–577n.1, for a list of researchers who provided the data for this table.

*An unavoidably broad category. It includes manufacturing and service corporations with the exception of those listed separately, such as private utilities and oil and gas companies. These and other business corporations were listed separately because of their frequency of presence across the states.

†Another unavoidably broad category. It includes chambers of commerce as well as specific trade associations, for example, the American Tobacco Institute, air carriers, manufacturers' associations, etc.

it is present. In both sections interests are listed in order of the estimated intensity of their lobbying efforts across the states.

Almost all the interests listed as being present in more than forty-five states (close to 60 percent of all interests) are present in all fifty states. Although not all are continually active, it is clear that a broad range of interests, both public and private, operate in the states today. As much as 75 percent of the time and money spent in the lobbying effort is attributable to the nineteen interests that are continually active.

The increasing prominence of several interests that are active in more than forty-five states is worthy of special mention. We have already mentioned individual cities and special local government districts and state agencies. The most prominent of state agencies in all states are the Departments of Education, Transportation, and Welfare and state universities and colleges. Associated with this rise in government lobbying has been the increased prominence of public sector unions, particularly unions of state and local employees, including police and firemen, as well as teachers' unions. Ideological groups, which are also often single issue groups like antiabortionists and the religious right, have also become quite active in recent years. Public interest organizations—particularly, good government and, most of all, environmentalist groups—and senior citizens are other forces that now have a significant presence in almost all state capitals.

Interests that are present in twenty-five to forty-five states and in fewer that twenty-five states tend to be newly formed groups, such as consumer and animal rights groups, or those representing an interest concentrated in certain states, such as Native Americans and Latinos. The general trend for most interests is to expand to more and more states. Since 1989, several interests, particularly gaming interests, Latinos, and pro- and antismoking groups, have expanded their presence in the states. And more groups, senior citizens and Native Americans, for example, have become continually active (Gray, Jacob, and Albritton 1990, 132–33).

One final word about groups active in the states today: It is important not to equate presence with power. Just because a group or interest is active in state politics does not by itself ensure its success in achieving its goals. As we shall see later in this chapter, some of the interests listed in the table are often very effective, while others have little influence.

THE PRIVATE GOALS AND THE PUBLIC ROLES
OF INTEREST GROUPS

This recent expansion in group activity might seem contradictory, given the generally negative attitude toward interest groups among Americans or, as one political scientist has expressed it, the "triple tension" of the "inevitability, indispensability, and dangers of interest groups" (Petracca 1992, xx). Given this public ambivalence, it is useful to explore the function of interest groups in a democratic society, including their functions in the American states. In doing so it is instructive to make a distinction between the private goals of interest groups and the public role that they play, particularly their contribution to the functioning of American democracy. There is an interesting contradiction between these private goals and public roles, as there is in the attitudes of Americans toward interest groups.

The Private Goals of Interest Groups

Unlike political parties, which originate and exist primarily for political purposes, most interest groups are not primarily political organizations. They usually develop from a common economic or social interest, as, for example, workers forming a trade union, clothing manufacturers or book publishers forming a business trade association, or religious or minority groups forming self-help associations. Such organizations promote programs and disseminate information to enhance the professional, business, social, or avocational interests of their members. Much of this activity is nonpolitical, as when the American Medical Association publishes its journal or provides cut-rate life insurance for its members.

However, many nonpolitical interest groups are forced to become politically active because there is no other way to protect or promote the interests of their members (Walker 1991, 41–55). Workers' movements did so in the late nineteenth century in order to establish the legality of trade unions and to promote child labor and worker safety laws. Employers' organizations became politically active to counter both union power and to resist government regulation. Farm groups used the political process to secure and preserve import tariffs and farm subsidies. As we noted above, greater government involvement in the economy and in society in general since the 1960s has brought a plethora of new groups into the political arena to protect themselves from government regulation, to secure a piece of the government budget, or to promote some value or belief.

Therefore, while most interest groups have many nonpolitical goals, they have one overriding goal when they become involved in politics—to influence the political process and particularly public policy in their favor. Despite the rhetoric of many groups that their goals are "in the public interest," these goals are often narrow and sometimes very self-serving: gaining a tax break, getting an exemption from a regulation, securing a budget appropriation, and so on. If one considers that a democracy like the United States is a myriad collection of interests, attitudes, and values, there is nothing wrong with such narrow, special interest representation. In fact, it is essential to the functioning of pluralist democracy.

The Public Roles of Interest Groups

In promoting their private goals, interest groups perform certain indispensable public roles. Five of these roles are particularly important, and we discuss them in turn.

The Aggregation and Representation of Interests. Together with political parties, interest groups are one of the primary means by which people with similar interests and concerns are brought together, or aggregated, and their views articulated to government. Thus, interest groups are an important vehicle of political participation; they act as major intermediaries between the governed and the government by representing the views of their members to public officials, especially between elections.

Facilitating Government. Groups contribute to the substance of public policy by being significant sources of both technical and political information for policy makers. In most instances groups help to facilitate the process of bargaining and compromise essential to policy making in a pluralist system. And in some cases they aid in the implementation of public policies, as, for example, when the Arkansas Farm Bureau disseminates information about a state or federal agricultural program.

Political Education and Training. To varying degrees, interest groups educate their members and the public on issues. They also provide opportunities for citizens to learn about the political process and to gain valuable practical experience for seeking public office.

Candidate Recruitment. Groups often recruit candidates to run for public office, both from within and outside their group membership.

Campaign Finance. Increasingly these days groups help to finance political campaigns, both candidate elections and, at the state and local level, ballot measure elections (initiative, referendum, and recall).

Certainly, each of these five functions is subject to abuse by interest groups, particularly campaign finance. But that does not make them any less essential to the working of democracy or lessen the importance of the public role of interest groups. What is contradictory or paradoxical about the relationship between these private political goals and public roles of interest groups is that the positive public roles are purely incidental. As we noted above, in their private capacity interest groups do not exist to better the democratic process or to improve the functioning of the political process. Thus the positive public role of interest groups is a paradoxical byproduct of the sum of their selfish interests.

Furthermore, as vehicles of representation, interest groups are far from ideal (Schattschneider 1960, 20–46; Schlozman and Tierney 1986, 58–87; Zeigler 1983, 99, 104–106). The most important problem is that they do not represent all segments of the population equally. Their bias is toward the better-educated, higher-income, white, and male segments of the population; and therefore minorities (including women) and the less-well-educated and lower-income segments are underrepresented in the political process by interest groups. As umbrella organizations embracing a host of groups and interests, political parties are far more representative political organizations.

THE CONNECTION BETWEEN INTEREST GROUPS
AND POLITICAL PARTIES

Setting aside the nonpolitical functions of interest groups, it is their political roles, and particularly those roles in connection with political parties, that are fundamental determinants of politics and policy making in any democratic society. Several scholars have noted and examined this party-group relationship in the states (Morehouse 1981, 116–18, 127; Zeigler 1983, 111–117; Zeigler and van Dalen 1976, 94–95; Zeller 1954, 190–193). The relationship of groups and parties affects the power distribution in the society, what gets on the policy agenda, which policies get enacted, and which ones do not. What exactly is the group-party relationship in the states and what are its consequences for understanding interest group activity and public policy making?

In most cases parties form around some broad view—political philosophy— of the role that government should play in society. At one end of the political spectrum is the liberal perspective of government as a promoter of social and economic well-being; at the other end is the conservative perspective, which places the emphasis on individual initiative rather than on government. Political parties are formed by certain interests and thus gather under their umbrella like-minded interests and groups: liberal causes—environmentalists, gay rights groups, certain labor organizations, and so forth—associating with liberal parties; more conservative interests—business, many professional groups, fundamental religious interests, and so forth—associating with more conservative parties. Thus there is a fundamental political linkage between parties and interest groups.

The stronger the party, the more control it has in determining the policy agenda and ensuring its passage. Strong parties also control the access of interests and interest groups to the policy-making process. Parties in the United States have been relatively weak, although the extent of their strength or weakness varies across the fifty states. The weaker a party is, the more leeway is given to other elements of the political system to fill the power vacuum. Because of the close linkage between parties and interest groups, this vacuum is filled largely by the groups themselves.

The general weakness of parties has given a greater role to interest groups in the policy-making process in many states than is the case in Washington, D.C., and certainly in other Western democracies. The effect of this greater role of interest groups has been to increase the fragmented nature of policy making in the states. Power is more fragmented among various interests and less concentrated in one place—the party. Political parties have less control over the policy agenda, and certain groups have the ability to affect the content of that agenda; groups have many more options and avenues of access—including election campaign activity, lobbying, playing the legislature against the administration, using clientele groups—than they would have if parties were strong; and groups have more effect on what gets enacted in the states. Again, this situation varies across the states, the greatest impact of interest groups on policy making having been in the South and West. The general trend, however, is that groups are gaining strength and political parties are getting weaker (see Morehouse 1981, 101–118; Thomas and Hrebenar 1990, 147–148).

A major reason for the political power of interest groups in the states is that their relatively homogeneous constituency and narrowly defined goals make them more effective agents of representation for specific interests than parties. Parties have been less effective because they are essentially broad coalitions of interests and tend to pursue broad issues and policies, as opposed to the concerns of small and very narrow group interests. Consequently, those seeking specific policy goals in the states, particularly in the South and West, have been more likely to use an interest group than a political party. Also, over the years, the narrower constituency and policy focus of interest groups have enabled them to adapt easily to their political environment. In addition, interest groups have often filled the void in many state political systems by taking over essential political functions, such as candidate recruitment and financing election campaigns, that parties would not or could not perform. It is, in fact, the increased role of groups in the financing of elections that has been primarily responsible for their greater prominence and power in recent years.

This does not mean, however, that parties can be completely ignored by groups and their lobbyists. Parties still play an important role in organizing legislatures, especially in some northeastern states, and in coordinating policy demands. This is where the entrepreneurial skill of lobbyists and group leaders comes in. They need to support each party, not to the extent that they antagonize the other, but enough to ensure access after an election.

VARIATION IN STATE INTEREST GROUP SYSTEMS: TWO EXAMPLES

So far in this chapter we have focused on the similarities in interest group activity across the states. But we have also noted that there are many differences in the makeup and operation of state group systems. To illustrate these differences in a specific way, let us look at two state group systems that are quite different.

New Jersey: A Highly Developed System

On a par with states like California, Florida, Massachusetts, and New York, New Jersey has one of the most developed interest group systems in the nation today. In 1990 more than 600 registered businesses, industries, and associations employed 444 legislative agents, or registered lobbyists, in Trenton. Virtually every interest listed in Table 4-1 operates in New Jersey. Trenton has a highly professional lobbying corps, and the role of contract lobbyists and multiservice lobbying firms is well established. State law requires that both legislative and administrative agency lobbyists register. Techniques such as coalition building, public relations campaigns, and grass-roots lobbying have reached sophisticated levels. Of particular importance is the recent rapid increase in the use of political action committees (PACs). In the period 1990–1994 the most effective groups in the state were the Business and Industry Association, the New Jersey Education Association, the New Jersey Trial Lawyers Association, Johnson and Johnson, Prudential Insurance, the Alliance for Action (a business-labor road construction coalition), and the casino industry. Within a state in which political parties were seen as weak, the influence of interest groups was seen as moderate, or complementary to other political institutions (Salmore and Salmore 1993).

Wyoming: A "Friends and Neighbors" Interest Group System

Wyoming has a much less developed group system than New Jersey. Although a variety of groups operate in Cheyenne, few manufacturing groups are in evidence, liberal social issue groups are much less active than in New Jersey, and few out-of-state interests are active. The groups that are prominent are those connected with agriculture, natural resources, government, and some services, particularly tourism. Wyoming has the smallest population of any state (less than 500,000), and there exists an intimate atmosphere among the players in state politics, what V. O. Key, Jr. (1949), called "friends and neighbors politics." Consequently, the small lobbying community still contains many "good old boys" and wheeler-dealers but few multiservice lobbying firms, and there is less need for sophisticated tactics and the use of PACs than in most states. Lobby laws are minimal and laxly enforced. In the early 1990s among the most influential interests were the mining lobby, the Stockgrowers Association and the Farm Bureau, schoolteachers, the oil and gas lobby, municipalities, environmentalists, truckers, physicians, tourism groups, and banks and financial institutions. The overall impact of groups on public policy was seen as greater than the moderate or complementary influence in New Jersey. Parties were seen as exerting moderate influence (Clark and Walter 1987).

These examples reveal many differences between the two group systems, especially the range of groups operating, the professionalism of lobbyists, the extent and use of lobby techniques, and the power of individual groups as well as of the group system as a whole. In fact, there are variations of some type in all fifty state group systems.

EXPLAINING DIFFERENCES IN STATE INTEREST GROUP ACTIVITY

How, then, do we explain these differences? What we need is a framework within which we can analyze the development and contemporary dynamics of interest group systems. Such an analytical framework should help us to explain their ability to influence public policy within individual states and their similari-

Table 4-2   Ten Major Factors Influencing the Development and Dynamics of Interest Group Systems in the States

Factor	Influence on state or political figures
Socioeconomic and political environment	
1. Level of socioeconomic development	*Increased diversity:* Produces a more diverse and competitive group system Results in decline in the dominance of one or an oligarchy of groups Results in use of more sophisticated techniques of lobbying Results in a rise in the professionalization of lobbyists
2. Political attitudes (esp. political culture and ideology)	Affect the level of integration and professionalization of the policy-making process Influence criteria for acceptability of lobbying techniques Influence the comprehensiveness and stringency of enforcement of public disclosure laws, including lobbying laws
3. Strength or weakness of political parties	*Strong parties:* Exert greater control over policy making, resulting in greater centralization of the policy-making and implementation process Mean more limited avenues of access and fewer strategies open to interest groups
4. Level of campaign costs and sources of support	Increased costs put pressure on candidates to raise funds More support directly to candidates from groups and PACs makes candidate more beholden to them
Government institutional factors	
5. Level of professionalization of state government (state legislatures and bureaucracy, incl. governor's staff)	*Greater professionalization:* Means more varied sources of information available to policy makers Results in higher demand for information by policy makers, including information from groups of lobbyists
6. Extent and enforcement of public disclosure laws (including lobbying laws, campaign finance laws, PAC regulations, conflict-of-interest provisions)	*Extensive and well-enforced laws:* Result in greater public information about lobbying activities, which affects the methods and techniques of lobbying Mean less power for certain individual groups and lobbyists, although not necessarily for system groups
State policy-making process	
7. State policy domain	Defined as the state's constitutional and legal authority and constitutes the areas over which it can formally exercise policy decisions Determines which interests will attempt to affect state policy Expansion of policy authority results in increase in number and types of groups lobbying
8. Level of integration or fragmentation of the policy process	The extent to which the policy-making process is centralized or dispersed within a state Affects patterns of group access and influence Greater integration generally means fewer options available to groups Greater fragmentation means a greater number of access points and available methods of influence
9. Intergovernmental spending and policy-making authority	Refers to the policies exercised and the amount of money spent by state governments in contrast to the policies and spending by federal and local governments. Changes in responsibilities between levels of government affect the types of groups that lobby the particular level of government and the intensity of their efforts.
10. State public policy and spending priorities	Refers to the policies and spending that governments emphasize at a particular time, as opposed to their general constitutional and statutory responsibilities. Groups directly concerned with and affected by the areas of policy priority are often given preferential access by government. The extent of this preferential access is related to the degree to which the group is needed by policy makers for advice in policy development and implementation. Shifts in priorities affect access and influence of certain groups and the relative power of groups within specific policy areas.

SOURCES: Developed from data in Hrebenar and Thomas 1987, 1992, 1993a, 1993b, and by reference to Elazar 1984; Erikson, Wright, and McIver 1993; Francis 1967; Gray and Lowery 1988; Gray and Lowery 1993; Hunter, Wilson, and Brunk 1991; Hyde and Alsfeld 1985; Morehouse 1981; Olson 1982; Rosenthal 1992; Thomas and Hrebenar 1991b; Wahlke et al. 1962; Wilson 1990; Zeigler 1983; Zeigler and Baer 1969; and Zeigler and van Dalen 1976.

ties and differences across states. The framework set out in Table 4-2 sheds new light on four key aspects of group activity: the development of state group systems; the types of groups that are active; the methods they use in pursuing their goals; and the power they exert.

The ten factors and their components in this framework are very much interrelated in that they influence each other. A change in one may reflect or lead to a change in one or more of the other factors. Major changes will have a significant effect on the interest group and lobbying scene in a particular state. To be sure, the variables are numerous, and we have only begun to understand how they interact with one another. Nevertheless, this framework does provide the first comprehensive approach to systematically understanding the otherwise rather complex and often confusing world of state interest group politics. Its value can be seen by the references made here to the two case studies presented in the last section. In the following sections we also see how the framework helps us understand group regulation, strategy and tactics, intergovernmental activity, and group system power.

REGULATING INTEREST GROUP ACTIVITY IN THE STATES

Although corrupt and underhanded dealings by interest groups and lobbyists have likely never been as widespread as commonly believed, some groups have been willing to use almost any means, including illegal ones, to gain access to and to influence government. And on the uneven playing field of American politics, those possessing large financial resources have always had an advantage. So even though abuses are relatively rare, from the heavy-handed and sometimes blatantly illegal political activities of railroad lobbyists in the years following the Civil War to the scandals involving legislators and lobbyists in Arizona, California, and South Carolina in the early 1990s, there have been enough incidents to reinforce public skepticism of moneyed political interests. Then, in recent years, the demand for openness in the policy-making process has increased, resulting in the so-called sunshine-in-government movement. When these circumstances and attitudes are taken together, it is obvious why pressure for government regulation and public disclosure of lobbying activity in the states has been increasing. Yet, while lobby regulation and disclosure laws have existed in some states for decades (Zeller 1954, 217–225), only since the mid-1970s have these laws become widespread and more stringently enforced.

To put the development of lobby regulations in perspective, we should not judge interest group and lobbyist activity of the past by the standards of today or apply the same standard to all states over the last hundred years. The sunshine-in-government era that followed Watergate makes all previous eras of lobbying activity look suspect, and in many cases corrupt. Certainly, there were many instances of corruption and unsavory dealing. The exploits of Artie Samish, a lobbyist who "ran California politics" in the 1930s and 1940s from his office in the

Senator Hotel across the street from the capitol, provide a prime example (Samish and Thomas 1971; Syer 1987, 34, 36, 38–39). Some lobbyist activities that today appear suspect, however, were probably quite acceptable to previous generations in most states.

Today the dominance of a state by one or a few powerful interests—particularly one or a handful of businesses—is viewed with great suspicion by the public. This is because the interests of industry are often viewed, in a populist mindset, as opposed to those of the public. Yet, in the developmental stage of most states the interests of the dominant business (lumber in Oregon, automobiles in Michigan, and the railroads in almost all states) were often viewed by politicians and citizens alike as identical with the interests of their state. For this and other reasons, in the past, political corruption and unsavory activities by lobbyists and interest groups were often perceived differently. And largely because of differences in political culture (described in Chapter 1), what was viewed as corrupt or unsavory in one state might be quite acceptable in another. A much more tolerant attitude to political corruption and unsavory dealings existed in the South, for example, than was prevalent in the upper midwestern states.

Today, four types of legal provisions provide for the regulation and public disclosure of lobbying activity in the states. Lobby laws are the most important, but these are supplemented by three other types of provisions. We briefly describe the other three provisions first and then focus on lobby laws.

Conflict of interest and personal financial disclosure provisions required of public officials are intended to disclose the financial connections that public officials have with individuals, groups, organizations, and businesses. Sometimes these laws prohibit certain types of financial relations or dealings. In several states, in an attempt to reduce corruption of administration officials, public ethics laws prohibit certain officials from being employed by an interest group within a specified period of time after their being involved in governmental decisions that directly affected that interest (COGEL 1990, 129–148).

Campaign finance regulations provide for public disclosure, to a varying extent, of campaign contributions from individuals and organizations. These laws often impose limits and prohibitions on such contributions and restrict the period during which such funds can be contributed. For example, some states prohibit contributions being made during the legislative session (COGEL 1990, 87–128).

The regulation of political action committees is another aspect of campaign finance. All states now have laws relating to the activities of PACs. As with campaign finance regulations, states often impose limits and sometimes prohibitions on the contributions of PACs. Many states, for example, limit the contributions to PACs that can be made by corporations, labor unions, and regulated industries, particularly public utilities (Thomas and Hrebenar 1991b).

Lobby laws now exist in all fifty states and provide for the registration of lobbyists, their clients, or employers, as well as the reporting of lobbying expenditures. These laws sometimes prohibit certain types of lobbying activities, such as lobbyists contracting with a group for a contingency fee—a percentage of the amount of money that the lobbyist secures for the group he or she represents. Yet while lobby laws often impose certain restrictions, their major purpose is to provide public information and throw light on group activities rather than to restrict or control these activities. Indeed, because of the provisions relating to the right to "petition government" in the First Amendment to the U.S. Constitution and similar provisions in many state constitutions, attempts to restrict lobbying would run into serious constitutional problems.

State lobby laws vary considerably, however, in their inclusiveness, their reporting requirements, and the stringency with which they are enforced (COGEL 1988, 157–168; COGEL 1990, 149–171; Opheim 1991). For example, while all states include contact with the legislature within their definition of lobbying, only a handful include contact with administrative officials within that definition. Similarly, some states require public officials (state or agency personnel) to register when they lobby, although most do not. States also vary in their reporting requirements and in the stringency with which they enforce lobby laws.

How do we explain such differences across the nation between lobby laws? Morehouse has argued that states with the most stringent lobby laws tend to be those with weaker interest group systems (Morehouse 1981, 130–131). This is more or less confirmed by the Hrebenar-Thomas study. Ironically, these are the states that have suffered relatively few abuses at the hands of interest groups over the years, and thus have less need of such laws. The weakest laws exist in the South, where some of the largest abuses have taken place. For example, one reason for the weak laws is the South's traditionalistic and individualistic political culture. Still, a state like North Dakota, which has a predominantly moralistic political culture, also does not have extensive public disclosure provisions. In this case, however, it is probably for the opposite reason. That is, a political culture that looks with strong disapproval on unsavory and illegal activities by interest groups may not feel the need for such extensive regulations and, indeed, may not need them.

Given variations among the states in the extent and in the stringency of enforcement of lobby laws, can we make any generalizations about their effect on interest group activity in the states? Assessing their impact is difficult because it is virtually impossible to isolate regulatory from other influences on the conduct of politics in the states since the mid-1970s. Nevertheless, research from the Hrebenar-Thomas study enables us to make some observations about the effect of these laws.

We noted earlier that lobby laws cannot restrict the right of citizens and groups to lobby government. What they can do is limit certain activities in connection with such representation, such as limiting the dollar amount spent on gifts to public officials and on entertaining them. The greatest value of lobby laws is in providing public information on who is lobbying whom. Public disclosure is the most important element in all four types of lobby regulations. Such disclosure increases the potential for public and, particularly, press scrutiny of lobbying. Increased public information has probably been the element of lobby regulation that has had the most significant effect on state politics and government. We can briefly comment on three aspects of this effect: who the beneficiaries of public disclosure of lobbying are; the effect of lobby regulations on the conduct of business by established interest groups and lobbyists; and how public officials, particularly elected officials, have been affected by these regulations.

According to regulatory officials, it is not the public but rather the press, candidates seeking election, and interest group personnel and lobbyists who make the most use of lobby registration and related information. The bulk of the information about lobbyist expenditures and activities is disseminated by the press. So while the public has benefited from these provisions, the extent of these benefits is largely determined by the press. What might be termed *outsider interests* may also have benefited from lobby regulations. Public information has made the activities of their entrenched opponents more visible and as a result more restrained in many instances.

This brings us to the effect that these regulations have had on the established interests and lobbyists in the states. Restraint in dealings with public officials, greater concern for their group's public image and increased professionalism of lobbyists appear to be the three major effects in this regard. Lobbyists, especially those representing powerful interests are much less likely to use blatant strong-arm tactics. Even dominant interests, like the Boeing Aircraft Company in Washington State, prefer to use low-key approaches, buttressed by public relations campaigns. The more public disclosure of lobbying in a state and the more stringently these laws are enforced, the more open is the process of group attempts to influence public policy.

Public exposure and disclosure of lobbyists and lobbying is also partly the reason for the apparent disappearance of the old wheeler-dealer lobbyist from state politics and the increased professionalism of lobbyists in general. In turn, public disclosure of lobbying activity has changed the way elected officials deal with interest groups and lobbyists. Much more cognizant of their public image than in the past, legislators and elected executive officials alike are much less likely to tolerate unsavory practices by interest groups and their representatives.

INTEREST GROUP STRATEGY AND TACTICS: CONTINUITY AND CHANGE

The terms *strategy* and *tactics* are often used interchangeably, but there is an important difference between them. A *strategy* is an overall plan for gaining access and influence; *tactics* are the specific means for achieving these goals. For example, the strategy of an advocacy group for the mentally handicapped might involve building up good relations with legislators, the governor, and with bureaucrats, as well as educating voters. The group's specific tactics for executing this strategy might involve group members' joining political parties, contributing money to the campaigns of like-minded candidates, providing information to public officials, and running advertisements in newspapers to increase public awareness of the group's concerns.

Interest groups today employ a much wider range of methods in their never-ending quest to gain access to and to influence public officials than they did in the 1970s or even the 1980s. Yet, while modern technologies such as computers and television have expanded their options, group strategy and tactics are still very much an art rather than a science. The essence of this art is an exercise in interpersonal communications from an advocacy perspective between group members and leaders on one side and policy makers on the other. Effective personal contacts are the key to lobbying success and form an enduring element of any group's involvement in politics, despite the development of modern techniques. In fact, the new techniques are simply more sophisticated methods for increasing the effectiveness of group contacts in the policy arena. In this section we briefly consider the strategies and tactics available to groups and what influences their choice of particular ones. Then we examine lobbyists as the key element of group tactics.

Choosing a Group Strategy and Deciding on Specific Tactics

Choosing a Strategy. The essence of any group strategy is the ability to marshal group resources to achieve the goal at hand. Exactly how these resources should be marshaled and managed varies according to the nature of the group, its available resources, the way it is perceived by policy makers, the issue it is pursuing, and the political circumstances at the time. Consequently, no one strategy is a guarantee of success for all groups or for any one group at all times. This situation provides a continual challenge to lobbyists and group leaders and gives interest group politics its variety and fascination.

Two other basic factors about a group's choice of a strategy are important to bear in mind. The first is that particular strategies are largely determined by whether the group is currently involved in a defensive, maintenance, or promotional situation. In order to be successful, a group trying to stop the passage of a law need only halt it at one point in its tortuous journey to enactment. Therefore it is likely that the group will concentrate on a particular point in the system—such as a sympathetic committee chair. In contrast, to achieve enactment, the group must clear all the hurdles in the process, and thus a more broadly based strategy is required. Between these two situations are those groups that are simply working to maintain good relations with policy makers for the time when they will need to fight for their interests. Maintenance lobbying requires yet another strategy, which varies from group to group.

Probably one of the most important changes in state capital lobbying since

1960 has been the great increase in the number of groups pursuing promotional strategies. Before 1960 most lobbying was defensive. Generally, more resources and greater sophistication in their use are required to promote something than to kill it.

The second basic factor is that most lobbying campaigns require a multifaceted approach. Certainly, the bulk of time and resources in most campaigns is still spent in dealing with legislators and their staffs; but increasingly, effort is being directed toward the executive branch—the governor's office and state agencies. Few lobbyists deal solely with the legislature. This is because a successful lobbying campaign, especially one that seeks to promote something, requires the cooperation and often the active support of one or more executive agencies. Without this support the chances of even partial success are considerably reduced. So today, as in the past, to focus solely on the legislative forum provides only a partial understanding of group strategy.

Deciding on Tactics: Direct and Indirect Approaches. It has become common in academic writing about group tactics to divide them into direct and indirect tactics. Although the distinction is not always a clear one, direct tactics are those involving direct contact with public officials to influence their decisions, such as lobbying the legislature and executive and using the courts. Indirect lobbying includes activities aimed at getting access to and influencing the environment in which officials make decisions, such as working on election campaigns and contributing money to them, trying to influence public opinion through public relations campaigns, and even mounting demonstrations, boycotts, and sit-ins.

By far the most common and still the most effective of direct group tactics is the use of one or more lobbyists. In fact, until very recently it was the only tactical device used by the vast majority of groups; and it remains the sole approach used by many today. Since the 1960s, however, increased competition between groups as their numbers expanded, the changing needs of public officials, and an increased public awareness of both the activities and potential of interest groups have spawned other tactical devices. These include mobilizing grass-roots support through networking (sophisticated member contact systems); building coalitions with other groups; and, as we shall see later in the chapter, intergovernmental lobbying activities. It is important to note, however, that such tactics are not viewed as a substitute for lobbyists. Rather they are employed as a means of increasing the ability of the group's lobbyists to gain access to public officials and to influence them. Shrewd and experienced group leaders and lobbyists choose the most cost-efficient and politically effective method that they can to achieve their goals. The increased use of two tactics is particularly worthy of note: the use of PACs and the use of the courts.

PACs have become major campaign fund providers in the states. By 1980, PACs provided 45 percent of all contributions of more than $100 to California state legislative candidates (Sabato 1985, 117). Arizona PACs by the early 1980s were providing more than half the campaign funding for legislative races. And

PACs in New York State accounted for 60 percent of the contributions to legislative campaign committees of both major parties. While evidence is mixed regarding the effect of PAC contributions on the voting behavior and actions of members of Congress (Evans 1986), evidence from the Hrebenar-Thomas study strongly suggests that those organizations that make the biggest contributions to campaign chests also wield most of the influence. There also appears to be a strong relationship between the percentage of campaign contributions coming from groups and the impact of groups on the political system. This is not the only reason why groups are successful; but it does appear to be an important contributing factor. Regardless of the strength of party in a state, the power triangle of elected official, lobbyist, and PAC is becoming increasingly significant.

Because of the role that state courts—like their federal counterparts—have acquired in interpreting their respective constitutions, some interest groups have increasingly turned to the courts to achieve their goals. The business community often challenges the constitutionality of regulations. And groups that cannot get the legislature to act or the administration to enforce mandated functions, such as certain mental health provisions, also often use the courts. One of the most recent publicized uses of the courts was their overthrow of a statewide initiative passed in Colorado in 1992 to limit the rights of gays and lesbians (Thomas and Hrebenar 1994).

Lobbyists

Few, if any, occupations are held in such low regard by the general public as that of the lobbyist. For a hundred years following the Civil War the flamboyance and flagrant abuses of many lobbyists gave ample justification for this attitude. Yet, while the images linger the reality has changed drastically. The fundamental changes in American government and politics since 1970 have had a significant effect on the types of people who make up the lobbying community, the skills required of them, and their styles and methods of doing business. The developments in the state capital lobbying community have been even more dramatic than those in Washington, D.C.

Differentiating between the categories or types of lobbyists is particularly important in the study of state lobbyists. Previous studies have rarely done this, but the reasons for doing so are compelling. Perhaps the most important reason is that it helps throw light on the relationship between the lobbyist and the public official. Different types of lobbyists have different assets and liabilities and thus are perceived differently by public officials. Such perceptions will determine the nature and extent of the lobbyist's power base. In turn, the nature and extent of this power base will affect the way a lobbyist approaches his or her job of gaining access to and influencing public officials.

Today's state capital lobbying community is composed of five categories of lobbyists. These categories, the sources from which they are recruited, their ap-

Table 4-3   The Five Categories of Lobbyists

Category of lobbyist	Description	Recruitment source	Gender	Share of total lobbying community
Contract	Hired on contract; often represent more than one client; approx. 20% represent five or more clients.	Former officials, usually legislators or political appointees; former in-house lobbyists; attorneys from capital law firms; public relations and media specialists.	80–90% male; over 90% in less developed systems.	15–20%; higher in less developed systems.
In-house	Employees of a group who lobby as part of employment, representing only their employer.	Experienced professionals, business people, etc.; less likely to have been public officials.	Approx. 75% male; 25% female.	40–50%; largest category in most state capitals.
Government; legislative liaisons	State, local, and federal agency employees who, as part of their job, represent agency to legislative and executive branches of state gov't; represent only their employer; include state gov't agency heads, elected and appointed local officials, and some federal officials. To monitor relations with the legislature, most state agencies, some local gov'ts, and federal agencies appoint a "legislative liaison."	Career bureaucrats with broad experience in the agency or gov't unit they represent; political appointees; legislative staffers.	Approx. 25–35% female; more women in more economically and socially diverse states.	Difficult to estimate because gov't personnel not required to register in many states. Approx. 25–40%; higher in states with higher state and local gov't employment, esp. in the West.
Citizen, cause, volunteer	Unpaid persons acting on ad hoc basis, representing citizen and community organizations or informal groups, only one at a time.	Varied. Most are committed to cause.	Difficult to estimate because many not required to register as lobbyists. Apparently majority female—up to 75% in some states.	10–20%.
Private individual; "hobbyist", self-styled lobbyist	Acting on own behalf; not designated by any organization as official representative. Usually lobby for pet projects or direct personal benefits, or against a policy or proposal they find objectionable.	Self-recruitment; no common pattern.	Difficult to estimate because many not required to, or do not, register as lobbyists. Probably most male; varies with time and state.	Difficult to estimate, but probably less than 5%.

SOURCES: Developed from data in Hrebenar and Thomas 1987, 1992, 1993a, 1993b.

proximate makeup of male and females, and their approximate percentage of the state capital lobbying community across the states are set out in Table 4-3.

It is the contract lobbyist about whom the public hears most through the press. This is partly because some such lobbyists earn six-figure incomes (although by our estimates less than 10 percent of the total) and partly because most of them represent the interests that spend the most money and have the most political clout—mainly business and professional associations. Often they represent more than one client at a time, approximately 20 percent of them representing five or more clients. Their percentage in the makeup of the state capital lobbying community has increased steadily since contract lobbyists began to appear in the 1930s; and it has increased markedly since the late 1960s. Often, contract lobbyists are called professional lobbyists; but since some of them may not be full-time lobbyists or even obtain the greatest part of their income from lobbying, this label is not very useful. Besides, in-house lobbyists and legislative liaisons are also usually paid lobbyists and are no less professional or sophisticated in their jobs, sometimes even more so.

In-house lobbyists are the executive directors, presidents, and employees of a host of organizations and businesses from farm bureaus, schoolteachers, and trade associations to oil companies, International Business Machines Corporation, and environmental groups. These were the first type of lobbyists, appearing initially in the mid-nineteenth century when big business and especially the railroads became a significant part of the American economy. As a group they have probably always constituted the largest segment of the state capital lobbying community. Probably because of the negative connotations raised in the public's mind by the word *lobbyist,* in-house lobbyists are often given a euphemistic title by their organizations, such as *representative, agent, advocate, government relations officer* or *specialist,* or, more often, *legislative liaison.*

Probably for this same reason—plus the fact that governments attempt to maintain at least a façade of unity—to our knowledge no state officially refers to those lobbying for government agencies as lobbyists. Instead they, too, most often use the designation *legislative liaison.* Yet, as we noted earlier, in practice they are very much lobbyists. They include heads and senior staff of state government agencies, both elected and appointed officials of local governments, and some federal officials.

Citizen, cause, or volunteer lobbyists tend to represent small nonprofit organizations, social welfare groups, or community organizations. Because they usually receive reimbursement only for their expenses, if that, as a group they tend to be committed to their cause. As to private individual, "hobbyist," or self-styled lobbyists, most states have at least one colorful character lobbying for a pet project or direct personal benefits or against a policy or proposal he or she finds particularly objectionable. In Florida, for example, such a character stalked the capitol for thirty-seven years. Armed with the concept that "knowledge is power," Nell Foster "Bloomer Girl" Rogers (so named for her distinctive attire) took up issues that affected the lives of "ordinary folks" (Kelley and Taylor 1992, 134).

The common denominator of lobbyists is that they provide information and seek to build a reputation for honesty, trust, and credibility with public officials so that their information will be more effective. It is important to be aware of the different types of lobbyists if we are fully to appreciate their methods of access and influence.

Technical knowledge is often not the greatest asset of contract lobbyists, who, as political insiders, are hired primarily for their knowledge of the system and their close contacts with public officials. What they usually possess is special knowledge of certain parts of the governmental process—for example, the budget or a particular department—and so they may be used by legislators and other officials to assist in the policy-making process. Often, they have a great influence on the disbursement of campaign funds on behalf of their clients. Many contract lobbyists also organize fund-raisers for candidates and work to help them get elected or reelected. Because they usually represent clients with important economic influence, this fact is not lost on public officials.

The major political asset of many in-house lobbyists is their unequaled knowledge of their particular interest. This knowledge is often supplemented by campaign contributions from their association or business in cash and in kind and by their ability to mobilize their membership. Government lobbyists, in contrast, have only one important weapon—information—although they can, and often do, surreptitiously use their client groups to their advantage. For example, state departments of education often work, unofficially, with state parent-teacher associations and other client groups, such as those for handicapped or gifted children, to secure increased funding or to promote legislation. As voters and members of the public, these client groups can add political clout to the department's attempt to achieve its policy agenda. Volunteer lobbyists usually rely on moral suasion to sell their cause to public officials. They may also provide information not available elsewhere, but they usually lack the status of political insiders or access to big campaign contributions and sophisticated organizations. Self-styled lobbyists have the fewest political assets of all, unless they have been major campaign contributors. These differing assets and liabilities very much shape the way that public officials view these lobbyists, and that view in turn partly determines their power base.

Overall, the state capital lobbying community has become much more pluralistic and has advanced greatly in its level of professionalism since the early 1960s. Contract lobbyists appear to have made the greatest strides in professionalism, but in-house lobbyists, particularly those representing associations, have also made such advances. While the level of professionalism varies from state to state, its general increase among contract lobbyists is evidenced by several developments. These include an increase in the number of those working at the job full time, the emergence of lobbying firms that provide a variety of services and represent as many as twenty-five clients, and an increase in the number of specialists among contract lobbyists in response to the increasing complexity of government. One contract lobbyist, for example, specializes in representing several California agricultural commodity and agribusiness groups such as the California Avocado Commission and the Agricultural Chemicals Association (Syer 1987, 42). Other contract lobbyists specialize in representing such interests as health care, education, and local governments.

Does this mean that the old wheeler-dealer has entirely passed from the lobbying scene in state capitals as we suggested earlier? In the raw form in which he used to exist, as in the shape of an Artie Samish, the answer is probably yes. Today's issues are much more complex than they were in Samish's time, and many more campaigns are promotional than in the past. The old wheeler-dealer was not much of a technical expert and was more adept at killing than promoting legislation. Still, under a more sophisticated guise, wheeler-dealers do exist today and are the most successful lobbyists. Like the old wheeler-dealers, they realize the need for a multifaceted approach to establishing and maintaining good relations with public officials. This includes everything from participating in election campaigns to helping officials with their personal needs. But in addition, the modern-day wheeler-dealer is aware of the greater importance of technical information, the higher degree of professionalism and the changing needs of public officials, and the increased public visibility of lobbying. The result is a low-key, highly skilled, and effective professional who is a far cry from the old public image of a lobbyist.

THE NATIONALIZATION OF LOBBYING ACTIVITY IN THE UNITED STATES

To this point in the chapter we have discussed state interest group activity as though it were isolated from other levels of government. Yet one aspect of state group activity that has become increasingly important since the early 1980s is, in fact, its interaction with affiliate and like-minded organizations in other states and at other levels of government.

While differences exist between the levels of the American interest group system, a nationalization, or homogenization, of interest group activity is taking place, particularly in the areas of strategy and tactics, group organization, and professionalism of lobbyists. The trend is especially evident in state group systems, as they become more and more like the system in Washington, D.C. (Thomas and Hrebenar 1991a). This nationalization is part of a general homogenizing trend in American society, brought about by the increased communications ability offered by computers, fax machines, and fiber optics; greater media attention to politics, which works to nationalize issues that were once purely local; and greater mobility and contact among Americans from all parts of the country. In addition, on the political front, the expanding role of states in policy making and implementation has fostered cooperation between groups at the three levels of government and thus the exchange of ideas and techniques. Competition between a larger number of groups has also encouraged a search for new, effective strategies and tactics.

Today, few organizations confine their activities to one level of government alone. More and more, groups and organizations as diverse as the National Education Association (NEA), American Telephone and Telegraph (AT&T), the League of Women Voters, and the American Legion are finding it necessary to have a presence at more than one level of government. In many cases, largely because of greater overlapping of jurisdictional authority among levels of government, they must attend all three levels. For example, many national groups that once operated only in Washington, D.C., find themselves having to operate in states and communities. This is true, for example, for the beleaguered tobacco industry as it tries to ward off antismoking provisions across the country. Such needs have spawned a new breed of political consultant in Washington, D.C.: middlemen who set up lobbying operations in state capitals (Watson 1989).

This integration of the American interest group system is also a product of more sophisticated group tactics. Lack of success at one level may lead a group, such as the Right-to-Life movement, to pursue its goals at another level. Or success at one level, such as that achieved by gay rights groups, may prompt the group to try to repeat its successes in other jurisdictions. More and more, groups operate simultaneously at all three levels of government.

THE TWO FORMS OF INTEREST GROUP POWER IN THE STATES

To be successful in the policy process an interest group and its lobbyist must possess *influence,* or *power.* We need to be aware, however, that the term *group power* as used in interest group studies has two connotations. It may refer to the ability of an individual group or lobby to achieve its policy goals. Alternatively, it may be used to refer to the strength of interest groups as a whole within a state in relation to other organizations or institutions, particularly political parties. We refer to the first connotation as *individual group power* and to the second as *group system power*. Political scientists have long realized that power is far less of a simple phenomenon than the press or the public would like to believe. In particular, scholars have found power to be one of the most elusive aspects of interest groups to study, particularly the measurement of group power.

Problems in Measuring Interest Group Power

Both individual and group system power present problems in measurement. First, political scientists agree that the acquisition and exercise of power encompass many factors. Second, it is hard to compare groups whose activity varies from issue to issue and over time. Given these problems, researchers have used many different methods to assess individual group power. In the past, these ranged from sending questionnaires to public officials and conducting interviews with them, to consulting academic and popular literature on the states, to intuition and guesswork. Since the mid-1980s, however, more empirical assessments have been attempted. For our assessment we employ the Hrebenar-Thomas study, which used a combination of quantitative and qualitative techniques. The results plus the major trends that were revealed are set out in the next section.

Group system power is even more difficult to assess than individual group power because of the multiplicity of variables involved. The method most frequently used to do so has been to garner the observations of political practitioners and political scientists regarding the importance of the players involved in the policy-making process in each state (Morehouse 1981, 107–117; Zeller 1954, chap. 13 and 190–193). The results from the Hrebenar-Thomas study enable us to suggest an alternative way of understanding group power. We explain this after considering our findings on individual group influence.

Individual Group and Lobby Power

What do we know about the bases and exercise of individual interest group power? Research has identified certain elements as essential to the foundation and exercise of political power by groups. The three most important elements are the possession of resources (money, members, and so forth), the ability to mobilize these resources for political purposes, and political acumen or leadership (Stone, Whelan, and Murin 1986, 196–208). The Hrebenar-Thomas study broke these three general elements down into ten specific factors:

1. *The degree of necessity of group services and resources to public officials.* The more government needs the group the greater the group's leverage will be to use sanctions against government to achieve its goals, through strikes, withholding cooperation, withholding campaign contributions, and the like. This is one of the bases of business power in the states.

2. *Whether the group's lobbying focus is primarily defensive or promotional.* Because it is much easier to stop a policy than to promote one, groups like business associations, which work to prevent tax hikes and regulations, have an advantage over groups such as environmental organizations, which attempt to promote policies. They have, in other words, the "advantage of the defense" (Zeigler and van Dalen 1976, 125–127).

3. *The extent and strength of group opposition.* The more extensive and organized the opposition, the harder it will be for a group to achieve its goals. Some interests have natural enemies—such as business is to labor and developers are to environmentalists and vice versa—whereas other interests—doctors, for example—have no natural political enemies.

4. *Potential for the group to enter into coalitions.* This gives it more flexibility of action.

5. *Group financial resources.* Because financial assets are the most liquid of resources, they can readily be used to hire lobbyists and other staff to promote the lobbying effort as well as mount public relations campaigns and set up networking systems. Financial resources are also increasingly important for setting up PACs and making campaign contributions. Thus, the greater a group or organization's financial resources, the better it will likely be able to compete in the political arena.

6. *Political, organizational, and managerial skill of group leaders.* The level of their skills will determine how well the group's financial and other resources are mobilized to achieve political goals.

7. Size and geographical distribution of group membership. The larger the membership and the more widely distributed it is, the more pressure the group can bring on elected and appointed officials.

8. Political cohesiveness of the membership. If public officials see a group divided, they will not want to act for fear of alienating some members.

9. Timing and the political climate. The timing and the political climate must be right to promote certain policies.

10. Relations between lobbyist and policy maker. These include the closeness and trust between lobbyists and policy makers, as well as public officials' dependence on lobbyists and their groups for information, campaign contributions, and so on.

It is difficult to place these ten factors in any order, but the first factor, the extent to which a group's services and resources are necessary to public officials in the performance and maintenance of their jobs is perhaps the most important. The more necessary or indispensable a group is, the greater its political clout will be. The last factor, relations between lobbyist and policy maker, is also crucial.

Table 4-4 is a list of the forty most effective interests across the fifty states according to the Hrebenar-Thomas study. The interests are ranked as of spring 1994 on the basis of their effectiveness in the early 1990s. We can make some brief observations about the table, and by making comparisons with Table 3.2 in Morehouse 1981 and our own 1989 table (Table 4.2) in Gray, Jacob, and Albritton 1990, we can identify some longer-term trends in individual group power.

In the power they are perceived to have, two interests, schoolteachers' organizations and general business organizations, far outstrip any other interest in the fifty states. Few interests are considered to be effective in a large number of states. Only the top thirteen ranked interests are mentioned as effective ("Most effective" and "Moderately effective") in more than half of the fifty states. This survey confirms once again what we have known since the first study of state interest groups, performed by Zeller (1954): business and the professions remain the most effective interests in the states (as they do in Washington, D.C.).

The interest making the main advance since 1989 is the health care industry (although this is included under three categories in our survey). Physicians moved up in the ranking as did health care organizations (hospital associations and so forth). A rise in the ranking of insurance is due to the increased power of medical underwriters, such as Blue Cross/Blue Shield. The reason for this rise is probably the salience of the issue of health care as a national and state issue. Other noteworthy advances were made by utilities, lawyers, environmentalists, and gaming, senior citizen, and taxpayer groups. Some social issue groups are beginning to exert influence in the states, certainly more so than in 1989. As yet, however, their influence is relatively minimal.

Viewing the ten major attributes of individual group power together clarifies why schoolteachers, general business organizations, utility companies, and various other business interests are continually so successful across the states and

Table 4-4 Ranking of the Forty Most Influential Interests in the Fifty States in the Early 1990s

Rank	Interest group	Ranking in states		
		Most effective (no. of states)	Moderately effective (no. of states)	Less effective (no. of states)
1	Schoolteachers' organizations (predominantly NEA)	43	5	2
2	General business organizations (chambers of commerce and the like)	37	16	1(2)
3	Utility companies and associations (electric, gas, water, telephone, cable TV)	23	24	7
4	Lawyers (predominantly trial lawyers and state bar associations)	26	14	14
5	Traditional labor associations (predominantly the AFL-CIO)	22	13	15
6	Physicians and state medical associations	22	12	16
7	Insurance: general and medical (companies and associations)	21	15	16
8	Manufacturers (companies and associations)	20	15	21
9	Health care organizations (mainly hospital associations)	15	24	14
10	Bankers' associations (includes savings and loan associations)	21	11	18
11	General local government organizations (municipal leagues, county organizations, and so forth)	16	21	15
12	State and local government employees (other than teachers)	18	14	21
13	General farm organizations (mainly state farm bureaus)	14	20	17
14	Individual banks and financial institutions	14	8	28
15	Environmentalists	9	16	26
16	Universities and colleges (institutions and personnel)	7	16	28
17	Realtors' associations	8	12	30
18	Individual cities and towns	8	12	32
19	Gaming interests (race tracks, casinos, lotteries)	7	11	33
20	Contractors, builders, developers	7	10	34
21	Liquor, wine, and beer interests	7	10	35
	K-12 education interests (other than teachers)	7	10	35
22	Retailers (companies and trade associations)	6	11	34
23	Senior citizens	1	19	30
24	Mining companies and associations	6	7	38
25	Truckers and private transport interests (excluding railroads)	5	8	37
26	Taxpayers' interest groups	5	7	38
27	State agencies	5	7	39
28	Individual traditional labor unions (Teamsters, UAW, and other unions)	6	4	40

(table continues)

Table 4-4 *(continued)*

Rank	Interest group	Ranking in states		
		Most effective (no. of states)	*Moderately effective (no. of states)*	*Less effective (no. of states)*
29	Sportsmen, hunting and fishing (including anti–gun control groups)	3	10	37
30	Miscellaneous social issue groups	2	11	37
31	Oil and gas (companies and associations)	3	7	40
32	Women and minorities	3	7	41
33	Religious interests (churches and religious right)	2	9	39
34	Miscellaneous professional occupational groups	2	9	40
35	Public interest and good government groups	1	12	38
36	Agricultural commodity organizations (stockgrowers, grain growers, and the like)	4	4	42
37	Railroads	2	7	41
38	Forest product companies	3	4	43
39	Pro-choice groups	3	2	45
	Pro-life groups	2	2	46
40	Tourist industry groups	2	3	45

SOURCES: Compiled from Hrebenar and Thomas 1987, 1992, 1993a, 1993b and the 1994 update of the Hrebenar-Thomas study of interest group power in the states. See note at end of chapter.

NOTE: This table is based on a ranking of individual interests in the fifty states performed by political scientists during the spring of 1994. Each researcher was asked to rank groups into two categories: a "most effective" and a "second level of effectiveness" category. Rankings were calculated by allocating 2 points for each "most effective" ranking and 1 point for each "second level of effectiveness" placement and adding the totals. Where a tie in total points occurs, where possible, interests are ranked according to the number of "most effective" placements or the overall number of states in which they are effective.

In some cases the totals for an interest add up to more than 50. This is because specific groups within an interest category sometimes appear within both the "most effective" and the "second level of effectiveness" category in a particular state. For example, utilities are ranked in both categories in Colorado. Therefore, they are counted once for each category.

why physicians, trial lawyers, and other interests can be particularly effective when they decide to become politically active. They all have extensive financial resources, which they use to hire full-time political staffs and lobbyists, and in many cases they contribute to election campaigns. Their membership also tends to be spread geographically and is fairly politically cohesive. All this, plus the services they provide, makes public officials dependent on them to a high degree. Not possessing these attributes to the same degree, many other interests, such as women's and good-government groups, enjoy only limited success. And some groups, such as those for the arts and some minority groups, which lack many of these attributes, achieve little lobbying success at all.

It is difficult to determine whether an interest is declining in power because it has no immediate issues (this may be the case with banking associations and oil and gas interests) or because the interest is actually declining in power over time (which is likely for agricultural commodity organizations and individual traditional labor unions).

In fact, of the five so-called traditional interests, agriculture and traditional labor unions are in a long-term decline, while white collar workers (particularly public employees) have advanced their power since the 1960s. Business has at least maintained its power, although some businesses, such as railroads, have declined while others, especially those in the service sector, have expanded their power. Education—including schoolteachers, other K-12 interests, and higher education—has advanced in power, as has the local government lobby, especially individual cities, towns, and special districts.

The results from the 1994 survey clearly show that there has been an expansion in many states in the number of groups considered powerful since 1989. The upshot is that, as in Washington, D.C., there is less certainty of political outcomes in the states. The survey also confirms that individual group power is much more volatile than group system power, which changes much more slowly, over several years or even decades. This is because individual group power is so dependent on the possession and exercise of the ten specific factors listed above, and these can change rapidly.

Interest Group System Power in the States

Whereas the power of individual groups and coalitions is observed in their political mobilization and their ability to achieve their goals, group system power is much more of an abstraction. Never do all the groups in a political system act in concert to achieve one goal. Nonetheless, understanding and trying to assess group system power can be enlightening in the study of state politics.

What, then, can we say about what factors determine group system power? Reference back to the analytical framework presented in Table 4-2 can help us here. It was observed in the Hrebenar-Thomas study that there is likely a connection between the political culture of a state and the extent of group system power (factor 2 in the table). States that have moralistic political cultures, such as Maine and Vermont, are likely to have less powerful group systems than states that have more individualistic cultures, such as Nevada and New Mexico. Socioeconomic development (factor 1 in the table) also has its effects, usually by increasing the number of groups and reducing the likelihood that the state will be dominated by one or a few interests.

There is one factor, however, that appears to affect group system power more than any other. This is the relationship between the group system as a whole and the strength of political parties (factor 3 in the table). It used to be believed that there was an inverse relation between group system power and political party power: when groups were strong, parties would be weak and vice versa. The researchers in the Hrebenar-Thomas study found that this is not entirely the case. We concluded that, while weak (noncompetitive) party systems are invariably accompanied by strong interest groups, as demonstrated in the South, strong parties are also often accompanied by strong groups, as Illinois and New York attest. It may be that in states that have strong party systems, groups use different, less

Table 4-5 Classification of the Fifty States according to the Overall Impact of Interest Groups

	Impact of interest groups			
Dominant (7)	Dominant/ complementary (21)	Complementary (17)	Complementary/ subordinate (5)	Subordinate (0)
Alabama	Arizona	Colorado	Delaware	
Florida	Arkansas	Connecticut	Minnesota	
Louisiana	Alaska	Indiana	Rhode Island	
New Mexico	California	Maine	South Dakota	
Nevada	Georgia	Maryland	Vermont	
South Carolina	Hawaii	Massachusetts		
West Virginia	Idaho	Michigan		
	Illinois	Missouri		
	Iowa	New Hampshire		
	Kansas	New Jersey		
	Kentucky	New York		
	Mississippi	North Carolina		
	Montana	North Dakota		
	Nebraska	Pennsylvania		
	Ohio	Utah		
	Oklahoma	Washington		
	Oregon	Wisconsin		
	Tennessee			
	Texas			
	Virginia			
	Wyoming			

SOURCE: Compiled from the 1994 update of the Hrebenar-Thomas study focusing on interest group power in the states. See note at end of chapter.

visible, techniques of influence, and that this lack of visibility has been mistaken for weakness.

Given this situation, we need more informative category designations than *strong, moderate,* and *weak* to describe interest group system power. A more accurate and informative way to designate the effect of groups is to use a terminology that conveys the degree of their significance in state public policy making in relation to that of other political institutions. One way to do this is to specify the impact of the group system as being dominant, complementary, or subordinate to other aspects of the system. In Table 4-5 we show in which of these categories each state group system can be placed as of 1994.

States listed as dominant are those in which groups as a whole are the overwhelming and consistent influence on policy making. Groups in states listed as complementary tend to have to work in conjunction with or are constrained by other aspects of the political system. More often than not this is the party system; but it could also be a strong executive branch, competition between groups, the political culture, or a combination of all these. The group system in states listed as subordinate would be one that was consistently subordinated to other aspects of the policy making process. The absence of a "Subordinate" column indicates that groups were not consistently subordinate in any state either in 1994 or in

1989. The "Dominant/complementary" and the "Complementary/subordinate" columns include those states whose group systems alternate between the two situations or are in the process of moving from one to the other.

What can the comparisons between the 1989 and 1994 surveys tell us about group system power in the states? First, as we noted above, group system power changes much more gradually than does individual group power—changes on a large scale take longer than changes on a small one. In total, eleven states (22 percent) changed categories between 1989 and 1994. All changes were movements of one category only—to the next category up or down. Five states rose a category, while six fell. Most activity involved the dominant/complementary and the complementary categories, the dominant/complementary category showing the only increase in the number of states (from 18 to 21) since the 1989 survey. The losers were the dominant category, dropping from 9 to 7 states, and the complementary category, dropping from 18 to 17. The complementary/subordinate category was unchanged from 1989 with five states. The South remains the region with the most powerful interest group systems, followed by the West and the Midwest; the Northeast remains the region with the least powerful interest group systems. These regional rankings are all unchanged from 1989.

Two aspects of group power are apparent from the Hrebenar-Thomas study and the comparisons between the 1989 and 1994 surveys. First, although there are some common influences across the states—namely, those identified in the analytical framework shown in Table 4-2—the impact of groups in a particular state is a product of the unique ways in which these influences interact and change. The factor that appears to have an increasing influence in strengthening the effect of groups is campaign contributions. The larger the number and the greater the percentage of contributions that are given directly by groups to candidates, the more impact the group system appears to have. Second, and partly because of the rise of PACs and the decline of parties, the most frequent change is movement toward the dominant/complementary category and not the subordinate end of the scale. Overall, however, there is no clear movement in any one direction. This gives further credence to our contention that while broad movements can be identified, change in group system power depends on the individual circumstances in a state.

CONCLUSION: STATE INTEREST GROUP SYSTEMS YESTERDAY, TODAY, AND TOMORROW

Over the years interest groups have proved to be resilient and adaptable to changes in their political environment. In addition, when it comes to securing immediate and tangible benefits, interest groups have been effective as political organizations. As a result, interest groups have been the preferred means for those seeking specific policy goals in the states, especially those with significant financial interests at stake. This has been the case for decades; but it has become a particularly significant phenomenon in the last twenty years. Besides this, in several states interest groups have taken over many of the tasks that weak political parties were unable or unwilling to perform, such as the recruitment of candidates. A major reason for the recent rise in the power of interest groups has been their expanded role in financing the rapidly escalating costs of election campaigns.

It has been largely their resilience, adaptability, performance of essential political functions, and unparalleled success in securing benefits that have made interest groups such a prominent feature of state politics. Consequently, in many states they remain the most significant influence on public policy making. This has certainly been the case in most western and southern states.

The years since the 1960s have wrought some major changes in the importance of interest groups in all fifty state capitals. A greater variety of interests are active than at any time in the past, and today many more citizens in each state are represented by interest groups. Interest group leaders and lobbyists have become much more professional and the techniques of lobbying more wide-ranging and more sophisticated, partly as a result of government's need for more technical information and an increasing number of promotional as opposed to defensive lobbying campaigns. More and more nontraditional interests are scoring political successes. And the whole lobbying process has been opened up to much greater public scrutiny through increased press coverage and the passage of public disclosure laws.

Yet, we must be careful not to assume that these changes have revolutionized interest group activity in the states in every respect. Many changes have occurred, but two things remain more or less the same. First, although modern technologies, such as computers and television, have expanded the options of groups, strategy and tactics remain very much an art and not a science. In the highly personalized world of group access and influence, the most important avenue to success remains, as always, the relationship between the lobbyist and the public official. This is an intricate, symbiotic relationship involving trust, information exchange, pressures, and obligations. Moreover, effective personal contacts will likely always be the key to lobbying success.

Second, we must be careful not to assume that recent changes in group activity have produced radical change in the factors that determine success in the lobbying game. The inescapable fact is that resources, and especially money, are at least three-fourths of the battle in building and maintaining good relations between lobbyists and public officials and in securing the other essential elements that lead to influence. In this regard, business and other well-financed lobbies are unsurpassed. In fact, in state after state our research indicates that business has consolidated and in many circumstances expanded its power. An important reason for this is that it has "the advantage of the defense." Another reason, however, is the experience of business groups and the resources they can employ; experience and resources have enabled business groups to adapt more easily than the new interests to the new circumstances and demands of state political systems.

The predictions of many writers a decade or so ago, that increased political pluralism brought about by socioeconomic diversity and other advances would result in a general diminution of group power (and especially the power of business) in the states, have only partially materialized. In fact, a good case can be made that individual groups are now more powerful than ever. Group systems as a whole, however, may be gradually exerting less influence on their state political systems as groups cancel out each other's power. Thus, even though some individual groups have increased their power, they are less certain of the political outcome than they were in the 1960s, and group system power has gradually diminished.

What does all this mean for the immediate future? First, our research suggests that the great increase in the number of groups is preventing group systems from becoming dominant. Thus there may be a self-regulating mechanism in the political system to prevent interest groups from running the states. Still, as Olson (1982) has argued with respect to Western nations, a combination of entrenched interests, such as labor and business, combined with a rapid expansion in the number of groups, can lead to a political stalemate that seriously inhibits policy making and the ability to deal with social and economic problems. We can see some parallels of this situation on the state level, such as in California, and this may be only the beginning of a trend across the states.

Second, money, both as a means of buying access through campaign contributions and as the essential element in organizing and maintaining a sophisticated lobbying operation, will continue to play a significant role in group access and influence. And because they have so much at stake, we should not underestimate the tenacity and resourcefulness of entrenched interests like business to adapt to changing circumstances. Third, the success of groups that were formerly outsiders, such as environmentalists, is evidence that if other groups want to become part of the entrenched group system they may do so if they become professional. Finally, the increasing professionalization and sophistication of interest group activity will move it closer and closer to the way that the interest group game is played in the nation's capital.

CONTRIBUTORS TO UPDATE OF HREBENAR-THOMAS PROJECT

Alabama: David L. Martin (Auburn University); *Alaska:* Clive S. Thomas (University of Alaska, Juneau), Tom Ackerly, Dan Austin, Eric Musser, and Diana Rhoades (Alaska State Legislature); *Arizona:* David R. Berman (Arizona State University); *Arkansas:* Arthur English (University of Arkansas at Little Rock); *California:* Beth Capell (California Nurses Association) and John H. Culver (California Polytechnic State University); *Colorado:* John A. Straayer (Colorado State University); *Connecticut:* Richard C. Kearney (University of Connecticut, Storrs); *Delaware:* Janet B. Johnson (University of Delaware); *Florida:* Anne E. Kelley (University of South Florida); *Georgia:* Charles S. Bullock III (University of Georgia); *Hawaii:* Anne F. Lee (Honolulu); *Idaho:* James Weatherby and Stephanie Witt (Boise State University); *Illinois:* David H. Everson (Sangamon

State University); *Indiana:* David J. Hadley (Wabash College); *Iowa:* Don Hadwiger (Iowa State University); *Kansas:* Allan J. Cigler (University of Kansas); *Kentucky:* Penny M. Miller and Malcolm E. Jewell (University of Kentucky); *Louisiana:* Wayne T. Parent (Louisiana State University); *Maine:* Douglas I. Hodgkin (Bates College); *Maryland:* Laura Wilson-Gentry (University of Baltimore); *Massachusetts:* John C. Berg (Suffolk University); *Michigan:* William P. Browne (Central Michigan University); *Minnesota:* Craig H. Grau (University of Minnesota, Duluth); *Mississippi:* Thomas H. Handy (Mississippi State University; retired); *Missouri:* James W. Endersby and Gregory Casey (University of Missouri, Columbia); *Montana:* Thomas Payne (University of Montana; retired); *Nebraska:* John C. Comer (University of Nebraska, Lincoln); *Nevada:* Dennis L. Soden (University of Nevada, Las Vegas) and Eric B. Herzik (University of Nevada, Reno); *New Hampshire:* Michelle A. Fistek (Plymouth State College); New Jersey: Stephen A. Salmore (Eagleton Institute, Rutgers University); *New Mexico:* Gilbert K. St. Clair (University of New Mexico); *New York:* David L. Cingranelli (State University of New York at Binghamton); *North Carolina:* Jack D. Fleer (Wake Forest University); *North Dakota:* Theodore B. Pedeliski (University of North Dakota); *Ohio:* Kent P. Von Der Vellen (University of Akron) and David C. Saffell (Ohio Northern University); *Oklahoma:* Robert E. England (Oklahoma State University) and David R. Morgan (University of Oklahoma); *Oregon:* William M. Lunch (Oregon State University); *Pennsylvania:* Michael R. King (Legislative Office for Research Liaison, Pennsylvania State Legislature), Michael E. Cassidy (Office of the Democratic Whip, Pennsylvania State Legislature), and Patricia McGee Crotty (East Stroudsburg State University); *Rhode Island:* Ronald D. Hedlund (University of Rhode Island); *South Carolina:* Robert E. Botsch (University of South Carolina at Aiken); *South Dakota:* Robert V. Burns (South Dakota State University); *Tennessee:* David M. Brodsky (University of Tennessee, Chattanooga) and David H. Folz (University of Tennessee, Knoxville); *Texas:* Keith E. Hamm (Rice University); *Utah:* H. E. "Bud" Scruggs (Brigham Young University); *Vermont:* Rodney Christy (Saint Michael's College); *Virginia:* John T. Whelan (University of Richmond); *Washington:* Stephen F. Johnson (Washington Public Utilities Districts Association); *West Virginia:* James R. Oxendale (West Virginia Institute of Technology); *Wisconsin:* Ronald D. Hedlund (University of Rhode Island, formerly of the University of Wisconsin at Milwaukee); *Wyoming:* James D. King (University of Wyoming) and Janet Clark (West Georgia College, formerly of the University of Wyoming).

REFERENCES

Clark, Janet M., and B. Oliver Walter. 1987. "Wyoming: Populists versus Lobbyists." In *Interest Group Politics in the American West,* edited by Ronald J. Hrebenar and Clive S. Thomas. Salt Lake City: University of Utah Press.
COGEL (Council on Governmental Ethics Laws). 1988. *Campaign Finance, Ethics, and Lobby Law Blue Book, 1988–89: Special Report.* Lexington, Ky.: COGEL through the Council of State Governments.
———. 1990. *COGEL Blue Book: Campaign Finance, Ethics and Lobby Law.* Lexington, Ky.: COGEL through the Council of State Governments.
Elazar, Daniel J. 1984. *American Federalism: A View from the States.* 3d ed. New York: Harper and Row.
Erikson, Robert S., Gerald C. Wright, and John P. McIver. 1993. *Statehouse Democracy: Public Opinion and Policy in the American States.* New York: Cambridge University Press.
Evans, Diana M. 1986. "PAC Contributions and Roll-Call Voting: Conditional Power." In *Interest Group Politics,* 2d ed., edited by Allan J. Cigler and Burdett A. Loomis. Washington, D.C.: CQ Press.
Francis, Wayne L. 1967. *Legislative Issues in the Fifty States: A Comparative Analysis.* Chicago: Rand McNally.
Gray, Virginia. 1984. "Fundamental Changes in Group Life at the State Level." Paper presented at the annual meeting of the American Political Science Association, Washington, D.C., September.
Gray, Virginia, Herbert Jacob, and Robert B. Albritton, eds. 1990. *Politics in the American States: A Comparative Analysis.* 5th ed. Glenview, Ill: Scott, Foresman/Little, Brown.
Gray, Virginia, and David Lowery. 1988. "Interest Group Politics and Economic Growth in the American States." *American Political Science Review* 82:109–131.

————. 1993. "The Diversity of State Interest Group Systems." *Political Research Quarterly* 46:81–97.

Hrebenar, Ronald J., and Clive S. Thomas, eds. 1987. *Interest Group Politics in the American West.* Salt Lake City: University of Utah Press.

————. 1992. *Interest Group Politics in the Southern States.* Tuscaloosa: University of Alabama Press.

————. 1993a. *Interest Group Politics in the Midwestern States.* Ames: Iowa State University Press.

————. 1993b. *Interest Group Politics in the Northeastern States.* University Park: Pennsylvania State University Press.

Hunter, Kennith G., Laura Ann Wilson, and Gregory G. Brunk. 1991. "Societal Complexity and Interest Group Lobbying in the American States." *Journal of Politics* 53:488–502.

Hyde, Mark S., and Richard W. Alsfeld. 1985. "Role Orientations of Lobbyists in a State Setting: A Comparative Analysis." Paper presented at the annual meeting of the American Political Science Association, New Orleans. September.

Kelley, Anne E., and Ella L. Taylor. 1992. "Florida: The Changing Patterns of Power." In *Interest Group Politics in the Southern States,* edited by Ronald J. Hrebenar and Clive S. Thomas. Tuscaloosa: University of Alabama Press.

Key, V. O., Jr. 1949. *Southern Politics in State and Nation.* New York: Alfred A. Knopf.

Morehouse, Sarah McCally. 1981. *State Politics, Parties, and Policy.* New York: Holt, Rinehart and Winston.

Olson, Mancur. 1982. *The Rise and Decline of Nations: Economic Growth, Stagflation, and Social Rigidities.* New Haven: Yale University Press.

Opheim, Cynthia. 1991. "Explaining the Differences in State Lobby Regulation." *Western Political Quarterly* 44:405–421.

Petracca, Mark P., ed. 1992. *The Politics of Interests: Interest Groups Transformed.* Boulder, Colo.: Westview Press.

Rosenthal, Alan. 1992. *The Third House: Lobbyists and Lobbying in the States.* Washington, D.C.: CQ Press.

Sabato, Larry. 1985. *PAC Power: Inside the World of Political Action Committees.* New York: W. W. Norton.

Salmore, Stephen A., and Barbara G. Salmore. 1993. "New Jersey: From Political Hacks to Political Action Committees." In *Interest Group Politics in the Northeastern States,* edited by Ronald J. Hrebenar and Clive S. Thomas. University Park: Pennsylvania State University Press.

Samish, Arthur H., and Bob Thomas. 1971. *The Secret Boss of California: The Life and High Times of Art Samish.* New York: Crown.

Schattschneider, E. E. 1960. *The Semisovereign People: A Realist's View of Democracy in America.* New York: Holt, Rinehart and Winston.

Schlozman, Kay Lehman, and John T. Tierney 1986. *Organized Interests and American Democracy.* New York: Harper and Row.

Stone, Clarence N., Robert K. Whelan, and William J. Murin. 1986. *Urban Policy and Politics in a Bureaucratic Age.* 2d ed. Englewood Cliffs, N.J.: Prentice-Hall.

Syer, John C. 1987. "California: Political Giants in a Megastate." In *Interest Group Politics in the American West,* edited by Ronald J. Hrebenar and Clive S. Thomas. Salt Lake City: University of Utah Press.

Thomas, Clive S., and Ronald J. Hrebenar. 1990. "Interest Groups in the States." In *Politics in the American States: A Comparative Analysis,* 5th ed., edited by Virginia Gray, Herbert Jacob, and Robert B. Albritton, Glenview, Ill: Scott, Foresman/Little, Brown.

————. 1991a. "Nationalization of Interest Groups and Lobbying in the States." In *Interest Group Politics,* 3d ed., edited by Allan J. Cigler and Burdett A. Loomis. Washington, D.C.: CQ Press.

————. 1991b. "Political Action Committees in the States: Some Preliminary Findings." Paper presented at the annual meeting of the American Political Science Association, Washington, D.C., September.

————. 1994. "Lobbying through the Courts by State Interest Groups: A Fifty State Comparison." Paper presented at the annual meeting of the Western Political Science Association, Albuquerque, N.M., March.

Wahlke, John C., Heinz Eulau, William Buchanan, and Leroy C. Ferguson. 1962. *The Legislative System: Explorations in Legislative Behavior.* New York: John Wiley and Sons.

Walker, Jack L., Jr. 1991. *Mobilizing Interest Groups in America: Patrons, Professions, and Social Movements.* Ann Arbor: University of Michigan Press.

Watson, Tom. 1989. "Have Lobbyist, Will Travel." *Governing,* February, 32–38.

Wilson, Graham K. 1990. *Interest Groups.* Oxford: Basil Blackwell.

Zeigler, L. Harmon. 1983. "Interest Groups in the States." In *Politics in the American States: A Comparative Analysis,* 4th ed., edited by Virginia Gray, Herbert Jacob, and Kenneth N. Vines. Boston: Little, Brown.

Zeigler, L. Harmon, and Michael Baer. 1969. *Lobbying: Interaction and Influence in American State Legislatures.* Belmont, Calif.: Wadsworth.

Zeigler, L. Harmon, and Hendrik van Dalen. 1976. "Interest Groups in the States." In *Politics in the American States: A Comparative Analysis,* 3d ed., edited by Herbert Jacob and Kenneth N. Vines. Boston: Little, Brown.

Zeller, Belle. 1954. *American State Legislatures,* 2d ed. New York: Thomas Y. Crowell.

SUGGESTED READINGS

Cigler, Allan J., and Burdett A. Loomis, eds. *Interest Group Politics,* 4th ed. Washington, D.C.: CQ Press, 1995. A collection of essays presenting the latest thinking about interest group formation and influence at national and state levels.

Hrebenar, Ronald J., and Clive S. Thomas, eds. *Interest Group Politics in the Southern States.* Tuscaloosa: University of Alabama Press, 1992. This is one of the four books in which Hrebenar and Thomas analyze the interest group systems in each of the fifty states in the late 1980s.

Morehouse, Sarah McCally. *State Politics, Parties, and Policy.* New York: Holt, Rinehart and Winston, 1981. In Chapter 3, "Pressure Groups versus Political Parties," the author extensively explores the relationship between groups and parties and provides a listing of the most significant interests in the fifty states.

Rosenthal, Alan. *The Third House: Lobbyists and Lobbying in the States.* Washington, D.C.: CQ Press, 1992. Good descriptive account of the role and techniques of contract and in-house lobbyists in the states.

Zeigler, L. Harmon, and Michael Baer. *Lobbying: Interaction and Influence in American State Legislatures.* Belmont, Calif.: Wadsworth, 1969. Comparative analysis of interest groups in four states (Massachusetts, North Carolina, Oregon, and Utah) and one of the best early treatments of state lobbying.

CHAPTER 5

Legislative Politics in the States

SAMUEL C. PATTERSON

James Bryce, a turn-of-the-century British commentator on American political life, was a stern critic of the politics of the American states. Of their legislatures he pronounced, "It need scarcely be said that the state legislatures are not high-toned bodies" (Bryce 1906, 539). Although it is still true that many citizens harbor negative perceptions about their legislatures, and the legislatures are by no means perfect organizations, those of today are a far cry from what they used to be. One of the leading students of state legislatures testifies, "Years ago state legislatures merited much of the criticism that is aimed at them today" but "lately . . . they have proved to be more deserving; now they merit commendation rather than blame" (Rosenthal 1981, 3).

Nowadays the state legislatures are much more effective bodies than they were two decades ago. Many have become highly professional. More and more legislators acquire expertise by serving several terms, during which they receive full-time pay in a legislature that meets annually and has developed a complex system of committees and staff organizations. In the aftermath of the U.S. Supreme Court's historic decision in *Baker v. Carr* (369 U.S. 186 [1962]), the legislatures have been reapportioned on the principle of one person, one vote. The reapportionments in many states rectified the imbalance between rural and urban interests, brought new and younger members to the legislatures, and stimulated a variety of efforts to renew the vigor of legislative processes. Procedures and rules were modernized; committee systems were streamlined; leadership was strengthened; salaries and benefits for members were improved; the capacity of legislatures to engage in oversight of executive agencies was expanded; and staffs grew in size and professionalism. For many members, serving in the legislature became a career because a growing number of people, once elected to the legislature, relinquished their careers as lawyers, accountants, morticians, nurses, or whatever and became full-time legislators.

It is desirable in a democratic society for governing institutions to have the support and good opinion of citizens. Nevertheless the state legislatures were not brought into the world merely as objects of blame or commendation. They were intended to make laws and establish policies within the proper constitutional realm of the states in a manner that would be responsive to, and representative of, the people of the states. The legislatures are representative institutions. Their memberships may not have universal appeal, but legislators are chosen in free and open popular elections. Legislative enactments may not always be wise, but they are responsive to citizens' wishes and demands. That the legislatures now perform more effectively and represent the people more adequately makes them more interesting to analyze. They are more complex and more durable bodies, with more intricate linkages to their constituencies (Hickok 1992). Because the legislatures are more formidable, they are more capable of responding to the policy demands made on them, and so their work takes on greater importance. Ironically, the modernization of the state legislatures is poorly appreciated, and legislatures are generally under attack from those who seek to limit the terms of their members and weaken the institutions.

RUNNING AND GOVERNING

Understanding the legislative process of a state requires a grasp of two interrelated, but nevertheless distinctive, dynamics. One of these is running for the legislature; the other is governing the state. Running for the legislature is not the normal thing to do; most Americans never contemplate becoming legislative candidates. The few thousand who do are those who are especially interested in politics, who are highly active in political parties or other political groups, and who have some political ambitions. Many have served in local political offices; some have been party leaders; some have been drawn into politics by significant political events or issues. All have strong local ties, and the vast majority run in districts in which a single person is chosen to represent a district's interests in the legislature.

Almost all legislative candidates are chosen in party primary elections. Then, in contested districts, candidates vie for the electoral pluralities that will win them legislative seats. Campaigning can require intensive effort in the district—raising campaign money, advertising, going on handshaking tours, leafleting at factory gates, appearing on radio and television, attending kaffeeklatsches in supporters' homes, and making speeches to church, civic, economic, and social groups. On Election Day, candidates may cap their campaign efforts with frenetic last-minute activity, making final appeals to voters, encouraging campaign workers to get out the vote, and then nervously waiting for the electoral verdict. Running for the legislature puts a premium on personal ambition and drive, attention to the locality and its special needs, and identification or exploitation of the political issues that can help to mobilize voter support.

Governing the state, in which the legislature takes an important part, differs from campaigning in the electoral arena. In a sense, governing involves translating what is desired into what is most needed and possible. Doing this requires establishing rules to expedite business and ensure fair play. It requires a division of labor for the consideration of, and the bringing of expertise to, important questions of public policy. It requires leadership on the part of political parties and groups. It requires an intricate network of relationships between the legislature and the executive branch.

Above all, legislative deliberation and policy making entail collective action. No legislator, no matter how deep his or her conviction and commitments, can make public policy. Rather, the legislator must win the support of other members so as to form a majority that can act collectively. So legislative governance must involve bargaining, negotiation, give-and-take, and compromise. In taking on its collective form, the legislature acquires a group life, grounded in networks of interpersonal relationships among its members, written and unwritten rules of the game, recognition of obligations among members, and formal and informal leadership. Accordingly, "the tyro who reaches the capitol breathing fire after a vigorous campaign soon finds that he can accomplish nothing until he learns how to get along with his colleagues" (Truman 1971, 345).

Running for the legislature and governing the state are not mutually exclusive. Many who run do so in order to govern. But running and governing are not always compatible. Winning the support of constituents in a district and winning the support of colleagues in the legislature involve different processes and put a premium on somewhat different skills and motivations.

Elected representatives respond to the tensions involved in differences between running and governing in different ways. Some effectively combine the skills necessary for aggressive campaigning and the defining of local political issues with deep commitments to the substantive tasks of the legislature, adjusting readily to the strains of both constituency and legislature. But others respond more hesitantly. They nurse their districts, responding to immediate constituency demands while mainly serving as spectators in the legislature. They concentrate their energies on enhancing their occupation or profession at home and focus their activity in the legislature more on their desire to advertise themselves than on the legislature's substantive work. In addition, they are often reluctant to engage in the extended work of either their constituencies or the legislature, content to perform a limited and brief civic duty (Barber 1965).

This dilemma of legislative representation—serving the constituency and making policy for the state—provides the strain and the conflict that make legislative life interesting to experience and interesting to study. We need to investigate both of these dynamics, not just with a view to resolving the attendant tensions but also in order to move toward a better understanding of the legislative process.

THE ELECTORAL ARENA

The context in which running for the legislature takes place is not created anew for every election. The basic rules within which candidates run are part of the stage and setting, and they are not within the control of the candidates in any given election. Two fundamental sets of rules govern the electoral arena. One set of rules controls how the legislators are to be distributed over the state's territory by drawing legislative district boundary lines. The other set of rules has to do with the conditions under which legislative seats are won by the contestants. Legislative *apportionment* refers both to constructing legislative districts in a state and to assigning one or more legislative seats to be filled in these districts. The decision rule in the legislative elections within these districts is, in general, the plurality vote rule, whereby the winning candidate in a given contest has received more votes than any other candidate in that contest.

Reapportionment Politics

Since the mid-1960s, state legislative apportionment has been a source of major political controversy. Before the 1962 decision of the U.S. Supreme Court in the case of *Baker v. Carr,* many state legislatures were egregiously malapportioned, so some legislators represented districts with much larger populations than did other legislators. The apportionment rule, sometimes followed in practice before the *Baker* decision and subsequently enforced by the courts, is that of one person, one vote. The rule means that, barring persuasive claims to extenuating circumstances, legislative districts within a state must be equal in population according to the most recent census.

In some cases the courts have permitted a state legislative apportionment to stand despite departures from exact population equality, so as to permit legislative district boundary lines to coincide with the boundaries of cities or counties. In contrast, state legislative districts nearly equal in population have been declared to be inappropriate by the courts if they could be shown to exclude minority groups from representation. It is fair to say that the courts have not developed a clear and consistent standard by which to determine the adequacy of a state's apportionment. This appears to be the case, not because it is impossible to draw district boundary lines embracing equal populations, but rather because the proper basis for and extent of tolerable inequality have not been established.

In the aftermath of the Supreme Court's *Baker* decision, federal and state courts entered into apportionment decisions in many states. By 1967, after all states had been reapportioned, legislative districts within states were reasonably equal in population according to the 1960 census (on the "reapportionment revolution" of the 1960s, see Dixon 1968). The completion of the 1970 census prompted a renewed round of adjustments in state legislative district boundary lines. In order to avoid the intervention of federal or state courts, the new reapportionments tended to be done by the legislatures in accord with the criterion of one person, one vote. As a consequence, the number of state legislators from urban and suburban areas increased, and sea changes in legislative memberships transpired, bringing into membership younger, better-educated legislators, many more women, and more members from ethnic minorities, notably blacks. Generally speaking, the reapportionments also reshaped the partisan coloration of the legislatures, giving an advantage to the Democratic party in the northern states and to the Republican party in the South. In addition the reapportionments contributed to the greater responsiveness of the legislatures, especially where city dwellers had been greatly underrepresented.

Reapportionments in the 1980s and 1990s

The 1980 census brought into sharp relief the enormous population shifts that occurred during the 1970s. The most dramatic changes were the decline of population growth in the northeastern states and the galloping growth of states in the West, the Southwest, and the South—the so-called Sun Belt. The reapportionments of the 1980s primarily featured adjustments in legislative district boundaries in order to reflect population growth and the shift of population to the suburbs. In the early 1990s, as the legislatures considered the population changes revealed by the 1990 census, the impetus for redistricting had changed, as well. The major new feature of the 1990s was the emphasis on the representation of ethnic and racial minorities. The U.S. Supreme Court (in *Thornburgh v. Gingles*, 478 U.S. 30 [1986]) interpreted the 1982 amendments to the Voting Rights Act to mean that states must draw legislative district boundaries so as to produce minority districts (where the majority among voters is a racial or ethnic minority) whenever this is possible. Adherence to this constraint produced political and legal controversy over racial gerrymandering, and it culminated in drawing some districts of very irregular geographical shape. But in 1995 the Court put the brakes on minority redistricting; in *Miller v. Johnson* (63 USLW 4726 [1995]) the Court said race cannot be the "predominant factor" in drawing boundaries. Coupled with the creeping abolition of districts with more than one representative, multiple-member districts, deliberate efforts to draw boundaries that would maximize black candidates' chances of winning produced substantial increases in the numbers of African-American state legislators, especially in the South (see Bullock and Gaddie 1993; Coleman 1993).

State Electoral Systems

The American system for electing legislators is often called a "single-member district, plurality vote" electoral system. But the single-member district system still is not universal in the states. The proportion of legislators from multimember districts has declined since 1970, but as recently as the mid-1980s fully a fourth of lower-house members were elected in such districts (Jewell and Patterson 1986, 21). However, the proportion of multiple-member districts has declined sharply, especially in the South (see Niemi, Jackman, and Winsky 1991). Whether voters in a legislative district elect one representative, or two or more, makes a difference. Blacks are more likely to be elected in single-member districts, at least in urban areas. In contrast, multiple-member districts seem to enhance the chances that women will be elected (see Darcy, Welch, and Clark 1994; Moncrief and Thompson 1992).

In the electoral system through which legislators are chosen, political parties accumulating large proportions of the popular vote tend to acquire even larger percentages of the legislative seats, and parties with relatively small proportions of the vote tend to get even smaller percentages of seats. It is easy to see how this happens: in a single-member district, a party's candidate may win only a bare 51 percent of the popular vote, but in that district the party will win all the seats, there being only one seat to win. In multimember districts, the majority party in a district tends to sweep all or most of the seats available. This regularity in the performance of the electoral system is called the *Matthew effect,* after the words of Matthew 13:12 in the Revised Standard Version of the Bible: "To him who has will more be given, and he will have abundance; but from him who has not, even what he has will be taken away." Thus, it is generally true in state legislative elections that a party that wins 55 to 60 percent of the votes in a state wins roughly 65 to 70 percent of the legislative seats, while a party that wins only 40 to 45 percent of the statewide vote wins only about one-third or fewer of the seats in the legislature.

Why is this disparity between the popular votes for a party's candidates and the seats a party captures so large? Malapportionment can contribute to this disparity if differences in the populations of constituencies systematically favor one party over the other (for example, if all rural districts are both predominantly Republican and smaller in population than all urban districts, which are predominantly Democratic). Again, systematic gerrymandering (drawing legislative district boundary lines for partisan advantage) could make the Matthew effect greater. If, for example, district boundary lines were drawn so as to ensure that 51 percent of the voters in every district were Democrats, the Democrats could win 100 percent of the legislative seats!

Nevertheless, the Matthew effect is substantial even in well-apportioned states where deliberate gerrymandering has not rigged the outcomes. Since legislative districts have a tendency to be politically homogeneous, consistently leaning to one party or the other, and since the voters for the losing party's candidate in a single-member district (or individual contests in a multimember district) elect no representatives, disparities between votes and seats occur regardless of the adequacy of apportionment or the absence of gerrymandering (Tufte 1973). For instance, in Ohio in the 1980s Democratic house candidates together averaged 54 percent of the popular vote, but they captured an average of about 60 percent of the legislative seats. For some state legislative bodies this disparity between votes and seats is even greater than it is for the Ohio House.

The upshot of state electoral systems is that they create "manufactured majorities" in the legislative houses. The political party winning the largest proportion of the statewide vote in the legislative election tends to be endowed by the electoral system with a substantial legislative majority. In states where there is a traditional and stable dominant party, this electoral magnification will have protected that party's domination of the legislature. The Matthew effect thus benefits the majority party, whether Democratic or Republican.

The system of legislative apportionment and the payoff of the electoral system are important parts of the electoral environment in which candidates run for legislative office. The conditions thus brought about provide the broad controlling factors governing who can win and who will lose.

RUNNING FOR THE LEGISLATURE

No one really knows how many people run as candidates for the state legislatures, or why. One of the peculiarities of a federal, highly decentralized system like ours is that no one agency keeps track of such things. Approximately 14,000 people run for a state legislative seat every two years; the only way to find out for sure is to get the primary and general election results from each of the fifty states. Why they run is harder to discern (for the best speculation, see Rosenthal 1981, 18–19).

Years ago, four political scientists began a pioneering study in which they personally interviewed a large proportion of the members of the legislatures in California, New Jersey, Ohio, and Tennessee (Wahlke et al. 1962). They found that, by and large, people who run for the state legislature acquired a deep interest in politics early in their lives, and many come from highly politicized families. Many become party activists or serve in local public offices before launching an effort to capture a legislative berth. These are people with considerable political skill who, largely for personal reasons, find politics fun and challenging. Some are ambitious; for them, service in the legislature is seen as a steppingstone to more prominent political office. More recently, scholars have studied women's decisions to run for the legislature; women seem to run for very much the same reasons as men (Carroll 1985, 121–37; Kirkpatrick 1974, 59–84).

Self-Starting as Opposed to Sponsorship

No politician is an island. All are affected by others—family, friends, political cronies, party, or group associations—in their decisions about becoming candidates for office. This influence is a matter of degree, however. Some who decide to run for the legislature are self-starters. They have strong entrepreneurial instincts, and they seek legislative office largely out of their own personal drives and ambitions. Others, perhaps no less willing to serve, are nonetheless pressed into service by those who urge candidacy upon them. Research on this aspect of running for the legislature has produced wildly varying estimates of the incidence of self-starting candidacies as opposed to ones that were sponsored by others. The estimates vary partly because times and places are different and partly because much depends on how the question is asked.

Amid the congeries of data about self-starting candidacies, one finding stands out: in states where political parties are strong, party leaders tend to play a prominent role in recruiting candidates to run for the legislature. For example, a study of legislative candidates in Pennsylvania, a state in which the parties are relatively strong, demonstrated that party leaders initially recruited a majority of the candidates (Sorauf 1963, 102). Where party organization is only moderately strong, party and nonparty recruitment agencies tend to share in the instigation of legislative candidacies.

In a study conducted in Iowa, it was found that in addition to party leaders, who were involved in candidate recruitment to a significant degree, interest group leaders and other nonparty recruiting agents played an important role in initiating candidacies (Patterson and Boynton 1969). Similarly, a study of women candidates in 1976 indicated that even though party leaders played a substantial role in recruitment, "the encouragement of primary groups, including both family and friends, was a more frequent influence on candidates' decisions" (Carroll 1985, 32). The importance of the candidates' families in decisions to run for legislative office is underscored by a study conducted in 1994 of 900 legislators in sixteen states: 70 percent strongly indicated that the support of their spouses and families played a major role in their decision to run (Woo 1994).

Finally, in states where party organization is weak or highly fragmented, legislative candidate selection tends to be a free-for-all in which self-recruitment plays a major role. An Oregon study of candidate recruitment showed, for example, that as many as half of the legislative candidates were self-starters (Seligman et al. 1974, 47). Similarly, Nebraska's nonpartisan legislative elections give party leaders a minor role in soliciting candidates and provide a much more important role for sponsors in the private sector, especially people in business and business groups (Kolasa 1978).

Party Recruitment and Nominating Systems

But more is involved in getting people to run for the legislature than merely the strength of a state's political parties. The method of nominating candidates plays an important part as well. States with restricted nominating processes (such as closed primaries, in which a voter must declare a partisan preference upon registering and may vote only in that party's primary) tend to encourage party-sponsored candidacies, while states with more open nominating systems (such as the open primary, in which any registered voter may participate in any one primary) probably foster a greater degree of self-starting for legislative office.

Scholars have not invested much effort in analyzing the incidence and effects of political party sponsorship of legislative candidates. But one study of four states—Connecticut and Pennsylvania (which have relatively closed nominating systems) and Minnesota and Washington (which have more open nominating systems)—did reveal the expected relationship between party sponsorship and nominating systems (Tobin and Keynes 1975). More legislative candidates in Connecticut and Pennsylvania tended to be sponsored by the party than in the other two states. In both Connecticut and Pennsylvania, parties played a more active role in candidates' decisions to run. These differences developed despite the vigorous political party competition found in all four states. Nevertheless, party sponsorship of candidacies is of some consequence in all these states, and party recruitment probably is underrated in an age in which it is fashionable to believe that political parties are disappearing in this country.

Deciding to run is one thing; conducting an effective campaign is something else. A complex group of factors affect the act of campaigning for the legislature, much of which political scientists have not studied carefully; but certain factors are of major importance. Two such factors loom largest to legislative candidates—the conditions under which a campaign must be conducted and the resources available to deal with those conditions.

Factors That Determine a Campaign

What factors determine the type of campaign run by a candidate for a state legislature? In truth, there are many. Whether the district is a single-member or multiple-member district may have a large effect on a candidate's strategy. An incumbent legislator—a legislator seeking reelection—whether in a primary or a general election, is a major factor. The population density of the district—whether it is urban or rural—may substantially affect campaign effort. Traditional political party strength and party organization in a district have an important impact too. These kinds of factors are present in almost any legislative contest and are not especially susceptible to the manipulations of the campaign itself.

It is easy to appreciate that political conditions like these vary widely across the house and senate districts into which the fifty states have divided themselves. In their population sizes alone, these districts are disparate. The largest house districts, those in California, include, on average, more than 300,000 people, while the smallest, those in New Hampshire, include an average of only about 2,000 people. Senate districts in California contain more than half a million people, about the same size as congressional districts; Wyoming senators represent only about 11,000 people.

To run for the legislature in New Hampshire is quite different from running in

California. In New Hampshire, candidates can personally meet most of the voters in a district, and campaigns can be conducted at modest cost. In California, campaigning must be undertaken on a much larger scale, very much like that of running for a congressional seat. The campaign must be professional and highly organized, and it must depend heavily on mass mailings and radio and television advertising. Such campaigning involves substantial costs and puts a premium on the ability of candidates to raise substantial sums of money.

Raising Campaign Money

In many states, especially small, less urbanized ones, it does not cost a lot of money to conduct an effective campaign for the legislature (see Jewell 1982, 38–42). In the 1988 election in Montana, for example, the average campaign spending for house candidates was only $2,692 (the median spending was $2,265). The average candidate for the Kansas House in 1988 spent less than $2,000 in the primaries, and less than $7,000 in the general election (Hogan 1994). But in large states like California, New York, or Texas, campaigning for the legislature is much more costly, and growing more so (Jewell and Patterson 1986, 36–38). In 1988, Texas House candidates on average spent $11,000 in primary contests and $14,517 in general elections (Hogan 1994). But California's legislative elections are the most expensive in the nation: in 1988, for example, the average campaign expenditure for the lower house in California was more than $370,000.

Although New York is the second largest state in population, the amount spent on campaigns in legislative politics is relatively modest. In 1984 the 140 incumbent assemblymen running for reelection raised only about $35,000 each, on average (challengers raised only about $8,300). In addition, the New York Democratic and Republican parties raised and spent about $1.1 million on assembly candidacies (Stonecash 1988). In Table 5-1, I provide selected illustrations of the costs of state legislative electioneering, showing average and median campaign expenditures for several states. Among other things, this comparison dramatizes the extraordinary costs of running for the California Assembly, even taking into account the large population of that state.

Where does state legislative campaign money come from? Its sources vary a great deal among the states. Where campaigns are relatively inexpensive, individual citizens' contributions make up a sizable proportion of campaign war chests. But increasingly, campaign money comes to candidates from political action committees (PACs) and from political party leaders or caucus committees. In the large urban states like California, party organizations, party leaders, and PACs are major sources of money for rank-and-file candidates for the legislature.

Studies of state legislative election campaigns consistently show that PACs contribute preponderantly to incumbents. For instance, it was stated in a recent analysis of the 1988 elections in three states that "PAC contributions constitute more than half of all contributions to incumbents in Pennsylvania, almost 40

Table 5-1 The Costs of Campaigning for State House Seats, 1988

| State | Campaign expenditures | |
	Average $	Median $
California	370,722	302,128
Idaho	4,425	2,244
Minnesota	13,244	13,144
Missouri	9,618	6,921
Montana	2,692	2,265
New Jersey	48,033	33,670
North Carolina	12,085	10,025
Oregon	35,982	30,333
Pennsylvania	18,462	13,944
Washington	25,811	20,145
Wisconsin	14,868	11,812

SOURCE: These spending data were collected in the course of a research project conducted by David Breaux, William Cassie, Anthony Gierzynski, Keith Hamm, Malcolm E. Jewell, Gary Moncrief, and Joel Thompson. They are reported in Beyle 1993, 50.

percent in North Carolina, and over one-fourth in New Jersey; they represent only about one-fifth of the contributions to challengers in Pennsylvania and New Jersey and one-fourth in North Carolina" (Thompson, Cassie, and Jewell 1994, 228). PAC expenditures give the advantage to incumbents in legislative contests; the increasing return rate of incumbents has transpired in part because of the growing support PACs have been prepared to accord to incumbent candidates. Moreover, PACs in at least some states contribute heavily to the campaigns of legislative leaders, including Speakers and committee chairs (Thompson and Cassie 1992).

Political party organizations and party leaders are important sources of campaign money for legislative candidates in some states. In highly partisan states like New York, party funding is a major consideration (Stonecash 1988, 484–487). In California, about a fourth of legislative campaign receipts in 1986 came from the parties, mostly from party leadership and caucus funds (Sorauf 1988, 268). In New Jersey, North Carolina, and Pennsylvania elections in 1988, the party organizations contributed significant amounts to legislative candidates of their party. In New Jersey and North Carolina, party money was largely Republican money, but in Pennsylvania the Democrats far outspent the Republicans (see Thompson, Cassie, and Jewell 1994, 230). In addition, twenty-four states have some form of public funding for political campaigns, and in most of them public funds may be used for legislative candidates, either directly or through the state party organizations (Sorauf 1988, 274–284). In New Jersey, where public funding of gubernatorial contests has existed for several years, a new campaign finance law requires that contributions from PACs be made to the state political parties, which may, in turn, allocate funds to legislative candidates (Hansen 1994b).

Because state and local party organizations often have not been willing or able to raise campaign funds for legislative contests, the legislative parties have come to take a substantial role in campaign finance (Gierzynski 1992). In more than three-fifths of the states the legislative leaders engage in fund-raising and determine how campaign support will be distributed among campaigns. Legislative party leadership PACs, formed by house Speakers or senate presidents, have taken on growing importance. One of the most successful was organized by former Speaker Vernal G. Riffe, Jr., for the Democratic majority in the Ohio House of Representatives. Through his birthday party and other fund-raising efforts, Speaker Riffe was able to ensure campaign funding for members of his caucus (Patterson 1994, 246). According to a report in the *Columbus Dispatch* on January 16, 1994, in 1992, Riffe's House Democratic Committee spent $5.1 million for Democratic candidacies.

Perhaps more impressive has been the success of Speaker Willie Brown, leader of the California Assembly who, "for most of the 1980s . . . was the single largest contributor to Assembly races, outspending the two major external parties and the state's largest political action committees" (Clucas 1992, 269). In Illinois, chamber party committees and Democratic and Republican leaders in the House and Senate raised about $7.1 million during the 1990 election cycle, more than $6.7 million of which was distributed directly to state legislative candidates, used to support party organizational activities, or spent for related political purposes (Redfield and Van Der Slik 1992). Party leaders and caucus committees distribute campaign money so as to maintain or acquire partisan advantage in the legislature. This partisan campaign effort tends to make legislative elections more competitive, as party money is funneled into open-seat and marginal races (see Gierzynski and Breaux 1993).

LEGISLATIVE ELECTIONS

Electoral Competition

Deciding to be a candidate and raising the campaign money only begin the process of running for the legislature. In the main, to be a candidate in the general election a person must be nominated in a primary election. The extent to which these primaries are competitive varies a good deal among states and among legislative districts within states. Because the Democratic party has been dominant in state legislative elections, contests (elections in which there is more than one candidate) have taken place substantially more often in Democratic than in Republican primaries, and the Democratic races have tended to be closer. Moreover, metropolitan districts, and those where no incumbent is entered in the race, have more competitive primaries. As the prospects for general election victory improve, primary contesting tends to increase, so competition is greater in the primary of the party more likely to win the seat in a district (Grau 1981; Key 1956, 172).

If the nomination of legislative candidates is normally not a matter involving much competition, in general elections the legislative races are much more wide-ly contested. Nevertheless, although contested, the bulk of legislative races in most state elections are not, in fact, very competitive (see, for instance, Tucker and Weber 1992). In many states, contested legislative districts produce lopsided general election victories. Across the states, usually about three-quarters of the incumbent legislators win reelection (see Breaux and Jewell 1992; Tucker and Weber 1992). The so-called incumbency advantage has apparently not grown in re-cent years, but the victory margin attained by incumbents has increased (see Cox and Morgenstern 1993; Jewell and Breaux 1988; and Shan and Stonecash 1994). In the South most legislative districts are safe, readily won by the candidate of the incumbent party. Republican candidates for president or governor may have been successful in southern states, but Democratic hegemony still prevails in the state legislatures of that region even though the Republican proportion of state legislative seats has grown markedly.

Typically, state legislative elections are about as competitive as congressional elections, but in most states the majority of legislative seats are electorally safe. The political implications of this fact, however, could be exaggerated. Noncom-petitive elections in a state's legislative district can produce a competitive legisla-ture if one-half of the districts are safe for one party and one-half safe for the other. In fact, traditions of party dominance and the operation of the electoral system tend to produce one-sided legislatures. In 1993, for example, only four-teen state senates and twelve houses contained representatives of the Democratic and Republican parties in so close a balance that the stronger party had no more than 55 percent of the membership.

The Effects of Party Strength

Partisanship is an important factor in state legislative elections, although its significance varies greatly among states. Certainly in the more competitive states, the strength of the political parties in legislative districts plays an important part in shaping election results. In some elections this shows up with special empha-sis, as when the parties make unusual efforts to stimulate turnout or absentee voting (see Patterson and Caldeira 1985). The Democratic and Republican parties now enjoy about equal shares of the seats in the state houses and senates (see Fig-ure 5-1). The 1994 elections produced a historic surge in Republican representa-tion in the legislatures, including striking gains in the legislatures of the formerly solid Democratic South. In the aftermath of the 1994 elections, Republicans en-joyed majorities in both legislative houses in nineteen states, Democrats con-trolled both houses in eighteen states, and the parties split chamber control in a dozen states. The decline in Democratic legislative hegemony has accrued largely out of Republican electoral successes in the southern states, where, in 1994, Re-publicans won 669 state legislative seats (up from 538 Republican-held seats in 1992 and 474 seats held in 1990).

Figure 5-1 Party Control of State Legislatures after the 1994 Elections

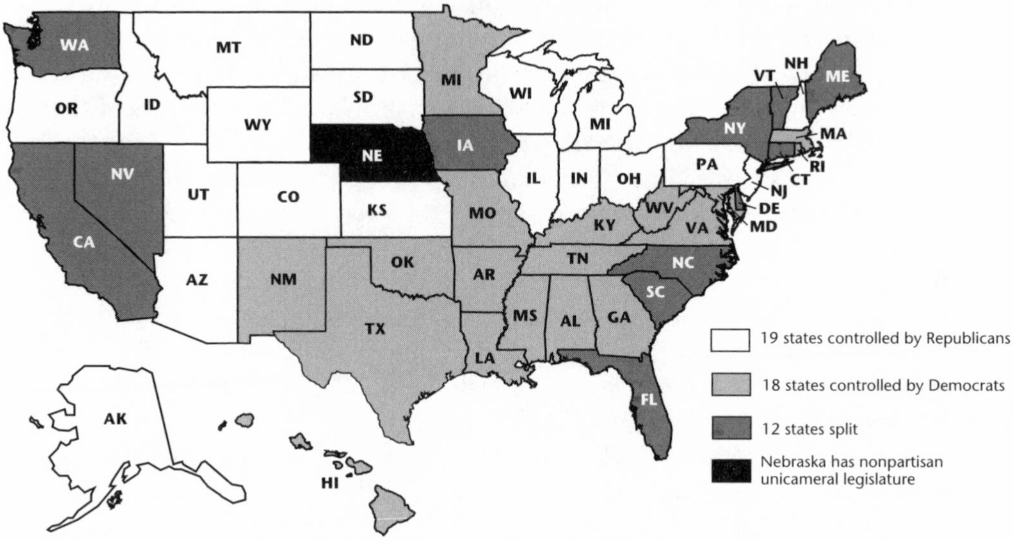

19 states controlled by Republicans

18 states controlled by Democrats

12 states split

Nebraska has nonpartisan unicameral legislature

SOURCE: Data from National Conference of State Legislatures, printed in *State Legislatures* 21, no. 1 (1995): 20.

In competitive states the outcome of elections can depend substantially on the partisan complexion of the districts. The one-sidedness of legislative elections arises partly because those districts carry long traditions of strength for one of the political parties. For example, in districts where Democratic party strength is traditionally robust, Democrats will tend to be elected and reelected time and time again. Despite apparent changes in state partisanship since the 1970s, partisan strength remains an important factor in legislative election outcomes. A detailed study of elections in California and Iowa indicated that, on average, a 10 percent increase in the proportion of voters registered for a party in legislative districts would yield a 5 to 6 percent increase in the vote for that party's legislative candidates (Caldeira and Patterson 1982).

And yet nothing about partisan change is more dramatically demonstrated than the substantial shifts to the Republican party that occurred in the 1994 elections. After the 1992 elections, the Democrats still enjoyed one-sided control of the state legislatures. In half the states, they held majorities in both legislative houses, while the Republicans enjoyed majorities in both houses in only eight states. In sixteen states, the Republicans controlled one house, the Democrats the other. In short, after the 1992 elections the Democrats controlled at least one house of the state legislatures in most of the nation. The 1994 elections brought about striking changes in party control. For the first time in four decades the Republicans captured nearly half of the state legislative seats in the land, and the map of partisan control changed sharply. As indicated in Figure 5-1, the number of Republican-controlled legislatures more than doubled, from eight legislatures to nineteen; Democratic-controlled legislatures diminished from twenty-five to eighteen; and split legislatures declined from sixteen to twelve. Republicans captured full control of the Great Lakes states—Illinois, Indiana, Michigan, Ohio, Pennsylvania, and Wisconsin. Republicans won the West, adding control over the legislatures in Alaska, the Dakotas, Montana, and Oregon to their strength in that region. Moreover, Republicans gained ground in the South, holding their control of the Florida Senate and adding control of the house in the Carolinas. Indeed, the 1994 elections greatly altered the electoral map of the United States, increasing Republicans' numbers among members of the U.S. Congress and state governors as well as providing majorities for fifty state legislative bodies (both houses in nineteen states, one house in twelve).

The Effects of Incumbency

A legislator who wishes to continue representing his or her constituency is unlikely to be challenged in the party primary or defeated in the general election. Even with the substantial party changes that occurred in 1994, most incumbents who ran won reelection. To a large extent, legislative primaries go uncontested because aspiring candidates do not wish to challenge incumbent legislators of their own party. General election outcomes are lopsided mainly because challengers are not able to overcome the advantages incumbents have in visibility in their districts, because voters believe the incumbent has represented them well and should be returned to the legislature, or both (Holbrook and Tidmarch 1993).

Judging from research on elections from 1968 to 1986 in single-member districts in fourteen states, the propensity of incumbents to run for reelection to the legislature and to win has increased, but not a great deal, in the last two decades. Incumbent return rates were high in the 1960s, and they have remained so (Jewell and Breaux 1988). The successes of incumbents at the polls do not necessarily mean there is no competition. In 1988, for instance, the parties targeted many incumbent-occupied seats in several states for special election effort as part of their jockeying for the reapportionment struggle to come after the 1990 census.

Moreover, opportunities for newcomers to win legislative seats do arise because incumbents do decide at some point not to run again. Also, incumbents can be defeated, and with some frequency they are. Moreover, reapportionment upsets patterns of incumbent reelection to some extent, changing the composition of incumbents' districts or pitting two incumbents of the same party against one another so that they "kill each other off" in the primary. And sometimes the coattails of a popular presidential or gubernatorial candidate can sweep incumbents out of office. But "a contest for [a seat that is up for grabs] has been compared to Halley's comet; it does not come around often" (Rosenthal 1981, 24).

The Effects of Campaign Spending

Campaign funds are spent to activate voters, to win visibility for candidates, and to mobilize voter support for candidates. Research on the impact of campaign spending on legislative election outcomes in two states—California and Iowa—revealed that even when party strength, incumbency, and the closeness of races were taken into account, candidates were substantially helped by their own campaign spending or else were undermined by the spending of their opponents (Caldeira and Patterson 1982; for similar results in Florida, see Giles and Pritchard 1985).

Just as in congressional elections, campaign spending in state elections is primarily beneficial to challengers. Incumbents are already so visible in their districts and have such well-established partisan support that campaign spending adds little or nothing to their election prospects. They need only to maintain an already heavy advantage, and many incumbents probably spend more than they need to in order to be reelected. Challengers usually are little known in their districts and need to campaign aggressively and advertise themselves. Campaign spending up to a point of diminishing return substantially helps challengers win support. For challengers, a campaign war chest makes possible the activities and effort necessary for a competitive race. But the efforts of challengers rarely suffice to overcome the advantages of incumbents.

THE STATE LEGISLATORS

Who Are They?

Candidates who win legislative seats find themselves in the company of people like themselves when they attend their first meeting of the legislature. The vast majority are business and professional people, the largest occupational group being lawyers, although the percentage of lawyer-legislators has declined somewhat in the past twenty years. But the prevalence of lawyers varies greatly among the legislatures of the states, with the largest proportion in the South and the fewest in the West and Northeast (see, for example, Bryan 1981, 191–227; Ingram, Laney, and McCain 1980, 49–60).

The occupations of state legislators are presented in Table 5-2. In 1993 more than a third of the legislators were lawyers or other professionals, and nearly a third were in business occupations. It is quite striking how few clerical and blue-collar workers serve in the legislatures, even in the industrial states that have large labor union memberships. It is easy to understand why business and professional people dominate the legislative memberships. They have the personal resources that make it possible for them to pursue political interests and to make the sacrifices that legislative service may involve. What is not readily understood is why a third to half of the legislators in some of the states are lawyers, while in other states, lawyers have not usually been attracted to legislative service.

Although the vast majority of state legislators are citizen-legislators—com-

Table 5-2   Occupations of State Legislators, 1993

Occupation	% of members	
	Houses	Senates
Full-time legislator	15.3	13.9
Lawyer	14.3	22.6
Other professionals*	18.6	17.2
Business owner, executive, employee	21.6	20.6
Real estate, insurance	6.5	6.0
Agriculture	7.4	9.4
Government employee	2.8	1.9
Labor union employee	.3	.3
Homemaker	1.4	1.0
Retired	8.3	4.1
Other	3.5	3.0
Total	100.0	100.0

SOURCE: Calculated from data in Gordon 1994, 27.
* Includes educators, consultants, physicians, engineers, scientists, architects, clergy, accountants, employees in communications and the arts, and students.

bining their service as legislators with another occupation—a growing proportion of members are full-time legislators. By 1993, 15 percent of state representatives and senators nationally considered themselves full-time legislators. In nine states, more than a fourth of the members of the legislature avow that they are serving full time; in New York, Pennsylvania, and Wisconsin, full-time legislators make up more than 60 percent of the membership (Gordon 1994). In the large urban states like California, New York, and Pennsylvania, citizen demands on the legislature are so staggering that most members cannot avoid full-time service. In contrast, in small rural states like North Dakota and Vermont, representation and the scope of public business permits the retention of a citizen legislature.

In recent decades, the state legislatures have become professional bodies. Differences among the states in levels of legislative professionalism are portrayed in Figure 5-2. At the high end of the scale are legislatures whose members work at their task full time, are relatively highly paid, and enjoy substantial staff support; at the other end of the scale are legislatures whose members are mostly part time, relatively poorly paid, and minimally staffed. In Figure 5-2, states are classified into three categories: those with highly professional legislatures, mainly large urban states; those with moderately professional legislatures; and those with less professional legislatures, mainly in New England and the midwestern and western agricultural states. The level of professionalization of the legislatures is indicative of the development of settled legislative career lines. Some state representatives seek to acquire seniority in order to achieve positions of committee or party leadership within the legislature; some members' careers unfold in the form of movement from service in the house of representatives to the senate;

Figure 5-2 Professionalism of the State Legislatures

Professional: full-time, large staff, high pay

Hybrid: in-between

Citizen: part-time, small staff, low pay

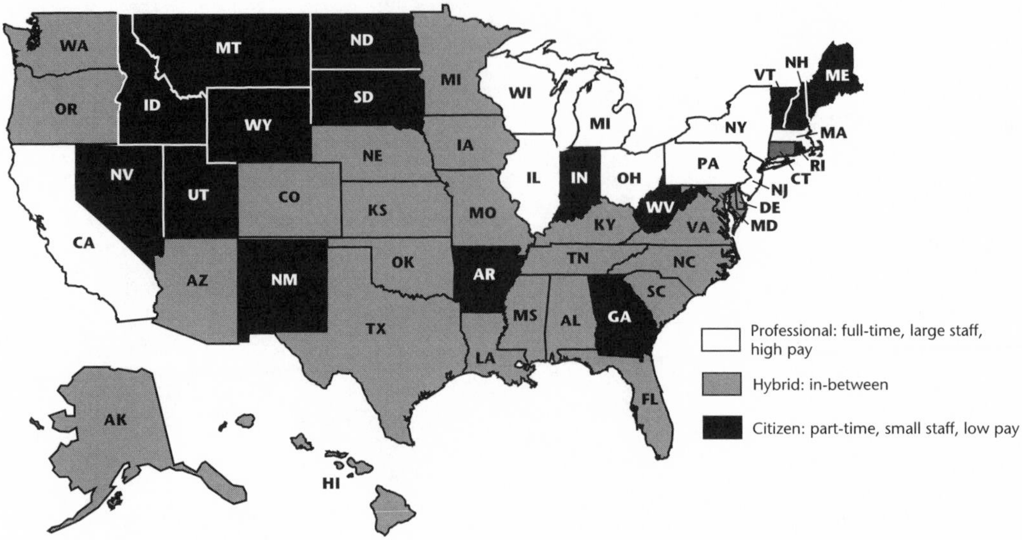

SOURCE: Adapted from the classification of states developed by the National Conference of State Legislatures, printed in *State Legislatures* 20, no. 11 (1994): 5.

some members seek a career move from the state legislature to the U.S. Congress (see Berkman 1993; Francis 1993).

In the last decade women and members of racial and ethnic minority groups have been winning legislative seats in increasing numbers. This growth for women and African Americans is depicted in Figure 5-3. In 1993 some 1,517 women, about 60 percent of whom were Democrats, served in state legislatures, more than one-fifth of the total number of members (Thaemert 1994).

But sheer percentages understate the influence of women in the legislatures (Thomas 1994). Women's caucuses have been organized in at least sixteen states. Moreover, in several legislatures women have achieved major leadership posts (such as Oregon House Speaker Vera Katz, or Arizona House Speaker Jane Dee Hull). In 1995, women won numerous leadership posts. For instance, Republicans in Alaska chose Gail Phillips as Speaker of the house and Drue Pearce as senate president; in Ohio, the Republican Jo Ann Davidson was elected Speaker; and in Colorado the minority house Democrats elected a full slate of women leaders, including Peggy Kearns as minority leader.

It is a mistake to assume that the electoral fortunes of women are inferior to men's. At least since the mid-1980s, women candidates for the state legislatures have been as successful as men candidates. From 1986 to 1992, 21 percent of state house candidates and 17 percent of senate candidates were women. The success rates for women and men candidates were the same. An exhaustive study by the National Women's Political Caucus showed that, of these candidates, "incumbent women won 95 percent of their elections, as compared to 94 percent for incum-

Figure 5-3   Women and African-American State Legislators

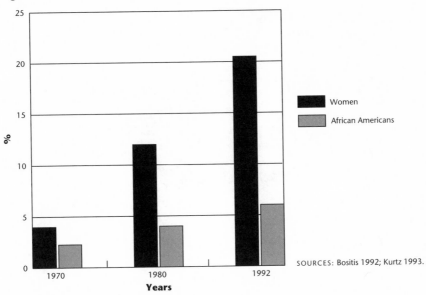

SOURCES: Bositis 1992; Kurtz 1993.

bent men; women running for open seats won 52 percent of their elections, compared to 53 percent for men; and women challengers won 10 percent of their elections, compared to 9 percent for men" (Newman 1994, 9). The comparable election success rates of women and men holds over time, whether the opponent was a man or a woman, and in multimember as well as in single-member districts.

In 1994, women made up about 22 percent of the state representatives and 17 percent of the state senators, proportions virtually identical to the gender composition of legislative candidates (Newman 1994, 23–24). A state-by-state count in 1993 showed that women formed more than 30 percent of the overall legislative membership in seven states, including Arizona (36 percent), Colorado (34 percent), Idaho, Maine, New Hampshire, Vermont, and Washington (40 percent). The proportion of women legislators was smallest—less than 10 percent—in Alabama, Kentucky, Louisiana, and Oklahoma. The variations among the states in the representation of women in the houses of representatives can be seen in Figure 5-4, confirming that there are relatively more women legislators in the West, New England, and the upper Midwest and generally fewer in the South and mid-Atlantic states.

Membership in the legislatures also has increased in recent years for ethnic and racial minority groups, especially in districts where such groups make up a considerable proportion of the voting population. The proportion of blacks in the legislatures, indicating growth in African-American membership over three decades, can be seen in Figure 5-3. In 1992, 459 blacks were elected to the state legislatures, constituting somewhat over 6 percent of the total number of legislators. Gains in minority representation were especially marked in the South. By

Figure 5-4 Women in State Houses of Representatives, 1993

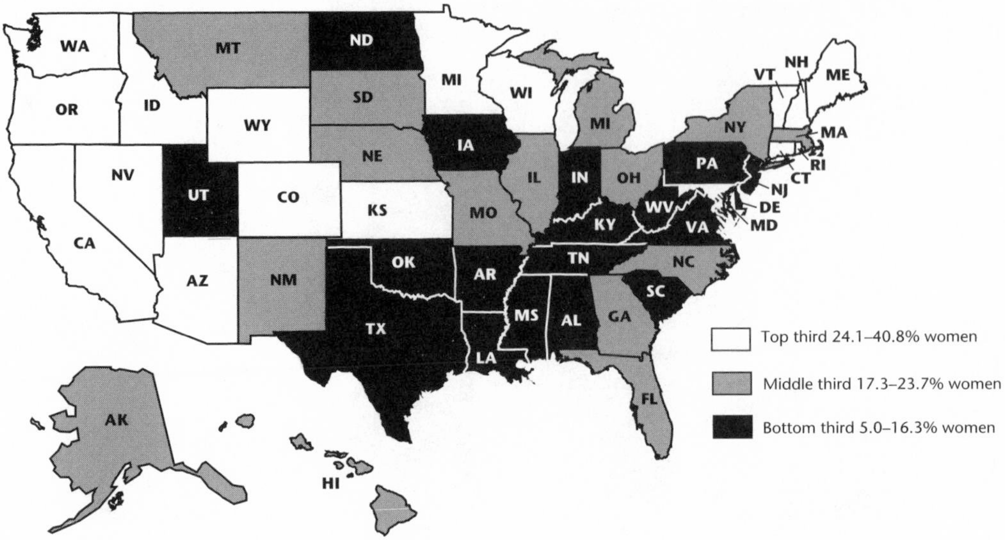

Top third 24.1–40.8% women

Middle third 17.3–23.7% women

Bottom third 5.0–16.3% women

SOURCE: Darcy, Welch, and Clark 1994, 58. Reprinted by permission.

1993, blacks held nearly a fourth of the seats in the Mississippi legislature, and more than 15 percent in Alabama, Georgia, Louisiana, Maryland, and South Carolina. To a considerable extent black gains in representation in southern state legislatures can be attributed to the effects of stronger enforcement of the Voting Rights Act of 1965 and to redistricting. Of course, African Americans are not the only important racial and ethnic minority; they are just the largest group. Hispanics and Asians are also winning an increasing number of state legislative seats, although the successes of these groups are not monitored and publicized as widely as are black gains. Some Hispanics serve as members of the legislatures in the states with the largest Hispanic populations—California, Florida, New York, and Texas (Bullock 1992).

Party Complexion

Democrats held a stable share of state legislative seats until the redistrictings following the 1990 census. Until then, their overall proportion of seats in houses of representatives and senates hovered around the 60 percent mark, as shown in Figure 5-5. But Democratic fortunes slipped in 1992, when Democrats won about 57 percent of house and senate seats, and dropped even more in 1994, when they won only about 52 percent.

The Democrats' share of legislative seats has undergone a monotonic decline in the South. The political changes in the South have been dramatic over the past thirty years, and it can be seen in Figure 5-5 how this transformation has been re-

Figure 5-5 Democratic Party Seats in the State Legislatures

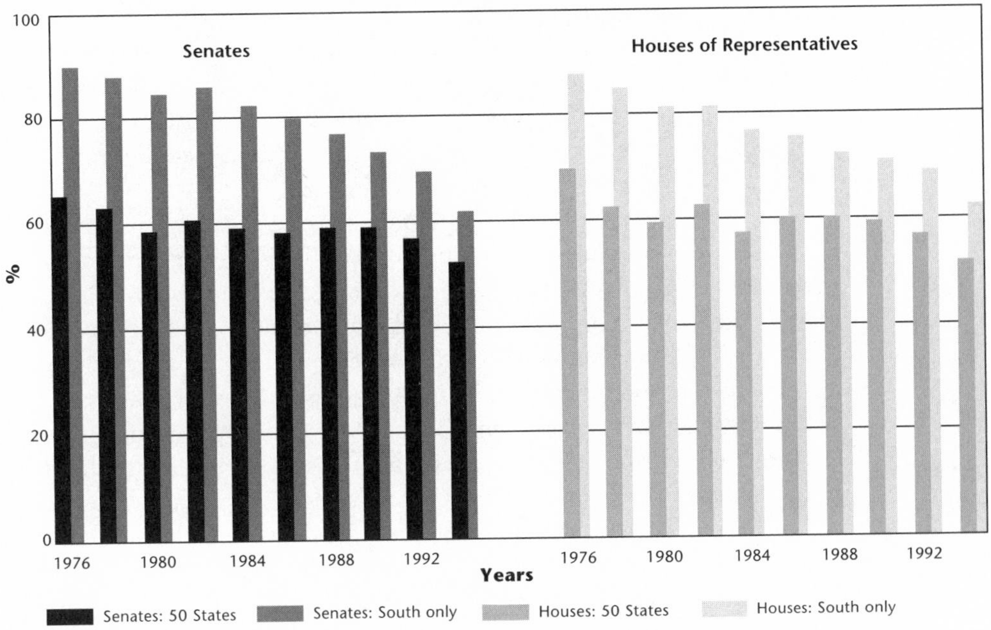

SOURCES: CSG, Various years; for 1994 results, data from the National Conference of State Legislatures.

flected in the party complexion of the state legislatures. In the mid-1970s, Republicans held only 10 percent of southern state legislative seats; by the early 1980s, the Republican share had jumped to about 17 percent; after the 1992 elections, the Republicans occupied almost 30 percent of these seats (Kurtz 1993, 16). In the aftermath of their victories in the South in 1994, Republicans held about 37 percent of the seats in the legislatures. These gains meant majority control of the Florida Senate and the lower houses in the Carolinas, and significant gains in other southern state legislative chambers. In South Carolina, the Republican edge of four seats (62 to 58) developed when two members elected as Democrats decided to switch sides and become Republicans (Boulard 1995).

Legislative Turnover

Even though the satisfactions of serving as a member of a legislature can be great, the sacrifices made by these mainly business and professional people can be great as well. Legislative salaries and benefits have improved in recent years, but even so, many legislators suffer some financial disadvantages. Family life can be disrupted by heavy travel and weeks away from home in the state capital.

The job of a legislator has become much more demanding and time consuming in the last twenty years; today even part-time legislators are spending more than half their time engaged in legislative work. The job can leave members frustrated, feeling that they are confronted by too many demands. Many state legislators expect to serve in office for a limited period of time and then return to their private lives. But others find serving in the legislature sufficiently rewarding to stay on over several terms, and they find that they can accommodate themselves to the strains and frustrations of serving. Still others, ambitious to advance their political careers, see serving in the legislature as but a steppingstone to higher and more satisfying public offices (see Squire 1988).

Some states have improved the job of being a legislator by raising pay, providing professional staff help, improving office facilities, paying retirement benefits, streamlining the processing of legislative work, and so forth. The California legislature is a good case in point. In 1992 the annual salary for California legislators was $52,500 plus $92 per day for living expenses. Members have adequate staffs, district offices, good office facilities in the capitol, and travel allowances and other benefits. Despite improvements of this kind, a high proportion of California legislators do not stay in the job very long; from the beginning to the end of the 1980s, 70 percent were new members. Similar developments in other states have meant that, in general, turnover of state legislative memberships is relatively high.

The state legislative turnover rate over the last three decades is shown in Figure 5-6. The peaks in turnover are brought about by reapportionments—notice

Figure 5-6   Membership Turnover in State Legislatures

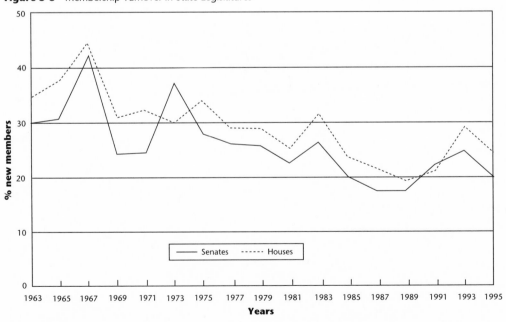

SOURCES: For 1963–1971, Rosenthal 1974, 611; CSG, Various years; for 1991–1995, data from the National Conference of State Legislatures.

these peaks for 1967, after the U.S. Supreme Court and state courts mandated the elimination of malapportionment, and for 1973, 1983, and 1993, the years following redistrictings after the decennial censuses. Notice also the gradual decline in state legislative turnover throughout the thirty-year period. Even though the 1994 elections brought about significant increases in Republicans' state legislative representation, turnover of membership actually was only moderate. In states where legislators were chosen in 1994, only about one-fifth of senators and one-fourth of representatives were new to their chambers. Those who continue to serve over many terms acquire expertise and seniority, and opportunities for committee or party leadership in the legislative body are available to them. The more ambitious seek election or appointment to more prestigious and more secure offices (Rosenthal 1981, 57).

Adapting to Legislative Life

A person newly elected to the legislature enters an institution that has a well-established organizational structure: complex rules of procedure, a division of labor that is largely preordained, patterns of leadership, unwritten rules of the game, and time-honored traditions. New members have to adjust themselves to operating within this new group—they have to "learn the ropes," make new friends, and adapt themselves to conflicting demands and pressures. Most new legislators understand how to make the necessary adjustments because they have been raised in politicized families and have had considerable political experience before they enter the legislature.

Naturally, adaptation to the legislative institution also involves the emergence of patterns of interpersonal contact, friendship, and mutual respect. Legislators find kindred members who share their own life experiences (such as education), have similar attitudes and beliefs, share affiliations, or are geographically or spatially close to them. These affinities help members to exchange political or legislative information and voting cues. The most pervasive basis for bonds of friendship among legislators, and for the development of respect, is partisan similarity (see Caldeira, Clark, and Patterson 1993; Caldeira and Patterson 1987, 1988).

The first part of a legislative session is a whirlwind of activity for new members; they must adjust their personal affairs to the life of the capital, attend orientation sessions led by staffs and leaders, participate in party caucuses, and engage in the flurry of political activities, such as electing a Speaker or other leaders, that organizing a session involves. New members learn how to "get along" and learn their roles as legislators rather quickly, although, of course, not all new members adapt themselves to legislative life in the same ways (Bell and Price 1975; Jewell and Patterson 1986, 78–110).

Adaptation to legislative life involves such complexity of personal and political behavior that it cannot be summarized or generalized in any easy way (Barber 1965; Wahlke et al. 1962). To simplify, it may be said that some members emerge from campaign and legislative experience as professional lawmakers, prepared to make careers as legislators and dedicated to full immersion in the lawmaking process. Such professionals are to be found most frequently in the full-time, professional legislatures of states like California, Illinois, Massachusetts, New Jersey, New York, Ohio, Pennsylvania, and Wisconsin, although any state legislature may have its cadre of pros. Other legislators are primarily amateurs who serve only part time, who are preoccupied to some extent with maintaining a private business or profession, and who may not think of legislative service as a career but only as an interesting pastime or a temporary obligation of public service.

Legislators' Constituency Roles

In taking on the role of state legislator, a new member may perform the job in various ways. For example, some legislators are deeply committed to their constituencies and view themselves as delegates from their districts, obliged to act and vote in accordance with what they understand to be their constituents' wishes and desires. Others try to perform in a manner more detached from the particular demands of their own districts, believing that the dictates of their conscience or the needs of the state as a whole should provide the guiding stars for their actions. These trustees may feel that they must act according to what they believe is in their constituents' best interest and, if necessary, to educate people in their districts to understand what their best interest is. And then, of course, some legislators are delegates on some issues and trustees on others (these legislators have been dubbed *politicos*), depending on factors such as the character of their districts, their sense of party loyalty, their reelection prospects, the intensity of their own views about issues, or their personalities.

But whatever the legislator's adaptation to legislative life, however the legislator approaches problems of formulating public policies, the constituency is ever present. For most, the district they represent is home, the place where their families and friends live and where they pursue their private occupations. Many state legislators are partly nomads, traveling back and forth from their constituency to the capital. Almost all states now provide travel allowances for the legislators so they can make regular trips from their homes to the legislature. Moreover, many state legislators maintain legislative offices in their districts, and a dozen states provide regular staffing for these district offices. In recent years, legislators have been in greater touch with their constituents through the mail, particularly through the use of newsletters.

A growing number of legislators are providing a variety of services to their constituents, much of it in the form of *casework*—helping constituents with problems they have in dealing with state agencies, such as securing food stamps, unemployment compensation, drivers' licenses, and government jobs. Legislators' casework efforts vary substantially across the states, depending on the professionalism of the legislature and the availability of staff (see Elling 1979; Freeman and Richardson 1994; Jewell 1982). Legislators do not need to have explained the political advantages that casework may give them—assisted citizens are likely to be loyal supporters. The demands of constituents for the legislator to intercede with the state bureaucracy on their behalf and the recognition by legislators that constituency service may ensure reelection have been the main stimuli for the growth of district staffing.

Oftentimes, constituents do not respond to legislators' efforts as legislators would like. Many legislators find a large proportion of their constituents to be ill-informed, not very interested, and even highly cynical about the work of the state legislature. Citizens' confidence in the people running the state legislature and their evaluations of legislative performance undoubtedly vary from time to time and state to state.

Empirical studies of citizens' attitudes toward the legislature are rather rare. But a study in one state, Ohio, is illustrative. In 1988 in a poll conducted by the Polimetrics Laboratory of Ohio State University, Ohioans were asked to rate the job performance of their state legislature. About 60 percent of Ohioans approved of the job their state legislature was doing, and nearly half rated the Ohio legislature higher than the U.S. Congress. Ohioans rated their state legislature more or less favorably, depending on their appraisal of the performance of the governor—those who approved of the work of the Democratic governor Richard Celeste also tended to give favorable ratings to the legislature, with its large and visible Democratic majority in the Ohio House of Representatives. Moreover, Ohioans who generally exhibited some faith in the government system were more likely to take a favorable view of the legislature than was true for those who believed the government was unresponsive to citizens (see Patterson, Ripley, and Quinlan 1992). The results of a survey in seven states conducted in 1989 by the Heartland Poll at the University of Iowa indicated that citizen evaluations of the state legislatures are partly a matter of partisan affinity—individuals whose own political party identification corresponds to the party majority of the legislature give the legislature more favorable evaluations. The study results also revealed that citizens' assessments of the performance of the legislature depend on their appraisal of the governor's performance (see Squire 1993).

The mixed assessments furnished by citizens about the performance of their state legislature do not mean that Americans lack support for the legislature as a political institution or even that they favor significant changes in the nature of these institutions (Patterson, Hedlund, and Boynton 1975). Nor do they mean that citizens in substantial degree are not favorably disposed to and relatively satisfied with the work of their own individual legislator, whom they are likely to return to the legislature election after election if the member is willing to run.

THE LEGISLATURES

Organizational Features

Legislatures are not the ordinary, everyday kind of human group, nor are they occasional and informal convocations. Legislatures are political institutions, long-standing collective decision-making bodies that mold and shape the behavior of their members. These institutions have long histories and well-established traditions, some of which go back to the seventeenth century (Campbell 1980; Loewenberg and Patterson 1979). As political institutions, they exhibit a high degree of stability, uniformity, and complexity. Their principal organizational features are committee structure, political party organization, and leadership. But the significance of these organizational features varies widely among the states.

All but one of the state legislatures are bicameral, composed of a house and a senate. In the bicameral states, the larger body is most often called the house of representatives, but in California, Nevada, New York, and Wisconsin it is called the assembly; in New Jersey, the general assembly; and in Maryland, Virginia, and West Virginia, the house of delegates. The smaller body is called the senate. The Nebraska legislature is unicameral, and its members are referred to as senators.

All the legislatures are apportioned on the basis of population. In many states the houses are twice as large as the senates and senate districts are made up of two house districts. The size of these bodies varies a good deal among states, however. The smallest houses are in Alaska (40 members), Delaware (41 members), and Nevada (42 members); the largest are in Pennsylvania (203 members) and New Hampshire (400 members). In 1979 the Massachusetts House of Representatives was reduced from 240 to 160 members, and in 1983 the Illinois House was shrunk from 177 to 118 members. Minnesota has the largest senate (67 members); the smallest senates are in Alaska (20 members) and Nevada and Delaware (21 members each).

Differences between houses of representatives and senates go beyond mere size: houses are likely to be more partisan, and senates are likely to have a more sedate, clublike atmosphere. Each may guard its status and independence jealously, and, since different parties may have the majority in house and senate, interhouse conflict may be substantial.

Party Leadership

Except for the nonpartisan Nebraska unicameral body, all the state legislatures have a party organization of some sort. Historically, in the Deep South states the Republican minority was so small that party organization played a minimal role, but today Republican party leadership is important in these states. Most state legislatures are very partisan bodies, and they have developed hierarchical partisan structures, complete with top leaders, secondary leaders made up of committee chairmen and key committee members, an outer circle of supporters, and, finally, rank-and-file followers. A case in point is the Democratic party organization of the Massachusetts House of Representatives (Carroll and English 1981, 20). There, an inner circle of leaders clusters around the primary leadership group, with the Speaker playing the dominant leadership role (McNitt and Brazil 1993). The house Speaker, as both the presiding officer of the house and the leader of the majority party, can have pervasive influence on the work of the house. Here, for instance, is the way one Michigan legislator described the role of Speaker William Ryan:

> Nothing happens without the Speaker's approval. He works through the various committee chairmen to carry out his mandates. He gets his own way about all the time. He wears down the Governor. Well, the Governor has got a few other things to do and he spends so much time at it. But Ryan—he's got unlimited time, seven days a week. It makes no difference to him. He'd just wear the opposition. . . . What he wants, he gets. . . . He's at least number two man in the state, if not number one man when it comes to determining what's going to happen (Stollman 1978, 75).

So important is the speakership that winning it frequently involves a hotly contested race. In 1980, Willie L. Brown, Jr., a Democrat, won the speakership of the California Assembly after a vigorous contest, and with the support of several Republicans (see Salzman 1981). He has been reelected subsequently, although in 1989 Republican assemblymen did not support Speaker Brown and instead voted for the dissident Democratic "Gang of Five" member Charles Calderon (Zeigler 1989). After the 1994 election, the Republicans held a 41-to-39 vote margin in the assembly, foreshadowing the election of the Republican Jim Brulte as Speaker. But when the opening session convened, one Republican member of the assembly switched sides in the Speaker contest, leaving the vote equally divided—40 votes for Brulte, and 40 votes for the incumbent Speaker Willie Brown, stalemating the outcome and leaving Speaker Brown in the chair (Clucas 1995).

When the Indiana House of Representatives met after the 1988 election to choose a Speaker, the evenly divided house deadlocked (Traub 1989). The two-day stalemate was broken when Republicans and Democrats agreed to a unique plan by which the Republican leader Paul S. Mannweiler and the Democratic leader Michael K. Phillips were named co-Speakers, and each was scheduled to preside on alternative days (the plan is called "Speaker du jour"—Speaker of the day!). The 1992 Florida state senate elections yielded twenty Democratic and twenty Republican members. After three days of haggling and nine votes without a break in the partisan deadlock, the Florida senators finally agreed that the Republican leader Ander Crenshaw would serve as president of the senate for 1993 and the Democratic leader Pat Thomas would be presiding officer during 1994 (Moss 1993). And when the two parties each captured fifty-five seats in the Michigan House of Representatives in 1992, it was agreed that the Democrat Curtis Hertel and the Republican Paul Hillegonds would serve as co-Speakers (called "stereo Speakers"), alternating each month (Weeks and Weeks 1993).

These power-sharing resolutions to partisan deadlock are hammered out after arduous interparty conflict and negotiation. Often they are followed by continuing partisan maneuvering to win supporters to one side or the other on ideological grounds to break the tie. After the 1992 Pennsylvania state senate election produced a 26-to-24 margin of Republicans to Democrats, Senator Frank Pecora defected to the Democrats, permitting the Democratic lieutenant governor and presiding officer Mark Singel to break a tie vote and thereby allowing the Democrats to organize the senate (Reeves 1993).

The 1989 session of the North Carolina House of Representatives opened to a revolt against the incumbent Speaker. Republicans and maverick Democrats voted together to elect Speaker Josephus L. Mavretic, a Democrat, who then announced he would name several Republicans as subcommittee chairmen (*Winston-Salem Journal,* January 12, 1989, 1,6). The four-term Speaker of the homa House of Representatives Jim Barker, a Democrat, was ousted in 1989 by a coalition of Republicans and dissident Democrats led by a dozen conspirators (called the "T-Bar 12," after the name of the bar where they met; see *Washington Post,* June 8, 1989, A6). In Connecticut, the Democratic Speaker Irving Stolberg was deposed in 1989 by a coalition of Democrats and Republicans (Ehrenhalt 1990). In May 1990, Louisiana Democratic senators ousted the senate president Allen Bares in a coup engineered by the former senate president Sammy Nunez (Hill 1990). In the Kansas House of Representatives, a cross-party attack on Speaker Jim Braden in 1989 left him still in office, but rules changes significantly reduced his capacity to serve as a leader (Loomis 1994, 56–65). These occasions, however, are the exception, not the rule. Speakers and senate presidents are, in effect, normally chosen in the majority party pre-session caucus and approved by a party-line vote at the beginning of a new session of the legislature. Moreover, rebellions against the authority of Speakers and senate presidents are rare.

In the state senates, the principal officer is called president (except in Tennessee, where the title of *Speaker* is used in both houses). In twenty-eight states, this office is filled by the lieutenant governor; in twenty-two states, the president of the senate is elected or confirmed by the senate members. The leadership position of the lieutenant governor, when he or she is president of the senate, is somewhat anomalous, since the lieutenant governor is, formally, within the executive branch of state government. Nevertheless, in some states, such as Texas, the lieutenant governor wields great legislative power; in others, the lieutenant governor is relegated to a very limited role, and the real leadership is in the hands of an elected president pro tempore or majority leader. This especially occurs when the senate majority party differs from that of the lieutenant governor. Where the senate president is elected by senators, leadership contests may develop, as in California, where David Roberti unseated veteran James R. Mills as president pro tempore in 1980, and where a challenge was a recurrent possibility thereafter (LaVally 1989).

If the governor's party commands a legislative majority, he or she can exert influence on the selection of house and senate leaders. Kentucky, where the governor traditionally handpicked the house Speaker (the lieutenant governor presides over the senate), was the last state in which the governor personally selected legislative leaders. In 1980, Governor John Y. Brown, Jr., refrained from entering into the choice of Speaker, ending this quaint Kentucky tradition (Jewell and Miller 1988, 228–239).

When the 1981 session of the Illinois Senate opened, the Republican governor James R. Thompson was constitutionally required to preside until the senate elected its president. The new senate was closely divided, with thirty-one Democrats and twenty-nine Republicans. While the contentious Democrats caucused elsewhere, and with only the Republican senators on the senate floor, the governor declared that a quorum was present and permitted the minority Republicans to elect Senator David "Doc" Shapiro as president. Three weeks later, the Illinois Supreme Court voided the election. The Democrats had assembled in the senate chamber a week before the court's action, electing Senator Philip J. Rock as president by the constitutional majority of thirty votes. The court's decision had the effect of ousting Shapiro, and confirming Rock, as senate president. This bizarre skirmish was one in a series of highly controversial leadership contests in the Illinois legislature (Ross 1981). Another Republican-led assault on Rock's leadership transpired in 1989, when the so-called Sturdy Thirty, a group of insurgent Democrats and Republicans, sought to overturn Rock's rulings from the chair (Wheeler 1989). In general, it is probably fair to say, nonetheless, that the governor's role in influencing the choice of legislative leaders has diminished in the past decade.

Party leadership is central to the organization of most state legislatures. Although house Speakers and senate presidents are the principal leaders, in most legislatures majority leaders, minority leaders, and whips have an important role to play as well. In some Deep South states (and in Nebraska because the legislature is nonpartisan) no floor leaders have been chosen, reflecting a lack of partisanship. However, in recent years in some of these states, like Louisiana, where the Republican minority has grown, Democrats and Republicans have begun to caucus and elect party leaders (Jewell and Olson 1988, 232–234). By the same token, Democrats in the Texas House of Representatives organized a caucus in 1981, and by 1987 the Speaker and his team had joined the Democratic caucus; a Republican caucus was organized in 1989 (Hamm and Harmel 1993).

Party caucuses play an important role in the party organization of most state legislative houses; they are relatively unimportant only in Alabama, Arkansas, Florida, Maryland, Mississippi, Nebraska, and New Hampshire. In general, house Speakers are chosen in the majority party caucuses. In about two-fifths of the states, the party caucuses are presided over by a legislator elected to be caucus chairman; in about a third of the states, the caucuses are presided over by majority or minority party floor leaders; in the remainder of the states, caucus leadership is provided by the house Speaker, the senate president, the party whips, or, in a few cases, the senior party member.

The operating role of the caucuses varies a good deal among the state legislatures. In a few of them the caucuses are major locales in which public policy decisions are hammered out. In many, the caucuses serve to stimulate and foster cohesion among party members. In some states, the caucus serves as an important vehicle through which party leaders disseminate information or as a mechanism for the election of officers. In the most partisan of the state legislatures, caucuses may meet daily, particularly late in the legislative session, and binding votes on major bills, such as appropriations or revenue bills, may come frequently (see Jewell and Olson 1988, 235–244).

The truth of the matter is that legislative leadership is only dimly understood. To complicate matters, leadership in the legislatures is undergoing change. Professionalization brought more commanding and effective leadership to the legislatures, and partisan polarization altered the strategic role of legislative leaders. Changes in party composition and party control shape and reshape leaders' powers, and term limitations add constraints to leadership performance. As has been remarked by two students of legislative leadership who interviewed leaders in twenty-two states in 1991: "It is impossible to interview leaders in twenty-two state capitols without recognizing that there are differences in styles and methods of leadership and in the institutional and political environment in which they operate" (Jewell and Whicker 1994, 191).

Committees in the Legislatures

The principal work groups of legislatures are their substantive committees (see Francis 1989). The states' committee systems vary in size; for instance, the Massachusetts and Rhode Island legislatures have only a handful of standing committees; the Missouri and North Carolina houses have had large committee systems (see Table 5-3). All committees in Connecticut and most in Maine and Massachusetts are joint committees, made up of members of both house and senate. Several other legislatures employ one or more joint committees as well. In the main, the assignment of legislators to committees and the selection of committee chairpersons are controlled by house Speakers and senate presidents, and in some legislatures, committees on committees advise the leadership about committee appointments. But in many legislatures the preferences of the members are taken into account, and their own strategic calculations tend to prevail in committee assignments (see Hedlund and Patterson 1992).

State legislative committees have an important role in screening legislation and studying policy problems, but in general these committee systems are relatively weak, especially in comparison to the powerful committee system of the U.S. Congress (Hamm 1980; Rosenthal 1974a). This is so for a variety of reasons. First, state legislative committees tend to be under the control of the party leadership of the houses—the house Speakers and senate presidents who dominate the committee assignment process. Second, rules and procedures may thwart

Table 5-3 Committees in State Legislatures, 1992–1993

Number of standing committees	Number of states*	
	Houses	Senates
10 or fewer	6	11
11–20	20	28
21–30	17	8
31–50	5	2
Total	48	49

SOURCE: Calculated from data in CSG 1992, 191–192.

*All legislative standing committees in Connecticut (22), and most committees in Maine (19) and Massachusetts (21), are joint committees, consisting of members from both houses. The legislatures of twenty-four other states have a few joint standing committees. The Nebraska unicameral is counted with the senates.

committee power by permitting bills to be considered on the house floor without a committee stage, or by requiring that all bills referred to committees be reported out of them, thereby not allowing committees to use discretion or pigeonhole bills. Third, because turnover in the membership of committees and in their chairmanships is generally high, they lack stability (see Basehart 1980).

State Legislative Staffing

Perhaps the most dramatic change in state legislative organization since the 1960s has been in the provision of clerical and professional staff for members, leaders, committees, and party caucuses. Although all legislatures have improved their staffs, the most remarkable development has occurred in the highly professionalized legislatures, notably in California and New York. Spending for legislative staff support in California more than doubled in the 1980s. Fiscal constraints arising mainly from voter approval of a proposition setting a ceiling on legislative expenditures brought about a major reduction in the staff (more than 600 staff members were laid off) of the California legislature during the early 1990s (Jones 1992, 131–132). The staff of the New York legislature mushroomed in the early 1970s, and then stabilized.

A survey by the National Conference of State Legislatures counted 33,396 staff assistants for all the legislatures in 1988, 45 percent of them professional staff and the remainder clerical aides (Weberg 1988). For all fifty states, from 1979 to 1988 legislative staffs grew by about 24 percent. The New York and California legislatures employed the largest staffs by far in 1988 (4,157 and 2,978 staff members, respectively). In contrast, legislatures in small states like Vermont and Wyoming managed with diminutive staffs (71 and 113, respectively). In the past decade, the largest increases have occurred in the staffs of individual members and political parties (Weberg 1988).

Some staff assistance is provided to legislators in all states, although in most the members share staff assistants or have staff help only during legislative sessions. About a dozen legislatures provide full-time professional staff to members of both houses, and in nine states, full-time staffs for members' districts are available as well. All states provide staff assistance for legislative committees, although committee staffing is best developed in California, Florida, Pennsylvania, and New York. In addition, some states provide professional staffs to party caucuses and party leaders, and to house officials (Speaker, president, and parliamentarians).

The prevailing system for staffing legislative committees is through a central agency, often under the aegis of a joint legislative committee called a legislative council. Often called *legislative reference service* or *legislative research bureau,* these central staff agencies provide a wide range of technical and professional services to leaders, committees, and individual legislators.

Overall, developments of the last ten years in legislative party organization, committee structure, and staffing have made the state legislatures more effective, professional bodies. These legislatures are processing a growing workload of public policy issues and oversight of administrative agencies. The legislator's own work has become more technical and complex, and thus more demanding. Typically, legislators who can paint with a broad brush on the canvas of their election campaign find that they must confront difficult questions of great complexity when they enter the legislature.

THE LEGISLATURE AT WORK

The main work of the state legislatures involves processing bills and engaging in oversight of the executive branch. Nearly 250,000 bills and resolutions are introduced every biennium, and approximately 30 percent are enacted into law. But the workload varies among states. In the 1990–1991 sessions, the California legislature enacted 3,197 bills and resolutions, while 8,998 were enacted in New York; but in Missouri and Ohio the legislatures passed fewer than 400 laws. Twenty-six states now have generally applicable sunset laws, requiring some arm of the legislature to engage in extensive evaluation of the performance of executive agencies, and in ten other states sunset clauses in legislation control selected programs. All but a handful of states have some form of legislative review of administrative regulations propounded by executive agencies.

The Lawmaking Process

The enactment of bills involves a rather complex process guided by detailed and often complicated rules of procedure. While the process of passing bills into law is not the same in every state, differences are found mainly in detail. In a general way, the legislative process is similar from state to state and can be summarized rather easily (a detailed illustration of the process in California is provided in Figure 5-7). Bills may actually be drafted by legislative staff, executive agencies,

Figure 5-7 The Legislative Process in California

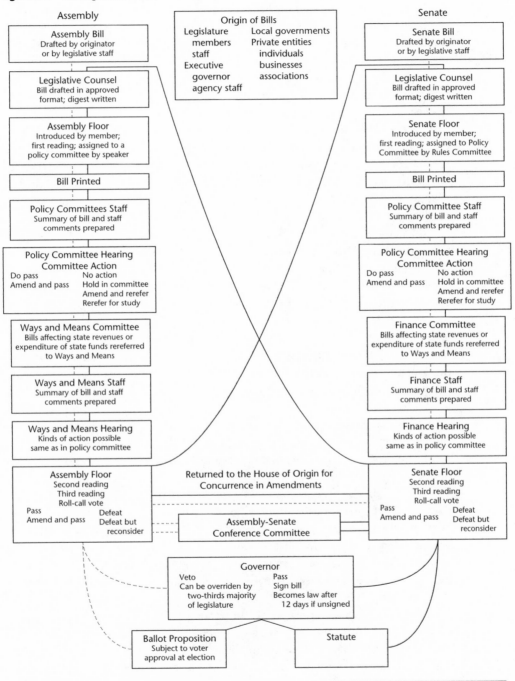

SOURCE: BeVier 1979, 257.

or lobby groups, as well as by individual legislators, but they can be introduced in the legislature only by members. Introduction begins when a member gives a properly typed copy of the draft of a bill to the appropriate person, a "clerk," on the staff of the house or senate. The title of the bill is read aloud by the clerk during a session, a ritual referred to as the *first reading*. Then the bill is sent to the relevant legislative committee. The committee may hold a public hearing on the bill and then decide whether or not to recommend the passage of the bill by the house.

Bills involving the expenditure of money may, in addition to being considered by a substantive committee, be referred also to a revenue, finance, or ways and means committee for an assessment of costs. For example, a bill affecting the state university may be considered by the higher-education committee of the legislature, and its spending provisions considered by a fiscal committee. When a bill is reported from committee to the floor of the legislative house, this fact is noted by reading the title of the bill a second time (the *second reading*). In some state legislatures, this is the occasion for a debate on the merits of the bill and the proposing of amendments; in other states, general debate and consideration of amendments do not occur until later. Once the bill in question has been debated and amended, it may be given a third reading, after which a final vote is taken.

Then, in the bicameral states, the bill will be considered by the other house in much the same manner as in the originating house. If the versions of a bill passed by the two houses are different, these differences are reconciled either by the concurrence of one house in the amendments of the other, or by the appointment of a conference committee composed of members of both houses whose job it is to iron out differences. Once both houses have passed a bill in the same form, it is ready to go to the governor for approval. If the governor disapproves, the legislature may override his veto by a two-thirds majority vote.

The environment of the legislature greatly constrains what it can do in public policies. Rich states like New York and California can consider policy alternatives that are unthinkable in poor states like Mississippi. If the electoral system is such that rural and suburban Republicans, or metropolitan Democrats, have disproportionate legislative majorities, policy alternatives may be limited. Relatively brief legislative sessions and insufficient staff support impinge on possibilities for policy making. If the voters return the same members to office election after election, and these members come to dominate the committee leadership, policy alternatives may harden.

Past legislative policies may limit future alternatives through the incremental character of the budgetary process or the demands of standing commitments to state programs or agencies. Some of these conditions, if not all, are themselves part of the political struggle. When they are taken as givens, however, it is possible to examine the effects of more immediate, more proximate influences on legislative decisions.

Influences on Legislative Policy Making

The policy-making behavior of state legislators may be affected by any of the factors generally known to influence human behavior, perhaps even including what they had for breakfast! But six factors seem most systematically to influence legislators when they make decisions on policy: (1) their party and party leaders, (2) committees, (3) staff, (4) lobbyists representing private interest groups and executive agencies, (5) the governor, and (6) constituents in their legislative districts. Some of these influences on legislators have been the target of voluminous research by political scientists; here, only general conclusions can be discussed (Jewell and Patterson 1986, 202–239).

In many states, political party leaders can mobilize or count on the support of the members of their own party in the legislature. Some of the legislatures are consistently partisan in voting on policy issues—those in states like Connecticut, Massachusetts, and New York. Other state legislatures are moderately partisan or have exhibited a pattern of partisanship that waxes and wanes over the years. States like California, Iowa, Ohio, Montana, and Vermont fall into this category. In some states, party is not a significant factor—Nebraska is officially nonpartisan—but in Alabama, Arkansas, Louisiana, Mississippi, and South Carolina, Democrats have so overwhelmed Republicans in sheer numbers that partisanship has been neither meaningful nor possible (Bryan 1981, 229–262; Comer and Johnson 1978, 101–111; Kirkpatrick 1978, 136–161; Theodoulou 1985, 140–147).

The extent of party voting in state legislatures varies, depending on the nature of the policy issues involved. Studies of party voting indicate that partisan behavior is most pronounced on bills having to do with elections and legislative organization, which directly affect party interests; labor legislation; and appropriations and revenue bills. In some states, welfare issues produce strong partisan divisions, but in other states they do not. Issues such as business regulation, liquor, crime control, and conservation are particularly unlikely to evoke party voting.

Why are some legislatures more partisan than others? The answer to this question is not fully understood, but partisan legislatures do seem to develop most readily in the urban and industrial states. In such states, metropolitan districts elect Democrats, while suburban and rural communities elect Republicans. In the more rural states, Democrats and Republicans tend to be elected from about the same kinds of constituencies; the parties are less likely to be programmatic; and legislators are likely to be elected more for their personal abilities or because of local voting traditions than because of their party's program. But other factors come into play, too. Party voting is higher in the legislatures of states where party competition in elections is brisk and where the political parties are organizationally strong and issue oriented. Consequently, when party voting cues are provided by legislative leaders who are active and aggressive in leading party caucuses, partisan strength in the legislature is likely to be more pronounced. Indeed, partisanship and intraparty cohesiveness probably do not develop naturally; more than from any other source, legislators get voting cues from other legislators and from leaders (Patterson 1972).

Decisions in legislative committees, often guided by the majority party leadership, can have an enormous effect on the verdict of the legislature as a whole. Committees tend to screen out, and thus not report to the floor of the legislatures, highly controversial bills. Since much legislation considered by the state legislatures is not controversial and does not stimulate partisan differences, legislators usually acquiesce in committee judgments on their merits, and committeereported bills tend to be approved (Hamm 1980). Legislators rely on the greater expertise of committee members.

Legislative staffs have a major effect on policy making because of their proximity to the legislators and the centers of legislative power and because of their key role in processing and providing the information legislators require. Staffs are also in a position to provide a buffer between legislators and outside influences, such as the executive or interest groups, that members may wish to avoid or keep under control. The legislative staff can shape and modify the channels of information to legislators and their committees. In the state legislatures, such staff influence has grown measurably in recent years and probably is most pronounced in regard to fiscal and budgetary policies.

In highly staffed legislatures like California's, where there are a half-dozen professional staff people for each legislator, much of the handling of legislation is in the staff's hands. One California staff member who worked on housing bills expressed his own awe at the staff's influence: "The most remarkable discovery I made during my tenure as a staff member was the amount of power I had over the bills on which I worked. The members relied almost entirely on staff to accurately summarize the legislation and also to develop compromises among the many interests which were brought into conflict by these bills" (BeVier 1979, 229).

Political interest groups can substantially influence legislative policy making. In states where there is a single or major economic interest, legislative policy is likely to be bent favorably toward that interest whether interest groups engage in lobbying or not. Agricultural interests in Iowa, the oil companies in Oklahoma, the automobile industry in Michigan, and the lumbering industry in Oregon do not need to engage much in lobbying the state legislature. The legislature would not contemplate legislation inimical to the state's principal industry. Lobbying can, of course, be an important source of influence on the legislature. As Alan Rosenthal has nicely observed, "Lobbyists play an important role in the drama of legislation" (1993b, 207). Recently, business groups have become more active in attempting to wield legislative influence. Education and labor groups are perceived by state legislators as among the most powerful lobbying influences with which they deal, largely because both types of groups have large memberships in all or many legislative districts.

Lobbying groups commonly seek to influence political affairs outside the legislature or the state capital, engaging in grass-roots lobbying in the legislature's constituencies. The most visible of this kind of lobbying takes the form of PAC contributions to candidates for the legislature. Although commentators often imply that PAC campaign spending places legislators at the lobbyists' beck and call, careful research has demonstrated that PAC contributions do not translate directly into roll-call voting support for an interest group's policy agenda (see Dow and Endersby 1994).

Legislatures with strong internal party organization tend to be less amenable to direct interest group influence. Where the legislative parties are weak—or nonexistent, as in Nebraska—lobbying by interest groups is likely to be more influential in lawmaking (for example, see Rodgers, Sittig, and Welch 1984, 80–82). A study conducted in three states—California, Iowa, and Texas—demonstrated that when interest group influences were pitted against party influences on legislators, the party influences substantially prevailed (Wiggins, Hamm, and Bell 1992). Moreover, the more professional the legislature is, and particularly the better staffed it is, the more impervious its members are to interest group pressures. A professional staff provides legislators with their own source of information, freeing them from dependency on information from lobbyists and thereby partly insulating them from lobbyists.

As state legislatures become more professional, lobbyists tend to make their contacts with the staffs of members and committees and with legislators who strongly identify with the interest group's views from the beginning. It is very much to the advantage of the lobbying groups to elect legislators sympathetic to their interests, who will not need to be pressured while the legislature is in session. In recent years, the proliferation of PACs engaged in electioneering and fund-raising in legislative elections on behalf of business, labor, professional, or public interest groups indicates the view of interest groups that they can more effectively influence the legislature by electing their friends to it than by lobbying after the election.

The governor of a state is an integral part of the legislative process. Governors recommend legislative programs to their legislatures and seek adoption of those programs. If the legislature enacts legislation distasteful to the governor, he or she may veto it (except in North Carolina, where the governor has no veto power). In those states where governors may veto bills the legislature passes, gubernatorial veto power varies, from merely the ability to strike out particular items from appropriations bills to the so-called amendatory veto, which gives the governor substantial power to rewrite legislative provisions. Indeed, the governor's influence may pervade the entire legislative session if gubernatorial wishes are followed in the selection of legislative leaders and in the appointment of members and chairmen of committees (as in Louisiana; see O'Connor 1982, 58–59). When the party majorities in the legislative houses are from the same political party as the governor, legislators' support for the governor's legislative program may be impossible to disentangle from their partisan voting behavior (see Bernick 1978). When the governor is a member of one political party and one or both houses of the legislature are controlled by the other party, the influence of the governor may be diminished considerably.

Constituencies certainly exert a profound influence on the behavior of their legislative representatives. Such influence turns up when some attribute of the legislative districts, like their rural or urban character, comes to provide the major source of voting cleavage in the legislature (Broach 1972). More detailed studies of the extent of policy agreement between state legislators and their constituents, and the extent to which legislators perceive their constituents' opinions correctly have produced mixed results (Erikson, Luttbeg, and Holloway 1975; Uslaner and Weber 1979).

The translation of constituents' attitudes into legislative policy depends heavily on the role orientation of the legislators. Legislators who are delegates are much more likely to reflect constituency opinions in their behavior than are trustees or politicos, very strongly so if the policy issue is highly salient in the district and constituents tend to have highly consistent attitudes with regard to the issue (Kuklinski and Elling 1977; McCrone and Kuklinski 1979).

Legislators vote on many issues concerning which their constituents have no opinions and little interest. Even when constituents have opinions, it is difficult for a legislator to represent his or her constituents' attitudes if the constituency is deeply divided or fragmented on issues (Ingram, Laney, and McCain 1980). Many state legislative constituencies, however, are quite homogeneous, containing citizens with highly consistent opinions on major issues of concern to the district. Insofar as such districts elect legislators who believe it is their duty to represent constituents' wishes, constituency influence in the legislature is substantial.

Analyzing the effects on legislators' voting of all the variables that may be at work is difficult (Uslaner and Weber 1977). Many confounding influences are at work in legislative decision making. Interest group influence may be felt through the legislator's constituency; the governor's influence may develop through the legislative party; committee influence may reflect decisions of party leaders; various influences may coagulate through the influence on a member of his seatmates or members of his district or county. Legislators may be influenced in a variety of ways, some direct, others indirect.

One approach to a more general assessment of influences on legislative decision making has been to map out and analyze the voting cues that legislators receive from various actors in the policy-making situation in which they find themselves. When Ohio legislators were interviewed in 1993, they were asked whom they consulted in making their decisions about how to vote on legislation.[1] Their responses are shown in Figure 5-8. Most Ohio legislators responded that they consulted their constituents. But lobbyists, party leaders, com-

---

1. During March through June 1993, a team of political scientists at Ohio State University conducted extensive interviews with 126 of the 132 members of the Ohio House of Representatives and Senate. This study was part of the continuing research of the Ohio Legislative Research Project.

Figure 5-8   Whom Do Ohio Legislators Consult in Evaluating Legislation?

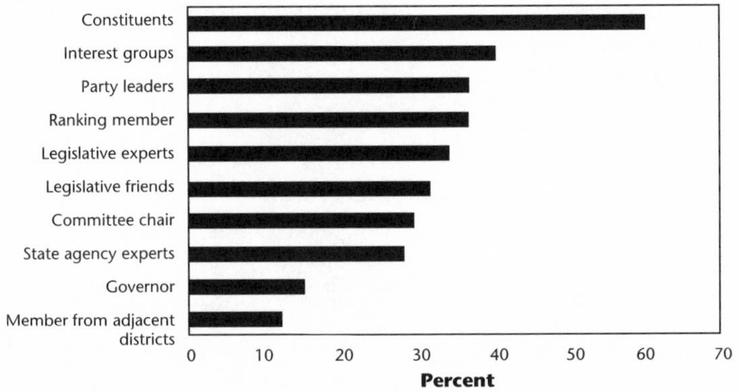

SOURCE: Data from interviews with Ohio legislators conducted by the Ohio Legislative Research Project in 1993.

mittee leaders and substantive policy experts, and the representative's friends in the legislature were consulted by a third of the members or more (legislators could mention more than one influence agent). A similar study, drawing its data from a sample of 1,256 legislators from all states who served in 1973, indicated that the Ohio results were fairly typical (Uslaner and Weber 1977). Both the national and the Ohio studies suggest that, except for consultation with interest group spokesmen, legislators draw mainly on influence agents within the legislature itself, so that party and committee leaders are prominent sources of cues for decision making.

The governor is more remote in the consultation process than might have been expected, but gubernatorial cues may be conveyed to legislators through party leaders and experts on the subject matter from state administrative agencies. Finally, constituents do not, by themselves, constitute a large component in the cue-giving process when it comes to policy making, although constituency influence is likely to be much more pervasive than the incidence of direct consultation would suggest. Constituents' desires are internalized by the individual legislator and reinforced by friends in the legislature, or by fellow partisans from the same or nearby districts (compare Songer 1988).

Overseeing the Administration

As the state legislatures have streamlined the effectiveness of the legislative organization, improved their facilities, come to draw on wider and more adequate forms and sources of information, and enlarged their professional staffs, they have expanded their supervision and control of administrative agencies. This expansion has taken different forms, including committee staff investigations of agency effectiveness in carrying out the intent of the legislature; the enhancement of the so-called postaudit efforts of the legislature; an increase in the capacity of the legislature to audit agency books; greater legislative staff efforts in the realm of more general fiscal management; and more ready handling by legislators' of constituents' requests for help in dealing with executive agencies (Elling 1980).

Two types of legislative oversight have grown dramatically in recent years: regulatory review and sunset legislation. Forty legislatures now have adopted legislation providing for the review of administrative regulation through legislative committees. In many of these states, the joint committee consideration of rules is only advisory, but in a growing number of legislatures the committee may suspend the implementation of administrative regulations. The fairly typical review process in Michigan illustrates how this form of oversight works:

> The first step in the rule-making process does not include the legislature directly. Agencies draft proposals, hold public hearings as required by law, and subsequently draft their regulations. . . . After the rules are past all clearances, they are submitted to the Joint Committee on Administrative Rules. If the committee approves the rules, the agency can adopt them formally, and they become effective shortly thereafter. If the committee disapproves the rules, they are void and cannot become effective unless legislation is passed to overturn the committee's disapproval. If the committee takes no action, a resolution of approval must still be introduced which must be approved by the legislature if the rule is to become effective. (Ethridge 1981b, 12)

In recent years, state legislatures have tended to enact regulatory legislation conferring very general powers upon executive agencies and then to oversee the implementation of these enactments through review of administrative rules. Such a development underscores the growing tendency for legislative and executive branches of state government to share much more intimately in the legitimation of public policy (Hamm and Robertson 1981).

Most state legislatures have adopted sunset laws in some form since the mid-1970s, and several have terminated them after a period of time. These laws require a periodic review of the adequacy of an executive agency's performance; if the agency's programs are found wanting, they may be permitted to terminate—the sun may set on them. The provisions of these laws vary. Some laws apply to all state agencies, others only to regulatory agencies, and a few to a limited number of specific agencies.

The effectiveness of these laws in facilitating legislative oversight remains uncertain. In some states—Arkansas, Mississippi, Nevada, New Hampshire, North Carolina, Rhode Island, South Dakota, and Wyoming—the sunset laws themselves have set. In Illinois the sunset law remains on the statute books, but staff support for agency reviews ended in 1985. Kansas's sunset law is inactive. The effectiveness of sunset legislation is open to doubt. In several states a few small administrative agencies and licensing boards were eliminated or reorganized, and some organizational reform may be attributed to these laws. But many legislators and others have criticized sunset laws as unnecessary, administratively expensive, ineffective, and inappropriate encouragement to politically motivated legislators to intrude unduly into the administrative processes of state agencies (Ethridge 1981a).

THE ATTACK ON THE LEGISLATURES

Despite the modernization of the state legislatures since the mid-1960s, these institutions have come under widespread attack, most directly through the term limitation movement. Arguing that the legislatures are dominated by corruption-prone and entrenched incumbents who have lost touch with their constituents, advocates of limiting legislators' terms of office have used the initiative procedure to get citizen enactment of term limits (see Benjamin and Malbin 1992). The first successful efforts occurred in 1990 in California, Colorado, and Oklahoma, followed by a dozen successful state initiatives in 1992 and five more in 1994. The total number of legislative term limitation states stands at twenty. A term limitation initiative enacted in Nebraska in 1992 was invalidated by that state's supreme court because the petitions were found to have insufficient numbers of signatures, but the state's voters reinstated term limits in 1994. Utah's legislature was the first to pass a bill limiting members' terms; in other states, limits were adopted in the form of propositions submitted to voters (see Table 5-4).

"The current drive to limit the terms of state legislators," says Alan Rosenthal, "probably is the most serious assault on the legislature in years" (1993b, 42). Strongly promoted and supported by conservative business interests and Republican activists, the ostensible purpose of legislative term limitations is to restore a citizen legislature peopled by amateurs, increase membership turnover, control and restrict government activity, and curtail political corruption. Republicans' advocacy of term limits is part and parcel of their efforts to uproot the Democratic majorities in many of the legislatures (see Donovan and Snipp 1994).

It is not easy to predict the ultimate consequences of legislative term limits in the states where they have been adopted. In states with relaxed limits, as in Oklahoma or Utah, the consequences for legislative turnover are likely to be small (Copeland 1993; Moncrief et al. 1992). But where limits of two or three two-year terms have been imposed, a substantial proportion of state legislators will be forced out of office sooner than in states that have no limits. Legislators and their leaders will be newer to the job, and the rotation in office will tend to weaken the legislative institution, acceding relatively more power to bureaucrats in the executive branches and to lobbyists speaking for private or special interests (Opheim 1994; Rosenthal 1993a, 143).

The low esteem in which state legislators are held by the public, and the concomitant propensity of voters in the states to endorse term limitation initiatives on Election Day, surely stems partly from the media notoriety given to instances of corruption, and the demands these have engendered for new ethics legislation. The scandals have been juicy. In 1990 and 1991 an investigation by the Federal Bureau of Investigation and local police in South Carolina resulted in the indictment of eleven lawmakers for selling their votes; and in Arizona, investigations

Table 5-4   Term Limitations for State Legislators

States	Year term limitations adopted	Term limits		Explanation
		Rep.	Sen.	
Arizona	1992	8	8	Consecutive years.
Arkansas	1992	6	8	Lifetime limit of 14 years.
California	1990	6	8	Lifetme limit.
Colorado	1990	8	8	Consecutive years.
Florida	1992	8	8	Consecutive years.
Idaho	1994	8	8	8 years in a 15-year period.
Maine	1993	8	8	Consecutive years; takes effect for 1996 election.
Massachusetts	1994	8	8	Four consecutive terms in 9 years.
Michigan	1992	6	8	Lifetime limit of 14 years.
Missouri	1992	8	8	16 years total service permitted.
Montana	1992	6	8	House members may serve 6 years in a 12-year period; senators, 8 out of 16 years.
Nebraska*	1992, 1994	—	8	Consecutive years; 1992 initiative invalidated by the Nebraska Supreme Court.
Nevada	1994	12	12	Lifetime limit.
Ohio	1992	8	8	Consecutive years, unless there is a 4-year break.
Oklahoma	1990	12	12	12-year lifetime limit for either or both houses.
Oregon	1992	6	8	Lifetime limit of 12 years.
South Dakota	1992	8	8	Consecutive years.
Utah	1994	12	12	Consecutive years; lifetime limit; enacted by the legislature.
Washington	1992	6	8	House members may serve 6 years in a 12-year period; senators, 8 out of 14 years; service prior to 1992 not counted.
Wyoming	1992	6	12	House members may serve 6 years in a 12-year period; senators, 12 of 24 years.

SOURCE: Compilation supplied by the National Conference of State Legislatures.
* Legislature is unicameral, and all legislators are called senators.

led to charges of bribery, extortion, and money laundering against seven legislators (Gurwitt 1991; Moore 1992). In 1992 the headlines featured a federal investigation of corruption in the Kentucky legislature, climaxing in the conviction of the former Speaker of the House Don Blandford on charges of extortion and racketeering (Loftus and Cross 1993). Charges of corruption and ethics violations have arisen in other states, as well—in New York and Texas, house Speakers were indicted in 1991, and in New Mexico a legislator was convicted on charges of corruption in 1992. These and other violations of ethical standards have precipitated enactment of new and tougher ethics legislation in many of the state legislatures. But despite enacting ethics legislation, creating ethics committees, requiring legislators to recite the codes of ethical conduct, convening ethical training sessions, and sharply restricting lobbyists, the public and the media remain markedly suspicious and cynical. Because the legislatures' ethical problems often stem from the handling of campaign funds, much of the new round of reform legislation concerns campaign finance regulation. In New Jersey the legislature restricted special-interest contributions to candidates and provided that contributions be made to party leadership committees; in Nebraska a program of public funding of campaigns was adopted (Hansen 1994a). Campaign finance reform remains high on the agenda of most legislatures.

CONCLUSION

The state legislatures have become much more formidable policy-making bodies than they used to be, and running for the legislature has become a more complex and expensive proposition than it was only a few years ago. The American state legislator struggles to resolve the demands of the constituency and the requirements of serving in the legislature. "Tuggings from the constituency are ever-present stimuli in the life of the legislator" (Keefe 1966, 69). The members' needs, explored and stimulated during the legislative race, are not necessarily the same as the needs of the legislature as an institution.

Men and women run for the legislature for many reasons—excitement, power, the deference given them, personal gain, a chance to advertise themselves, a need for self-esteem, the challenge of making good public policy, or a sense of loyalty to their political party. Serving in the legislature does not necessarily satisfy these needs, and, indeed, outstanding performance as a legislator may jeopardize the member's chances for reelection or advancement. If members perform in the legislature with an eye primarily to their reelection, the needs of the legislature and the state may be woefully slighted. But the temptation is great, especially so since Americans have a well-known tendency to respect and admire their own legislator more than the legislature as an institution.

Life in the legislature is often too ambiguous, too inconclusive, too harassing, and too disruptive of personal lives to satisfy highly qualified persons for long. Running for the legislature is not enough. And yet, the very act of running for office may influence the type of life a legislator lives in the legislature if, in the process, he or she comes to appreciate human failings and needs, human potential, and the diversity of conditions under which people live. The education of running for the legislature may help prepare good men and women for the task of compromise and the complexity of policy making that is part of legislative life.

In the legislature, all members are more or less equal and are not electorally responsible to one another. But to make laws, legislators must form coalitions large enough to make up a majority, "to find through the art of compromise a way of life in which nobody will escape some share of common burdens and in which everybody will get some share of the benefits of life which we together create" (Smith 1940, 55). That ideal, if practiced, can bridge the experiences of running for the legislature and legislating. And, in the practice, it may be possible to restore the balance between what can be reasonably expected of and admired in individual legislators and what the legislature can do through collective action. It has wisely been said that "if the legislative way can but keep the qualities of its defects, we must continue to allow it the defects of its qualities" (Smith 1940, 91).

REFERENCES

Barber, James D. 1965. *The Lawmakers.* New Haven: Yale University Press.

Basehart, Hubert Harry. 1980. "The Effect of Membership Stability on Continuity and Experience in U.S. State Legislative Committees." *Legislative Studies Quarterly* 5:55–68.

Bell, Charles G., and Charles M. Price. 1975. *The First Term: A Study of Legislative Socialization.* Beverly Hills, Calif.: Sage Publications.

Benjamin, Gerald, and Michael J. Malbin, eds. 1992. *Limiting Legislative Terms.* Washington, D.C.: CQ Press.

Berkman, Michael B. 1993. "Former State Legislators in the U.S. House of Representatives: Institutional and Policy Mastery." *Legislative Studies Quarterly* 18:77–104.

Bernick, E. Lee. 1978. "The Impact of U.S. Governors on Party Voting in One-Party Dominated Legislatures." *Legislative Studies Quarterly* 3:431–444.

BeVier, Michael J. 1979. *Politics Backstage: Inside the California Legislature.* Philadelphia: Temple University Press.

Beyle, Thad L. 1993. *State Government, 1993–1994.* Washington, D.C.: CQ Press.

Bositis, David. 1992. *Black State Legislators.* Washington, D.C.: Joint Center for Political and Economic Studies.

Boulard, Garry. 1995. "Seismic Shift in the South." *State Legislatures* 21, no. 1:16–21.

Breaux, David, and Malcolm Jewell. 1992. "Winning Big: The Incumbency Advantage in State Legislative Races." In *Changing Patterns in State Legislative Careers,* edited by Gary F. Moncrief and Joel A. Thompson. Ann Arbor: University of Michigan Press.

Broach, Glen T. 1972. "A Comparative Dimensional Analysis of Partisan and Urban-Rural Voting in State Legislatures." *Journal of Politics* 34:905–921.

Bryan, Frank M. 1981. *Politics in the Rural States.* Boulder, Colo.: Westview Press.

Bryce, James. 1906. *The American Commonwealth.* Vol. 1. New York: Macmillan.

Bullock, Charles S., III. 1992. "Minorities in State Legislatures." In *Changing Patterns in State Legislative Careers,* edited by Gary F. Moncrief and Joel A. Thompson. Ann Arbor: University of Michigan Press.

Bullock, Charles S., and Ronald K. Gaddie. 1993. "Changing from Multimember to Single-Member Districts: Partisan, Racial, and Gender Consequences." *State and Local Government Review* 25:155–163.

Caldeira, Gregory A., and Samuel C. Patterson. 1982. "Bringing Home the Votes: Electoral Outcomes in State Legislative Races." *Political Behavior* 4:33–67.

———. 1987. "Political Friendship in the Legislature." *Journal of Politics* 49:953–975.

———. 1988. "Contours of Friendship and Respect in the Legislature." *American Politics Quarterly* 16:466–485.

Caldeira, Gregory A., John A. Clark, and Samuel C. Patterson. 1993. "Political Respect in the Legislature." *Legislative Studies Quarterly* 18:3–28.

Campbell, Ballard C. 1980. *Representative Democracy.* Cambridge: Harvard University Press.

Carroll, John J., and Arthur English. 1981. "Governing the House: Leadership of the State Legislative Party." Paper presented at the annual meeting of the Midwest Political Science Association, Cincinnati, Ohio, April 15–18.

Carroll, Susan J. 1985. *Women as Candidates in American Politics.* Bloomington: Indiana University Press.

Clucas, Richard A. 1992. "Legislative Leadership and Campaign Support in California." *Legislative Studies Quarterly* 17:265–283.

———. 1995. *The Speaker's Electoral Connection: Willie Brown and the California Assembly.* Berkeley: Institute of Governmental Studies, University of California.

Coleman, Mary DeLorse. 1993. *Legislators, Law, and Public Policy: Political Change in Mississippi and the South.* Westport, Conn.: Greenwood Press.

Comer, John C., and James B. Johnson. 1978. *Nonpartisanship in the Legislative Process: Essays on the Nebraska Legislature.* Washington, D.C.: University Press of America.

Copeland, Gary W. 1993. "Legislative Career Planning under Term Limitations." Paper presented at the annual meeting of the American Political Science Association, Washington, D.C., September 2–5.

CSG (Council of State Governments). 1992. *The Book of the States, 1992–93.* Lexington, Ky.: Council of State Governments.

———. Various years. *The Book of the States.* Lexington, Ky.: Council of State Governments.

Cox, Gary W., and Scott Morgenstern. 1993. "*The Increasing Advantage of Incumbency in the U.S. States.*" Legislative Studies Quarterly 18:495–511.

Darcy, R., Susan Welch, and Janet Clark. 1994. *Women, Elections, and Representation.* 2d ed. Lincoln: University of Nebraska Press.

Dixon, Robert G., Jr. 1968. *Democratic Representation.* New York: Oxford University Press.

Donovan, Todd, and Joseph R. Snipp. 1994. "Support for Legislative Term Limitations in California: Group Representation, Partisanship, and Campaign Information." *Journal of Politics* 56:492–501.

Dow, Jay K., and James W. Endersby. 1994. "Campaign Contributions and Legislative Voting in the California Assembly." *American Politics Quarterly* 22:334–353.

Ehrenhalt, Alan. 1990. "A Coup in Connecticut: The Unmaking of a Leader—and Its Consequences." *Governing,* August, 74–79.

Elling, Richard C. 1979. "The Utility of State Legislative Casework as a Means of Oversight." *Legislative Studies Quarterly* 4:353–379.

———. 1980. "State Legislative Casework and State Administrative Performance." *Administration and Society* 12:327–356.

Erikson, Robert S., Norman R. Luttbeg, and William V. Holloway. 1975. "Knowing One's District: How Legislators Predict Referendum Voting." *American Journal of Political Science* 19:231–246.

Ethridge, Marcus E. 1981a. "Legislative Administrative Interaction as `Intrusive Access': An Empirical Analysis." *Journal of Politics* 43:473–492.

———. 1981b. "Legislative Participation in Policy Implementation: An Analysis of the Michigan Experience." Paper presented at the annual meeting of the Midwest Political Science Association, Cincinnati, Ohio, April 15–18.

Francis, Wayne L. 1989. *The Legislative Committee Game: A Comparative Analysis of Fifty States.* Columbus: Ohio State University Press.

———. 1993. "House to Senate Career Movement in the U.S. States: The Significance of Selectivity." *Legislative Studies Quarterly* 18:309–320.

Freeman, Patricia K., and Lilliard E. Richardson, Jr. 1994. "Casework in State Legislatures." *State and Local Government Review* 26:21–26.

Gierzynski, Anthony. 1992. *Legislative Party Campaign Committees in the American States.* Lexington: University Press of Kentucky.

Gierzynski, Anthony, and David A. Breaux. 1993. "Money and the Party Vote in State House Elections." *Legislative Studies Quarterly* 18:515–533.

Giles, Micheal W., and Anita Pritchard. 1985. "Campaign Expenditures and Legislative Elections in Florida." *Legislative Studies Quarterly* 10:71–88.

Gordon, Dianna. 1994. "Citizen Legislators—Alive and Well." *State Legislatures* 20, no. 1:24–27.

Grau, Craig H. 1981. "Competition in State Legislative Primaries." *Legislative Studies Quarterly* 6:35–54.

Gurwitt, Rob. 1991. "Deadly Stings and Wounded Legislatures." *Governing,* June, 26–31.

Hamm, Keith E. 1980. "U.S. State Legislative Committee Decisions: Similar Results in Different Settings." *Legislative Studies Quarterly* 5:31–54.

Hamm, Keith E., and Robert Harmel. 1993. "Legislative Party Development and the Speaker System: The Case of the Texas House." *Journal of Politics* 55:1140–1151.

Hamm, Keith E., and Roby D. Robertson. 1981. "Factors Influencing the Adoption of New Methods of Legislative Oversight in the U.S. States." *Legislative Studies Quarterly* 6:133–150.

Hansen, Karen. 1994a. "Our Beleaguered Institution." *State Legislatures* 20, no. 1:12–17.

———. 1994b. "Two Ways to Restrict the Campaign-Money Flow." *State Legislatures* 20, no. 3:13.

Hedlund, Ronald D., and Samuel C. Patterson. 1992. "The Electoral Antecedents of State Legislative Committee Assignments." *Legislative Studies Quarterly* 17:539–559.

Hickok, Eugene W., Jr. 1992. *The Reform of State Legislatures and the Changing Character of Representation.* Lanham, Md.: University Press of America.

Hill, John. 1990. "Louisiana Senate Unseats Governor-Backed Leader." *State Legislatures* 16, no. 7:17.

Hogan, Robert E. 1994. "Expenditure Patterns in State Legislative Campaigns." Paper presented at the annual meeting of the Southern Political Science Association, Atlanta, Ga., November 2–5.

Holbrook, Thomas M., and Charles M. Tidmarch. 1993. "The Effects of Leadership Positions on Votes for Incumbents in State Legislative Elections." *Political Research Quarterly* 46:897–909.

Ingram, Helen M., Nancy K. Laney, and John R. McCain. 1980. *A Policy Approach to Political Representation: Lessons from the Four Corner States.* Baltimore, Md.: Johns Hopkins University Press.

Jewell, Malcolm E. 1982. *Representation in State Legislatures.* Lexington: University Press of Kentucky.

Jewell, Malcolm E., and David Breaux. 1988. "The Effect of Incumbency on State Legislative Elections." *Legislative Studies Quarterly* 13:495–514.

Jewell, Malcolm E., and Penny M. Miller. 1988. *The Kentucky Legislature: Two Decades of Change.* Lexington: University Press of Kentucky.

Jewell, Malcolm E., and David M. Olson. 1988. *Political Parties and Elections in American States.* 3d ed. Homewood, Ill.: Dorsey Press.

Jewell, Malcolm E., and Samuel C. Patterson. 1986. *The Legislative Process in the United States.* 4th ed. New York: Random House.

Jewell, Malcolm E., and Marcia L. Whicker. 1994. *Legislative Leadership in the American States.* Ann Arbor: University of Michigan Press.

Jones, Rich. 1992. "The State Legislatures." In *The Book of the States, 1992–93,* vol. 29. Lexington, Ky.: Council of State Governments.

Keefe, William J. 1966. "The Functions and Powers of the State Legislatures." In *State Legislatures in American Politics,* edited by Alexander Heard. Englewood Cliffs, N.J.: Prentice-Hall.

Key, V. O., Jr. 1956. *American State Politics.* New York: Alfred A. Knopf.

Kirkpatrick, Jeane J. 1974. *Political Woman.* New York: Basic Books.

Kirkpatrick, Samuel A. 1978. *The Legislative Process in Oklahoma.* Norman: University of Oklahoma Press.

Kolasa, Bernard D. 1978. "Party Recruitment in Nonpartisan Nebraska." In *Nonpartisanship in the Legislative Process,* edited by John C. Comer and James B. Johnson. Washington, D.C.: University Press of America.

Kuklinski, James H., and Richard C. Elling. 1977. "Representational Role, Constituency Opinion, and Legislative Roll-Call Behavior." *American Journal of Political Science* 21:135–147.

Kurtz, Karl T. 1993. "The Election in Perspective." *State Legislatures* 19, no. 1:16–19.

LaVally, Rebecca. 1989. "In Control of the Legislature's Quiet Side." *California Journal* 20:19–22.

Loewenberg, Gerhard, and Samuel C. Patterson. 1979. *Comparing Legislatures.* Boston: Little, Brown.

Loftus, Tom, and Al Cross. 1993. "Lies, Bribes, and Videotape." *State Legislatures* 19, no. 7:42–47.

Loomis, Burdett A. 1994. *Time, Politics, and Policies: A Legislative Year.* Lawrence: University Press of Kansas.

McCrone, Donald J., and James H. Kuklinski. 1979. "The Delegate Theory of Representation." *American Journal of Political Science* 23:278–300.

McNitt, Andrew, and Edward Brazil. 1993. "Speakers of the State Houses: 1960–1989." *Comparative State Politics.* 14 (February): 31–42.

Moncrief, Gary F., and Joel A. Thompson, eds. 1992. "Electoral Structure and State Legislative Representation: A Research Note." *Journal of Politics* 54:246–256.

Moncrief, Gary F., Joel A. Thompson, Michael Haddon, and Robert Hoyer. 1992. "For Whom the Bell Tolls: Term Limits and State Legislatures." *Legislative Studies Quarterly* 17:37–47.

Moore, Richard. 1992. "The New Scalawags: How the South Carolina Legislature Really Works." In *The Reform of State Legislatures and the Changing Character of Representation,* edited by Eugene W. Hickok, Jr. Lanham, Md.: University Press of America.

Moss, Bill. 1993. "Sunshine State Detente." *State Legislatures* 19, no. 7:27–33.

Newman, Jody. 1994. *Perception and Reality: A Study Comparing the Success of Men and Women Candidates.* Washington, D.C.: National Women's Political Caucus.

Niemi, Richard G., Simon Jackman, and Laura R. Winsky. 1991. "Candidacies and Competitiveness in Multimember Districts." *Legislative Studies Quarterly* 16:91–109.

O'Connor, Patrick F. 1982. "The Legislature." *Louisiana Politics: Festival in a Labyrinth,* edited by James Bolner. Baton Rouge: Louisiana State University Press.

Opheim, Cynthia. 1994. "The Effect of U.S. State Legislative Term Limits Revisited." *Legislative Studies Quarterly* 19:49–59.

Patterson, Samuel C. 1972. "Party Opposition in the Legislature: The Ecology of Legislative Institutionalization." *Polity* 4:344–366.

———. 1994. "Legislative Politics in Ohio." In *Ohio Politics,* edited by Alexander P. Lamis. Kent, Ohio: Kent State University Press.

Patterson, Samuel C., and G. Robert Boynton. 1969. "Legislative Recruitment in a Civic Culture." *Social Science Quarterly* 50:243–263.

Patterson, Samuel C., and Gregory A. Caldeira. 1985. "Mailing in the Vote: Correlates and Consequences of Absentee Voting." *American Journal of Political Science* 29:766–788.

Patterson, Samuel C., Ronald D. Hedlund, and G. Robert Boynton. 1975. *Representatives and Represented.* New York: John Wiley and Sons.

Patterson, Samuel C., Randall B. Ripley, and Steven V. Quinlan. 1992. "Citizens' Orientations toward Legislatures: Congress and the State Legislature." *Western Political Quarterly* 45:315–338.

Redfield, Kent D., and Jack R. Van Der Slik. 1992. "The Circulation of Political Money in Illinois Legislative Elections." Paper presented at the annual meeting of the Midwest Political Science Association, Chicago, April 9–11.

Reeves, Tim. 1993. "Power Plays in Pennsylvania." *State Legislatures* 19, no. 7:36–37.

Rodgers, Jack, Robert Sittig, and Susan Welch. 1984. "The Legislature." In *Nebraska Government and Politics,* edited by Robert D. Miewald. Lincoln: University of Nebraska Press.

Rosenthal, Alan. 1974a. *Legislative Performance in the States.* New York: Free Press.

———. 1974b. "Turnover in State Legislatures." *American Journal of Political Science* 18:109–616.

———. 1981. *Legislative Life.* New York: Harper and Row.

———. 1993a. "The Legislative Institution—In Transition and at Risk." In *The State of the States,* 2d ed., edited by Carl E. Van Horn. Washington, D.C.: CQ Press.

———. 1993b. *The Third House: Lobbyists and Lobbying in the States.* Washington, D.C.: CQ Press.

Ross, Diane. 1981. "The Day the Republicans Stole the Senate." *Illinois Issues* 7, no. 4:4–6.

Salzman, Ed. 1981. "The Powder-Keg Speakership: How Long Can Brown Hold It?" *California Journal* 12:5–9.

Seligman, Lester G., Michael R. King, Chong Lim Kim, and Roland E. Smith. 1974. *Patterns of Recruitment: A State Chooses Its Lawmakers.* Chicago: Rand McNally.

Shan, Chao-Chi, and Jeffrey M. Stonecash. 1994. "Legislative Resources and Electoral Margins: New York State Senate, 1950–1990." *Legislative Studies Quarterly* 19:79–93.

Smith, T. V. 1940. *The Legislative Way of Life.* Chicago: University of Chicago Press.

Songer, Donald R. 1988. "The Influence of Empirical Research: Committee vs. Floor Decision Making." *Legislative Studies Quarterly* 13:375–392.

Sorauf, Frank J. 1963. *Party and Representation: Legislative Politics in Pennsylvania.* New York: Atherton Press.

———. 1988. *Money in American Elections.* Glenview, Ill.: Scott, Foresman.

Squire, Peverill. 1988. "Member Career Opportunities and the Internal Organization of Legislatures." *Journal of Politics* 50:726–744.

———. 1993. "Professionalization and Public Opinion of State Legislatures." *Journal of Politics* 55:479–491.

Stollman, Gerald H. 1978. *Michigan State Legislators and Their Work.* Washington, D.C.: University Press of America.

Stonecash, Jeffrey M. 1988. "Working at the Margins: Campaign Finance and Party Strategy in New York Assembly Elections." *Legislative Studies Quarterly* 13:477–493.

Thaemert, Rita. 1994. "Twenty Percent and Climbing." *State Legislatures* 20, no. 1:28–32.

Theodoulou, Stella Z. 1985. *The Louisiana Republican Party, 1948–1984: The Building of a State Political Party.* Tulane Studies in Political Science. New Orleans: Tulane University.

Thomas, Sue. 1994. *How Women Legislate.* New York: Oxford University Press.
Thompson, Joel A., and William Cassie. 1992. "Party and PAC Contributions to North Carolina Legislative Candidates." *Legislative Studies Quarterly* 17:409–416.
Thompson, Joel A., William Cassie, and Malcolm E. Jewell. 1994. "A Sacred Cow or Just a Lot of Bull? Party and PAC Money in State Legislative Elections." *Political Research Quarterly* 47:223–237.
Tobin, Richard J., and Edward Keynes. 1975. "Institutional Differences in the Recruitment Process: A Four-State Study." *American Journal of Political Science* 19:667–682.
Traub, Patrick J. 1989. "Speakers du jour in Indiana." *State Legislatures* 15, no. 7:17–22.
Truman, David B. 1971. *The Government Process.* 2d ed. New York: Alfred A Knopf.
Tucker, Harvey J., and Ronald E. Weber. 1992. "Electoral Change in U.S. States: System versus Constituency Competition." In *Changing Patterns in State Legislative Careers,* edited by Gary F. Moncrief and Joel A. Thompson. Ann Arbor: University of Michigan Press.
Tufte, Edward R. 1973. "The Relationship between Seats and Votes in Two-Party Systems." *American Political Science Review* 67:540–554.
Uslaner, Eric M., and Ronald E. Weber. 1977. *Patterns of Decision Making in State Legislatures.* New York: Praeger.
———. 1979. "U.S. State Legislators' Opinions and Perceptions of Constituency Attitudes." *Legislative Studies Quarterly* 4:563–585.
Wahlke, John C., Heinz Eulau, William Buchanan, and Leroy C. Ferguson. 1962. *The Legislative System.* New York: John Wiley and Sons.
Weberg, Brian. 1988. "Changes in Legislative Staff." *Journal of State Government* 61:190–197.
Weeks, George, and Don Weeks. 1993. "Taking Turns." *State Legislatures* 19, no. 7:19–25.
Wheeler, Charles N., III. 1989. "Was This Nebraska?" *Illinois Issues* 15, no. 6:6–7.
Wiggins, Charles W., Keith E. Hamm, and Charles G. Bell. 1992. "Interest-Group and Party Influence Agents in the Legislative Process: A Comparative State Analysis." *Journal of Politics* 54:82–100.
Woo, Lillian C. 1994. "Today's Legislators: Who They Are and Why They Run." *State Legislatures* 20, no. 4:28–33.
Zeigler, Richard 1989. "The Road to Legislative Hell." *California Journal* 20:11–14.

SUGGESTED READINGS

Benjamin, Gerald, and Michael J. Malbin, eds. *Limiting Legislative Terms.* Washington, D.C.: CQ Press, 1992. Authors of chapters in this anthology address the emergence and development of the term limitation movement and assay the effects of term limitations on legislative behavior and performance.
Jewell, Malcolm E., and Samuel C. Patterson. *The Legislative Process in the United States.* 4th ed. New York: Random House, 1986. This general treatise on American legislative politics includes much information about state legislatures and emphasizes comparisons between state legislatures and Congress.
Muir, William K., Jr. *Legislature: California's School of Politics.* Chicago: University of Chicago Press, 1982. California, the most populous state, has a highly institutionalized state legislature, more like Congress than the legislature of any other state. Muir's analysis is based on his close personal observation of the California legislature at work.
Thomas, Sue. *How Women Legislate.* New York: Oxford University Press, 1994. From a survey of women legislators in a dozen states, Thomas demonstrates how women have come to influence the lawmaking process in the state legislatures.
Uslaner, Eric M., and Ronald E. Weber. *Patterns of Decision Making in State Legislatures.* New York: Praeger, 1977. From a survey of state legislators in all fifty states, Uslaner and Weber probe the ingredients influencing legislators' decision-making behavior.

CHAPTER 6

 Governors
The Middlemen and Women in
Our Political System

THAD BEYLE

Greatest job in the world, as most Governors, I suspect, tell you.
—Michael Dukakis, *Governor of Massachusetts, 1975–1979, 1983–1991*

At the top of each state's political and governmental hierarchy is the governor—the person who personifies the state to many. He or she is seen as the most powerful political personality in most states; the state's legislature, bureaucracy, press, politics, and policies are affected by or bear the imprint of the governor.

These major actors in our states are supposed to fill a long roster of roles. A handbook written just for governors lists the following: head of the executive branch, legislative leader, head of party, national figure, family member, and ceremonial chief (NGA 1978). Other roles are equally broad in responsibility, such as those of intergovernmental actor and policy leader, and some appear to be narrower in scope, such as those of manager and chief crisis manager (Morehouse 1981; NGA 1981).

How a governor responds to and handles unexpected crises greatly influences how we perceive his or her overall performance as a governor. Gov. Pete Wilson (R-Calif., 1991–) has repeatedly faced crises, from earthquakes to fires to massive budget deficits, and his reactions have helped frame the public's view of him as a governor. As former governor Scott M. Matheson (D-Utah, 1977–1985) argues, "[T]he public expects the governor to take a lead . . . and a governor found wanting in a crisis situation rarely recovers politically" (Matheson 1986, 200).

How a governor performs in day-to-day administrative actions can also influence how we perceive his or her performance in office. Most governors perform admirably and their administrations are well respected; others do not perform well and struggle as they govern. In the early 1990s, several governors lost their constituents' support and respect and left office before they wanted to. One example is former governor Joan Finney (D-Kan.), who was elected in 1990 and soon proved to be a poor governor in many observers' eyes. Generally considered the weakest Kansas governor for several decades, she declined to seek her party's 1994 nomination for a second term. Another such case is that of former governor David Walter (D-Okla.), also elected in 1990, who fought allegations of political corruption from the day he took office and finally pled guilty to a misdemeanor and announced he would not seek reelection in 1994.

Governors have not always been at the top of the pecking order in their states, nor have they always been at the center of most state activities. The negligible powers and responsibilities given to the earliest state governors reflected the basic antipathy the citizens of the colonial period felt toward executive power—a dislike carried over from their relations with imposed colonial governors. Over the next two centuries, the governors gradually gained more power, and many of the early restrictions placed on them were removed or greatly reduced. This did not happen in an orderly fashion; rather, it happened in a series of incremental steps and in varying degrees across the states. And in many states, new restrictions or new problems and challenges faced the governors as state governments evolved.

Beginning with the democratization movement in the early nineteenth century, the selection of governors moved from the legislature to the people. This "pursuit of representativeness" also added new restrictions on the governor as other state administrative officials came to be selected by direct popular election (Kaufman 1963, 36). Thus, some of the administrative functions were placed outside the control of the governor and into the hands of others directly responsible to the people.

As it became apparent following the Civil War that legislative bodies could not run the states or administer programs, and as patronage and corruption increased, more changes occurred. Restrictions were placed on gubernatorial and legislative powers, and a drive began to raise the competence of state government—like governments at all levels—through the use of merit systems and civil service personnel procedures in which "what you know" became more important than "who you know." Further, as new problems and responsibilities arose, agencies, boards, and commissions were established to handle them—again, often outside the direct control of any executive official. These efforts to obtain something called "neutral competence" in running government were an attempt to separate politics from administration. The governors and legislators were obviously on the political side, and these reforms were meant to maintain that separation.

In the twentieth century, constitutional revision and executive branch reorganization have changed state governments and clarified lines of authority. Governors now have longer terms of office, can succeed themselves, and have more staff for assistance. In addition, they have been given considerable budget authority to help control the executive branch and more veto power to use in their legislative negotiations. At the same time, however, the strength and reach of the civil service and merit systems have increased, providing state employees with a degree of protection and even insulation from the governor.

In this chapter, I examine the current status of the American governorship and discuss the following questions. First, who are the governors and how do they become governors? What is the nature of gubernatorial politics? Second, what powers do our states provide to the governors so they may fulfill their roles? To what extent do these powers vary across the fifty states and by individual governors? Third, what are the major roles that all governors must perform? How do these roles provide governors with greater informal powers to achieve their goals? Last, what do governors do after the governorship? What options are available to these key state actors following their tenure in office? In a sense, I follow the trajectory of the individuals who seek to be governor, win the election, serve as governors, and move on from the governorship. Throughout the chapter, I present the differences between states, governorships, and governors to point out the diversity inherent in the fifty-state federal union. This should not overshadow the larger point of understanding, which is how similar these actors, their offices, and their responsibilities are, despite the diversity.

BECOMING GOVERNOR

The First Job Makes a Difference

A basic clue to what a particular public office is all about, and its position within any political-power hierarchy, is who seeks and fills that office. In 1949 one critic moaned that "there are some enlightened, honest, and well-intentioned governors . . . but they are pathetically few in number" (Allen 1949, xi). More recently, an observer has argued that the "new breed" of governors that arose between 1950 and 1975 are no longer ill-prepared to govern or lead. They are, he said, "vigorous, incisive, and thoroughly trained leaders" who are younger and better educated than their predecessors (Sabato 1978, 1, 57).

Of interest here are the career patterns that the governors pursued prior to the governorship. What are the public office steps on the gubernatorial ambition ladder? "Frequency trees" for the 225 elected governors serving between 1970 and 1994 are presented in Table 6-1.

This table should be read from right to left. For example, forty-three, or 19 percent, of the governors in office between 1970 and 1994 held a state legislative seat as their "penultimate office," their last public office before election as governor. Moving leftward to the "Office experience" column, we find that 100 percent of those in the state legislative category had, by definition, experience in the state legislature, and seven, or 16 percent, had also had law enforcement experience. Moving left to the "First office" column, we find that thirty-two, or 74 percent, of

Table 6-1 Prior Office Careers of Serving Governors, 1970–1994

Those following path %	No.	Office	First office* %	No.	Office experience† %	No.	Penultimate office‡ %	No.
14	32	Legislative	74	32	100	43	State legislative§ 19	43
3	7	Law enforcement	16	7	16	7		
0	0	Statewide elective	0	0	5	2		
0	0	Congress	0	0	0	0		
<1	1	Administrative	2	1	5	2		
1	3	Local elective	7	3	7	3		
0	0	Party position	0	0	9	4		
0	0	Other office	0	0	5	2		
2	5	Legislative	16	5	22	7	Law enforcement‖ 14	32
10	22	Law enforcement	69	22	100	32		
0	0	Statewide elective	0	0	3	1		
0	0	Congress	0	0	0	0		
<1	2	Administrative	6	2	9	3		
0	0	Local elective	0	0	3	1		
0	0	Party position	0	0	0	0		
1	3	Other office	9	3	9	3		
12	28	Legislative	47	28	65	39	Statewide elective# 27	60
3	7	Law enforcement	12	7	13	8		
2	5	Statewide elective	8	5	100	60		
0	0	Congress	0	0	2	1		
<1	2	Administrative	3	2	12	7		
5	11	Local elective	18	11	12	7		
2	4	Party position	7	4	12	7		
1	3	Other office	5	3	5	3		
7	16	Legislative	53	16	40	12	Congress** 13	30
<1	2	Law enforcement	7	2	10	3		
0	0	Statewide elective	0	0	10	3		
2	4	Congress	43	13	100	30		
<1	2	Administrative	7	2	3	1		
2	5	Local elective	17	5	20	6		
<1	1	Party position	3	1	3	1		
0	0	Other office	0	0	3	1		
8	18	No prior office††					Governor 8	18
2	4	Legislative	29	4	36	5	Administrative‡‡ 6	14
<1	2	Law enforcement	14	2	14	2		
0	0	Statewide elective	0	0	14	2		
0	0	Congress	0	0	0	0		
2	5	Administrative	36	5	100	14		
<1	2	Local elective	14	2	14	2		
0	0	Party position	0	0	7	1		
<1	1	Other office	7	1	7	1		
<1	1	Legislative	8	1	17	2	Local elective§§ 5	12
<1	1	Law enforcement	8	1	17	2		
0	0	Statewide elective	0	0	8	1		
0	0	Congress	0	0	0	0		
0	0	Administration	0	0	0	0		
3	6	Local elective	50	6	100	12		
<1	1	Party position	8	1	8	1		
<1	1	Other office	8	1	8	1		

Table 6-1 (*continued*)

Those following path %	No.	Office	First office %	No.	Office experience %	No.	Penultimate office %	No.
0	0	Legislative	0	0	0	0		
<1	1	Law enforcement	17	1	17	1		
0	0	Statewide election	0	0	0	0		
0	0	Congress	0	0	0	0	Party position‖‖	
0	0	Administrative	0	0	0	0	3	6
0	0	Local elective	0	0	0	0		
2	5	Party position	83	5	100	6		
0	0	Other office	0	0	0	0		
0	0	Legislative	0	0	0	0		
<1	2	Law enforcement	20	2	20	2		
0	0	Statewide election	0	0	0	0		
0	0	Congress	0	0	0	0	Other office##	
<1	2	Administrative	20	2	30	3	4	10
<1	1	Local elective	10	1	10	1		
<1	1	Party position	10	1	10	1		
2	4	Other office	40	4	100	10		
Total							99	225

SOURCES: The design of this "office frequency tree" has been developed from Sabato 1983, 33–45, and Schlesinger 1966, 91.

NOTE: This figure excludes governors who succeeded to office because of the death, resignation, or impeachment of their predecessor, but who failed to win election in their own right.

*The first public office in a politician's career.

†An office held sometime in a politician's career.

‡Last office held prior to election as governor.

§A seat in the lower or upper house of the state legislature.

‖County and city attorneys, district attourney, U.S. attorney, judges at all levels, CIA and FBI personnel, and state attorney general (even if elected by statewide vote).

#All offices elected statewide by the voters with the exception of the attorney general. The number and kind of statewide office differ from state to state.

** Seats in the U.S. House of Representatives or U.S. Senate.

††The governor never held any public or political office, as defined above, before election as governor.

‡‡All public offices on local, statewide, and federal levels that are not elective. These are sometimes appointive and other times career positions. (No law enforcement offices are included in this category.) At the state level, elective offices in some states (such as the state auditor) are "administrative" in others.

§§All elective offices at the local level except county and city attorneys or district attorneys.

‖‖A position of formal leadership at the local, state, or national level of a political party.

##Public or political office not falling into the preceding categories.

these "legislative office" governors first began their public careers as state legislators, and seven, or 16 percent, began in law enforcement. The column farthest to the left gives the percentages of all governors who followed each particular office path to the governorship: thus, thirty-two, or 14 percent, of the 225 governors held a legislative seat both as their first office and as the penultimate office, while seven, or 3 percent, began public life in law enforcement and then advanced through state legislative service to the governor's chair.

The most frequent paths followed to become governor between 1970 and 1994 were the state legislature (thirty-two, or 14 percent, who entered as a state legislator later became governor and twenty-eight, or 12 percent, who entered as a legislator later won a statewide office and then become governor) and law enforcement (twenty-two, or 10 percent, who entered through law enforcement then become governor). Other paths, such as no prior elective office experience (8 percent), entry as a legislator but with subsequent service in Congress (7 percent), or beginning in local elective office and moving to the governorship via another statewide elective office (5 percent), are less frequent. As shown in Table 6-1, the most significant entry point is the state legislature, where 86 of the 225 governors (38 percent) began their careers.

Several other major patterns are evident. First, looking just at all previous public office service, we see that 108 of the 225 governors (48 percent) had some state legislative experience, and 73 of them (32 percent) had held a statewide elective office at some point in their careers.[1] Thus, an elective state government position is an important rung on a gubernatorial career ladder. For 57 of the 225 governors, law enforcement is a significant office experience (25 percent). The other types of office experience—Congress, administrative, local elective, party position—were held by between 9 and 14 percent of the governors.

Second, elective statewide positions—whether lieutenant governor, secretary of state, state treasurer, state attorney general, or state auditor—provide a strong jumping-off position for candidates for the governorship. In addition to the sixty who moved up from a statewide office, there were the fourteen elective state attorneys general in the law enforcement category, the twenty former governors who won their seats back after sitting out a term or two, and the four U.S. senators who won the governorship in the period. Thus, we see that ninety-eight of the governors advanced from elective statewide offices (44 percent).

Of the incumbent governors in 1994, twenty-one moved up from a statewide elective position, five others were former governors, and three were former U.S. senators. Another, Gov. Christine Todd Whitman (R-N.J.), had run a nearly successful U.S. Senate campaign against Senator Bill Bradley (D-N.J.) in 1990. Thus, thirty of the fifty governors serving in 1994 had had statewide elective and service experience prior to their successful run for the governor's chair. Seven of the other incumbents had had no prior office experience, five were former U.S. congressmen, three had moved up from the legislature and three from local government positions, and one each came from a law enforcement, a political party role, or an administrative position.

Within the 1970–1994 period the penultimate office varied somewhat among the states according to party and region. Among the 128 Democratic governors, 53 percent used statewide and state legislative offices as the penultimate office. By contrast, of the 95 Republican governors, only 38 percent used those spring-

1. The number 108 and percentage (48) were determined by adding the frequencies for each office in the "Office experience" column. For example, the state legislative frequencies are 43 + 7 + 39 + 12 + 5 + 2 = 108, which, divided by the 225 governors who served in the period involved, equals 48 percent. The number 83 and percentage (37) were determined by adding the frequencies for each statewide elective office in the "Office experience" column (2 + 1 + 60 + 3 + 2 + 1 = 69), and adding to that total the 14 elected attorneys general (not shown separately in table) from the law enforcement category.

boards. Some distinct regional patterns also emerge. Only 35 percent of the forty-three northeastern governors used these state offices as their springboards, compared with 52 percent in the Midwest, 47 percent in the South, and 46 percent in the West.

There has also been fluctuation in the number of governors moving from the U.S. Congress to the state house, from 9.5 percent between 1900 and 1958 (Schlesinger 1966, 91), down to 6.3 percent in the 1960s (Sabato 1983, 40), and up to 13.3 percent between 1970 and 1994. The growth in this avenue is most pronounced in the South, and smallest in the Midwest and West.

A part of the political calculus involved in making this type of move is the ability to do so without jeopardizing one's current congressional seat. Some states have off-year gubernatorial elections, which allow members of Congress to campaign while retaining their federal seat. In some other states, such as Connecticut, the timing of the party nominations permits a member of Congress to hold the seat until the nomination is won and then resign in time for the election campaign (Sabato 1983, 41).

By and large, the evidence suggests that previous electoral experience (with the attendant visibility) at the statewide, congressional, or state legislative level is one of the most important steps to the governorship. Such experience was had in the penultimate office of most of the governors. The career ladders of those who ran and failed to win the governorship are missing here. Would their paths to defeat be substantially different from the paths of those who won? It is an interesting question to consider.

There are a few hints if we reverse our perspective and look at a few specific elective positions in the states and see how successful the occupants have been in moving from them to the governorship. Using a shorter time frame (1977–1994), we look at those lieutenant governors, attorneys general, state treasurers, and Speakers of the house who sought the governorship. In these 216 races, lieutenant governors were the most likely to run for governor (in 28 percent of the races), followed by attorneys general (in 25 percent), state treasurers (in 12 percent), and Speakers of the state house (in 4 percent). State treasurers were the most successful when they ran (35 percent) and Speakers the least successful (22 percent); lieutenant governors (28 percent) and attorneys general (26 percent) fell in the middle (Beyle 1994). Their success rates are considerably less than incumbent and former governors but higher than for those in some of the offices noted in Table 6-1.

The Election Campaign: It Costs Money

Will Rogers once said, "Politics has got so expensive that it takes a lot of money to get beat with." Like other political campaigns described in Chapter 3, during the last few decades the costs of running for and winning the governor's seat have escalated rapidly. In 1956, the average cost of a gubernatorial campaign was estimated to be $100,000 (up to $300,000 in the more populated states); any "political skullduggery" would be on top of that (Ransone 1956, 105–106). Those 1956 dollars would be equal to just over a half million dollars and nearly $1.6 million, respectively, in 1993 dollars.[2] By 1990, the average cost of the thirty-six gubernatorial elections had leapt to $10.6 million; in the two campaigns held in 1993, the average cost was just under $18 million.

The 1990 election in California cost nearly $58.8 million, and in Texas it cost $55.9 million in officially reported expenditures—no one knows how much more was spent and not reported. While more populous states such as California, Texas, and New York might be expected to have expensive races, ten of the eighteen most expensive races were in southern states, where one-party Democratic dominance is declining and being replaced by costly candidate-oriented campaigns. In the same period, twelve gubernatorial candidates spent more than $15 million each in their quest for the governor's chair—seven of these candidates won.

The reasons for such costs and their continuing escalation are many. Changes in the style of campaigning are the most significant among them. With the transformation of state political parties and the decline of party identification among voters, candidates cannot afford to sit back and work with the party regulars to deliver the votes needed for winning. Going from county to county and meeting with the local politicos may solidify some votes and bring together part of a winning coalition, but doing so takes time, hits too few people, and does not deliver enough votes.

The most direct path to the potential voters is through the mass media, and that costs a lot of money. Opinion polls, political consultants, media consultants, direct-mail persuasion and fund-raising, telephone banks, and rapid travel throughout the state are all expensive, but all are needed in contemporary campaigns. The 1988 gubernatorial election in Utah provides a good example of the cost of media in a campaign. The four major candidates spent nearly $4.3 million, of which over 46.5 percent, or nearly $2 million, was spent for communications media. For the not-so-well-known candidate in a party primary or the general election, "electronic advertising is the only way to gain visibility" (Morehouse 1987). As one political consultant noted, "[E]veryone knows that half the money spent in a political campaign is wasted. The trouble is that nobody knows which half" (North Carolina Center 1989).

What, in effect, all this money adds up to is the cost of building a winning coalition. As Sabato has suggested, this involves the creation of a party "substitute," through which the candidate constructs his own campaign organization for his or her race (Sabato 1978).

Why do so many candidates spend so much of their own and other people's money to become governor? One reason might be the salary a governor receives,

2. All dollar amounts are 1993 dollars unless otherwise specified.

a proposition suggesting that a candidate does so for the money he or she can make while being governor. In 1993, gubernatorial salaries averaged $87,166, ranging from $130,000 in New York to $54,254 in Montana. Adjusted for inflation, this average is slightly less than the average salary governors made in 1955 (Beyle 1995). These may be goodly sums but scarcely warrant the amounts spent in the campaign to become governor.

Salary is not the only monetary reward a governor can receive: upon leaving office, some former governors can obtain high-paying positions in the private sector. Those who are lawyers often open or join a law firm in the state capital and receive large retainers to serve as legal representatives or lobbyists for various interests that purchase the former governor's unique access to state officials and agencies. Thus some candidates may spend the money in campaigns for the money they can make after being governor.

A third reason is tied to the political ambitions of the gubernatorial candidates. The governorship can serve as a launching pad for the individual to seek other offices, such as a seat in the U.S. Senate or even the presidency. In the twentieth century, more than 120 governors moved on to the U.S. Senate; in the 103d Congress (1993–1994) sixteen former governors had Senate seats, and one former governor was sitting in the House of Representatives. Sixteen former governors have become president, and governors have been candidates for either the presidency or the vice presidency in forty-four of the nation's fifty-one presidential elections. Most governors, however, go no further than the governorship; more than 2,000 have served in the office, and for most it is the final elective office they hold (Beyle 1988a, 134–135).

Of course, any listing of the reasons for spending large amounts of money in a political campaign must include the desire to perform public service for the good of the state and its citizens. Even so, it still costs a great deal to become a statesman or stateswoman. The cost of gubernatorial campaigns is summarized in Table 6-2. In the sixteen years from 1977 to 1993, the average cost of gubernatorial campaigns was $8.6 million per state. Over that period, this amounted to an average expenditure of $3.87 for every voter registered in 1992.

In seven states (four in the South plus California, New Jersey, and New York), an average of $18 million or more was spent on winning gubernatorial campaigns in the 1977–1993 election period; and in nine states (five in the South, three in the Midwest, and one in the Northeast), the average was between $10 and $18 million. The size of the state in population is clearly related to these costs: eleven of these sixteen states are among the sixteen most populous states. The five anomalous states according to population rank were in the South— Louisiana ($24.7 million), Kentucky ($19.3 million), Tennessee ($11.7 million), West Virginia ($10.5 million), and Alabama ($10.4 million).

Seven of these expensive states have also seen rather equal partisan competition for the governors' offices because the Democrats and Republicans have either split the races evenly or almost evenly over the period. In the other nine

Table 6-2 The Average Cost of Campaigns for Governor, by State and Cost Category (in 1993 dollars)

State and cost category	Average cost* Campaigns as reported (millions of $)	Average cost* Per no. of registered voters† ($)	Region	Size rank Pop.‡	Size rank Land	Party % of Republican wins
Over $18 million						
Texas§	39.6	4.69	South	3	2	33
California‖	28.6	1.90	West	1	3	71
New York#	25.1	2.78	Northeast	2	30	29
Louisiana**	24.7	10.98	South	21	31	14
Florida§	22.3	3.41	South	4	22	29
Kentucky**	19.3	9.31	South	24	37	14
New Jersey††	18.7	4.60	Northeast	9	46	50
Between $10 million and $18 million						
Illinois§	14.9	2.25	Midwest	6	24	86
Pennsylvania§	11.9	1.99	Northeast	5	33	57
Tennessee§	11.7	4.28	South	17	34	57
Michigan§	11.5	2.65	Midwest	8	23	71
Virginia††	11.5	3.77	South	12	36	50
Ohio‡‡	11.4	1.74	Midwest	7	35	57
North Carolina§§	11.1	2.92	South	10	28	43
West Virginia‖‖	10.5	10.93	South	35	41	43
Alabama§	10.4	4.38	South	22	29	29
Between $5 million and $10 million						
Massachusetts#	8.8	2.62	Northeast	13	45	43
Missouri##	8.4	2.75	Midwest	15	19	57
Georgia§	7.7	2.42	South	31	32	14
Alaska§	7.3	23.82	West	48	1	43
Mississippi***	7.3	4.43	South	31	32	14
Indiana##	6.4	2.02	Midwest	14	38	71
Minnesota§	6.4	2.00	Midwest	20	12	43
Hawaii§	5.9	12.66	West	40	47	0
Washington##	5.7	2.02	West	16	20	57
Connecticut§	5.4	2.78	Northeast	27	48	14
Oklahoma§	5.4	2.36	South	28	18	43
Maryland§	5.4	2.19	South	19	42	14
Arizona§	5.3	2.72	West	23	6	75
Kansas§	5.2	3.80	Midwest	32	14	22
Between $2 million and $5 million						
South Carolina§	4.5	2.91	South	25	40	43
Nebraska§	4.2	4.39	Midwest	36	15	43
Wisconsin§	4.0	1.12	Midwest	18	26	63
Iowa§	4.0	2.38	Midwest	30	25	89
Rhode Island§	3.8	6.93	Northeast	43	50	43
Colorado§	3.7	1.87	West	26	8	29
Maine§	3.6	4.39	Northeast	39	39	29
Arkansas§	3.6	2.72	South	33	27	25
New Mexico§	3.5	4.91	West	37	5	50
Oregon#	3.3	1.86	West	29	10	71
Nevada§	3.2	4.98	West	38	7	43
Utah##	2.8	2.91	West	34	12	43
Montana##	2.3	4.33	West	44	4	29
Less than $2 million						
Wyoming§	1.8	7.87	West	50	26	29
Idaho§	1.8	2.99	West	42	13	14
New Hampshire§	1.7	2.54	Northeast	41	44	79

Table 6-2 *(continued)*

State and cost category	Average cost*		Region	Size rank		Party
	Campaigns as reported (millions of $)	Per no. of registered voters† ($)		Pop.‡	Land	% of Republican wins
Less than $2 million *(continued)*						
South Dakota§	1.6	3.67	Midwest	45	16	67
Delaware##	1.3	3.83	Northeast	46	49	71
Vermont§	0.9	2.47	Northeast	49	43	50
North Dakota‖‖	0.8	1.70	Midwest	47	17	29
Average	8.6	3.87				44

SOURCES: Calculated by the author. Registered voter data from Barone and Ujifusa 1993; estimated population figures from SPR 1993, table A-1; land rankings from Barone and Ujifusa 1987.

NOTE: Calculation of 1993 dollars based on the consumer price index for all urban consumers, U.S. Department of Labor, Bureau of Labor Statistics, using the 1982–1984 average value, with the 1993 dollar equal to 100.

*Determined by converting the costs for all gubernatorial elections for which expenditure data are available to 1993 dollars, adding these costs, then dividing the total by the number of elections involved.

†Determined by dividing the average cost of the elections by the number of registered voters in the state (1992).

‡Estimated population rank as of 1992.

§All elections between 1978 and 1993.

‖All elections between 1958 and 1993.

#All elections between 1966 and 1993.

**All elections between 1975 and 1993.

††All elections between 1965 and 1993, except 1969.

‡‡All elections between 1974 and 1993.

§§All elections between 1968 and 1993.

‖‖All elections between 1980 and 1993.

##All elections between 1976 and 1993.

***All elections between 1979 and 1993.

states, the governors' races been dominated by one party; indeed, in two states, Illinois and New York, by one individual, James R. Thompson (R-Ill., 1977–1991) and Mario M. Cuomo (D-N.Y., 1983–1995).

At the low end of the scale are seven states in which the campaign for the governor's chair costs less than $2 million. All are among the least densely populated, and in all but Vermont one party tended to dominate their governors' races.

If we control for the size of the registered voting population in each state, however, another picture appears. The most expensive gubernatorial election state is Alaska ($23.82 per voter registered in 1992), followed by Hawaii ($12.66), Louisiana ($10.98), West Virginia ($10.93), Kentucky ($9.31), and Wyoming ($7.87). Three of these six states are in the South, but the other three—Alaska, Hawaii, Wyoming—have small populations spread about in some unique ways. It costs more to reach the voters in these states. Furthermore, nine of the sixteen most expensive states actually have costs per registered voter below the average cost of $3.87 for all fifty states. So geography also plays a considerable role in the cost of gubernatorial elections.

Which of these factors is the most significant probably varies not only by state but by candidate and by circumstances. Individual governor's races are generally more expensive when political parties are weak, an open seat is up, the race is highly contested from nomination to general election, there is a partisan shift due to the election, or an incumbent is unseated (Beyle 1988b, 21–22). A time factor may also be involved: in the 1980s, more states (thirty-one) saw the costs of their races escalate than decline (twelve); in the 1990s more states (thirty-one) have seen their races cost less than in the 1980s, although the much higher costs of the 1994 elections (in 1994 dollars) in at least seventeen states reversed this trend.

How Much Opportunity Is There to Become Governor?

Another constraint on individuals wishing to become governors is the availability of opportunities to do so.[3] Just how often do the governors' chairs have new occupants?

The twentieth century has seen a decline in the number of such opportunities. One of the causes is obviously the executive reform movement, which has increased most gubernatorial terms from two years to four and has allowed more governors to seek reelection. In fact, several recent governors have effectively made the office their career, thereby closing off opportunities for others for more than a decade.

To demonstrate this change, the data in Table 6-3 indicate that there was a much greater opportunity to become governor after the Civil War, when the thirty-seven states averaged 4.2 governors per state in the 1870s, than in the 1980s, when the fifty states averaged 1.1 new governors per state. In the 1980s only two states—Kentucky and Mississippi—had three new governors, while four—Idaho, Massachusetts, Minnesota, Oklahoma—did not see a new governor in the decade (Beyle ["Term Limits"] 1992, 164, 166). Longer terms, the ability to succeed to another term, and former governors reentering the office have greatly reduced the opportunities for outsiders to be elected to governorships.

This state of affairs is significant for politically ambitious individuals in various states, because it suggests a further tightening of electoral opportunities at the top of the states' political ladders. An earlier study by Schlesinger (1966) indicated that only the U.S. Senate seats tended to be career offices and that congressional seats and the offices of state attorney general, secretary of state, and state auditor were intermediate offices (held for more than four years). Now, with some governorships becoming, at a minimum, intermediate offices, if not career offices, political opportunities are being restricted.

Important here is the concept of political time, or window of opportunity—that moment in a person's political career when he or she can or should move to run for a higher office. It is not easy to define exactly when one's political time occurs, how long it lasts, or for whom it really does exist. It is much easier to define when it is not the right political time for someone to seek a higher office: the person is too young and his or her time will come, or the person is too old and his or her time has passed. For some, there will be a time for such an upward political move, for others there may never be. Clearly, the concept of political time varies from state to state and from individual to individual.

Generally, political time is relatively short from the individual's perspective. There are several reasons for this. As already noted, longer terms and succession have cut back the number of times available. Term limits on how long someone

3. Portions of this section are taken from Beyle ("Term Limits") 1992.

Table 6-3 Number of Governors in Selected Decades, 1800–1989

Decade	No. of states	No. of governors	Average no. of governors per state
1800–1809	17	56	3.3
1820–1829	24	92	3.8
1850–1859	31	124	4.0
1870–1879	37	154	4.2
1900–1909	46	154	3.3
1920–1929	48	185	3.9
1950–1959	48	108	2.3
1960–1969	50	102	2.0
1970–1979	50	93	1.9
1980–1989	50	55	1.1

SOURCE: Adapted from Beyle ("Term Limits") 1992, 164.

can hold an office, where they exist, create periodic openings for those seeking an office and a time schedule of when these openings will occur. But the political time of others on the ladder may conflict with a person's own political time. In addition, the new variable of money in the political process allows political interlopers to interrupt an otherwise ordered process of political advancement by buying their way into the system at the very top.

Obviously, with the average number of new governors per state per decade dropping to 1.1, there are very few openings. What do ambitious politicians do when this happens? Many move their ambitions elsewhere, even if it means leaving the political arena. The reform goal of longer terms for governors, with the ability to succeed themselves, may have led to the unanticipated result of shunting off into other careers individuals who might have sought the governorship or some other higher office. This shift is difficult to measure, but the cries that there are too few good candidates in many states suggest that something like this may be happening (Beyle ["Term Limits"] 1992, 172–173).

While the term limits movement of the 1990s has been mainly aimed at state legislatures and Congress, some of the states have also included provisions restricting how long their governors may serve. Of the twenty-one states that adopted term limits through 1994, eleven placed limits on their governors. All went from no limits on how long a governor might serve to either two four-year terms or eight years in a specific time period (Beyle 1995; Beyle and Jones 1994). These limits should now produce more openings in these states.[4]

Sometimes idiosyncratic political situations can either severely restrict an individual's access to office or overly enhance it. Alabama is an example. For three decades gubernatorial politics revolved around George C. Wallace (D). After his unsuccessful campaign for governor in 1958, his successful candidacies in 1962, 1970, 1974, and 1982 gave him sixteen years in office. In addition, his first wife, Lurleen, ran in his stead in 1966 and won, but she died after serving less than six-

4. The states are Arizona, Arkansas, California, Colorado, Idaho, Massachusetts, Michigan, Montana, Utah, Washington, and Wyoming.

teen months, thereby short-circuiting his attempt to govern through his wife. In 1994 the Alabama governor was Jim Folsom, Jr. (D), who succeeded to the office when his predecessor was ousted because of a felony conviction. The junior Folsom is the son of former Gov. "Big Jim" Folsom who served as governor from 1955 to 1959.

Similarly, in California the Brown family has long played a dominant role. Edmund G. "Pat" Brown served two terms (D, 1959–1967); his son Edmund G. "Jerry" Brown, Jr., served two terms (D, 1975–1983); and his daughter and Jerry Brown's sister, Kathleen, sought the office unsuccessfully in 1994. In Kansas, it was the Dockings—father George (D, 1957–1961) and son Robert B. (D, 1967–1975); George Docking's grandson Tom R. (D) became lieutenant governor and then tried for the governorship in 1986 but lost in a close race.

In addition to the rule that money can buy the best campaign for the winners (it is obviously wasted or ill-spent in the campaign of a loser), another political rule has gained importance in the last decade: incumbency provides the best campaign platform. Even in the anti-incumbent mood of the 1994 elections, incumbent governors won at about the same rate as usual.

Between 1970 and 1994, there were 362 separate elections for governor in the states; 282 incumbent governors (78 percent) were eligible to run for reelection, and 216 did so (77 percent of those eligible). Of these 216 governors, 72 percent won their races, while 7 percent lost in their party's primary and 21 percent lost in the general election (CSG 1994, 37). As noted earlier, this does not leave many seats available for those with gubernatorial ambitions.

From Campaigner to Governor

A major hallmark of our political system is the concept of an orderly transition of power from one elected official to another once the election results are known. Even when an incumbent governor is beaten in a bitter and personally acrimonious campaign, the reins of power are turned over at the appointed time—although not always easily or with complete grace. There are no coup d'états led by colonels of the state's highway patrol or members of the state National Guard; the vehicle of change in our executive chairs is the vote of the electorate.

The keys to a successful transition are planning and communication. When both sides have thought ahead to the transition period and the potential problems of leaving or entering office, many of the difficulties can be reduced. When both sides strive to communicate rather than continue the election campaign or start another conflict, we seldom hear of difficulties during this period (NGA 1990a, 1990b). The National Governors' Association (NGA) has developed a series of materials to assist in gubernatorial transitions and holds a "New Governors' Seminar" in the even years to let incumbent governors pass on their accumulated wisdom to those who are about to enter office (NGA 1978, 1990b).

But there are always some deviations from any general rules, and the Blanton-Alexander transition in Tennessee in 1978–1979 is an example. Federal law enforcement officials had reason to believe that the outgoing Democratic governor, Ray Blanton, was "about to release some state prisoners who [were believed to have] bought their way out of prison." One of the prisoners allegedly involved in the governor's pardon-selling scheme was James Earl Ray, the convicted assassin of Martin Luther King, Jr. The newly elected Republican governor, Lamar Alexander, agreed to be sworn in three days early without the knowledge of the incumbent Blanton and the locks to the governor's office were changed so that Blanton could not gain access. Blanton was later convicted of selling pardons and served time in prison (Alexander 1986, 22, 24).

THE POWERS OF THE GOVERNORS: A COMPARISON

As Schlesinger (1965, 1971) has shown us, some governors are strong, some are weak, and some fall in between. Reasons for strength can derive variously from personality, personal wealth, electoral mandate, party or interest group structure, state statute, or the formal powers of the office itself. The ability to be strong can vary within a particular state; for example, a governor may have considerable power over the executive branch but little in working with the legislature. A governor may have little power with either of these but have a close relationship with the president, which confers some significant power in the intergovernmental arena and even in the state.

The governors of the most populous states—California, New York, Texas—are important and powerful in political circles. They have greater influence in national political conventions and larger congressional delegations. They are often elevated to potential presidential candidacy just because they are the governors of these states. The national press covers them closely, giving their state activities a national tinge. In short, these governors have national power because of the states they head.

Here, we are more interested in the powers the governors have within their own state: those powers they bring to the office themselves and those powers provided them by state constitution, state statute, and the voters. Let us turn first to those powers the governors bring with them.

The Personal Power of Governors

Each individual serving as governor has his or her own set of personal attributes that can be turned into either strength (power) or weakness, depending on the situation.[5] Here we will look at six separate indicators of the personal strength of the governors serving as of the summer of 1994.

5. In the summer of 1994, I conducted a fifty-state survey of nearly 400 political scientists, working journalists, and others with experience in the states on how they viewed the performance of their state's governor. That survey will be cited as the Summer 1994 Survey in this chapter. All quotations in this chapter whose sources are not otherwise identified are taken from responses to the Summer 1994 Survey. Scores for individual state governors presented in the tables are the average score on that item from all responses in the state.

Electoral Mandate. This indicator can be considered the margin of victory by which the governor won the seat. The premise is that the larger the margin of victory, the stronger the governor will be in the view of other actors in the system. Governors with a wide margin can use that margin politically by declaring that the people overwhelmingly wanted him or her in office so that a particular goal could be achieved. Governors who won by a narrow margin or by a plurality in a three- or four-way race and those who succeeded to office on the death, removal, or resignation of the elected governor cannot use this argument.

In the calculations of the extent of a governor's mandate, a five-point scale is used, ranging from those governors who won in a relative landslide on the high side to those who succeeded to office and thus were not elected on the low side. As indicated in Table 6-4, a majority of the governors (twenty-six) won their most recent election rather handily, another six comfortably. At the other end of the spectrum are the governors who won by less than 2 points or were plurality winners (nine), or succeeded to office (three). The average score for the 1994 governors is 3.9 on the five-point scale.

Table 6-4   The Personal Power of Governors: The Electoral Mandate, Rated on Five-Point Scale, Summer 1994

Score	Category	Point spread	No. of governors
5.0	Landslide win	11+	26
4.0	Comfortable majority	6–10	6
3.0	Narrow majority	3–5	6
2.0	Tight win or plurality win (<50%)	0–2	9
1.0	Succeeded to office		3
Average score: 3.9			

SOURCE: Calculated from data in Barone and Ujifusa 1993.

The governor with the greatest margin of victory was Howard Dean (D-Vt.), who more than doubled his 1992 Republican challenger's vote. The squeakers were Govs. Arne Carlson (R-Minn.), who won by 0.6 percent (17,595 votes), Ben Nelson (D-Neb.), who won by 0.7 percent (4,030 votes), and Christine Whitman (R-N.J.), who won by 1.3 percent (33,000 votes). Does it make a difference? As one Virginia survey respondent said of the newly elected governor George Allen: "The reason [his legislation passed] is not that Assembly members liked him, but that they can count votes and understand Allen's mandate."

Position on the State's Political Ambition Ladder. This indicator places the 1994 governors on the state's political ambition ladder in relation to their previous positions. The premise is that a governor progressing steadily up from substate to statewide elective office to the governorship will be stronger than those who start at the top with the governorship as their first office. They have worked their way through each level and have learned en route what to expect and what is expected of them. They also have developed friends and allies who will support them (as well as enemies and ingrates who will not). The governor for whom it is the first elective office must build such understanding and relationships on the job.

A five-point scale is used, running from those who moved upward in a steady progression from substate to statewide office to governor on the high side to those for whom the governorship was their first elective office on the low side. As shown in Table 6-5, nearly half of the governors (twenty-four) did follow a steady progression up the rungs in their state's political ambition ladder, while at the other extreme nearly one-quarter of them (twelve) started at the top. Former governors, those who moved up from legislative leadership or congressional posts, and those moving up from substate positions (mayors and legislators) fall between these two end points. The average score for the 1994 governors is 3.5 on the five-point scale.

Table 6-5 The Personal Power of Governors: Position on Ambition Ladder, Summer 1994

Score	Category	No. of governors
5.0	Steady progression	24
4.0	Former governors	5
3.0	Legislative leaders or Congress members	7
2.0	Substate position to governor	2
1.0	Governorship is first office	12

Average score: 3.5

SOURCE: Calculated from data in NGA 1994.

The five former governors who regained their seats took distinctive paths to their first terms: it was Walter Hickel's (I-Alaska) first elective office; Cecil Andrus (D-Idaho) moved from a four-term stint in the state legislature; Edwin W. Edwards (D-La.) went from city council to state legislature to Congress to governor; Bruce King (D-N.M.) moved from the legislature and the speakership to become governor; and James B. Hunt (D-N.C.) jumped from the lieutenant governorship to the higher office. Andrus and Edwards have served four terms, while Hunt and King are in their third terms. The advantages that former governors bring to the office were summed up by two observers of Hunt: "[H]e returned to office with a very focused agenda" and "is a competent, polished chief executive [who] understands the issues and how to make the system work."

The Personal Future of Governors as Governors. The premise behind this indicator is that governors who are near the beginning of their terms and who have the ability to run again have more power than governors who are nearing the end of their terms in office or are retiring or are term limited. The reason is that governors up for reelection are able to go out to the voters again and seek the elec-

Table 6-6 The Personal Future of Governors as
Governor, Summer 1994

Score	Category	No. of governors
5.0	Early in term, can run again	10
4.0	Late in term, can run again	19
3.0	Early in term, term-limited	3
2.0	Succeeded to office, can run	2
1.0	Late in final term	16
Average score: 3.1		

SOURCES: Calculated from data in NGA 1994; Beyle 1995.

toral mandate they can provide and at the same time possibly help supporters and hurt detractors. Governors who cannot run again become lame ducks with little political potential remaining.

A five-point scale—ranging from those, on the high side, who are early in their terms and can seek reelection to those, on the low side, who are late in their final terms—was used to indicate the personal future of governors as governors. As shown in Table 6-6, in 1994 most governors (thirty-one) were able to run again and therefore still had some political potential. Nineteen, however, were lame ducks in their final terms, sixteen of them late in those terms. The average score for the 1994 governors is 3.1 on the five-point scale.

Lame duckism is a frustrating malaise for governors. They have the trappings and formal powers of office but lack the political power and wallop they once had. As noted earlier, in the summer of 1994 Governor Edwards announced his exit from Louisiana's politics a year and a half before his fourth term would end. According to one observer, he then found an immediate change in the political environment around him as the decision "left him a lame duck and largely ineffective in the legislature[,] with no political clout to speak of and no money with which to reward loyal legislators with projects and patronage." Another observer stated that he would be surprised if Edwards "were able to get anything important through the legislature during the rest of his term."

The Personal Style of Governors. Often it is the intangibles that matter the most in how well a political actor such as a governor performs. The ability to charm and lead the voters, the media, and others can overcome deficits in other areas. A warm and enticing personality can obscure problems that might be quite deleterious to an administration. Conversely, those without these qualities often suffer because they cannot throw the blanket of their personal style and skills over problems.

To measure the personal style of governors, the Summer 1994 Survey asked: "How would you characterize (his/her) personal style?" A five-point scale with half-point increments was used in which the end points were "charismatic" and "dull." As can be seen in Table 6-7, most governors were placed midway between the two extremes of these end points. No governor was characterized as being

Table 6-7 The Personal Style of Governors,
Summer 1994

Score	Category	No. of governors
5.0	Charismatic	0
4.5		5
4.0		2
3.5		11
3.0		15
2.5		5
2.0		11
1.5		1
1.0	Dull	0

Average score: 3.0

SOURCE: Calculated from data from Summer 1994 Survey.

charismatic or dull. The average score for the 1994 governors is 3.0 on the five-point scale.

The five governors who were rated as most charismatic were Lowell P. Weicker, Jr. (I-Conn.), Andrus (Idaho), Edwards (La.), Cuomo (N.Y.), and Ann Richards (D-Texas). At the other end of the scale was Bob Miller (D-Nev.). But these personal style extremes can be misleading. For example, although Cuomo was widely seen as charismatic, most New York respondents indicated that his performance did not match his style rating. And while Terry Branstad (R-Iowa) was rated near the dull end of the scale, one observer noted that "dull works in Iowa," because "Midwesterners tend to distrust anyone with slick or charismatic qualities."

Other governors also were rated as fitting their state's political culture well. For example, several observers rated their governor's style as typical for the South: a "them vs. us approach" (said of Kirk Fordice, R-Miss.); "feuds with own partisans in the legislature, often embarrassing" (said of David Walters, D-Okla.); "matches the rather traditional political culture" (said of Ned Ray McWherter, D-Tenn.); and has "Cajun charm and wit" (said of Edwards, La.). Mike Sullivan's (D) "style fits the Wyoming culture well," and Evan Bayh (D-Ind.) was rated as "strictly Hoosier."

Gubernatorial Performance Ratings. Their performance as governor is another aspect of the personal power of governors. There are several ways to measure the performance of the governors of the fifty states. Two of them rely on asking people—involved observers and the public—just how well they think the governor of their state is performing. The premise here is that those governors who are seen as performing in a relatively positive way add to their own personal power and will be more effective than those who are not performing well.

In the Summer 1994 Survey, respondents were asked to rate the governor's overall performance on a five-point scale of "excellent, good, average, fair, poor." As can be seen in Table 6-8, no governor achieved either extreme of an excellent

Table 6-8   Gubernatorial Performance: Summer 1994

Score	Category	No. of governors
5.0	Excellent	0
4.5		7
4.0	Good	6
3.5		11
3.0	Average	17
2.5		4
2.0	Fair	4
1.5		1
1.0	Poor	0

Average score: 3.3

SOURCE: Calculated from data from Summer 1994 Survey.

or poor performance. The curve of responses tilted toward the higher side, with forty-one evaluations of the governors falling in the 3-point (average) to 4.5-point (good to excellent) range. The average score for the governors is 3.3 on the five-point scale. Several of the governors at the low end of these evaluations obviously understood their low rankings and took themselves out of the race to seek reelection: Finney (Kan.), Edwards (La.), Walters (Okla.), and Barbara Roberts (D-Ore.).

But what constitutes a good performance by a governor? On what basis do these observers make their judgments? One factor in some of the evaluations was that the governor had achieved some level of success in economic development efforts. This was especially important because the country and most states had experienced a weak economic period during the governors' terms in office, and thus successes in seeking and obtaining new businesses and new jobs were important.

A second factor in a few cases was how well the governors compared to their predecessors. On the negative side one was nominated as the "poorest governor in a long time." In another state, which had a history of serious ethical, moral, and legal problems among its elected leaders, one observer stated that the governor had "been a strong governor in a state that desperately needed political and governmental leadership of the highest ethical standards and of noble purpose."

Another factor was their ability to keep things on an even keel and to be in tune with what the voters wanted. For example, one was cited for running "a tight fiscal ship and that is what [citizens] want"; another was called "consistent and competent"; and still another was "elected to be a custodian and he has done this better [this] term." Some governors' ratings were based on rather lukewarm assessments: "average, which means good for [this state]" and "could have done more, but mostly status quo." Finally, there were the assessments of those at the bottom end of the performance scale: "a disaster" and "lack of ethics."

The second way to measure gubernatorial performance is by the proliferating

Table 6-9 Gubernatorial Performance according to
Public Polls Taken in or about Summer 1994

Score	Approval rating	No. of governors
5.0	Over 60%	12
4.0	50–59%	15
3.0	40–49%	7
2.0	30–39%	8
1.0	Less than 30%	8

Average score: 3.3

SOURCES: Poll results obtained from *The Hotline, The Polling Report, The Rothenberg Political Report,* Mason-Dixon Opinion Research, and other reports of state polls in the media and from the National Network of State Polls, Institute for Research in Social Science, University of North Carolina at Chapel Hill, 1994.

state-level public opinion polls, which have led to some fairly consistent results being published on how the citizens, registered voters, or likely voters feel their governor is performing. These results are usually made public by the media paying for the polls or by the university center conducting the polls.

In such polls the reasons for the respondents' assessments are obscure, but how they rate their governor's performance becomes part of the politics around the governor. The categories of responses used vary from "approve, disapprove" to "excellent, good, average, fair, poor." What everyone looks for is the percentage of positive responses in the ratings of the governor, although most political consultants believe that the negative assessments are more meaningful.

To compare these performance ratings across the fifty states, we used a five-point scale, ranging from those governors who had a positive rating of 60 percent or higher to those who had a rating of less than 30 percent. These are all snapshot ratings taken at one point in time. Most of these polls were taken between June and September 1994. The results presented in Table 6-9 indicate that more than half the governors had a positive rating of 50 percent or higher in their state; twelve of these governors had a rating above 60 percent and fifteen between 50 and 60 percent. At the lowest end of the scale were eight governors with ratings below 30 percent. Four of these eight governors declined to seek reelection, another was constitutionally barred from seeking another term, and another lost his bid for his party's renomination. Two others, Fife Symington (R-Ariz.) and Pete Wilson (R-Calif.), were reelected to a second term in 1994 despite their low ratings with the public in the polls. The average score for the 1994 governors is 3.3 on the five-point scale.

While the reasons for these ratings are not always clear, their impact is. For those at the low side of the scale, their administrations are jarred, and their political future is unclear, if not damaged beyond repair. For those at the high side of the scale, these public opinion poll ratings become part of their political and personal arsenal in their attempt to achieve results. But, as an observer noted about Governor Whitman of New Jersey, "as long as she has 70 percent approval ratings, they (the old boy network) need her and will never bring her down. But once those ratings drop, watch out! The knives will be out."

The Personal Power of Governors: Summary. To make an assessment and comparison of how the fifty state governors fare in their personal power, the scores of each of the above indicators were brought together into one index. The scores for each governor in the six separate indicators were totaled and that total score was then divided by six to keep within the framework of the five-point scale.

As indicated in Table 6-10, three-quarters of the governors (thirty-eight) fell in the range between 3.0 and 4.5 points, with an average score of 3.3. The two governors with the most personal power on this scale at 4.5 were Roy Romer (D-Colo.), at the end of his second term, and Mel Carnahan (D-Mo.), eighteen months into his first term. At the other end of this index were governors John R. McKernan, Jr. (R-Me.), at the end of his second and final term; Walters (Okla.), at the end of his first, stormy, and only term; and Bruce Sundlun (D-R.I.), at the end of his second and final two-year term, having been defeated for his own party's renomination in 1994.

Table 6-10   Summary of Personal Power of Governors, by State, Summer 1994

5.0	4.5	4.0	3.5	3.0	2.5	2.0	1.5	1.0
	Colorado	Delaware	Florida	Arkansas	Alabama	Maine		
	Missouri	Georgia	Illinois	California	Alaska	Rhode Island		
		Idaho	Minnesota	Connecticut	Arizona			
		Indiana	Nevada	Hawaii	Kansas			
		Iowa	New Hampshire	Louisiana	Kentucky			
		Montana	New Jersey	Maryland	Mississippi			
		New York	North Dakota	Massachusetts	Oklahoma			
		North Carolina	South Carolina	Michigan	Oregon			
		Ohio	Tennessee	Nebraska	South Dakota			
		Texas	Utah	New Mexico	West Virginia			
		Vermont	Virginia	Pennsylvania				
		Wisconsin	Washington	Wyoming				

Average score: 3.3

SOURCES: Calculated from data in Tables 6-4 through 6-9; Beyle 1995.

In summary, it would appear that most governors do bring, and continue to hold, their own brand of personal power to the governorship. While there are some who fall on the weak side, there are more who are on the stronger side.

The Institutional Powers of Governors

The institutional powers of the governorship are those powers given the governor by the state constitution, state statutes, and the voters when they vote on constitutions and referenda. In a sense, these powers are the structure into which the governor moves upon being elected to office.

Separately Elected State-Level Officials. The concept of a plural executive is alive and well in many of the states. Instead of following the presidential model,

Tables 6-11 Separately Elected Executive Officials

Score	Category	No. of governors
5.0	Governor or governor–lieutenant governor team only	5
4.0	Governor–lieutenant governor team with some process officials elected (atty. gen., sec. of state, treasurer, auditor)	9
3.0	Governor–lieutenant governor with some process officials elected, plus a major policy official (education, public utilities); or governor (no team) and four or more process and minor elected officials (agriculture, insurance, labor)	21
2.0	Governors (no team) with six or fewer officials elected, plus a major policy official	6
1.0	Governors (no team) with seven or more process and major policy officials elected	9

Average score: 2.9

SOURCE: Calculated from data in CSG 1994, 55–56, 72–76.

which we see at the national level with a president and vice president as the only elected executive branch officials, the states have opted to allow voters to select a range of state officials.

Over the course of the twentieth century, however, one of the most consistent reforms advocated for the states has been to reduce the number of separately elected executive branch officials. The results of such reforms, however, are not impressive, nor do they look promising in the future. Since 1955, the number of separately elected officials at the state level has dropped from 514 in the then forty-eight states to 511 in the now fifty states. The average has only dropped from 10.7 per state to 10.2 per state (Beyle 1995).

Each of these separate offices has its own political support network that is quite resistant to any changes in how leadership is selected. And as noted earlier, some of these offices serve as launching pads for individuals seeking higher elective offices such as the governorship and are tightly woven into the state's political ambition ladder. It is often just not worth the struggle to change how they are selected; too much political effort and capital would be expended for too little real political gain.

As shown in Table 6-11, only five states come close to mirroring the presidential model. The remainder have a variety of other elected officials, ranging from a few process-type offices (attorney general, secretary of state, treasurer, auditor) to some major policy offices (K-12 education, university boards, and public utility authorities). On this five-point scale, the average score is 2.9.

For the governor, this means working with other officials who have similar claims to a statewide political constituency. And while process-type officials seem to be more innocuous by definition, they can cause a governor considerable problems. For example, tensions between governors and lieutenant governors have led to bizarre political situations in which governors have been wary of leaving their states lest their lieutenant governor sabotage their programs while serving as acting governor.[6] In another situation, the Republican governor of

6. For examples of such difficult situations, see "The Executive Branch" section of recent issues of the Council of State Governments' biennial publication *The Book of the States.*

North Carolina once found himself being sued by the separately elected Democratic attorney general in one case while being represented by the attorney general in another (CSG 1992, 29).

Tenure Potential. Obviously, how long governors can serve and whether they
can succeed themselves for more than one term are important factors in determining just how much power they have. One argument is that those having the
possibility of a longer stay in the office are able to carry out their programs. But
this can cut both ways: if limits were put on gubernatorial terms, governors
might move faster and more decisively to achieve their goals and not be afraid of
the voters' retribution at the ballot box when a necessary yet unpopular decision
had to be made.

Initially, ten of the governors of the thirteen original states had one-year
terms, another a two-year term, and two had three-year terms. Gradually, states
moved to either two- or four-year terms, and one-year terms finally disappeared
early in the twentieth century.

Table 6-12   The Tenure Potential of Governors, Summer 1994

Score	Category	No. of governors
5.0	4-year term, no restraint on reelection	11
4.5	4-year term, only 3 terms permitted	1
4.0	4-year term, only 2 terms permitted	35
3.0	4-year term, no consecutive reelection	1
2.0	2-year term, no restraint on reelection	2
1.0	2-year term, only 2 terms permitted	0

Average score: 4.1

SOURCE: Calculated from data in CSG 1994, 30, 50–51.

Another significant shift has been taking place since 1960: the borrowing by
the states of the presidential succession model, as embodied in the Twenty-second Amendment to the U.S. Constitution, adopted in 1951, which states: "No person shall be elected to the office of President more than twice." This was a direct
reaction to the four terms to which President Franklin D. Roosevelt was elected.
In 1960 only six states restricted their governors to two four-year terms
(Schlesinger 1965, 220). By 1969 this number had increased to eleven states
(Schlesinger 1971, 223); and by 1988, to twenty-five states. With the rise of the
term-limits movement, more states acted to impose such a restriction, and by
1994 a total of thirty-five had done so (see Table 6-12). On this five-point scale,
the average score is 4.1.

The Power of Appointment. One of the first set of decisions facing governors-
elect on the morning after their election is the appointment of personnel to key
positions in their administration. This power of appointment is fundamental to
a governor's administration, especially in relation to the state bureaucracy. But
the appointive power also extends to the governor's legislative role, for promises

Table 6-13 The Appointive Power of Governors, Summer 1994

Score	Category	No. of governors
5.0	Governor appoints, no other approval needed	1
4.5		1
4.0	Governor appoints; board, council or legislature approves	4
3.5		6
3.0	Someone else appoints; governor approves or shares appointment	15
2.5		13
2.0	Someone else appoints; governor and others (legis.) approve	5
1.5		2
1.0	Someone else appoints; no approval or confirmation needed	3
0.0	All officials separately elected or selected by legislature	0

Average score: 2.8

SOURCE: Calculated from data in CSG 1994, 72–76.
NOTE: The scores are based on the governor's power of appointment in six major functions and offices in each state: corrections, K-12 education, health, highways, public utilities regulation, and welfare.

of appointments to high-level executive positions and to the state judiciary are often the coin spent for support for particular legislation.

The history of state governors' appointment powers is one of growth from weak beginnings. The increase of separately elected officials during the nineteenth century and the ad hoc proliferation of state agencies, often headed by boards and commissions, added to the problem of gubernatorial control. This diluted gubernatorial power was the background for twentieth-century reforms to increase gubernatorial appointive power. The assumption underlying these reforms is that governors who can appoint officials without any other authority involved can be held accountable for these officials' actions. Such governors are more powerful than those who must have either or both houses of the legislature confirm an appointment. Governors who only approve appointments rather than initiate them have even less appointive power. Weakest are those governors who neither appoint nor approve but have a separate body do so and those who have no opportunity to appoint because the officials who head agencies are elected.

As shown in Table 6-13, which indicates who selects the heads of the agencies providing the six major functions in each state—corrections, K-12 education, health, highways or transportation, public utilities regulation, and welfare—governors face constraints in their appointment power. A majority of the states fall in the middle of the scale, that is, someone else appoints these individuals to their positions with the approval of the governor or the legislature or both. On this five-point scale, the average score is 2.8.

On the high side is Ohio, where the governor appoints all six of these officials with no confirmation involved, closely followed by Pennsylvania, where four of the six gubernatorial appointees must receive senatorial confirmation. At the other end of the scale is Oklahoma, where two of the officials are elected separately, three others are appointed by boards, and one is a civil service appointee, supposedly not subject to political influence.

One caveat on this appointive power index; a politically shrewd governor with an efficient political operation in the governor's office can probably orchestrate many of the selection decisions made by boards and commissions. Thus, the governor might not be as powerless as the constitutional or statutory language might suggest.

Control over the Budget. The executive budget, centralized under gubernatorial control, is a twentieth-century response to the chaotic fiscal situations found in state government at the turn of the century. An executive budget seeks to bring into one document under the chief executive's control all the agency and department requests for legislatively appropriated funds; it also reflects the governor's own policy priorities. This document is then transmitted to the legislature for its consideration and ultimate passage. By putting governors at the top of this process in the executive branch and making them the chief lobbyist for the budget in the legislature, the centralized budget places much power in their hands.

What the governor can do in developing and presenting the state budget as the fiscal road map for the next fiscal year or biennium, however, the legislature can often undo as the budget bill works its way through the legislative process. In some states the governor's proposed budget is described as "DOA" (dead on arrival) because the legislature intends to build the state's next budget on their own. Moreover, when there are conflicts over the budget within the executive branch agencies and between the agencies and the governor, the legislature is where agency grievances can be heard and gubernatorial decisions changed. The greater the power of the legislature to make changes in the governor's proposed budget, the less potential budget power for the governor. I use the word *potential* advisedly, because not all gubernatorial-legislative relationships are adversarial in nature, and what the governor proposes usually does set the agenda for debate and decision.

State legislatures have been seeking even more involvement in the budgetary process in order to regain some of the budgetary powers lost to governors. They have developed legislative oversight procedures, tried to require legislative appropriation or approval of federal grant funds flowing into the state, and sought to have legislative committees involved in administrative budgetary shifts made during the fiscal year.

But there are some limitations on the budgetary powers of both these executive and legislative branch actors. For example, most states earmark their gasoline taxes for highway or mass transportation uses, and some earmark taxes on alcohol for various purposes or allot a fraction of their sales taxes to local governments. Tolls and fees for bridges, highways, and other state-established public authorities are retained by the agencies collecting them to finance their activities and projects. In recent decades, states have been facing more and more federal mandates on how much they should be spending on Medicaid, certain environmental problems, prisons, and the handicapped. A governor's budgetary power is

Table 6-14 The Budgetary Power of Governors, Summer 1994

Score	Category	No. of governors
5.0	Governor has full responsibility; legislature may not increase executive budget	2
4.0	Governor has full responsibility; legislature can increase by special majority vote or subject to item veto	2
3.0	Governor has full responsibility; legislature has unlimited power to change executive budget	40
2.0	Governor shares responsibility; legislature has unlimited power to change executive budget	4
1.0	Governor shares responsibility with other elected official; legislature has unlimited power to change executive budget	2

Average score: 3.0

SOURCES: Calculated from data in CSG 1994, 55–56, 317–319, 320–321; NASBO 1992, 10, 26.

thus reduced when appropriated funds are earmarked or otherwise diverted by legislative prescription, when public authorities raise or expend independent income, or when federal mandates direct state expenditures.

A five-point scale is used to measure the budgetary power given to each governor and the legislature's authority to change the governor's budget. At the top of the scale were the states whose governors have full responsibility for the executive budget and whose legislatures have no ability to increase the executive budget; at the bottom of the scale were the states whose governors share responsibility for developing the executive budget with others and whose legislatures have unlimited power to change the executive budget.

It can be seen in Table 6-14 that most states provide their governors with full budget power and their legislatures with unlimited authority to change that budget. Hence, the average score for the fifty states is very close to the midpoint of the scale at 3.0.

The Veto Power. Governors have been provided the formal power of being able to veto bills, and in most cases parts of bills, passed by the legislature. This is the most direct power the governor can exercise in relation to the legislature. There are many differences in the veto power extended to governors: total bill veto, amendatory veto, item veto, item reduction power, or no veto power at all, as in North Carolina.

The veto, while a direct power over the legislature, also provides governors with some administrative powers because it gives them the ability to stop agencies from gaining support in a legislative end run around their governor's or their budget office's adverse decision. This is especially true in those forty-three states in which the governor can veto particular items in an agency's budget without rejecting the entire bill (Benjamin 1982, 11; Moe 1988, 4).

Some states have provided a more refined form of the item veto for their governors; ten states provide a line item veto in which the governor can reduce the amounts in the lines of a budget rather than having to veto the entire line; seven go further by allowing the governor to condition his or her approval of the bill with amendments to the bill or rewording of the lines (Moe 1988, 3–5).

The veto and its use involve two major actors: the governor and the legislature. Obviously, it is a legislative act that a governor must sign or veto; however, the legislature has the opportunity to vote to override the veto and thus make a law without the governor's signature. In fact, thirty-three states even allow their legislatures to recall bills from the governor prior to his or her action, thereby creating a negotiating situation, sort of an informal alternative to the veto (Benjamin 1982). This latter tactic can allow the governor to become part of the legislative process with de facto amendatory power as the governor and the legislature negotiate over the bill's contents (Benjamin 1982, 12; Moe 1988, 13–14).

The requirements for legislative override range from only a majority of members present and voting to a special majority, such as a three-fifth's vote. While the threat of a legislative override has not been great in the past, the number of gubernatorial vetoes overridden by legislatures has grown somewhat. In 1947, governors vetoed approximately 5 percent of the bills passed by legislatures and were overridden on only 1.8 percent of them (Wiggins 1980, 1112–1113). In 1992–1993, governors vetoed about 5.6 percent of the bills passed by legislatures but were overridden 3.2 percent of the time (CSG 1994, 148–150). But this overall rate masks some of the extremes; in 1992–1993, Governor McWherter (Tenn.) signed all 1,262 bills presented to him into law, whereas Governor Wilson (Calif.) vetoed over 21 percent of the 2,681 bills presented to him and none of these vetoes were overridden (CSG 1994, 148–150).

Some would argue that the use of the veto is a sign of gubernatorial weakness rather than strength because strong governors win the battle through negotiation rather than confrontation with the legislature. In a slightly different vein, one governor argued that a governor should "avoid threatening to veto a bill. You just relieve the legislature of responsibility for sound legislation" (Beyle and Huefner 1983, 268–269). Moreover, a governor using a veto risks embarrassment at the hands of the legislature. It is a power to be used sparingly (NGA 1987, 8).

A study done in the late 1980s suggests that there are at least four consequences following the use of a line item veto in any of its variants: it profoundly alters the relationship of the legislature to the governor to the benefit of the latter; it increases the number of formal confrontations between the two branches; it spawns procedures to neutralize its impact; and it precipitates litigation between the two branches, thereby introducing the third branch of state government, the courts, into the lawmaking process at an early stage in its role as umpire (Moe 1988, 1–2).

A recent battle in Wisconsin over the governor's *partial veto* demonstrates most of these points. The Republican governor Tommy Thompson startled the Democratic legislature in 1987 by creatively using the partial veto to change legislative intent: he excised isolated digits, letters, and words to the point of creating new words and meaning. The legislative leaders sought relief from the state's supreme court only to have the court back the governor's actions in a four-to-three decision (*State ex. rel. State Senate v. Thompson* 144, Wis.2d 429, 424 N.W.2d 385, 386, n.3 [1988]; see also Hutchison 1989). The legislature placed a constitutional amendment on the ballot in 1988 prohibiting such vetoes; it was approved by a 62 percent vote. In 1991 a federal appeals court, in upholding a lower-court decision, found the partial veto "quirky" but not unconstitutional. By mid-1993, Thompson had executed more than 1,300 vetoes (Farney 1993, A16).

The governors' veto power is measured on a five-point scale whose high side has governors with an item veto requiring an extraordinary legislative vote to override it (three-fifths or two-thirds) and whose low side has the one governor with no veto power at all. In between are variations on the type of veto and the size of the majority needed to override a governor's veto. As indicated in Table 6-15, most states do provide their governors with considerable veto power; three-quarters of the states are in the top category. North Carolina with no veto and Indiana with no item veto and only a simple majority needed to override the veto are at the low end of the scale. On this five-point scale, the average score is 4.4.

NC & IN
↓
no veto

Table 6-15　The Veto Power of Governors, Summer 1994

Score	Category	No. of governors
5.0	Item veto; three-fifths of legislators elected or two-thirds of legislators present needed to override	37
4.0	Item veto; majority of legislators elected needed to override	6
3.0	Item veto; majority of legislators present needed to override	0
2.0	No item veto; special legislative majority needed to override	5
1.0	No item veto; only simple legislative majority needed to override	1
0.0	No veto of any kind	1

Average score: 4.4

SOURCE: Calculated from data in CSG 1994, 55–56, 141–142.

The veto can also be used in what might be called an affirmative way. During the 1991 legislative session, Governor Weicker of Connecticut, an Independent, had no one of his party in the legislature; yet he was able to use the veto over the state's budget as a positive weapon. By continually vetoing the budget bill because it did not contain an income tax, he assisted those who favored the imposition of a state income tax and opposed those who would rather have turned to an increase in the state sales tax as a way to balance the state's growing budget deficit. In the end, an income tax was adopted, the first in the state's history (Murphy 1992, 69).

Party Control. Partisanship is a key variable in the governors' relationship with the legislatures. If the governor's party also controls the legislature, then partisan conflicts can be minimized and the governor's ability to achieve his or her agenda is more likely to be successful. Cooperation should be the style of their relationship. If the governor and the legislative leadership are not of the same party,

Table 6-16   Gubernatorial Party Control, Summer 1994

Score	Category	No. of governors
5.0	Governor's party substantial majority (75%+) in both houses	7
4.0	Governor's party has simple majority in both houses, or a simple majority in one house and a substantial majority in the other	12
3.0	Split-party control in the legislature, or a nonpartisan legislature	18
2.0	Governor's party in simple minority in both houses, or a simple minority in one and a substantial minority in the other	9
1.0	Governor's party in substantial minority in both houses	4

Average score: 3.2

SOURCE: Calculated from data in CSG 1994, 113–114.

then partisan conflicts all too often become the style of the relationship, and the ability of the governor to achieve his or her goals is lessened. Since there are two houses in the legislatures of each state, except Nebraska, it is quite possible that at least one house will be controlled by the opposition party.

Recent decades have seen a growing trend toward a "power split" in state governments (Sherman 1984). In 1984, sixteen states had a power split; in the summer of 1994 there were thirty. V. O. Key, Jr., called this a "perversion" of separation of powers allowing partisan differences to present an almost intractable situation (Key 1956, 52), but not all view this situation with alarm. In 1984 Governor Alexander of Tennessee indicated that "it makes it harder, sometimes much harder; but the results can be better, sometimes much better" (Sherman 1984, 9).

At least three factors help to determine just how harmonious the power-split relationship will be: how great a majority the opposition party has in the legislature; the style and the personalities of the individuals involved—the governor and the legislative leaders; and whether an election year is near (Sherman 1984, 10).

When the governor's party is in the minority but controls a sizable number of seats, it is more difficult for the opposition majority to change the governor's budget or override his or her veto. However, open and easygoing personalities can often overcome partisan differences or, as Alexander says, "If you have good, well-meaning leaders, it's likely to be much better than any other process" (Sherman 1984, 12).

These variations in the governor's party control were measured on a five-point scale, in which the highest score is for states where a governor's party controls both houses by a substantial majority, and the lowest score is for states where the governor faces a legislature controlled by a substantial majority of the opposing party in both houses. Given the fact that there were thirty states in which a power split existed in 1994, it is no surprise to see in Table 6-16 that only seven governors have a legislature in which their party has a substantial majority. Nebraska's governor faces a unicameral (one-house) legislature elected on a nonpartisan basis. Two governors, both Republicans, faced a legislature controlled by a substantial majority of the opposition party (William F. Weld of Massachusetts, and Fordice of Mississippi), and the two Independent governors faced a legislature in which there were few if any of their party members (Hickel of Alaska and Weicker of Connecticut). On this five-point scale, the average score is 3.2.

The Institutional Powers of the Governors: Summary. To make an assessment and comparison of how the fifty governors fare in their institutional powers, the scores of each of the above indicators were brought together into one index. The scores in each of the six indicators were totaled for each state governor and that total score was then divided by six to keep within the framework of the five-point scale. As can be seen in Table 6-17, all but three governorships fell in the 3- to 4-point range on the scale, and the average score was 3.4. The nine governorships with the most institutional power on this scale at 4.0 were spread throughout the country with three in the Northeast, three in the mid-South, two in the Midwest, and one in the Far West. At the other end of this index were the governorships of both North and South Carolina and Vermont. A few institutional changes in each of these states (a veto for North Carolina, a four-year term and a stronger veto power for Vermont, fewer separately elected officials in both Carolinas, and more budgetary power in South Carolina) would move these states into the same range as all the other states.

Table 6-17 Summary of Institutional Powers of Governors, by State, Summer 1994

5.0	4.5	4.0	3.5	3.0	2.5	2.0
		Hawaii	Alaska	Alabama	North Carolina	
		Iowa	Arizona	California	South Carolina	
		Maryland	Arkansas	Colorado	Vermont	
		New Jersey	Connecticut	Florida		
		New York	Delaware	Georgia		
		Ohio	Illinois	Idaho		
		Pennsylvania	Kansas	Indiana		
		Tennessee	Kentucky	Maine		
		West Virginia	Louisiana	Massachusetts		
			Michigan	Mississippi		
			Minnesota	Nevada		
			Missouri	New Hampshire		
			Montana	Oklahoma		
			Nebraska	Texas		
			New Mexico	Virginia		
			North Dakota	Washington		
			Oregon	Wyoming		
			Rhode Island			
			South Dakota			
			Utah			
			Wisconsin			

Average score: 3.4

SOURCE: Calculated from Tables 6-11 through 6-16.

Overall Gubernatorial Powers in the Fifty States. Finally, the two sets of gubernatorial powers were combined into one overall 10-point index. The results, presented in Table 6-18, suggest a normal curve with forty-one states in the 6.0 to 7.5 range. At the high side of this combined index are three midwestern states (Iowa,

Table 6-18 Summary of Personal and Institutional Powers of Governors, by State, Summer 1994

8.0	7.5	7.0	6.5	6.0	5.5	5.0
Iowa	Colorado	Georgia	Arkansas	Alaska	Alabama	Maine
Missouri	Delaware	Hawaii	Connecticut	Arizona	Mississippi	
New York	Montana	Idaho	Florida	California	Oklahoma	
Ohio	New Jersey	Illinois	Louisiana	Kansas	Rhode Island	
	Tennessee	Indiana	Michigan	Kentucky		
	Wisconsin	Maryland	Nebraska	Massachusetts		
		Minnesota	Nevada	Oregon		
		North Dakota	New Hampshire	South Carolina		
		Pennsylvania	New Mexico	South Dakota		
		Texas	North Carolina	Wyoming		
		Utah	Vermont			
			Virginia			
			Washington			
			West Virginia			

Average score: 6.6

SOURCE: Calculated from data in Tables 6-10 and 6-17.

Missouri, and Ohio) and New York. At the low end of the scale are three southern states (Alabama, Mississippi, and Oklahoma) and two northeastern states (Maine and Rhode Island). Much of this may change as incumbents are replaced with a new group of men and women, who carry with them their own personal styles and strengths or weaknesses.

BEING GOVERNOR

The true measure of governors and their administrations is how well they actually perform the various roles for which they are responsible. Are they able to translate their potential powers into effective action? What additional informal powers must they use to achieve the goals of their administrations?

As governor of Tennessee, Lamar Alexander argued that a governor's role was to "see the state's few most urgent needs, develop strategies to address them, and persuade at least half the people that he or she is right" (Alexander 1986, 112). Clearly, to Alexander, the governor's main role concerns policy. A former governor of Vermont, Madeleine Kunin (D, 1985–1991), agreed and asserted that "[t]he power of a governor to set the tone and define the values of a state administration is enormous." She also felt that "[a]s governor, I had the incredible luxury to dream on a grand scale" (Kunin 1994, 11–12).

The Governor as Policymaker

The goals of a gubernatorial administration are those policy directions a governor wishes to emphasize during his or her tenure in office. The types of policy priorities vary greatly across the activities of state government and depend on several factors, including the governor's own personal interests and outside events.

In a series of interviews with former governors, several themes emerged concerning how they believed they exerted policy leadership. Most saw their role as that of an issue catalyst, picking the issue up from the public, focusing it, and seeking to take action on it. Some others saw their role as that of a spectator viewing policy issues arising out of conflicts between actors on the state scene, whether they were special interest groups, the bureaucracy, or the mayor of the state's largest city. Finally, a few saw the governor as a reactor to accidents of history and other unanticipated events. In the eyes of these governors, leadership was more a process of problem solving and conflict resolution than agenda setting (NGA 1981, 1).

Obviously, issues and policy needs flow from many sources and provide governors with both flexibility in choice and restrictions on choice. The events of the late 1980s and the early 1990s demonstrate just how governors can be forced to address issues and concerns not of their own choosing. The national recession of those years hit almost every state budget hard and some states, such as California, extremely hard. The main issue facing governors then were how to keep the state budget balanced in the face of falling revenues, and how to provide the services people needed in such an economy and that were normally provided in the states. The options available to the governors, and by extension the state legislatures, were to increase taxes, cut services, or both. Many states had to follow the third option, which was not a pleasing prospect for these leaders and the citizens of the states (Beyle, ed. 1992).

In the mid-1990s, as the economy recovered in most states, governors were freer to post their own agendas on the wall. Among the issues on the current agendas are economic development, education quality and reform, health cost containment, welfare reform, children's policies, and crime control. In fact, because some of the issues that seem to bedevil our national leaders threaten to bankrupt the states or cause even greater problems, governors and other state leaders in many of the states are already taking steps to address them.

But the results of the 1994 elections may serve to return governors and state leaders to the problems they faced earlier in the decade. The policy agenda that the Republican congressional leaders put forward during the 1994 campaign and sought to implement has potentially severe consequences for the states. If a balanced budget is ultimately achieved, many governors fear that the federal budget will be balanced at the expense of the states. If welfare programs are consolidated into block grants, the states will face serious problems establishing service levels and paying for them.

Several recent developments have aided governors in exerting policy leadership. The first level of change has taken place in the governor's office itself. In recent years the office has increased greatly in size, ability, functions, and structure. What used to amount to a few close associates working together with the governor has now been transformed into a much larger and more sophisticated bureaucratic organization in many of the states.

Table 6-19 Administrative Performance of
Governors, Summer 1994

Score	Category	No. of governors
5.0	Excellent	0
4.5		3
4.0	Good	8
3.5		11
3.0	Average	14
2.5		11
2.0	Fair	2
1.5		0
1.0	Poor	1

Average score: 3.2

SOURCE: Calculated from data from Summer 1994 Survey.

There have also been changes in the governor's extended office, the budget and planning agencies, which are increasingly being moved closer to the governor. In the most recent changes, governors have developed more aggressive offices of policy management, often following the federal model by creating a state-level Office of Management and Budget. One of the most critical roles of these agencies is "to provide the governor an independent source of advice on a broad range of state policy issues" (Flentje 1980, 26). They can also assist by reaching into the departments and agencies to help them implement policy directions and decisions.

These changes, and others, highlight the basic fact that governors have had to improve their policy capacity substantially in order to govern, especially in administering their state's executive branch. But governors can vary on how they use this capacity, how much they believe it really helps them, and how well they perform in this role. In the Summer 1994 Survey, respondents were asked how they would characterize their governor's overall administrative abilities, from "excellent" to "poor" on a five-point scale. As can be seen in Table 6-19, almost three-quarters of the governors are given scores of "average" to nearly "excellent" for their administrative efforts. The average score on this five-point scale is 3.2.

The two governors with the highest scores were Andrus (Idaho), who was finishing his fourth term of service, which had been interrupted by his appointment as U.S. Secretary of the Interior in the administration of President Jimmy Carter, and Jim Guy Tucker (D-Ark.), who succeeded to the governorship upon the election of the incumbent governor Bill Clinton as president. At the other end of the scale was Governor Finney (Kan.); one observer stated, "[T]he state is fortunate to survive her and her failed policies and appointments."

The Governor and the Legislature

Governors' relations with the legislature and their success in dealing with it often determine the success of their administrations. While the governor takes the lead, it is still the legislature that must adopt the state budget, set or agree to basic policy directions, and, in many cases, confirm major gubernatorial appointments. A governor and legislature at loggerheads over a tax proposal, budget, policy direction, or a major department head's confirmation can bring part or all of state government to a halt.

Added to the constitutional separation of powers are the political facts of life in many states where the governor is of one party and one or both the legislative houses are controlled by another party. Ideological factions can splinter a majority party's control of the legislature and be just as debilitating to a governor. While governor, Michael Dukakis (D-Mass.) found himself under greatest fire from his own party members: "And when you've got majorities of four to one in the Legislature—I'm sure you recognize that is by no means an unmitigated blessing—you've got conservative Democrats, you've got liberal Democrats, you've got moderate Democrats, you've got suburban Democrats, you've got urban Democrats, and you don't have any Republicans." He also noted that he was beaten in his 1978 reelection bid by a Democrat who was "philosophically miles away from him" (NGA 1981, 65).

The members of each of these two major branches bring quite different perspectives to state government. In terms of constituency, the governor represents the whole state; the legislature is a congeries of individuals representing much smaller parts of the state. The governorship is a full-time job, and complete responsibility is placed on the shoulders of one person; the legislature is not a full-time job, although the time involved varies among states, and responsibility is diffused widely among many leaders and many more members. The governor's chair sits atop the state's political ambition ladder; legislative seats are some of the rungs available in climbing the ladder.

Most new governors face their legislatures within the first month of their administration. The state-of-the-state address, the governor's budget message, specific programmatic legislation, special messages on high-priority programs, oversight of agency bills, and responses to bills introduced by individual legislators are high on the governor's agenda. Over the course of an administration, the governor gradually reduces his or her relations with the legislature to a routine in order to lessen the personal burden and the burden on the governor's office in general.

The resources available to governors in their relations with the legislature can be formidable. Gubernatorial patronage appointments can be attractive to legislators either for themselves or for an important ally or constituent. Attractive, too, can be the allocation of certain state contracts for services and facilities or support for local projects. These political plums or "gifts" can be provided by a governor as payment for support, either already rendered or anticipated later, in the form of legislative votes for gubernatorial priorities.

Many governors develop elaborate legislative efforts under the direction of a legislative liaison. The governor's program is watched over by the liaison from its formative stages through its introduction as a bill, legislative consideration in committee and on the floor, debate, and vote. Meetings with individual legislators and breakfast sessions at the governor's mansion with the governor serve to keep legislators aware of the governor's position and interest in issues.

But the governor should never try to be the *chief* legislator, according to those who have sat in the chair. This advice captures a very simple point: the governor can do much to set the agenda of the legislature, can try to direct the l ture's consideration and action on bills of concern to him or her, and can use the veto and other tools to redirect a legislative decision. But the governor should never intervene in purely legislative political processes such as leadership selection.

Why? First, if the governor attempts to do so and loses this key legislative political decision at the outset of the legislative session, the governor's political power is often irretrievably diminished well before the key policy and budgetary issues are considered. Thus, this step should never be taken, unless the governor is certain to win. Second, such an intrusion is perceived as a step across the separation-of-powers line set in most state constitutions and in most state government practices. Third, and most important according to those who have been there, "a governor successful in managing the leadership selection gains a Pyrrhic victory" (Beyle and Huefner 1983, 268). All those on the losing side will be looking for a chance for revenge, and those on the winning side will not have their own strong political coalition on which they can count to run the legislature— without the governor's support.

Finally, whatever negative situations occur in the legislature can be tracked back to the governor and that political intrusion. Most governors find there are enough problems and explosive issues in the executive branch and elsewhere for them to cover and that there is no need for the added burden.

How well do governors perform their crucial legislative role? Are they able to handle both their own agenda and that of the many legislators who come to the capital to serve? In the Summer 1994 Survey, respondents were asked how they would characterize their governor's relations with the state legislature. While the fifty-state average on the five-point scale is right in the middle at 3.0 in Table 6-20, there is a much greater spread of gubernatorial abilities in this relationship than in other areas analyzed in this chapter. While the ratings for twelve governors were "good" to "excellent," those for eleven were "poor" to "fair," with an average of 3.0. Previous service in a state legislature did not necessarily seem to be a positive factor in how well a governor's legislative relations were perceived (average score: 3.1), nor was service in the U.S. Congress (average score: 3.0).

Having been a legislative leader did seem to be an experience that assisted governors in this role (average score: 3.3). But not all of them; one governor who had been a legislative leader was characterized as someone who "did not seem to remember her time in the legislature, and how that body operates."

Table 6-20 Relations of Governors with the
Legislature, Summer 1994

Score	Category	No. of governors
5.0	Excellent	0
4.5		4
4.0	Good	8
3.5		10
3.0	Average	8
2.5		9
2.0	Fair	5
1.5		5
1.0	Poor	1

Average score: 3.0

SOURCE: Calculated from data from Summer 1994 Survey.

The Intergovernmental Middleman

The world that a governor must address is not constrained by the boundaries of the state. In an earlier time, out-of-state efforts made by governors were limited to occasional trips to attract industry, to attend the more socially oriented governors' conferences, and to participate in the presidential nominating conventions every four years. In recent decades, however, the states and the governors have found a need to focus on the issues, problems, and governmental activities that are part of the larger intergovernmental system in which individual states are lodged. Some of these issues concern several states at once, such as a common river pollution problem. Others are regional in scope, such as higher education in the South following World War II or, more recently, the need to dispose of hazardous waste materials. Still others, like health and welfare reform, are national in scope, and thus all states and governors have a stake in the actions of Congress and the national executive branch.

Governors were slow to move in these circles, tightly limiting their concerns and interests to their own states and leaving national government concerns to the state's congressional delegation. But in the last three decades, governors and states have been forced to develop their intergovernmental relations roles at varying levels of government: national, regional, state, substate, and local. This development has generally coincided with the rapid expansion in national programs since the administration of President Lyndon B. Johnson in the 1960s, and it is also tied to the increasingly articulated demands of state citizens and interests for the government to do more about a wider range of concerns. Most recently, in the face of a reduced federal domestic effort, governors have worked to lessen the impact of federal cutbacks and unfunded federal mandates on their states and citizens, because the consequences of such cutbacks and programmatic shifts land on their own desks.

During the past two decades, governors have taken several significant steps to enhance their intergovernmental role. One was the establishment of a joint gubernatorial presence in Washington in the form of the National Governors' Association. The NGA is now considered one of the major public interest associations on Capitol Hill, with a lobbying, research, and state service staff of ninety—a marked increase from its staff of three in the late 1960s (Weissert 1983, 52). Ironically, the governors and other state officials have had to increase their representation on Capitol Hill as it has become increasingly clear that state congressional delegations often do not have the state's overall interest in mind as they pass budgets and policy initiatives. So the states must join the crowd of interest groups pressing their needs on their own states' representatives.

Gubernatorial relations with a state's congressional delegation are complex and subject to different types of difficulties. At the purely political level, a governor can be seen as a potential challenger for a U.S. senator's seat or even a congressional seat, and we have seen that more members of Congress are eyeing gubernatorial chairs. On policy matters, a governor may have an interest in particular issues for his or her own state or for states in general. Congressional delegation members also have their own interests—both of a national, specific, or constituent nature—which may or may not coincide with the governor's expressed interests. Therefore, the degree of cooperation between these two sets of political actors can vary greatly; some governors find their delegations remote, inaccessible, and suspicious of any joint venture, while others find camaraderie.

Beginning ten years ago, the NGA took another step to increase the governors' influence on public policy. The governors began a series of year-long, fifty-state assessments of specific issues of concern to each of them and their states. In the first year, NGA addressed public education and set an agenda for each state's governor to follow, building in an annual updating on certain measures. In succeeding years the NGA focused on economic development and job creation, the changing balance in the federal system, international trade, health and welfare reform, and children's policies.

What has this meant for the NGA annual meetings? In a subtle, backhanded compliment, two observers complained that the NGA "just ain't what it used to be. All the governors seem to talk about anymore are serious, important issues . . . . It's a hell of a note. . . . The conferences undoubtedly are worthwhile. They just aren't as much fun anymore" (Germond and Witcover 1988, 19A).

In recent years a new factor entered the politics of intergovernmental relations. Longer tenure is important in the governor's intergovernmental role. The relations need time to mature and the activities undertaken are complex and take time to perform effectively. Furthermore, leadership in the NGA provides a platform for views to be made known and the opportunity for governors actually to affect policy. Term limitations, therefore, restrict governors in their ability to fulfill this intergovernmental role, especially in holding leadership positions. Thus, states may be short-changing themselves by limiting the tenure they allow their governors (Grady 1987). As one observer suggested: "Our state changes the team captain and key players just about the time we get the opportunity and know-how to carry the ball and score" (Farb 1977, 18). As the movement to limit terms of public officials grows and succeeds, this particular role of governors may also be curtailed.

Working with the Media

Probably the most significant source of informal power available to governors is their relationship with the public through the media and through other modes of contact. Most of the governors used media contact with the people to gain election to office, so they are well aware of the potency of this informal power. However, once in office, the governor's relationship with the press undergoes a subtle yet important change. The governor is no longer the head of the army of attack but is the head of the army of occupation, the new administration in the state capital.

The media watches the governor with a keen eye, evaluating his or her performance not only against the promises but against previous gubernatorial efforts and the needs of the state. Furthermore, the media watches in the same manner all those whom the governor has brought into the administration. Stories of official misconduct sell newspapers and make the evening news more exciting.

Governors have the opportunity to dominate the news from the state capital by carefully planning when press conferences are held during the day and when press releases are distributed. If they time it right, their news is on the evening TV news programs and in the morning papers, where there are greater audiences to reach. A governor's communications or press relations office (every governor has one) can in large part determine a portion of the news the citizens of a state receive about a gubernatorial administration.

Governors do vary, however, in their approach to and openness with the media. Press conferences are held routinely by some and only on specific occasions by others; individual interview sessions with members of the press are regular fare for some governors, whereas others are more protective of their time and interactions with the media.

The advice provided new governors by incumbents indicates just how sensitive they all are to this relationship: "The media expects you to do well. Thus, doing well isn't news"; "When you hold a press conference and are going to face the lions, have some red meat to throw them or they'll chew on you"; "Never make policy at a news conference"; and "Never argue with a person who buys ink by the barrel" (Beyle and Huefner 1983, 268).

How well do the governors actually do in this relationship? Do the new governors heed the advice of their more experienced peers? Are they able to make that switch from campaigner to governor in a manner that helps to continue their relationship with the media, voters, and other constituencies? In the Summer 1994 Survey, respondents were asked about their governor's relations with the media. Table 6-21 indicates that for the most part it appears that governors work well with the media. The fifty-state average on the five-point scale is 3.3, and one-third

Table 6-21 Relations of Governors with the Media, Summer 1994

Score	Category	No. of governors
5.0	Excellent	0
4.5		7
4.0	Good	10
3.5		15
3.0	Average	6
2.5		6
2.0	Fair	3
1.5		2
1.0	Poor	1

Average score: 3.3

SOURCE: Calculated from data from Summer 1994 Survey.

of the governors (seventeen) were rated as having good to excellent relations with the media. Those with the top ratings come from all over the country—three in the West, two in the South, and one each in the Northeast and the Midwest.

But of the six governors in the poor-to-fair range, four decided not to run for reelection in 1994 (Finney of Kansas, Walters of Oklahoma, Roberts of Oregon) or in 1995 (Edwards of Louisiana), one was beaten in his bid for his party's nomination in the primary after succeeding to the office on the death of the governor (Walter B. Miller, R-S.D.), and one could not run because of a term-limit restriction (William D. Schaefer, D-Md.). Governors seeking reelection do not need poor media relations, which are hard to overcome. After all, the media is one of the primary vehicles by which voters get a reading on how their governor is performing.

The reasons given for governors having very good relations with the media included their skills in working with the media. The survey is sprinkled with comments such as "he is a PR guy," "an example of 'the harder you work at something, the luckier you get' in the media," "very media savvy," and a "very skillful" media staff. Poor relations with the media are the product of gubernatorial lack of skills—"He is media shy, which makes him tongue-tied with us often," "He's a little stand-offish, seems a little self-conscious about his lack of 'polish'"—or governors' injecting an adversarial tone into the relationship.

Then there are the governors who work well in one media situation but not in others. One is "good with editorial boards, poor with working press," another is "excellent with electronic media, fair with print media." Respondents from two midwestern states indicated a more complex problem for state governments and governors and their relations with the media. The comment of one of them sums it up: "Difficult to be excellent in this state, prime media are in the metro areas, less interested in state politics."

Another part of a governor's public role is primarily reactive. The governor's office receives many letters, visits, and telephone calls, each with a request, a critical comment, or question of some kind. All of them must be answered. Each response probably affects two to five people among the extended family and friends of the recipient. Thus, the number of contacts between the governor or the governor's staff and the public, either directly or indirectly, is very high. How well these letters and requests are handled can make up an important part of the public's perception of the governor's performance.

Some governors take an activist stance with regard to the public and generate citizen contacts through a variety of approaches. Some capitalize on their ceremonial role by appearing at county fairs, cutting ribbons at shopping centers, attending dedication ceremonies, and crowning beauty queens. These activities often can require a considerable investment of time.

Sometimes governors use structured approaches to stimulate and maintain contacts with their statewide constituency. In a survey of the states done in 1980, eight states reported having a "Capital for a Day" program in which the governor makes a particular city or county the state capital for that day, interacting with citizens and local public officials in carefully planned meetings. The overall goal in such programs is to cover the whole state (Olander and Duncombe 1981). These types of approaches allow for two-way communications, the governors not only hearing from constituents but also being able to carry their message and priorities to the people.

The governor, through this public role, has the potential to set the state's public agenda and focus attention on it. A governor's priorities can become the state's unless unforeseen crises or problems arise or the media itself is inadequate to the task.

Priorities on the Job: The Personal Factor

Being governor is a time-consuming and busy undertaking. Many who have been governors or served with governors find that discussions and analyses of gubernatorial roles, power, and responsibilities do not provide the sense of what being a governor really means. In an attempt to capture the pace of a governor's life and show how time, or lack of time, affects gubernatorial actions, the NGA developed a case study called "A Day in the Life of a Governor" for newly elected governors (Beyle and Muchmore 1983, 32–42). That case cannot be recreated here, but based on a survey of those who scheduled gubernatorial time and from the estimates of sixteen incumbent governors, some indication can be given about where they spend their time (Beyle and Muchmore 1983, 52–66).

Both governors and their schedulers basically agreed on how much time was allocated to the various roles governors perform. Including recruiting and appointing personnel to positions in the executive branch, half their time was taken up just in running state government and working with the legislature. Another large segment of time was spent in their public roles, either directly interacting with the public, participating in ceremonial functions, or indirectly working with the media. Their schedulers estimated that over one-third of the schedule was devoted to these public roles; the governors had a lower estimate, one-fifth of their time. The governors' intergovernmental activities, divided equally between federal and local governmental issues, took up slightly more than one-eighth of their time.

In sum, we find what most of us would hope to find—governors serving primarily as chief executives and working with the legislature, relegating their public roles to second place, and giving their intergovernmental concerns less but not inconsiderable attention. They spend less time on politics by these estimates, although much that is politics is present in ceremonial, legislative, and other activities.

What gets squeezed in these official priorities is the governor as a person and his or her ability to maintain some semblance of a private life. As the NGA case study suggests, a governor in those few, short moments of reflection when alone with family "may find that his campaign did not result in his capturing the office, but in the office capturing him" (NGA 1978, 115). Nearly half of the fifty-one former governors responding to a 1976 NGA survey cited interference with their family life when asked what they considered the most difficult aspects of being governor. Being governor exacts a personal toll on the individual (Beyle and Muchmore 1983, 23–27).

LEAVING THE GOVERNORSHIP

The former Vermont governor Madeleine Kunin suggests "[t]here are two climaxes in political life: rising to power and falling from it" (Kunin 1994, 19). At the end of a gubernatorial term, a governor usually has several options available for the future. Many can and do choose to seek reelection to the governor's chair. In recent decades, we have seen some governors virtually turn a gubernatorial chair into their own private property as they served for several terms. While seeking reelection as an incumbent usually provides a major campaign advantage, winning reelection (sometimes renomination by their own party) is not always an easy task, as was noted earlier.

The Unplanned Departure

Why do incumbent governors lose? In a few situations a single issue can be pinpointed as the cause of a governor's defeat. In many cases, a defeat is the result of an accumulation of several issues and concerns. But certain constants come into focus when we look at the situations of all the defeated governors over a period of time.

First, between 1951 and 1993, over half of the gubernatorial defeats seemed to be tied to the voters' desire for a new governor. This meant defeating incumbent governors in their party's primary (31 percent) in order to ensure that someone new would be their party's nominee, or electing candidates of the opposing party in the general election (28 percent), ensuring a partisan change in the governorship. In the fifteen election years from 1980 through 1994, this desire was even greater: 35 percent of the incumbents were defeated in their party's primary, and

48 percent were defeated in the general election as the opposing party claimed the governor's chair. Part of the reason for these upsets was the increasing two-party turmoil in the formerly one-party, Democratic southern states.

Second, the long-suggested concept of the tax-loss governor—those who raise taxes will feel the voters' wrath—was found to be a major element in more than one-fifth of the defeats from 1950 through 1994 and 29 percent of the defeats from 1980 through 1994. Taxes bedevil governors, especially when additional funds must be raised to provide for state facilities and services. Seven of the fifteen gubernatorial losses in the 1990 through 1994 elections, when state budgets were in considerable distress, could be attributed at least partly to some aspect of a tax issue.

Scandals and incompetence, either administrative, political, or personal, are also significant issues in the defeat of governors seeking reelection and former governors seeking to return to office. In sum, governors seeking to stay in office, or to regain office, are vulnerable to the ambitions of others within their party and state, to a desire on the part of voters for a change to someone new, to issues directly affecting the electorate's wallets (taxation) or lives (jobs, the economy, the environment), and to allegations of misconduct or poor performance.

Onward and Upward

Staying in office is only one of many options that an incumbent governor may weigh. As noted earlier, for some governors, the position is one step on a ladder that they hope leads to a higher office, such as the U.S. Senate or even the presidency, as in the cases of three of our last four presidents: Carter, Ronald Reagan, and Clinton.

Some move on to appointed national-level positions, such as cabinet offices, as Interior Secretary Bruce Babbitt (D-Ariz., 1978–1987) and Education Secretary Richard Riley (D-S.C., 1979–1987) did in the Clinton administration. Two New Hampshire governors became chief-of-staff for a president—Sherman Adams for Dwight Eisenhower and John Sununu for George Bush. Why did New Hampshire governors do so well in these presidential administrations? The early New Hampshire presidential primary is crucial to the presidential nomination process; winning candidates remember the help given them by the governor.

Some other governors move into leadership positions in the corporate world or in higher education, as did the former governor of North Carolina Terry Sanford (D, 1961–1965), who became president of Duke University; Lamar Alexander, who became president of the University of Tennessee; and the former New Jersey governor Tom Kean, who became president of Drew University. However, we must be impressed most with the large number of governors for whom the governorship was their ultimate public office. They sought the office, served, and returned to their private lives—often to a lucrative law practice that may have included representing clients before the state legislature, state agencies, or state courts—their old home turf.

Unfortunately, some governors were prosecuted for their misconduct in office, and some later served terms in prison. Two recent governors who fell on hard ethical times after leaving office were Arch A. Moore (R-W.Va, 1967–1977, 1985–1989) and Edward DiPrete (R-R.I., 1985–1991).

Leaving There

Most governors find a good life after being governor. But, as former Michigan Governor William Milliken (1969–1983) observed, they must take pains in planning their leave-taking and "take advantage of the lessons learned by those who have already gone down the path." This means taking steps to prepare for the new administration while winding down the old and preparing for their own new life (Weeks 1984, 77). The NGA has developed a "worst case scenario" to alert them to what can happen without such planning and to suggest some strategies to follow to avert such problems (NGA 1990a).

This sounds most rational, but in the white heat of politics, and especially in the worst of all situations—being unseated as governor—these steps are not easy to take, nor does there seem to be enough time to plan them. Although states generally make provisions for their incoming governors, they tend to ignore their outgoing governors. The exiting governors suddenly lose all the perquisites of being governor: staff, cars, drivers, schedulers, office equipment, telephones, and so forth. This is seen in the lament of former governor Calvin L. Rampton (D-Utah): "I never realized how much of a man's life he spends looking for a parking place" (Weeks 1984, 73).

CONCLUSION

The American state governorship is the highest elective office in a state and, in some cases, the steppingstone to an even higher office. The governor symbolizes the state to many, and when state government falters or errs, the public often holds the governor accountable. The states have refurbished their governments, bidding "Goodbye to Goodtime Charlie" and, in doing so, have generally obtained a new breed of very capable people to serve as governor (Sabato 1978). Sabato has, however, questioned whether there may not be some slippage in caliber of some of our recently elected governors (Rosenthal 1988, 37).

This chapter provides a view of the governorship through the eyes of the governors themselves and of those who watch what governors do. In it are described the politics of becoming governor, the tools available to the governor—both personal and institutional—the major roles now being performed by governors, and how, in performing these roles, governors have informal powers of considerable magnitude. Governors not only sit atop our state governments and the state political system, but through their informal powers, they can set and dominate the state's policy agenda and have an impact on regional and national agendas as well.

REFERENCES

Alexander, Lamar. 1986. *Steps Along the Way: A Governor's Scrapbook.* Nashville, Tenn.: Thomas Nelson.

Allen, R. 1949. *Our Sovereign State.* New York: Vanguard Press.

Barone, Michael, and Grant Ujifusa. 1987. *The Almanac of American Politics 1988.* Washington, D.C.: National Journal.

———. 1993. *The Almanac of American Politics 1994.* Washington, D.C.: National Journal.

Benjamin, Gerald. 1982. "The Diffusion of the Governor's Veto Power." *State Government* 55:99–105.

Beyle, Thad L. 1988a. "The Governor as Innovator in the Federal System." *Publius* 18, no. 3:131–152.

———. 1988b. "Incumbency and Money in Gubernatorial Campaigns." *Election Politics* 5, no. 4:18–23.

———. 1992. "Term Limits in the State Executive Branch." In *Limiting Legislative Terms,* edited by Gerald Benjamin and Michael Malbin. Washington, D.C.: CQ Press.

———. 1994. "The Speaker's Office as a Political Stepping Stone?" *North Carolina Insight* 15, no. 1:30–31.

———. 1995. "Enhancing Executive Leadership in the States." *State and Local Government Review* 27, no. 1: 18–35.

———, ed. 1992. *Governors and Hard Times.* Washington, D.C.: CQ Press.

Beyle, Thad L., and Robert Huefner. 1983. "Quips and Quotes from Old Governors to New." *Public Administration Review* 43:268–270.

Beyle, Thad L., and Lynn Muchmore. 1983. *Being Governor: The View from the Office.* Durham, N.C.: Duke University Press.

Beyle, Thad, and Rich Jones. 1994. "Term Limits in the States." In *The Book of the States, 1994–95.* Lexington, Ky.: Council of State Governments.

CSG (Council of State Governments). 1992. *The Book of the States, 1992–93.* Lexington, Ky.: Council of State Governments.

———. 1994. *The Book of the States, 1994–95.* Lexington, Ky.: Council of State Governments.

Farb, Robert L. 1977. *Report on the Proposed Gubernatorial Succession Amendment, 1977.* Chapel Hill, N.C.: Institute of Government.

Farney, Dennis. 1993. "When Wisconsin Governor Wields Partial Veto, the Legislature Might as Well Go Play Scrabble." *Wall Street Journal,* July 1, sec. A.

Flentje, H. Edward. 1980. *Knowledge and Gubernatorial Policy Making.* Center for Urban Studies, Wichita State University, Wichita, Kan.

Germond, Jack, and Jules Witcover. 1988. "Once-Wild Governors' Conferences Now a Tame Show." *News and Observer* (Raleigh, N.C.), July 13, sec. A.

Grady, Dennis. 1987. "Gubernatorial Behavior in State-Federal Relations." *Western Political Quarterly* 40:305–318.

Hutchison, Tony. 1989. "Legislating via Veto." *State Legislatures* 18 (January): 20–22.

Kaufman, Herbert. 1963. *Politics and Policies in State and Local Governments.* Englewood Cliffs, N.J.: Prentice-Hall.

Key, V. O., Jr. 1956. *American State Politics.* New York: Alfred A. Knopf.

Kunin, Madeleine. 1994. *Living a Political Life.* New York: Alfred A. Knopf.

Matheson, Scott M. 1986. *Out of Balance.* Salt Lake City, Utah: Peregrine Smith Books.

Moe, Ronald C. 1988. *Prospects for the Item Veto at the Federal Level: Lessons from the States.* Washington, D.C.: National Academy of Public Administration.

Morehouse, Sarah M. 1981. *State Politics, Party, and Policy.* New York: Holt, Rinehart and Winston.

———. 1987. "Money versus Party Effort: Nominating the Governor." Paper presented at the annual meeting of the American Political Science Association, Chicago, September 4–7.

Murphy, Russell D. 1992. "Connecticut: Lowell P. Weicker, Jr.: A Maverick in 'The Land of Steady Habits.'" In *Governors and Hard Times,* edited by Thad Beyle. Washington, D.C.: CQ Press.

North Carolina Center for Public Policy Research. 1989. *Report on Campaign Financing in North Carolina.* Raleigh: North Carolina Center for Public Policy Research.

NASBO (National Association of State Budget Officers). 1992. *Budget Processes in the States, 1992.* Washington, D.C.: National Association of State Budget Officers.

NGA (National Governors' Association). 1978. *Governing the American States.* Washington, D.C.: National Governors' Association.

————. 1981. *Reflections on Being Governor.* Washington, D.C.: National Governors' Association.

————. 1987a. "The Institutional Powers of the Governorship, 1965–1985." *State Management Notes.* Washington, D.C.: National Governors' Association.

————. 1990a. "The Governor's Final Year: Challenges and Strategies." *State Management Notes.* Washington, D.C.: National Governors' Association.

————. 1990b. "Organizing the Transition Team." *State Management Notes.* Washington, D.C.: National Governors' Association.

————. 1994. *Governors of the American States, Commonwealths, and Territories, 1994 Directory.* Washington, D.C.: National Governors' Association.

Olander, Frank H., and Sydney Duncombe. 1981. "Capital-for-a-Day Program: A New Approach to Public Contact." *State Government* 54, no.1:21–27.

Ransone, Coleman B. 1956. *The Office of Governor in the United States.* University: University of Alabama Press.

Rosenthal, Alan. 1988. *The Governor and the Legislature.* New Brunswick, N.J.: Eagleton Institute of Politics, Rutgers University.

Sabato, Larry. 1978. *Goodbye to Good-Time Charlie: The American Governorship Transformed.* Lexington, Mass.: Lexington Books.

————. 1983. *Goodbye to Good-Time Charlie: The American Governorship Transformed.* 2d ed. Washington, D.C.: CQ Press.

Schlesinger, Joseph A. 1965. "The Politics of the Executive." In *Politics in the American States,* edited by Herbert Jacob and Kenneth N. Vines. Boston: Little, Brown.

————. 1966. *Ambition and Politics: Political Careers in the United States.* Chicago: Rand McNally.

————. 1971. "The Politics of the Executive." In *Politics in the American States,* edited by Herbert Jacob and Kenneth N. Vines. 2d ed. Boston: Little, Brown.

Sherman, Sharon. 1984. "Power-split: When Legislatures and Governors Are of Opposing Parties." *State Legislatures* 10, no. 5: 9–12.

SPR (State Policy Reports). 1993. *States in Profile: The State Policy Reference Book, 1993.* Columbus, Ohio: State Policy Reports.

Weeks, George. 1984. "Gubernatorial Transitions: Leaving There." *State Government* 57, no. 3:73–78.

Weissert, Carol S. 1983. "The National Governors' Association: 1908–1983." *State Government* 56, no. 3:44–52.

Wiggins, Charles W. 1980. "Executive Vetoes and Legislative Overrides in the American States." *Journal of Politics* 42:1110–1117.

SUGGESTED READINGS

Blair, Diane. *Arkansas Politics and Government.* Lincoln: University of Nebraska Press, 1988. One of the best single-state studies of a state political and governmental system masquerading as a textbook.

Herzik, Eric B., and Brent W. Brown. *Gubernatorial Leadership and State Policy.* Westport, Conn: Greenwood Press, 1991. A multiauthored book focusing on the governors' policy roles. Case studies on both the policy processes around the governor and specific policy areas that concern governors.

Kunin, Madeleine. *Living a Political Life.* New York: Alfred A. Knopf, 1994. A governor's view of the path to the governorship, how the governorship operates, and what governors can accomplish when they have a clear focus on their goals.

Rosenthal, Alan. *The Governor and the Legislature.* Washington, D.C.: CQ Press, 1988. A fifty-state analysis of the relationship of the two major governmental actors in the states. Based on extensive interviewing and participant observation.

Sabato, Larry. *Good-Bye to Good Time Charlie.* 2d ed. Washington, D.C.: CQ Press, 1983. One of the best studies of modern governors and the governorships of the fifty states. Based on extensive research and interviewing of participants in the governorship.

CHAPTER 7

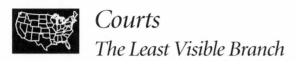 *Courts*
The Least Visible Branch

HERBERT JACOB

A casual observer might conclude that courts have little significance in state politics. In some states, judges are not on the ballot; and even in states where they are, judicial elections rarely capture the imagination of the electorate. Those news reports that do feature the courts usually emphasize matters far removed from the turbulence of ordinary politics, such as the drama of a criminal trial or the legalistic elements of a decision.

In addition, the myth that courts should be nonpolitical is prominent in American culture. Courthouse friezes portray justice as a blindfolded woman holding the scales of justice in her hand. Most Americans firmly believe that courts should be blind to political bias; fairness, it would seem, requires neutrality.

Yet there is another theme running through American political thought: that all public officials should be responsive to the electorate, especially if they play prominent roles in molding and implementing public policy. Although some judges deny it, courts occupy a significant position in the policy-making process by ratifying choices made by legislatures and governors, by interpreting their policies (and thus adding or subtracting to their substance), and by vetoing policies when the courts declare them to be unconstitutional. Moreover, they routinely exercise discretion as they impose the norms specified by statutes and administrative regulations while ruling on the disputes brought before them. Thus, judges are very much the kind of officials who might be held responsive to the electorate.

These two views of the courts constantly compete in both theory and practice. Those holding the view that courts should be nonpolitical argue that they should be treated separately from ordinary political analysis, yet those who maintain that they should be responsive to the electorate claim that courts should be analyzed as an integral part of the politics and government of the states.

Everyday experience supports both perspectives because the state judiciary performs two distinct functions. On the one hand, *appellate courts* are particularly visible in their policy role because they continuously provide guidance to other government officials and private individuals about the meaning of state legislative enactments, sometimes declaring them or executive actions unconstitutional. Appellate courts, especially the supreme courts of the states, often play a significant *policy-making* role in state politics. On the other hand, the principal task of *trial courts* is to apply the law to such disparate matters as divorce, debt collection, personal injuries, insurance disagreements, and challenges to government decisions, as well as criminal cases of all kinds. In implementing policy, trial courts are one of the most important *social control* instruments available to state governments. While this implementing role is perceived to require evenhanded, unbiased decisions, it nevertheless has significant ramifications in the political arena.

The functions of trial and appellate courts are so distinct that this chapter contains a separate section on each. First, however, some of the important structural characteristics of state courts and the traits of the principal participants in judicial policy making and norm enforcement are examined.

STRUCTURAL ATTRIBUTES OF STATE COURTS

Organization

Courts in some states are organized in two tiers and in others, in three. Every state has trial courts and at least one supreme court. Thirty-nine states have intermediate appellate courts; those that do not are compact, like Rhode Island, or sparsely populated, like Wyoming (CSG 1994, 186–187). However, the relations between courts are not as simple as suggested in Figure 7-1. In the figure the courts are shown as a hierarchy, and indeed, appellate courts are usually called *higher* courts and trial courts are called *lower*. However, the hierarchy works only in a limited way. Judges in lower courts are not actual subordinates of those in higher courts. The higher-court judges do not hire, fire, set compensation, or normally assign judges in lower courts. Judges in lower courts often retain authority to develop some of their own procedures and rarely are under the daily supervision of higher courts. Still, the decisions of higher courts bind lower courts, and many higher courts issue rules and procedures that lower-court judges must follow.

Another complication hidden in the diagram is that trial courts should usually not be represented by single boxes. Only when they are fully unified, as in Illi-

Figure 7-1   Structure of State Courts

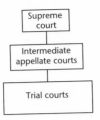

nois, where there is only one trial court in each county (sometimes with many branches and divisions), can a single box accurately represent them. In most states, many different kinds of trial courts exist. Some hear the more important cases, while others hear cases involving small disputes or lesser crimes. Some specialize in particular kinds of disputes, such as those involving families or the probate of wills or traffic tickets. Each state has its own set of boundaries for these trial courts; they often constitute a maze that only lawyers who practice in a particular locale fully understand.

An attribute implicit in the diagram is that each level of courts operates in a different-sized jurisdiction. The highest court of a state has jurisdiction over the entire state; trial courts typically have jurisdiction only in a single city, a single county, or a circuit composed of several counties. Intermediate appellate courts sometimes have jurisdiction over an entire state and sometimes are limited to one region of it. Important consequences flow from these jurisdictional differences. The highest courts of states respond to the political environment of the entire state, whereas trial courts are typically quite local in their outlook. One may expect quite different perspectives on crime, for instance, from the Superior Court of Los Angeles and from the Superior Court of Sierra County, although both are in California. Such differences sometimes generate conflicting rulings by trial courts, which appellate courts then must reconcile.

Finally, the titles of the courts are not as simple as the diagram suggests. Trial courts may be called superior courts, district courts, circuit courts, courts of common pleas, municipal courts, and many other names. A state's highest court is usually called the supreme court, but in New York, supreme courts are trial courts and the highest court is called the court of appeals. In addition, Oklahoma and Texas do not have a single highest court; they have a supreme court for civil cases and a criminal court of appeals for criminal cases. Simplicity and streamlining are not among the virtues of American state courts!

Procedure

The procedures that produce decisions in courts are quite different from those that do so in legislatures or in the executive branch. Adversarial proceedings govern American courts. That means that judges depend on adversaries to bring disputes to them and that every case involves people on two sides who argue their respective positions before the court. In criminal cases, the two sides consist of the state (represented by the prosecutor) and the defendant; in civil cases, the two sides are the plaintiff (who initiates the court case) and the defendant. The two adversaries attempt to persuade the judge or jury to rule in their favor. They do so by presenting information in ways that accord with complicated rules of evidence and by citing legal authorities. The exact manner in which these arguments are made varies from state to state and even within states. Moreover, evidence can normally be presented only at the trial; appellate courts take the trial record and then consider arguments about how the law should be applied to the situation revealed at trial. Because the process is driven by adversaries, the litigants control both the agenda of courts and the pace of litigation. In criminal cases, the prosecutor determines who shall be charged with a crime; prosecutor and defense attorneys exercise great influence over how rapidly the charges will be tried. In civil cases, such as contract disputes and personal injury claims, plaintiffs (and their attorneys) bring the disputes to the courts and together with defendants and their lawyers determine the pace of the litigation.

In trial courts, judges are not the only decision makers. A trial may be heard by a jury of ordinary citizens; in such cases the jury determines which side should win. Jury trials, however, are the exception; most cases are heard by judges alone or are settled after the court has made some preliminary decisions but before they actually come to trial. Appellate courts never use juries; in those courts several judges (usually at least three) make the decision collectively. In both kinds of courts, decisions are usually announced in open court, although the deliberations producing the decisions remain secret. There is no "sunshine" law for courts that forces appellate or trial judges or juries to deliberate in public.

In many other ways, the decisional process in courts is much more closed than in legislative or executive arenas. Interest groups enjoy only limited access. Moreover, ordinary citizens cannot intervene in cases unless they have an immediate interest in the outcome. No one may telephone the courthouse to attempt to sway a judge's decision in a pending case; all arguments must be made in open court.

The Scope of Law

Lawyers frame disputes in court cases in ways that highlight the legal aspects of the problem. Courts then apply the law to disputes to impose at least a temporary solution. The typical disagreements that reach a court are different from those handled by legislatures in that they usually concern only single individuals or corporations; they do not normally involve large-scale social conflicts around which mass movements have organized. Of course, in exceptional circumstances social conflicts find their way into courtrooms, as when disputes over civil rights, abortion, or religious liberty come to court. Even in those circumstances, however, lawyers frame the case as if the conflict involved an individual or small group of litigants. The characteristics and problems of these litigants then become the focus of the litigation, not the characteristics or problems of the entire social group whom they represent. Moreover, although social conflicts often have many sides, the judicial process compresses them into two: plaintiff and defendant.

Litigants choose the courts as the arena in which to bring their disputes because they think the law offers a remedy that the courts can set in motion, such as a judgment of compensation, an order requiring the other party to "cease and desist" from certain actions or to restore prior conditions, an order that establishes a new status for the parties (as in divorces or adoptions), or a judgment that imposes punishment on the other party. Consequently, the law plays a much more prominent role in courtroom decisions than in legislative or administrative proceedings, where political and economic considerations may be more prominent.

State law is a rich source of authority for state courts. Although federal statutes have become much more numerous, the states remain the primary source of law in the United States. State law provides most of the remedies for problems that bring people to court, but while legal remedies have the same general form across the states, the details vary enormously from one state to another.

Each state has its own constitution, and these constitutions vary on many dimensions. Some are quite old; for instance, the constitution of Massachusetts predates the U.S. Constitution, having been adopted in 1780, and two others were adopted before 1800. All but the newest state constitutions have been amended much more frequently than the federal charter. The large number of amendments reflects the enormous detail contained in state constitutions. While the federal Constitution has only 7,800 words, the median length of state constitutions at the beginning of 1994 was 22,500 words (CSG 1994, 19; Janda, Berry, and Goldman 1987, 100).

The verbiage in state constitutions has been inserted purposively. Much of it imposes specific limits on state or local governments, such as the requirement for a balanced budget or special procedures for passing tax laws. Much of the language, however, provides remedies for specific situations that are not available in the federal Constitution (Galie 1982). For instance, whereas the federal Constitution has no explicit provision protecting the right to privacy, the Montana Constitution reads: "The right of individual privacy is essential to the well-being of a free society and shall not be infringed without the showing of a compelling state interest" (section 10). Indeed, eighteen states include some form of the Equal Rights Amendment, which failed ratification to the federal Constitution (Galie 1982, 745).

Such provisions of state constitutions, which differ both in substance and in the amount of detail from the federal Constitution, sometimes allow state courts to offer different remedies from those offered in the federal courts. For instance, while the U.S. Supreme Court in the 1980s began to whittle away the protected status of early term abortions by upholding congressional mandates to prohibit federal funds from paying for abortions for the indigent, the California, Connecticut, and Massachusetts supreme courts ruled otherwise on the basis of their interpretation of their state constitutions ("Developments in the Law" 1982, 1442; Wermiel 1988, A1).

It has long been a principle of American federalism that state law and state courts could provide rights to their citizens beyond those guaranteed by the federal government. The opposite is not true: states cannot deny rights granted by the federal Constitution. State courts are not consistently more liberal than the U.S. Supreme Court, however (Esler 1994).

A second major source for legal remedies lies in state law. Some of this law originates from court interpretations of common usage—so-called common law. In the twentieth century, however, most state law originates from statutes passed by the state legislature or, in rare cases, by popular initiative and referendum. Statutes reflect political compromises reached in the legislature, often after vigorous contention by opposing interest groups.

The volume of state law has grown enormously during the twentieth century. In 1930 the average state legislature passed laws filling about 206 printed pages; by 1982, according to my tabulation, that figure had risen to 1,486 pages. In addition, many state agencies issue regulations that also become part of the body of state law.

Legislation and regulations may be quite broad, giving courts considerable leeway in applying them to specific situations. Much legislation, however, is very detailed. Many state laws incorporate both tendencies. For instance, state laws minutely regulate the procedures that must be followed in order to obtain a divorce, prescribing such details as the number of days a couple must be separated before being eligible for one. In contrast, the standards for child custody are often framed in general terms, requiring courts only to act in the child's "best interests." The fixed length of separation clearly tells courts when they have the power to grant a divorce, and almost no disputes arise about this matter. The vague "best interest of the child" standard, however, spawns many disputes about whether the mother, father, stepparent, or someone else should have custody.

Each state handles such details somewhat differently. For example, in some states no mention of fault may be made in any divorce decision; the law is simply blind to whether one party or another "caused" the breakdown of the marriage. In other states, fault may play a large role in determining who has the best claim to custody of the children and who gets most of the property, even when the divorce itself is granted in a no-fault proceeding (Jacob 1988). Similar variations exist in the law governing how much control patients, their families, doctors, and hospitals may exercise during the final days of a person's life—may a patient in unbearable pain, for instance, direct a physician to give him or her a fatal dose of a medicine (Glick 1992)? Parallel variations also exist in state criminal statutes (see Chapter 10). Because of these differences, the rights of litigants and the remedies available to them vary greatly from state to state.

These bodies of state law constitute the raw materials that courts use to process disputes that are brought to them. When a litigant petitions for judicial intervention, the court must decide whether the law provides a remedy for the circumstances involved. For instance, if an automobile owner alleges that the car he or she bought was defective, the courts must first determine whether the law provides any remedy should the allegation prove true. Some states have passed "lemon laws," which provide protection for consumers in such circumstances; if no such law exists, the case is thrown out. If the court decides that the law affords a remedy, it then turns to the factual questions of the case (whether the alleged defects were the fault of the manufacturer or of the purchaser's failure to maintain her car) and its interpretation of the law (whether the circumstances fit the statute).

Most legal remedies in the United States depend on such provisions of state law and are litigated there rather than in federal courts. This is true, for instance, of the myriad cases that arise from disputes about contracts, whether they concern the purchase of land and buildings, the sale of wholesale or retail goods, or the borrowing of money. The same is true of most cases involving disputes about injuries resulting from auto accidents, medical malpractice, or improperly designed products. In addition, all divorces go through state courts because there is no federal divorce statute. Finally, most allegations of crime come before state rather than federal courts because the bulk of American criminal law is the product of state legislatures.

Consequences of the Legal Focus

We tend to take the legal focus of courts for granted. Many of its consequences are so obvious that they scarcely merit mention. The procedures of courts are distinctive, inhibiting the freewheeling behavior typical of legislative bodies or the bureaucratic style of administrative agencies. Likewise, the language of the law has become the jargon of lawyers, encapsulating legal technicalities in terms that only attorneys fully understand.

Other consequences, however, are not so obvious. One lies in the form of decisions that emanate from courts. Courts often do not just announce their decision but accompany it with opinions in which the judge or judges articulate the reasons supporting it. Judicial opinions often pay little attention to the wider repercussions of a case's outcome and they pay no heed at all to its political attractiveness. Judges intend opinions to persuade litigants to obey their decisions by showing that the decision accords with the requirements of the law. They also want their decisions to inform lawyers about the meaning of the decision for later cases. Opinions of a court are authoritative documents that command considerable respect. They have no close parallel in the legislative or administrative process.

Another consequence of the legal focus is an enormous concern for procedural correctness. A decision that accords with the substance of the law but has been made through procedural errors is often fatally flawed. Correct procedure is important because procedures are designed to ensure fairness. Consequently, judges consider the neglect of required procedures to be a serious violation of legality.

PARTICIPANTS IN THE JUDICIAL PROCESS

Three sets of participants dominate the judicial process: litigants, lawyers, and judges. A fourth set, interest groups, plays a less prominent role than in the other branches of government. Each set varies in different ways among the fifty states.

Litigants

Litigants play the essential role of bringing disputes to the courts. Without litigants, there are no disputes for the courts to process and the courts sit idle. This arrangement makes courts somewhat like executive agencies, such as a state university or welfare department, whose existence depends on demands for services from a clientele. Many litigants bring cases to court in response to their private needs, but sometimes they play a role analogous to that of political activists in raising public issues and making demands that otherwise would have remained dormant (Zemans 1983). The contrast may be illustrated by comparing a homeowner who files a court case about a neighboring garbage dump with a group of environmentalists who sue to stop use of the dump because of the public health hazards it presents. The homeowner uses the court as a public facility to handle his or her private dispute arising from the discomfort caused by the odors created by the dump. The environmentalists are mobilizing politically, just as if they had taken their demands to the state legislature; they have concluded that the courts are more likely to be receptive to their plea than the legislature, and taking their case to a trial court is the first step in their quest for a favorable outcome. In both instances, judges exercise little or no initiative in deciding which kinds of cases come to the courtroom; they wait for litigants to propel them into activity.

How many litigants crowd into court depends on a large number of variables that are as yet poorly understood because the seemingly simple task of counting litigants is in fact complicated and has not yet been fully mastered. The reason for this is that the act of filing a suit has multiple meanings. Some attorneys do it to show their client that they are working on their case and to signal the other side that their client is serious about the claim; but the dispute may eventually be negotiated and never require any significant time from a judge. In other instances, litigants repeatedly come before judges, actively exercise all the options that courts provide, and insist on a trial.

It is unclear whether litigation has become more common in recent years; many academics and judges differ over whether the United States has witnessed an explosion of litigation (Galanter 1983; Marvell 1987). According to the best national data that are available, it appears that the volume of civil cases (disputes involving individuals and companies) brought to court has been rising at about the same pace as the population or slightly faster (Roper 1986; Marvell 1987). The number of case filings seems to respond to fluctuations in economic activity; some types of cases increase during bad times and other kinds decline (Marvell 1985, 153; Stookey 1986). In addition, changes in the type of economic activity have been reflected in altered caseloads. For instance, there is less commercial and real estate litigation today than fifty years ago (McIntosh 1980–81, 1983). And although personal injury cases arising from automobile accidents have remained stable during recent decades, suits involving claims of medical malpractice and product liability have increased dramatically (Hensler et al. 1987).

The inclination to litigate varies from state to state, although we do not have enough data to analyze this phenomenon systematically. For instance, Arizona, California, and Connecticut have the highest per capita rates of cases involving claims for injuries, while Colorado, Kansas, North Carolina, and North Dakota have the lowest rates (Roper 1986, 280); however, neither regional characteristics nor the degree of urbanization is systematically associated with these rates. States with high rates of tort litigation are scattered across the United States, and some highly urbanized states—such as Michigan, New York, and Ohio—experience relatively low rates. Moreover, states with high rates of one kind of case do not necessarily have high rates for other kinds. There is no evidence, for instance, that personal injury litigation rates move in step with divorce rates or contract cases.

Criminal cases, which represent a large portion of the courts' business, come to court for entirely different reasons from those that bring civil cases. In part, the number of criminal cases reflects the number of crimes committed in a state. As shown in Chapter 10, how crime is defined and measured influences the count, but the number also varies very much with the density of the population; states with large metropolitan populations have more crime than rural states. In addition, the vigor of the police (which are locally controlled) and the exertions of prosecutors contribute to a state's quantity of criminal cases. It is just as difficult to enumerate criminal cases as civil cases because the definition of what is a crime and how serious it is varies among the states. Moreover, states begin counting cases at different stages in the criminal process. Consequently, no valid comparisons can be made between states based on currently available information (National Center for State Courts 1987, 45–51, table 10). However, across the country, the number of criminal cases, even if imperfectly counted, has clearly risen during the past few decades. Most such cases go to state courts because most crimes violate state law rather than federal statutes. Unlike many civil cases, every criminal case requires considerable time from court personnel. Within hours after an arrest the person charged must be brought before a judge to hear the charges and to receive a hearing that determines eligibility for pretrial release. Many other court hearings occur until the case is dismissed, a guilty plea is entered, or a trial occurs. Thus criminal proceedings are quite intensive consumers of court resources.

There are many important differences between civil and criminal cases. Complainants in civil cases use the court system to settle grievances that often involve their private lives, for example, debts, family squabbles, or disputes arising from injuries. Occasionally, civil cases are instituted to seek remedies for damages done to large groups of people, as when a product has caused injury to many of its users. In most civil cases, complainants are private citizens who must pay for litigation out of their own pockets. All these characteristics make most civil cases appear to be private affairs, yet they have important public consequences. In the aggregate, personal injury suits, for instance, transfer hundreds of millions of dollars from insurance companies to injured parties. In divorce cases, families restructure their living and financial arrangements in ways that accord with the norms established by law. Perhaps most important, civil cases provide safe procedures for processing disputes that might otherwise lead to violence. In all these ways, state courts contribute to social order in civil cases, even though private parties motivated by private interests take the initiative in bringing the cases to court.

Criminal cases involve the government more directly. Complainants in criminal cases always rely on public prosecutors to handle court proceedings. Moreover, criminal proceedings threaten to impose severe sanctions on defendants, such as imprisonment and even death. Therefore, criminal proceedings are enveloped with greater safeguards against unfair decisions by the courts; this is particularly evident in the greater availability of free legal assistance for indigent defendants in criminal than in civil cases as well as a greater burden of proof of guilt that is required of the government.

Thus far we have considered two categories of litigants: complainants (plaintiffs) in civil cases, who are often private parties, and prosecutors in criminal cases, who are always government officials. Together, they determine the agenda of the courts. In addition, of course, every case also has defendants. Defendants are reluctant participants in the judicial process. However, they play a significant role in determining the speed of the judicial process and the resources that courts must devote to cases. An O. J. Simpson presents a quite different kind of defense from that of the ordinary defendant charged with murder; a Microsoft Corporation mounts a much more vigorous defense in a civil case than would a small business.

The characteristics of litigants have important consequences for their ability to use courts. Money speaks loudly in courts, as it does in most spheres of life; it is needed to hire the lawyers and to pay the court fees that are required in most cases. Indigents receive some free services, but all others must pay their own way. For instance, divorced mothers who need additional child support often do not return to court to seek a new child support order because the lawyer's fee would consume much of what she might gain if she were successful. In contrast, a corporation believing unfavorable newspaper coverage is libelous may spend millions pursuing a libel suit. Consequently, the rich are more successful than the poor in using the courts. Indeed, some lawyers and judges perceive the courts as being principally an institution for the affluent and have sought to push "small" cases out of the courts because they were unworthy of court attention (Nelson 1988).

Despite considerable efforts to remove the effects of discrimination based on race and gender, ethnic minorities and women also remain at a disadvantage in many state courts. Women are taken less seriously than men of comparable social standing according to many reports about gender discrimination in state courts (Schafran 1993). Ethnic minorities, especially African Americans, suffer from disparate treatment, chiefly in criminal courts (Mann 1993).

Another personal characteristic of litigants that is important in understanding their role in litigation is the degree to which they are repeatedly involved in court cases (Galanter 1974). Most individuals seldom use the courts and usually appear only once. The typical claimant in a personal injury case, for instance, has never before been in court about an injury claim. Contrast this with "repeat players" like insurance companies, who use the courts regularly. Such regulars enjoy considerable advantages. They know the informal routines and can accommodate their own practices to them; they develop personal acquaintances in courtrooms and deal with court personnel as familiars rather than as strangers; and they sometimes are involved in so much litigation that they can use the courts strategically, settling cases that they consider minor while litigating those that they believe to be particularly important (Jacob 1969; Ross 1970). Not all repeat players are wealthy corporations; some are relatively small businesses, such as realty companies that manage rental housing and are frequently in court to evict tenants, or debt collectors, who use the courts repeatedly to obtain judgments against delinquent creditors.

All the characteristics of litigants that have been considered here have important consequences for the manner in which courts operate. The fact that most civil litigation arises from private motives makes courts responsive to different agendas from those of concern to legislatures and executive agencies. The courts' reliance on litigants gives a decided advantage to those who have financial resources to invest in litigation. Repeat players can more easily use the courts for their purposes than occasional users. Government officials fully control only the criminal justice process, but that control is exerted by local police and prosecutors rather than by state officials.

Lawyers

Attorneys play a central role in all courtrooms in the United States. They have a monopoly on representing clients. Although individuals may go to court without a lawyer, only the poor, those with small claims, and the stubborn do that—the adage that an attorney who represents himself has a fool for a client is widely respected.

Lawyers perform many functions for their clients. They know the deadlines that court rules prescribe and the forms that official pleadings must follow. They have an insider's knowledge of courtroom personnel and procedures, including an understanding of the "going rate" (or usual outcome) for particular cases and other information that is essential for successfully negotiating settlements. If cases go to trial, lawyers know the rules for presenting evidence and all the other procedural matters that are important in trials.

In urban courts that handle minor cases, it is not uncommon for lawyers to have little knowledge of their particular client or case because the client hired the attorney just moments before a hearing; some lawyers even patrol courthouse hallways in search of clients just before their cases come before the judge. This is particularly true outside courtrooms handling traffic offenses, misdemeanor complaints, housing offenses, and the like. The matters these courts handle require very little preparation because most of the cases involve routine complaints. Although it is unlikely that an attorney will procure a better outcome for a client in such a case than the client would without the attorney, courtroom rituals appear so mysterious that they easily intimidate occasional litigants. Consequently, in these courtrooms lawyers often do little more than present barely prepared cases in a routine manner.

In other courtrooms attorneys perform much more substantial functions. In serious criminal cases attorneys frequently allocate considerable time for interviewing their client and witnesses and for seeking physical evidence to substantiate their case. In large civil cases attorneys may spend hundreds of hours taking depositions from likely witnesses, searching through records, and researching the law.

Often what lawyers do outside the courtroom is even more important than what they do inside it. For them, a courtroom appearance is either an unusual exception or it simply marks the ratification of agreements reached before coming to court. This is typical of the common criminal case, the usual divorce, the normal personal injury suit, and most commercial litigation. Lawyers bring these cases to court either because they are required to obtain court approval of negotiated outcomes (as in criminal cases and divorces) or because filing the case is a signal to the other side that the plaintiff is serious about pursuing the complaint. After the suit is filed, however, the attorneys for the two sides usually negotiate an acceptable agreement that avoids a trial. Both lawyers and clients often wish to avoid trials because they are costly and time consuming, and their outcome is unpredictable, since trials place the final decision in the hands of strangers on the bench or in the jury box (Rosenthal 1974; Ross 1970). Therefore, the task of the attorney is to pilot clients through negotiations; often the lawyers are the principal negotiators themselves because they know the other attorneys involved,

Table 7-1   Number of People per Practicing Attorney, 1991

State	No. of people per attorney	State	No. of people per attorney
North Carolina	795	Ohio	509
Arkansas	789	Montana	496
South Carolina	757	New Hampshire	496
West Virginia	750	Georgia	494
South Dakota	706	Oregon	490
Alabama	703	Texas	478
North Dakota	701	Florida	472
Mississippi	696	Missouri	471
Indiana	681	Washington	463
Tennessee	646	Maryland	456
Iowa	630	Minnesota	453
Kentucky	629	Pennsylvania	451
Wisconsin	624	Oklahoma	449
Delaware	620	Vermont	441
Utah	614	Rhode Island	439
Nevada	596	Hawaii	411
Idaho	576	Louisiana	403
Wyoming	564	Alaska	380
Virginia	562	California	373
Michigan	558	New Jersey	357
Arizona	550	Illinois	351
Nebraska	529	Colorado	337
Kansas	528	Connecticut	312
Maine	527	Massachusetts	280
New Mexico	517	New York	261

SOURCE: Curran and Carson, 1994, 238.

are familiar with the "going rate" of settlements, and have developed specialized negotiating skills.

As shown in Table 7-1, the number of people potentially served by every practicing attorney varies greatly among the states. Near one extreme, Arkansas, there are 789 persons for each attorney; at the other, New York, there are only 261 persons for every attorney. However, in Arkansas, lawyers working alone or in firms with fewer than five lawyers—the kind of lawyer serving individual clients—constituted 74 percent of all practicing lawyers; in New York only 57 percent were such attorneys. Thus, the number of lawyers likely to serve individuals is not quite as disparate as it first seems, but there still were 2.35 times more people per attorney likely to serve individuals in Arkansas than in New York (Curran and Carson 1994, 43, 159, 238).

One other kind of attorney needs to be considered. This is the public prosecutor (the title varies across states), who represents the state in criminal cases, and the public defender, who represents indigent defendants. They are public officials. In most states, every county has at least one prosecutor. Larger counties have one chief prosecutor and many assistant prosecutors. The chief prosecutor is often a highly visible and powerful politician, for this post is frequently a step-pingstone to higher elective office. The assistants are usually young attorneys who serve for a few years in order to accumulate trial experience before going into private practice. On the defense side, in some states most of the defendants are represented by public defenders who are employed full time by the government; in others, most indigent defendants are represented by private attorneys who receive their fees from the court. In addition, in big cities some private lawyers specialize in criminal defense and represent clients who can afford their services (Eisenstein and Jacob 1977). Small communities furnish less opportunity for attorneys to specialize in criminal law, and the attorneys defending alleged criminals often have a more general practice (Eisenstein, Flemming, and Nardulli 1987).

Judges

Judges epitomize the courts. They govern the courtroom; in many instances they decide cases. All other courthouse participants treat them with enormous respect. They are not a cross section of the population. As we shall see, they do not even accurately reflect the characteristics of the bar from which they are drawn.

The Composition of the Bench. All but the lowest level of judges (for example, justices of the peace) possess a legal education and were practicing lawyers before ascending the bench. However, there is no special educational program for would-be judges in law school. Nor do law school graduates start on a judicial career just after graduating. In the United States, unlike most other Western countries, men and women become judges midway through their legal career. They often begin as assistant states' attorneys or public defenders; many then have substantial careers as private attorneys. When they become judges, they are typically in their forties or fifties.

Most judges are white males despite substantial efforts by minorities and women to penetrate the black-robed fraternity. Women, who for many years have constituted a substantial proportion of law school classes, have made in-roads to the state judiciary. They have served as chief justices on some of the most prestigious state supreme courts (for example, California and New York). However, they still fall far short of occupying half of all state judgeships. In a personal communication to me the National Center for State Courts reported that in 1991 they occupied only 10 percent of all supreme court seats and 12 percent of the intermediate appellate judgeships. By 1985 every state had *some* women on trial courts (Henry et al. 1985). African Americans have had less success. While the number of African-American judges has gradually increased in the last decade, the number of states with black trial judges declined from thirty-eight to thirty-five between 1985 and 1991 (Henry et al. 1985; Joint Center 1991, 5–6). In addition, only twelve states had African Americans sitting on their supreme courts in 1991; seven of those were southern states (Joint Center 1991). As recently as

1985 most states did not have a single Hispanic judge; Hispanics have won judge-ships in appreciable numbers only in the Southwest, with New Mexico at 18.7 percent having the largest proportion (Henry et al. 1985).

These facts reflect the social and economic screening that occurs as people seek to become attorneys. To become an attorney, one must graduate from col-lege and from an accredited law school and then pass a state bar examination. These are considerable hurdles for anyone without substantial financial backing. Such factors have been important in keeping the access of minorities to the judi-ciary low because only a small proportion of them have had the resources and social opportunities to obtain an attorney's license. The situation for women is somewhat different because they face fewer strictly economic barriers, although socially ascribed family obligations often create equally substantial hurdles. An-other reason that only a small number of women and minority members hold judgeships is that attorneys must accumulate half a lifetime's experience practic-ing law before most have a serious chance to become judges. A high proportion of women and members of minority groups did not enter the legal profession until the 1980s and are likely not to have the desired experience before the year 2000.

It is important to note that not all lawyers wish to become a judge. Both the economics of the judiciary and the work involved in being a judge lead most lawyers to eliminate themselves from consideration. Low salaries discourage many high-income, high-prestige attorneys. In 1993 the average trial judge earned approximately $81,000, and the average supreme court justice's salary was about $93,000 (CSG 1994, table 4.6). These are not paltry sums when compared with the 1992 median family income of about $41,000 (U.S. Bureau of the Census 1993, 467), but they are low when compared with salaries of top-flight lawyers, who often earn more than $250,000 ("What Lawyers Earn" 1994, C5). Conse-quently, the highest paid lawyers in large cities rarely seek a judgeship. Only in small communities, where lawyers earn much less, do judgeships compete with prestigious private practice in economic terms. The tasks that many judges per-form also repel some of the best lawyers. While judges exercise much authority and garner considerable respect, their everyday work is often tedious, especially in cities where courtrooms are specialized. Except at the supreme court level, state courts usually do not regularly provide intellectually challenging tasks. Consequently, judgeships do not attract the best attorneys as measured by the fees they collect or the intellectual cast of their mind. Rather, judicial careers more often appeal to middle-echelon lawyers whose practice brings them fre-quently to court.

Judicial Selection and Retention. Selection procedures reinforce these tenden-cies (Dubois 1980). The route to a judgeship is often convoluted and varies markedly from state to state. In Table 7-2 the states are grouped according to the formal procedures they use for selecting judges. The table reflects the division of the states between those in which judges are selected through popular elections

Table 7-2 Judicial Selection Procedures

State	Election			Appointment		
	Major trial courts	Intermediate appellate courts	Supreme courts	Major trial courts	Intermediate appellate courts	Supreme courts
Alabama	P	P	P			
Alaska				M	M	M
Arizona	NP (small counties)			M (large counties P)	M	M
Arkansas	P	P	P			
California	NP (varies)			G (retention election)	G (retention election)	G (retention election)
Colorado				M	M	M
Connecticut				L (merit)	L (merit)	L (merit)
Delaware				G	—	G
Florida	NP				M	M
Georgia	NP	NP	NP			
Hawaii				M	M	M
Idaho	NP	NP	NP			
Illinois	P (retention election)	P (retention election)	P (retention election)			
Indiana	P (except Marion County)			G (Marion County)	M	M
Iowa				M	M	M
Kansas				M	M	M
Kentucky	NP	NP	NP			
Louisiana	NP	NP	NP			
Maine				G	—	G
Maryland				G (then election)	M	M
Massachusetts				G	G	G
Michigan	NP (partisan primary)	NP (partisan primary)	NP (partisan primary)			
Minnestoa	NP	NP	NP			
Mississippi	P	—	P			
Missouri	P (some counties)			M (some counties)	M	M
Montana	NP (retention election)	—	NP (retention election)			
Nebraska				M	M	M
Nevada	NP	—	NP			
New Hampshire				G	—	G
New Jersey				G	G	G
New Mexico				M (then partisan election)	M (then partisan election)	M (then partisan election)
New York	P	P				G
North Carolina	P	P	P			
North Dakota	NP	NP	NP			
Ohio	NP (partisan primary)	NP (partisan primary)	NP (partisan primary)			
Oklahoma	NP	NP				M
Oregon	NP	NP	NP			
Pennsylvania	P (retention election)	P (partisan election)	P (partisan election)			
Rhode Island				L	—	L
South Carolina				L	L	L
South Dakota	NP	—				M
Tennessee	P		P		M	
Texas	P	P	P			
Utah				M	—	M
Vermont				G	—	G
Virginia				L	L	L
Washington	NP	NP	NP			
West Virginia	P	—	P			
Wisconsin	NP	NP	NP			
Wyoming				M	—	M

SOURCE: CSG 1994, 190–192.

NOTES: P = partisan election; NP = nonpartisan election; M = merit selection; G = gubernatorial appointment; L = legislative selection; dashes = no intermediate appellate court. Variants and exceptions noted in parentheses; thus, "partisan election" after M means that judges run for second term in a partisan election.

and those in which they are appointed. Within each category, there are several variants.

Elections are of two sorts: partisan and nonpartisan, the latter being more common. To win a judgeship on a partisan ballot, one must first win a political party's nomination in a primary election or a caucus and then overcome the opposing party's candidate at the general election. Election is simpler in states using a nonpartisan procedure; candidates must obtain a required number of signatures on petitions in order to gain a place on the ballot and achieve a plurality of the votes in a single election to win office. Nonpartisan elections tend to be held at off-beat times—for example, in the spring, when few other officials face the electorate. Because the media pays little attention to such elections and there are few if any heated contests to capture the electorate's imagination, not many voters participate. In contrast, partisan elections are usually held in the fall, at the same time as high-profile gubernatorial or presidential elections, which tend to overshadow the judicial contests placed at the end of long ballots; the fortunes of candidates at the top of the ticket—those for the presidency, the governor's office, or a Senate seat—may sweep judicial candidates of the same party into office (Kiel, Funk, and Champagne 1994, 290–293; Tarr and Porter 1988, 124–183). Consequently, in both nonpartisan and partisan elections, voters pay little heed to their opportunity to select judges. In most circumstances, incumbent judges win, but when they lose, their defeat may have little to do with their records as judges or their qualifications as judicial candidates. When incumbent judges are not on the ballot, the outcome in partisan elections seems to be most influenced by the coattail effect of other candidates, whereas the outcome in nonpartisan elections seems to depend on more random factors (Hojnacki and Baum 1992; Johnson, Schaefer, and McKnight 1978; Sheldon and Lovrich 1983). Only in special circumstances, as discussed below, are judicial elections hotly contested.

Understanding judicial elections is further complicated by the variants of electoral procedures some states have adopted, as the statements in parentheses in some of the entries in Table 7-2 indicate. In Ohio, for instance, candidates must win a partisan primary in order to be placed on the nonpartisan general election ballot. In Illinois, judges are initially elected on a partisan ballot but must win 60 percent of the votes in a noncompetitive retention election to stay in office. In a different, but not uncommon variant, Arizona uses nonpartisan elections in all but the largest counties to select trial judges; in the most populous counties (where most of the litigation occurs) an appointive procedure is employed.

The second category of selection procedures encompasses appointments. As the data in Table 7-2 show, more states use appointive procedures than elections, but there are many more variants in this category. One principal variant is some form of "merit" selection, sometimes called the Missouri Plan, used at least partially by fifteen states in 1994. This kind of selection system is usually urged on states by reformers who wish to reduce the influence of politicians, but in practice it simply substitutes private politics for public politics (Watson and Downing 1969). Merit selection procedures depend on screening committees usually composed of bar association officials and judges, although lay people also occasionally serve. The task of these screening committees is to nominate several highly qualified persons for each vacancy, but they operate with quite loose definitions of what constitutes high qualification. The governor makes the final selection (Watson and Downing 1969). Once appointed, a new judge serves for a year or until the next election, when he or she must run on a retention ballot; the question on the ballot is whether the judge should be retained, and the voters indicate yes or no. If a majority grants the judge an affirmative vote, the judge retains his or her position; if a majority votes No, the judge is replaced by another merit appointee. At the end of each term of office, these judges face another such plebiscite.

States use many variants of this merit procedure. The size and composition of the nominating commissions are different in almost every state; the number of nominees from which the governor chooses varies. In New Mexico, after their initial term, merit-selected judges must run for their second term in competitive partisan elections; when they seek a third term, they run in noncompetitive retention elections. Other variations center on the number of years judges serve before facing a retention election.

A second major appointive variant, employed by ten states in 1994, is gubernatorial appointment without mandated participation by a nominating commission. In most instances, such appointments require ratification by the upper house of the legislature. In many states that use some form of elective procedure, governors may fill vacancies pending the next election. Such appointments usually do not require ratification by the state senate (Stumpf 1987, 172–173).

The third appointive variant is selection by the legislature. Only four states employ legislative selection, a method popular in the early nineteenth century but abandoned by most since then.

Each method establishes special hurdles for some categories of aspirants. Merit appointive procedures tend to produce fewer women and minority judges than gubernatorial or legislative appointments (Graham 1990); that may be the result of the lack of contact of women and members of minorities with the elite lawyers who tend to sit on nominating commissions (on characteristics of members of such commissions see Henschen, Moog, and Davis 1990). The success of minorities in elections depends very much on the characteristics of the district in which elections are held. Rarely are minority judges elected in at-large elections in which the proportion of minorities in the electorate is small. Thus, if judges are elected on a statewide basis or even in large districts, such as a whole metropolitan county, African Americans rarely succeed even though they might constitute as much as one-third of the total population. If districts are smaller and drawn to encompass neighborhoods with high concentrations of minority populations, however, many more minorities are likely to be elected.

Consequently, elective procedures in several states have been challenged in federal courts as violating the Voting Rights Act of 1965, and the Supreme Court has recognized that the provisions of that act apply to judicial elections (*Chisom v. Roemer*, 501 U.S. 380 [1991] and *Houston Lawyers v. Texas Attorney General*, 501 U.S. 419 [1991]). In 1994, Alabama, Arkansas, Florida, Georgia, Illinois, Louisiana, Mississippi, New York, Ohio, and Texas faced such challenges (Luskin et al. 1994, 316). In North Carolina in 1987 the legislature eliminated many of the large multijudge districts in favor of smaller districts that each elected a single judge; these were designed to elect African Americans (Drennan 1993, 27–33, 42–43). In Illinois, the legislature created electoral subdistricts in Cook County, carving out safe districts for minority candidates (Smith and Garmel 1992, 156). Both Georgia and Louisiana have struggled with the difficult political choices these pressures created (Haydel and Ferrell 1993, 93–116; Smothers 1994, A8). In each of these states, not only racial but also partisan politics played a large role in the design of judicial selection procedures. Republicans, who also had been at a disadvantage in many of these states, joined African Americans in challenging existing procedures. That alliance produced the subdistricts for Illinois's Cook County, since some subdistricts were created in Republican suburban areas and others in African-American central city neighborhoods. In North Carolina, in contrast, Republicans became less interested in reform once their growing electoral strength began to bring them judgeships under the existing arrangements.

One common theme runs through the various selection procedures: being known by the right people is invaluable to the potential judge. In states where judges are initially elected, public prominence gained through prior successes in winning and holding elective offices is important. Former prosecutors and legislators have an advantage because they have the contacts to get party endorsements in primary elections and also enjoy name recognition among voters. Where judgeships are filled by gubernatorial appointment, prior public activity at the state level or campaign assistance in the incumbent governor's election are likely to prove helpful (Dubois 1985, 23). Where merit commissions make initial recommendations, bar association activities and professional contacts with the bar elite can be useful.

Remaining on the bench requires a different combination of circumstances. Judges who engage in controversial practices and alienate members of the bar are likely to stir opposition in the form of disapproval in bar polls in retention elections or in the form of opposition in competitive elections. However, judges cannot control their fate entirely. Where judges depend on gubernatorial action for reappointment, the election of a new governor may erase the ties that brought the original appointment, and the new governor may choose to reward one of his or her political friends rather than reappoint the incumbent judge. Where judges must stand for reelection in partisan elections, bad luck in the form of an unpopular presidential or gubernatorial candidate at the head of the ticket may doom the judge's reelection bid. Only in retention elections do judges enjoy con-

siderable assurance that extraneous events will not substantially affect their opportunity to win another term, for very few judges lose retention elections. Between 1964 (when such elections were first held) and 1984 only 22 of the 1,864 trial judges on the ballot were defeated (Hall and Aspin 1987, 343); if Illinois had
not required an affirmative vote of 60 percent, nine of the ten defeated Illinois
judges would have been retained. The average affirmative vote for judges was
more than 75 percent (Hall and Aspin 1987, 342–343). However, even in these circumstances, many judges approach elections with considerable trepidation (Aspin and Hall 1994).

The experience of three justices of the California Supreme Court in 1986 illustrates some of the circumstances that lead to vigorous opposition to incumbent
judges. A concerted campaign against Chief Justice Rose Bird of the California
Supreme Court and two of her associates did not allege incompetence but focused on their opposition to the death penalty. Television advertisements urged
people to vote "three times for the death penalty: vote no on Bird, Reynoso,
Grodin" (Grodin 1987, 367). More than this slogan lay behind the campaign,
however, for it was also part of a strategy to give a recently elected Republican
governor the opportunity to appoint more conservative jurists in order to
change the direction of the California court on many issues (Grodin 1987; Wold
and Culver 1987).

A somewhat different kind of campaign was waged in 1988 in Chicago against
the chief judge of the Cook County Circuit Court. A number of black community organizations first threatened a campaign called "Just Vote No" against all
judges on the November retention ballot if the court did not appoint more black
associate judges. When only nine blacks were appointed for twenty-six positions,
just before the election, the black community groups turned their wrath against
the chief judge, targeting him for defeat (Mount 1988, sec. 1, p. 1; Tybor 1988, sec.
2, p. 1). Since they only needed a 40 percent negative vote, their threat was credible and was perceived as a stern warning to consider race in selecting judges, although, as the *Tribune* reported on November 10, 1988, it failed to defeat the chief
judge.

The occasional venture of judges into the arena of competitive elections can
be personally painful. The three California Supreme Court judges challenged by
their conservative opposition found it necessary to raise $4.5 million for their
campaign (Grodin 1987, 368); judges who face no opposition typically spend
nothing but their filing fee. One of the defeated California judges, Joseph Grodin,
reflected on his experience:

> To begin with, it was a novel experience, and one for which nothing in my back-
> ground had particularly prepared me. I had been a candidate for a local city council
> years ago—and my practice representing labor unions was hardly reclusive. I had
> been politically active to a degree—in the McCarthy for President campaign, for ex-
> ample. But I had had no experience with a statewide campaign, and for ten years I
> had been judging and teaching in relative political isolation. To put together a cam-

paign organization, to hire a political consultant, to raise nearly a million dollars statewide, to spend time away from the court visiting newspaper editorial boards and giving interviews to television reporters for 60 seconds on the evening news—that is not exactly what I thought I had bargained for.

I did not fully appreciate, when I was appointed to the court, the handicaps that canons and traditions of legal ethics and decorum impose upon a judge in such an election. Unlike most political candidates, I could make no campaign promises, nor could I state my position on any legal issue pending or likely to be pending before the court, unless I had already done so in an opinion. . . . In short, I felt I was in the ring with at least one hand tied behind my back. (Grodin 1987, 367–368)

The 1986 California campaign and the events of the 1988 judicial campaign in Chicago, as well as similar campaigns in other states, highlight the uncomfortable position of the judiciary in the political arena. It may seem unfair to hold a judge's feet to the fire as Justice Grodin's were because it may lead to individual litigants being treated unfairly in order to protect the jurist from reprisal by powerful interests. Yet it is undeniable that such campaigns articulate public concern about judicial policies, whether it is expressed with regard to judicial decisions in criminal cases or in uneasiness about minority representation among judges.

Examination of selection procedures, however, does not demonstrate that any particular formal selection procedure leads to better judges. People use varying standards of quality. For some, ethnic identification—all other things being equal—is an important consideration. For others, intellectual ability ranks highest, although no simple test is available for judicial nominees. Still others believe the most significant attribute for a judge is a judicial temperament, by which they mean such qualities as politeness, evenhandedness, integrity, and coolheadedness. In addition, some prefer having judges with life experiences that are somewhat like those of the persons who will appear before them.

No aggregate measures of these qualities exist, and observers often come to different conclusions in evaluating judges on such vague criteria. Nevertheless, we do possess information on the backgrounds of judges. Studies of their education and experience show that judges selected by various procedures do not systematically vary (Canon 1972; Glick and Emmert 1987). For instance, merit system judges are neither more nor less likely to have gone to an elite law school or to have had a long legal career before becoming a judge. Moreover, neither the general public nor legal professionals appear to have a higher opinion of a state's judiciary if it was appointed under a merit system than if it was elected (Wasmann, Lovrich, and Sheldon 1986).

Interest Groups

The final set of participants we need to consider are interest groups. As indicated in Chapter 4, groups play a significant role in state politics. Their role is quite attenuated, however, in judicial decision making.

One reason for their diminished role lies in the institutional culture of courts.

The free-wheeling attempts to influence policy that are an integral part of the legislative process because legislatures are representative institutions are impermissible in the courts. Courts are not representative institutions. The norms governing the judicial process require that judges be disinterested and their decisions be impartial. Those norms do not preclude interest group activity but they severely throttle it.

Several legitimate paths exist for interest groups to become active in the state judicial process. As we have already seen, the legal profession takes an active interest in the question of who becomes a judge. Other groups also sporadically participate in that process. That is particularly true of states where supreme court justices are elected in competitive elections and the cost of those election campaigns far exceed the personal resources of the candidates (on the cost of campaigns, see Moog 1992). In Texas, for instance, the Texas Medical Association in 1988 spent considerable sums in support of a slate of supreme court candidates (Champagne 1993, 107–108). Efforts to influence judicial selection, however, are less intense than those to influence the election of legislators and governors.

Interest groups may also sponsor litigation to bring cases to the courts that will allow courts to interpret the law in ways they favor. The plaintiffs in challenges to state abortion laws, to welfare policies, to educational expenditures, and the like are individuals, but those individuals are often supported financially and recruited by the groups whose broader interests are involved.

A third tool that interest groups may employ is filing amicus curiae briefs before the court in cases in which the groups are not directly involved as plaintiff or defendant. Such briefs are normally filed only during appeals, and most are directed to supreme courts. Epstein (1994) has shown that the number of such briefs and the number of groups participating in each brief increased substantially between 1965 and 1990, indicating that groups have become more active before state judiciaries. Moreover, a larger variety of groups, such as health organizations, labor unions, education associations, and legal groups, participated in 1990 than had done so earlier.

The pattern of interest group activity, however, is not uniform across all states. Illinois, Kansas, Michigan, and New Jersey had far more groups participating in amicus curiae briefs than Nevada, South Dakota, or Tennessee. The states with much amicus activity are not those where the overall impact of interest groups in state politics is dominant (see Chapter 4). Conversely, states with little amicus activity are not necessarily those where groups are subordinate. They include Nevada, where interest groups are dominant, Tennessee, where interest groups in general are somewhere between dominant and complementary, and South Dakota, where they are somewhere between complementary and subordinate (see Chapter 4). Although not much research has been published on state interest group activity before courts, Epstein's study suggests that such activity is not part of a larger pattern of interest group activity in the states but rather is driven by concerns that stem from the peculiarities of the judicial process.

TRIAL COURTS AND SOCIAL CONTROL

The principal task of trial courts is to impose social control over seriously deviant behavior and in disputes. Criminal courts judge offenders and dictate punishment for those found guilty of criminal acts. Civil courts referee disputes and follow legal norms in resolving them.

We have already noted one trait of trial courts: their roots in localities; their localism has many consequences. Although trial courts are agents of the state government whose judges are often paid with state funds, many of their resources come from city and county governments. If trial judges want additional judges, they generally have to look to the state legislature for authorization. However, if they want a new courthouse, an additional clerk, or computers, they must go to their city or county for the funds. In addition, trial courts work closely with other local officials, especially the police and prosecutor. Finally, trial courts depend on the local population and its situation to bring cases to them. Not only the pace but also the content of litigation in a rural county in Montana is quite different from that in Los Angeles or Chicago. The authors of one study of rural courts noted:

> The web of interrelationships in rural areas affects the court and community alike. The judge's car may be in for a brake job at the only repair shop around, which is being sued by a dissatisfied customer. The court clerk may sing in the choir with the prosecutor and have the public defender's daughter in her Brownie troop. . . . The parties and victims, too, may have some relationship with those who work in the justice system. The disposition of a particular case must take into account and accommodate all of the ways in which the court, attorneys, and parties relate or expect to relate in the future. (Fahnestock and Geiger 1993, 258, 262)

Such a web of relationships is unthinkable in large metropolitan areas. Courthouses are justice factories often located in places remote from much of the population and inhabited by specialists who disappear into their private worlds at the end of their work day. In metropolitan areas, courts render detached judgments untempered by personal relationships. Thus differences among courts *within* states are probably larger than those *between* states.

There are, however, some important commonalities among trial courts. One is the importance of routine driven by specialization. In large cities, courts themselves are specialized according to the types of cases they hear; in rural areas certain days are set aside for particular kinds of cases. Although litigants may think their dispute is unique, courtroom personnel tend to perceive it as commonplace and have difficulty distinguishing one case from another. Every trial court develops routines for handling most cases and "going rates" for disposing of them.

Within each courtroom there is further specialization of tasks. Judge, prosecutor (or plaintiff's attorney), defense attorney, witnesses, litigants, clerk, and bailiff all have their assigned roles. When those people work together for long periods of time, they develop informal relationships that play a prominent role in courtroom operations. This is particularly striking in criminal courts, where the judge, attorneys, clerk, and bailiff share many weeks together and form a courtroom work group (Eisenstein and Jacob 1977). Courtroom work groups share goals and standard operating procedures. In a criminal court the goals are to dispose of the caseload as expeditiously as possible and to achieve justice while maintaining group cohesion and reducing uncertainty about the results (Eisenstein and Jacob 1977, 25). Pursuing justice is what the external society demands; it requires adherence to socially defined standards of fairness. A court that is perceived as unfair will lose public support, and its principal officials may face political opposition. At the same time, the court must meet the demand of its users for expeditious case disposition, and courtrooms that are plagued by endless delay lose public confidence as surely as those that are manifestly unfair. Maintaining group cohesion is essential so that the courtroom participants can develop the mutual trust and confidence necessary to dispose of cases quickly and fairly. Reducing uncertainty is also important. If procedures are made definite and fixed, with little left to chance, courtroom participants gain control over their work flow.

In criminal courtrooms the pursuit of these goals leads to a high rate of plea bargaining, while in civil courtrooms it produces a high rate of settlement before trial. Plea bargaining, by which a defendant agrees to plead guilty to a lesser charge in exchange for a lighter sentence, particularly meets the needs for the swift disposition of a case and the reduction of uncertainty. It permits rapid action while allowing the courtroom principals to decide outcomes without sharing power with witnesses and jurors, who do not belong to the courtroom work group and who may perform erratically. Plea bargains reached among courtroom regulars are likely to be kept within the bounds demanded by group cohesion; demands that undermine the position of either the judge or one of the attorneys are unlikely to win acceptance. For instance, some district attorneys keep a tight rein over their assistants with respect to plea bargains on heinous crimes. Everyone in the courtroom understands that an assistant prosecutor cannot agree to a plea to a lesser charge in such a case; however, the prosecutor may be expected to accommodate the defense attorney in another case where no such constraints are imposed. Nevertheless, plea bargains usually meet the criterion of justice in most instances because they dispense penalties within the accepted "going rate" for the offense involved in the case.

In civil cases, pretrial settlements serve the same purposes. The standard procedure in many civil trial courtrooms is to provide opportunities for settlement before a trial begins (Zeisel, Kalven, and Buchholz 1959). As in some criminal courtrooms the judge may participate in that effort. The result is similar. Pretrial settlements dispose of most cases, which allows the parties to control dispositions without having to share power with witnesses, jurors, or a judge. As long as the outcomes are not far from what might reasonably be expected if a trial had occurred, they are likely to be perceived as just.

The work group concept helps us place the judge in his or her appropriate position. The courtroom is formally a judge's domain—in fact, many courtrooms are known informally by the judge's name. However, if we look carefully at the dynamics of decision making, we will see that judges do not unilaterally impose decisions but rather only contribute to them. Although judges announce decisions, they are based on information provided by attorneys. The amount of information attorneys supply and the manner in which they frame it go far in molding a judge's decision. For example, an attorney's decision about whether to call a witness affects the amount and kind of information available to the judge and can have a significant effect on the judge's rulings during the trial and final decision.

On the other hand, the discretion of trial courts is constrained by the rulings of appellate courts. Trial courts are explicitly obligated to adhere to those decisions; if they do not, attorneys for the aggrieved party will take their case to the appellate court with the request that the errant decision be overturned. This obligation is taken for granted by trial judges; it is embedded in their training and experience as lawyers before ascending the bench.

The manner in which trial courts impose social control varies across states as well as within them. This dimension of their work has not been widely explored by scholars, but several indicators of such variations exist for criminal justice. The data in Table 7-3 show the state-by-state variation in the number of persons serving life sentences in 1992 and the number sentenced to death between 1990 and 1992. According to these data, there are marked variations in the harshness of the criminal courts by these measures of social control. Many of the southern states are among the highest in their use of life sentences, although the very highest are Nevada and Delaware. Among the states that have a death penalty on their statute books, California, Florida, and Texas imposed it more frequently than others in the three-year period 1990–1992. Note that this is not a function of their large population, since the measure in Table 7-3 holds population constant. Some southern states that have long been considered to have particularly punitive criminal courts, such as Georgia, Louisiana, and South Carolina, are in the middle range of the states in their imposition of the death penalty. Nor is the imposition of the death penalty related to the incidence of crime in a state; the correlation between the violent crime rate and the death penalty rate is an insignificant .23. There is, however, a moderate correlation between the frequency with which states impose life sentences and their violent crime rate ($r = .67$).

Some scholars (Mather 1991) argue that trial courts also are significant policy makers. In some instances, trial courts are the first to proclaim a new interpretation of a law or constitutional provision, and their decision is later ratified but not significantly altered by an appellate court. In another sense, one may think of the accumulation of trial court decisions in what Galanter (1990) has called a "congregation of cases" as the development of policy. No single decision may have widespread significance or visibility, but looking backward after a period of time, observers can point to the emergence of a definite policy that is the product

Table 7-3 The Application of Social Control by Criminal Courts in the States

State	No. of lifers per 100,000 Pop.*	Death penalty per 100,000 Pop.†	State	No. of lifers per 100,000 Pop.*	Death penalty per 100,000 Pop.†
Alabama	64.4954	0.8910	Montana	3.3788	0.2503
Alaska	NA	—	Nebraska	5.3218	0.0634
Arizona	20.1626	0.9004	Nevada	77.7168	1.0817
Arkansas	21.0150	0.3829	New Hampshire	2.5241	—
California	39.5396	0.3192	New Jersey	11.7720	0.0259
Colorado	15.5415	0.0607	New Mexico	10.8904	0.0000
Connecticut	4.6241	0.0608	New York	52.6778	—
Delaware	60.4923	0.7505	North Carolina	33.7477	0.7392
Florida	37.9660	0.8270	North Dakota	2.0351	—
Georgia	52.1904	0.4168	Ohio	28.3762	0.3319
Hawaii	0.2707	—	Oklahoma	31.5043	0.8266
Idaho	19.3702	0.4967	Oregon	16.2544	0.2815
Illinois	4.9429	0.3849	Pennsylvania	20.3424	0.3787
Indiana	NA	0.1804	Rhode Island	8.2711	—
Iowa	14.1890	—	South Carolina	38.9193	0.3155
Kansas	20.4634	—	South Dakota	14.6552	0.1437
Kentucky	15.9010	0.1899	Tennessee	26.4496	0.5741
Louisiana	52.8436	0.3555	Texas	24.9433	0.4533
Maine	3.4431	—	Utah	2.3797	0.0580
Maryland	NA	0.1046	Vermont	2.4876	—
Massachusetts	15.7736	—	Virginia	20.5741	0.3071
Michigan	34.3507	—	Washington	12.4931	0.1027
Minnesota	3.6571	—	West Virginia	14.4968	—
Mississippi	1.9042	0.6995	Wisconsin	10.6914	—
Missouri	23.8025	0.4886	Wyoming	24.4709	—

SOURCES: Data for lifers: U.S. Department of Justice 1992, table 6.81; data for death penalty: Greenfeld and Stephan 1993.
NOTE: NA = data not available; dash = state had no death penalty.
*As of December 31, 1992.
†As of December 31, 1992, for prisoners sentenced in 1990, 1991, or 1992.

of a series of trial court decisions. There is no doubt that trial courts engage in policy making in both of these ways. However, both are exceptional products of trial court activities. The vast bulk of the work of trial courts concerns itself with the imposition of legal norms in the pursuit of social control.

APPELLATE COURTS AS POLICY MAKERS

Appellate courts wield more power than trial courts in legal and political arenas. Much of their work involves routine decisions (like that of a supervisor in an administrative setting), but appellate courts also have an opportunity to lay down new policy with each case.

Appellate courts possess the potential for policy making because appeals center on interpretive issues rather than factual ones. It is a fundamental tenet of American law that appellate courts possess the right to interpret statutes, to alter past judicial rulings, and even to declare legislative enactments as contrary to the Constitution. Many appellate judges, therefore, perceive their role as interpreters of the law rather than simply as implementers of legislative and administrative decisions (Glick and Vines 1973, 61).

Every litigant who appeals a trial court decision does so with the assertion that the trial judge misapplied the law. In many cases it is simply alleged that the judge made a mistake; such appeals serve to keep the rulings of trial courts throughout a state relatively uniform. In some instances, however, new laws, unusual situations, or novel legal arguments provide appellate courts with the opportunity to formulate new legal and social policies. For instance, many state legislatures have adopted laws providing for the automatic suspension of a driver's license if the driver refuses a breath analyzer test when suspected of driving while under the influence of alcohol. These laws have frequently been challenged before appellate courts and provide those courts with an opportunity to decide whether the statute is specific enough in setting the level of alcohol, whether too much discretion is given to police officers or the licensing authority, and whether the period of suspension is appropriate.

Such questions reflect the large amount of discretion that arises from the criteria that appellate courts typically apply in their interpretive task. Appellate judges ask such broad questions as, Is this rule reasonable? Is it sufficiently linked to a legitimate governmental purpose? Does it adhere to due process of law?

These standards are not quite as loose as they may appear at first because they are based on a long tradition of constraints that appellate judges accept as a matter of course. The most important of these constraints is the preference for following past decisions (the rule of *stare decisis*). Appellate courts do not slavishly follow that rule, of course, for that would vitiate their interpretive role entirely, but they begin their task with a presumption that precedent should be followed. Only when they are convinced that doing so violates some other important standard—such as a statutory or constitutional mandate or their own sense of justice—do they overturn past decisions. Moreover, most appellate interpretations do not involve overturning precedents; appellate judges much more frequently distinguish the present case from past ones or change only the fringes of past policy. Thus, most appellate policy making is incremental, creating only small alterations in past interpretations and moving tentatively in a new direction.

Two other features of state appellate courts bring them into the policy arena. The first is their power to issue advisory opinions. Unlike the U.S. Supreme Court, which refuses to respond to requests for opinions except when a case or controversy comes before it, some state supreme courts issue advisory opinions at the request of the governor or other state officials. Such advisory opinions thrust appellate courts into policy controversies.

In addition, many state supreme courts possess the power to make rules for all courts in the state (Glick 1982). To the lay person such rules are dry procedural matters with little apparent consequence. Such a perception, however, underestimates the influence of procedures upon outcomes. The rules that state supreme courts issue involve such matters as the ways in which evidence may be presented, the deadlines that litigants and attorneys must meet, and the procedures that other courts must follow in making decisions. Attorneys representing particular interests sometimes vigorously contest proposed rule changes because they recognize that they alter their chances of winning cases for their clients. Such rule changes thus also thrust state supreme courts into the policy arena.

State supreme courts have in recent years made important policy decisions in many different areas. One that has attracted particular attention is the definition of what has popularly been called "the right to die" (see Glick 1992). When persons are mortally ill, they sometimes wish to stop all medical procedures; if they are unconscious, they may have left instructions to family members requesting that they be permitted to die without further medical intervention. Such situations have presented many novel and serious legal problems. Some physicians fear liability if they comply (or fail to comply) with such instructions. Those instructions run counter to the deeply held beliefs of many physicians and some hospitals. In addition, those involved need guidance about the documents that are needed to assure them that the patient really intended to leave such instructions.

These issues sometimes go to state legislatures, where legislators must reconcile opposing interest groups. However, in many instances, they first come to the courts because in a particular case a doctor or hospital has refused to carry out the wishes of a patient or the patient's family. The leading case involved a young woman, Karen Quinlan, who lay for years in a vegetative state in a New Jersey hospital. Finally, in 1976, the New Jersey Supreme Court decided that on the basis of a person's right to privacy and the right of parents to act as guardians, they could order the removal of the respirator that was assisting her breathing (*In re Quinlan*, 355 A.2d 647 [N.J. 1976]). Between 1976 and 1990, appellate courts in sixteen states decided such issues (Glick 1992, 143–145). In many instances, those decisions came in the absence of specific legislation; in others, court decisions led to legislation that was then further interpreted by the courts.

Perhaps the most visible example of judicial policy making has come in controversies about the funding of public schools. In most states, schools depend heavily on the property tax. Some districts are able to endow their schools generously because they have a large assessed property base, while other districts, with low assessed valuations, can afford only small budgets for their schools. By 1994, inequalities in spending had been challenged in twenty-six states (Gray 1994, A12). Such a challenge led New Jersey's supreme court to force the legislature to impose an income tax in 1973 (*Robinson v. Cahill* 111, 303 A.2d 273 [1973]); however, that 1973 case did not end the litigation. In 1994 the court once again declared that students in poor districts were not getting what the New Jersey Constitution required: "a thorough and efficient" education. The court gave the legislature three years to erase the inequities that existed in thirty districts, including Newark and Camden (Gray 1994, A12; "New Jersey Justices" 1994, A8). Similar rulings had occurred in twelve other states (Gray 1994, A12).

Thus, appellate courts, especially supreme courts, occupy a position of considerable importance in the policy-making process. However, not all participants in state politics perceive them that way. A study of Massachusetts legislators, for instance, found that the "Massachusetts Supreme Judicial Court is perceived by most members of the legislature as an extremely passive actor in state politics" (Miller 1993, 37). One legislator captured this feeling with the statement: "For us to react to the courts, it takes a combination of media attention and strong public sentiment. Usually we don't react at all to court decisions, because the courts create little controversy in this state" (Miller 1993, 38). In other states, courts are much more visible policy makers. We have already noted the storm of controversy surrounding the California Supreme Court's decisions on death penalty cases in the mid-1980s. In Ohio, another study found that most legislators paid attention to the decisions of the Ohio Supreme Court (Felice and Kilwein 1993). Most attentive were partisan opponents of the court, as reflected by one Republican: "I only watched a lot when [the former Democratic chief justice] was over there. They used to act like a second legislature" (Felice and Kilwein 1993, 45) One significant difference between the two states was that most state offices in Massachusetts were held by Democrats and there was no partisan division between the supreme judicial court and the legislature or governor's office. In Ohio, however, state offices were hotly contested by both parties and the supreme court was led by a chief justice who was perceived to be a strongly partisan Democrat. In all likelihood, the power and influence of appellate courts in most states rise and fall as such circumstances change, but we have no indicator to measure the changing power of state supreme courts.

The immersion of appellate courts into the political arena through their policy-making decisions emphasizes the questions at the beginning of this chapter: the degree to which judges are or ought to be responsive to the citizens of their states. The empirical side of this question may be roughly tested with measurements recently devised by several scholars. On the one hand, we have a measure of the ideological direction of the mass public in the states, as developed by Erikson, Wright, and McIver (1993). On the other, we have a measure of the innovative thrust of state courts in the area of the privacy rights as developed by Domino (1990). The two scales have a simple correlation of .48 for the forty-seven states for which we have the two measures; this indicates a moderate relation between the degree to which a state's mass public is liberal and the speed with which a state's supreme court expanded privacy rights.[1]

A more intriguing result, however, occurs when we run this correlation separately for states that elect their supreme court justices and those that appoint them. Those who advocate the election of judges point to the likelihood that the judges will be in step with public opinion. The results of a correlational analysis, however, show the opposite. The data in Table 7-4 show the correlations between privacy innovation and the ideological bent of the states for those states that have elective systems and those that have appointive systems. The correlation is slightly greater for those with appointive systems; if we limit our analysis to the states

1. Alaska, Hawaii, and Nevada are omitted because of missing or insufficient information.

Table 7-4 Correlation between Privacy Innovation by State Supreme Courts and Ideological Liberalism of State Mass Publics

	All states (N = 47)	States electing justices (N = 22)	States appointing justices (N = 25)	States with large samples and electing justices (N = 12)	States with large samples and appointing justices (N = 1)
Privacy innovation and ideological liberalism	.48	.43	.56	.40	.75

SOURCES: Calculated from data in Domino 1990, 28; Erikson, Wright, and McIver 1993, 16, 77.

for which the measure of ideological bent is most reliable (those with large samples in Erickson, Wright, and McIver's study), the difference between the two (.40 and .75) is much greater. In addition, when we correlate privacy innovation by the courts with the liberal bent of state policies (also as measured by Erikson, Wright, and McIver), we find similar relations. The courts in states where judges are appointed are more in step with their state's policy inclination than those in states where judges are elected, and the difference doubles when we consider only those states with the most reliable measure of ideological tendency.

There is an explanation for these counterintuitive findings. It seems plausible that judicial elections do not keep judges in step with their state's electorate because, as we saw earlier, those elections are rarely competitive. Judges are not permitted to discuss their policy inclinations, and the elections usually attract little attention from the electorate. Governors, however, when making judicial appointments are sensitive to the possible political fallout of their appointments. Liberal governors are likely to appoint liberal judges and conservative governors are likely to appoint conservative judges. I hasten to add, however, that these analyses rely on less than perfect measures. At this point they merely suggest this intriguing result rather than confirm it.

CONCLUSION

Courts are complex institutions that readily disguise their participation in state politics. Yet the conclusion is inescapable that courts are significant participants in state political arenas on many occasions. They implement thousands of laws while routinely hearing millions of cases at the trial level. By doing so, they translate these laws from dormant pieces of paper into robust policies that alter the lives of every resident of their state. Courts also create new policies in their role as interpreters of the law. Every day, some appellate court in one of the states is likely to issue a decision that alters state policy.

Although courts possess these significant powers, they remain shielded from much of the political turmoil that routinely surrounds legislators and governors. Made remote by abstruse rituals and complex selection procedures for judges, state courts operate in the shadow of social conflict, which is more readily portrayed by the mass media.

REFERENCES

Aspin, Larry T., and William K. Hall. 1994. "Retention Elections and Judicial Behavior." *Judicature* 77:306–315.

Canon, Bradley C. 1972. "The Impact of Formal Selection Processes on the Characteristics of Judges." *Law and Society Review* 6:579–594.

Champagne, Anthony. 1993. "Judicial Reform in Texas." In *Judicial Reform in the States,* edited by Anthony Champagne and Judith Haydel. Lanham, Md.: University Press of America.

CSG (Council of State Governments). 1994. *The Book of the States, 1994–95.* Lexington, Ky.: Council of State Governments.

Curran, Barbara, and Clara N. Carson. 1994. *Lawyer Statistical Report: The U.S. Legal Profession in the 1990s.* Chicago: American Bar Foundation.

"Developments in the Law: The Interpretation of State Constitutional Rights." 1982. *Harvard Law Review* 95:1324–1502.

Domino, John C. 1990. "Judicial Innovation in the Fifty States: The Diffusion of Seven Privacy Doctrines." Paper presented at the annual meeting of the Midwest Political Science Association, Chicago, April 5–7.

Drennan, James. 1993. "Judicial Reform in North Carolina." In *Judicial Reform in the States,* edited by Anthony Champagne and Judith Haydel. Lanham, Md.: University Press of America.

Dubois, Philip L. 1980. *From Bench to Ballot: Judicial Elections and the Quest for Accountability.* Austin: University of Texas Press.

———. 1985. "State Trial Court Appointments: Does the Governor Make a Difference?" *Judicature* 69:20–28.

Eisenstein, James, Roy B. Flemming, and Peter Nardulli. 1987. *The Contours of Justice: Communities and Their Courts.* Boston: Little, Brown.

Eisenstein, James, and Herbert Jacob. 1977. *Felony Justice: An Organizational Analysis of Criminal Courts.* Boston: Little, Brown.

Epstein, Lee. 1994. "Exploring the Participation of Organized Interests in State Court Litigation." *Political Research Quarterly* 47:335–351.

Erikson, Robert S., Gerald C. Wright, and John P. McIver. 1993. *Statehouse Democracy.* Cambridge: Cambridge University Press.

Esler, Michael. 1994. "State Supreme Court Commitment to State Law." *Judicature* 77:25–32.

Fahnestock, Kathryn, and Maurice D. Geiger. 1993. "'We All Get Along Here': Case Flow in Rural Courts." *Judicature* 76:258–263.

Felice, John D., and John C. Kilwein. 1993. "High Court-Legislative Relations: A View from the Ohio Courthouse." *Judicature* 77:42–48.

Galanter, Marc. 1974. "Why the 'Haves' Come Out Ahead: Speculations on the Limits of Legal Change." *Law and Society Review* 9:95–160.

———. 1983. "Reading the Landscape of Disputes: What We Know and Don't Know (and Think We Know) about Our Allegedly Contentious and Litigious Society." *UCLA Law Review* 31:1–71.

———. 1990. "Case Congregations and Their Careers." *Law and Society Review* 24:371–396.

Galie, Peter J. 1982. "The Other Supreme Courts: Judicial Activism among State Supreme Courts." *Syracuse Law Review* 33:731–1023.

Glick, Henry R. 1982. "Supreme Courts in State Judicial Administration." In *State Supreme Courts: Policymakers in the Federal System,* edited by Mary Cornelia Porter and G. Alan Tarr. Westport, Conn.: Greenwood Press.

———. 1992. *The Right to Die.* New York: Columbia University Press.

Glick, Henry R., and Craig F. Emmert. 1987. "Selection Systems and Judicial Characteristics: The Recruitment of State Supreme Court Judges." *Judicature* 70:228–235.

Glick, Henry R., and Kenneth N. Vines. 1973. *State Court Systems.* Englewood Cliffs, N.J.: Prentice-Hall.

Graham, Barbara Luck. 1990. "Do Judicial Selection Systems Matter: A Study of Black Representation on State Courts." *American Politics Quarterly* 18:316–336.

Gray, Jerry. 1994. "New Jersey School Financing Ruling Is Seen as Push toward More State Control." *New York Times,* July 14.

Greenfeld, Lawrence A., and James J. Stephan. 1993. "Capital Punishment 1992." *Bulletin* (U.S. Department of Justice, Bureau of Justice Statistics), December.

Grodin, Joseph R. 1987. "Judicial Elections: The California Experience." *Judicature* 70:365– 369.

Hall, William K., and Larry T. Aspin. 1987. "What Twenty Years of Judicial Retention Elections Have Told Us." *Judicature* 70:340–347.

Haydel, Judith, and Tom Ferrell. 1993. "Judicial Reform in Louisiana." In *Judicial Reform in the States,* edited by Anthony Champagne and Judith Haydel. Lanham, Md.: University Press of America.

Henry, M. L., Jr., Estajo Koslow, Joseph Soffer, and John Furey. 1985. *The Success of Women and Minorities in Achieving Judicial Office: The Selection Process.* New York: Fund for Modern Courts.

Henschen, Beth M., Robert Moog, and Steven Davis. 1990. "Judicial Nominating Commissioners: A National Profile." *Judicature* 73:328–335.

Hensler, Deborah R, Mary E. Vaiana, James S. Kakalik, and Mark A. Peterson. 1987. *Trends in Tort Litigation: The Story behind the Statistics.* Special Report. Santa Monica, Calif.: Rand Corporation.

Hojnacki, Marie, and Lawrence Baum. 1992. "Choosing Judicial Candidates: How Voters Explain Their Decisions." *Judicature* 75:300–309.

Jacob, Herbert. 1969. *Debtors in Court: The Consumption of Government Services.* Chicago: Rand McNally.

———. 1988. *Silent Revolution: The Transformation of Divorce Law in the United States.* Chicago: University of Chicago Press.

Janda, Kenneth, Jeffrey M. Berry, and Jerry Goldman. 1987. *The Challenge of Democracy.* Boston: Houghton Mifflin.

Johnson, Charles A., Roger C. Shaefer, and R. Neal McKnight. 1978. "The Salience of Judicial Candidates and Elections." *Social Science Quarterly* 59:371–378.

Joint Center for Political and Economic Studies. 1991. *Elected and Appointed Black Judges in the United States.* Washington, D.C.: Joint Center for Political and Economic Studies.

Kiel, J. Douglas, Carol Funk, and Anthony Champagne. 1994. "Two Party Competition and Trial Court Elections in Texas." *Judicature* 77:290–293.

Luskin, Robert C., Christopher N. Bratcher, Christopher G. Jordan, Tracy K. Renner, and Kris S. Seago. 1994. "How Minority Judges Fare in Retention Elections." *Judicature* 77:316–321.

McIntosh, Wayne. 1980–1981. "150 Years of Litigation and Dispute Settlement: A Court Tale." *Law and Society Review* 15:823–848.

———. 1983. "The Private Use of a Public Forum." *American Political Science Review* 77:99–1010.

Mann, Coramae Richey. 1993. *Unequal Justice: A Question of Color.* Bloomington: Indiana University Press.

Marvell, Thomas B. 1985. "Civil Caseloads: The Impact of the Economy and Trial Judgeship Increases." *Judicature* 69:153–156.

———. 1987. "Caseload Growth—Past and Future Trends." *Judicature* 71:162–168.

Mather, Lynn M. 1991. "Policy Making in State Trial Courts." In *The American Courts: A Critical Assessment,* edited by John B. Gates and Charles A. Johnson. Washington, D.C.: CQ Press.

Miller, Mark C. 1993. "Lawmaker Attitudes toward Court Reform in Massachusetts." *Judicature* 76:34–41.

Moog, Robert. 1992. "Campaign Financing for North Carolina's Appellate Courts." *Judicature* 76:68–76.

Mount, Charles. 1988. "11 Minority Judges Chosen; Critics Unmoved." *Chicago Tribune,* October 28.

National Center for State Courts. 1987. *State Court Caseload Statistics: Annual Report, 1985.* Williamsburg, Va.: National Center for State Courts.

Nelson, Robert L. 1988. "Ideology, Scholarship, and Sociolegal Change: Lessons from Galanter and the 'Litigation Crisis.'" *Law and Society Review* 25:677–693.

"New Jersey Justices: Poor Schools Shortchanged." 1994. *National Law Journal,* July 25, A8.

Roper, Robert T. 1986. "The Propensity to Litigate in State Trial Courts." *Justice System Journal* 11:262–281.

Rosenthal, Douglas E. 1974. *Lawyer and Client: Who's in Charge?* New York: Russell Sage Foundation.

Ross, H. Laurence. 1970. *Settled Out of Court: The Social Process of Insurance Claims Adjustment.* Chicago: Aldine Publishing.

Schafran, Lynn Hecht. 1993. "Gender Equality in the Courts: Still on the Judicial Agenda." *Judicature* 77:110–114.

Sheldon, Charles H., and Nicholas P. Lovrich, Jr. 1983. "Knowledge and Judicial Voting." *Judicature* 67:234–245.

Smith, Nancy J., and Julie Garmel. 1992. "Judicial Election and Selection Procedures Challenged under Voting Rights Act." *Judicature* 76:154–156.

Smothers, Ronald. 1994. "Court Overturns Georgia Accord on New Judges." *New York Times,* March 9, sec. A.

Stookey, John A. 1986. "Economic Cycles and Civil Litigation." *Justice System Journal* 11:282–301.

Stumpf, Harry P. 1987. *American Judicial Politics.* San Diego: Harcourt Brace Jovanovich.

Tarr, G. Alan, and Mary Cornelia Aldis Porter. 1988. *State Supreme Courts in State and Nation.* New Haven: Yale University Press.

Tybor, Joseph R. 1988. "Pressure by Minorities Pulls Judges Races to Center Stage." *Chicago Tribune,* October 13.

U.S. Bureau of the Census. 1993. *Statistical Abstract of the United States, 1993.* Washington, D.C.: U.S. Department of Commerce.

U.S. Department of Justice, Bureau of Justice Statistics. 1992. *Sourcebook of Criminal Justice Statistics, 1992.* Edited by Kathleen Maguire, Ann L. Pastore, and Timothy J. Flanagan. Washington, D.C.: U.S. Government Printing Office.

Wasmann, Erik, Nicholas P. Lovrich, Jr., and Charles H. Sheldon. 1986. "Perceptions of State and Local Courts: A Comparison across Selection Systems." *Justice System Journal* 11:168–185.

Watson, Richard A., and Rondal G. Downing. 1969. *The Politics of the Bench and Bar: Judicial Selection under the Missouri Nonpartisan Court Plan.* New York: John Wiley and Sons.

Wermiel, Stephen. 1988. "State Supreme Courts Are Feeling Their Oats about Civil Liberties." *Wall Street Journal,* June 15.

"What Lawyers Earn—A Special Supplement." 1994. *National Law Journal,* May 30, C1–C12.

Wold, John T., and John H. Culver. 1987. "The Defeat of the California Justices: The Campaign, the Electorate, and the Issue of Judicial Accountability." *Judicature* 70:348–355.

Zeisel, Hans, Harry Kalven, Jr., and Bernard Buchholz. 1959. *Delay in the Court.* Boston: Little, Brown.

Zemans, Frances Kahn. 1983. "Legal Mobilization: The Neglected Role of the Law in the Political System." *American Political Science Review* 77:690–703.

SUGGESTED READINGS

Eisenstein, James, Roy B. Flemming, and Peter Nardulli. *The Contours of Justice: Communities and Their Courts.* Boston: Little, Brown, 1987. An analysis of criminal courts in small cities and rural areas in Illinois, Michigan, and Pennsylvania. This book and *Felony Justice,* below, provide a realistic view of how criminal courts operate in a large variety of contexts in the United States.

Eisenstein, James, and Herbert Jacob. *Felony Justice: An Organizational Analysis of Criminal Courts.* Boston: Little, Brown, 1977. An examination of criminal courts in Baltimore, Chicago, and Detroit, showing how they work in large cities. *Felony Justice* and *The Contours of Justice,* above, provide a realistic view of how criminal courts operate in a large variety of contexts in the United States.

Glick, Henry R. *The Right to Die.* New York: Columbia University Press, 1992. Glick provides a fascinating account of how states formulate policy in an area in which the technology is rapidly changing. He shows how court decisions affect legislative consideration of the same issues and how courts respond to legislative initiatives.

Stern, Gerald M. *The Buffalo Creek Disaster.* New York: Vintage Books, 1976. Stern provides a compelling description of the ways in which state politics and litigation mix when a major economic interest in a state is challenged in court.

Tarr, G. Alan, and Mary Cornelia Aldis Porter. *State Supreme Courts in State and Nation.* New Haven, Conn.: Yale University Press, 1988. An excellent description of the work of several state supreme courts.

CHAPTER 8

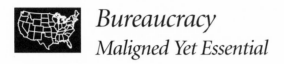

Bureaucracy
Maligned Yet Essential

RICHARD C. ELLING

With responsibilities ranging from A (agriculture, the arts, aviation) to Z (zoos), state bureaucracies do most of what state governments do.[1] For most citizens, state government is as often a state agency and one of its employees as the governor or the legislature.

Citizens interact most frequently with lower-level state bureaucrats. Welfare caseworkers, conservation officers, probation and parole agents, college financial aid workers, public health inspectors, state police officers, and unemployment compensation clerks can significantly affect the fortunes of those with whom they deal. Higher-level administrators make less routine decisions, determine standards to guide the actions of subordinates in accomplishing agency objectives, and supervise the performance of subordinates. They also interact with numerous external institutions, officials, and groups.

Two examples can hardly capture the diversity of tasks performed by the 4.6 million full-time and part-time employees of state government. But since the "bashing" of public bureaucrats and bureaucracies is a national sport, they may at least challenge the stereotypes of some readers.[2]

Scott Alisoglu has been an analyst in the Budget Division of the Kansas De-

1. I use the term *bureaucracy* as a synonym for a large, complex organization, like a government department.
2. The quotations from Scott Alisoglu and Kristine Kelly that follow are from personal communications to me in June 1994.

partment of Administration since 1993. His primary responsibility is to assist the governor in preparing the executive budget, which is submitted to the legislature each January. He also assists agencies with management and budget-related issues at their request. Concerning the rewards of his job, Scott observes: "As a 24 year-old recent college graduate, I was amazed at the responsibility I was given. This job requires that the work that is done be as accurate as possible because this work may be used by the Governor in making his or her policy/management decisions. This job gives me the opportunity to be involved in a wide range of areas on both the legislative and gubernatorial sides."

Dr. Kristine Kelly works in the Air Resources Division of the New York State Department of Environmental Conservation. Kristine, who supervises a staff of ten as the head of the Program Development and Services Section, describes the work of the section this way: "Basically, we work with division management to secure enough resources to ensure that we can meet our responsibilities under the federal Clean Air Act Amendments of 1990 and the New York State Clean Air Compliance Act of 1993—that is, controlling air pollution. We establish workplan priorities, oversee the hiring and recruitment of personnel, develop the state budget, prepare new legislative proposals and conduct program evaluations." The rewards and the frustrations in Kristine's job lie in the fact that the task of regulating air pollution is a daunting one: "The regulatory decisions that we make affect the quality of everyone's life—cleaner cars and industries, and better air to breathe. Working within a state bureaucracy that has this kind of influence is both exhilarating and frustrating. . . . [T]he chance to do something to improve the air for millions of people . . . is a thrill—the ability to make a difference. The frustration is how to accomplish this equitably."

State bureaucrats are important because they implement state programs. But the federal government also uses them to implement many of its programs. This occurs frequently because state agencies participate in numerous federal grant-in-aid programs. A major part of the work of Dr. Kelly's department involves implementing federal air pollution laws.

State bureaucracies also matter because they are involved in more than just "administration," narrowly defined. After a policy is established, many questions remain about how best to deliver services or how to secure the compliance of those affected by a policy. Decisions on these matters, which can have significant consequences for policy success, are largely in administrative hands.

State administrative agencies also help set the policy agenda. Elected officials are often made aware of problems, or deficiencies in existing programs, by those administrators who regularly deal with those problems or programs. Administrators may also help develop solutions to problems on the policy agenda and provide information on the merits of policy options to the elected officials who formally adopt them. Recall, in this regard, Kristine Kelly's mention of the development of new legislative proposals as one of the tasks of her section in New York's Department of Environmental Conservation.

THE CHALLENGING ENVIRONMENT OF
STATE BUREAUCRACIES

Governors, legislators, the courts, the federal government, and interest and clientele groups are but some of the external actors who constitute an important element of the environment of state bureaucracies. These actors seek to influence state administrative affairs, contending among themselves for "custody" of agencies and their programs (Gormley 1989). Other developments since the mid-1970s have made the environment in which state agencies function more challenging. As discussed in other chapters, these developments include fiscal stringency, continued strong demand for existing services, and the emergence of new problems. In the 1990s, state bureaucracies have often been forced to do more with constant or shrinking resources.

The data in Table 8-1 make this point, as well as others, about the significance of state bureaucracies and their environment. In 1992, states employed nearly one out of every four civilian public employees. Although more populous states employ many more workers, the ratio of state employees to state population is lower in these states, as the fifth column of Table 8-1 discloses. The balance of responsibilities between state and local governments also affects state employment. Less populous, less densely settled, geographically smaller, and poorer states all tend to rely more heavily on state agencies for the delivery of services (Hanson 1990; Stephens 1985). For example, note that Arkansas ranks thirty-third in population but sixteenth in number of state employees per 10,000 Arkansans.

Some states have more employees because they do more in certain functional areas. On average, one-third of all state employment is in higher education. But public higher-education systems are more extensive in some states than others, as indicated in the fourth column of Table 8-1. Notable here are several midwestern states that are home to one or more "Big Ten" public universities.

Although state employment grew by 30 percent between 1978 and 1992, such growth was uneven across states, as revealed in the seventh column of Table 8-1. The biggest increases were in states whose populations were growing most rapidly. Periods of employment growth are often followed by contractions. Layoffs occurred in a majority of states in both the early 1980s and the early 1990s (Hall 1992; Lewin 1983). For example, New York eliminated 10 percent of its positions in the early 1990s. Employment growth sometimes trailed population growth, however. Thus, between 1978 and 1992 the number of state employees per 10,000 residents decreased in ten states. Moreover, employment increases were concentrated in just two functional areas. Across all fifty states, employment in higher education grew by 42 percent. Most states embarked on a correctional facilities building spree during the 1980s and early 1990s. As a result, employment in such state facilities was 148 percent higher in 1992 than it had been in 1978.

While fiscal stringency is a more recently salient element in the environment of state bureaucracies, public dissatisfaction with the performance of bureaucra-

Table 8-1 State Government Employment

State	Pop. rank in 1990 (1)	State employees, all functions, (FTE, thousands) 1992* No. (2)	Rank (3)	% of state work force in higher education (4)	State employees, all functions, per 10,000 residents, 1992 No. (5)	Rank (6)	% of change in employment all functions, 1978–1992 (7)
Alabama	22	81	18	37	196	15	31
Alaska	49	24	39	24	413	1	55
Arizona	24	54	27	35	141	44	49
Arkansas	33	47	32	32	194	16	41
California	1	322	1	33	104	50	29
Colorado	26	53	28	52	153	33	18
Connecticut	27	54	26	23	165	31	19
Delaware	46	20	42	32	293	3	38
Florida	11	165	11	29	122	47	63
Georgia	11	114	11	29	170	26	50
Hawaii	41	51	29	14	437	1	48
Idaho	42	20	41	35	190	19	34
Illinois	6	137	8	34	117	49	21
Indiana	14	95	14	47	168	27.5	53
Iowa	30	47	34	39	168	27.5	9
Kansas	32	48	31	42	190	19	26
Kentucky	23	76	20	37	203	13	28
Louisiana	21	89	15	31	207	11.5	30
Maine	38	22	40	26	178	25	27
Maryland	19	82	17	25	167	29.5	14
Massachusetts	13	85	16	24	142	43	18
Michigan	8	138	7	51	146	39	15
Minnesota	20	67	24	49	150	35	26
Mississippi	31	47	33	31	181	23	29
Missouri	15	74	22	28	143	42	16
Montana	44	17	45	33	207	11.5	14
Nebraska	36	29	38	35	179	24	2
Nevada	39	19	44	31	144	41	58
New Hampshire	40	16	47	32	147	38	22
New Jersey	9	116	10	24	149	36	39
New Mexico	37	42	35	40	267	4	52
New York	2	267	2	16	148	37	40
N. Carolina	10	109	12	36	159	32	23
N. Dakota	47	16	46	41	259	5	42
Ohio	7	140	6	47	127	46	26
Oklahoma	28	67	25	35	209	10	32
Oregon	29	50	30	28	167	29.5	18
Pennsylvania	5	144	5	34	119	48	9
Rhode Island	43	20	43	29	198	14	32
S. Carolina	25	78	19	34	216	9	8
S. Dakota	45	14	48	32	190	19	20
Tennessee	17	76	21	38	151	34	45
Texas	3	240	3	34	136	45	46
Utah	35	40	36	48	219	8	21
Vermont	48	13	49	34	227	7	24
Virginia	12	116	9	37	182	22	44
Washington	18	98	13	41	191	17	13
W. Virginia	34	34	37	34	185	21	31
Wisconsin	16	73	23	50	145	40	30
Wyoming	50	11	50	28	242	6	30
Total		3,856		33	219		30

SOURCES: Council of State Governments 1980 and 1994, 446.
*Full- and part-time employees expressed as full-time equivalents.

cies is a long-standing concern. Yet, little systematic evidence exists on state bureaucratic performance. One reason for this is the multidimensional nature of bureaucratic performance. We hold administrative agencies to several, often contradictory, standards. Even if we can agree on a single performance standard, arguments continue because of the difficulty in measuring performance. This is so because most agencies produce services rather than physical products.

Three broad standards of public bureaucratic performance are efficiency, effectiveness, and political and public accountability. The first two standards can be applied to public, private, and nonprofit organizations alike. Indeed, we have typically wanted public agencies to attain levels of efficiency and effectiveness similar to those that private enterprises are presumed to achieve.

An efficient organization gets the most out of a given amount of resources. If a greater volume of highway litter is collected at a comparable or lower cost, efficiency has increased. Effectiveness is goal oriented. An effective organization gets the job done. It also asks the question, So what? However well administered, does a given program solve or ameliorate a problem? For example, does vocational training for incarcerated felons improve their chances of securing jobs on release and reduce the likelihood that they will engage in future criminal activity? A moderately inefficient organization may still be reasonably effective. Still, while efficiency may enhance effectiveness, it cannot ensure it.

Accountability as a standard has two dimensions. A *process* dimension is concerned with the constitutionality or legality of administrative actions—with honesty, observance of due process, impartiality, and decency in dealing with the public. More demanding expectations concerning this standard distinguish public from private administration. A second dimension of accountability is *responsiveness*. Whose goals do bureaucracies attempt to achieve? Since few state bureaucrats are elected, their role in government troubles many. Specifying to whom unelected administrators should be responsive is difficult, however. Should they simply follow the orders of administrative superiors? Is primary responsibility owed to the governor or to the legislature? What about responsiveness to those served by an agency's programs? Disagreement also exists on exactly how to ensure accountability.

The existence of conflicting performance standards means that difficult trade-offs abound. Efforts to ensure process accountability often increase costs and erode efficiency or effectiveness. Although requiring bureaucrats to follow detailed procedures in service delivery puts limitations on arbitrary action by them, it may generate much despised red tape. In the public sector we often sacrifice some degree of efficiency or effectiveness in order to increase bureaucratic accountability to elected officials. Perhaps this is as it should be in a democracy. Nonetheless, clear thinking about administrative performance requires awareness of the tensions between these performance standards.

PERSPECTIVES ON STATE
BUREAUCRATIC PERFORMANCE

For this section I have drawn on disparate sources of evidence in order to assess state bureaucratic performance. Surveys suggest Americans are relatively satisfied with their encounters with state bureaucracies. Thus, more than 80 percent of the 6,000 Wisconsin residents surveyed about their contacts with state transportation employees (highway patrol officers and driver's license examiners) described these contacts as either good or excellent as far as "courtesy of treatment" and "helpfulness of employees" were concerned (Goodsell 1985). Other clientele surveys paint a similar picture (Goodsell 1994, esp. 25–39; Michigan Department of Civil Service 1987; and Schmidt 1977). Recorded statistics on agency operations also suggest satisfactory performance. A study of the administration of the Aid to Families with Dependent Children program found that errors in determining eligibility occurred in just 5 percent of cases across the states (Campbell and Bendick 1977). A study of state unemployment compensation operations found that 90 percent of claims were paid within three weeks (Goodsell 1985).

Unfortunately, data of the sort discussed in the two preceding paragraphs are available for only a few states, agencies, or programs. I adopted a different approach in a mid-1980s survey of state managers in Arizona, California, Delaware, Indiana, Michigan, New York, South Dakota, Tennessee, Texas, and Vermont (Elling 1992; hereafter referred to as the ten-state study). The focus was on the specific problems of state bureaucracies as viewed through the eyes of 847 middle- and upper-level administrators in them. They assessed the severity of fifty-two conditions, circumstances, and practices that might exist in their state, or in their administrative unit, and that might impede the "efficient and effective administration of the programmatic responsibilities" of their units. Certainly some administrators may dissemble or misperceive reality. But it is useful to assess administrative performance from the perspective of those "in the trenches."

Only about one-fourth of the fifty-two potential impediments were considered to be severe by even 20 percent of the managers surveyed. These problems are listed in Table 8-2. Eight of the ten most serious problems concern the availability or use of human and fiscal resources. In contrast, problems that only about one manager in ten considered to be serious included lazy employees, ineffective communication with subordinates or difficulties supervising them, having a complex organizational structure, media hostility toward a unit, legislative or gubernatorial "meddling" in a unit's operations, and agency employees treating clients badly.

In sum, state bureaucracies face difficulties as they seek to do what their state's citizens want done. Few seem overwhelmed by their problems, however. Most do a decent job in the eyes of those citizens. While not perfect, most state bureaucracies "manage to manage."

Table 8-2   State Managers' Judgments regarding Major Problems
Hindering Bureaucratic Performances (in percent)

Problem	Managers reporting problem as "serious"*
Adequately rewarding outstanding employees	51
Insufficient appropriations	45
Legislative program expansion without additional funding	40
Difficulty disciplining and dismissing employees	34
Civil service procedures for recruiting and selecting staff	34
Filling key vacancies and retaining key staff	33
Complex process for promulgating rules or regulations	30
Paperwork and clearance requirements on decisions	28
Organizational resistance to change	24
Excessive restrictions on expenditures of agency funds	23
Unpredictable federal grant funding	23
Ineffective organizational planning	22
Inadequate facilities	20

SOURCE: Elling 1992. Reprinted with permission of Greenwood Publishing Group.
*Column entry is based on the responses of high-level managers surveyed in ten states. These managers were asked to assess the severity of some fifty-two potential impediments to the effective performance of their units. The response options were "no problem," "minor problem," "serious problem," or "very serious problem." Only those problems considered to be serious or very serious by 20 percent or more of the managers are listed here. The total number of respondents was 847. The number of responses regarding the severity of particular problems ranged between 794 and 845.

IMPROVING STATE BUREAUCRATIC PERFORMANCE: REORGANIZATION, REINVENTION, OR PRIVATIZATION?

Although state bureaucracies often perform better than their critics recognize, their performance is not ideal. In this section, I discuss some approaches to improving the performance of state bureaucracies.

The Anatomy of State Administration: Dynamics of Organization and Reorganization

The Bureaucratic Form of Organization. The structure and operations of state administrative agencies are generally consistent with an organizational model called *bureaucracy.* Bureaucracies are found in both the public and the private sector. The characteristics of bureaucracies include:

• Extensive subdivision of the responsibilities of the organization in various ways. Bureaucracies emphasize *division of labor and specialization of function.*

• The arrangement of organizational units in a hierarchy. Authority flows down from a single head at the top of the organization, and responsibility flows upward to this individual. Bureaucracy embodies the principle of *monocratic authority.*

• Employment of persons based on their possessing technical competence relevant to the organization's tasks rather than considerations such as their political beliefs or family connections.

• An elaborate set of rules governing the operations of the organization.

Organizations based on these principles are thought by many to be capable of delivering services reliably and consistently while treating citizens fairly. The ability of elected officials to hold such organizations accountable is increased by the hierarchy of authority within them.

The structure and processes of individual agencies, as well as the overall organization of a state's administrative apparatus, frequently deviate from the bureaucratic ideal, however. Organizational structures reflect disagreements over how much say various nonadministrative actors ought to have. Some reformers believe effective administration demands the insulation of day-to-day operations from meddling by partisan elected officials. Others favor the direct election of officials with largely administrative duties as a way to ensure administrative accountability. Contemporary examples include treasurers, superintendents of public instruction, and commissioners of public lands or agriculture. In addition, most states rely on boards or commissions to direct the operations of some agencies. Such "plural executives" violate the bureaucratic precept of monocratic authority.

In short, state organizational patterns embody classic bureaucratic precepts tempered by antibureaucratic values. In addition, as states took on new tasks, these were commonly assigned to single-purpose agencies, thus further complicating the overall structure of state bureaucracies. By the 1950s state bureaucracies often contained 100 or more units (Conant 1992b).

The Religion of Reorganization: Believers and Heretics. Organizational restructuring is a commonly prescribed strategy for improving bureaucratic performance. Consolidating the responsibilities of numerous separate agencies into a small number of broadly functional ones such as transportation, natural resources, or human services supposedly reduces wasteful duplication of services and uncoordinated service delivery. Reorganizers support centralization of authority in the hands of department heads. Gubernatorial authority is then increased by making these agency heads subject to gubernatorial appointment and removal. This requires eliminating independently elected officials with largely administrative functions, along with boards and commissions. Reducing the number of agencies reporting to the governor further clarifies his or her administrative authority. Concentrating authority in the governor's hands is viewed as a way of increasing bureaucratic accountability because the voters can hold the governor responsible for administrative mistakes.

The tenets of this religion were so persuasive that twenty-six states undertook major reorganizations between 1965 and 1991 (Conant 1992b). Few reorganizations achieved all that their proponents desired, however, in part because the goals of efficiency, effectiveness, and accountability are valued differently by various participants in the reorganization effort. Governors embrace reorganization because it promises to concentrate authority in their hands. Business interests, the media, and "good government" groups such as the League of Women Voters often endorse it because they believe it will result in a more "businesslike" administrative process.

Not everyone is an adherent of the religion of reorganization, however. Legislators, especially those not of the governor's own party, may see reorganization as threatening valuable legislative ties with particular state agencies. Agency heads may resist reorganizations that jeopardize their relations with the legislature or clientele groups, or that reduce their unit's visibility. Elected agency heads and members of elected or appointed boards are often vociferously opposed. Finally, interest groups or agency clientele typically reinforce legislative and agency opposition. Groups instrumental in the establishment of "their" agency have special working arrangements with it. They believe that fish and wildlife, veterans, or education programs are best administered by semiautonomous agencies insulated from gubernatorial control.

Assessing the Effects of Reorganization: The Bottom Line and Other Standards. Reorganization rarely generates substantial administrative savings (Conant 1992a). Reducing the number of agencies may save little money either because many eliminated units had minuscule budgets or their functions continue to be performed by other agencies. Today's reorganizers stress gains in efficiency or effectiveness more than saving money. Most administrators feel reorganization improves agency performance (Elling 1992; U.S. Advisory Commission 1985). Reorganization does not, however, guarantee gains in efficiency or effectiveness. It may simply transform a situation in which the relationships between numerous separate agencies have hampered effective service delivery into one that features a smaller number of internally unmanageable "superagencies." Such "garbage can" agencies are not necessarily models of administrative effectiveness (Hult 1987).

The clearest effect of reorganization is to increase bureaucratic accountability, particularly to the governor (Elling 1992; Hebert, Brudney, and Wright 1983). The proportion of agencies headed by gubernatorial appointees has grown. In some states the number of agencies has been reduced by as much as 80 percent, and these agencies have often been combined into a smaller number of larger, multifunctional departments (Conant 1992a). Examples include natural resources and transportation departments. Simplifying the administrative structure may make it easier for both elected officials and citizens to determine who does what. In short, reorganization can make a difference, but it is a mistake to pin all of one's hopes for improving bureaucratic performance on it.

Reinvention: Contracting and the Role of State Bureaucracies

Some critics dismiss structural reorganization of the bureaucracy or the reform of personnel processes, to be discussed later in this chapter, as mere tinkering. For them nothing less than a reinvention of how governments and bureaucracy do business will do. This argument is made most enthusiastically by Osborne and Gaebler in their book, *Reinventing Government: How the Entrepreneurial Spirit Is Transforming the Public Sector* (1993).

One element of the reinvention paradigm is its call for *catalytic government,* which is defined as governments that "steer but do not row" (Osborne and Gaebler 1993, chap. 1). Governments must determine what is to be done, what services will be provided, and how they will be paid for, but the actual implementation of those policies should not necessarily be accomplished by government bureaucracies. Closely related is the model's call for *competitive government*—for "injecting competition into service delivery" (1993, chap. 3). While reliance on private or nonprofit organizations to deliver services is an obvious implication of these two principles taken together, Osborne and Gaebler are not extreme privatizers. In addition to competition among private service providers, they recommend that public agencies compete with private providers as well as with other public agencies. An example of the latter might be competition among colleges in a state system of higher education. Moreover, Osborne and Gaebler believe public bureaucracies can compete effectively with private providers.

Privatization and Contracting for Services

The "reinvention" perspective stresses that governments should "steer but not row" and that they should seek to inject competition into the delivery of public services. Various forms of privatization are consistent with this argument, and states have made increased use of each of these since the mid-1970s. Here I examine the most commonly used form of privatization—contracting with private or nonprofit organizations for the provision of particular services (see Hatry 1989, 3, for a discussion of other privatization options).

States have long relied on private contractors for highway construction. Building maintenance services are currently contracted out in twenty-one states, food services in fifteen, clerical services in thirteen, and security services in ten (Olberding 1994). All but two of New Jersey's twenty-one departments contract for at least some services, with half or more of the budgets of several—including Transportation, Commerce and Economic Development, and Health—spent on contracts with various providers (Van Horn 1991). Recent decades have seen contracting extended from "hard" services—like road construction—to "soft" services—such as the provision of day care, adoption and foster care services, mental health services, child care support enforcement, drug and alcohol abuse treatment, Medicaid claims management, and employee training and placement. A few states have experimented with privately run correctional institutions (Lemov 1993).

The most common rationale put forth for contracting out is that private providers can deliver services of equal or better quality more cheaply than can government bureaucracies, which are monopoly suppliers. Moreover, when a government has only a limited or short-term need for certain services, hiring those who can provide them for only as long as is needed makes sense. Finally, private providers operating in several jurisdictions may have lower unit costs of production (Hatry 1989a).

In addition to these "official" reasons for contracting out, other considerations also drive this process. Having campaigned on a platform favoring the downsizing of the state bureaucracy, elected officials may see contracting as a way to reduce state employment while maintaining levels and quality of service. Even if total program costs do not decline, the number of state employees does. Since many government services are labor intensive, employee wages and fringe benefits are a big part of service costs. In many states the proportion of state employees that collectively bargain exceeds the proportion in the private sector. Hence, contracting may be a way to lower labor costs, if not also "bust the unions." Public sector unions argue that this is often the only reason that jurisdictions shift from in-house to contracted service delivery.

Contracting does not always work as well as its proponents assert. Costs have often declined, but sometimes this is so because the quantity or quality of service being provided has also declined. A multistate study of contracting concludes that most states lacked sufficient evidence on how costs or quality changed to be able to determine if that contracted service provision was superior (Allen et al. 1989). Private contractors may operate more cheaply because they compensate employees less well (Kettl 1993). Lower pay and benefits sometimes translate into less qualified employees.

Although competitive forces may cause private providers to deliver more or better service at lower costs, the need to make a profit may also encourage contractors to skimp on quality (Hatry 1989a). Moreover, competition among qualified providers is often absent, especially in less populated areas and for various social services (De Hoog 1984; Smith and Lipsky 1993; Van Horn 1991). Even when there are competing bidders, corruption can short-circuit the process. Bid rigging, bribery, and kickback scandals are common in the history of contracting. Indeed, contracting corruption prompted many governments in the late nineteenth and early twentieth centuries to move to direct service provision by civil service employees. Ensuring high-quality services requires that specific performance standards be written into contracts and that there be effective monitoring of contractor performance. But writing precise performance criteria is difficult, especially when the services involved are complex (Kettl 1993). As for monitoring of contract compliance, it is often done badly, if it is done at all (De Hoog 1984; Rehfuss 1989; Van Horn 1991). The costs of effective monitoring may exceed 10 percent of the value of a contract (Rehfuss 1990). When monitoring costs are added to other contract administration costs, any financial advantage of contracting is significantly reduced.

Finally, some critics of contracting would argue that—even if it results in greater efficiency or effectiveness—it sacrifices too much in the way of accountability to the public and reduces citizen access. Contracting complicates the chain of command. It now runs not just from a governor or the legislature to an agency head and then down to the level at which services are delivered in an agency, but to private concerns charged with delivering certain services as well.

The contracting agency may suggest that a disgruntled citizen contact the contractor; the contractor may refer the citizen to the contracting agency. Contracting also raises liability issues. The ultimate power of government is to deprive an individual of his or her life, liberty, or property. Whether to give private actors such power is controversial. This is a major reason that few states have contracted for the operation of maximum security correctional institutions (Allen et al. 1989; Lemov 1993).

So where does this leave us? Certainly contracting for services often works well. I found that 76 percent of state managers familiar with contracting said it had positive effects on the performance of their units (Elling 1992). One lesson is that contracting works best for services whose quality is more easily judged by both citizens and agency officials (Bendick 1984). Liability, accountability, and service continuity concerns suggest that tax collecting; regulation designed to control the behavior of citizens or corporations; and "critical services" such as public safety, perhaps corrections, and care for the severely mentally ill be provided directly by state bureaucracies (Becker and Mackelprang 1990). This leaves a wide range of state government services as candidates for privatization, however.

Even if particular services are good candidates for contracting, success demands that significant resources be devoted to contract administration, especially the drafting of specific contract language and the vigorous monitoring of contract compliance. Paradoxically, contracting may increase rather than decrease the managerial responsibilities of state bureaucracies, since it imposes heavy information and oversight demands on them (Kettl 1993).

THE FACE OF THE STATE BUREAUCRACY

The face of the bureaucracy is its thousands of employees. Although contracting out may reduce the number of employees directly involved in service delivery, state governments will have to hire others to perform the tasks that ensure that a system of catalytic government works well—employees skilled in the writing, letting, monitoring, and enforcing of contracts. Hence, the performance of state bureaucracies will continue to be significantly affected by how they are staffed.

Following the Civil War, civil service reformers attacked political patronage and argued that effective government required the hiring and retention of public employees on the basis of merit—that is, on the basis of their education, experience, or actual job performance, rather than their political or family connections. A civil service commission, independent of elected officials and political parties, would ensure that merit principles were observed. The result would be a competent corps of politically neutral civil servants. State civil service systems represent another manifestation of the belief in the desirability of a separation of politics and administration.

Today, nearly three-fourths of the states have comprehensive civil service systems, while the remainder have more limited coverage. Yet despite civil service reform—and sometimes because of it—state personnel systems confront challenges. In this section, I examine some of these challenges.

State Personnel Processes: Competence, Organizational Effectiveness, and Accountability

Advocates of civil service reform argued that it would ensure that "only the best shall serve the state." Critics charge that, today, civil service systems often fail to achieve this goal. Securing able employees is sometimes hampered by unimaginative recruiting, examinations whose job-relatedness has not been validated, and hiring practices so complex and slow that qualified applicants accept jobs elsewhere. In seeking to eliminate patronage politics by protecting the competent from dismissal for inappropriate reasons, civil service rules have made it difficult to fire the objectively incompetent. When even high-ranking administrators are covered by civil service, governors may find it difficult to impress their policy priorities on state bureaucracies.

Each of these criticisms has some merit. Each is also subject to qualification. A fifty-state survey found that few of those administering state hazardous waste clean-up programs felt civil service rules hindered their effectiveness (Cohen and Ingersoll 1985). In my ten-state study, however, I found that four of the six most serious impediments to effective agency management were personnel related (Table 8-2). On the positive side, few managers complained that their employees were lazy or incompetent or that political patronage was a problem.

Although some criticize supposedly excessive levels of compensation for state employees, the concerns of managers in the ten-state study about difficulty in rewarding outstanding performance suggests a different conclusion. State personnel directors believe that their states have had only average success in providing competitive salaries and benefits (Hays and Kearney 1992). In fact, assessing levels of state employee compensation, both among the states and between the states and the private sector, is difficult. Many public sector jobs have no equivalents in the private sector. Nonsalary compensation, such as health care and retirement benefits, must be considered as well. Comparisons must also take differences in cost of living into account. A much-cited study by Cox and Brunelli (1992), arguing that states' fiscal difficulties resulted from excessive pay for their employees, failed to take various of these considerations into account (Gold and Ritchie 1993).

With these complexities in mind, how does the compensation of state government employees compare across states and with that paid to private sector employees? The data in Table 8-3 indicate that in October 1992 the monthly pay of a full-time state employee not employed in education averaged $2,487—or $29,844 annually. Although not shown in Table 8-3, the average when state education employees are included tends to be one or two hundred dollars per month higher.

Table 8-3 Average Monthly Earnings, Full-Time Noneducation State Employees, October 1992

State	Rank	Average monthly earnings	State	Rank	Average monthly earnings
Alaska	1	$3,526	Utah	27	2,216
California	2	3,282	North Carolina	28	2,215
Connecticut	3	3,222	Arizona	29	2,185
New York	4	3,088	Texas	30	2,180
Michigan	5	3,068	Montana	31	2,162
New Jersey	6	2,945	New Mexico	32	2,108
Minnesota	7	2,915	Nebraska	33	2,103
Wisconsin	8	2,888	Virginia	34	2,100
Colorado	9	2,850	Alabama	35	2,084
Rhode Island	10	2,814	Florida	36	2,080
Nevada	11	2,729	North Dakota	37	2,060
Washington	12	2,712	Kentucky	38	2,043
Ohio	13	2,641	Indiana	39	2,024
Iowa	14	2,585	Louisiana	40	2,013
Massachusetts	15	2,553	Tennessee	41	2,012
Illinois	16	2,540	South Dakota	42	2,007
Maryland	17	2,474	Arkansas	43	1,981
Pennsylvania	18	2,470	Wyoming	44	1,965
Oregon	19	2,444	Oklahoma	45	1,930
Vermont	20	2,408	South Carolina	46	1,891
Hawaii	21	2,305	Georgia	47	1,885
Maine	22	2,350	Missouri	48	1,882
New Hampshire	23	2,345	Mississippi	49	1,781
Idaho	24	2,264	West Virginia	50	1,756
Delaware	25	2,248	50 state average		2,487
Kansas	26	2,226			

SOURCE: U.S. Bureau of the Census 1992.

Great interstate disparities in pay exist. In 1991 the average monthly earnings of noneducation employees exceeded $2,800 in seven states but was below $1,900 in eight. Cost-of-living differences explain some of this variation. By adjusting earnings for cost of living using 1989 data for noneducation state employees, the pay ranking of some states changes dramatically (Gold and Ritchie 1993). When Alaska's high cost of living was taken into account, its pay rank dropped from first to thirteenth. In contrast, Vermont emerged as the best-paying state even though it ranked twenty-second in unadjusted pay. Still, although adjusting for cost of living narrows interstate variation in pay, it does not eliminate it. Before adjustments, noneducation state employees in West Virginia earned, in 1989, only 46 percent as much as their counterparts in the best-paying state, Alaska. After cost of living was factored in, West Virginia remained the worst-paying state, its noneducation employees earning just 48 percent as much as their counterparts in the best-paying state (Vermont).

In addition to wages or salary, employee compensation includes important fringe benefits, such as pensions, vacation and sick leave, and, most important, health care coverage. The value of these benefits averaged 24 percent of salaries and wages for all states in 1987 (Stevens 1992). The 1989 study cited earlier also factored in fringe benefits. Generally, states ranking high in regard to average monthly salary also rank high when the value of fringe benefits is factored in, although a few states become either more or less competitive when this is done.

Debate over compensation often concerns whether public employees are better paid than persons performing comparable jobs in the private sector—the implication being that they should not be. Available data suggest that state employees performing jobs requiring lower levels of skill are typically compensated as well as similar employees in the private sector. State employees in middle- and upper-level technical, professional, and administrative jobs, however, often earn much less than their counterparts in the private sector. In 1984, compensation for jobs at the high end of the scale lagged in relation to compensation given for comparable jobs in the private sector by 20 to 25 percent (Hay/Huggins 1984).

The adequacy of the salaries paid to agency heads and other high-level managers has been of particular concern. A 1990 study calculated the average annual salary of eight top-level state executives in each of the fifty states in 1989 (Council of State Governments and the National Association of State Personnel Executives 1990). The average salary of these executives ranged from $49,602 in Arkansas to $105,164 in New York. Yet a 1984 study concluded that private sector executives with comparable responsibilities earned from $230,000 to $600,000 (Hay/Huggins 1984). The values of our capitalist society are unlikely to cause us to triple the salaries of top state executives. But many current or potential state employees have the choice of whether to work in the public or the private sector, and state governments must pay salaries that are at least in the ballpark if they are to be able to attract and retain competent persons for these jobs.

Many Americans do not care if state employees are poorly paid. They are much more concerned about how hard it is for state governments to fire employees who are not doing a good job. Data that I have collected for one or more years in the early 1990s for nine states (Iowa, Kansas, Maryland, Michigan, Minnesota, Missouri, Nevada, Pennsylvania, and West Virginia) disclose annual dismissal rates ranging from less than 0.5 percent to 1.7 percent of a state's workforce. Many citizens may believe that more than 2 percent of any state's workforce deserve the ax every year. Recall, however, that most Americans are also reasonably satisfied with the quality of services provided by state employees. Moreover, lazy or incompetent employees ranked twenty-sixth out of fifty-two potential impediments to effective management in my ten-state study.

Most state personnel directors think that their state's personnel system does a good job of protecting employees from adverse personnel actions unrelated to their actual ability to perform and of ensuring the political neutrality of the state workforce (Hays and Kearney 1992). This is a significant accomplishment of civil service reform. But it comes at the price of rules that make it difficult to discipline or discharge public employees who are performing poorly. In recent years many states have streamlined procedures for disciplining or dismissing employees so as to make a better balance between employee rights and the public's right to a productive workforce (Walters 1994). But giving high-level managers, who are often political appointees, greater freedom to remove employees for "legitimate" performance-related reasons risks opening the door to dismissals based on political considerations or other irrelevancies.

Other personnel system changes seek to increase the accountability of the career civil service to governors or their appointees. Nearly every state has shifted personnel management responsibilities from semiautonomous civil service commissions to central personnel agencies often headed by gubernatorial appointees (National Association of State Personnel Executives 1992). Many states have removed some high-level administrative positions from the classified civil service on the grounds that those in these positions are involved in shaping policies as well as administering programs. These officials now serve at the "will and pleasure" of the governor (Roberts 1991).

Reforms like these may have increased the competence or responsiveness of state bureaucracies. State personnel directors give their states' systems good marks for "aiding in effective administration" and "implementing the governor's program" (Hays and Kearney 1992). Others worry, however, that various "reforms" risk excessive politicization of state personnel systems.

The Challenge of Equal Opportunity and Diversity

Civil service's stress on "objective merit" has reduced discrimination based on race, ethnicity, age, gender, and disability. Nonetheless, state governments have been forced—in response to state and federal laws and court rulings—to address discriminatory practices or effects in their personnel systems.

Frederickson makes a distinction between *block inequality* and *segmented inequality* (1990). The former refers to the overall proportion of jobs held by a particular group in a governmental jurisdiction or institution. *Segmented inequality* refers to disparities in the type and quality of jobs that are held by groups of employees in a given agency or jurisdiction. Block inequality is declining in most states with the proportion of female and, to a lesser extent, minority state employees closely approximating their presence in the total state labor force. From 1973 to 1989, African Americans as a proportion of all full-time state employees grew from 10 to 18 percent, the proportion of other ethnic minorities increased from 3 to 7 percent, and the proportion of female employees went from 43 to 49 percent (Hebert, Wright, and Brudney 1992).

The major problem today is segmented inequality. Male and white employees have a larger share of higher-level jobs that pay better and have more responsibility. To be sure, women and minorities hold a growing share of such jobs. Between 1964 and 1990 the proportion of female state agency heads grew from 2 percent to 19 percent. During the same period the proportion of African-American agency heads grew from 1 percent to 5 percent. The proportion of all minorities combined grew from 8 percent in 1978 to 11 percent in 1988 (Bullard and Wright 1993; Hale and Kelly 1989; Wright, Yoo, and Cohen 1991). Still, given current rates of changes, it will be fifty to a hundred years before the proportion of female or minority agency heads will match their present share of the total state government workforce.

Moreover, women and members of minorities who attain the upper reaches of state bureaucracies remain concentrated in agencies with certain functions. Bullard and Wright (1993) classified fifty-two types of state agencies in terms of the presence of female agency heads. In 1988 there was a "significant female presence" in just four: aging, library, public assistance, and treasury. Minorities remain concentrated in agencies with health, social services, employment security, personnel, and correctional responsibilities (Bayes 1989).

The employment circumstances of women and minorities are by no means entirely due to discrimination. But racism and sexism continue—especially in the promoting of employees to higher-level positions (Hopkins 1980). Stereotypes about the abilities of women and minorities are a key part of the "glass ceiling" that limits advancement. Among a sample of high-level state administrators in Texas, women were about twice as likely as men to report having experienced discriminatory actions based on gender (Stanley 1989).

One form of discrimination against women is sexual harassment. A five-state study found that the percentage of female employees who had experienced "requests for sexual favors" ranged from 11 to 24 percent; those reporting "offensive physical contact" ranged from 14 to 36 percent; and those encountering "offensive verbal behavior" ranged from a "low" of 33 percent, among female employees in Texas, to 60 percent in Wisconsin (Kelly and Stambaugh 1992). Sexual harassment discourages women from pursuing opportunities in male-dominated occupations or may cause them to leave jobs to escape it. Fortunately, by the late 1980s, nearly three-fourths of the states had sexual harassment policies applying to state employees (Ross and England 1987).

Efforts to improve the employment circumstances of women and minorities have been controversial, especially when they have taken the form of affirmative action. Critics allege that affirmative action discriminates against better-qualified white males. While this may sometimes be so, several studies find no evidence that female or minority candidates for promotion are being leapfrogged over better educated or more experienced white or male state employees (Bullard and Wright 1993; Dometrius 1984; Duke 1992). The slow increase in the proportion of minorities or women in higher-level public jobs suggests that affirmative action constitutes, at most, a gradual revolution. Moreover, affirmative action gains can be quickly wiped out by seniority-based layoffs caused by fiscal stringency. The courts have upheld such layoffs even when they disproportionately affect female or minority workers (*Firefighters Local 1784 v. Stotts* 467 U.S. 561 [1984]; *Wygant v. The Jackson (MI) Board of Education* 476 U.S. 267 [1986]).

As occupational segregation by gender or race has declined, so has the gap in pay between male and female and between white and minority employees. Still, these gaps remain substantial (Dometrius and Sigelman 1984; Guy 1992; Kelly 1993). Advocates of equity in pay argue that holding different jobs, being less well trained, or having less experience does not adequately explain the disparities in monetary compensation between male and female or majority and minority employees. In addition, jobs that disproportionately employ women (and to a lesser extent, minorities) have lower pay scales because employers undervalue "women's work" or rely on "market factors" that are themselves biased. Hence, advocates insist, pay scales for such jobs must be revised to equal those for jobs of "comparable worth" that disproportionately employ men.

Opponents of comparable worth argue that pay disparities are not primarily due to gender or racial discrimination (Rhoads 1993). Among other arguments, they contend that it is the surplus of women seeking certain jobs (teaching, nursing, social work, librarianship) that depresses pay. Others, while agreeing that gender bias exists, argue that the solution to the problem lies in vigorous enforcement of existing employment discrimination laws along with more aggressive affirmative action (Aaron and Lougy 1986). Since the courts have refused to accept statistics on pay disparities for job classes disproportionately employing men as opposed to women as sufficient evidence of intentional employment discrimination (*California State Employees Association v. State of California*, 682 F.Supp. 1044 [1987]), pay equity battles are primarily fought out in state legislatures or at the bargaining table. By 1990, twenty states had adjusted pay scales to eliminate sex or race biases (Kelly 1991). Not coincidentally, most are states in which collective bargaining by public employees is well developed. Those employed in affected job classes have sometimes received wage increases of 10 percent or more. Pay equity efforts can be expensive. Funding Minnesota's pay equity program required an amount equal to 4 percent of total state payroll costs, and Washington's program cost nearly $500 million (Chi 1986; Mangum and Mangum 1986).

The Challenge of Collective Bargaining

The employees of thirty-two states engage in some form of structured negotiations with their employer (Ban and Riccucci 1993). Forty percent of full-time state employees belong to an employee organization or a union. In twenty states, 70 percent or more of state classified employees are covered by union contracts (*classified employee* generally means one covered by a state's civil service provisions).[3] Most of these states have a history of strong private sector unionization. With a few exceptions, such as Florida, state employee unions are weak or nonexistent in southern and southwestern states as well as most of those of the Moun-

3. These states are Alaska, California, Connecticut, Florida, Hawaii, Illinois, Iowa, Maryland, Massachusetts, Michigan, Minnesota, Nebraska, New Hampshire, New Jersey, New York, Ohio, Oregon, Pennsylvania, Rhode Island, and Vermont.

tain West, such as Idaho, Nevada, Utah, and Wyoming. Following rapid growth in the 1960s and 1970s, state employee unions now confront a less hospitable environment. Fiscal stringency has changed the contours of bargaining. The threat to contract out the provision of services has sometimes been used to wrest concessions from unions.

The consequences of collective bargaining for state administration are far from clear. The diversity of state laws on the matters subject to negotiation, and the differing political and economic environments in which collective bargaining occurs, suggest highly variable effects (Loney 1989). Still, collective bargaining has affected the operation of civil service systems, the costs of state government, and bureaucratic performance.

Collective bargaining and civil service practices often coexist (Ban and Riccucci 1993; Lewin and Horton 1975). Unions join civil service advocates in opposition to patronage practices and support protections against dismissal for non-work-related reasons. Merit principles are most threatened by the preference of unions for seniority as the primary criterion for promotion, salary increases, or layoffs. This preference also hampers efforts to increase the diversity of the state workforce.

Some critics allege that wage and fringe-benefit settlements resulting from collective bargaining inflate budgets and may lead to tax hikes. What limited research exists on this issue suggests a modest impact, however. Kearney and Morgan (1980) found that unionized state employees across the country were compensated approximately 4 percent better than their nonunionized counterparts. Public sector unions representing women in health care and clerical jobs are in the vanguard of the pay equity movement. Adjustments for particular classes of employees may significantly increase the pay of these employees while having substantial budgetary implications. Tight state budgets have prompted union flexibility on compensation, often in return for guarantees that there would be no layoffs (Lewin 1983; Mitchell 1986). In 1991, for example, twenty-six of twenty-seven state bargaining units in Connecticut gave up pay increases in order to save jobs (Kearney 1992).

Other critics believe that collective bargaining negatively affects bureaucratic performance as employees gain a greater say in decisions traditionally reserved for managers. This may sometimes be so, but the findings of the ten-state study suggest otherwise. Even in highly unionized states such as California, Michigan, and New York few managers considered "bargaining on inappropriate matters such as program planning" or "limits on managerial authority due to collective bargaining" to be serious impediments to effective management. In these same states, unions were seen, on average, to have only "some impact" on the conduct of daily operations. Moreover, collective bargaining can be viewed as a vehicle for achieving the sort of participative management much touted by management scholars and practitioners alike (Kearney and Hays 1994).

Public unions sometimes defend inefficient work practices. But there is little systematic evidence that collective bargaining hampers productivity or reduces the quality of government services (Crane, Lentz, and Shafritz 1976; Loney 1989; Perry, Angle, and Pittel 1979). A major effort to improve state government productivity in New York was initiated as part of a union contract (Jarrett 1985). In Minnesota, members of the American Federation of State, County, and Municipal Employees were key actors in efforts to restructure the state's services for persons with developmental disabilities (National Commission on the State and Local Public Service 1993).

The emergence of collective bargaining, like efforts to increase the diversity of the state government workforce, has changed how state bureaucracies perform. Sometimes this has been a change for the worse. At least as often, in my view, it represents a change for the better.

ADMINISTRATORS AND OTHERS: STATE BUREAUCRATIC PERFORMANCE IN A POLITICAL CONTEXT

The dichotomy between politics and administration posited by Woodrow Wilson in the 1880s held that efficient and effective administration would result if trained professionals with considerable job security handled administrative tasks. For their part, elected officials were to establish agencies, authorize their programs, and specify the amounts of dollars and personnel to be made available to them. As a description of contemporary reality, such a dichotomy is seriously flawed. The difficulty of crafting complex policy in the modern era, combined with the fact that nonadministrators control resources crucial to administrative success, cause many administrators to believe that policy making cannot remain the sole preserve of elected officials. Hence, it is not surprising that state administrators devote as much as one-fourth of their time to policy development activities (Elling 1992; Wright, Yoo, and Cohen 1991). At the same time, elected officials seek to influence agencies to ensure that policies are implemented appropriately. These agencies make too much difference in the lives of constituents for elected officials to allow them to function in splendid isolation.

State Bureaucrats as Policy Shapers

Bureaucratic influence in policy making stems from several sources. First, career bureaucrats often know best, in a technical sense, how to deal with problems. Public health officials, for example, know more than anyone else in state government about a state's health problems and its public health programs.

Second, bureaucrats have a certain amount of discretionary authority. No law can be so precisely drafted as to eliminate completely the need for choice in applying it. Moreover, it is unwise for elected officials to limit administrative discretion unduly, since policy implementation is often improved if administrators can respond to feedback and make adjustments according to the circumstances in individual cases. In deference to bureaucratic expertise, elected officials often grant

Table 8-4   The Impact of Selected Actors on Decisions Affecting, or Actions of, State Bureaucracies in Ten States

Influence actor	Determination of overall agency budget level	Budget levels for specific programs	Major policy or program changes	Content of rules and regulations	Establishing administrative procedures	Daily operations
The Agency Itself	2.8	2.9	3.1	3.3	3.5	3.7
Governor and Staff	2.7*	2.6*	2.5*	1.7*	1.5*	1.1*
State Legislature	3.2*	3.1	2.8*	2.2	1.7*	1.2
State Courts	1.0	0.7	1.2	1.4	0.9	0.7
Federal Agencies/Congress	1.6	1.5	1.6	1.4	1.1	1.1
Federal Courts	0.8	0.7	1.0	1.1	0.7	0.6
State Budget Office	2.9*	2.8*	2.0*	1.0*	1.4*	1.4*
State Personnel Office	1.3*	1.0*	1.0*	0.8*	1.4*	1.3*
Other State Agencies	1.0	0.9	0.9	1.1*	1.1*	1.0
Local Governments	0.8*	0.7*	0.8	0.8*	0.6	0.8
Professional Associations	0.7	0.7	0.8	0.9*	0.6	0.6
Agency Clientele	1.2	1.2	1.4	1.4	1.1	1.6
State Employee Unions	0.8*	0.7*	0.6*	0.6*	0.7*	0.7*
Political Parties	0.7*	0.6	0.6	0.4	0.3	0.3
Communications Media	0.9	0.8	0.9	0.7	0.5	0.8
Interest Groups	1.3	1.3	1.4	1.4*	1.0	1.1*

SOURCE: Elling 1992.
NOTE: Each column shows the mean attributed impact for an actor on a given decision or activity based on responses in all ten states. Response options were (0) no impact, (1) some impact, (2) moderate impact, (3) great impact, (4) very great impact. Depending on an actor or the area of decision or activity, the number of respondents ranged between 780 and 821.
*Statistically significant difference in the mean impact of influence actor across the ten states (F-test, .01 level).

agencies broad authority to develop the procedures and regulations necessary to implement programs.

Finally, administrative influence in policy making increases to the extent that the beneficiaries of the programs an agency administers become supporters of those programs and the agency itself. Agencies sometimes develop constituencies, which contribute to administrative influence in policy making. The alliance between an administrative unit, its clients, and supportive legislators may constitute a subgovernment, dominating policy making in an area.

The first row of Table 8-4 illustrates the "policy-shaping" role of state bureaucracies. Administrators not only see their agencies as dominant actors in administrative realms, but many say that their agencies also influence in an important way the content of major decisions that are formally made by political institutions (also see Miller 1987). Indeed, 40 percent of the managers reported that they originated half or more of the legislation affecting their units. Although these managers may be exaggerating their importance, it is striking that they see their agency as the dominant player in making major policy decisions affecting their units.

State Bureaucratic Influence in Context

If the politics-administration dichotomy has been breached from the administrative side, does this mean that we are confronted with runaway bureaucracies? Such a conclusion is as wrong as believing that state bureaucracies and bureaucrats leave policy making entirely in the hands of elected officials while passively awaiting their marching orders. It is easy to overgeneralize. Every agency's situation is different. Administrative influence is also relational. As more nonadministrative players get into the act, the relative power of an agency itself declines. Although agencies are reservoirs of power, rarely is such power completely mobilized in support of particular goals. Moreover, bureaucrats are appointed officials in a political system in which popular election is a powerful source of legitimacy. Administrators taking unilateral action are likely to be harshly admonished for exceeding their authority. Most administrative power is "derivative power," exercised at the sufferance of others. The abolition of an agency or the transferring of some of its programs is rare. But both occur. More common is the narrowing of administrative discretion in response to elected officials' displeasure with how that discretion has been used.

The data in Table 8-4 suggest the complexity of state administrative influence relationships. State legislatures and governors have a significant effect on agency budgets. Although the governor is seen as slightly less influential than the legislature, the governor's role becomes substantial when the influence of the budget office—which is highly attuned to gubernatorial interests—is factored in. The governor and legislature also have a significant voice in basic policy decisions affecting state bureaucracies. In addition, the federal government, agency clientele, and interest groups have moderate influence in these three arenas.

Most nonadministrative actors have less say in the promulgating of rules and regulations, the determination of administrative procedures, or daily operations, although a few actors have moderate impact. The governor, legislature, federal agencies, state budget and personnel offices, other state agencies, agency clientele, and interest groups even have some impact on daily operations.

The statistics reported in Table 8-4 also indicate that the impact of certain actors varies from state to state. This is particularly so for governors, legislatures, budget and personnel offices, and state employee unions. Within a given state the influence of nonadministrative actors may vary as a function of agency responsibilities or other factors. In the ten-state study, agencies that depended on the federal government for a large proportion of their funding reported much greater federal agency or congressional influence. Federal and state courts importantly influence agencies with certain responsibilities. Those with criminal justice, environmental, transportation, and regulatory responsibilities report that state courts have greater impact on broad policies affecting them. The federal courts have forced states to increase funding for, and modify the operations of, correctional institutions and facilities for the mentally ill, developmentally disabled, and children (O'Leary and Strassman 1993).

Contending for Custody of State Bureaucracies

The years since the mid-1970s have witnessed increased efforts by nonadministrative actors to influence state administration, with competing political sovereigns sometimes waging bitter battles for "custody" of particular state bureaucracies (Gormley 1989, 1993). As states took on new or expanded responsibilities, as the federal government's role in certain policy areas diminished, and as state budgets became tighter, concern for the performance of state bureaucracies grew and caused various actors to increase their ability to influence them. New types of interest groups, often less tied to administrative agencies and their programs, emerged. The knowledge possessed by administrative agencies was less persuasive in an era of "policy volatility" in which modest alterations in existing programs seemed insufficient (Rourke 1991, 122–126). Here I will explore the changing dynamics of influence that surround state bureaucratic relations with the governor, the state legislature, and the public in various guises—organized interest groups, clients of agencies, and ordinary citizens.

The Governor as Chief Bureaucrat

To be successful, governors often need their state's bureaucracy. Although gubernatorial relations with state bureaucracies are sometimes conflictual, more often they are not (Elling 1992, chap. 7). The Republican governor of Michigan, John Engler, is no fan of big government. Yet one of his aides had this to say about Michigan's bureaucracy: "The biggest surprise we faced when moving to the governor's office . . . was in working with the bureaucracy. We now had to recommend programs that could be effectively implemented and we needed state agency assistance on that. We were surprised at how many really good people were over there" (Elling and Kobrak 1995).

Until quite recently governors were often chief executives in name only. This is true for relatively few states today, however. Administrative reorganization is one reason. Governors in more than half of the states can initiate and make organizational changes that take effect unless the legislature objects within a specified time period (Rosenthal 1990). Personnel system reform has also increased gubernatorial power over the bureaucracy. Many governors now have greater authority to appoint and remove key administrators (Beyle 1988; Roberts, 1991; see Chapter 6 in this book for other ways in which gubernatorial authority has been strengthened).

While governors are more powerful than ever in formal terms, vigorous gubernatorial direction of a state's bureaucracy is still more the exception than the rule. Governors sometimes fail to exploit formal resources, such as their appointment power (Haas 1989). Governors also have other tasks than functioning as chief bureaucrat. These other obligations, such as providing policy leadership for the legislature, may be both more pressing and more interesting. Bureaucratic complexity also discourages involvement. Given these realities, involvement with state bureaucracies is very much a matter of governors picking their spots.

What prompts gubernatorial interaction with one or another state agency? Sometimes governors concentrate on agencies with the biggest budgets or those administering programs central to the goals of their administrations (Hebert, Brudney, and Wright 1983; Weinberg 1977). Often, governors intervene only if a "crisis" arises in the administration of a particular program and if it has the potential for serious political fallout (Weinberg 1977). Nearly two-thirds of the managers in the ten-state study felt this was true of gubernatorial involvement in their state.

Crises can provide opportunities for expanding gubernatorial influence. One example arose in Michigan as the state's Department of Agriculture (MDA) dealt with a 1973 incident in which the highly toxic fire retardant PBB was erroneously mixed into cattle feed sold to farmers across the state. This had dire consequences not only for cattle but also for Michiganians as PBB entered the food chain. Some of the anger of farmers about this disaster was directed at Gov. William G. Milliken (R), even though the director of the MDA was appointed by a commission (Coyer and Schwerin 1981). In response to the department's perceived failure, the governor sought to bring it under closer control. Milliken made it known after the 1978 election that he would use his two 1979 appointments to the Agriculture Commission to change MDA policy, starting with the replacement of B. Dale Ball as director. Ball resigned before he could be fired (Coyer and Schwerin 1981, 719).

Waiting for crises to occur is a risky management strategy. But even a governor with strong formal powers often must embrace it to function effectively as chief bureaucrat.

The Legislature as Bureaucratic Overseer

Although the say of most governors in the conduct of state administration has grown, state legislative influence often rivals that of the governor, as suggested in Table 8-4. This is consistent with the findings of other studies (Abney and Lauth, 1986; Brudney and Hebert 1987; Miller 1987). Legislatures can tap an impressive array of resources in seeking to influence bureaucracies. These include approving agency budget requests, modifying agency programs or organization, investigating agency practices, and confirming at least some of the governor's appointments to top administrative posts. Legislatures have also adopted some newer tools for impressing their will on state agencies. These include requiring legislative review or approval of proposed agency rules and regulations, and the creation of legislative audit offices.

Although legislatures delegate significant authority to administrative agencies to promulgate the technically complex, specific rules or regulations giving operational effect to general statutes, they also fear that agencies will distort legislative intent. Hence, forty states mandate legislative review of proposed regulations or regulations before they take effect (Rosenthal 1990). Much more controversial are provisions in about one-third of the states that permit the legislature as a whole, a single house, or, in a few states, a legislative committee to invalidate an administrative rule or regulation (Gormley 1993).

Administrative agencies dislike such arrangements. Only 34 percent of the managers in the ten-state study saw the legislative veto of agency rules as having positive effects for agency performance (Elling 1992, 90). Nor are governors fond of the process. Fortunately for governors, state courts have invalidated legislative vetoes in eight states on the grounds that they violate the separation of powers enshrined in state constitutions (Levinson 1987). Hence, the legislative veto may be in decline as a vehicle of influence (Rosenthal 1990).

Legislative auditors represent a more systematic form of legislative oversight of state bureaucracies. Legislative audit offices are found in nearly every state (Rosenthal 1990). What has made these offices increasingly influential is a shift from narrowly oriented financial auditing to "performance auditing" (Wheat 1991). Performance auditing extends beyond concerns for financial rectitude to questions of how well agencies are implementing programs for which they are responsible and how successful those programs are in solving problems. An audit shines the harsh light of legislative and public attention on particular agencies and programs. Although not seen as being as effective as other strategies, such audits had positive effects for the performance of their units, according to 62 percent of the managers in the ten-state study (Elling 1992).

In assessing the influence of the legislature on state administration it is important to understand that legislators are especially interested in the specific actions of specific agencies as they affect specific individuals, groups, or interests. This is why the exercise of oversight by handling the complaints and questions of constituents—known as casework—is so attractive to them. Among a sample of Minnesota and Kentucky legislators, at least half claimed that addressing the specific problems of constituents alerted them to more general administrative problems (Elling 1979). Administrators surveyed by Abney and Lauth (1986) said constituent complaints relayed by legislators often improved service delivery. Unfortunately, casework can undermine administrative impartiality. One-quarter of the Minnesota administrators and almost half of the Kentucky administrators I interviewed felt that "most of the time legislative requests on behalf of constituents amount to asking for special favors or exceptions" (Elling 1980, 336).

State Bureaucracies and Organized Interests

Since state agencies do things that make a difference in citizens' lives, these citizens, whether organized or unorganized, have a stake in how those agencies operate. Interest groups—well-organized but not broadly representative—may exert undue influence on state administration. Especially in the case of agencies created to regulate segments of the economy, the result has sometimes been a "captured" agency—one that is highly solicitous of the interests of the targets of regulation but forgetful of the interests of the broader public that is supposed to benefit from regulation.

Excessive interest group influence on state administration may be less common today than in the past, however. Table 8-4 indicates that state managers do not consider organized groups to be extremely influential. Other research paints a similar picture (Abney and Lauth 1986; Brudney and Hebert 1987; Miller 1987).

High levels of both group and agency-initiated interaction were certainly evident in the ten-state study as well as in Abney and Lauth's fifty-state study (1986). But interaction does not automatically translate into influence. Several studies find very low correlations between intensity of agency interaction with groups and perceptions of group influence (Abney and Lauth 1986; Elling 1992). One reason for this is that most administrators are appointed rather than elected officials, and those below the top levels of an agency are often protected from dismissal by civil service rules. They are thus less vulnerable to some forms of interest group pressure.

Agencies and interest groups interact because each has resources useful to the other. In the ten-state study, I found that agencies often contacted interest groups to acquire information on the effects of their programs, to get advice on proposed regulations, and to gain technical information needed for agency operations. Groups contacting agencies often sought information about agency programs or tried to influence the content of rules and regulations.

Interest groups may also hamper administrative performance, or, more precisely, may want agencies to do things that are not good for the rest of us. They may encourage partiality in rule application or distort agency priorities (Abney and Lauth 1986). Such problems are more likely if fewer groups contend for influence. Bureaucracies that interact with a larger number of groups are less likely to be beholden to any single one and can play them off against one another. This is more likely today because, as discussed in Chapter 4, the state interest group universe has grown more diverse. The ten-state study revealed that half of the agencies interacted with six or more groups, and these groups varied widely in their degree of support for agency actions.

Gormley (1986b, 1989) speaks of the "representation revolution" in the states that aims to make agencies—especially those with regulatory responsibilities—more accountable to "broad, diffuse, interests" by facilitating public representation in administrative decision-making processes (1986b, 180). Representation has been increased by requiring public hearings on environmental issues and mandating the appointment of public members to state occupational licensing boards. More than half of the states have established "proxy advocacy" offices to represent consumers in public utility regulatory proceedings.

As a consequence of changes such as these, the capture of state administrative agencies by organized interests is increasingly rare. But these state agencies still find life difficult. As Wilson (1989, 81) remarks:

> For one thing, anything they do will be criticized by somebody. . . . For another, their political superiors in the executive branch and the [legislature] will tilt, depending on the political winds, first toward one interest group and then toward another. Under these circumstances it will be hard to know what one is supposed to do; things that were once rewarded are now penalized, and vice versa.

These are, however, different problems from those raised when groups and agencies are locked in loving embrace. A state government filled with agencies like those described by Wilson would seem preferable, from the point of view of the average citizen, to one filled with captured agencies.

State Bureaucracies and the Public Encounter

The success of a public bureaucracy is often judged by how well it meets the needs of its clients—those individuals or groups that often are why the organization exists. The data in Table 8-4 indicate that clients matter. State managers see their agency's clientele as having more impact than any other nonagency actor on the daily operations of their agency.

One of the supposed virtues of the bureaucratic model is that similar cases are treated similarly. Once a client has satisfied the criteria for receiving services, the ideal bureaucrat draws on his or her professional skills to provide services irrespective of the client's race, age, gender, social status, or political connections. This optimistic view is challenged by those who argue that a bureaucracy's emphasis on reliability and consistency causes bureaucrats to overemphasize the importance of formal rules. "Going by the book" becomes an end in itself so that the bureaucrat "never forgets a single rule binding his action and hence is unable to assist many of his clients" (Robert Merton, quoted in Goodsell 1985, 89). Even worse, the ideal of equal treatment may get perverted so that bureaucrats treat all clients in an equally nasty manner. This theme runs through some of the arguments of those urging the reinvention of government. Osborne and Gaebler (1993) see a need to move from "agency-driven" to "customer-driven" government. As they remark, "The greatest irritant most people experience in their dealings with government is the arrogance of the bureaucracy. People today expect to be valued as customers—even by government" (167).

Denunciations of client-hostile bureaucracies must be taken with a grain of salt, however. The various studies of citizens' contacts with state agencies summarized earlier in this chapter suggest that most citizens are well-treated and that the bureaucrats that they deal with are helpful. Citizens who have been unfairly treated by a state agency can pursue several avenues of redress. The roles played by legislative casework and interest group intervention have been discussed earlier. State agency actions are also regularly challenged in the courts, although the costs of and possibilities for delay inherent in the judicial process limit its value as an avenue of appeal for the average citizen. All states have open records or freedom-of-information laws designed to facilitate citizen access to materials upon which state agencies base their actions. A few states have adopted variants of the Scandinavian institution of the ombudsman—an official who investigates citizens' complaints about problems with government agencies.

Moreover, bureaucracies do not necessarily resent citizen or clientele input (Miller 1987). Many agencies have pursued changes designed to make them more user-friendly. Surveys of those who use their services are increasingly common. The ten-state study indicates that, even ten years ago, 38 percent of the units had surveyed those whom they served. As part of Minnesota's STEP program to improve agency performance, managers sit in the service areas of their offices to talk with "customers" and ask employees who regularly deal with them what they are hearing and how service delivery can be improved. Arkansas, Minnesota, and Wisconsin provide their employees with customer service training (Osborne and Gaebler 1993).

The "customer" analogy must be applied carefully to the work of public agencies. State governments often regulate the behavior of economic interests or individuals. Citizens can be forced to become customers of some government bureaucracies. Most prisoners would just as soon not be "valued customers" of a state's correctional system. This is not to say that the rights and the welfare of prisoners should be ignored. But it does suggest a rather different link between producer and customer. Unlike the situation in the private sector, even when an agency has willing consumers, those who consume services do not necessarily pay for them, or pay only some of the costs of the service being provided—as in the case of students at state universities. Battle and Nayak (1994, 12) assert that "customer satisfaction for public-sector agencies needs to be replaced by a broader stakeholder analysis." Stakeholders include elected officials, professional associations, and taxpayers, among others. Such an analysis reveals how difficult it is for an agency just to focus on its customers. Agencies may be less user-friendly than they should be because other stakeholders are sending different messages. For example, via budget cuts, the state legislature is in effect asking agencies to try to provide good service but to do it with fewer personnel. Sometimes this is possible, often it is not.

State bureaucracies must always be mindful of who their customers are. It may well be possible to make a few easy and inexpensive changes that will improve the quality of service that they provide. But we must realize that true improvements in the quality of service may require something as old-fashioned as hiring more staff.

STATE BUREAUCRACIES IN A CHALLENGING WORLD: SOME CONCLUSIONS

Concerns about government performance quickly become concerns about bureaucratic performance, since bureaucracies do much of the work of government. I have focused on organizational structure and personnel processes as important determinants of administrative performance. But many other factors, including the quality of organizational leadership and the nature of an agency's clientele, also affect bureaucratic performance. The increasing complexity of state bureaucratic environments in the 1980s and 1990s raised additional obstacles to effective performance. Budget reductions occasioned by fiscal stress forced many managers to become experts at "cutback management." According to the ten-state survey, managers considered insufficient appropriations and the legislature's penchant for expanding programs without additional funding to be the second and third most serious impediments to their agency's ability to discharge its responsibilities effectively (Table 8-2).

The ideas of those who would "reinvent" government seem worth trying in an effort to improve bureaucratic performance. But this should be done tentatively. One reason is that "reinventors" are often insufficiently sensitive to the appropriateness of their prescriptions in a public setting. Another reason is that evidence of the benefits of various reinvention prescriptions is not as compelling as one might like. Although a state such as Minnesota has experienced some success in applying such strategies as part of its STEP effort (Barzelay and Armajani 1992), other observers reach less positive conclusions about the utility of these strategies (Gurwitt 1994; Weimer 1994).

State administrators are important policy shapers who have breached any wall that may once have limited their involvement in the broader policy-making process. Yet, the increasing complexity of the administrative influence matrix, combined with the efforts of governors, legislatures, the courts, and the public to exert greater influence over the affairs of state bureaucracies, suggest that runaway agencies are rare.

Policy making is clearly improved by the involvement of bureaucrats and bureaucracies in it. While we rightfully prefer that the governor and the legislature make major policy decisions, elected officials are fallible. Often they find it hard to look beyond the next election. With greater security of tenure, and the benefit of professional expertise, administrators can broaden the horizons of elected officials and point out deficiencies in proposed policies that those officials may wish to ignore.

That most state agencies operate on a short leash may be taken as good news. But the intervention of various nonadministrative actors in administrative affairs raises the question of how much efficiency and effectiveness to sacrifice in return for increased accountability or responsiveness. As Gormley (1986a, 6) points out: "Without some external pressure, bureaucrats will be less responsive, less efficient, and less innovative than they might otherwise be. However, if external pressure becomes excessive, bureaucrats will also be less innovative, responsive and efficient than they could be."

State bureaucracies carry out their responsibilities reasonably well. Unfortunately, the greater scope of state administrative responsibilities means that even if bureaucracies perform better than in the past, the aggregate costs of inefficiency or ineffectiveness remain great. The incompatibility of the standards to which we hold state bureaucracies means their performance can never be good enough. Instead, changes will occur in the trade-offs that elected officials and citizens will accept. Sometimes improving efficiency and effectiveness will be emphasized. But often we will value accountability or responsiveness more highly.

REFERENCES

Aaron, Henry, and Cameron Lougy. 1986. *The Comparable Worth Controversy.* Washington, D.C.: Brookings Institution.

Abney, Glenn, and Thomas Lauth. 1986. *The Politics of State and City Administration.* Albany: State University of New York Press.

Allen, Joan, Keon Chi, Kevin Devlin, Mark Fall, Harry Hatry, and Wayne Masterman, eds. 1989. *The Private Sector in State Service Delivery: Examples of Innovative Practice.* Washington, D.C.: Urban Institute Press.

Ban, Carolyn, and Norma Riccucci. 1993. "Personnel Systems and Labor Relations: Steps toward a Quiet Revitalization." In *Revitalizing State and Local Public Service,* edited by Frank Thompson. San Francisco: Jossey-Bass.

Barzelay, Michael, and Babak Armajani. 1992. *Breaking through Bureaucracy: A Vision for Managing Government.* Berkeley: University of California Press.

Battle, Byron, and P. Ranganath Nayak. 1994. "Going Public." *Spectrum: The Journal of State Government* 67, no. 2:16–22.

Bayes, Jane. 1989. "Women in the California Executive Branch of State Government." In *Gender, Bureaucracy, and Democracy,* edited by Mary Hale and Rita Kelly. New York: Greenwood Press.

Becker, Fred, and A. J. Mackelprang. 1990. "Attitudes of State Legislators toward Contracting for Public Services." *American Review of Public Administration* 20:175–189.

Bendick, Marc. 1984. "Privatization of Public Services: Recent Experience." In *Public Management,* edited by J. Steven Ott, Albert Hyde, and Jay Shafritz. Chicago: Nelson-Hall.

Beyle, Thad L. 1988. "The Institutionalized Powers of the Governorship: 1965–1985." *Comparative State Politics Newsletter* 9, no. 1:23–29.

Brudney, Jeffrey, and F. Ted Hebert. 1987. "State Agencies and Their Environments: Examining the Influence of Important External Actors." *Journal of Politics* 49:186–206.

Bullard, Angela, and Deil Wright. 1993. "Circumventing the Glass Ceiling: Women Executives in American State Governments." *Public Administration Review* 53:189–202.

Campbell, Roby, and Marc Bendick, Jr. 1977. *A Public Assistance Data Book.* Washington, D.C.: Urban Institute.

Chi, Keon. 1986. "Comparable Worth in State Government, 1984–85." In *The Book of the States, 1986–87.* Lexington, Ky.: Council of State Governments.

Cohen, Steven, and Thomas Ingersoll. 1985. "The Effects of Personnel Rules on Line Managers: The Case of State Hazardous Waste Clean-Up Organizations." *Public Personnel Management* 14:33–39.

Conant, James. 1992a. "Executive Branch Reorganization: Can It Be an Antidote for Fiscal Stress in the States?" *State and Local Government Review* 24:3–11.

———. 1992b. "Executive Branch Reorganization in the States, 1965–1991." In *The Book of the States, 1992–93.* Lexington, Ky.: Council of State Governments.

Council of State Governments. 1980. *The Book of the States, 1980–81.* Lexington, Ky.: Council of State Governments.

———. 1990. *The Book of the States, 1990–91.* Lexington, Ky.: Council of State Governments.

———. 1994. *The Book of the States, 1994–95.* Lexington, Ky.: Council of State Governments.

Council of State Governments and the National Association of State Personnel Executives. 1990. *1989 United States Governmental Wage and Salary Survey.* Sacramento, Calif.: California Department of Personnel Administration.

Coyer, Brian, and Donald Schwerin. 1981. "Bureaucratic Regulation and Farmer Protest in the Michigan PBB Contamination Case." *Rural Sociology* 46:703–723.

Cox, W., and S. A. Brunelli. 1992. *America's Protected Class: Why Excess Public Employee Compensation Is Bankrupting the States.* Washington, D.C.: American Legislative Exchange Council.

Crane, Edgar, Bernard Lentz, and Jay Shafritz. 1976. *State Government Productivity: The Environment for Improvement.* New York: Praeger.

De Hoog, Ruth. 1984. *Contracting Out for Human Services: Economic, Political, and Organizational Perspectives.* Albany: State University of New York Press.

Dometrius, Nelson. 1984. "Minorities and Women among State Agency Leaders." *Social Science Quarterly* 65:127–137.

Dometrius, Nelson, and Lee Sigelman. 1984. "Assessing Progress toward Affirmative Action Goals in State and Local Government: A New Benchmark." *Public Administration Review* 44:241–246.

Duke, Lois. 1992. "Career Development and Affirmative Action." In *Women and Men of the States: Public Administrators at the State Level,* edited by Mary Guy. Armonk, N.Y.: M. E. Sharpe.

Elling, Richard. 1979. "The Utility of Legislative Casework as Means of Oversight." *Legislative Studies Quarterly* 4:353–379.

———. 1980. "State Legislative Casework and State Administrative Performance." *Administration and Society* 12:327–356.

———. 1992. *Public Management in the States: A Comparative Study of Administrative Performance and Politics.* Westport, Conn.: Praeger.

Elling, Richard, and Peter Kobrak. 1995. "The Bureaucracy: An Ambiguous Political Legacy." In *Michigan Politics and Government: Facing Change in a Complex State,* edited by William Browne and Kenneth Verburg. Lincoln: University of Nebraska Press.

Frederickson, H. George. 1990. "Public Administration and Social Equity." *Public Administration Review* 50:237–238.

Gold, Steven, and Sarah Ritchie. 1993. "Compensation of State and Local Employees: Sorting Out the Issues." In *Revitalizing State and Local Public Service,* edited by Frank Thompson. San Francisco: Jossey-Bass.

Goodsell, Charles. 1985. *The Case for Bureaucracy: A Public Administration Polemic.* 2d ed. Chatham, N.J.: Chatham House.

———. 1994. *The Case for Bureaucracy: A Public Administration Polemic.* 3d ed. Chatham, N.J.: Chatham House.

Gormley, William. 1986a. "Muscles and Prayers: Bureau-Busting in the 1970s." Paper presented at the annual meeting of the American Political Science Association, Washington, D.C., August 28–31.

———. 1986b. "The Representation Revolution: Reforming State Regulation through Public Representation." *Administration and Society* 18:179–196.

———. 1989. "Custody Battles in State Administration." In *The State of the States,* edited by Carl Van Horn. Washington, D.C.: CQ Press.

———. 1993. "Accountability Battles in State Administration." In *The State of the States,* 2d ed., edited by Carl Van Horn. Washington, D.C.: CQ Press.

Gurwitt, Rob. 1994. "Entrepreneurial Government: The Morning After." *Governing,* May, 34–40.

Guy, Mary. 1992. "The Context of Public Management in the States." In *Women and Men of the States: Public Administrators at the State Level,* edited by Mary Guy. Armonk, N.Y.: M. E. Sharpe.

———. 1993. "Three Steps Forward, Two Steps Backward: The Status of Women's Integration into Public Management." *Public Administration Review* 53:285–291.

Haas, Peter. 1989. "Public Policy and Administrative Turnover in State Government: The Role of the Governor." *Policy Studies Journal* 17:788–803.

Hale, Mary, and Rita Kelly, eds. 1989. *Gender, Bureaucracy, and Democracy: Careers and Equal Opportunity in the Public Sector.* New York: Greenwood Press.

Hall, Wayne. 1992. "State Management and Administration: Doing More with Less." In *The Book of the States, 1992–93.* Lexington, Ky.: Council of State Governments.

Hanson, Russell. 1990. "Intergovernmental Relations." In *Politics in the American States,* 5th ed., edited by Virginia Gray, Herbert Jacob, and Robert Albritton. Glenview, Ill.: Scott Foresman/Little, Brown.

Hatry, Harry. 1989. "Introduction." In *The Private Sector in State Service Delivery: Examples of Innovative Practice,* edited by Joan Allen, Keon Chi, Kevin Devlin, Mark Fall, Harry Hatry, and Wayne Masterman. Washington, D.C.: Urban Institute Press.

Hay/Huggins Company and Hay Management Consultants. 1984. *Study of Total Compensation in the Federal, State and Private Sectors.* Washington, D.C.: Hay Company.

Hays, Steven, and Richard Kearney. 1992. "State Personnel Directors and the Dilemmas of Workforce 2000: A Survey." *Public Administration Review* 52:30–38.

Hebert, F. Ted, Jeffrey Brudney, and Deil Wright. 1983. "Gubernatorial Influence and State Bureaucracy." *American Politics Quarterly* 11:243–264.

Hebert, F. Ted, Deil Wright, and Jeffrey Brudney. 1992. "Challenges to State Governments: Policy and Administrative Leadership in the 1990s." *Public Productivity and Management Review* 16:1–21.

Hopkins, Anne. 1980. "Perceptions of Employment Discrimination in the Public Sector." *Public Administration Review* 40: 131–137.

Hult, Karen. 1987. *Agency Merger and Bureaucratic Redesign*. Pittsburgh, Pa.: University of Pittsburgh Press.

Jarrett, James. 1985. "An Overview of Productivity Improvement Efforts in State Governments." *Public Personnel Management* 14:385–391.

Kearney, Richard. 1992. *Labor Relations in the Public Sector*. 2d ed. New York: Marcel Dekker.

Kearney, Richard, and Steven Hays. 1994. "Labor-Management Relations and Participative Decision Making: Toward a New Paradigm." *Public Administration Review* 54:44–51.

Kearney, Richard, and David Morgan. 1980. "Unions and State Employee Compensation." *State and Local Government Review* 12:115–119.

Kelly, Rita. 1991. *The Gendered Economy*. Newbury Park, Calif.: Sage Publications.

———. 1993. "Diversity in the Public Workforce: New Needs, New Approaches." In *Revitalizing State and Local Public Service*, edited by Frank Thompson. San Francisco: Jossey-Bass.

Kelly, Rita, and Phoebe Stambaugh. 1992. "Sexual Harassment in the States." In *Women and Men of the States: Public Administrators at the State Level*, edited by Mary Guy. Armonk, N.Y.: M. E. Sharpe.

Kettl, Donald. 1993. "The Myths, Realities, and Challenges of Privatization." In *Revitalizing State and Local Public Service*, edited by Frank Thompson. San Francisco: Jossey-Bass.

Lemov, Penelope. 1993. "Jailhouse Inc." *Governing*, May, 44–48.

Levinson, L. H. 1987. "The Decline of the Legislative Veto: Federal/State Comparisons and Interactions." *Publius* 17:115–132.

Lewin, David. 1983. "Implications of Concession Bargaining: Lessons from the Public Sector." *Monthly Labor Review* 106, no. 3:33–35.

Lewin, David, and Raymond Horton. 1975. "The Impact of Collective Bargaining on the Merit System in Government." *Arbitration Journal* 30:199–211.

Loney, Timothy. 1989. "Public Sector Labor Relations Research: The First Generation." *Public Personnel Management* 18:162–175.

Mangum, Garth, and Stephen Mangum. 1986. "Comparable Worth Confusion in the Ninth Circuit." *Labor Law Journal* 37:357–365.

Michigan Department of Civil Service. 1987. *Public Perceptions of State Employment in Michigan*. Lansing: Michigan Department of Civil Service.

Miller, Cheryl. 1987. "State Administrator Perceptions of the Policy Influence of Other Actors." *Public Administration Review* 47:239–245.

Mitchell, Daniel. 1986. "Concessional Bargaining in the Public Sector: A Lesser Force." *Public Personnel Management* 15:23–40.

National Association of State Personnel Executives and the Council of State Governments. 1992. *State Personnel Office: Roles and Functions*, 2d ed. Lexington, Ky.: Council of State Governments.

National Commission on the State and Local Public Service. 1993. *Hard Truths/Tough Choices: An Agenda for State and Local Reform*. Albany, N.Y.: Nelson A. Rockefeller Institute of Government.

Olberding, Julie. 1994. "Reforming State Management and Personnel Systems." In *The Book of the States, 1994–95*. Lexington, Ky.: Council of State Governments.

O'Leary, Rosemary, and Jeffrey Straussman. 1993. "The Impact of the Courts on Public Management." In *Public Management: The State of the Art*, edited by Barry Bozeman. San Francisco: Jossey-Bass.

Osborne, David, and Ted Gaebler. 1993. *Reinventing Government: How the Entrepreneurial Spirit Is Transforming the Public Sector*. New York: Penguin Books.

Perry, James, Harold Angle, and M. E. Pittel. 1979. *The Impact of Labor-Management Relations on Productivity and Efficiency in Urban Mass Transit*. Washington, D.C.: U.S. Department of Transportation.

Rehfuss, John. 1989. *Contracting Out in Government*. San Francisco: Jossey-Bass.

———. 1990. "Contracting Out and Accountability in State and Local Governments: The Importance of Contract Monitoring." *State and Local Government Review* 22:44–48.

Rhoads, Steven. 1993. *Incomparable Worth: Pay Equity Meets the Market*. Cambridge: Cambridge University Press.

Roberts, Deborah. 1991. "A Personnel Chameleon Blending the Political Appointee and Careerist

Traditions: Exempt Managers in State Government." In *Public Personnel Management: Current Concerns—Future Challenges,* edited by Carolyn Ban and Norma Riccucci. New York: Longman.

Rosenthal, Alan. 1990. *Governors and Legislatures: Contending Powers.* Washington, D.C.: CQ Press.

Ross, Cynthia, and Robert England. 1987. "State Governments' Sexual Harrassment Policy Initiatives." *Public Administration Review* 47:259–262.

Rourke, Francis. 1991. "American Bureaucracy in a Changing Political Setting." *Journal of Public Administration Research and Theory* 1:111–129.

Schmidt, Stuart. 1977. "Client-Oriented Evaluation of Public Agency Effectiveness." *Administration and Society* 8:403–422.

Smith, Steven, and Michael Lipsky. 1993. *Nonprofits for Hire: The Welfare State and the Age of Contracting.* Cambridge: Harvard University Press.

Stanley, Jeanie. 1989. "Women in the Texas Executive Branch of Government." In *Gender, Bureaucracy, and Democracy,* edited by Mary Hale and Rita Kelly. New York: Greenwood Press.

Stephens, G. Ross. 1985. "State Centralization Revisited." Paper presented at the annual meeting of the American Political Science Association, New Orleans, La., August 29–September 1.

Stevens, Alan. 1992. "State Government Employment in 1990." In *The Book of the States, 1992–93.* Lexington, Ky.: Council of State Governments.

U.S. Advisory Commission on Intergovernmental Relations. 1985. *The Question of State Government Capability.* Washington, D.C.: U.S. Government Printing Office.

U.S. Bureau of the Census. 1992. *Public Employment in 1991.* Washington, D.C.: U.S. Government Printing Office.

Van Horn, Carl. 1991. "The Myths and Realities of Privatization." In *Privatization and Its Alternatives,* edited by William Gormley. Madison: University of Wisconsin Press.

Walters, Jonathan. 1994. "The Fine Art of Firing the Incompetent." *Governing,* June, 35–39.

Weimer, David. 1994. Review of *Reinventing Government,* by David Osborne and Ted Gaebler. *Journal of Policy Analysis and Management* 13:187–192.

Weinberg, Martha. 1977. *Managing the State.* Cambridge: MIT Press.

Wheat, Edward. 1991. "The Activist Auditor: A New Player in State and Local Politics." *Public Administration Review* 51:385–392.

Wilson, James Q. 1989. *Bureaucracy: What Government Agencies Do and Why They Do It.* New York: Basic Books.

Wright, Deil, Jae-Won Yoo, and Jennifer Cohen. 1991. "The Evolving Profile of State Administrators." *Spectrum: The Journal of State Government* 64, no. 1:30–38.

SUGGESTED READINGS

Abney, Glenn, and Thomas Lauth. *The Politics of State and City Administration.* Albany: State University of New York Press, 1986. Especially Part 1. Based on a survey of agency heads in all fifty states, the book explores the interactions between state bureaucracies and governors, legislators and interest groups.

Elling, Richard. *Public Management in the States.* Westport, Conn.: Praeger, 1992. Drawing on a survey of administrators in ten states, this study examines the problems confronting state bureaucracies, how managers have sought to address those problems, and how a wide range of actors affect the administrative process.

Gormley, William. "Accountability Battles in State Administration." In *The State of the States,* 2d ed., edited by Carl Van Horn. Washington, D.C.: CQ Press, 1993. Assessment of recent efforts to limit the discretion of state bureaucracies and the battles among political sovereigns for influence over them.

Guy, Mary, ed. 1992. *Women and Men of the States: Public Administrators at the State Level.* Armonk, N.Y.: M. E. Sharpe. Examination of the status of female managers in six states and the challenges they confront.

Thompson, Frank, ed. *Revitalizing State and Local Public Service.* San Francisco: Jossey-Bass, 1993. Noted experts explore challenges to effective management in states and localities and discuss how to meet those challenges. The book is a companion to the first report of the National Commission on the State and Local Public Service, *Hard Truths, Tough Choices,* which is reprinted in an appendix.

CHAPTER 9

 The Politics of Taxing and Spending

RICHARD F. WINTERS

The rapid growth of American governments in this century has sharpened debate on how these governments tax, how much they tax, and how much they spend on what goods and services. Government spending has increased nearly sixtyfold in this century, while per capita spending increased nearly twenty times over this period. In relation to the size of the economy as a whole, government spending in 1990, which amounted to nearly 40 percent of the gross national product (GNP; defined as the total value of all goods and services produced in the United States), was five times greater than in 1902, when it was 7.7 percent. Government has grown; it has grown by means of increased taxes, and more taxes have led to heightened citizen concern and debate over the size and role of government. By the time of the 1992 presidential election, four out of every five Americans with an opinion believed that American government "wastes a lot of tax money" and that "government was run for the benefit of a few big interests" (Gold 1994, table 4).

If the public agrees on the wasteful size of American governments and that few benefit from such waste, how, then, did we get into this situation? The argument in this chapter is that voters do, in fact, prefer and, therefore, vote for larger budgets by their selection of executives and representatives. But factors other than voters' directly expressed preferences also explain the growth in government. Now the question arises, if voters believe government taxes too much and wastefully spends, can they exert control over taxing and spending? As will be

319

seen, voters in the American states have taken many recent steps to control the growth of their governments.

A CLOSER LOOK AT GROWTH OF GOVERNMENT

All levels of government—national, state, and local—are responsible for growth. Simple data concerning the size and growth of American governments from 1902 until 1990 are set out in Table 9-1. The absolute growth in federal and state and local spending is shown in the first two columns. At the turn of the century, the federal government was barely half the size of our state and local governments; ninety years later it was almost 50 percent bigger. At the federal level, the years that included the two world wars (1913–1922 and 1940–1950) show the greatest growth, closely followed by the years of the Great Depression (1932–1940). The comparable growth figures for these two eras in state and local spending show lower overall rates of growth. During the depression the federal government more than doubled in size, while state and local governments grew by barely 20 percent. Outside of years of war or economic depression, the growth rate of state and local governments (4.2 percent) is about the same as that of the federal government (4.1 percent).

Per capita spending has also increased. In 1902, federal, state, and local governments combined spent about $374 per person, the sum of $129 and $245, shown in Table 9-1. We now spend about $7,000 per person, a nearly 1,800 percent increase since 1902. Population, of course, grew during the ninety years of this table, but government grew five times faster during this period than did population. From another perspective, at the beginning of the century less than 10 percent of all goods and services were provided by the government; currently, that figure is about 40 percent.

Table 9-1   Federal, State, and Local Expenditures (1982 Constant Dollars)

Year	Millions of dollars of spending		Per capita spending		As percentage of GNP	
	Federal	State and local	Federal	State and local	Federal	State and local
1902	10,214	19,429	129	245	2.6	5.0
1913	14,265	33,015	147	340	2.4	5.7
1922	33,009	48,544	300	441	5.1	7.5
1932	46,370	88,815	371	711	7.3	14.0
1940	105,905	109,011	800	823	10.0	10.3
1950	266,667	151,994	1,751	998	15.7	9.0
1960	390,699	216,888	2,172	1,206	18.9	10.5
1970	546,430	327,546	2,679	1,606	20.5	12.3
1980	719,789	401,448	3,168	1,767	22.4	12.5
1990	1,036,135	615,034	4,155	2,466	24.9	14.8

SOURCES: Adapted, recalculated, and updated from Borcherding 1985. GNP figures: 1902–1950, U.S. Bureau of the Census 1975, part 1, table F 1-5; 1960–1990, *Economic Report of the President* 1994, table B-1. Federal, state, and local spending figures: Tax Foundation 1992, table A9. Price deflator: 1902–1950, U.S. Bureau of the Census 1975, part 1, table F 1-5; 1960–1990, Tax Foundation 1992, table B37. Population figures: U.S. Bureau of the Census 1993, 8; 1902–1940, U.S. Bureau of the Census 1975, part 1, table A 6-8.
NOTE: Population figures for 1940–1990 are for resident population.

Why Do Governments Grow?

Inflation. The figures in Table 9-1 have been calculated using the value of the 1982 dollar as the base, thus taking into account the effects of inflation. Several analysts argue, however, that the costs of delivering government goods and services likely rise faster than the simple rate of inflation (Baumol 1967; Olson 1973). Government must compete with the private sector for its administrative personnel; thus government wages and salaries for secretaries, laborers, and administrators must roughly equal the salaries and wages paid for these positions in private business. But employee productivity in government is harder to measure than that in the private sector because government usually does not produce goods and services in measurable unit quantities with accompanying information about prices. Lacking information on how efficiently an agency can deliver a difficult-to-measure service such as "public health" makes productivity comparisons among government agencies difficult to measure and, therefore, cost savings from heightened efficiency hard to achieve. If such information is lacking, then the cost of delivering government might well rise at a steady, inexorable rate. By this logic, delivering even the same amount of government goods and services may well get more and more expensive; thus the cost of government goes up to cover these expenses.

Population. Many services that state governments offer their populations—colleges and universities, health and hospital beds, welfare payments, and so forth—grow as the populations of college students, the sick, and needy grow. But the per capita spending data in Table 9-1 indicate that government goods and services grew at a rate greater than simple population growth. Thus, while increasing population accounts for some growth, there must be more explanations than inflation or population growth.

Increasing Income and Changing Voter Preferences. Voters' desires and preferences for government goods and services change and expand as their personal incomes and wealth grow. As citizens in our society became better paid and wealthier, they turned to governments to provide the goods and services that the wealthier or better paid prefer—education in colleges and universities is an excellent example. Middle-class parents want their children to go to college; further, they argue that colleges and universities ought to be at least partially publicly supported through tax payments. And, as the population in the middle class expands, so will voters' interest in more spending on higher education. Rising income and wealth provide a second likely cause of greater government spending. States with rapidly growing economies, and therefore rising personal incomes, are those with rapidly diversifying and industrializing economies. These traits of rapidly developing economies, in turn, lead to an "expanded need for law and order, . . . regulation, etc. . . . arising from the increased complexity of industrialized society" (Larkey, Stolp, and Winer 1981, 176; Berry and Lowery 1987).

The results of opinion polls give evidence of the voter demand for growth of government. When quizzed about whether they believe that "government spends 'too little' or 'too much,'" more people routinely say that state governments spend too little on law and order, too little dealing with drugs, too little on health care, too little on protecting the environment, too little on education, and so on. Only on issues such as welfare is there ordinarily agreement that we are spending too much (Crocker 1981). There is widespread voter support for many of the particulars of what governments do.

Behavior of Elected Leaders. The choices politicians make and the way their choices are presented to voters also shape the growth of government. This argument takes two paths. First, "the politics of the budgetary process" may lead politicians to choose systematically the path of government enlargement. The institutional practices that increase government growth appear on both the gubernatorial side of the budgetary process as well as on the legislative side (see the discussion under "Spending and Taxing and the Budgetary Process," later in this chapter; Chubb 1985). Second, political leaders couch alternatives in ways that lead voters to choose the path of greater government spending (Riker 1986; Winters 1990). The bulk of the enlargement of American state government has been approved by legislators and signed into law by governors. In turn, these elected officials seek reelection, and in most cases, they are returned to office by voters. Contrary to what one might expect, given conventional wisdom, voters reelect politicians who are "taxers and spenders" (Kone and Winters 1993). The list of big-taxing, big-spending governors is legendary and contains surprising names: Republicans such as Nelson A. Rockefeller of New York, John A. Volpe of Massachusetts, and Ronald Reagan of California and Democrats such as Brendan Byrne of New Jersey, Philip H. Hoff of Vermont, and Kenneth Curtis of Maine.

Since 1945, twelve states have instituted brand-new income tax programs, and twenty states have instituted new general sales taxes. Few of the governors who put these programs into place were defeated at the polls. The fundamental lesson of budgetary politics is clear—taxing more and spending more does not lead inevitably to electoral defeat. Exactly how politicians transform the burdens of new taxes and bigger government on voters into positive approval is complex and subtle.

Variability and Change in States' Taxes

Let's look more closely at variability and change in state taxing. Levels of per capita taxation among the states at three different points in time are displayed in Table 9-2. Taxation by all of the states increased during this period. Even the least-taxed state increased its levies threefold between 1950 and 1970 and fourfold between 1970 and 1990. This state, New Hampshire, had the third lowest tax burden in 1950 and the lowest in 1970 and 1990. The tax issue has dominated the politics in this small state, which has neither a general sales tax nor a broadly based personal income tax. It is also one of the more Republican states in the Union, embracing well-organized and relatively strong conservative political move-

Table 9-2 Per Capita Taxation in the American States, 1950, 1970, 1990

| | 1950 | | 1970 | | 1990 | |
State	per capita taxes	rank	per capita taxes	rank	per capita taxes	rank
Alabama	36.84	2	191.09	11	945.29	7
Alaska	—	—	290.20	44	2811.44	50
Arizona	67.00	39	273.04	41	1194.13	31
Arkansas	46.10	14	183.72	8	961.80	9
California	78.48	44	278.91	42	1459.98	42
Colorado	69.08	40	217.13	23	931.71	6
Connecticut	51.99	22	247.26	35	1602.62	47
Delaware	81.57	46	362.31	50	1695.59	48
Florida	63.82	35	213.99	22	1027.17	14
Georgia	37.49	4	206.84	17	1092.62	20
Hawaii	—	—	200.37	16	2106.78	49
Idaho	52.72	23	220.49	26	1131.11	26
Illinois	43.86	11	259.87	37	1127.72	24
Indiana	51.26	21	194.91	13	1100.55	21
Iowa	56.80	28	224.00	28	1193.15	30
Kansas	62.00	32	192.74	12	1077.26	19
Kentucky	37.69	5	219.84	25	1156.13	27
Louisiana	91.45	48	231.77	29	968.42	11
Maine	46.10	15	209.29	20	1271.14	35
Maryland	56.45	27	279.75	43	1349.99	41
Massachusetts	49.54	20	246.66	34	1557.26	44
Michigan	62.07	33	267.06	38	1220.34	32
Minnesota	64.26	36	271.67	40	1558.65	45
Mississippi	41.94	9	218.81	24	931.08	5
Missouri	41.79	8	176.91	5	965.23	10
Montana	52.99	24	185.62	9	1073.36	18
Nebraska	41.52	7	177.28	6	958.53	8
Nevada	69.76	41	310.68	48	1317.39	36
New Hampshire	37.18	3	130.89	1	536.67	1
New Jersey	30.25	1	187.77	10	1349.76	40
New Mexico	79.30	45	270.49	39	1329.34	37
New York	59.88	30	337.84	49	1590.54	46
North Carolina	54.39	25	236.59	31	1186.49	29
North Dakota	65.68	38	195.89	14	1059.97	16
Ohio	47.59	17	161.19	2	1054.32	15
Oklahoma	75.17	43	198.08	15	1105.31	22
Oregon	69.76	42	208.87	19	980.15	12
Pennsylvania	42.29	10	236.57	30	1112.61	23
Rhode Island	47.81	18	245.36	33	1229.05	33
South Carolina	44.37	12	211.55	21	1128.40	25
South Dakota	60.10	31	168.72	3	718.52	2
Tennessee	46.29	16	176.27	4	870.38	4
Texas	41.34	6	178.82	7	866.36	3
Utah	65.00	37	240.30	32	1026.20	13
Vermont	55.35	26	309.33	47	1183.00	28
Virginia	44.68	13	207.14	18	1066.77	17
Washington	87.86	47	307.52	46	1525.29	43
West Virginia	48.72	19	220.50	27	1243.25	34
Wisconsin	58.26	29	304.42	45	1340.57	38
Wyoming	63.77	34	256.76	36	1349.39	39

SOURCE: Tax Foundation 1992, table E21.
NOTE: Figures are in current dollars; rankings are from the least to the most taxed.

ments. The state's most influential newspaper—the *Union-Leader* of Manchester—has taken up the slogan "No broad-based taxes" as its editorial battle cry (Winters 1980).

Note, however, that there are states with substantial changes in their relative tax levels. Louisiana fell from the most heavily taxed state in the 1950s to the eleventh in burden by 1990. This is, in part, an artifact of that state's tax policies in the 1950s, which relied on the oil and gas severance tax—a tax on natural resources as they are extracted—the largest part of which falls on consumers of oil and gas in the other states. This is a classic case of a state exporting its tax burden to the consumers in other states. It is in the interest of a state's leaders and voters to shift as much of the state's tax as is administratively and constitutionally possible onto out-of-staters. Note that many states export tax burdens in one way or another. A frequently encountered example are hotel and meals taxes (Fisher 1988, 20). Other states with rapidly lightening tax loads over recent decades include Colorado, Oregon, South Dakota, and Utah. States that experienced sharp increases in taxes between 1950 and 1990 include New Jersey, which went from the least taxed (first in rank), to fortieth—followed by Connecticut, Massachusetts, Kentucky, and Maine. Four of these five states experienced at least one new major source of taxation during this period—new income taxes in Maine (1969) and New Jersey (1976) and new sales taxes in Massachusetts (1966) and Kentucky (1960).

Some states bounced back and forth over the forty-year time span. Vermont started off in the middle of the pack in 1950 and then rocketed to the rank of forty-seventh, becoming the fourth most heavily taxed state by 1970. Since then, it has settled back into the middle. The rise and fall of its taxes parallel changes in its income tax during the Democratic and liberal Hoff administration and, shortly after, the institution of the sales tax in 1971 by his Republican successor. Since then, its tax legislation has been relatively quiet. Vermont is a moderate state ideologically and a relatively Republican state by conventional public opinion standards (see Erikson, Wright, and McIver 1993, figures 2.1 and 2.2). Neither the prevailing Republican party attachments nor the professed moderate ideological stands of its population would appear to explain the radical changes in its tax structure. Its leadership behavior, however, does explain its taxing and spending choices, as discussed later.

Growth, Change, and Variability in States' Personal Incomes and States' Taxes

The data in Table 9-3 show how state taxes and personal income in the states have varied over the past half century. They vary in counterintuitive ways; there are increasing similarities among states in the distribution of personal income but scarcely any convergence at all in their taxes. States are becoming more like one another in social and economic ways but remaining fairly distinctive in their tax policies.

Table 9-3 Personal Income and Taxes in the States in Current Dollars: Selected Years from 1939–1940 to 1990

	1939–1940*	1950	1960	1970	1980	1990
Per capita income						
Average ($)	540	1,401	2,058	3,663	9,391	17,590
Standard deviation						
of per capita income	190	324	407	540	1,312	2,859
Coefficient of variability	.35	.23	.20	.15	.13	.16
Per capita taxes						
Average ($)	23	56	103	230	594	1,160
Standard deviation						
of per capita taxes	6	14	24	49	118	236
Coefficient of variability	.26	.25	.23	.21	.20	.20
"Outlier" analysis ($ and rank)						
New Hampshire	26 (32)	37 (3)	69 (3)	131 (1)	301 (1)	537 (1)
Vermont	28 (36)	55 (26)	113 (35)	309 (45)	540 (16)	1,183 (28)
North Dakota	17 (9)	66 (38)	97 (24)	196 (14)	566 (22)	1,060 (16)
South Dakota	23 (22)	60 (31)	78 (7)	169 (3)	392 (2)	718 (2)

SOURCES: Data on income, 1940: U.S. Bureau of the Census 1948, 279; 1950, 1960, and 1970: U.S. Bureau of the Census 1973, 326; 1980 and 1990: U.S. Bureau of the Census 1993, 451. Data on taxes: Tax Foundation 1992, 248.
*Income figures are for 1940 and per capita tax figures are for 1939. Data are for forty-eight states only.

As shown in Table 9-3, citizens in the American states got richer over the past fifty years. The average of all states' personal incomes in 1990 amounted to more than thirty-five times the 1940 average (though in constant dollars it is only two and one half times). The poorer states got richer faster than the richer states. The standard deviation of states' per capita incomes is the amount by which roughly one-third of the states vary above and one-third below this average figure. In 1940, the average per capita income in two-thirds of the states was between $730 and $350. The per capita income coefficient of variability is the standard deviation as a fraction of the personal income average. In the table, this figure shrinks from left to right, which indicates that, over time, differences in personal income among the states diminished. States are more like one another now than they were in earlier periods—a substantial convergence effect has occurred. One reason is that the economies of the southern states boomed while wealthier non-southern states experienced slower growth during this period. Other forces, too, produced convergence among the states: increased mobility of population; the homogenizing effects of an integrated national economy, and technological and communications innovations. But social convergence has not necessarily produced the same amount of tax policy convergence.

An analysis of states' tax collections calculated on a per capita basis can also be viewed in Table 9-3. The average annual tax collected from every person in the typical state was $23 in 1939; that figure rose by a factor of fifty to almost $1,200 in 1990 (though in constant dollars it is only a factor of three and one half). The standard deviation of taxes collected was about one-fourth that average figure in 1939 (at $6 per person collected), and that variation declined ever-so-slowly to about one-fifth the states' average by 1990. Thus, states are becoming like one another in their taxing practices, but at a glacially slow rate. In the early and middle parts of the century, great variation existed in states' taxing practices, and that variation has continued to the present day at almost the same rate.

A further trait of state variability is how states change their taxing practices over time, as we saw in Table 9-2. The "outlier analysis" in Table 9-3 tracks four states in the amounts of taxes that they collected for each of these years and their rank among the forty-eight continental states; the lowest number (1) is given to the state with the least amount of taxes collected per person and the highest number (48) to the state with the most. As we saw in Table 9-2, states like New Hampshire and Vermont start to diverge in tax policy. In 1939, Vermont and New Hampshire collected about the same amount in taxes per person ($28 and $26 per person, respectively) and were ranked close to one another. By 1950, Vermont remained more or less positioned near the middle of the distribution, while New Hampshire began to drift downward in rank from thirty-second to third— among the least taxed. By 1970, New Hampshire had the lowest per capita tax burden of any of the states with the rank of one, and Vermont's citizenry was one of the most heavily taxed in the nation, with the rank of forty-five. In succeeding years, Vermont again drifted toward the middle.

A similar pattern occurred in North Dakota and South Dakota, two other states that, in the opinion of this outsider, appear to be quite like one another and yet end up, over time, with quite different tax policies. A reader might speculate that small states might be more vulnerable to economic fluctuations. This may be true, but a closer examination demonstrated that the relative changes occurred because of purposeful tax choices made by political leaders that have been affirmed time and again by voters (Winters 1980). In the 1960s Governor Hoff accelerated spending in Vermont. He was succeeded by the Republican Deane C. Davis, who convinced voters of the need for a brand-new sales tax in that state. Davis's sales tax now accounts for about one-sixth of Vermont's tax revenues. In this case, purposeful choice determined tax policies, not simple demographic factors.

An Analysis of Causes of Changing Taxes and Spending

Three corollary questions arise when one asks the question, Why do states have the taxing and spending policies that they do? The first is, What accounts for the origin of the policy? The second, Once a tax policy is in place, what forces maintain it? And finally, How is a tax policy altered or changed?

In responding to the causal questions of origins, maintenance, and change, in turn, three levels of analysis are important:

• *Within-state causal factors:* Most of us carry around in our minds the notion that politics in Louisiana, New Jersey, or South Dakota are largely determined by particular, idiosyncratic determinants that set these states apart from one another, that is, that there is a within-state explanation. What accounts for Louisiana's apparent willingness to tax (especially, other states' citizens), New Jersey's variability, and South Dakota's reluctance to tax is determined by political forces operating within the state. States, by this line of reasoning, are sui generis, one-of-a-kind, and the peculiarities of each state's politics determine the adoption of certain tax policies.

• *Horizontal causal factors:* All states exist within a horizontal set of across-state relationships that condition the choices they make. Adoption of a policy by one state may make adoption of that policy by a nearby state easier or more difficult. Some states may be consistent leaders in taxation, usually setting rates at a high level, yet not so high as to lose customers to adjacent states. Other states then set their rates at some fraction of the leading state's tax. The adoption of or increase in a general sales tax may ease or make more difficult a change in another state's tax policy. It is easier if a state is bounded by other states with sales taxes at least as high as the prospective new tax rate. But, no sales tax at all in an adjoining state probably constrains a state's political choices in increasing its tax rate.

• *Vertical causal factors:* Finally, states exist within a vertical arrangement of relations with the federal government. As discussed in Chapter 2, the federal government can make spending on some kinds of activities more attractive by altering the rate of matching funds by which it assists the state. One dollar of state highway funds is often matched by nine dollars of federal funds, whereas in welfare, for many states one dollar of state money will generate only one dollar of federal aid. State officials, when faced with a menu of federal matching rates, must consider how their decisions on spending have implications both in the flows of federal matching funds and their state appropriations for programs raised by the states' own taxes.

Interactions among factors at the differing levels of analysis probably account for the largest fraction of tax changes (Winters 1990). The ordinary occasion for changing taxes is a two-step process. Leaders initiate costly new programs within a state, calculating that the new spending will gain them votes and will be financed, in the short-term, by expected ordinary gains in revenue or through minor tax and revenue changes. As the full costs of new programs become apparent after a few years, it also becomes apparent that other programs cannot be trimmed nor can minor revenue changes be found to finance increasing demands for spending. New taxes are needed in order to balance the budget. The political value of continuing already established programs outweighs the political costs of new taxes even in economically tough times.

HOW STATES COLLECT REVENUE AND SPEND

Spending on programs that directly help and assist people, that create the high quality of day-to-day life that Americans cherish and appreciate, is largely a state and local responsibility. If all spending on the biggest items in the federal budget—interest, national defense, international affairs, social security, and pensions—is separated out, one finds that the federal share of domestic programmatic spending amounts only to about half of what is spent at the state and local levels.

How Do State Governments Finance Their Activities?

Federal, state, and local governments gain revenues in different ways. The revenue obtained from the important sources available to American governments is ranked by order of importance to state governments in Table 9-4. Distinctive patterns emerge. The federal government overwhelmingly relies on two sources of revenue: the individual income tax and individual contributions to the social security and Medicare programs. Together, revenues from these two programs constitute more than four-fifths of federal revenues.

About 40 percent of local government revenue comes from a single source, a tax on property, which is an easy-to-calculate tax on an immobile form of wealth. During the twentieth century, a gradual division of revenue specialization occurred among the three levels of government, which yielded this source of revenue to local governments. In 1900 the property tax was the largest single revenue source for the states, but by 1991 it had shrunk to less than 1 percent (Hansen 1990, 339). During the course of worsening property values at the time of the Great Depression, states gave up this taxing power to local governments. In reaction to the need for new sources of revenue, the period of the Great Depression saw sixty separate state adoptions of the three major taxes—the individual income tax, the corporation income tax, and the general sales tax. During the legislative year following the climactic 1932 elections, 1933–1934, at the height of the depression, there were twenty-three adoptions (Tax Foundation 1992, 249).

State governments rely on a larger number and more even mix of revenue sources than the federal and local governments. This situation came about, in part, because the states gave up certain taxation powers—the property tax to local governments and the bulk of the personal income tax to the federal government. There are other reasons, as well. States rely on a broad mix of taxes in order to spread the burden of taxation onto as many people and activities as possible. Lawmakers regard reliance on diverse revenue sources as desirable.[1] One virtue of the diversity is that it insulates a state's total revenue from the vagaries of short-term economic fluctuations that affect some regions and not others; spreading revenue sources spreads the risk of revenue fluctuations. In addition, lawmakers create a virtue from what voters see as multiple sins. Making numerous small changes in different tax programs in order to balance the state

---

1. Some of the material in this chapter comes from a series of interviews with New Hampshire and Vermont legislators and state officials first begun in 1973.

Table 9-4 Major Revenue Sources by Level of Government (percent)

Type of revenue	Federal	State	Local
Sales and gross receipts taxes	0	23	8
Federal intergovernmental revenue	0	22	3
Social insurance and other insurance	38	16	4
Individual income tax	44	15	2
Charges, fees, and miscellaneous	0	15	30
Corporation income taxes	9	3	0
Excise taxes	4	0	0
Customs duties	2	0	0
Property	0	1	39
Other	3	6	15

SOURCE: Calculated from data in U.S. Bureau of the Census 1993, tables 510 and 480.

budget is proof positive to legislators that many citizens are fairly sharing the burden of the costs of government. Finally, because there are strong political imperatives for states to balance their budgets, the larger the number of revenue sources, the more evenly spread and difficult to detect will be the revenue changes that are required to bring taxes in line with required spending.

Bringing Budgets into Balance

In twenty-four states the imperative of final legislative passage and gubernatorial approval of a balanced budget is a constitutional one. In eight states the necessity for a final balanced budget is a weaker, statutory requirement (CSG 1992, 355–356). While eighteen states do not require that the final budget signed by the governor be balanced, all states, except for Vermont, have some sort of statutory or constitutional budget requirement for balance at either the stage of the gubernatorial budget, the legislative budget, or on final passage. California, for example, constitutionally requires only that the governor submit a balanced budget; it does not require that the final budget itself be balanced. Colorado, conversely, does not require gubernatorial submission of a balanced budget, but it does require that the budget passed by the legislature with final gubernatorial action be balanced. Note the logic of each position. For California lawmakers, requiring a balanced budget from the governor informs them of the basic priorities of the governor—what programs must be cut or what taxes raised so as to finance necessary programs. The legislature may, as the year unfolds, find a greater wisdom in a short-term deficit, depending on revenue performance. In contrast, Colorado's less constraining procedure allows that state's governor to inform the legislature of gubernatorial priorities regarding new initiatives and possible alternative policies and to leave the question of financing increased spending—balancing the budget—for later negotiation.

Sixteen states require that the budget be balanced at all three stages: submission of governor's budget, submission of legislative budget, and final passage with gubernatorial approval. This process forces revelation of spending and taxing preferences of the governor and legislature, and mandates that their preferences ultimately be reconciled.

Another factor pushes leaders to balance state budgets. A strong reputation for fiscal integrity and budgetary balance will reduce the costs of borrowing for long-term, capital-intensive projects. States finance projects with long-term benefits, such as highways, hospitals, and university and college buildings, by a *capital budget.* Capital budgets set out a schedule of projects and the ways of financing those projects that almost invariably mean borrowing in the long-term bond markets. Borrowing large amounts for expensive construction projects implies large interest charges over the long-term life of the borrowing, and these interest charges are paid out of the current operating budget. States with reputations for fiscal integrity typically have interest charges that are lower than those with more suspect fiscal reputations. Private financial firms (Standard and Poor's, and Moody's) rate states and assign them grades according to their fiscal reputation. Poor ratings by these firms result in higher interest rates and greater pressures on the annual operating budget. What makes one state fiscally upright and another suspect is both the estimates of their economic strengths and their fiscal—spending and taxing—reputations. Forthrightness in balancing the budget is an important ingredient of the latter.

Raising Revenue to Meet States' Programmatic Needs

Sales taxes make up the largest single source of revenue for states, followed by intergovernmental aid, the bulk of which is aid from the federal government. The personal income tax is also important. Like local governments, the states also rely on user fees and charges for substantial revenue.

Figure 9-1 is a chart of the changing revenue mix for the most important state revenue sources for 1942 through 1990. The largest (in 1990) of the various state revenue sources is at the bottom of the chart and the smallest is at the top. The "big four" sources in 1990—aid from the federal government; sales taxes; charges, fees, and licenses; and the personal income tax—account for almost 80 percent of state revenue. Note that this combined figure grew from about 50 percent forty-eight years earlier. The most dramatically shrinking revenue source is that of selective sales and receipts taxes, which is discussed below.

How can we judge taxes? First of all, there is a *state economic standard.* Does a tax so burden the choices of individuals and of businesses that citizens are worse off after the tax even after calculating the benefits of the added government goods and services?

Asking who bears the burden of paying the tax yields the answer to who bears the *equity burden,* or *incidence,* of the tax. The easiest way to think about tax inci-

Figure 9-1   State Taxes, 1942–1990

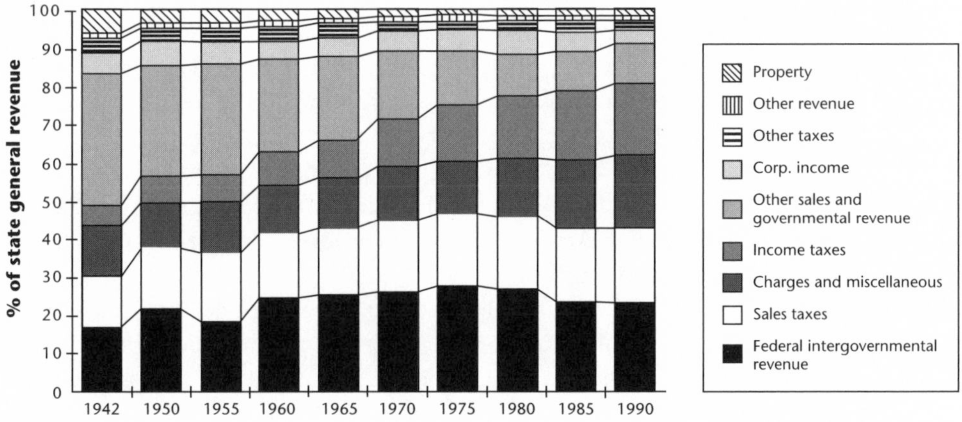

SOURCE: Calculated from U.S. Bureau of the Census, various years.

dence is by personal income or wealth. If those who are best off shoulder more than a simple proportional share, then taxation is considered *progressive*—a person's taxes rise faster than his or her income rises. Advocates of progressive taxation argue that poorer citizens have greater difficulty in carving out a share of income to give to government. Necessities of life—food, housing, clothing—dominate the poor person's budget. Others argue that taxation ought simply to be *proportional* to income—the so-called flat tax. While it is difficult to argue that the poor should shoulder a share that is heavier than proportional, many state taxes are *regressive*—the share of a person's income given up in taxes actually rises as income falls, thereby disproportionately burdening the poor.

Elastic taxes rise along with personal incomes in the state. Some would argue that state governments ought to share in the increasing income that citizens obtain. After all, costs for government go up, as does the demand for government services; thus, more money is needed to satisfy these increasing demands.

State governments are also concerned with *ease of administrative application and collection*. Taxes ought to be easy to calculate and easy to collect. If a tax is costly to apply and collect, then governments have less money raised for revenue purposes and may have alienated citizens, as well.

Finally, there is the judgment and assessment of the *political costs* of new taxation. This is discussed in later sections of this chapter, but because taxes come with direct costs to citizens, they also likely have political and electoral costs for leaders in terms of diminished voter support. Now let's review the major taxes in regard to the first four standards above.

General Sales Tax. The general sales tax—that most familiar of all state and local taxes—is applied to consumer purchases of merchandise in forty-five of the fifty states.[2] As was shown in Figure 9-1, the general sales tax is the states' major tax and has been so for the last half century. The data in Table 9-5 indicate that it accounts for a low of 21 percent of state tax revenue in Massachusetts to a high of 62 percent in Florida. In principle, a sales tax is a general tax applied to a wide range of merchandise; it is a tax on consumption and on retail sales; and it is applied at an established rate. In practice, none of these statements generally holds. For example, the sales tax base is usually a general one only on some kinds of merchandise. In practice, states exempt a wide range of items from the sales tax, food being the major exemption. Only a few states tax services, none taxes housing, and many exempt drugs.

With the passage of time, the sales tax base is gradually eroded. Either the consumers of particular items or the purveyors of those goods pressure state legislators to exempt them. One compelling argument for exemption is that the item is not truly a "consumption" good, but rather it is an intermediate good used in the production of some other item. The net effect of the gradual erosion of the sales tax base is pressure on lawmakers gradually to increase the rate on the remaining nonexempted items (Mikesell 1992). Recently, states have attempted to address this problem by extending the sales tax to services; however, such moves have been met by strong resistance from voters and service providers.

To the extent that the sales tax is applied to some goods, and to goods but not services, it has distortionary effects on economic performance and, therefore, on simple economic efficiency. Because the sales tax applies only to a fraction of all goods and services sold, consumers may substitute, if possible, untaxed products or services for the taxed products. Still another distortionary effect is the time-consuming behavior of citizens who avoid the sales tax by shopping in a nearby state with a lower sales tax or none at all. Examples of tax migrations abound, most directly in customer travel to such sales-tax-free states as Delaware, New Hampshire, and Oregon.

The sales tax is regressive; it more severely affects low-income citizens (Fisher 1988, 187–188). Those whose incomes are on the low end of the scale devote a larger share of their income to consumption—as opposed to saving or investing—and thus the tax falls more heavily on them. Regressivity can be diminished by not taxing food, drugs, and other necessities of life (Mikesell 1992, 85). A summary statistic of one estimate of the overall regressivity or progressivity of state tax systems is in the final column of Table 9-5.

The sales tax can better be thought of as cyclical and responsive as opposed to elastic. The revenue yield varies with business conditions; when times are good and consumers are flush with cash, sales tax coffers fill quickly. In recessionary times or in periods of economic and job anxiety, reluctant consumers don't spend and states don't collect. And, as the base of items that are taxable shrinks over the years to a less representative list of goods (and services), then the predictability of the sales tax revenue decreases, but its elasticity increases as slow-

2. Alaska, Delaware, Montana, New Hampshire, and Oregon do not levy a sales tax.

Table 9-5 The Tax Distribution by State (percent)

	General sales	Selective sales	Personal income	Corporation income	Severance taxes	Overall regressivity*
Fifty state average	33	16	32	7	2	—
Alabama	27	25	29	5	2	194
Alaska	—	5	—	12	71	171
Arizona	44	15	24	4	—	160
Arkansas	37	16	33	6	1	142
California	31	8	39	11	—	111
Colorado	27	17	44	4	—	150
Connecticut	46	20	12	13	—	193
Delaware	—	14	40	10	—	87
Florida	62	18	—	5	—	328
Georgia	37	12	41	7	—	148
Hawaii	50	13	30	4	—	94
Idaho	34	15	35	6	—	121
Illinois	31	18	33	6	—	208
Indiana	42	13	34	6	—	179
Iowa	28	16	38	6	—	139
Kansas	33	15	32	8	3	161
Kentucky	26	19	28	7	5	137
Louisiana	31	19	18	9	10	187
Maine	33	17	37	4	—	106
Maryland	24	18	44	5	—	111
Massachusetts	21	11	52	9	—	133
Michigan	28	11	35	16	—	154
Minnesota	27	16	42	7	—	101
Mississippi	45	20	18	5	2	162
Missouri	38	12	36	4	—	174
Montana	—	21	33	9	11	99
Nebraska	34	21	33	5	—	168
Nevada	51	35	—	0	1	327
New Hampshire[†]	—	46	7	21	—	215
New Jersey	32	21	28	1	—	132
New Mexico	42	15	18	3	15	134
New York	21	12	53	3	—	116
North Carolina	23	18	43	8	—	117
North Dakota	34	22	16	7	12	172
Ohio	31	19	36	6	—	124
Oklahoma	24	20	29	3	11	144
Oregon	—	14	66	5	2	102
Pennsylvania	32	18	24	1	—	211
Rhode Island	32	20	35	6	—	129
South Carolina	37	18	35	4	—	117
South Dakota	50	31	—	6	2	308
Tennessee[†]	55	22	2	8	—	307
Texas	52	29	—	0	7	339
Utah	40	12	37	5	2	147
Vermont	20	28	38	4	—	87
Virginia	20	19	47	5	—	141
Washington	60	15	—	0	1	326
West Virginia	34	19	23	10	7	127
Wisconsin	30	15	40	7	—	141
Wyoming	27	9	—	0	42	258

SOURCE: Figures in the first five columns were calculated from data in Tax Foundation 1992, table E18. The overall regressivities were calculated by the author from data in Citizens for Tax Justice 1991.

NOTE: Dashes indicate that there is no such tax program.

*The figures represent the income, in percent, extracted in taxes from the lowest 40 percent of income earners as a percentage of the income, in percent, extracted from the top 5 percent of income earners in each state. The larger the figure, the greater the burden on the lowest income classes.

[†]Income tax is on interest and dividend income only.

growing sectors of "necessities and essentials" such as food and clothes are elimi-nated (Duncombe 1992, 308–309).

The sales tax is applied at the final stage of sales—at the retail level—so the ease of application of the tax is dependent on the efforts of the retail merchant community. A fraction of the sales tax that each retail merchant collects as part of the transaction is paid out to the merchant for administrative costs.

Personal Income Tax. In 1942 the individual income tax accounted for about 5 percent of state revenues (see Figure 9-1). But by 1990 it accounted for nearly 19 percent. Forty-four of the fifty states have some form of income tax.[3] As indicat-ed in Table 9-5, states that rely heavily on the income tax include Oregon, New York, and Massachusetts, with 66 percent, 53 percent, and 52 percent, respectively, of their revenue coming from the income tax.

Three different ways of assessing the state income taxes bear on the issue of incidence. Three of the states (Colorado, Rhode Island, and Vermont) use the federal income tax form as a basis for the state income tax. In Vermont, for ex-ample, the state income tax liability is 28 percent of the federal tax liability. And because the federal government taxes citizens on the basis of income, in that those with higher incomes fall into a higher tax bracket and thus pay a higher percentage of their income in taxes, the income taxes in these states are fairly progressive. Still other states—Connecticut, Illinois, Indiana, Massachusetts, and Pennsylvania—levy a flat tax on personal incomes. In principle, this is a propor-tional tax, but with the large number of exemptions, deductions, and credits, the flat tax can take on progressivity, as it has in Massachusetts, or be almost perfect-ly proportional, as it is in Pennsylvania (Citizens for Tax Justice 1991).

Most states with income taxes adopt some form of the "ability to pay" princi-ple. Steep progression in income brackets occurs in California, where a 1 percent rate is applied to those with less than $5,000 in annual income, while those with $200,000 or more in income pay taxes at an 11 percent rate. The highest rate is 12 percent, applied in North Dakota to its residents who earn more than $50,000 per year (see Tax Foundation 1992, table E23). Note that the estimates of regres-sivity supplied by the Citizens for Tax Justice in Table 9-5 are strongly affected by a personal income tax and by the progressivity of such a tax.

The income tax tends to be responsive to changes in personal income in states; thus it is considered an elastic tax. Revenues in states with progressive in-come taxes that include several income brackets and increasing rates applied to increasing incomes tend to be more elastic, but they also tend to be more vari-able—that is to say, they rise rapidly in good economic times but fall rapidly in poor times. There seems to be a trade-off at work; states with steeply progressive taxes have tax systems that are highly responsive to economic change, but the yield is more difficult to predict (Dye and McGuire 1991).

3. Alaska (which abolished its income tax in 1980), Florida, Nevada, South Dakota, Texas, Wash-ington, and Wyoming do not have income taxes. New Hampshire and Tennessee tax limited forms of income and are not considered to have general income taxes (Tax Foundation 1992, 249).

The income tax may require substantial costs of application at the government level and at the taxpayer level. Forms have to be prepared, information on personal income checked and verified by state revenue administrators, likely taxable amounts withheld from paychecks, and delinquents and malingerers pursued. Taxpayers also bear personal costs in time spent preparing the return and the use of accountants and tax services in assisting in preparation. Note that state income taxes that are calculated as a fraction of the federal income tax liability can, in principle, be collected by a very simple form at a low cost of preparation to the citizen.

There is conflict about the economic efficiency of the income tax. Of particular concern to state politicians is the *local efficiency,* that is, how the income tax and its progressivity affects the residential choice of citizens and of businesses. States with high, punitive income tax codes may drive individuals with high taxable incomes into nearby or adjacent states that have lower or no income taxes.

Selective Sales and Excise Taxes. Selectively taxing the sale of a set of particular items is jokingly labeled by state legislators as "taxing the five bees"—taxes on selective sales of "butts, beer, booze, bellies, and beds" (that is, cigarettes, beer, wines and liquors, restaurant meals, and room occupancy in hotels and motels). They are often referred to as "sin taxes" and are popular because they satisfy so many political interests. One important interest is the effect on efficiency. State legislators believe that they can easily raise the tax rate on cigarettes or beer or wine without affecting consumption of the items. Even if consumption of cigarettes or beer slowly declines with ever-higher taxes (and at some point consumption must decline with ever-higher taxes), legislators believe that the resulting diminished consumption actually benefits the state. Higher taxes will lead to declines in "sinful" consumption, which will lead to less sickness and to fewer drunk drivers, and so on.

One inefficiency in sin taxing derives from its interstate variability. Cigarette taxes are the best example—they vary from a low of 2 cents, 2.5 cents, and 3 cents per pack in the tobacco-producing states—North Carolina, Kentucky, and Virginia—to highs of ten times or more of those tax rates in non-tobacco-producing states. The difference in price due to the higher taxes sets up interstate smuggling of cigarettes.

Selective sales taxes are generally thought to be regressive. Most analysts believe that the reasonable way to figure out the burden of sin taxes is to assume that they are distributed by the consumption of the item taxed. Thus, motor fuels are thought to be regressive because the poor make heavier use of older, inefficient automobiles. Increases in liquor and wine taxation, however, may be relatively progressive because of the heavier consumption of these items by middle- and upper-income individuals.

Selective sales taxes are not thought to be elastic taxes. The consumption of beer, tobacco, and motor fuels, while responsive to changes in personal income, doesn't increase significantly more rapidly than personal income.

Selective sales are one of the best-established bases of taxation in the states. States have cooperated with the manufacturers and wholesalers of items that are selectively taxed, most especially the tobacco and beer and liquor distributors, so as to ensure ease of administrative application. Even at the retail level of hotels, motels, and restaurants, vendors are easily detectable and procedures relatively straightforward. Very often consumers are not even aware that selective sales taxes are applied to the goods that they purchase—gasoline and liquor are examples.

No chapter on taxing and spending in the states written in the mid-1990s would be complete without a discussion of what is now a small but the fastest growing source of revenue in the states—a selective sales and gross receipts tax on gambling. The reasons for the rapid growth are increases in demand by consumers for gambling activities; enormous growth in the availability of gambling sites; the decline in opposition to legalized gambling on the part of lawmakers and voters; and, finally, a constitutional anomaly in American law. Gross revenues of gambling businesses increased by 300 percent per year to $30 billion from 1982 to 1992, while box office revenues in many other entertainment sectors barely budged. In Louisiana, in the first six months of legalized gambling, gross business revenues from gambling went from zero to $100 million per month, and taxes paid to the state went from zero to nearly $20 million per month. Nevada has long relied on direct revenue from casino and other gambling to finance about one-sixth of its activities.

One proximate cause of the rapid growth in gambling is the federal courts' rulings on how state and local governments must handle lands held by recognized American Indian tribes (Johnson 1993, sec. 4, p. 6). If a state—for example, Connecticut—allows some forms of gambling, such as bingo nights sponsored by charitable or nonprofit activities, then the semisovereign tribes gain even more general rights and can open up a casino. In one case, Connecticut authorities, recognizing the inevitable, allowed the Mashantucket Pequot tribe to open the enormously successful Foxwood Casino in Ledyard, Connecticut. A large fraction of revenues from slot machines (expected to exceed $100 million per year) is given to the state in lieu of other tax payments to the state. The success of the Mashantucket tribe has been emulated elsewhere; sixty-five tribal casinos have opened in seventeen states since 1989, and "80 more tribes have gambling plans in a dozen other states" (Clines 1993, sec. 1, p. 1).

One important within-state effect of successful tribal gambling is to create internal pressures on other recognized tribes within the state to open competing casinos. Tribal gambling success also creates incentives for nontribal private entrepreneurs and local officials who see the economic development potential of local casino gambling operations. (Judson 1994, sec. 4, p. 5). Today, "more than 20 river boats [ply] the Mississippi and other rivers in the Midwest [and] are expected to generate more than $1 billion in revenues this year—40 percent more than is generated in Atlantic City" (Feder 1993, sec. 3, p. 5).

Corporation Income Taxes. Although important sources of revenue for the states, corporation income taxes are neither large nor growing. This tax amounted to about 5 percent of state revenues in 1942 and about 4 percent nearly fifty years later in 1990. One possible reason why it is not a growing source of revenue is the complexity of the tax. Ordinarily, one would think of the corporate income tax as equivalent to the personal income tax and apply the appropriate tax rate much like the ordinary citizen does to personal income. In fact, this would be a gross receipts tax. However, if it is assumed, quite reasonably, that the greatest fraction of the total receipts that businesses receive for sales is used for the direct costs of production—for labor, materials, financing, and so on—then the company should not be taxed on its total receipts but rather on receipts less the costs of production, sales, and so on. Basing the corporate income tax on income net of costs, then, brings up the question of what is, justifiably, a cost of production? Still another complication is the following: If a business is headquartered in California but has half of its production operations in Nevada and half in Malaysia and sells only 10 percent of its goods in California, what state (or nation) taxes what?

State decision makers are faced with conflicting interests in assessing efficiency considerations of the corporation income tax. On the one hand, corporations are "good citizens" of states and therefore corporations ought to share in the financing of services that benefit them. On the other hand, to the extent that corporate taxes are low, a state will be seen as a more attractive place to continue to do business or to move one's business. State legislators must ask themselves if, by lowering such taxes, more businesses with more jobs can be lured to the state and if the state's revenue picture is thus ultimately improved.

Are corporation income taxes progressive? Corporate taxation becomes another cost to the company, which hopes to shift that cost onto the consumer. It may not be able to do so, however. For example, if a rival is in business in another state with low corporate taxation, a company may be constrained by the competitive market to pass on the tax cost to shareholders or to employees in reduced corporate benefits, pay, and so on.

Corporation taxes ought to be elastic and probably are quite volatile as they track the economic performance of the state and nation. But such taxes pose profound problems of application and collection. One of the main reasons is, as the discussion above suggests, that it is difficult to calculate what fraction of a corporation's activities and its income ought to be taxed.

Charges, Fees, and Miscellaneous Revenues. A somewhat smaller rate of growth is seen in charges, fees, and miscellaneous revenue that is collected by the state for those activities for which it can reasonably expect users to pay. This category of revenue can be likened to government endeavoring to apply pricing to the production of its own goods and services. Well-known examples would be entrance fees to parks and museums, tuition at colleges, charges for drivers' and automobile licenses, water and sewer fees, and so on.

The simple analysis of the efficiency of such fees suggests that these fees are a simple benefit tax—those who benefit from use pay for its provision. Even though everyone actually benefits from the provision of certain state and local services, those who are direct beneficiaries, such as park users and homeowners who have a hookup to the sewer system, ought to pay a fair share of the costs. It is not often possible, however, to price a government's goods and services directly and fully (Olson 1973). All citizens benefit from governments' provision of services such as parks and sewer systems through the park's contributions to an attractive and beneficial environment and from the sanitary sewers' contribution to public health. In economic terms, these are positive externalities associated with these goods and services—positive effects of a service the benefits of which cannot be reasonably captured through a user fee or personal charge. Thus, there is no simple linkage between the cost of a service, its user fee as a price, and a tax on all beneficiaries.

The calculation of how progressive or regressive such fees are is difficult to assess. While governments that charge for their services can be praised for allocating the costs of government to those who benefit, another task of government is to ensure that all citizens can obtain some fair share of public services regardless of wealth or income. Many states now require telephone companies, as state-regulated public utilities, to provide elementary "lifeline" phone service to all consumers at a price less than the cost of the service. In effect, all telephone users pay a higher fee for telephone service (a hidden user tax) to ensure that this service is available and distributed to all citizens.

Charges, licenses, and miscellaneous fees are not elastic. Fees are usually set by statute at a particular figure and remain unchanged until the law itself is changed. Revenue thus fluctuates as a function of the number of users, licensees, or beneficiaries. Administrative application of this source of revenue, however, is easy. Users and licensees are charged by formula.

Intergovernmental Aid. The second largest source of revenue for state governments in 1991 was intergovernmental aid, about 95 percent of which was aid from the federal government (*Statistical Abstract of the U.S.* 1993, 300). In 1991, about $135 billion in federal moneys were employed by states to advance their programs. About one-half of this supported welfare programs, 20 percent supported education, and 15 percent supported highway building.

Severance Taxes. Although severance taxes do not amount to much in the way of revenues in the fifty American states (at 2 percent of total revenue collected by the states), for a handful of states they loom large—71 percent of Alaska's revenues and 42 percent of Wyoming's. States with large oil and coal extractive industries rely on such a tax as a way of exporting the burden onto the consumers of such resources, almost all of whom live in other states. From the perspective of the state's economy the burden is exported to out-of-state (nonvoting) citizens. Thus, having other states' citizens finance their government is seen as a tax windfall by lawmakers. A major concern about the severance tax, however, is that it is a highly volatile source of revenue. Because the severance tax is levied as a percentage of the value of the resource extracted and sold, the amount the severance tax yields is a function of production and price. Oil, especially, has been highly volatile in both production and price. In 1970, Alaska earned $10 million in severance taxes; in 1980, $506 million; in 1986, $1.4 billion; and in 1987, $667 million. In effect, the Alaskan revenue system fluctuates just about as wildly as the world market price of oil.

HOW TAXES GET ADOPTED AND GET CHANGED

New tax programs are adopted and existing ones increased in order to allow more spending in the states. We also know, however, that politicians are reluctant to tax, for "tax adoptions are nearly always unpopular and pose great risks for politicians hoping to win re-election" (Berry and Berry 1992, 716). Several studies have analyzed factors explaining how new taxes get adopted or tax rates get changed. In brief, significant changes in tax laws are more likely when fiscal woes hit the state; less likely late in the gubernatorial term; more likely in wealthy states; and more likely if a state is bounded by other states with similar programs (Berry and Berry 1992; Brace 1994; Hansen 1983, 1990). But the story is actually more complicated and politically more interesting.

Let's narrow our focus on innovations to the most broadly based taxes, defined as new programs of general sales taxes, new personal income tax programs, or rate changes in either of these two existing taxes. These are the tax programs that are most likely to galvanize public sentiment. The dates and states of original adoption for these two taxes can be seen in Figures 9-2 and 9-3. As the data in both figures indicate, tax innovations have been frequent, and all but a handful of states now have one or both of these programs. The data offer several lessons bearing on what causes innovations in the forty-one states with income taxes and the forty-five states with sales taxes.[4]

The nonfederal income tax was first adopted by law when the remote U.S. possession of Hawaii was first organized as a territory in 1901. Among the then-existing states, Wisconsin and Mississippi first adopted the tax in 1911–1912, and it slowly spread to other nonadjacent states over the next two decades. The pace of income tax adoptions rapidly accelerated during the Great Depression. In this time of great personal and governmental hardship, property taxes and selective sales and excise taxes were either hard to collect or did not amount to enough revenue to be useful. A new revenue source was needed, and states' leaders saw that the income tax had established itself as administratively workable. Also, burdening the better-off was politically a more acceptable solution to revenue shortfalls in those difficult economic times. But as the years of the Great Depression

---

4. States with no broadly based income taxes are Alaska, Florida, Nevada, New Hampshire, South Dakota, Tennessee, Texas, Washington, and Wyoming. Alaska instituted an income tax in 1949 but repealed it in 1980. States with no sales tax include Alaska, Delaware, Montana, New Hampshire, and Oregon.

Figure 9-2   Dates of Adoptions of State Income Tax Programs

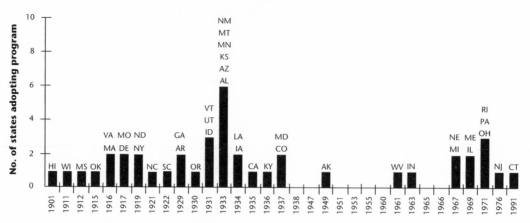

SOURCE: Calculated from data in Tax Foundation 1992, 249.

Figure 9-3   Dates of Adoptions of State Sales Tax Programs

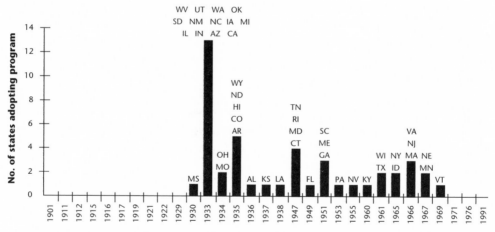

SOURCE: Calculated from data in Tax Foundation 1992, 249.

drew to an end, so also did adoptions of the income tax. Nevertheless, the data in Figure 9-2 reveal the most important factor in explaining tax changes—hard times.

The situation in which *budgetary woes* determine tax adoptions or rate changes is a classic within-state causal factor. Nevertheless, other budgetary choices are available to a state's political leaders. Governors and legislators could, after all, reduce expenditures. Thus, while the state's budgetary troubles are a necessary condition for tax increases, such troubles are not a sufficient condition to produce taxes. Leaders focus on how many votes will be lost because of the imposition of new taxes in relation to how many will be lost if expenditures for programs are cut (Downs 1957; Hansen 1983). New taxes are attractive if the vote loss from program cuts is formidable. The actions of the states' leaders during the Great Depression suggest that large gaps between expenditure needs and revenues lead to new tax programs. The most recent example of this phenomenon is the imposition of an income tax in Connecticut in 1991.

The pattern of sales tax adoptions in Figure 9-3 also appears to be strikingly affected by the factor of difficult financial situations. Nearly one-half of the American states adopted the general sales tax in the years of the Great Depression. Politically competitive states that fell under the control of the Democratic party in the Roosevelt era were much more likely to be among those that did (Hansen 1990, 359). But a second pattern found in sales tax adoptions differs from the pattern in income tax adoptions. Every four years or so, usually in the years immediately following the gubernatorial elections, new sales tax programs were adopted. *Timing,* defined as passage early in a gubernatorial term, then, is a second general factor in adoptions, in addition to hard times and the resultant budgetary woes.

Berry and Berry (1992) argue that tax innovations are more attractive the further the temporal distance to the next election. Politicians count on the short memories of voters to diminish the pain of increased taxes, and they also count on voters' myopic vision to put into sharp focus the beneficial stream of services present at election time.

As the term of a governor nears its end, not only do the incentives to put the state into budgetary balance diminish, so also does that capacity of the incumbent to mobilize legislators to balance the budget. The will of all political actors to raise new taxes weakens as the election approaches because of the fear of voter wrath and simply to postpone the needed fiscal stringency until later. Gubernatorial incumbents reason that if they can hold off on new taxes for the next year and if they are reelected, they will be in a stronger position with the legislature; if they are not reelected, then their successors can bite the tax bullet.

Politicians avoid broad, general tax changes in an election year, but that may not be true for all taxing activities. Mikesell (1978) discovered that in the third and fourth year of a gubernatorial term, minor taxes are more likely to get changed, sin taxes increased, and the taxes not easily ascertainable by voters increased.

Vermont's adoption of a brand-new 3 percent general sales tax in 1969 is a classic case of timing. In the 1968 Vermont gubernatorial election, a businessman and longtime Republican activist, Deane Davis, succeeded the three-term Democratic incumbent, Philip Hoff. Hoff, who was the first Democrat to be elected as Vermont's governor in 100 years, was widely recognized as the state's most activist governor. He was responsible for many new expenditure programs and for the expansion of countless others, while leaving his Republican successor with a resulting large gap between expenditure obligations and expected revenues. In January 1969, nine minutes after being sworn in, Davis recommended in his inaugural address a 3 percent general sales tax as a solution to Vermont's fiscal problems. One analyst commented that Davis began to lose the 1970 election in that ninth minute of his term. His own views on the effects of the new sales tax on his reelection chances were more optimistic. He noted that former governor Hoff congratulated him on his sales tax message immediately after the inauguration, claiming that Davis "was doing the right thing" (interview with Davis, July 18, 1990). Davis obtained passage of his new 3 percent general sales tax; he also won reelection with a greater margin of victory than he had had in his first election.

The concept of timing of tax legislation is further entangled in two other important determinants of adopting taxes. Democratic party control, in the public's view, is related to increasing taxes. Democrats are seen as representing voters who favor larger government, which provides many more, and expensive, services (CBS-NYT poll as reported in Oreskes 1988, 32). The Democratic party is also seen as the party more favorable to special interests in need of governmental assistance. All of these perceptions suggest upward pressure on spending that may irresistibly produce Democratic tax increases. But if party control is related to timing of tax increases, then that control ought to manifest itself early in the period of control, not later. A new Democratic governor coming into office with a newly Democratic legislature is under great pressure to produce programs that demonstrate the worth of the Democrats' control of government. If that entails a tax hike, then it will occur early so as to finance the noteworthy additions that the Democrats bring to the government establishment.

Several analysts of American state politics have reviewed the effect of party control of the governor's office on budgetary politics. It turns out to be difficult to predict unambiguously the kinds of changes that occur with a change in the party holding the governorship. Garand (1985) provides evidence that a new administration means general changes in the budgetary activities of states. Plotnick and Winters (1990) found that politically liberal states were more generous in their welfare programs, an effect that was magnified when the liberal party was in control and when that control was highly uncertain or tentative because of heightened party competition. Others have noted that change in party control and electoral realignments are also associated with changing taxes (Hansen 1983). An interesting example of timing, party control, and election consequences occurred in 1971, when the newly elected Democratic governor John J. Gilligan put into place the Ohio income tax. Gilligan replaced a tough-minded, fiscally conservative Republican governor, James A. Rhodes. Gilligan campaigned and won, in part, on his success in putting Ohio's fiscal house in order and his promotion of state assistance to programs aiding localities, the poor, and those with special needs. A large new tax source was needed, and Gilligan obtained early in his term passage of a new income tax program. Three years later, Gilligan lost in his reelection bid. Many more examples of tax increases for programmatic ends occur in the states. New taxes for increased funding for education is a particularly popular item. Two well-known examples resulted in more salutary outcomes for Governors Terry Sanford of North Carolina and Bill Clinton of Arkansas, each of whom increased their respective sales taxes for education programs and went on to win reelection.

A final factor related to timing is the *public mood*. In some time periods (but certainly not the 1990s), voters want bigger government; it is as if there is a demand for government, which governors and legislators endeavor to satisfy. The adoption of new income and sales tax programs in the 1960s and early 1970s are examples of such a period. An outstanding example exists in the behavior of a former Republican governor of Massachusetts, John Volpe. In his first reelection campaign for the governorship in 1964, Volpe signaled to the voters that he might proceed with a new sales tax. Volpe gained the passage of the new sales tax by transforming it into a positive electoral issue by the time of his reelection. Like Vermont's Davis, Volpe brought the positive features of efficiency and no-nonsense business practices to politics (he owned a large construction company), but he also established a reputation as a progressive and reform-oriented governor. In recalling the sales tax fight, Volpe's lieutenant governor, Elliot L. Richardson, noted, "There was no fiscal crisis as such, we just wanted to be able to do more" (Black 1990, sec. A, p. 21).

Volpe endeavored to establish the public benefits of new programs financed by the new sales tax. His strategy was enormously successful. State legislators remember walking in Memorial Day holiday parades (in mid-spring when the legislature was still in session) with people shouting from curbside, "Pass the tax!"—certainly puzzlingly quaint behavior by today's standards (*Boston Sunday Globe,* May 27, 1990). Ultimately, legislators widely agreed on the need for new taxes in order to support new state spending. But this was a period when the positive possibilities of government were thought to be great.

An important within-state causal factor that shapes gubernatorial and legislative receptiveness to new taxes is the income and wealth of the state. Richer states are more generous in their spending programs, in part, because they can afford to tax more (Dye 1966; Plotnick and Winters 1985). The law of diminishing marginal returns suggests that voters are more generous when they have high incomes and that they are more willing to tax themselves in rich states; thus politicians may have less to fear at the polls. A parallel causal factor is that wealthy states are the most socially and economically diverse states and have the most closely competitive electoral systems. The net effect of wealth in combination with greater diversity of social and economic interests is to increase political pressures on governors and legislators alike to help groups in need of assistance. As diversity increases in a competitive state, more and more groups can reasonably claim that each provided the last crucial voting bloc to the victor's winning coalition. "In the diverse states, party leaders will lack precise information on the validity of the claims of group influence and will become captive to the pleas of many of them" (Plotnick and Winters 1985, 463).

A final within-state causal factor that helps to explain tax adoptions is the equilibrium outcome, one that is agreeable to more than a simple winning coalition. Republican fiscal conservatives like Davis in Vermont and Volpe in Massachusetts advocate a new tax as the one solution to the state's problems. And by personally advocating the tax and pushing for it, they mute criticism from fiscal conservatives. But note that programs already in existence have many advocates for their continuation, such as government bureaucrats who deliver the services, those working in the private sector who benefit from a particular program (doctors, social workers), and the direct beneficiaries of the services (welfare clients, farmers, students). Governors can make this same argument to every group that is assisted by government: "Get on board with this tax now or put your program in peril." Threats of budgetary cutbacks mobilize a diverse coalition of groups. All that they agree on is the need for new revenue, but that is all the governor needs.

A classic example of the equilibrium nature of new and expanded tax programs comes from the first term of Governor Kenneth Curtis of Maine. The Democratic Curtis narrowly defeated the incumbent governor, John H. Reed, in the 1966 election, campaigning on behalf of his "Maine Action Plan." Two years later, some of the costs of action came due, and Curtis pushed for and won a general income tax. The tax passed the house and the senate by a margin of one vote; the crucial votes were cast by the Republican leadership in the two chambers. In effect, a bipartisan tax plan was passed in Maine. Curtis went on to win reelection, having mooted the ability of his Republican opponent to use the new taxes effectively against him.

A final factor that eases the way for new taxes is the behavior of one's neighbors, a horizontal factor affecting state politics. Berry and Berry (1992, 722) argue that information that voters get about the practice of a tax in a nearby state alleviates the "uncertainty" about possible consequences. A large number of nearby states with the same tax "should diminish the fear that adopting the tax would seriously hurt a state's ability to compete for business, thereby reducing the political costs of doing so." Having many nearby neighbors with the tax, however, also works in the opposite direction—increasing the marginal value to states' leaders of being among the very last tax holdouts. Not having the sales tax when one's neighbors do or the income tax when other states do is an important horizontal causal reason for not adopting them. The tax-less state becomes more attractive as a residence and business location. Many states currently benefit from this tax-free situation: Florida, Nevada, New Hampshire, Texas, and Washington benefit from citizens fleeing the income taxes in other states. Delaware, New Hampshire, and Oregon, particularly, benefit from their sales-tax-free environment that lures shoppers from nearby states with its guarantees of saving 5 percent or more on each purchase.

Both propositions—emulating one's neighbors and holding out against them—probably obtain. In the early and midpoint of the diffusion of tax programs across the states, a nearby state's positive experience with a tax program probably counted in favor of its adoption and expansion. However, as the diffusion of tax adoptions proceeds, the value of not adopting the tax—of holding out—becomes more politically and economically profitable for a state. It is unclear what the final stages of this emulation process will look like in regard to adopting sales and income taxes among all fifty states. It is reasonable to speculate, however, that the five states that now have no sales taxes and the nine states that have no general income taxes may never adopt these taxes. The longer the tax-less state holds out, the larger the numbers of citizens and groups that actively benefit from that tax-less situation. States with no sales taxes have significant numbers of owners of small businesses who aggressively lobby to keep their state tax-free, while states with no income tax attract a sizable retired and wealthy population who are politically active in safeguarding the advantages of their tax-free residency.

IF TAXES ARE UNPOPULAR, DO VOTERS PUNISH "TAXERS"?

The political wisdom of activists and leaders says that the relation between new or increased state taxes and voting is direct and negative. The electoral plights of Gov. James Florio in New Jersey in 1993 and of Gov. Lowell P. Weicker in Connecticut in 1994 confirm the conventional wisdom of electoral vulnerability. The link between taxes and voting has strong informal and anecdotal evidence, as well (Beyle 1992; Sabato 1978). An excellent study that merged aggregate data with exit polls of voters confirmed the voter-tax link. Niemi, Stanley, and Vogel (1994) merged the 1986 ABC News/*Washington Post* exit polls with data on statewide economic performance and tax changes for thirty-four gubernatorial elections. They discovered that "raising a visible tax was sufficient for a governor or his party to lose votes" and that each new tax that was hiked in the four-year period "had an added effect" (16). Their conclusions are consistent with the view of discriminating voters who are sensitive and aware of state taxes and are knowledgeable about state officials who tax, especially those who increase the most objectionable taxes (Bowler and Donovan 1995).

Yet, many political scientists share Pomper's earlier ambivalent conclusions that "contrary to the rules of political folklore, governors who lead in increasing taxes do not suffer at the polls significantly" (1968, 133–134). Eismeier (1979, 1983) examined 389 elections between 1950 and 1980 and argued that "governors, gubernatorial candidates and state parties that urged higher taxes faced greater risks of electoral defeat," yet "these risks are not overwhelming in all cases" (Eismeier 1983, 379). In an examination of the tax-vote link, a colleague and I proposed a model of a rational electorate wreaking retribution against a party and its candidates for changes in tax policy—new or additional taxes—in which the party's incumbent chief executive was directly involved (Kone and Winters 1993). We included in the model factors that plausibly account for the vote received by the incumbent: changes in national economic indicators (income, unemployment) and changes in statewide economic indicators of income and unemployment that are also relevant to the plight of voters.

We argued that while the gubernatorial outcome will favor the party traditionally strong within the state, voters are also swayed by national and other electoral bandwagons and tides. Our results indicated that while passing new tax programs did have the predicted negative effects on the electoral outcomes, the modest-sized coefficients had sufficiently large standard errors to be judged not significant. Further examination turned up only a few cases in which electoral defeats could reasonably be traced to new tax programs, and for every tax-related election loss like those of Norbert T. Tiemann in Nebraska and John J. Gilligan of Ohio, there were equally powerful counterexamples of new tax programs put into place and election gains that followed—the reelections of Deane C. Davis of Vermont and Milton Shapp of Pennsylvania are examples (Winters 1990). My finding that many governors adopt a new sales or income tax program and their vote margins are only 2 percent or 3 percent less, on the average, than governors who don't tax leads to the next question: What electoral strategies are available to the candidates for turning the sow's ear of new taxes into the silk purse of the successful reelection campaign?

TAXING AND GETTING REELECTED

How can governors who tax get reelected or get their party successors reelected? Governors act to reduce large vote losses from taxing by attracting support on other grounds. For governors, political damage is not a foregone conclusion. Following are some of the conditions that either heighten the impact of taxing on voting or dampen or attenuate losses.

Voter evaluation of the present revenue system ought to affect the vote. Changing already-existing low rates of an existing tax—a sales tax, for example—by a small increment to a still lower rate ought to have minimal electoral retribution, but there should be increasing marginal political cost of raising taxes. Changing high rates to higher rates probably increases voter anger, as demonstrated by the political experiences of the former Democratic governor Florio in New Jersey, who lost his reelection bid after passing many new taxes in an already heavily taxed state.

A reasonable but untested hypothesis is that there are "era effects," such that tax increases since 1981 have been more politically costly for incumbent politicians than they were in earlier eras. This should follow from the changing political climate engendered, in part, by the efforts of the Reagan administration to sensitize voters to the size of current tax levies. Retributive, antitax political climates have fallen most heavily on politicians who have undertaken tax changes in states with already high levies of taxes.

Invidious comparisons with nearby states make taxation politically costly. Differences in taxes from neighboring states set up powerful arguments regarding the loss of business and flights of the wealthy to adjacent states. Further, some political debates about new taxes are cast in more politically costly terms for the taxing governor and his or her followers. To the extent that changes in subsequent spending are focused on unpopular programs, for example, Ohio Governor Gilligan's embracing more welfare spending, the greater the electoral retribution.

Still, electoral support for those initiating new taxes or increasing existing ones may be greater than expected because the candidates who did the taxing will make compensating changes in their campaign behavior. If the chances for punishment are high for new tax programs, then the political investments governors make in attenuating the likely punishing effects are going to be proportionally higher. Because they expect punishment at the polls, governors ensure that all possible efforts are made to limit the electoral effects of their new tax initiatives. Governors, by strategy or tactics, try to turn what ought to be a barnyard mess into chicken salad at the polls.

The positive traits of the taxing governor, too, may lessen electoral retribution. For example, the likelihood is high that Republican candidates are seen as more fiscally conservative and, therefore, "more responsible." For this reason, Republicans may be less vulnerable than Democrats to electoral retribution, especially in the case of sales tax adoption. The personal activism of the incumbent is also a crucial variable in gaining the final electoral win. Taking the case to the voter aggressively is the key, as Volpe and Davis discovered. Following are some other strategies that appear to be viable for compensating for new taxes.

• Generating bipartisan, pro-tax coalitions, as Curtis did in Maine, limits between-party sniping.

• Signaling the likelihood of new taxes early is important in vitiating the initial effects of the new tax program. Although one does not have to say while campaigning for office, as Walter Mondale did when he campaigned for the presidency, that new taxes are needed, having to retreat from language such as George Bush's "read my lips, no new taxes" is electorally damaging.

• If new taxes become a contentious partisan issue, then the taxing incumbent must first frame the tax issue in terms of the positive goods associated with the benefits of new spending before trying to neutralize the negative traits of new taxes in voters' minds. Then, the positive traits of the incumbent can be enhanced and attacks made on the challenger.

• A coalition of intense minorities favoring reelection of the taxing incumbent can be generated by a strategy of exaggerating the consequences of budget shrinkage if the new taxes are not adopted.

The strategy most often used by governors and legislators is to tighten their belts and work out the balance between spending and revenue through the ordinary politics of the budgetary process.

SPENDING AND TAXING AND THE BUDGETARY PROCESS

Every two years in about one-third of the states with biennial sessions, and every year in the remaining states, the appropriations bill is introduced into the states' legislative chambers.[5] How a bill becomes a law is discussed in Chapter 5 of this volume, but the appropriations and tax bills differ in significant ways from an ordinary bill. More time and energy and more people's cumulative knowledge are devoted to the appropriations bill than to any other in state politics. Even though the size and sophistication of staffs of governors and legislatures vary across the states, both of them usually have their own staffs at work on their versions of the appropriations or budget acts. The companion revenue bill also receives close attention—sometimes, even closer attention—but generally by fewer people. The appropriations bill is closely scrutinized because so many important decisions are wrapped up in this one bill; it is presented to the legislature as the governor's program; it is considered by multiple subcommittees and committees of the states' legislative chambers, amended (at times, substantially so), and approved by the legislature. Once signed into law, the bill sets the limits on what can be spent by the state—program by program and agency by agency—for the coming fiscal year. The revenue bill is subject to close scrutiny, as well, because of the dramatic impact simple changes in revenue codes can have on the activities of concerned individuals and groups.

The appropriations bill is also the object of attention because the personal future and well-being of so many are dependent on it. The livelihood of administrators depends on successfully defending or advancing the interests of their particular program (Clynch and Lauth 1991). Administrators believe in what they are doing, and they have a professional stake in claiming the importance of the goods or services that they deliver. And, because the number, size, and benefits of state government activities have grown during the past several decades, legislators and their constituents have come to value what the state provides (Chubb 1985). One of the inevitable consequences of the growth of state government has been, then, the rise of groups that are attentive to changing government activities. These interest groups pressure legislatures and governors to avert cuts (in their worst case) and (better yet) to increase appropriations in beneficial programs (Winters 1980).

An important lesson is that the appropriations power is not simply divided between the governor and legislature; it is shared. Officials rarely have the power to act independently without the approval or consideration of the interests of other individuals or institutions. The amount of sharing of power varies among the states, however. Some states, such as Illinois and California, have powerful governors with strong powers of initiation, approval, and change. Other states, such as Florida, Mississippi, and South Carolina, have powerful legislatures that

5. This section contains a general description of the appropriations process in state governments. The discussion is of practices in those states with which I am most familiar.

are active in budget formulation and action. Since the mid-1970s, legislative involvement and influence in budgeting have increased as a result of the rising professionalism of those bodies (Squires 1992).

Preparing the Administrative Budget. In a typical budget year, six (or more) months before the legislature considers the budget and a year before the final budget takes effect, the orders go out from the governor's office to begin preparing the *administrative budget.* The process begins at the front lines of each agency as officials document what is needed to provide the current level of goods and services for which they are responsible. This *current-services budget* level is the level calculated to deliver what the legislature has already ordered the agency to provide by law. The current-services budget is also supported by all of the work and analysis that went into the current year's appropriation as the *baseline budget.* The current-services budget differs from the baseline budget in at least two ways. First, the costs of providing the same level of services will move upward incrementally because of changes in wages and salaries paid to government employees and because of upward (usually) changes in the cost of goods and services required for executing the policy as set out by law. Second, the demand for the government good or service may have changed for the forthcoming year. For example, if there is a downturn in the economy, the Department of Welfare (or its equivalent) will ask for more money to handle the greater expected demand for welfare assistance.

The head of the department or his or her budgetary staff collects the requests from lower-level administrators of agencies and assembles them as a draft of the department budget. This budget can be thought of as the administrators' and department heads' summation of the current-services budget, that is, the current year's budget adjusted by changes in costs and expected demand. Administrators are at the same time asking their departmental colleagues about new initiatives and programs that will likely catch the governor's or legislators' eyes as politically feasible and desirable (see Wildavsky 1980, chap. 3). We can speculate on what might determine how expansionary an administrator could be. In times of economic growth, bureaucrats in states with responsive revenue systems generate forceful efforts in claiming their "fair share" of the booming revenues. States with consistently growing revenues may attract individuals who could be termed *bureaucratic entrepreneurs,* individuals who are highly ambitious and who recognize that the fastest route to personal advancement in their chosen fields is to build programs that become nationally noteworthy among their peers (Winters 1980). Yet, the constraints concerning precisely how much to request are high on departmental officials. In states where there is a balanced budget requirement, all participants have to recognize that in the end expenditures cannot exceed revenues; that their preferences for larger budgets must have a limit. Administrators realize that it makes little sense to request an increase greatly in excess of the expected change in total revenues; bureaucrats are sensitive to the need for "political credibility" (Wildavsky 1980).

Each department's budget, however, is calculated in the absence of knowledge of what other departments are doing. Given poor information, it is in the self-interest of each department head to scrutinize closely what new initiatives might be attractive in light of the interests of the governor and legislators. This scrutiny is also in the self-interest of governors and legislators who rely on administrators to inform them of possible programmatic opportunities. Nevertheless, all elected officials realize that the information that agency officials provide is biased in favor of the case for continued or greater appropriations for their program.

The vertical arrangement also affects bureaucratic budgetary behavior. Some agency officials may gain an advantage in their efforts to shape their budget by exploiting federal aid matching requirements. As noted in Chapter 2, the federal government matches state efforts in a variety of ways, from a match of dollar for dollar to a match of nine dollars of federal aid for one dollar of state appropriations. The bureaucrat who can enroll a larger federal match has an advantage in budgetary negotiations with governors and legislators. There are also across-state variations in acquiring federal aid. Some states have aggressively sought such aid. Other states have been more suspicious of federal entanglements in state policy making, fearing the strings that may accompany federal aid in the form of eventually expensive federal mandates.

Preparing the Executive Budget. In the fall, several months before the legislature gathers for the new year, the governor and his or her budgetary staff begin to scrutinize the budget requests of department heads and their agencies. In many states, formal representations of the budget requests of department heads are made either to the governor or his or her budget staff and advisers. Much time is devoted to the budget because it is a key indicator of gubernatorial priorities and a signal to electoral supporters of the delivery of commitments. Ordinarily, the amounts in the executive budget are smaller than what was asked for by agency and department officials. Governors, like presidents, believe that agencies pad their budgets with requests that are not necessary and that agencies engage in acquisitive behavior (Thompson 1987).

When the budgets of states are examined closely, it appears that new administrations make few significant changes in them (Lowery, Konda, and Garand 1984). The political value of the current programs leads governors, even those who may be hostile to particular programs, to decide that it is not worth the political effort to reduce or abolish the programs. Statutory commitments mandating the outlays of moneys double the difficulties of legislative alteration—both the statute and the budget have to be changed. In addition, budgets are fixed because of strings associated with federal matching aid; because of the political commitments that legislators have made to various programs; and because new governors often get elected in times of economic distress, precisely when the demand for government assistance is the greatest. Basically, newly elected governors find fixed budgets that they can change only incrementally because the political consequences of change are too costly. New endeavors, they often find, must be financed out of new taxing initiatives.

Profound changes, however, do sometimes occur in taxing and spending policies following elections, as demonstrated by the election in 1990 of the Independent candidate Lowell Weicker in Connecticut and the election in 1993 of the Republican Christine Todd Whitman in New Jersey. Whitman, who succeeded Governor Florio, campaigned on the basis of rolling back the Florio tax increases. She interpreted her victory as a mandate for shrinking New Jersey's spending, which she and the Republican legislature immediately began doing. Whitman is discovering, however, that it is more difficult than anticipated to alter spending and taxing in New Jersey, even though significant changes have already occurred.

The Revenue Bill. A companion bill to the appropriations bill sets out changes in the tax and revenue code required to balance the state's budget. Revenue bills follow appropriations bills because what the state needs in revenue is determined by the appropriations act. This act also establishes the bounds of what the state can expect in some revenue streams—for example, what can be expected in federal aid is often determined by how much is appropriated as the state's share. As the legislative session unfolds, the governor, the executive budgetary staff, and the legislative revenue committees have three crucial pieces of information before them. First, there are increasingly finer estimates of the revenue requirements that the final budget act entails. A clearer picture appears of the likely shape of the appropriations bill and, therefore, of what changes are required in the tax and revenue code. Second, a somewhat clearer picture is also obtained—an estimate—of what the present array of taxes, charges, and federal aid will produce in the way of revenue. Revenue estimation is part science and part art. Much of what a state can expect depends on the performance of the national, regional, and state economies and on the public's reaction to economic news.

The final set of figures that governors and legislators have available to them is the likely yield of incremental changes to existing taxes and the yield that will accrue as a result of enacting new taxes or increasing present ones. Schedules prepared for the revenue and tax committees will, for example, note that a one cent increase in the sales tax would yield so many millions in new revenue, while the extension of that same tax to the heretofore exempt "all retail grocery food" would yield other tens of millions. The committee might also consider smaller changes, such as an increase of one mill on cigarettes or a new tax on, say, boat moorings and services.

One interesting device used by many states is to combine the appropriations and revenue committees and their bills. By linking the two actions directly, legislators are compelled to justify increased expenditures with the new taxes or revenues needed to finance them (Miller 1994).

Submitting the Budget. The final gubernatorial recommendation to the legislature can probably best be characterized by the calculus that governors will add expenditures up to the point where the vote gain from the next expenditure just balances the vote loss of the new revenue programs needed to finance new programs (Downs 1957, 1960). But what is crucial for the budgetary process is that this electoral calculus—what makes sense politically in terms of taxing and spending—for the governor is not necessarily the same calculus that makes sense for state legislators. They have their own electoral interests, which may or may not be congruent with the governor's. Legislatures in the past two decades have increased their scrutiny of the executive budget and more closely reshaped it for their own ends (Chubb 1985; Clynch and Lauth 1991, esp. chap. 9). State legislators see that their own electoral fortunes are affected by state taxing and spending; the institutional changes described in Chapter 5, such as greatly increased staffing and computerized retrieval of appropriations and revenue data, strengthen them in bargaining with the governor about the budget (Squires 1992).

The Legislature Acts. The legislature receives the budget in the form of enormously detailed information about all government spending, including that of each department, agency, and program. How the legislature handles the budget varies from state to state, but the typical state legislature receives the budget by a letter or formal speech by the governor outlining his or her priorities as set out in the accompanying budget documents. The governor's budget is given a bill number by the leadership of the legislative chambers and is then assigned to the committees responsible for appropriations in the chambers. The house of representatives ordinarily begins earlier action, holding hearings with department heads on their overall views of spending in their departments. Subsequent hearings with agency and program officials are often carried out at a subcommittee level, where the budget is parceled out to numerous smaller subcommittees for even more detailed scrutiny. Seats on committees responsible for appropriations are widely seen by legislators to be prestigious yet time-consuming legislative assignments. These ordinarily attract the more serious and more committed legislators.

For a variety of reasons already discussed, the total of the many departmental and agency requests submitted to the appropriations committees are larger, on the average, than the current year's appropriations. If automatic revenue gains do not match the increases in requests, then the members of the committee begin considering strategies for cutting budgets. One observer has classified such cuts as "soft" as opposed to "hard" (State Policy Research 1990, 9). Favorite soft cuts include freezes in hiring new personnel thereby allowing the number of state employees to decline via normal retirement and resignation, freezes on out-of-state travel for state employees, deferring spending from one fiscal year to the next, and across-the-board cuts. The last strategy is an oft-encountered one because it appears so politically attractive—all share equally in the burden and no specific hard choices of penalizing one program and favoring another have to be made. Harder cuts that are more politically costly are those that entail real penalties for people by layoffs and reduction of personnel and cutting specific benefits and programs.

Efforts are often made to fashion a broad, bipartisan consensus on the budget. Such efforts often fail because of significant party differences in spending and taxing priorities. In the typical state, each subcommittee sends back to the appropriations committee a majority report on its section of the bill (which is usually made up of majority party members), and the majority party on the committee is then charged with reconciling the sum of all subcommittee operations within the revenue constraint. Because each subcommittee often attracts to it members with personal or constituency stakes in its appropriations, the appropriations figures may still be too large, thus entailing further cutting at the full committee level. The appropriations committee reports its bill to the full chamber, where it is voted on and often amended. More frequently, a series of opposing party amendments are dutifully voted down by the majority party, and the bill is sent on to the senate. In some states, in order to promote more regularized procedures, the house votes to bind itself to a particular date for the approved bill to "cross" to the senate.

The senate, with its smaller committees, often operates at a more leisurely pace than the house and without subcommittees. It is continually aware in a general sense of progress in the other chamber, and it continuously refashions its hearings with agency officials in light of developing events in the house. It eventually has the house bill before it, and that bill focuses hearings in the senate on whether and where to depart from the house figures. The senate committee bill is usually in the form of amendments—either increases or decreases—to the house bill. The senate committee must finally come to agreement, an agreement made easier because the house vote settles many issues. Discussion and voting then occur at the floor level, and the final bill is sent to the governor for approval, veto, or some intermediate action.

The Governor Acts. In forty-two states, governors have some form of intermediate item veto, by which they can veto parts of bills, lines, or particular items in a bill. Governors with these powers often take some care in examining the budget bill and alter it in important ways. Several scholars have studied the use of the item veto in the American states in expectation of establishing evidence of its efficacy (Abney and Lauth 1985; Alm and Evers 1991; Berch 1992). The topic is of particular importance because eight of the last twelve presidents have endorsed the idea of a veto power that allows the executive selectively to excise single lines from appropriations bills (Thompson and Boyd 1994, 38). In principle, this ought to be a particularly powerful weapon in the hands of those governors because, as Fisher notes (1985, 7), most state budgets are written in highly specific line item form that spells out spending for the most minute outlay. This is unlike the federal budget, where large items are budgeted in lump sums. The conclusion of the state studies is that having the item veto has a negligible impact on spending in the states. States in which the governor is empowered to burrow into the budget and selectively cut it do not have smaller budgets than states with less-empowered governors. Alm and Evers (1991), confirming other studies, did note a very small effect—about 1 percent smaller than expected budget—when the governor was of one party and the legislature of the other.

The findings that the governor's item veto had no overall impact and that it had only a small effect under divided control of government may be explainable by the same causal process—the item veto sets up a situation in which governors and legislatures engage in sophisticated political games. For example, if the legislature prefers a larger amount of spending for an item than it knows the governor wishes, then it will pad, or increase, the amount it desires to allot to an item in an effort to preserve it. One sophisticated method of padding is to combine line items known to be favored by the governor with line items that are not favored, which usually will mean that both items are preserved. Under the condition of divided partisan control of the government the stakes and sophistication of the games increase. Legislatures heighten their efforts to protect favored programs, while governors subject the budget to even greater scrutiny and broader excision, thereby reducing slightly the overall budget. Gamesmanship reached new heights when Governor Tommy Thompson of Wisconsin "vetoed words, including 'shalt' and 'not,' punctuation such as commas and periods, and 'then cobbled together the surviving words into whole new sentences—and new law'" (quoted in Beyle 1994, 44).

Fiscal Caps on State Spending and Taxing

Voters have a chance to register their reactions to particular budgets when legislators and governors appear before them as candidates for reelection. In many states that power is enhanced by the referendum process, in which voters can take some of the budgetary powers into their own hands.[6] Since 1978, when the first great tax revolt proposition was voted in California, states and localities across the country have adopted devices that endeavor to constrain the size of their governments. The assessment of the effect of various tax limitation devices on state taxing and spending is scarcely more favorable than the assessment of the item veto. A cap on the size of the budget in relation to the size of the state economy or total personal income has been favored by state electorates. Fiscal "caps are explicitly designed to restrict public sector size to some proportion of the size of the total economy" by the conservative political movement, which desires to constrain "excessive government growth" (Cox and Lowery 1990, 492). In an interesting comparison of three states that had caps of varying degrees of porosity with three other states, matched in terms of region, population size, and wealth, that had no fiscal caps, Cox and Lowery found no differences between the capped and uncapped states in various measures of taxing and spending (1990, 507). The most likely interpretation of this finding is that all states' economies grew fast enough to allow for comparable government growth in the capped and uncapped states. Still, the caps do constitutionally exist in many states, and it is possible that a prolonged decline in statewide personal income would force the budget up to the level of the cap.

6. The important story of voter referendums on taxing and spending propositions is ably told in the fifth edition of this book (see Hansen 1990). Also, see Sears and Citrin (1985); Lowery and Sigelman (1981).

Emulation and Competition. Cox and Lowery (1990) mention in passing a more general process at work in the states that dampens rises in tax revenues—a horizontal causal process. While legislators in the states that have caps may be reluctant to increase revenues rapidly and thereby approach the limit of the cap, the restraint may constrain legislators in the nearby states that have no caps. After Tennessee adopted its cap, legislators in uncapped Kentucky may have learned two lessons. First, constraint in tax increases now may reduce public pressure for imposing a cap in Kentucky. And second, constraint in revenue and tax rises may prevent Kentucky's losing businesses and other mobile residents to Tennessee.

The Economy—the 1990–1991 Recession and Taxing and Spending. State political leaders have little control over the timing of economic booms or recessions that affect their states; they are subject to economic decisions made in Washington and elsewhere. Yet, they must come to grips with the effects of recessions, namely, diminishing revenue from sales taxes and from personal and corporate income taxes and increased demand for state services from the jobless or disadvantaged. One response, as we noted, was to diversify revenue sources so as to reduce the effects of economic fluctuations. A second strategy is to be "risk-averse." To do that, state legislators and governors must make special efforts to resist the pleas of special interests for benefits because they may not always be able to finance those benefits. State political leaders have generally become more cautious in yielding to entreaties for help because historical experience suggests unpredictable variability in economic booms and recessions.

The economic recession from early 1990 to early 1991 illustrates the variable effect of recessions across the states. For the country as a whole, the year-long recession saw a loss of about 1 percent in employment. States in the West South Central region, such as Oklahoma and Arkansas, saw the least effect of the recession, averaging a 1 percent gain in employment, whereas the New England states averaged a 4.6 percent loss of employment. If the loss of jobs is tracked by region from recession to recession over the past two decades, only the East North Central great industrial states, such as Illinois, Indiana, Michigan, Ohio, and Wisconsin, seem to be uniquely vulnerable to economic downturns. Yet, in the 1990–1991 recession, these states' economies performed just about as well as the nation as a whole (Brauer 1993, table 2).

Even within regions, there is great variability. Although the Pacific Coast states did about as well as the nation during the recession of the early 1990s, California has grappled with as many unpredictable social and economic calamities as have hit any state in recent decades. A series of earthquakes, mud slides, and rainstorms has damaged buildings, highways, and public facilities and has resulted in both a loss of revenue from diminished economic activity and a need for increased public outlays to rebuild the state's infrastructure. Further, the nation's economic troubles in the early 1990s hit California the hardest of all the states. California had typically added hundreds of thousands of jobs per year to its economic rolls, but the depression that hit this state cost it more than 700,000 jobs.

Exacerbating these difficulties, the growth in population caused by illegal immigrants from Mexico and other Central American countries added to the demand for public services (Barone 1994). The cumulative effect of the immigration was to create great uncertainty among political leaders about how much revenue was needed or might be expected so as to satisfy increasingly difficult-to-predict public demands for government services.

Variable economic performance leaves states unpredictably vulnerable to forces beyond their control, which leads them to behave in a risk-averse, conservative fashion.

FUTURE DIRECTIONS

In this chapter I have examined the politics of taxing and spending, bearing in mind the question, How and why did state and local governments grow at the rates that they have in the modern era? The question is particularly relevant in the 1990s because of evidence of increasing voter disenchantment with financing the current production of government goods and services at the national, state, and local levels. The very significant gains that the Republican party made in the 1994 congressional races were mirrored in impressive gains also in governors' races and in state legislative races. These gains point toward the likelihood of a nationwide political focus on taxing and spending.

The evidence concerning government growth is unambiguous. We have ever-so-slowly but significantly enlarged government at all levels. Citizens and voters have contributed to this growth by their demands for government goods and services. Also contributing to this growth are the indirect, tentative links between taxing and instruments of voter control. Elections are ordinarily the means by which voters control elected officials, but the links between taxing and voter disapproval in this modern era are imperfect and indirect. We may not like our taxes, but we have not in the past disliked our legislators and our governors so much that we punished them directly at the polls when they taxed. And there is a certain logic to the weak electoral link. Only a handful of elected officials ever put themselves into the position of having their election become a referendum on a tax. Elected officials present more facets in their appeals to voters, and it is the complexity and diversity of determinants of voter choice that attenuates the link between taxing and voting. Nevertheless, the pressures of cutting spending and taxes appear inexorable.

There is a complementary argument, however, that voters can be presented with unambiguous choices of cutting taxes in referendums; California's Proposition 13 and the various tax caps installed by referendum in many states are examples. When faced with such direct and simple choices, voters often vote for direct tax cuts—self-interest is direct and straightforward (Sears and Citrin 1985). When admonitions from politicians such as "Vote for this proposition and watch your property taxes get cut by two-thirds" are commonly heard, it is difficult for voters to resist. What is much more difficult to achieve, however, is agreement on exactly which government program or service would get cut if the proposition passes. In fact, no such agreement could ever be reached among voters on a list of cuts. Each of us would list the programs that we want untouched, and each voter's list would be slightly different from that of the next person; no agreement on spending cuts would ever be reached by a direct voting process.

The ordinary institutions of representative government in America are structured so as to make those kinds of decisions—reconciling the demands of those seeking government goods and services with the interests of those seeking to minimize the costs of government. Ultimately, if control of government taxing and spending is to occur, it will have to be by means of these representative institutions—the governors and legislatures. The control has been ragged and inefficient to this point, but we may be entering an era of heightened voter awareness of the limits of what government can do and heightened sensitivity to the costs of government action. Politicians, because of their vote-seeking natures, are sensitive to the voters' signals. In the coming years, better means of control on government spending probably will be found by elected officials in the American states.

There is impressive rival evidence that, irrespective of voter pressures to cut taxes, budgets of the American states will continue to grow and possibly accelerate. Powerful voter pressure exists to increase spending on some items—corrections, transportation, and economic development programs, for example. Still other programs may well be forced on states; several states are under state supreme court orders to equalize per pupil educational expenditures by reducing reliance on the local property tax. States continue to rely on aid from the federal government for a large part of their revenue. Many states have exploited a loophole (now slowly closing) in the federal Medicaid statute to help balance their budget on non-Medicaid items, thereby growing even more dependent on federal largesse. Yet all of the signals emanating from Washington, D.C., suggest diminishing federal support. And if a balanced federal budget is ever achieved, one of the easiest places to cut the federal budget is in aid to the states. Cutting federal aid for state programs in welfare, highways, environmental protection, and law and corrections may reduce state revenues for such programs, but it will not diminish citizen interest in and pressures for program continuity. The next several years promise to be a particularly interesting period in the American federal system as states' political leaders wrestle with these dilemmas of conflicting interests of taxing and spending.

REFERENCES

Abney, Glenn, and Thomas Lauth. 1985. "The Line Item Veto in the States." *Public Administration Review* 45:372–377.

Alm, James, and Mark Evers. 1991. "The Item Veto and Government Expenditure." *Public Choice* 68:1–15.

Barone, Michael. 1994. *The Almanac of American Politics*. Washington, D.C.: National Journal.

Baumol, William. 1967. "Macroeconomics of Unbalanced Growth: The Anatomy of Urban Crisis." *American Economic Review* 62:415–426.

Berch, Neil. 1992. "The Line Item Veto in the States: An Analysis of the Effects over Time." *Social Science Journal* 29:335–346.

Berry, Frances Stokes, and William D. Berry. 1992. "Tax Innovation in the States: Capitalizing on Political Opportunity." *American Journal of Political Science* 36:715–742.

Berry, William, and David Lowery. 1987. *Understanding United States Government Growth: An Empirical Analysis of the Postwar Era*. New York: Praeger.

Beyle, Thad 1994. "The Governors—1992–1993," *The Book of the States, 1994–95*. Lexington, Ky.: Council of State Governments.

———, ed. 1992. *Governors and Hard Times*. Washington, D.C.: CQ Press.

Black, Chris. 1990. "The Sales Tax Revisited: Lessons from 1965." *Boston Sunday Globe,* May 27.

Borcherding, Thomas. 1985. "The Causes of Government Expenditure Growth." *Journal of Public Economics* 28:359–382.

Bowler, Shaun, and Todd Donovan. 1995. "Popular Responsiveness to Taxation." *Political Research Quarterly* 48:1.

Brace, Paul. 1994. "Choice and Consequence: The Politics and Economics of Tax Change in the American States." Department of Political Science, Florida State University, Tallahassee, Fla.

Brauer, David. 1993. "A Historical Perspective on the 1989–1992 Slow Growth Period." *Quarterly Review* (Federal Reserve Bank of New York), Summer, 1–14.

Chubb, John. 1985. "The Political Economy of Federalism." *American Political Science Review* 79:994–1015.

Citizens for Tax Justice. 1991. *A Far Cry from Fair*. Washington, D.C.: Citizens for Tax Justice.

Clines, Francis X. "Gambling, Pariah No More, Is Booming across America." *New York Times,* December 5.

Clynch, Edward J., and Thomas P. Lauth, eds. 1991. *Governors, Legislatures, and Budgets: Diversity across the American States*. Westport, Conn.: Greenwood Press.

Cox, James, and David Lowery. 1990. "The Impact of the Tax Revolt Era: State Fiscal Caps." *Social Science Quarterly* 71:492–509.

Crocker, Royce. 1981. "Federal Government Spending and Public Opinion." *Public Budgeting and Finance* 1:25–35.

CSG (Council of State Governments). 1992. *The Book of the States, 1992–93*. Lexington, Ky.: Council of State Governments.

Downs, Anthony. 1957. *An Economic Theory of Democracy*. New York: Harper and Brothers.

———. 1960. "Why the Government Budget Is Too Small in a Democracy." *World Politics* 12:541–563.

Duncombe, William. 1992. "Economic Change and the Evolving State Tax Structure: The Case of the Sales Tax." *National Tax Journal* 45:299–313.

Dye, Richard, and Therese J. McGuire. 1991. "Growth and Variability of State Individual Income and General Sales Taxes." *National Tax Journal* 44:55–66.

Dye, Thomas. 1966. *Politics, Economics, and the Public: Policy Outcomes in the American States*. Chicago: Rand McNally.

Economic Report of the President. 1994. Washington, D.C.: U.S. Government Printing Office.

Eismeier, Theodore. 1979. "Budgets and Ballots: The Political Consequences of Fiscal Choice." In *Public Policy and Public Choice,* edited by D. Rae and T. Eismeier. Beverly Hills: Sage Publications.

———. 1983. "Votes and Taxes: The Political Economy of the American Governorship." *Polity* 15:368–379.

Erikson, Robert S., Gerald C. Wright, and John P. McIver. 1993. *Statehouse Democracy: Public Opinion and Policy in the American States*. New York: Cambridge University Press.

Feder, Barnaby. 1993. "In a Bid for Casino, Chicago Comes Up with Snake-Eyes." *New York Times,* October 3.

Federation of Tax Administrators. 1993. *Tax Administrators News*. Washington, D.C.: U.S. Bureau of the Census.

Fisher, Louis. 1985. "The Item Veto: The Risks of Emulating the States." Presented at the annual meeting of the American Political Science Association. New Orleans, La., August 29–September 1.

Fisher, Ronald. 1988. *State and Local Public Finance.* Glenview, Ill.: Scott, Foresman.

Garand, James C. 1985. "Partisan Change and Shifting Expenditure Priorities in the American States, 1945–1978." *American Politics Quarterly* 14:355–391.

Gold, Howard J. 1994. "Third Party Voting in Presidential Elections: A Study of Perot, Anderson, and Wallace." Presented at the annual meeting of the American Political Science Association. New York, September 1–4.

Hansen, Susan. 1983. *The Politics of Taxation: Revenue without Representation.* New York: Praeger.

———. 1990. "The Politics of State Taxing and Spending." In *Politics in the American States,* edited by Virginia Gray, Herbert Jacob, and Robert B. Albritton. Glenview, Ill.: Scott, Foresman/Little, Brown.

Johnson, Kirk. 1993. "Tribal Rights: Refining the Law of Recognition." *New York Times,* October 17.

Judson, George. 1994. "Some Indians See a Gamble with Future in Casinos." *New York Times,* May 15.

Kone, Susan, and Richard Winters. 1993. "Taxes and Voting: Electoral Retribution in the American States." *Journal of Politics* 55:22–40.

Larkey, Patrick D., Chandler Stolp, and Mark Winer. 1981. "Theorizing about the Growth of Government: A Research Assessment." *Journal of Public Policy* 1:157–220.

Lowery, David, Thomas Konda, and James Garand. 1984. "Spending in the States: A Test of Six Models." *Western Political Quarterly* 37:48–66.

Lowery, David, and Lee Sigelman. 1981. "Understanding the Tax Revolt: An Assessment of Eight Explanations." *American Political Science Review* 75:963–974.

Mikesell, John. 1978. "Election Periods and State Policy Cycles." *Public Choice* 33:99–106.

———. 1992. "State Sales Tax Policy in a Changing Economy: Balancing Political and Economic Logic against Revenue Needs." *Public Budgeting and Finance* 12:83–91.

Miller, Penny. 1994. *Kentucky Politics and Government.* Lincoln: University of Nebraska Press.

Niemi, Richard, H. Stanley, and R. Vogel. 1994. "State Economies and State Taxes: Do Voters Hold Governors Accountable?" University of Rochester, New York.

Olson, Mancur. 1973. "Evaluating Performance in the Public Sector." In *The Measurement of Economic and Social Performance,* edited by Milton Moss. New York: National Bureau of Economic Research.

Oreskes, Michael. 1988. "The Republicans in New Orleans: The People in the Party." *New York Times,* August 14.

Plotnick, Robert D., and Richard F. Winters. 1985. "A Politico-Economic Theory of Redistribution." *American Political Science Review* 79:458–473.

———. 1990. "Party, Political Liberalism, and Redistribution: An Application to the American States." *American Politics Quarterly* 18:430–458.

Pomper, Gerald. 1968. *Elections in America.* New York: Dodd, Mead.

Riker, William H. 1986. *The Art of Political Manipulation.* New Haven: Yale University Press.

Sabato, Larry. 1978. *Goodbye to Good-time Charlie.* Lexington, Mass.: Lexington Books.

Sears, David O., and Jack Citrin. 1985. *Tax Revolt: Something for Nothing in California.* Cambridge: Harvard University Press.

Squire, Peverill. 1992. "Theory of Legislative Institutionalization and the California Assembly." *Journal of Politics* 54:1026–1054.

State Policy Research. 1990. "The Fiscal Crisis." *State Policy Reports.* Alexandria, Va.: State Policy Research.

Tax Foundation. 1992. *Facts and Figures on Government Finance.* New York: Tax Foundation.

Thompson, Joel. 1987. "Agency Requests, Gubernatorial Support, and Budget Success in State Legislatures Revisited." *Journal of Politics* 49:756–779.

Thompson, Pat, and S. R. Boyd. 1994. "Use of the Item Veto in Texas, 1940–1990." *Social Science Quarterly* 26:38–45.

U.S. Bureau of the Census. 1948. *Statistical Abstract of the United States 1948.* Washington, D.C.: U.S. Department of Commerce, Bureau of the Census.

———. 1973. *Statistical Abstract of the United States, 1973.* Washington, D.C.: U.S. Department of Commerce, Bureau of the Census.

———. 1975. *Historical Statistics of the U.S.: Colonial Times to 1970.* Washington, D.C.: U.S. Government Printing Office.

———. 1993. *Statistical Abstract of the United States 1993.* Washington, D.C.: U.S. Department of Commerce, Bureau of the Census.

————. Various years. *Statistical Abstract of the United States.* Washington, D.C.: U.S. Department of Commerce, Bureau of the Census.

Wildavsky, Aaron. 1980. *The New Politics of the Budgetary Process.* Glenview, Ill.: Scott, Foresman.

Winters, Richard. 1980. "Political Choice and Expenditure Change." *Polity* 12:598–622.

————. 1990. ""Forget All about That 'Read My Lips' Stuff, OK!"—Gubernatorial Election and Re-election Strategies in the Face of New Tax Programs, 1957–1985." Presented at the annual meeting of the American Political Science Association. San Francisco, August 30–September 2.

SUGGESTED READINGS

Clynch, Edward J., and Thomas P. Lauth, eds. *Governors, Legislatures, and Budgets: Diversity across the American States.* Westport, Conn.: Greenwood Press, 1991. A chapter-by-chapter survey of budgeting politics in thirteen states.

Fisher, Ronald C. *State and Local Public Finance.* Glenview, Ill.: Scott, Foresman, 1988. The standard public finance textbook presents the economist's view of taxing and spending in American state governments.

Hansen, Susan B. *The Politics of Taxation: Revenue without Representation.* New York: Praeger, 1983. The most comprehensive and interesting political science account of taxation in state politics.

Rubin, Irene. *The Politics of Public Budgeting: Getting and Spending, Borrowing and Balancing.* Chatham, N.J.: Chatham House, 1990. A very readable survey of budgeting in American local, state, and federal governments.

Wildavsky, Aaron. *The New Politics of the Budgetary Process.* 2d ed. New York: HarperCollins, 1992. Although this is a book about the federal government, it remains the classic account of the politics of budgeting.

CHAPTER 10

 Crime and Punishment

WESLEY G. SKOGAN

The criminal justice policies of the American states have been shaped by the nature of the crime problem; the division of responsibility among federal, state, and local governments for dealing with crime; and changing views of what we ought to do concerning crime and criminals. In the first section of this chapter, I describe the crime problems facing the states and explore the factors that differentiate high-crime from low-crime areas. I also describe some of the main features of state criminal justice systems and how much they cost. Most of the money is spent by cities. They are responsible for the police, which absorb the lion's share of the overall budget for criminal justice. Courts are also a significant expense item, and responsibility for them is shared by municipalities, counties, and the states. The second-largest slice of the criminal justice budget is devoted to prisons and jails, and the former are the responsibility of state governments. The focus in most of this chapter is on state policies and practices with regard to filling those prisons and jails—the kinds of sentences outlined in the states' criminal codes, the number of offenders they hold in custody, the construction and operation of prisons, and how the states have responded to rising crime rates since the 1960s. In the final sections of this chapter, I examine how these policies have in turn created new problems for states and their taxpayers, including massive overcrowding and pressure to build many new prisons.

TRENDS IN CRIME

In 1960, a little more than 285,000 violent crimes and about 900,000 burglaries were reported to the nation's police. That year there were about 190,000 inmates in state prisons across the country. These numbers had changed only a little since shortly after the end of World War II. A decade later, following the onset of an upward spiral in crime that haunts the nation to this day, the Federal Bureau of Investigation (FBI) recorded more than 2 million burglaries, and more than 700,000 violent crimes. By 1992, about 2 million violent crimes and almost 3 million burglaries were reported to the police. At the end of 1993 almost 950,000 people were locked in prison. To be sure, the population of the nation had increased over this period. Between 1960 and 1992, the U.S. population grew by 40 percent. But during the same time violent crime went up 600 percent, and the number of prison inmates had increased 400 percent.[1]

These were large increases. Both the level of crime and the rate of increase in crime and imprisonment has been higher in the United States than in any other industrial country (or for that matter, in any country that keeps reasonable crime statistics). Given the structure of American government, it was mostly up to the cities and states to do something about it.

As large as these numbers were, they also were far from a complete accounting of crime. We know from interviews with victims that a significant percentage of crimes are never reported to the police and remain uninvestigated. In fact, surveys by the Census Bureau point to about twice as much individual robbery and residential burglary as can be found in police statistics. (For a description of these surveys, see U.S. Department of Justice 1994a). However, the workload of the criminal justice system is made up of the crimes that are reported to the police, the arrests that they make, and the problems that face crime victims.

The crime problem is not the same everywhere. Throughout the world, levels of crime are highest in large cities and lowest in rural areas, while the suburbs and smaller cities stand in between; residents of the countryside typically report one-half as much violent crime and two-thirds the rate of property crime as do the inhabitants of big cities. Not surprisingly, crime rates are therefore highest in the metropolitan states—those whose populations are concentrated in and around big cities. The three least metropolitan states—Idaho, Montana, and Vermont—lie among the bottom 20 percent of states in regard to violent crime. In contrast, California, Massachusetts, and New Jersey are the most urbanized states, and in 1992 their crime rate was, on average, 450 percent higher than the three least metropolitan states. Social and economic factors that go along with metropolitanism naturally are related to crime rates as well. These include such factors as population density and household crowding, concentrations of immigrants, and larger numbers of renters than home owners. Data on metropolitanism and the total number of FBI index crimes (roughly, the most serious and

1. All the statistics on reported crime and arrests in this chapter come from yearly editions of the FBI's *Uniform Crime Reports for the United States.*

Table 10-1 Crime Rates and State Demography

State	Index crime 1992 (no.)*	Violent crime 1992 (no.)*	Property crime 1992 (no.)*	Metropolitan crime rate 1990 (%)	Pop. change 1980–1990 (%)	Single-parent families 1990 (%)
Alabama	5,268	872	4,396	67	4	14
Alaska	5,570	661	4,909	41	37	15
Arizona	7,029	671	6,358	85	35	14
Arkansas	4,762	577	4,185	44	3	13
California	6,680	1,120	5,560	97	26	15
Colorado	5,959	579	5,380	82	14	13
Connecticut	5,053	495	4,558	96	6	11
Delaware	4,849	621	4,227	83	12	13
Florida	8,358	1,207	7,151	93	33	12
Georgia	6,405	733	5,672	67	19	15
Hawaii	6,112	258	5,854	76	15	11
Idaho	3,996	281	3,715	29	7	11
Illinois	5,765	977	4,788	84	0	13
Indiana	4,687	509	4,178	72	1	12
Iowa	3,957	278	3,679	43	−5	10
Kansas	5,320	511	4,809	54	5	11
Kentucky	3,324	536	2,788	48	1	12
Louisiana	6,547	985	5,562	74	0	18
Maine	3,524	131	3,393	36	9	12
Maryland	6,225	1,000	5,225	93	13	14
Massachusetts	5,003	779	4,224	96	5	12
Michigan	5,611	770	4,841	83	0	15
Minnesota	4,591	338	4,253	69	7	10
Mississippi	4,283	412	3,871	30	2	18
Missouri	5,097	740	4,357	68	4	12
Montana	4,596	170	4,426	24	2	12
Nebraska	4,324	349	3,975	50	1	10
Nevada	6,204	697	5,507	84	50	14
New Hampshire	3,081	126	2,955	59	21	10
New Jersey	5,064	626	4,439	100	5	12
New Mexico	6,434	935	5,499	56	16	16
New York	5,858	1,122	4,736	92	3	15
North Carolina	5,802	681	5,121	65	13	13
North Dakota	2,903	83	2,820	40	−2	9
Ohio	4,666	526	4,140	81	1	13
Oklahoma	5,432	623	4,809	59	4	12
Oregon	5,821	510	5,311	70	8	12
Pennsylvania	3,393	427	2,966	85	0	11
Rhode Island	4,578	395	4,184	94	6	12
South Carolina	5,893	945	4,949	70	12	15
South Dakota	2,999	195	2,804	32	1	10
Tennessee	5,136	746	4,390	66	6	13
Texas	7,058	806	6,252	83	19	14
Utah	5,659	291	5,368	78	18	11
Vermont	3,410	110	3,301	27	10	12
Virginia	4,299	375	3,924	77	16	12
Washington	6,173	535	5,638	83	18	13
West Virginia	2,610	212	2,398	42	−8	11
Wisconsin	4,319	276	4,043	68	4	12
Wyoming	4,575	320	4,256	30	−3	12

SOURCES: U.S. Bureau of the Census 1993; U.S. Department of Justice, Federal Bureau of Investigation 1993.
* Per 100,000 population.

thoroughly recorded offenses) that were reported to the police in each state are presented in Table 10-1.

Another factor that is strongly associated with high levels of crime is population and other growth. States growing in population and jobs report more property crime but not more violent crime. Between 1980 and 1990, the states with the highest rates of growth were Alaska, Arizona, California, Florida, and Nevada; they showed double-digit expansion on several measures, including population (Table 10-1). Four of these five states also are among the top nine states in regard to property crime, and in 1992, Florida had the highest property and total crime rate of any state in the nation. Arizona, which ranked third in growth during the decade from 1980 to 1990 reported the second highest property crime rate of any state and ranked third on the combined property and violence list. The lowest-growth states were Iowa, North Dakota, West Virginia, and Wyoming. Their average property crime rate stood at about half that of the average for the highest-growth states. The most crime-prone low-growth states were Illinois, Louisiana, and Michigan; their population growth rate was zero between 1980 and 1990, yet their average property crime rate stood above that for the five highest-growth states. This discrepancy is explained in part by their high level of metropolitanism.

A third factor associated with crime is economic disadvantage. At the state level, disadvantage is strongly linked to both property and (especially) violent crime. States with high concentrations of single-parent families (which is reported in Table 10-1), high levels of infant mortality, many adults who never graduated from high school, and large African-American populations, tend to report higher levels of homicide, assault, robbery, auto theft, and burglary. The states with the most highly disadvantaged populations in 1990 included Louisiana, Michigan, Mississippi, New Mexico, and New York. Together their violent crime index averaged 3.6 times the average rate for the states with the least disadvantaged populations (Iowa, Minnesota, Nebraska, New Hampshire, and North Dakota).

Nevertheless, property crime is actually linked to many measures of *advantage;* burglary and theft rates are higher in states with more college-educated adults and higher individual incomes. These kinds of people are concentrated in the metropolitan states, which enjoy a disproportionate share of higher-paying jobs. Persons of Hispanic origin are overconcentrated in states that are high in both property and violent crime, but those are also growth states, where measures of both affluence (people are attracted by well-paying jobs) and other crime-related factors (for example, the divorce rate) are high as well.

CRIME AND THE CRIMINAL JUSTICE SYSTEM

Governments face two problems: how to prevent crime and how to respond to it once it occurs. Both are difficult tasks. Most crime prevention probably is not in the hands of the criminal justice system at all. Rather, the crime rate largely is a product of the strength of families, the cohesiveness of neighborhoods, the quality of schools, the availability of jobs, and the extent to which people think they are treated fairly by economic and political institutions. Responding when crime occurs by assisting victims and dealing with offenders, however, is to a great extent the responsibility of the criminal justice system.

In this chapter the focus is on the criminal justice responsibilities of the states. Principally, these responsibilities are to make criminal justice policy and to build and operate state prisons. In addition, the states supervise those who have been released from prison on parole, or who have been found guilty but placed on probation in lieu of serving time in prison. As this chapter will make abundantly clear, these are rapidly changing, controversial, and expensive responsibilities. It is important to recall, however, that the government agencies that deal directly with crime in this country are overwhelmingly local: police and sheriffs, criminal courts, and jails. Even following the passage of the widely debated 1994 crime bill, measured by spending, the federal government is involved in only a fraction of all criminal justice activity.

The most money is spent on police, whose funding is decentralized. About 84 percent of all uniformed police officers and sheriffs are employed by cities and counties; only 9 percent are state police (U.S. Department of Justice 1993b). Policing consumes about 20 percent of city expenditures, a budget share that has doubled in the past forty years. To put this figure in perspective, in 1990 there were about as many police employees as social workers or doctors, more than public health and hospital workers, and more than postal workers (U.S. Bureau of the Census 1993).

Although the number of police officers is large, the increases in their ranks have not kept abreast of crime. The amount of resources committed to crime control (like the number of criminal justice employees per thousand crimes) actually has fallen. Between 1965 and 1995, the number of crimes per police employee for the country as a whole rose by almost 50 percent. In a study of the politics of local justice in ten major cities, Jacob (1984) found that in many of them the share of the budget allocated to the police declined or remained constant while crime rates exploded. In the ten cities, the number of police officers fell in relation to the number of violent crimes by a factor of six, and expenditures declined by a factor of more than two, between 1948 and 1978 (Jacob and Lineberry 1982). This decline was almost unique to policing, as expenditures for many other municipal functions either kept up with or exceeded the growth of their workloads during the same period (Jacob and Swank 1982).

Criminal courts are also an important component of the criminal justice system, and courts in general are discussed in Chapter 7. Criminal courts are, for the most part, a function of county government, although municipal courts and justices of the peace abound and state governments contribute to the funding of some local courts. Many courts and judges hear both criminal and civil cases, so it is difficult to account separately for the resources devoted to each activity. The personnel and expenditures devoted to local prosecutors' and public defenders' offices and to criminal court staff members account for about 20 percent of the total local criminal justice budget. City jails, which hold suspects after arrest and those sentenced for short periods after trial, also are a local expense item.

The criminal court system handles a torrent of cases. In 1993, state and local police made about 14.2 million arrests of all kinds. (Millions of traffic citations were handed out as well, adding somewhat to the workload of those in the system.) While this is a large number of arrests, it is considerably less than the number of crimes that were reported to the police. Most crimes are never solved. This is particularly true in the case of property offenses like burglary, which typically do not involve an eyewitness or any useful clues. Across the United States, police claim to solve about 13 percent of burglaries; this is the official "clearance rate" for burglary. Studies of this process indicate that the real probability of arresting someone for a burglary is more like 5 percent. In contrast, face-to-face crimes like rape and assault, which frequently involve people who know one another, are solved more than 50 percent of the time, and about 65 percent of all murders (which also often involve related parties) lead to an arrest. The limited capacity of the criminal justice system to locate and arrest offenders in the first place should be an important consideration in discussions about how to control crime, although it is often lost from view. One justification for stiff criminal sentences is that they deter others from breaking the law. However, the low chances actually of being caught for many kinds of crime (a low "certainty of punishment") may undermine some of the deterrent value of the severe sentences that are meted out to those few who do fall within the grasp of the law.

Those who are arrested must be dealt with in some fashion or another by the system, with, it is hoped, fairness and some efficiency. Tracking those who enter the criminal justice system to see if they are dealt with fairly and efficiently, however, is difficult. Still, it is obvious that most of the 14.2 million or so who are arrested each year are not dealt with at great length.

Because people are often arrested multiple times in the course of a year, the number of arrests does not equal the number of arrestees. Unlike arrests, which are classified according to standard national definitions, courts account for their workload in diverse and confusing ways (see Eisenstein and Jacob 1974). The definition of what is a serious crime (a *felony,* for which people can be sent to prison) and what is not (which includes *misdemeanors* and traffic offenses, for which people may be fined or jailed for a short time) varies from state to state. Some state courts count and report on cases, which may involve multiple defendants; others publish statistics on indictments, and one individual may be faced with several of those; still others report on defendants. For management and analysis purposes it would be useful to follow arrestees through the criminal justice system to see what happens to them, but it is often impossible to do so. In eight states it is possible to glean some systemwide information on the flow of felony defendants through the process. In those states, about 80 percent of those arrested for a felony were prosecuted, 60 percent were convicted of something (but not necessarily a felony), 40 percent spent some time behind bars, and 10 percent went to prison. The last figure varied according to the crime, ranging from about 50 percent (for those arrested for homicide) to only 4 percent (for assault) (U.S. Department of Justice 1991b).

Organizational factors also cloud the meaning of such seemingly simple factors as the offense charged and the conviction rate. In some places, the police vigorously review their arrests and only pass on to the prosecutor serious cases that can legitimately be prosecuted. In other jurisdictions they pass on to the prosecutor's office virtually everyone they pick up and rely on that office to screen and reclassify cases. Some prosecutors do not do much of that and instead rely on the judge who holds the first hearing, called the preliminary hearing, of a case in court to decide what to do with it. As a result, the fact that there are about 14.2 million arrests, 1.5 million felony cases filed, and 830,000 felony convictions each year does not tell us very much at all.

Detailed national statistics on courts, prisons, and jails can be found in yearly editions of the *Sourcebook of Criminal Justice Statistics,* by the Bureau of Justice Statistics in the U.S. Department of Justice. The only reasonably solid figures on what happens after arrest are based on a sample of local criminal justice agencies that are monitored by the Bureau of Justice Statistics, and even the bureau keeps track only of felony arrests. It reports that in 1990 about 50 percent of the arrested felons who were turned over to prosecutors were convicted of something. Of that group, half were placed on probation. Probation is a form of supervised community living; probationers have been found guilty, but as long as they stay out of further trouble, follow the terms of their release, and report regularly to their probation supervisors, they can serve out their sentences while living at home and keeping their jobs. This is the most common disposition of criminal cases of all kinds; in 1990 more than 2,520,000 persons were on probation.

The remaining half of those convicted felons were incarcerated; about one-quarter each were sent to jail and prison. Whether offenders go to jail or prison largely depends, of course, on their offense: 91 percent of those convicted of murder, 67 percent of those convicted of rape, and 44 percent of those convicted of burglary went to prison.

Another large group of Americans under correctional supervision are parolees. They have been released from prison before the end of their original sentences, usually after state parole boards have reviewed their cases and judged them ready to return to the community. Like those on probation, they must stay out of trouble and report in regularly. In 1990 about 457,000 people were on parole. During the early 1990s about 2.6 percent of all adults in the United States (one in every forty-three) were living under some form of correctional supervision—either probation or parole.

THE COST OF CRIME TO THE STATES

Running this criminal justice system is expensive. Information on state and local finances takes longer than many other statistics to assemble, so discussions about dollars and cents refer to the early 1990s, the most recent years for which expenditure figures were available. All of the expenditure data reported here can be found in the *Sourcebook of Criminal Justice Statistics* and the Census Bureau's yearly *Statistical Abstract of the United States,* unless otherwise noted (U.S. Bureau of the Census, various years). In 1990, government units in the fifty states spent about $64.9 billion on police, judges and criminal court staff, jails and prisons, and other forms of punishment and supervision. This was about $261 for every person in the United States. Of this, about 20 percent went for judicial, prosecution, criminal defense, and other court services; 36 percent went for prisons and jails; and 43 percent went for policing. The federal government spent another $10 billion on criminal justice matters in 1990, spread over roughly the same categories; this brought the burden borne by each U.S. resident to just under $300. To set the total of all criminal justice expenditures in context, it was about 1.7 times the budget of the U.S. Postal Service that year and about 89 percent of what all levels of government spent on hospitals and health care. It was far less (three times less) than what was spent on elementary and secondary education in 1991, but it was not much of an investment in the future.

The current trend is to increase spending. Between 1970 and 1990, state and local spending on the police went up 420 percent and expenditures on punishment and supervision (known, for reasons we shall see shortly, as corrections) went up 978 percent. Of course, the value of the dollar went down during this period, but when these figures are expressed in constant dollars, taking into account the effects of inflation, the increases were about 125 percent for policing and 290 percent for corrections. Police expenditures grew the most during the late 1960s and early 1970s and have now leveled off; spending on corrections grew wildly after the mid-1970s and continues to skyrocket. The increase in total state and local spending on criminal justice was twice the increase in state and local public welfare expenditures during the same period and almost twice the increase in spending for hospitals and health care; only spending for education was up more.

As mentioned earlier, most of the cost of operating the criminal justice system is borne by state and local governments. In 1990 the federal government accounted for only 12 percent of all criminal justice expenditures, the states contributed 38 percent of the total, and local governments (principally cities and counties) 50 percent. Police and sheriffs account for the large local share, but since 1980, it has been the state share that has been growing. The growth in state spending is due to two factors: more states are contributing to the financing of local courts, and there has been a tremendous increase in the cost of constructing and operating state prisons. Prisons are the largest component of state criminal justice spending (60 percent in 1990), and this component is growing the fastest.

Figure 10-1 Index Crime Rate and Criminal Justice Expenditures, 1991

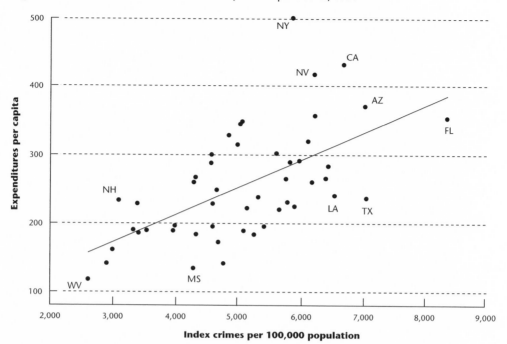

SOURCE: U.S. Department of Justice 1993e.
NOTE: Excludes Alaska.

High crime and arrest rates drive up state spending on criminal justice. In addition, factors that have little to do with crime (such as variations in wages in the public sector) also affect expenditure levels. There is a high correlation between crime rates and the workload of the components of the criminal justice system. Reported crime is the largest element of police workload, and the enormous jump in the crime rate during the late 1960s played an important role in boosting municipal public safety expenditures at that time. Police make arrests, and those in turn constitute the workload for judges, prosecutors, and public defenders. This creates pressure to hire more of them, which has been one of the forces behind increasing state funding of local courts in many jurisdictions. Finally, many arrestees also must be fed and housed in the local jail, which is a significant expense in urban counties.

Figure 10-1 illustrates how the total per capita cost of running the criminal justice system (including all state and local expenditures on police, courts, and corrections) reflects the burden of crime. Both were measured in the same year, 1990. Statistically, the correlation between the two measures was +0.60. It will be remembered that the states spend, on average, $261 per person on criminal justice operations. In 1991, Alaska and New York spent more ($600 and $499 per capita, respectively) than any other state, and more than their crime rates would

Table 10-2 Expenditures, Arrests, Police Employment, and Corrections, 1991

State	Total system expenditures per capita	Number of police per 10,000	Total arrests per 1,000	Rate in jail or prison*	Rate on probation or parole*
Alabama	185	25.5	47	7.3	11.3
Alaska	600	27.6	62	6.6	11.1
Arizona	372	29.6	66	7.9	12.3
Arkansas	142	21.5	72	5.1	11.5
California	432	28.4	54	7.6	17.0
Colorado	290	27.3	75	5.0	13.8
Connecticut	346	28.1	64	4.0	18.5
Delaware	328	28.1	28	6.1	26.8
Florida	354	33.9	51	7.5	21.1
Georgia	266	27.6	59	9.2	33.1
Hawaii	320	28.7	56	2.9	15.8
Idaho	197	25.8	58	5.3	6.6
Illinois	266	34.6	46	4.6	13.4
Indiana	173	23.3	43	4.8	17.7
Iowa	190	21.6	33	3.0	7.8
Kansas	239	26.5	67	4.0	15.4
Kentucky	190	21.0	79	5.1	3.9
Louisiana	241	27.9	66	9.2	13.1
Maine	189	23.8	45	3.9	8.2
Maryland	358	30.4	54	7.1	26.0
Massachusetts	315	28.9	35	3.0	16.6
Michigan	303	23.1	45	6.6	21.3
Minnesota	228	20.5	32	2.2	19.1
Mississippi	134	22.0	65	6.4	6.4
Missouri	189	28.3	58	5.1	13.6
Montana	196	24.2	39	4.1	8.5
Nebraska	183	24.1	47	3.5	13.3
Nevada	417	32.9	77	9.5	11.7
New Hampshire	233	26.6	33	2.9	4.4
New Jersey	349	39.4	49	5.3	16.1
New Mexico	284	29.3	74	5.3	7.0
New York	499	37.1	76	6.1	13.7
North Carolina	231	25.7	73	5.4	17.5
North Dakota	143	21.5	37	2.1	3.8
Ohio	249	25.0	52	5.1	11.3
Oklahoma	195	27.6	46	5.9	12.0
Oregon	288	22.2	53	4.5	21.5
Pennsylvania	229	24.4	38	4.3	16.9
Rhode Island	287	29.7	43	3.1	20.1
South Carolina	224	25.0	36	8.3	14.0
South Dakota	161	22.0	61	3.8	7.6
Tennessee	221	25.0	66	5.4	12.0
Texas	237	26.6	59	7.0	34.4
Utah	220	22.4	65	3.6	6.8
Vermont	185	21.7	16	2.4	14.8
Virginia	260	24.2	62	5.4	6.5
Washington	261	21.7	58	4.1	26.2
West Virginia	118	16.3	35	2.5	4.5
Wisconsin	268	25.8	78	3.7	9.3
Wyoming	300	33.2	59	4.7	10.4

SOURCES: U.S. Bureau of the Census 1993; U.S. Department of Justice 1993e; U.S. Department of Justice, Federal Bureau of Investigation 1993.
*Per 1,000 population.

predict (Table 10-2).[2] These excessive costs are due mostly to Alaska's high cost of living and New York's high public-sector wage level. The next highest-spending state (California) is quite high on the crime index, ranking fourth in crime per 100,000 population. The state with the most crime in relation to population, Florida, was seventh in spending. West Virginia and the two Dakotas had the lowest crime rates and did not spend much on criminal justice. West Virginia and Mississippi spent the least.

A key factor driving state government expenditures on criminal justice is the sentencing policies that legislators have written into criminal codes. State criminal justice agencies do other things, including patrolling the expressways on the lookout for speeders, but the largest percentage of state money goes to building and operating prisons. In 1990, states spent 60 percent of their criminal justice budgets on prisons and jails; 20 percent on their share of court costs, prosecutors, public defenders, and other legal services; and 19 percent on state police.

The cheapest sentencing policies are those that keep offenders under supervision but out of confinement. States that make liberal use of probation get off the easiest; in 1993 it cost about $775 per year to supervise a probationer at a normal level of intensity. More intensive probation supervision (see below) cost $2,700 per year, while electronic monitoring of probationers living at home cost $3,500. States also can save money by making extensive use of parole, releasing offenders from prison but keeping them under supervision for a period of time. In 1993 this cost only about $975 per year for each parolee, with further cost increments for intensive supervision or electronic monitoring. Locking people up is much more expensive. In 1993 it cost about $17,200 to hold someone in a local jail for a year, and to keep them in a minimum security prison that long cost $18,300. To build a maximum security prison cost about twice as much as constructing a jail (which in 1992 cost about $38,000 per bed), because jails have many fewer facilities. Placing someone in a residential care facility located in the community (a halfway house or work-release center) cost somewhat less than in a secure lockup, about $11,000. Expenditures on these alternatives vary from place to place, for factors such as construction and labor costs differ everywhere. However, states that hold more people in jail or send more to prison, or do so for longer periods, find that such a strategy for controlling crime is costly.

By the late 1970s, many had chosen this course. Rising crime rates generated incessant demands that governments "do something" about the problem. State, municipal, and county governments made choices about how to deal with those pressures, and many chose (consciously, or to their later surprise) criminal justice policies that cost more than others would have.

2. Figure 10-1 excludes Alaska; per capita expenditures there were so high that they distorted the picture presented by the other states. The data for Alaska are presented in Table 10-2, along with those for the other forty-nine states.

TRENDS IN STATE SENTENCING POLICY

For most of the twentieth century the American states lived with a policy of ambiguity concerning just how long convicted offenders would remain in prison. This policy was dubbed *indeterminate sentencing;* it was exemplified by states such as California and Washington, where judges could render sentences of "from one day to life." Almost everywhere, for most crimes, state criminal codes specified broad ranges of sentences (such as "2 to 10 years") for common classes of offenses. The actual decisions concerning how long individuals would remain behind bars were left to others, usually state parole boards. While in prison, inmates were to participate in educational and job training programs and to engage in group therapy and individual counseling sessions. The idea was that sentences should be tailored to the responsiveness of individual prison inmates to this treatment and how well behaved they were in custody; when they were "ready" (as determined by the staff and ratified by the parole board, and when their accumulated time off for good behavior was taken into account) they should be let go. The use of the generic term *corrections* to characterize the American system of punishment reflects this therapeutic and rehabilitative model of how the process should work.

The result was that the sentences handed down by judges had little to do with how long offenders actually spent in prison. By the mid-1970s, no one was happy with this system. Liberals attacked the seemingly arbitrary and bureaucratically determined length of sentences, pointed to apparent racial and class disparities in the actual time prisoners served, and objected to some of the treatments (especially those relying heavily on tranquilizers and personality-altering drugs) employed in prisons. Conservatives pointed with alarm to the often large discrepancy between how long prisoners were actually incarcerated and popular perceptions of how tough the system should be on murderers and rapists. They argued that one reason for this discrepancy was excessive leniency (from their point of view) on the part of parole boards and rehabilitation-oriented correctional officials. Indeterminate sentences also limited the ability of prosecutors to deliver on agreements they made in return for guilty pleas. Everyone was cynical about what a *sentence* actually meant.

In addition, a serious intellectual attack was mounted on the rehabilitative ideal that underlay the policy of indeterminate sentencing. A series of academic studies concluded that few if any therapeutic programs had any demonstrable effect on preventing future crimes, once inmates who had participated in them left prison (see Lipton, Martinson, and Wilks 1975; Sechrest, White, and Brown 1979). These findings were (and are to this day) widely heralded as signifying that "rehabilitation doesn't work." A great deal could be said that is critical about the quality of those studies, how their findings were interpreted, and how much they reflected not the principle but the actual operation of rehabilitation programs (which often was not very good). Nevertheless, their impact on the credibility of therapeutically inclined participants in the politics of criminal justice policy was far-reaching. For example, the Omnibus Crime Bill signed by President Clinton in 1994 actually *forbids* the awarding of federal grants supporting college classes for prisoners.

The collapse of consensus among legislators, prison administrators, and knowledgeable outsiders on what prisons were to do took place in a political environment that encouraged many politicians to try to "look tough" on criminals and do something about soaring crime rates. In the political scramble that resulted, the conservatives won some victories; for example, sentences got longer and more threatening. But in addition, some attention was given to the issue of racial disparities in the imposition of criminal sanctions, programs were inaugurated to focus special attention on the most dangerous offenders, attempts were made to limit the almost-invisible discretion exercised at the local level by prosecutors and judges, and new efforts were made to impose penalties more commensurate with the seriousness of particular offenses.

The Trend to Make Sentences Predictably Longer

One of the goals of sentencing reformers during the 1980s was to make sentences more predictable. A complementary goal of many of those involved in the politics of sentencing in both the 1980s and the 1990s was also to make them longer, but the indeterminacy of the existing system was widely perceived to be part of the reason that sentences were too short.

Many changes were made in state criminal codes that were designed to increase the predictability of time served. One strategy was to write determinate sentences into the criminal code by specifying exact sentence lengths for various crimes rather than broad sentencing ranges. Virtually every state now has at least some determinate sentences. A second strategy followed in some states was to abolish parole. In these states there is no administrative process for releasing prisoners before the end of their sentences. This is commonly called a *flat time* sentencing policy. Flat-time policies lend a great deal of predictability to sentences by eliminating the ambiguity associated with possible parole decisions later on. To achieve flat time in Illinois, felons are required to serve at least 85 percent of the sentence imposed by the court. Flat-time states are not necessarily determinate states; for example, Maine eliminated parole but left judges there with wide statutory ranges from which they could choose sentences. In addition, some of the presumed advantages of flat-time sentencing can be achieved by carefully standardizing parole decisions (see below). States can also pursue a mixed strategy. For example, Ohio's criminal statutes call for short, determinate sentences for first-time and property offenders, and longer, indeterminate sentences for repeat and violent offenders. The release of the latter thus remains in the hands of the state parole board.

An additional strategy for increasing the predictability of time served was to eliminate time off for good behavior, so-called good time. *Good time* is the common term for credit that can be accumulated for good behavior within prison. Days of good time are subtracted from prisoners' sentences, making them very valuable indeed. When combined with determinant and flat sentences, eliminating good time would make the period to be served entirely predictable on the day of sentencing. Most states have not adopted the whole package, however. California and North Carolina increased the ability of prisoners to earn good time at the same time that they moved toward determinate sentences. This was a relief to prison administrators in those states, for the ability of prisoners to get out early by accumulating good time (and related credits for working in prison industries) has long been seen as an important mechanism for controlling their behavior behind bars.

The final, and perhaps most difficult, target of state criminal law reformers was that of local judicial and prosecutorial discretion. The reformers were concerned that defendants routinely were being allowed to plead guilty to charges that did not reflect the seriousness of what they had done. In response, some legislatures attempted to impose mandatory sentences for offenses of particular kinds. Perhaps the best known is the Bartley-Fox Gun Control Law, which incorporated the now famous "Use a gun, go to prison" rule. In 1975 the Massachusetts legislature passed this law mandating a one-year minimum sentence for anyone convicted of a crime while carrying a firearm without a special license. The license was just a legal trick; the real idea behind the law was that many robberies and rapes involved the use of a gun and that by flagging that aspect of a case it would be more difficult to charge robbers and rapists with lesser offenses. The statute specified that sentences in gun cases could not be suspended, violators could not be granted probation, and parole boards could not consider their cases until those convicted under this law had served at least one year in prison. Almost all states now have some mandatory sentences on the books. Typically, they are reserved for weapons offenses, offenders with long prior records, and drug sales. For example, in Illinois, anyone convicted of the sale of five grams or more of cocaine receives an automatic six-year prison sentence.

Of course, mandatory sentencing policies will work only if police, prosecutors, and judges go along. Many are concerned that the imposition of new mandatory sentences will be circumvented at the local level because they will stand in the way of tailoring sentences to the perceived needs of individual defendants and the community. It is also widely believed that the threat of a stiff mandatory sentence will encourage more defendants to plead not guilty and demand jury trials. If it looks as though a charge that carries a mandatory sentence is going to stick, defendants seemingly will have little to lose by stalling and delaying their cases, as long as they are out on bail. Because additional cases would multiply the workload of the criminal courts, judges and prosecutors would be forced to work around mandatory charges in order to facilitate negotiated guilty pleas and keep cases moving.

Evaluations of sentencing reforms in several states suggest that these fears are unfounded, however. Tonry (1988) reports that, by and large, determinate, presumptive, and mandatory sentencing statutes are not being widely circumvented or manipulated by local officials. Such statutes probably increase the leverage of prosecutors in discussions leading to arranged guilty pleas, for defendants have a great deal to gain by pleading guilty to an offense that does not carry a stiff mandatory sentence. Evaluations in Minnesota and Pennsylvania indicate that bargaining over the charges that were filed in felony cases increased after determinate sentencing schemes were put in practice in those states.

All of these reforms have had some effect. Even though most states have not abolished parole entirely, the combination of abolishing parole and introducing flat and mandatory sentences has greatly reduced the percentage of prisoners being released on parole. In 1977, for example, 72 percent of all prisoners were discharged on parole before the end of their nominal sentences; by 1990 that proportion had shrunk to 40 percent (U.S. Department of Justice 1991a). Most of the reforms discussed here have been in place in a large number of states just since the early 1980s. We only know the actual sentences served by those who are now coming out of prison, and most of them went in under a different set of arrangements. Because of lengthening sentences, it will be a long time before we can be certain of the fate of prisoners who have been sentenced since the beginning of the 1980s.

Of course, there are other options available to judges at sentencing besides incarceration. The length of sentences and their predictability is relevant to those who are locked up, but most of those found guilty of criminal offenses do not go behind bars. At the end of 1991, when there were about 1,270,000 people incarcerated in jails, prisons, and juvenile facilities in the United States, more than 2.7 million others were on probation. When combined with the 532,000 people who had been released from prison but were still on parole, about 72 percent of all those under correctional supervision in the United States were walking the streets.

The Trend to Reduce Variation in Sentencing

As part of increasing the length and predictability of time served, the states also have moved in related ways to reduce case-by-case variation in the sentences imposed for seemingly similar offenses. States that have retained parole generally have mechanisms to automate that decision process as well. In order to reduce case-by-case variation, states have devised strategies to constrain the discretion of judges and prosecutors at the sentencing stage of the criminal process and that of parole boards later on. These measures were developed in response to charges of racial and class bias in the administration of justice. Legislators also suspected that local judges were using their discretionary powers to undermine the sometimes draconian intentions of sentencing reformers in the 1980s, and these mechanisms were handy in foreclosing that option as well.

Before these reforms, judicial decision making was extremely decentralized. Decisions about the guilt or innocence of accused parties and about the manner and length of time for which they must do penitence was traditionally left in the hands of the judges and juries that originally heard criminal cases. Judges enjoyed their independence from bureaucratic control (and even from one another) and liked to feel that they were bound in their decisions only by the law and the requirement that they employ it to find justice in the cases before them. In practice they were bound only by their states' rules of criminal procedure, for—within broad limits—the important decisions they made about the type of punishment and the length of prison stays were not subject to review by appellate courts. This left them free to choose the factors they weighed in making those decisions, and they could give those factors different weights from case to case.

Of course, this discretion inevitably meant that sentences did vary from case to case and judge to judge, even when they seemed similar in many important ways. Evidence of this could be found easily, and it lent credence to charges that sentencing practices were at best arbitrary and unfair, and at worst systematically discriminatory. In virtually every jurisdiction this perception was refueled at least occasionally by prominent instances of seeming abuse. In addition, massive social and legal studies documented the seemingly discriminatory fashion in which sentences were rendered and later reviewed. It was easy to point to evidence that African Americans and the poor (and even people who just did not dress properly in court) systematically were treated more harshly.

Under pressure from civil rights groups, social critics, and the courts, states devised strategies to cope with these charges. Several states organized sentencing commissions to formulate detailed guidelines for the disposition of cases. Prominent sentencing commissions were formed in Florida, Minnesota, Pennsylvania, and Washington. In other states, legislative committees took on the same task. Their purpose was to recommend (with the stamp of approval of the entire legislature) presumptive sentences. These are the sentences that judges are expected to give under circumstances that are described in detail in the legislation. In their most advanced form, these presumptive sentences are calculated using a case work sheet. The judge or a clerk refers to a scoring handbook to record elements of the offense; these commonly include weapon use, the extent of injury to the victim, the prior record of the defendant, and the established seriousness of the offense category. These are added together, and the number of months the offender should be incarcerated, given the total score, is indicated on a chart. This is his or her presumptive sentence. The states that have adopted such systems all leave judges some creative leeway around the presumptive sentence in order to take into account any aggravating or mitigating circumstances that were not reflected in the sentencing formula, but that leeway is always just a matter of months. The states also make it possible to render a sentence outside of that range, but only if judges submit a written statement detailing their reasons for doing so. In sum, presumptive sentencing serves to (a) specify exactly the factors that judges are to take into account when rendering judgment, and (b) standardize the weight given to each factor in all cases and by all judges.

Parallel moves have been made to constrain the discretion of boards authorized to release selected prisoners on parole, where such boards still exist. Point-scoring procedures and detailed parole guidelines have been inaugurated to reduce case-by-case variation in decisions about when prisoners are to be let free.

Some states (including Massachusetts, Michigan, and Wisconsin) have not gone so far as to legislate presumptive sentences. Instead, state and local sentencing councils have been formed to formulate and recommend model sentences for major classes of offenses and to conduct training sessions to imbue judges with the spirit of their recommendations. Unlike mandatory guidelines, the evidence suggests that voluntary ones do not have much effect on sentencing disparity. Sentences continue to vary widely, and only a low percentage fall within the recommended guidelines; they still are dominated by plea agreements made by prosecutors and the individual predilections of judges (Tonrey 1988).

The Trend to Incapacitate High-Rate Offenders

While pressure to increase the severity of criminal sanctions virtually has been across the board, there has been a great deal of interest in trying to identify individuals who pose a particular risk to society and to single them out for special treatment. Those who commit more serious crimes have always been subject to harsher sentences; however, it is also the case that a relatively small number of repeat offenders contribute disproportionately to the total crime count. High-repeat offenders can be found for violent and property crimes, drug offenses, drunk driving, and dangerous motoring violations. The policy of identifying them and imposing longer sentences so that society will experience fewer of their offenses in the immediate future is known as selective incapacitation.

An example of the importance of high-repeat offenders in violent and property crime rates can be found in two studies of youths in Philadelphia. In each case, researchers followed the records of boys, beginning at age fifteen; the first group was fifteen in 1960, the second in 1973. They found that most of them did not commit any serious crimes, and that most of those who did got into trouble only once or twice. However, the top 6 percent of the first group they studied got into so much repeated trouble that they accounted for 63 percent of all the serious offenses committed by the group. The second birth cohort they studied was much more crime prone, reflecting changes in society between the two periods. The second group committed more serious property offenses and more violent crimes, were more inclined to use weapons, and were more likely to harm or kill their victims. The most crime-prone 8 percent of them accounted for 68 percent of all serious offenses by the group (Tracey, Wolfgang, and Figlio 1985).

Beginning about 1975, prosecutors' offices began to develop what came to be known as career criminal programs. In principle, such programs were to target high-rate, criminally active offenders even if the offense with which they were charged was not very serious. Rather than routinely disposing of these cases with a slight penalty in return for a guilty plea, prosecutors and investigators were to develop and prosecute them to the hilt, taking advantage of the fact that they had a high-rate criminal in their grasp. Concentrating prosecution resources in this way was expensive, and the early programs were supported with federal funds by an agency (the Law Enforcement Assistance Administration) charged with promoting innovation in criminal justice. The same agency sponsored a great deal of research aimed at identifying appropriate targets for selective prosecution, based on such criteria as their past records as juveniles and adults, a pattern of drug use, and a history of involvement in assaultive violence (Forst 1983).

The politics of crime in the 1990s brought a new slogan to the battle against career criminals, "Three strikes and you're out!" Legislation building on this catchy metaphor, seemingly chosen more for its resonance with baseball than research on offending, calls for harsh and certain sentences for repeat offenders. In 1993, voters in the state of Washington approved a referendum (by 76 percent) mandating life prison terms for violent felons with two previous felony convictions. Under California's 1994 criminal sentencing act, a defendant with one previous conviction for a serious or violent crime, if found guilty of another felony, receives double the established penalty for the second crime, plus five additional years. An unfortunate Californian with two prior convictions must receive a prison sentence of at least twenty-five years. In neither case could they become eligible for parole. Observers estimated that these changes called for the construction of twenty new prisons in California, commencing almost immediately at a cost of about $10 billion. These kinds of harsh sentencing measures are encouraged by federal legislation that awards generous police and prison construction grants to states that change their sentencing codes to abide by the principles embodied in "Three strikes and you're out!" For example, in order for states to get the money, the 1994 Omnibus Crime Bill requires that they make serious offenders serve at least 85 percent of their sentences.

There has been considerable debate about the potential payoffs and liabilities of pursuing such selective incapacitation strategies. The discussion has largely been hypothetical, for in practice few career criminal programs have worked as they should; they have gravitated instead toward prosecuting those charged with more serious crimes even if they were not high-rate offenders. Still, it has been claimed that increasing the length of sentences given to a few chronic offenders and lowering those given to others (to balance the required prison bed space) could greatly reduce crime without increasing the need for new prisons. Others have argued that criminal careers may in fact be lengthened by prison stays, so that such dramatic benefits will not accrue simply by locking offenders up for a while. Finally, selective incapacitation raises deep questions about the purposes of punishment. Although offenders may be identified for special treatment by seemingly objective criteria, such as their record of past convictions, drug use, and the age at which they became criminally active, the real goal of these programs is to punish people for things they might do rather than for what they have done. This is a long way from one of the touchstones of the American system of justice, the presumption of one's innocence even of things that have already occurred.

The Trend to Use Executions More Often

One of the most visible changes in the sentencing policies of the states has been the reappearance of the death penalty. This may be the ultimate symbol that a state is being tough on crime. Between 1967 and 1976 it was impossible in practice for the states lawfully to execute anyone. Then the U.S. Supreme Court announced the conditions under which it would entertain the imposition of the death penalty (in the case of *Gregg v. Georgia,* 428 U.S. 153 [1976]), and many states quickly took advantage of the opportunity. By the end of 1992, 2,575 persons sat on death row in state prisons, and 188 had been executed since the *Gregg* decision (U.S. Department of Justice 1993a). The execution count had grown to 249 by August 1994.

Until the passage of the Omnibus Drug Bill of 1988, the possibility of employing the death penalty in *federal* offenses was confined to cases involving treason; espionage; deaths resulting from aircraft hijacking, train wrecking, bank robberies, or letter bombs; and the murder of the president, Supreme Court justices, or members of Congress. The 1988 act added major drug trafficking offenses to that list, but the death penalty has not yet been frequently used. At the end of 1992 only one federal nonmilitary prisoner awaited execution.

The number of state death row inmates has been growing by about 10 percent a year, and if past practice is any guide, they will be there for some time. The average waiting time for those who have been executed since 1977 has been seven and a half years. During the wait, 100 death row prisoners died, almost half of the number actually executed. Prisoners sentenced to death are entitled to a series of appeals through the state and federal courts regarding their conviction, the penalty, and how their cases were handled. To many observers, these appeals seem frivolous, expensive, and time consuming, and conservatives have made many proposals to limit and speed up these appeals. It is important to note in this regard that about 36 percent of those sentenced to death have had their convictions or sentences overturned on appeal, so moves to limit appeals are of considerable significance to those involved. Two percent have had their sentences of death commuted, another outcome worth a wait.

Table 10-3 identifies the thirty-six states that have devised new statutes calling for the death penalty, the number of executions they have carried out between 1977 and 1992, and the number of prisoners sitting on death row in each state at the end of that year. New Hampshire and Wyoming had the death penalty on the books in 1992 but no one on death row. Almost all death row inmates were male, half were black or Hispanic, and two were only seventeen years old. Texas (344), California (332), and Florida (312) had the largest death row populations, ac-

Table 10-3 Prison Crowding, Judicial Intervention, and Executions, 1992

State	Corrections depts. under court order* Entire department	Corrections depts. under court order* Some units	Percentage of prison capacity used 1992	Total inmates on death row 1992	Total executions 1977 to 1992
Alabama	No	No	111	124	10
Alaska	Yes	Yes	116	—	—
Arizona	No	Yes	106	103	1
Arkansas	No	Yes	104	32	4
California	No	Yes	191	332	1
Colorado	Yes	Yes	113	3	0
Connecticut	No	Yes	103	4	0
Delaware	No	Yes	99	11	1
Florida	Yes	Yes	88	312	29
Georgia	No	Yes	100	101	15
Hawaii	Yes	Yes	123	—	—
Idaho	No	Yes	106	23	0
Illinois	No	No	129	145	1
Indiana	No	Yes	95	50	2
Iowa	No	Yes	138	—	—
Kansas	No	Yes	91	—	—
Kentucky	No	Yes	107	29	0
Louisiana	Yes	Yes	95	44	20
Maine	No	No	112	—	—
Maryland	No	Yes	101	15	0
Massachusetts	No	No	144	—	—
Michigan	No	Yes	144	—	—
Minnesota	No	No	104	—	—
Mississippi	Yes	Yes	89	42	4
Missouri	No	Yes	100	82	7
Montana	No	No	106	8	0
Nebraska	No	No	150	12	0
Nevada	Yes	Yes	105	62	5
New Hampshire	No	Yes	113	0	0
New Jersey	No	No	131	3	0
New Mexico	Yes	Yes	95	1	0
New York	No	Yes	103	—	—
North Carolina	No	Yes	98	76	5
North Dakota	No	No	81	—	—
Ohio	No	Yes	177	121	0
Oklahoma	No	Yes	119	120	3
Oregon	No	No	101	11	0
Pennsylvania	No	Yes	149	153	0
Rhode Island	Yes	Yes	84	—	—
South Carolina	Yes	No	112	41	4
South Dakota	No	Yes	125	1	0
Tennessee	Yes	Yes	94	99	0
Texas	No	Yes	106	344	54
Utah	No	No	81	10	4
Vermont	No	No	147	—	—
Virginia	No	No	139	49	17
Washington	No	Yes	128	11	0
West Virginia	No	Yes	100	—	—
Wisconsin	No	Yes	139	—	—
Wyoming	No	Yes	105	0	1

SOURCES: U.S. Department of Justice 1993a, 1993e.
NOTE: Dashes indicate the state has no death penalty.
*Adult institutions only.

counting for 38 percent of the national total. Texas and Florida, followed by Louisiana, have executed the most inmates since 1977; the three states account for 55 percent of all the nation's recent executions. The city of Houston alone accounted for 10 percent of all the nation's executions since 1976. California ranked second to Texas in the number of sentences but by the end of 1992 had actually executed only one person. Arizona also had a particularly large discrepancy between the imposition of the death penalty and its actual use. Most executions and persons under sentence of death are in the South (as they were before 1967), while the thirteen states that have not reinaugurated the death penalty (plus Vermont, which did so and then repealed the law) are concentrated in the Midwest and the Northeast. All but one of the inmates sitting on death row was convicted of homicide (the exception was for the rape of a child). Two-thirds of them had previously been convicted of a felony; two-fifths were on probation, parole, in prison, or had other charges pending against them when they committed their capital offense; and one in ten had been convicted of killing someone before.

THE CONSEQUENCES OF STATE CRIME POLICIES

All of these new policies have had consequences for how state criminal justice agencies operate—and how much they cost. They have contributed to an explosive growth in the size of state prison populations, which in turn has led to mammoth prison overcrowding. This overcrowding then led to litigation that has passed control of important aspects of state criminal justice policy making to the federal courts. Pressure from the courts has led to the controversial practice of releasing jail and prison inmates without bail or before their sentences are completed. It has also put great financial pressure on the states by forcing them to dig deep into their pockets to build expensive new prisons. Other problems remain unresolved, including racial disparities in sentencing. In addition, the persistent political pressure to increase the certainty and severity of sentences for even more crimes will put more upward pressure on prison populations.

Growing Inmate Populations

Perhaps the most obvious consequence of changes in state criminal justice policy has been a vast increase in the rate at which Americans are being incarcerated. At the end of 1991, about 1,270,000 people were locked in about 3,300 jails, 3,300 juvenile facilities, and almost 1,000 state and federal prisons; 95 percent of the prisoners were male, 1 percent were juveniles, and more than 50 percent were African American or Hispanic. This accounted for 1 of every 200 Americans residing in the United States. Between 1991 and 1993 the prison population alone rose by almost 125,000.

This rate of imprisonment is unprecedented in modern times. The only accurate national trend statistics are on those confined in state and federal prisons, who currently make up about two-thirds of all the prison and jail inmates combined. In relation to the size of the population, the number of prisoners in the United States remained surprisingly stable from the late 1930s through the mid-1970s. Then their numbers began to explode. In 1970 there were 196,000 persons in prison; in 1975, 240,000; in 1980, 330,000; and in 1993, almost 950,000. The year 1993 was the nineteenth consecutive year to set a new record. The prison incarceration rate (prisoners per 100,000 in the population) in 1987 was 351. Adding together prisons and jails, it was 455. This is in sharp contrast to the incarceration rate of other nations. In the early 1980s, when the rate in the United States was 194, the rate for Sweden was only 16 (Blumstein 1988).

It is harder and more expensive to count people in jails than in prisons. Jails hold persons awaiting trial or trying to make bail, those sentenced for short periods, and some convicted state prisoners for whom there are no prison beds. As a result, most inmates do not stay in jail very long, and there is a large turnover in the jail population in the course of a year. In addition, in six states the same agencies run both the jails and the prisons, and they do not report separate inmate counts for the two. The combined figures for those states, all of which are small, are included among prison statistics.

In 1991 about 10,266,000 persons were admitted to jail in the United States and an almost identical number were released, because the jails are full. This does not mean that this many people went to jail, for even more so than prisons (because stays are shorter) these institutions are "revolving doors." People can easily reenter several times in the course of a year. We have no real idea how frequently individuals reenter jail in a year, so there is no way of estimating from admissions figures how many people have been jailed; we only know the average jail population in a year and the number of people in jail on a particular day (June 28) of each year.[3] In 1991 the latter number was 426,000, a figure that is only 4 percent of the yearly total of admissions. Estimates of average jail populations are included in the data in Table 10-2.

Those behind bars are a select group. First, they are disproportionately male. In June 1992, 94 percent of prisoners and 91 percent of jail inmates were men; twenty times as many men as women were incarcerated. Montana had so few women convicts that until 1982 it did not have a women's prison facility at all, finding it cheaper to pay to house female offenders in nearby states. The relatively few women who are in prison were sent there for reasons different from those that locked up their male counterparts. While men are most likely to be sentenced to prison for committing violent or drug offenses, women are there for drug offenses (33 percent of women as opposed to 21 percent of men), theft, fraud, and forgery. The increase in the female prison population has been higher than that for men, and has been so each year since 1981. For example, between 1986 and 1991 the number of male prisoners rose 53 percent and the number of females rose 75 percent, on a much smaller base (U.S. Department of Justice

3. June 28 was selected arbitrarily as "National jail census day" by the Bureau of Justice Statistics.

1994b). Prisoners are also disproportionately black and Hispanic. In 1991, 46 percent of prisoners were African Americans, 14 percent were of Hispanic origin, and about 36 percent were non-Hispanic whites; jail inmates were distributed in roughly the same way. Blacks and Hispanics make up a much smaller percentage of the general population, so as groups they have high incarceration rates (U.S. Department of Justice 1993c, 1993d).

Why are there are so many people in U.S. prisons? The main reason, of course, is that crime rates are high. In relation to the level of crime in the United States, we send people to prison with about the same frequency as many other industrial nations. We send so many people to prison because we have much more crime than they do. In a comparison of the number of people entering prison with the number of crimes that could result in a prison sentence, this country stands in the lower-middle range among industrial countries. The ratio of prisoners to homicides puts the United States at the same level as Australia, England, and West Germany; its ratio of prisoners to robberies is similar to those and other industrial nations as well (Blumstein 1988; Lynch 1988). As best it can be judged, the United States does not have a disproportionately high conviction rate; for example, Canada, Great Britain, and the United States send almost the same percentage of those arrested for robbery to prison, between 48 and 52 percent, and conviction percentages for burglary and theft in the three countries are just as similar (U.S. Department of Justice 1987).

Prison admissions have even lagged behind the growth of the crime rate. Crime was up so much in the United States that between 1967 and 1980 the number of prison admissions per 100 serious crimes was two and a half times less than in 1960. By this measure the incarceration rate did not slope upward again until after 1980, and it is still considerably below that for the early 1960s. In addition, some of the biggest increases in crime have been in categories of offenses that more easily get people into prison: violent personal crimes and those involving weapons. The Philadelphia studies mentioned earlier documented dramatic shifts in tendencies toward youthful violence, weapon use, and victim harm between the 1960s and the 1970s.

Another reason for skyrocketing prison populations is demography. Crime is disproportionately committed by young males. That was an important reason for the tremendous increase in the crime rate during the 1960s and 1970s, when members of the postwar baby-boom generation were in their teens. However, prison sentences generally are reserved for adult offenders who have substantial criminal records, so the peak prison-prone age group is those in their twenties. This group grew precipitously in size during the 1980s. In fact, much of the increase in the number of Americans entering prison during the 1980s can be attributed to the escalating crime rate and demography alone.

However, an important cause of the size of prison populations in the United States is the length of prison stays, which has been the subject of many recent policy changes in the states. As discussed earlier, during the 1970s and 1980s many states undertook measures that effectively increased the actual length of criminal sentences. They did so by abolishing parole and sometimes good time, by mandating prison sentences for special classes of offenses, and by tacking years onto sentencing guidelines. These measures had important consequences, for the size of the prison population is affected both by the number of people entering prison and by how long they stay. In the aggregate, someone sentenced to ten years occupies the same bed space as ten people sentenced to one year. The effect of increases in average length of stay can be dramatic. For example, a requirement proposed in Illinois in 1994 that felons serve at least 85 percent of their court-imposed sentences called for twenty-eight new prisons and a doubling of the state's prison capacity during the next decade because the state previously had a generous good-time policy. During the 1980s, the total size of the U.S. prison population was affected more by length of stay than by volume of intake. More people were coming in, principally as a result of crime rates and the number of offenders in their twenties, but they were also staying longer. When coupled with poor planning, this resulted in a prison overcrowding problem of crisis proportions.

Growing Prison Overcrowding

The prison overcrowding problem has become one of the major headaches facing American state governments. In 1992, thirty-seven states had more prisoners than the capacity of their prisons, some of them dramatically more (U.S. Department of Justice 1993d). During 1992, state prison populations increased so fast that more than 1,100 new beds were required each week to handle new admissions. In light of the scrutiny prisons were getting from the courts, these beds could not just be crowded in among the old ones. Space for them had to be supplied from new construction, or their previous occupants had to be leaving.

There are two ways to measure overcrowding. The first (and probably best) is the number of square feet of space that a prisoner has to live in. The only figures available are averages, for relatively few prison inmates live in a single-bunk cell. (In fact, about one-quarter of all prisoners live in barracks with more than fifty other people per room.) The average amount of living space allotted to inmates of U.S. prisons was fifty-six square feet. The amount of space varied considerably, however, and 30 percent of all prisoners had less than forty square feet (that is five by eight feet) of space to live in. Furthermore, these figures were lower than in earlier years; in 1979, the average living space was seventy square feet in size. Between 1979 and 1984, 138 state prisons were built, renovated, or expanded, adding 5.4 million square feet of housing space. This amounted to a 29 percent increase in the space prisoners had to live in. However, the prison population went up 45 percent during the same period, so the space for each inmate actually decreased (Innes 1986).

The second way to measure overcrowding—based on the capacity of a prison or jail—is slippery. There are several different ways of rating prison capacity. From one point of view, however many people can be crowded into a prison is its capacity. Texas once put tents in the exercise yard of its prison in Huntsville and wanted to count the cots in those tents as part of the prison's capacity. The data on prison crowding presented in Table 10-3 are based on the most favorable definitions of prison capacity that the states report. Even by these measures, the prisons in many states are overwhelmed. Forty-three states (plus the federal prison system) reported operating above capacity. Eleven states reported that at the end of 1992 their prisons were, in the aggregate, at more than 130 percent of capacity. The worst offender was California, which was operating at 191 percent of capacity. Prisoners in Hawaii had an average of thirty-six square feet of living space each. Only ten states were running at a comfortable 95 percent or less of capacity.

There is no clear agreement on the actual consequences of prison overcrowding alone. The dominant factor that is related to prison assaults and homicides, disturbances, and suicides is the type of prison. High-security prisons, which house the most dangerous offenders, are the worst on all these measures, almost regardless of their crowding or design characteristics, while low-security facilities come off best. Living in barracks seems to be worse than bunked cells, and there is some evidence that overcrowded prisons are more likely to have high assault rates. It certainly is reasonable to hypothesize that overcrowding increases levels of violence in prison. Crowding strains the recreational and educational capacities of a prison; as a result, the inmates are bored, and conflicts break out among them. It is easier for the staff to lose control of overloaded institutions. The only winners in this situation are gangs, which already control many aspects of prison life (see Ellis 1984; Gaes 1985; Innes 1986).

It also should not be forgotten that overcrowding also effectively increases the harshness of the sentences that are handed down by the criminal justice system, perhaps beyond the intent of legislators, judges, or society. At the extreme, overcrowding and its correlates can pervert a seemingly rational sentencing policy into something that is cruel and unusual in its application. Then prison living conditions become a constitutional question.

New Federal Supervision of State Prisons

One important change in state criminal justice policy since the 1970s has been the intrusion of the federal courts into the process. Before 1960 the federal courts had little to say about how prisons operated. Then, two waves of litigation swept through the system; the first had to do with prisoners' rights in matters of traditional constitutional concern, whereas the second had to do with the quality of their life behind bars. The results have been controversial and expensive (for a discussion, see DiIulio 1990).

During the 1960s, the basis of most of this court action was the First, Fifth, and Fourteenth Amendments, which guarantee freedom of religion, the right to fair administrative processes, and equal protection by the law. On these grounds the federal courts ruled against the denial of religious freedom to Muslim prisoners (who usually were black), found that prisoners had the right to meet with their attorneys and have access to legal materials, limited the censorship powers of prison administrators, insisted on fair procedures in prisoners' disciplinary hearings, and acted to soften often brutal disciplinary measures.

Beginning in the 1970s, the grounds on which important legal actions took place shifted from prisoners' rights to governments' responsibilities. Those law suits attacked crowded, unsanitary, and dangerous prison living conditions. Suits were brought against prisons that were in a deteriorated condition and against systems that did not provide adequate health care for prisoners. Federal district court judges frequently were appalled by the conditions of confinement that those suits revealed. Their general ground for imposing a remedy in those cases has been the Eighth Amendment to the Constitution, which forbids "cruel and unusual punishment." Since 1970, forty-five states have either been issued federal court orders or are still in litigation about such issues. In 1992 eleven entire state prison systems were operating under court orders or consent decrees specifying how they were to reduce crowding and deal with other prison problems; in thirty-seven states at least one major prison was operating under similar arrangements (Table 10-3). In an important sense the federal courts are governing state prisons.

The prisons are not directly run by the judges. Rather, the practice is for district court judges to appoint a *special master* to represent the courts in the matter. At one point about 1980, a Texan was serving as the special master overseeing state prison management in Oklahoma, while an Oklahoman was the special master for prisons in Texas. In 1992, seven state systems were under the supervision of a court-appointed master, as were individual prison units in thirteen states. Masters monitor conditions in the prison(s) in question and keep the courts abreast of progress toward their compliance with the judges' orders. Progress is not automatic. Even when there is a great deal of professional good will on both sides, state prison administrators often find it difficult to persuade legislators to approve the money they need to meet the requirements of the master. Judges frequently have to move the process along with injunctions, threats of contempt of court citations, and fines of $1,000 a day. The process is more difficult in states where the public must vote their approval of bond issues in order to pay for new prison construction; if they defeat the issue (which does not always happen, to be sure), states must scramble to find other sources for the money.

It is clear that "crowding them in" is no longer an acceptable response to the crisis generated by the growing stream of long-term inmates entering the nation's prisons. Judicial supervision of state prison conditions makes that impossible. Simple crowding is not, per se, unconstitutional. In fact, a line of U.S.

Supreme Court decisions has ruled to the contrary; evidence of other untoward conditions is required. This is why states can exceed the capacity for which their prisons were designed. For example, in 1992 Illinois housed 24,000 inmates in prisons intended to hold 20,800, but the state was not operating under court jurisdiction. However, evidence that conditions are unsanitary and dangerous has not been difficult to come by in many cases, and the federal district courts have also continued to be impressed by descriptions of crowded prison conditions. The problem is what to do about it. The short-term response has been simply to let out enough prisoners to get prisons down to their capacity; the long-term solutions have to be to build new prisons and to find politically acceptable alternatives to incarceration.

Mounting Pressure to Release Prisoners

While none of these alternatives is easy, perhaps the most controversial are the backdoor solutions to overcrowding employed by many states. They just let prisoners out. This happens at all levels of incarceration. In 1986 (the last year for which the data were published), fourteen states employed some kind of emergency release mechanism to rid themselves of excess prisoners, letting about 72,000 of them out early. California freed more than 37,000 prisoners before their time; Texas, almost 13,000; Illinois, 8,600; and New York and Maryland, 1,900 each. It worked: at year's end, the prison systems in all of these states were at or very slightly below 100 percent of capacity. But no one was happy with this solution.

Local jails face the same problem. In Cook County, Illinois (Chicago and its nearby suburbs), the local jail was forced to release 1,200 inmates in just November and December of 1986. By 1988 the situation had gotten worse. In the first eight months of the year, more than 6,000 persons charged with felonies who had been unable to make their assigned bail were released anyway because about 100 inmates were sleeping on the floor each night in the county's 5,500-bed facility. By November 1988 the release rate was up to 120 offenders a day, but there were still inmates sleeping on floors. The next month, a federal district court judge appointed a monitor to oversee the local corrections department, and jail officials were fined $1,000 per day for not reducing the jail's population or constructing new facilities.

As a temporary measure, some states are able to keep sentenced prisoners in local jails where there is some room. In 1992, twenty states held an additional 18,200 convicted felons in this manner. The difficulty with this is that jails are not designed or equipped to hold prisoners for long periods of time. They usually offer only rudimentary health services and have limited educational and recreational facilities, reflecting their short-term custodial role.

In principle these mandatory releasees are not simply dumped back into the community. Although they are not being released by parole boards, state prison emergency releasees are placed under the supervision of parole officers and acquire the responsibilities of parolees. How well this works in practice depends on the quality of the parole supervision system, which often is not very good. During the fiscal crisis of the 1980s, state parole agencies faced simultaneous increases in their caseloads and cuts in their budgets. Those released early from the Cook County jail effectively have no supervision at all. Their status just becomes a ground for setting a somewhat higher bail for them the next time they get into trouble.

Many states have shouldered the responsibility for reducing the size of prison populations. In statutes with titles like "The Forced Release Act" (to indicate that it was not *their* idea), these states have established uniform trigger mechanisms (such as an institution's capacity exceeding 105 percent for three consecutive months) and inmate-selection policies (for example, first release those near the end of their sentences, then free offenders incarcerated for property crimes rather than violent acts) to guide prison administrators. Some legislatures have attempted to hang the responsibility for making these decisions on the governor, making what happens appear to be his or her fault; when the state assembly did so in Michigan, the governor simply refused to release any prisoners, leading to further litigation. A few state legislatures have studiously ignored the issue, refusing to act and trying not to notice while their prison administrators proceed to release inmates without any statutory authority.

Mounting Pressure to Build New Prisons

One obvious response to the crisis of prison overcrowding is to build new prisons. Most states have done so; between 1984 and 1990 the number of prison beds increased by 52 percent. In 1995 the states and the federal government planned to spend $5.1 billion on prisons, up $200 million from the year before. A "build more" strategy, however, harbors several problems. First, keeping abreast of mounting and increasingly lengthy prison admissions is extremely expensive. In 1994, it cost an average of $75,000 per bed to build a new high-security prison; at the high end, Connecticut spent $147,000 per bed for a new high-security prison in the early 1990s. Juvenile facilities typically are smaller and provide more educational services, so they cost even more. Unfortunately, prisons (not to mention their inhabitants) do not have much of a political constituency. The construction of prisons is not a popular way to spend tax dollars, nor should it be. Not only is such construction expensive, but the states pay "opportunity costs" in the form of not being able to spend the money on other, more productive things like education and highways. If taxes are not to increase, more spending for criminal justice means less spending elsewhere. As a result, even in relatively progressive states the public has defeated measures for prison construction when given the opportunity. Voters have refused to approve bond issues to support prison construction in New York, Oregon, and Virginia, and in Michigan they rejected a proposed 0.1 percent increase in the state income tax to pay for new prisons (Petersilia 1987).

There has been a great deal of discussion about the privatization of prisons in the United States. Most media attention has focused on privately managed prisons and the controversial practice of delegating coercive (and potentially life or death) power over inmates to private contractors. By 1990, however, private contractors managed only twenty-one confinement facilities in the United States. From a political point of view, one of the most attractive features of privatization is financial. By leasing prison facilities from private developers who finance and oversee their construction, states can evade public referendums on bonds and taxes, and states, counties, and municipalities can avoid statutory or constitutional limitations on their bonded indebtedness. Using private investors to finance and own prisons lets the states meet their legal obligations out of current revenues.

The constituency problem also begets the problem of "Not in my back yard," or NIMBY—the response of many (but not all) communities to the proposal that a prison be built. The result is that prisons usually are built in inaccessible, thinly populated reaches of the state, where being a prison guard is regarded as a good job, but prisoners are far away from their friends and families.

Building new prisons is also an extremely slow response to the overcrowding problem. Planners must decide what kinds of prisons to build (high, medium, or low security) as well as how many, so they need to forecast the types of prisoners they will have on their hands in the future as well as how many there will be. They have to find locations for them, plan them in detail (looking forward to new standards for living space, health, and recreational facilities), and convince the legislature that building a prison is a good idea. Typically, this process takes about five years.

Anticipating future prison needs, therefore, is an integral part of the "build more" response to crime and overcrowding. The forecasting process relies in part on demography. As noted above, one reason for prison overcrowding during the 1980s has been the large size of the prison-prone population, males in their twenties. Demographic forecasts, however, call for caution in building new prisons, for following in the wake of the baby boom were dramatically fewer prison-age males; their numbers will not pick up again dramatically until after the turn of the century. Demography alone would lead many low-growth states to resist investing much more in prison construction. Other factors involved in the demand for prison space need to be included in forecasts as well. The National Council on Crime and Delinquency (NCCD) conducts prison forecasts for states, including California, Florida, Illinois, and Ohio. In addition to admissions, the predictions of the NCCD also take into account anticipated parole rates and parole violations (which bring releasees back in). The latter is an important component of capacity planning, for about two-thirds of all prisoners released on parole are rearrested within two years, most of them while they are still on parole. Thirty percent of all those admitted to U.S. prisons in 1991 were going back because they had violated their parole conditions.

Planners should also try to take into account anticipated sentence lengths for offenders entering prison, for their average length of stay is the largest determinant of a state's need for bed space. NCCD's estimates are steady-state forecasts; they "assume that arrest and court policies have stabilized and that new court admissions will be driven by demographic trends" (NCCD 1988, 3). This is unlikely, however, which is one reason why policy-related forecasting is an uncertain art. NCCD's 1988 forecast for California estimated that the state would need 102,550 beds by the end of 1993. But by the end of 1992 the state already had almost 110,000 prisoners. In 1991 the state of California forecast a need for 151,500 prison beds by 1995 but admitted that the state's own construction plan would fall far short of that total (U.S. Department of Justice 1993e). Changes in the criminal code can upset the most carefully thought out forecasts. Given the typical five-year plan-and-build cycle for new prisons, the ability of statutory changes to have such significant short-term consequences for the need for prison space makes it unlikely that new construction alone can suffice to respond to our changing prison needs.

An alternate view, one that is consistent with the Cook County, Illinois, experience, is that we can never build enough prisons. In 1983 a new 500-bed addition to the jail was hopelessly overcrowded within eighteen months despite court-ordered attempts to keep the jail's population under control. In the face of its mounting 1988 jail population, Cook County approved spending $60 million to add another 750 beds to its 5,500-bed facility. At the same time, however, the county was releasing enough inmates to have filled the new annex the month it opened. By 1994 the county jail had grown to 7,900 beds but housed an average daily population of 9,000. Once again, prisoners were sleeping on floor pads in large numbers. More than 700 prisoners were women, forcing the dedication of a wing of the facility for their use and the opening of a prenatal tier for women who were pregnant. Space needs for women prisoners were so tense that a special furlough program was devised that sent many of them out of jail each evening, so they could sleep elsewhere and not use up precious floor space. Nationally, while the number of prison beds increased 52 percent between 1984 and 1990, the number of prisoners went up 67 percent. In 1984, state prisons were 11 percent above capacity; in 1990, they were 22 percent above capacity.

Perhaps the states have gotten into trouble because they have been governed badly; it seems that the consequences of soaring crime rates and new sentencing policies should have been obvious. However, theorists on prison capacity argue that the limited willingness of political systems actually to spend money is how they cap their symbolic and emotional enthusiasm for increasing the scope and harshness of criminal sanctions. We hit our limits when symbolic crusades against crime overreach the scarce resources that the political system is willing to devote to crime control, and capacity thus provides a practical break on society's retributive impulses.

Mounting Pressure to Find Alternatives

Perhaps the only desirable element of the prison overcrowding problem is the opportunity it creates to explore alternatives to incarceration. It is neither possible nor desirable to throw the book at every offender who comes into court, and this is especially true now that the book has gotten heavier in many states. The sanctions outlined in criminal statutes serve many functions. They are presumed to have general deterrent value; that is, by sending the message that crime does not pay, punishing criminals should deter others from following in their path. Presumably the criminal justice system has some rehabilitative effect, and we have seen how close supervision of offenders is presumed to have an incapacitation value. The question is how to achieve these goals using sanctions that fall short of incarceration but at the same time respond to the public's demand that criminals be dealt with severely.

There are many correctional programs to which offenders can be diverted in lieu of prison. They range from residential care facilities, where offenders live (and often work) in the community, to detention programs that require that offenders serve their sentence by not leaving home. One important alternative to prison is intensive supervision probation (ISP). More than thirty states are experimenting with some version of ISP. In 1992, Florida had the largest program, one enrolling more than 12,000 of the state's 89,000 probationers. The next largest program was in Texas, where ISP enrollees numbered 6,000. In ISP, probationers are placed under heavy surveillance. They have frequent face-to-face meetings with their probation supervisors, and their supervisors independently monitor their status at work and conditions in their homes. ISP parolees typically face an early-evening curfew, and their supervisors make frequent home visits to make sure they are complying. They also must submit to urine tests to certify that they are staying off drugs. Often these programs require that parolees perform hundreds of hours of community service and participate in drug or alcohol treatment programs. The close supervision of ISP is used to justify releasing offenders who have committed relatively serious crimes but who appear to have a low risk of getting into serious trouble again. The savings to the state are considerable; Georgia estimated that in 1986 each ISP parole saved almost $11,000 in prison construction and operating costs per year (Petersilia 1987). There are benefits to offenders who participate in the program as well: those involved can keep or find a job and maintain contact with their families, two good predictors of probation success.

Shock incarceration programs (more commonly known as boot camps) put offenders in quasi-military confinement for short periods of time, followed by a more lengthy period of community supervision. These programs feature rigorous exercise, military drill, and hard and demeaning labor. Houston's program requires six hours of exercise and drill every day, two more working at a camp job, and some vocational training. Boot camp programs typically last for three to six months and are becoming the sentence of choice for drug offenders. The premise posed by supporters of boot camps is that participants will learn self-discipline and (depending on the program) be enrolled in educational and vocational training programs. Critics are unconvinced that lifelong behavior patterns will be changed by a few strenuous months of marching. Originally these programs were seen as less costly alternatives to state prison stays, and about half the states run them this way. Recently there has been increased interest in using boot camps as a sentencing alternative to jail. The best research to date has found no significant difference between boot camp graduates and former prison inmates in the rate at which they are rearrested or sent back to prison (MacKenzie 1994).

Other alternatives to incarceration include residential care in a halfway house or work-release center located in the community. In 1990 there were about 250 state-operated community-based correctional facilities in the United States, housing about one of every forty-three state prisoners. Residential care units also are operated by not-for-profit community groups, social welfare organizations, and churches. Halfway houses provide an opportunity to divert from incarceration those whose real problem is drug and alcohol abuse. Such facilities are also frequently used instead of prison to house parole or probation violators whose infractions are only minor or technical. They provide one of the better prospects for involvement by the private sector in the corrections business. Residential care contracts typically include the provision of counseling and training as well as managing the facilities but do not require extensive security arrangements.

Other offenders are sentenced to perform community service in lieu of jail time. In New York City, the courts can sentence offenders to community service projects supervised by the Vera Foundation, a nonprofit organization that runs and evaluates innovative criminal justice programs. In some jurisdictions, such as Minnesota, offenders can be released on probation if they agree to pay restitution to victims. It is also common for judges to hand down suspended sentences for violators who enroll in drug or alcohol treatment programs.

There is a great deal of interest in home detention programs as well. Those sentenced to home detention must serve out their sentences at home, and occasional spot checks are made to make sure they comply. Many states now use electronic-monitoring devices to provide low-cost supervision of home detention releasees. The number of states using home detention is growing rapidly because of its low cost; California and Illinois began doing so in 1989, using electronic monitoring.

As a practical and political matter, noncustodial alternatives to incarceration probably are open only to a selected group of convicted offenders. They are confined to those who have committed less serious offenses, first-time offenders, and those who appear to pose the least risk to the community. Furthermore, they will have to work (or least appear to) if they are to sustain the kind of support they need to become a viable alternative to incarceration for large numbers of people. Judges, prosecutors, crime victims, and the press all must be convinced that these

alternatives are appropriate for deterring, incapacitating, and perhaps even reha-
bilitating offenders.

Counterpressures to Impose New Sanctions

At the same time that states are searching for new alternatives to incarceration, opposing forces are at work that threaten to send even more people to jail
or prison. One is a new enthusiasm in the states for preventive detention. Many
people held in local jails (about 53 percent of the total) have not been found
guilty of a crime. Rather, they are being detained while awaiting trial because
they have not been able to deposit sufficient bail money to gain their freedom.
The traditional legal principle was that bail should be set in all but death penalty
cases, and that the bail demanded by the state should be set at a level just high
enough to ensure that the accused would show up in court later on. By the mid-
1980s, however, the criminal codes of thirty-two states had added provisions that
allowed judges to hold persons without bail if they believed that the alleged
offenders would be a danger to the community. To this end, preventive detention
usually is confined to cases involving violent crimes, weapons, major drug
offenses, and offenders with a prior record of convictions. The federal Bail Reform Act of 1984 included such preventive detention provisions; immediately af-
terward, the number of persons detained jumped about 20 percentage points
(U.S. Department of Justice 1988).

A second source of counterpressure is the nation's occasional enthusiasm to
crack down on "new" forms of crime. In an era generally characterized by a retributive stance toward criminals, as the media and other actors in the political
process focus attention anew on selected crime problems (frequently relabeling
them to gain notice), the easiest response seems to be to deal more harshly with
their perpetrators. Crimes in this category include spouse assault and child
abuse, elder abuse, child pornography, and garden variety crimes against the elderly. One important instance of this is the new criminalization of drunk driving.

Before the 1980s, driving while intoxicated (DWI) often drew a fine or a suspended driver's license. It also often drew just a wink and perhaps an escort
home by communities with service-oriented police departments. However,
about 50,000 Americans die each year as a result of drunk driving, and groups
like MADD (Mothers against Drunk Driving) have lobbied effectively for new
legislation and stricter enforcement of DWI statutes. It is now common for the
states to require mandatory confinement in these cases. By the mid-1980s, thirty
states had adopted more stringent penalties for DWI cases. Studies of the effect
of these statutes have documented their consequences for the criminal justice
system: arrests went up, and the workload of local courts increased. DWI cases
often involve middle-class defendants who engage private attorneys, and when
threatened with mandatory jail time they are more likely to challenge their indictment in court, maneuver to postpone their case, plead not guilty, and request

jury trials. Nevertheless, most defendants are convicted, and in those cases almost all are incarcerated. This in turn puts some strain on the correctional system. Mandatory DWI statutes typically require offenders to do their time on weekends, and these inmates are set apart from other prisoners in low-security facilities. Ohio had so many cases and was so short of weekend bed space that sentenced offenders often had to wait six or seven months before being locked up (Greenfield 1988; Heinzelmann et al. 1984).

Other important shifts have taken place in America's drug policy. There has been an explosion of drug arrests, and convictions for increasingly long periods, of a vast new group of offenders. In 1991 more than one million people were arrested for whom a drug offense was the highest charge against them, about 1.4 times the number who were arrested for all violent crimes. State statutes vary considerably in the stringency of penalties for drug trafficking and drug possession, but about 75 percent of those convicted of a drug offense are sentenced to prison or jail. By the end of the 1980s, 30 percent of all new state prison inmates were arriving to serve a drug offense sentence. In the federal prison system the total in 1994 was 62 percent. In the federal system they were also going in for longer sentences; for federal drug offenders the length of the average sentence to prison increased by 60 percent during the 1980s. In this group, 20 percent were convicted only of low-level drug offenses, had never been to prison before, and had no previous convictions for violent crime. The results of this influx as it relates to the need for new prison beds are obvious. The federal prison population is forecast to rise by 50 percent between 1994 and 2000, with more than 60 percent of all new prisoners going in for drug crime offenses (U.S. Department of Justice 1992).

Continued Racial Disparities

One of the greatest challenges to the system of justice in the American states remains the apparent racial disparities in how it operates. African Americans are disproportionately represented at every step in the criminal justice process, from arrest to imprisonment. In 1991, about 35 percent of those arrested for index crimes and 48 percent of those in state prisons were black. Based on 1979 data, it was estimated that 19 percent of blacks, but only 3 percent of whites, would serve a term in prison during their life time (Langan 1985). Blacks are also disproportionately likely to be executed; about 40 percent of those waiting on death row are African Americans.

We can track some of the reasons for this at every stage, from offending to sentencing. First, blacks commit (relatively) more crimes. Recent reports from the National Crime Survey, which directly questions representative samples of victims in the United States, found that blacks were more than twice as likely to commit rape, and almost five times as likely to be involved in a robbery, as their numbers in the population (about 12 percent of the total) would indicate (U.S. Department of Justice 1994a).

Second, black offenders are even more likely to be arrested. In 1991, 60 percent of all those arrested for robbery were black; the comparable figure for rape was 43 percent, and for murder 57 percent. Even more important, blacks are more likely to be arrested for the kinds of crimes for which people are more likely to be put into prison. While 49 percent of those arrested for violent crimes in 1991 were black, only 23 percent of those arrested for theft and burglary were black; property offenders generally must accumulate an extensive record before they are sent to prison. However, based on data on prison inmates, blacks are more likely to have a past history of felony convictions when they are up for sentencing; in addition, black offenders are more likely to carry guns (Block and Skogan 1986). This is important because violent, repeat, and weapon-carrying offenders typically get longer sentences as well as being sent to prison more readily. Sentencing figures are consistent with this: blacks are more likely to get longer sentences. This is true both overall and within every category of violent crime, for all types of drug offenses, and for most property crimes. Significantly, implementation of strict sentencing guidelines in federal criminal courts since 1989 has actually increased sentencing disparities between whites on the one hand, and black and Hispanic defendants on the other. This widening is due principally to the legal gravity of charges more typically brought against minority defendants, including trafficking in crack cocaine (McDonald and Carlson 1993).

Blacks, then, are both more likely to enter prison and to stay there longer when they do, which adds up to a disproportionate representation of them in U.S. prisons and jails. The numbers are large—Blumstein (1988) estimated that during the mid-1980s about one in twelve black males in their twenties was in jail or prison. The numbers vary from state to state, one obvious reason being the differences in the racial composition of the states. According to the latest available figures, over 70 percent of prisoners in Louisiana and Maryland and two-thirds of those in Mississippi are black. Black overrepresentation in prison, however, also varies dramatically between similar states. For example, the populations of Indiana and Connecticut are both about 8 percent black, but in Connecticut, 56 percent of prisoners were black, whereas in Indiana, 35 percent were black. In the main, the areas with the biggest discrepancies between population and prison figures are large, metropolitan states with high crime rates; the two states with the largest overrepresentation of blacks in their prisons are New Jersey and Illinois. The biggest discrepancies were not among rural southern states; the four southern states in which blacks were most overrepresented in prison compared to the population included three highly urban states—Florida, Maryland, and Virginia.

CONCLUSION

Crime rates in the United States doubled or tripled in the three decades following 1965, and the states were hard pressed to keep up in dealing with them. The highest levels of crime—and the biggest increases during that period—were concentrated in the metropolitan, high-growth states. Responding to the political and workload pressures generated by mounting crime rates proved to be expensive, and to a certain extent it came at the expense of other functions of government. Not only did state and local criminal justice budgets grow, but their slice of the total pie grew as well. Budgets and budget shares expanded most at the local level, largely to support policing; while federal involvement in crime control grew during this period, it still does not amount to very much.

The role of state government in the control of crime is limited, but state responsibilities include some of the most controversial elements of criminal justice policy making and some of the most expensive decisions. During the late 1970s and early 1980s, many states began to rely on longer and more certain imprisonment to control crime, and the early 1990s saw renewed enthusiasm for such hard-line measures. Average sentences got longer, and the elimination of parole and other mechanisms for releasing offenders before the end of their statutory sentences made it more certain that those sentences would be served in full. Often these stiffer penalties were combined with efforts to impose new sanctions on so-called career criminals, who presumably would otherwise continue to follow a life of crime.

One consequence of these policies has been an explosion in the size of prison populations. By 1994 more than one million people were in state and federal prisons, a number about equal to the population of Dallas or Detroit. If prisons were a city, they would be the ninth largest in the country. Some of the increase would have occurred anyway, driven by soaring crime rates and a growing pool of adult offenders seemingly fully qualified for prison. However, these events occurred at a time in which the old, liberal consensus on corrections, aimed at rehabilitation, was in retreat. The notion that prisons are about retribution and incapacitation was in the ascent, and more punitive policies resulted. The effects of this were to be multiplied by their extension into areas in which the criminal justice system hitherto had not relied heavily on incarceration, including such high-volume crime problems as drunk driving and drug possession or use.

The consequence of this new punitiveness remains a national crisis. People flooded into prisons and jails at an unprecedented rate. Crowding and underfunding, and their consequences (inadequate food and care, poor staffing, deterioration of buildings), soon caught the attention of the federal courts. The resulting litigation led to new rounds of fund-raising and prison construction and the release of sentenced prisoners to make room for others. The fiscal and political consequences of this quickly encouraged new thinking about punishment, and by the middle of the 1980s interest in alternatives to traditional forms of incarceration had been renewed. Finding large numbers of candidates for low-cost rather than high-cost treatment, and justifying this politically, has become the most popular topic in state criminal justice circles.

The issue of how to solve these problems in ways that seem fair as well as effective remains a source of great concern to those involved in criminal justice policy making. Efforts were made during the 1970s and 1980s to devise ways of reducing race and class discrimination in the imposition of criminal sanctions, principally through constraining the discretion of judges and parole boards by focusing their decisions on a few legally relevant criteria. However, there continue to be large discrepancies by race in the imposition of prison sentences and the death penalty. We have seen that some of these discrepancies are rooted in the distribution of crime and criminal careers, but whatever the reason, these dramatic racial disparities constitute the most serious—and potentially the most explosive—issue facing the American system of justice.

REFERENCES

Block, Richard, and Wesley G. Skogan. 1986. "Resistance and Nonfatal Outcomes in Stranger-to-Stranger Predatory Crime." *Violence and Victims* 1, no. 4:241–253.

Blumstein, Alfred. 1988. "Prison Populations: A System Out of Control?" In *Crime and Justice: An Annual Review,* edited by Michael Tonrey and Norval Morris. Chicago: University of Chicago Press.

DiIulio, John J., ed. 1990. *Courts, Corrections, and the Constitution: The Impact of Judicial Intervention on Prisons and Jails.* New York: Oxford University Press.

Eisenstein, James, and Herbert Jacob. 1974. "Measuring Performance and Outputs of Urban Criminal Courts." *Social Science Quarterly* 54 (March): 713–724.

Ellis, David. 1984. "Crowding and Prison Violence: Integration of Theory and Research." *Criminal Justice and Behavior* 11, no. 3:277–308.

Forst, Brian. 1983. "Prosecution and Sentencing." In *Crime and Public Policy,* edited by James Q. Wilson. San Francisco: ICS Press.

Gaes, Gerald G. 1985. "The Effects of Overcrowding in Prison." In *Crime and Justice: An Annual Review,* edited by Michael Tonrey and Norval Morris. Chicago: University of Chicago Press.

Greenfield, Lawrence A. 1988. *Drunk Driving.* Washington, D.C.: Bureau of Justice Statistics, U.S. Department of Justice.

Heinzelmann, Fred, W. Robert Burkhard, Bernard Gropper, Cheryl Martorana, Lois Mock, Maureen O'Connor, and Walter Travers. 1984. *Jailing Drunk Drivers: Impact on the Criminal Justice System.* Washington, D.C.: U.S. Department of Justice.

Innes, Christopher A. 1986. *Population Density in State Prisons.* Washington, D.C.: Bureau of Justice Statistics, U.S. Department of Justice.

Jacob, Herbert. 1984. *The Frustration of Policy: Responses to Crime by American Cities.* New York: Longman.

Jacob, Herbert, and Robert L. Lineberry. 1982. *Governmental Responses to Crime: Crime and Governmental Responses to American Cities.* Washington, D.C.: National Institute of Justice, U.S. Department of Justice.

Jacob, Herbert, and Duane Swank. 1982. "Police Expenditures And Public Policy: An Analysis of an Anomaly." Paper presented at the annual meeting of the Southwest Social Science Association, San Antonio, Texas, March.

Langan, Patrick A. 1985. *The Prevalence of Imprisonment.* Washington, D.C.: Bureau of Justice Statistics, U.S. Department of Justice.

Lipton, Dugan, Robert Martinson, and Judith Wilks. 1975. *The Effectiveness of Correctional Treatment.* New York: Praeger.

Lynch, James P. 1988. "A Comparison of Prison Use in England, Canada, West Germany, and the United States." *Journal of Criminal Law and Criminology* 79, no. 1:180–217.

McDonald, Douglas C., and Kenneth E. Carlson. 1993. *Sentencing in the Federal Courts: Does Race Matter?* Washington, D.C.: Bureau of Justice Statistics, U.S. Department of Justice.

MacKenzie, Doris Layton. 1994. "Shock Incarceration as an Alternative for Drug Offenders." In *Drugs and Crime,* edited by Doris Layton MacKenzie and Craig D. Uchida. Thousand Oaks, Calif.: Sage Publications.

NCCD (National Council on Crime and Delinquency). 1988. "The NCCD Prison Population Forecast: The Growing Imprisonment of America." *NCCD Focus,* April, 1–7.

Petersilia, Joan. 1987. *Expanding Options for Criminal Sentencing.* Santa Monica, Calif.: Rand Corporation.

Sechrest, Lee, Susan White, and Elizabeth Brown. 1979. *The Rehabilitation of Criminal Offenders.* Washington, D.C.: National Academy of Sciences.

Tonry, Michael. 1988. "Structuring Sentencing." In *Crime and Justice: An Annual Review,* edited by Michael Tonry and Norval Morris. Chicago: University of Chicago Press.

Tracey, Paul E., Marvin E. Wolfgang, and Robert M. Figlio. 1985. *Delinquency in Two Birth Cohorts.* Washington, D.C.: National Institute of Justice, U.S. Department of Justice.

U.S. Bureau of the Census. 1993. *Statistical Abstract of the United States, 1992.* Washington, D.C.: U.S. Government Printing Office.

———. Various years. *Statistical Abstract of the United States.* Washington, D.C.: U.S. Government Printing Office.

U.S. Department of Justice. Bureau of Justice Statistics. 1987. *Imprisonment in Four Countries.* Washington, D.C.: U.S. Government Printing Office.

———. 1988. *Pretrial Release and Detention: The Bail Reform Act of 1984.* Washington, D.C.: U.S. Government Printing Office.

———. 1991a. *Probation and Parole, 1990.* Washington, D.C.: U.S. Government Printing Office.

———. 1991b. *Tracking Offenders, 1988.* Washington, D.C.: U.S. Government Printing Office.

———. 1992. *Drugs, Crime, and the Justice System.* Washington, D.C.: U.S. Government Printing Office.

———. 1993a. *Capital Punishment, 1992.* Washington, D.C.: U.S. Government Printing Office.

———. 1993b. *Census of State and Local Law Enforcement Agencies, 1992.* Washington, D.C.: U.S. Government Printing Office.

———. 1993c. *Jail Inmates, 1992.* Washington, D.C.: U.S. Government Printing Office.

———. 1993d. *Prisoners in 1992.* Washington, D.C.: U.S. Government Printing Office.

———. 1993e. *Sourcebook of Criminal Justice Statistics.* Washington, D.C.: U.S. Government Printing Office.

———. 1994a. *Criminal Victimization in the United States, 1992.* Washington, D.C.: U.S. Government Printing Office.

———. 1994b. *Women in Prison.* Washington, D.C.: U.S. Government Printing Office.

U.S. Department of Justice. Federal Bureau of Investigation. 1993. *Uniform Crime Reports for the United States.* Washington, D.C.: U.S. Government Printing Office.

SUGGESTED READINGS

Eisenstein, James, Roy B. Fleming, and Peter F. Nardulli. *The Contours of Justice; Communities and Their Courts.* Boston: Little, Brown, 1988. An analysis of the operation of criminal courts and how they vary from community to community.

Goodstein, Lynne, and Doris Layton MacKenzie. *The American Prison.* New York: Plenum Press, 1989. A collection of essays that review most aspects of prison life and prison policy.

Morris, Norval, and Michael Tonry. *Between Prison and Probation: Intermediate Punishment in a Rational Sentencing System.* New York: Oxford University Press, 1990. The best treatment of theories of sentencing and how their social functions can be performed by alternative sanctions.

Scheingold, Stuart A. *The Politics of Street Crime.* Philadelphia: Temple University Press, 1991. An analysis of the policy choices facing municipal officials, and how those are confounded by the various ideologies that shape public and elite thnking about crime control.

Wilson, James Q. *Thinking about Crime.* 2d ed. New York: Basic Books, 1983. Although dated, an excellent series of essays on most of the important issues in crime and criminal justice.

CHAPTER 11

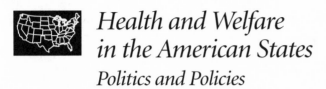

Health and Welfare in the American States
Politics and Policies

MARK ROM

America's health and welfare are tightly connected. Our health and welfare programs, unfortunately, are not. Traditionally, our health programs deliver medical treatment, and our welfare programs provide income support. Both types of programs deliver treatment or income to well-defined groups. Government-sponsored medical services go, in particular, to the elderly and to those with low incomes, as does income support. These programs have helped millions by staving off deprivation and disease, yet they have failed to create a nation of independent, prosperous, healthy individuals.

The problem is not a shortage of programs that affect our health and welfare; the United States has such programs beyond count. After all, there are more than 80,000 units of government around the country, and almost anything these governments do influences the health and welfare of their constituents. When governments fund or regulate agriculture, the environment, or transportation, for example, they affect our food, our water, and our air, surely the basic factors upon which our health is based. As governments fund or regulate education, housing, and commerce, they shape our knowledge, our shelter, and our jobs, all issues that determine our welfare.

In this chapter, however, I will focus primarily on the programs that deliver medical services and income support to the needy, especially as these programs

I wish to thank Nancy Schretzman for her able research assistance on this project and Virginia Gray for her insightful comments on an earlier draft.

involve state governments. I will attempt to answer five questions. First, what are the major health and welfare programs? Second, what are the politics of these programs? Third, what are the main patterns regarding program recipients, benefits, and expenditures? Fourth, what are states doing to reform their health and welfare programs? Finally, what are the states doing outside of these programs to promote personal health and economic independence?

There are many reasons to be hopeful regarding our nation's health and welfare. Although perhaps few readers will be encouraged by the politics and policies described in this chapter, it appears that state and federal governments are just now entering a period of vigorous experimentation as they attempt to improve the health and wealth of their citizens. The next edition of *The Politics of the American States* may depict programs far different—and, one hopes, more successful—than those described here.

THE PROGRAMS

Health and social welfare programs are the giants in our governments' budgets. In 1991, federal, state, and local governments spent over $1.1 trillion on social programs and another $330 billion on medical programs (U.S. Bureau of the Census 1994, 110, 372). State and local governments accounted for about 40 percent of social expenditures and one-third of medical expenditures; the federal government picked up the rest of the tab.

Social welfare programs either transfer income or provide services to individuals to improve the quality of their lives. The vast majority of social welfare spending is not aimed specifically at those in poverty. For example, Social Security, the largest national social welfare program, paid $420 billion to the elderly in 1992 (U.S. House 1994, 5). Medicare, a purely national program that provides medical benefits to the elderly, cost the federal government almost $130 billion in 1992 (U.S. House 1994, 124). The largest social welfare program funded by state and local governments—public education—cost these governments almost $260 billion in 1991 (U.S. Bureau of the Census 1994, 371).

Yet these social expenditures are not what is commonly known as welfare. *Welfare* usually refers to those programs that provide public assistance only to the poor. American governments spent $290 billion in 1992, or about one-fourth of their total social expenditures in that year, on these welfare programs. State and local governments, for their part, pay more than one-quarter of these welfare expenditures. The most important federal, state, and local welfare spending categories (including medical programs that target the poor) are presented in Table 11-1.

Medical programs are the largest welfare programs, consuming almost half (46 percent, or $134 billion) of the nation's welfare spending. States pay 40 percent of this amount. Note, in particular, that more than two-thirds of state spending on welfare is devoted to medical care. The vast majority of this spend-

Table 11-1   Cash and Non-Cash Benefits for Persons
with Low Incomes, 1992 (millions of dollars)

Program	Federal	State and local
Medical benefits	78,529	55,503
Medicaid	67,827	50,240
Veterans	7,838	0
General assistance	0	4,850
Indian Health Service	1,431	0
Maternal and child health	646	413
Cash aid	48,374	20,976
AFDC	13,569	11,354
SSI	18,744	4,030
Earned-income tax credit	9,553	0
Foster care	2,223	1,937
Pensions for needy veterans	3,954	0
General assistance	0	3,340
Food benefits*	32,661	1,446
Housing benefits[†]	20,535	0
Education aid[†]	15,423	614
Social services[†‡]	5,346	3,205
Jobs and training[†]	5,024	476
Energy assistance[†]	1,674	94
Total	207,566	82,314

SOURCE: U.S. Bureau of the Census 1994, 373.
*Food stamps; school lunch program; Women, Infants, and Children
(WIC); nutrition program for the elderly.
[†]Includes other programs not shown separately.
[‡]Nonfederal expenditure is a rough estimate.

ing is channeled through the Medicaid program. Indeed, states spend more on providing medical services to the poor than they do on all other health and medical programs combined. In 1991 the states spent $48 billion on Medicaid and general assistance (GA) medical payments and $40 billion on all other health and medical programs (U.S. Bureau of the Census 1994, 371).

Cash assistance programs make up the second largest block of welfare spending, accounting for about one-quarter of all welfare spending ($69 billion). The states, moreover, pay 30 percent of this amount ($21 billion). About one-quarter of state welfare expenditures goes to cash assistance programs. The largest such state programs are Aid to Families with Dependent Children (AFDC), Supplemental Security Income (SSI), and general assistance.

The states played a relatively minor role in all of the other welfare programs because more than 90 percent of state spending on benefits provided either medical or cash assistance. Notably, the states spent small amounts on such items as nutritional assistance, job training, or educational aid to the poor.

Medicaid, AFDC, SSI, and GA together soak up almost 90 percent of state welfare spending, while Medicaid and GA consume most state health expenditures. To understand state health and welfare programs, we must thus focus on the four big programs. What are their purposes? What do they do? How do they work?

Medicaid

Medicaid is the program that provides medical care to low-income persons who are aged, blind, disabled (primarily, SSI recipients), or in families with dependent children (AFDC recipients) and to certain other pregnant women and children (for a thorough discussion of Medicaid eligibility, services, and financing, see U.S. House 1994, 783–813). Medicaid is an entitlement program created as one of the Great Society efforts of the mid-1960s. The federal government and state governments share responsibility for it. The federal government establishes Medicaid guidelines (concerning eligibility, services, and financing), and the state governments design and administer the program. As with AFDC, federal and state governments split the cost of the program based on the federally established matching rate.

All states (except Arizona) must provide Medicaid to individuals in "categorically needy" groups (for example, those eligible for SSI or AFDC). Since 1982, Arizona has been running a medical program for low-income residents as a demonstration project and is thus exempted from the Medicaid program. The twelve states that offered Medicaid before SSI was implemented (Connecticut, Hawaii, Illinois, Indiana, Minnesota, Missouri, New Hampshire, North Carolina, North Dakota, Ohio, Oklahoma, and Virginia) may use their more strict Medicaid eligibility standards. States can also, at their option, provide coverage to those in "medically needy" groups, that is, those individuals who do not meet the income or resource standards of the categorically needy but otherwise meet the Medicaid standards. In 1993, thirty-eight states offered at least some services to the medically needy. States are required to provide more extensive services to the categorically needy than the medically needy.

Medicaid eligibility historically was linked to participation in AFDC or SSI. Beginning in the mid-1980s, however, the federal government gradually expanded coverage for other low-income pregnant women and children. For example, since 1988, states have been required to provide Medicaid for an additional year to families that leave AFDC because of rising income; since 1991, states must cover all children born after September 30, 1983, if their family income is below the federal poverty line, until they reach age nineteen (U.S. House 1994, 784–85). Eligibility for Medicaid is broadest for children in poverty; in 1992, 74 percent of poor children under five years of age received benefits, compared with only 30 percent of adults between the ages of forty-five and sixty-four (U.S. House 1994, 788).

The federal government requires that states provide a broad list of medical services within Medicaid, including inpatient and outpatient hospital services as well as physicians' services, to the categorically needy. States are allowed to offer additional services (such as the provision of drugs, eyeglasses, or psychiatric care), and they are also permitted to establish limits on recipients' use of the services (for example, on the number of hospital days reimbursed).

States reimburse health care providers who have delivered services to Medicaid recipients. The states decide, within federal guidelines, the reimbursement rates. Since 1989, states have been required to set reimbursement rates high enough so that Medicaid services will actually be available to recipients, at least to the extent that they are available to other residents in the state. Health care providers generally are required to accept these reimbursements as full payment for their services. In 1990 the Supreme Court, in *Wilder v. Virginia Hospital Association* (496 U.S. 498, 509), affirmed that institutions have the right to seek federal review of the state-set reimbursement rates, and hospitals and nursing homes in various states have since filed suit.

All individuals who are eligible for Medicaid are entitled to receive benefits. Federal and state governments are obligated to pay for the medical services obtained by eligible recipients. These governments thus can neither budget precisely how much they will spend on Medicaid each year nor limit expenses to a fixed amount. As a result, this open-ended entitlement program has become the glutton of state budgets—devouring all dollars in its path.

Aid to Families with Dependent Children

AFDC provides income support to needy children (and their guardians) when their principal wage earner is absent continuously, unemployed, incapacitated, or dead. Originally established in the Social Security Act of 1935 as a temporary program to provide assistance to widows and their families, more than fifty years later it provides income for more than 14 million Americans. Federal and state governments share responsibility for designing, financing, and administering AFDC (for a brief history of AFDC, see Peterson and Rom 1990).

States set benefit levels for AFDC in a roundabout way. First they calculate a needs standard, which the state regards as the amount necessary for a family to buy a reasonable amount of food, clothing, and shelter. Any family whose income is below the needs standard and is otherwise eligible (for example, because they have few assets) can receive assistance. The state then establishes the maximum amount it will provide eligible families by deciding how much of the needs standard it will supply. The actual grant is the difference between this maximum and the amount of income the family earns minus a certain amount for child care and transportation costs and, for a period of time, a percentage of the family's income. Federal law requires that AFDC mothers cooperate with state welfare officials to establish paternity of a child and to obtain child support; still, child support payments (except for the first $50 each month) go to the state. Adults lose their eligibility if their income rises above the needs standard; children lose eligibility on their eighteenth or nineteenth birthday at the state's option. Families receiving AFDC are automatically eligible for Medicaid.

The portion of the benefits paid by the federal government is established by the Medicaid matching rate. The matching rate is inversely proportional to state average per capita income; in the poorest states, the federal government will pay up to 80 percent of the benefits, while in the more affluent states it will pay 50 percent. For example, in 1994, the matching rate was 79.99 percent for Mississippi and 50 percent for the thirteen most affluent states (U.S. House 1994, 383–385). Administrative expenses are split fifty-fifty between federal and state governments.

In the past, AFDC was simply a "check writing" program; enrolled families received a monthly check from the government. Increasingly, however, AFDC has become a broader social service program, particularly since the enactment of the Family Support Act's Job Opportunities and Basic Skills (JOBS) training program in 1988. The purpose of JOBS is to help ensure that recipients obtain the education, training, and employment they need to become economically self-sufficient. In return for participating, recipients are provided supportive services such as child care and reimbursement for work-related expenses. In 1992, about 16 percent of the target AFDC population participated in JOBS. State welfare agencies administer AFDC, including JOBS, subject to extensive rules from the federal government.

AFDC, because it traditionally provided income only to single-parent families, had come under political attack for providing incentives for families to split up and for single women to become mothers. In response to these criticisms (and an economic recession), the AFDC-Unemployed Parents (AFDC-UP) program was established in 1961 so that families with jobless fathers could receive benefits. Until 1990, AFDC-UP was an optional program, and many states chose not to offer it; in that year, the federal government made the program obligatory for all states.

Supplemental Security Income

Established in 1972 as a replacement for several other federal programs that provided grants to the states, the SSI program provides cash payments to elderly, blind, or disabled persons who are also poor. The federal government establishes eligibility requirements, sets national benefit levels, and administers the program; states have the option of supplementing the federal benefit standard. All but seven states (Arkansas, Georgia, Kansas, Mississippi, Tennessee, Texas, and West Virginia) provide supplemental benefits. The federal government pays for federal benefits and administration; the state governments fund the supplemental benefits and their administrative costs.

In 1994 the federal SSI monthly benefit standard for an individual was $446; for a couple, $669. States set their own standards for supplemental benefits. SSI benefits are reduced as a recipient's earned income rises or if the recipient is living with another person. Federal SSI benefits are indexed to inflation, so recipients receive the same cost-of-living adjustments as do Social Security beneficiaries. SSI recipients may also be eligible for Social Security, Medicaid, and food stamps; they may not, however, also receive benefits from AFDC.

General Assistance

General assistance programs are purely state efforts designed to provide cash and medical assistance to low-income individuals who are not eligible for Medicaid, AFDC, or SSI. They receive no federal funds.

The term *general assistance* is a generic term for the entire group of state programs, which vary widely. Some GA programs cover broad categories of people who are not eligible for federal assistance, such as able-bodied adults without children, certain two-parent families with children, and the not quite elderly or disabled. Other states provide benefits only to narrow groups (for example, those who have applied for SSI but are not yet receiving benefits) or in special circumstances (as when a home is destroyed by a natural disaster). In 1992, twenty-two states administered statewide programs, and in twenty other states at least one county operated a GA program (in seven of these states, the state government requires all counties to offer GA). Eight states (Alabama, Arkansas, Louisiana, Mississippi, Oklahoma, Tennessee, and Wyoming) had no GA programs. Since 1992, at least one other state—Michigan—has abolished its GA program.

THE POLITICS

The Medicaid, AFDC, SSI, and GA programs together spend almost $200 billion each year to assist about 30 million recipients. Except for GA, the programs are a complex mix of federal and state designs, funds, and administrations. In this section I will examine the main factors that influence these programs.[1] While these elements include economic and demographic attributes, political factors ultimately dominate. The reasons for this are clear. Economic and demographic conditions provide policy makers with opportunities and constraints, but these conditions do not by themselves make policies: politicians do. The politicians make program decisions based on their electoral concerns, their ideological beliefs, and their pragmatic judgments about what is best for their constituents, state, and country.

Political Factors

Ours is a federalist country. Authority over health and welfare policy is thus shared—not always agreeably—among state and national governments. This has four main implications for state policies. First, states do not have sole jurisdiction over health and welfare policy: they are constrained by national laws. On the one hand, states must provide certain services and follow specific rules; on

---

1. Many scholars have written about the factors that influence state health and welfare programs, especially Medicaid and AFDC, in the United States. The analysis in the text briefly summarizes some main findings of these scholars. Those interested in studying the politics of health and welfare policies in the states would profit by turning to their research. For Medicaid, see Barrilleaux and Miller 1988; Buchanan, Cappelleri, and Ohsfeldt 1991; Grogan 1994a, 1994b; Hanson 1984; Reutzel 1989; and Schneider 1993. For AFDC, see Peterson and Rom 1990; Plotnick and Winters 1985; Shi 1994; Tweedie 1994. For GA, see Daniels 1991.

the other, they cannot adopt proposals they prefer if these conflict with federal law.

Second, state and federal governments each attempt to gain control over health and welfare programs while at the same time attempting to shift burdens to the other party. Efforts toward control can be seen in federal mandates on the states, in which the federal government requires the states to perform certain functions, and state requests for waivers from these mandates, whereby the states seek to escape from these requirements and establish their own standards. States, moreover, are often tempted to play these programs in such a way that they obtain the maximum federal financial support at minimum cost to themselves (Grogan 1994b). Note that states have greater incentives to manipulate welfare financing than does the federal government. Unlike the federal government, the states' constitutions prohibit them from running budget deficits, so the states literally cannot afford to be as generous as the federal government.

Third, state governments compete (and, at times, cooperate) with each other. As ambitious politicians strive to build their reputations, some of this competition is to become the policy leader among the states. More pervasive, however, is the economic competition of the states. As this competition has become increasingly intense, states have become more eager to cut their redistributive (that is, welfare) programs. Low welfare spending helps states attract businesses and avoid becoming so-called welfare magnets (Peterson and Rom 1990).

Fourth, state and federal governments each face other political, economic, and demographic factors (discussed below) that influence policy choice. Because these factors vary among state and federal governments, the policy choices of these governments also vary.

In addition to the influences of federalism, the political culture, ideology, institutions, and opinions of the states and the nation all affect health and welfare policies. These influences can differ across the states and change over time.

Political culture is "the particular pattern of orientation to political action in which each political system is embedded" (Elazar 1972, 84–85). This orientation "may be found among politicians and the general public, and it may affect their understanding of what politics is and what can be expected from government, influence the types of people who become active in politics, and influence the ways in which they practice politics and formulate public policy" (Sharkansky 1969, 67). In moralistic political cultures, "both the general public and the politicians conceive of politics as a public activity centered on some notion of the public good and properly devoted to the advancement of the public interest" (Elazar 1970, 174). Traditionalistic or individualistic political cultures, in contrast, view politics as a way of preserving the status quo or gaining personal enrichment, respectively, as explained in Chapter 1. Moralistic political cultures thus tend to be more activist and generous in their health and welfare programs than traditionalistic or individualistic states. A state's political culture changes only slowly, moreover, so it is the most stable of the political variables.

Political ideology involves the durable views of politicians about what the government should do and how it should do it. Most basically, Americans have either conservative or liberal ideologies regarding health and welfare programs; liberals are in favor of expanded benefits and more inclusive eligibility standards, and conservatives prefer more restrictive benefits and eligibility. Political culture thus is related to, but by no means identical to, political ideology. Moralistic states are not necessarily liberal, nor individualistic states invariably conservative, although traditionalistic states almost always are conservative. (For an excellent discussion of the relationship between ideology and political culture, see Erikson, Wright, and McIver 1993, 150–176; also see the brief description of ideology in Chapter 1.) Political conservatives in moralistic states might believe that governments best help the poor by making welfare difficult to obtain; liberals in individualistic states might seek to increase welfare spending merely to enhance their own political fortunes.

The political institutions of American governments—their legislatures, bureaucracies, political parties, interest groups, electoral systems—can also influence health and welfare policies. In general, governments with professional legislatures and competent bureaucracies may be more active in developing programs and openhanded in supporting them. Interest groups appear to be more involved, and more influential, in some states than in others and in some issues than others (Grogan 1994a; Hrebenar and Thomas 1987). States with more highly mobilized publics and more competitive elections are also more likely to support social welfare programs (Barrilleaux and Miller 1988; Buchanan, Cappelleri, and Ohsfeldt 1991; Peterson and Rom 1990; Plotnick and Winters 1985; Shi 1994).

Policy makers pay attention to public opinion, and these opinions vary across the states, over time, and among health and welfare issues. It should come as no surprise that the citizens of Minnesota and Mississippi, for example, have different opinions about the appropriate role of their governments in social policy and that state policies reflect in part these opinions. Still, the sentiments of the nation as a whole also change over the years, with the public looking more favorably on the recipients of welfare in the 1960s than in the early 1980s and mid-1990s. The American public also appears typically to be more sympathetic to programs that provide goods and services (like food and health care) to the poor rather than give them cash. Certain types of recipients are more politically popular. The "deserving poor" (for example, the disabled, children, and the elderly) are viewed sympathetically and provided greater support from health and welfare programs, while the "undeserving poor" (for example, young men and women bearing children out of wedlock) are scorned by the public.

Economic and Demographic Factors

The principal economic factors influencing health and welfare policies are both cyclical and structural. Whenever the economy goes into recession, the number of individuals eligible for these programs increase (as more people become poor) and program costs rise; when the economy is growing faster, fewer individuals receive benefits and costs are reduced. This cyclical effect, however, may be overshadowed by broader structural changes in the American economy and demography during the last couple of decades that have substantially increased the prevalence of poverty within certain groups (especially women and children) even during times of prosperity.

The causes for these economic and demographic changes are complex and hotly debated. They involve such issues as the decline in well-paying blue-collar jobs, the increase in single-parent families (through divorce and, particularly, childbearing out of wedlock), and the perceived rise in a more permanent underclass apparently locked in poverty. Nevertheless, it is important to note that the absolute wealth of the country—and so the potential resources available for health and welfare programs—has increased substantially every decade since the 1940s. These gains have not been shared equally by all groups or by all states, however.

Policy Implications

These political, economic, and demographic factors affect health and welfare policies in subtle and complex ways. All American governments are subject to their influence; however, because the exact weight of each factor differs for each state, varies between state and national governments, and changes over time, there is no single pattern of evolution for health and welfare policies. Still, a few observations might be offered.

In general, the federal government has expanded health and welfare eligibility criteria and benefit levels. States, in contrast, have been more concerned with restraining eligibility and benefits. With notable exceptions, the states are less generous with public assistance than the federal government. The most important political influence on the number of welfare recipients, for example, has been the federal government's tendency to expand program coverage (especially regarding Medicaid), with occasional moves by either federal or, more commonly, state governments to restrict it. Most notably, the federal government has substantially increased the availability of Medicaid to poor families and children. The states, meanwhile, have increasingly restricted GA. Still, the willingness of all levels of government to provide cash public assistance has declined in recent years.

Benefits are also higher for SSI than for AFDC, in part because SSI recipients are seen as more deserving of government support. These different perceptions of the relative merit of SSI and AFDC recipients have also probably contributed to the growing gap between the two programs, as the public has become increasingly hostile to the idea of government support for "welfare mothers."

Medicaid has also become more popular politically than AFDC because of differences in the goals and methods of each program. Medicaid's goal of remedying illness for the poor is easily seen as more concrete, specific, and feasible than AFDC's goal of reducing poverty. Public support is much higher for providing medical treatment to those who need it than for providing income to those who lack it. Furthermore, while both Medicaid and AFDC attempt to pay for essential needs, Medicaid does so directly (by purchasing services from health care providers), whereas AFDC does so indirectly (by providing cash to the poor). While it is clear that Medicaid buys health care, the public cannot be sure what AFDC buys.

Although the states in general are less willing and able than the federal government to support public assistance programs, there is nonetheless tremendous variation in the demand for and supply of these programs among the states. This variation again arises from economic, demographic, and political reasons. States differ in their economic circumstances; some are better able to afford public assistance than others. States also have diverse populations, with certain states having higher proportions of groups typically in greater need of public assistance (for example, single-parent families, the disabled, the elderly); policy makers in these states undoubtedly face greater political pressure to restrain program costs and reduce the number of beneficiaries. The states that have moralistic political cultures, highly professional institutions, mobilized parties and publics, and generously inclined publics have shown greater support for health and welfare programs than those states that do not have these characteristics.

It is worth remembering, however, that state health and welfare policy choices are far more complicated than a simple tallying of economic, demographic, and political forces would suggest. Policies vary among the states for unique historical reasons. An unusually forceful leader, a public scandal, a temporary surge in public opinion, can all have lasting effects on policy choice.

THE PATTERNS

Let us now turn to the patterns—and the anomalies—in health and welfare policies. First I examine trends since the mid-1970s in recipients, benefits, and expenditures nationally. After that, I discuss state program data.

Trends in Benefit Levels

Trends in benefits for the AFDC, Medicaid, and SSI programs are shown in Figure 11-1. The most important trend involves Medicaid. Real per-recipient Medicaid costs increased by nearly 120 percent (from $1,531 to $3,936) between 1975 and 1992, the last year for which data are available. While average Medicaid expenses were only three-fourths of AFDC benefits and two-fifths of SSI benefits in 1975, by 1993, Medicaid costs per beneficiary exceeded both AFDC and SSI. Moreover, real per-recipient Medicaid costs grew every single year during this period. Unlike AFDC and SSI, for which real benefits declined in at least some years, real Medicaid benefits grew by at least 2.4 percent every year, while average growth over these years was 5.7 percent.

Figure 11-1 Annual Welfare Benefits per Recipient, 1975–1993

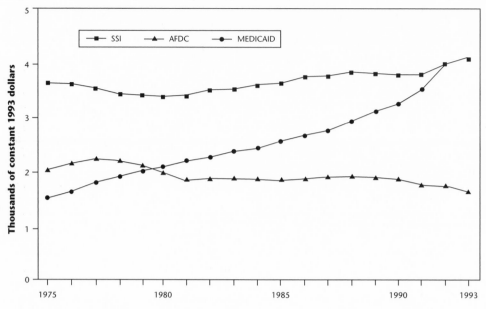

S O U R C E : Calculations from data in U.S. House 1994, 248, 262, 389, 796.

It is interesting to note that SSI benefits have been much larger than AFDC benefits for the entire period. In 1977, when the gap was narrowest, AFDC recipients received only about 60 percent as much as SSI recipients. By 1993, average AFDC benefits were only 40 percent as much as SSI benefits. Moreover, SSI and AFDC benefits have moved in different directions. By 1993, real average SSI benefits per recipient had grown by 20 percent (from $3,339 to $4,021) from their low point in 1980. In contrast, by that same year, real average annual AFDC benefits per recipient had dropped by almost 30 percent (from $2,215 to $1,576) from their peak in 1977. Yet these trends are neither automatic nor permanent. During the late 1970s SSI benefits were falling while AFDC benefits were increasing; after that, those patterns were reversed.

The differences in benefits between state and federal governments are even more striking. Average SSI benefits per person are much more generous than AFDC benefits, in large part because the federal government sets and fully funds a minimum benefit level for SSI. These federal benefits have also been indexed (and at times, overindexed) to inflation since the mid-1970s. While real federal SSI benefits grew at least slowly during these decades, rising by 0.5 percent annually on average between 1975 and 1993, state supplements declined sharply. Forty-three states supplement federal SSI benefits, yet real benefits declined in the median state by nearly 70 percent between 1975 and 1994 (U.S. House 1994, 224). Real state-supplemented benefits for aged individuals without countable income living independently fell by 63 percent; for aged couples, 75 percent. Not a single state maintained real benefit levels.

Real Medicaid benefits have also expanded enormously, especially in comparison with AFDC benefits. Although the state governments actually administer both programs, the federal government determines who will be covered by Medicaid and what services they are eligible to receive. Indeed, since Medicaid's inception, the federal government has continually expanded the program by requiring states to provide additional services to additional categories of individuals (U.S. House 1994, 783, 789).

Several factors have contributed to these trends. Program benefits set by the federal government (such as Medicaid and, mainly, SSI) have grown; benefit levels set by the states (such as for AFDC) have fallen. The states are clearly more eager to avoid paying for public assistance than is the federal government. Public opinion also supports these trends; hostility to providing cash to the "undeserving poor" (that is, AFDC recipients) has grown, whereas furnishing services (for example, Medicaid) to the needy has not. Inflation in medical fees has also contributed to the growth in Medicaid benefits. Finally, it must be noted, constituencies supporting higher benefits for SSI and Medicaid (for example, the elderly and doctors) have been more effective in voicing their support for these programs than have the supporters of AFDC.

Trends in the Number of Recipients

The number of recipients in the AFDC, Medicaid, and SSI programs annually between 1975 and 1993 are shown in Figure 11-2. All three programs have grown much faster than the U.S. population during this period. The number of SSI beneficiaries has grown an average of 1.5 percent annually, for example, while the number of AFDC and Medicaid recipients has risen 2 percent per year; the nation's population itself has increased at about 1 percent annually.

Program growth has not been steady, however. The number of AFDC recipients has fallen in seven of the eighteen years, and SSI rolls have declined in six. Program growth was especially rapid in the early 1990s, when SSI and AFDC grew by almost 7 percent annually and Medicaid by an extraordinary 10 percent. It is also worth noting that those enrolled in the SSI and AFDC programs have been gradually making up a smaller share of the Medicaid caseload. In 1975, 70 percent of those receiving Medicaid were also provided benefits by SSI or AFDC. By 1993, that figure was down to 62 percent as Congress expanded Medicaid eligibility.

Still, these trends do not mean that everyone who needs assistance is getting it. In 1975, over 70 percent of the elderly poor obtained SSI, and a similar proportion of poor children received AFDC; in 1993, only about half of the elderly poor received SSI, and 60 percent of children in poverty received AFDC. Most of this decline had occurred by 1982; since then, the coverage of each program has varied, but in neither case has coverage of the poor risen to the levels of 1975.

Figure 11-2 Welfare Recipients, 1975–1993

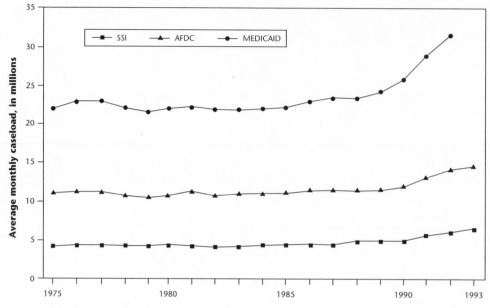

SOURCE: Calculated from data in U.S. House 1994, 248, 395, 798.

How can this be consistent with the growing number of SSI and AFDC recipients? For SSI, this figure reflects the growing number of the disabled (not elderly) poor; for AFDC, it indicates that the number of children in poverty has grown substantially since the 1970s.

Trends in Expenditures

Total real federal and state spending on AFDC, SSI, and Medicaid during 1975–1993 is shown in Figure 11-3. This figure illustrates the size of each program in relation to the others as well as the shares funded by federal and state governments. It can be clearly seen that state and federal spending on Medicaid dwarfs expenditures by either level of government on SSI and AFDC. Although it did so even in 1975, the gap between it and other programs had become much wider by 1993: in that year, total spending on Medicaid ($121 billion) was almost six times more than SSI ($22 billion) and AFDC ($23 billion). Federal and state expenditures on Medicaid rose 8 percent per year, on average, during these years; for SSI the average growth rate was 2 percent; for AFDC, 0.2 percent. If welfare spending is a problem, the problem is not AFDC but Medicaid.

Federal and state governments both shared in the growth of Medicaid's spending; the portion of the expense borne by each level of government was constant over the period (with the federal government carrying about 57 percent of the load). Medicaid's astonishing growth, fueled both by rising caseloads and

Figure 11-3   Welfare Spending, 1975–1993

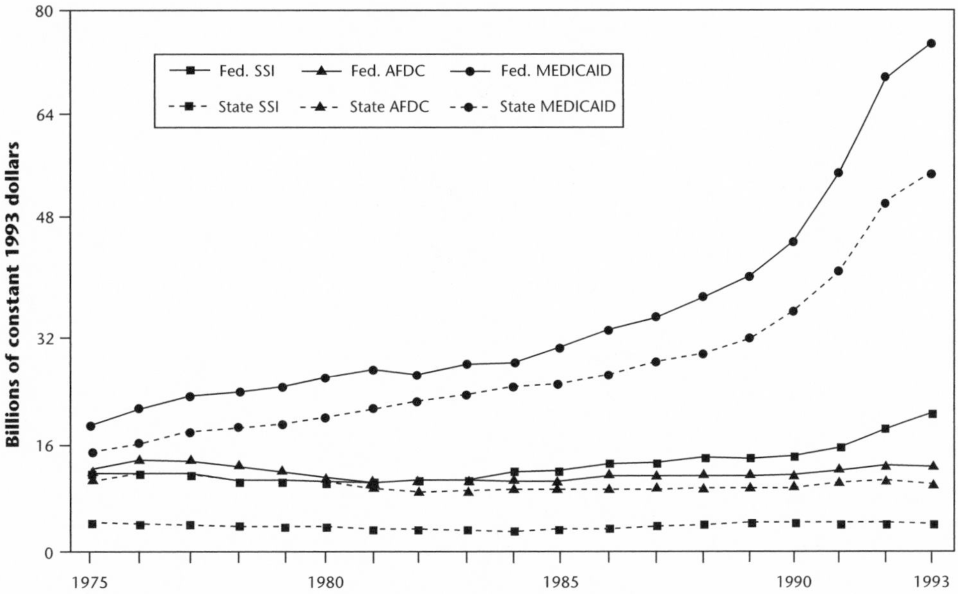

SOURCE: Calculated from data in U.S. House 1994, 262, 389, 796.

benefits, was thus a burden to both federal and state governments. The distribution of AFDC costs was unchanged during these years; the federal government picked up 55 percent of the cost every year. Only for SSI did the federal government assume an increasing portion of the costs; between 1975 and 1993 the federal share grew from 73 to 84 percent.

State Welfare Benefits and Recipients

The national trends since 1975 have thus featured growing recipient populations, especially for Medicaid; rising program expenditures, also especially for Medicaid; and diverging benefit levels (Medicaid grew and AFDC shrank). These trends have not affected all states equally, nor have all states responded in the same way to the changing times. Let us now examine the state of the states.

Benefits. Welfare benefits vary dramatically across programs and among the states (Table 11-2). The average annual benefit given by the states to each recipient in 1993 was $3,200 for Medicaid and $2,950 for SSI; the average annual AFDC benefit, $1,480, was less than half this amount. In almost every state, AFDC benefits were lower than SSI and Medicaid benefits—much lower in most states. In thirty-two states, average AFDC benefits per recipient were less than half the average SSI benefits per recipient. Only in California and Hawaii are average SSI benefits lower than AFDC benefits; only in California are Medicaid benefits lower.

Table 11-2   Mean Annual Welfare Benefit per Recipient, 1993

State	AFDC benefit	AFDC Rank	MEDICAID benefit	MEDICAID Rank	SSI benefit	SSI Rank
Alabama	684	48	2,261	44	2,994	21
Alaska	3,036	1	3,224	19	3,333	8
Arizona	1,368	28	520	51	2,771	32
Arkansas	828	45	2,757	30	3,043	16
California	2,376	4	1,938	48	1,958	51
Colorado	1,332	31	3,143	21	3,489	7
Connecticut	2,388	3	5,263	2	2,863	28
Delaware	1,428	23	3,590	17	3,030	18
Florida	1,164	38	2,287	43	2,952	24
Georgia	1,080	39	2,487	39	3,071	15
Hawaii	2,568	2	2,700	33	2,464	46
Idaho	1,344	30	3,161	20	3,091	13
Illinois	1,284	32	3,100	22	2,840	30
Indiana	1,056	41	4,389	7	2,695	35
Iowa	1,620	17	3,065	24	3,000	19
Kansas	1,428	25	2,731	31	2,870	27
Kentucky	936	44	2,647	37	2,759	33
Louisiana	672	50	3,531	18	2,453	47
Maine	1,740	13	3,963	11	3,590	5
Maryland	1,428	24	4,276	9	2,660	38
Massachusetts	2,304	5	4,735	4	2,551	42
Michigan	1,728	14	2,482	40	2,520	45
Minnesota	2,004	10	4,310	8	3,193	10
Mississippi	504	51	1,809	50	2,827	31
Missouri	1,080	40	2,437	41	2,967	23
Montana	1,416	26	3,617	14	2,857	29
Nebraska	1,356	29	3,099	23	3,699	4
Nevada	1,248	34	3,615	15	2,931	25
New Hampshire	1,896	11	4,789	3	3,947	3
New Jersey	1,536	18	4,020	10	2,572	41
New Mexico	1,248	36	2,255	45	2,920	26
New York	2,220	7	5,974	1	2,263	50
North Carolina	1,056	42	2,654	36	2,983	22
North Dakota	1,524	19	4,439	6	3,333	9
Ohio	1,368	27	2,988	26	2,545	43
Oklahoma	1,248	33	2,789	29	5,075	1
Oregon	1,716	15	1,894	49	3,509	6
Pennsylvania	1,512	20	3,019	25	2,408	48
Rhode Island	2,172	8	3,634	13	2,727	34
South Carolina	804	46	2,671	34	3,077	14
South Dakota	1,248	35	3,609	16	3,095	12
Tennessee	708	47	2,210	46	3,000	20
Texas	684	49	2,176	47	3,038	17
Utah	1,488	21	2,664	35	2,647	39
Vermont	2,304	6	2,846	28	2,667	37
Virginia	1,188	37	2,934	27	3,109	11
Washington	2,100	9	2,367	42	2,539	44
West Virginia	1,020	43	2,581	38	2,575	40
Wisconsin	1,860	12	3,811	12	2,299	49
Wyoming	1,452	22	2,714	32	4,118	2

SOURCE: Calculated from data in U.S. House 1994, 249, 391, 799, 801.

Within any single program, moreover, the states differ greatly in the benefits they offer. In 1993, Connecticut paid AFDC recipients an average of almost $2,400 per year, while Mississippi granted them just $500. Among the forty-eight contiguous states, average Medicaid benefits ranged from less than $2,000 (again, in Mississippi) to nearly $6,000 (in New York); mean SSI benefits were lowest in California ($2,000) and highest in Oklahoma ($5,100). The maximum (not average) annual GA benefit per person was $6,000 in Maine, while eight states provided no cash benefits. These differences are much greater than the cost-of-living variations in the states.

There is no simple relation among the benefits states offer. The correlations between the states' SSI benefits and their AFDC or Medicaid benefits are quite small (at 0.15 and 0.03, respectively, the correlation coefficients are not statistically significant). There is only a modest consistency between AFDC and Medicaid benefits among the states (the correlation coefficient [0.38] is statistically significant at $p < .01$). A strong relationship does exist between AFDC and GA benefits, however: states that are more generous with AFDC also tend to be liberal with GA benefits (the correlation coefficient is 0.68 [$p < .01$]; six states make benefit decisions on a case-by-case basis and so were omitted from the correlation). In other words, the states that are most generous with AFDC and GA are not necessarily openhanded with SSI (although they may be with Medicaid); the states most stingy with AFDC and GA need not be so miserly with SSI (although they may be with Medicaid).

As we have already seen, AFDC benefits have declined nationally since the mid-1970s. This trend toward lower real benefits has affected all states: once inflation is taken into account, no state had a higher maximum in 1993 than in 1975. (Interestingly, the two states whose real benefits changed the least were Alaska and Mississippi, the most and least generous states, respectively.) The decline has also been large. On average, state maximums fell by 36 percent during this period. Still, there was tremendous variation in the decline. Real maximum benefits fell by as much as 61 percent (in Idaho) and as little as 2 percent (in Alaska). Nor were declines concentrated among the most or least generous states. Benefits decreased by about the same amount, on average, in the most and least generous states, declining by an average of 33 percent in the fifteen most generous states and by 36 percent in the fifteen least generous states.

The more affluent states support more generous social welfare programs than do their poorer peers, as noted earlier. In general, a state whose median income is $1,000 higher than that of another state offers annual maximum AFDC benefits that are $280 higher.[2] This relation is not ironclad, however. Some states with higher incomes nonetheless have lower benefits, and vice versa. In Minnesota, for example, maximum AFDC benefits are $6,380 per year and median annual

2. This estimate is derived from a bivariate regression. The correlation coefficient is 0.76 ($p < .01$).

household income is $31,000; in Virginia, median household income is more than $7,000 higher than in Minnesota and maximum AFDC benefits are more than $2,000 lower. Moreover, the gap between AFDC benefits and household incomes grows larger as the benefits fall lower. In the most generous ten states, maximum AFDC benefits averaged 21 percent of household income (incomes averaged $36,500; benefits averaged $7,600), while in the stingiest ten states, maximum AFDC benefits averaged less than 10 percent of household income (incomes averaged $24,800; benefits averaged $2,400). The states with the highest (and lowest) incomes reveal a similar picture. In the ten states with the highest median incomes (averaging $38,700), mean AFDC benefits were $6,640, and AFDC benefits averaged 17 percent of median income. In the ten states with the lowest incomes (averaging $24,200), mean AFDC benefits were $2,920, and the average benefit was 12 percent of median income.

Nor does the relation between affluence and generosity hold true for SSI and income. For most states, there is no direct link between state incomes and SSI benefits. The reason for this is simple. The federal government has established the floor for SSI benefits, and so state supplements tend to be modest. Some of the more affluent states do provide larger supplements, however.

AFDC benefits are also as closely tied to a state's political ideology as to its income. States that are more liberal provide, on average, greater benefits. The correlation between ideology (as Erikson, Wright, and McIver [1993, 77] define it) and AFDC benefit is 0.75 ($p < .01$). Once again, there are strong exceptions. Delaware is much more liberal than its relatively low AFDC benefits would indicate; New Hampshire offers higher benefits than its conservative ideology suggests it would.

Ideology and income are not entirely independent of each other. In general, states with higher incomes were also more politically liberal (correlation coefficient, 0.60 [$p < .01$]). Yet income and ideology each are important influences on welfare; that is, knowing both a state's income and its ideology allows us to predict its welfare benefits better than if we knew only one of those factors. Together, income and ideology explain about 80 percent of the variation in AFDC benefits among the states (coefficients for both income and ideology are statistically significant [$p < .01$]).

State Welfare Recipients. As with benefits, the states vary greatly in the proportion of their residents receiving welfare (Table 11-3). California, the state with the highest proportion of its population receiving AFDC (almost 8 percent) has four times as large a welfare population as Idaho (less than 2 percent). The mean among the states is 4.8 percent. SSI beneficiaries range from a little less than 1 percent of the population (in Utah) to slightly more than 5 percent (in Mississippi). The mean among the states for SSI is 2.3 percent. Over 20 percent of the public receives Medicaid in Rhode Island, yet less than 6 percent of Nevadans are on the rolls. In all but two states (Alabama and Arkansas) the size of the AFDC population is greater than the size of the SSI population. GA programs tend to be

Table 11-3   Welfare Recipients as a Percentage of the Population, 1993

State	AFDC %	AFDC Rank	MEDICAID %	MEDICAID Rank	SSI %	SSI Rank
Alabama	3.33	42	11.15	24	3.80	5
Alaska	6.08	11	9.68	31	1.84	32
Arizona	4.99	22	10.21	28	1.62	37
Arkansas	2.98	45	13.24	11	3.75	6
California	7.90	2	14.37	8	3.18	10
Colorado	3.45	41	7.26	48	2.30	18
Connecticut	4.94	24	9.64	32	2.11	22
Delaware	3.97	35	8.71	42	1.43	45
Florida	5.05	19	11.24	21	2.24	20
Georgia	5.78	15	12.49	16	2.70	14
Hawaii	4.76	26	8.53	43	1.45	43
Idaho	1.93	51	7.92	45	1.55	39
Illinois	5.88	14	11.23	23	2.61	15
Indiana	3.73	38	8.87	39	1.45	42
Iowa	3.58	39	9.91	29	1.39	47
Kansas	3.48	40	8.97	36	1.30	49
Kentucky	5.92	12	15.39	7	4.01	3
Louisiana	6.13	9	16.34	5	3.96	4
Maine	5.43	17	13.08	13	2.26	19
Maryland	4.46	28	7.59	46	1.51	40
Massachusetts	5.41	18	11.41	19	2.48	16
Michigan	7.27	3	11.91	17	2.03	27
Minnesota	4.24	32	8.99	34	1.68	35
Mississippi	6.52	6	18.43	3	5.07	1
Missouri	5.02	21	10.58	27	2.22	21
Montana	4.13	33	7.15	49	1.43	44
Nebraska	3.01	43	9.40	33	1.68	36
Nevada	2.54	50	5.62	51	1.22	50
New Hampshire	2.63	49	6.31	50	1.33	48
New Jersey	4.45	29	8.85	40	1.70	34
New Mexico	5.91	13	13.12	12	2.48	17
New York	6.58	4	14.06	9	2.95	12
North Carolina	4.82	25	11.30	20	2.78	13
North Dakota	2.90	46	8.98	35	1.42	46
Ohio	6.46	7	13.00	15	1.93	30
Oklahoma	4.27	31	11.14	25	4.18	2
Oregon	3.89	36	13.03	14	1.98	28
Pennsylvania	5.04	20	9.75	30	1.96	29
Rhode Island	6.18	8	21.30	1	2.10	24
South Carolina	4.03	34	11.83	18	2.96	11
South Dakota	2.80	48	8.95	37	1.82	33
Tennessee	6.09	10	15.40	6	3.29	8
Texas	4.32	30	11.23	22	2.06	26
Utah	2.82	47	7.37	47	0.97	51
Vermont	4.95	23	13.54	10	2.08	25
Virginia	3.00	44	7.93	44	1.93	31
Washington	5.49	16	10.83	26	1.56	38
West Virginia	6.55	5	16.92	4	3.30	7
Wisconsin	4.71	27	8.73	41	2.10	23
Wyoming	3.88	37	8.94	38	1.49	41

SOURCE: Calculated from data in U.S. House 1994, 243, 249, 391, 799, 1215.

much smaller but are more variable; the median state of the thirty-nine for which data were available had about 4,000 GA recipients. Yet New York's GA program served almost 400,000 individuals each month in 1992, and South Carolina offered benefits to only 5 persons.

While there is only a weak relation between benefits for these three programs among the states, the size of the recipient populations is more closely linked. States with larger SSI populations tend also to have larger AFDC populations (correlation coefficient, 0.46 [p < .01]). And since those on SSI or AFDC are also eligible for Medicaid, the size of the Medicaid population in the states is directly proportional to the size of the populations for those two welfare programs. The variation in those two populations explains 70 percent of the variation in Medicaid populations across the states.

What is the relation between the generosity of a state's benefits and the size of its welfare rolls? While it might seem obvious that states that offered higher benefits would have greater shares of their residents receiving welfare, this is not true: there is little connection between benefit size and program rolls (correlation coefficient, 0.19 [p < .15]). The two states paying the lowest AFDC benefits (Mississippi and Louisiana) have proportionately more recipients than all but one of the seven states offering the highest benefits (California is the exception). An even looser connection exists between SSI and Medicaid benefits and their respective populations (correlation coefficients, 0.00 and 0.17, respectively). Paradoxically, the highest proportion of public assistance recipients are found in the more affluent states with higher benefits (such as California and New York) as well as in the poorer states with lower benefits (such as West Virginia and Mississippi).

THE PROPOSALS

During the 1960s and 1970s the federal government was the leading innovator in social welfare policy. It is no more. The states, once again, are where the main policy experiments are being conducted. The federal government is responsible for this by omission and commission: it failed to enact comprehensive health care reform in 1994, and it appears ready to delegate substantial control over welfare to the states in 1995. The states, for their part, are eager to gain control over these policy areas (as long as this control will not cost them too much) and willing to innovate to solve their problems.

Health Care Reform

The states are under tremendous financial pressure to reform their health care systems. State health expenditures (especially for Medicaid) have been rising rapidly. Because virtually all state constitutions require balanced budgets, the states, unlike the federal government, are unable to finance health programs by running deficits. The number of Medicaid recipients has also been growing quickly because of factors beyond the states' control (such as federal mandates and the growing number of people without private health insurance). Yet public demand for health services also continues to increase. As a result of rising costs, rising demand, and incomplete insurance coverage, many states are not waiting for the federal government to take the lead in health care reform.[3]

State health care reform proposals are usually built around two main goals. The first is to control costs, both for the state's citizens and for the state itself. The second is to provide access, so that the health care needs of all (or almost all) citizens are met. (Although the goal of quality care is also important, it is more controversial and difficult to define than the other two goals.) States are considering a variety of strategies to accomplish one or both of these goals. To control costs, states are examining such alternatives as centralized state planning agencies, global budgets, and increased regulation as well as market-based reforms that encourage managed care and reduce malpractice costs; shifting costs to the federal government or other providers is another popular alternative. To increase access, some states are focusing their efforts on particular groups (such as the poor in Minnesota and uninsured workers in Florida); other states (such as Hawaii and Oregon) are attempting to provide insurance for all residents. Some states are seeking to broaden insurance coverage by providing subsidies (Minnesota, Oregon, Washington); others, by enacting laws to make insurance more affordable and available (Colorado).

While almost all states are considering some type of health care reform, and the types of reforms being considered are quite diverse, it is worth briefly mentioning a few state programs or proposals that are among the most comprehensive or innovative. The success of these proposals is, of course, uncertain. All the political, economic, and demographic factors that influence their existing programs will also affect their reform efforts.

Two especially important federal barriers to state health care experiments stem from the Medicaid program and the Employment Retirement Income Security Act (ERISA).[4] ERISA preempts state authority to regulate self-insured firms and health insurance plans administered by third parties. As a result, states are unable to implement employer mandates or to limit employer-provided insurance benefits, for example, without receiving federal waivers. Likewise, states must receive waivers from the federal government if they plan to offer programs that differ from those specified by Medicaid. These are important barriers. Oregon's proposal for a Medicaid waiver was rejected by the Bush administration, and it would need an ERISA waiver to finance its program as planned. In Colorado, Gov. Roy Romer (D) vetoed a bill providing universal care because it

3. State initiatives are reviewed in Elliott 1993; GAO 1992; IHPR 1993; and Moon and Holahan 1992. For a historical perspective on state health reforms and a discussion of recent legislation, see Fox 1994.

4. Other impediments are discussed in Parmet 1993. Hawaii enacted its reform prior to ERISA and later became the only state to receive a federal exemption from it.

would have required both Medicaid and ERISA waivers; he called for legislation that would avoid this (Elliott 1993). The Clinton administration has promised to simplify and speed the waiver process; it remains to be seen whether it does (it has, however, approved Oregon's Medicaid waiver).

Hawaii was the first state to act (in 1974, long before the current health care crisis), when it enacted its successful Prepaid Health Care Act (PHCA; Lewin and Sybinsky 1993). It is still the only state with a comprehensive health care system. The PHCA, by requiring all employers to cover their employees with a standard, state-established package of health benefits and by subsidizing low-income families, has achieved a level of insurance coverage unprecedented in the nation; at the same time, it has not depressed business, increased unemployment, or proved too expensive. By the early 1980s, 95 percent of the residents of Hawaii had health insurance.

Oregon was the first state to attempt explicitly to ration health care. To expand its Medicaid coverage to more people, the state ranked 709 medical procedures in order of importance and effectiveness and planned to reimburse only the top 587 of them until the Medicaid budget was exhausted. Oregon also has an ambitious plan for ensuring universal coverage. Insurance is to be provided through the workplace, with the state extending services to those at or below the poverty line. It is to be a voluntary plan—employers are given tax incentives to insure their employees—with a mandatory "play-or-pay" component if enough workers are not covered. In play-or-pay programs, firms are required to pay a tax (pay) if they do not provide insurance (play) for their workers. Although Oregon has received its Medicaid waiver (necessary for its rationing scheme), as mentioned above, it will also need an ERISA waiver for its play-or-pay provisions, and it has not yet decided how to proceed.

Minnesota enacted and began implementing its HealthRight law in 1992. Instead of attempting to provide universal coverage, this law subsidizes health insurance for all residents earning less than 275 percent of the poverty line and who do not qualify for Medicaid. The program's main emphasis is on providing preventive and primary care in managed-care settings; its first target population is families with children and then adults without children. To control costs, a state-established commission was mandated to reduce health care inflation by 10 percent each year for the first five years. The plan is funded by new taxes on cigarettes (2 percent), hospitals and health care providers (2 percent), and insurers' gross revenues (1 percent). Minnesota is being sued for violating ERISA; it will also need a waiver if it is to incorporate the Medicaid program.

Florida has attempted to expand health insurance coverage through voluntary measures (although play-or-pay measures are to be used if coverage goals are not met by 1995). To encourage businesses to expand coverage while controlling costs, the state offers pooled health care purchasing arrangements. Florida is also attempting to develop a streamlined Medicaid benefit package that individuals and small businesses could purchase. Unlike Minnesota, then, the Florida plan focuses its efforts on its citizens who are already working; it does not attempt to assist the poor or unemployed.

Vermont, Colorado, and Washington, among other states, have also attempted to launch broad experiments in health care reform. Many other states have reformed their health systems along more conventional lines, such as by expanding care subsidies and regulating hospitals to contain costs (IHPR 1993).

Comprehensive reform does not come easily, however. In 1988, Massachusetts enacted legislation to provide universal coverage through a play-or-pay system, with the unemployed and impoverished covered by an expanded Medicaid program. Employer protests, an economic downturn, the need for an ERISA waiver, and a changed political environment have all delayed implementation of this program. It now appears unlikely that much of the 1988 law will ever go into effect.

Sweeping reform was soundly defeated in California, where the proposed California Health Security initiative was voted down in 1994. The Health Security Act would have given the state full responsibility for funding and managing health care. Each citizen would have been issued an identity card guaranteeing access to health care and medicines when necessary; the state would have controlled payments to providers, approved reimbursement levels, and set service standards. To pay for its universal care, California would have attempted to pool its Medicare and Medicaid payments, impose a payroll tax on all employers and an income tax surcharge on all individuals, and assess a tax of one dollar per pack on cigarettes.

While the prospects are good that at least some states will enact significant health care reforms in the coming years, one should not be too confident that the states by themselves can solve their health care problems (Gray 1994; Grogan 1994). The barriers are many, the challenges high, and the risks significant, especially for the poorer and weaker states. It is worth remembering that some of the states with the largest uninsured populations—like Texas, New Mexico, and Louisiana—are among the slowest moving on health care reform.

Welfare Reform

In contrast to health care, the drive to reform welfare (specifically, AFDC) comes neither from increased public demand for more welfare nor from increased program costs. Total real state and federal spending on AFDC has remained virtually unchanged since the mid-1970s; although state and federal budgets have grown considerably during this period, AFDC spending, as a share of those budgets, has diminished considerably. To be sure, the number of recipients has risen, especially since 1990, but falling real benefits have kept total program expenses from rising. Although policy makers and the public would no doubt like to reduce spending on welfare, the call for welfare reform comes not from the view that AFDC costs too much but rather that it fails to help the poor. The central criticisms of AFDC are that it creates dependency and encourages illegitimate births. The belief is widespread that AFDC has become a trap, not an open door.

Dependency is thought to be manifested in two ways. First, welfare recipients are seen as typically remaining on the dole for extended periods. Second, it is widely believed that welfare is passed from generation to generation, and thus, parents who cannot support their children will have children who cannot support theirs. Both claims have some truth, although it is important to understand the limits to these truths.

Many welfare recipients do indeed obtain benefits over long periods. At any given moment, 50 percent of the adults receiving AFDC have been on the rolls continuously for eight or more years. Yet many also obtain only short-term assistance; about 50 percent of AFDC recipients receive welfare benefits for less than two years at a time (and, over time, 80 percent receive them for less than eight years).[5] In other words, the AFDC program has essentially two groups of recipients—those who need (and use) short-term help and those who remain dependent for long periods. It is thus incorrect to argue that welfare recipients become dependent; many do, but most do not.

It is also true that there is an intergenerational aspect to AFDC. Daughters who grow up in homes highly dependent on welfare are more likely than others to receive AFDC when they become parents (see especially Gottschalk 1992 and U.S. House 1994, 447–449). "More likely" does not mean certainly. For example, one study found that over 60 percent of the daughters of heavily dependent mothers received no AFDC themselves (Duncan, Hill, and Hoffman 1988). Moreover, Gottschalk, after controlling for other relevant factors, found that the effect of welfare on dependency appears to be small (Gottschalk 1992). Because children receiving welfare grow up in poverty (and so have fewer educational, social, and economic opportunities than the more affluent), it is not surprising that many become poor adults (and so eligible for welfare). A final intergenerational finding may also surprise some: there is an apparent correlation between mothers and daughters on welfare for whites and Hispanics but not for African-Americans (Gottschalk 1992).

The problems of illegitimacy and child poverty have also grown dramatically during since the mid-1970s. Whatever one thinks about the morality of childbearing out of wedlock, it is clear that the large surge in illegitimate births is directly linked to the large increase in child poverty. In 1960, 5 percent of all children were born out of wedlock; in 1990, 30 percent were. In 1960, the child poverty rate was 15 percent; in 1990, it was just under 20 percent. The children most likely to be poor, furthermore, were those born to parents who were unmarried.

---

5. How can these seemingly contradictory facts be resolved? Assume that five people receive benefits during an eight-year period. One individual is on the rolls continuously. The other four are on the rolls consecutively for two-year periods. At any given time, then, half (one of two) the recipients are on the rolls for eight years. Over time, however, 80 percent (four of five) of the recipients receive benefits for less than eight years.

Yet the link between illegitimacy, child poverty, and welfare is far from clear. Some observers, such as the writer Charles Murray, have argued that welfare leads to illegitimacy and child poverty (Murray 1984). Yet few serious scholars believe that welfare has such a powerful effect on behavior. Indeed, real welfare benefits have been declining since the mid-1970s, while illegitimacy rose unabated; moreover, states offering higher benefits do not have higher levels of childbearing, nor are women on welfare more likely to have children than other women (Rank 1989). At most, welfare probably creates what the writer Mickey Kause has called an "economic life support system" for single mothers (Kause 1994).

Whether or not AFDC causes dependency and illegitimacy, numerous states appear eager to reform welfare in such a way that it discourages those traits. Reformers of all political stripes desire to change welfare so that it will foster work and marriage, independence and responsibility. Naturally, reformers disagree about the best way to obtain these goals. The most extreme view—although one that receives much publicity—is that no welfare program can do these things; the only way to eliminate problems in the welfare system is to eliminate welfare itself. More prudent reformers have sought ways to encourage recipients to engage in socially appropriate behaviors while still providing them essential support services.

Many recent state welfare reform proposals and programs consequently attempt to use monetary incentives (bonuses or, more often, punishments) to exact personal responsibility from welfare recipients. For example, states are using these incentives to promote school attendance, immunizations, work, marriage, and family planning (Levin-Epstein and Greenberg 1992). More dramatically, some states are preparing to introduce the ultimate economic incentive to encourage responsible behavior: welfare recipients may obtain benefits and services for only a specified period of time and, after that, they must leave the welfare rolls.

As is true of health care reform, states cannot conduct welfare experiments without limit. If a proposed state experimental, pilot, or demonstration project conflicts with federal law, the state must obtain a waiver for this program from the U.S. Department of Health and Human Services (HHS). The Clinton administration insists that, in order to encourage state innovation, it is willing to give waivers for experiments with which it does not necessarily agree. HHS has speeded the waiver process; indeed, some critics argue that waivers are often awarded without adequate public comment because they are processed so quickly (Levin-Epstein and Greenberg 1992, 3).

Workfare Programs. Workfare programs require welfare recipients to work in return for receiving welfare benefits. While federal law already requires states (through the JOBS program) to provide education, training, and employment services to a certain share of their welfare recipients, advocates of workfare insist that welfare recipients should be required to accept employment rather than just prepare for it.

No states currently have full-fledged workfare programs. This may soon change. The Republican governors George E. Pataki of New York, William F. Weld of Massachusetts, and Tommy G. Thompson of Wisconsin, for example, have all pledged in their campaigns to create workfare programs. The public, too, is sympathetic. Workfare will be no panacea, however. Studies of existing welfare-to-employment programs show that they have limited ability to help recipients obtain jobs (Bane and Ellwood 1994). Many welfare recipients, unfortunately, are among the least employable elements of the population, often lacking even such basic work skills as the ability to read. Serious workfare programs will thus have to provide employment to those unable to find private sector jobs. The political enthusiasm for workfare in general is tempered when it comes to creating and funding public sector employment for these recipients.

Learnfare Programs. Learnfare is the generic term for state efforts to reward or punish AFDC families for their children's school attendance. Before 1992, two states (Ohio and Wisconsin) had adopted Learnfare programs. In Wisconsin, benefits are cut for AFDC families whose teenage children fail to meet monthly attendance requirements, although the program has, like all others, exempt populations and excused absences. Ohio's Learning, Earning, and Parenting Program (LEAP) provides a bonus of $62 per month to pregnant and parenting teenagers who meet monthly attendance requirements and imposes a $62 per month penalty on those who fail to meet these requirements. California, Maryland, Missouri, and Virginia have also received approval to begin Learnfare programs. Legislation to create or expand Learnfare programs was rejected in fifteen other states (Levin-Epstein and Greenberg 1992, 10–15).

While Learnfare sounds like a good idea, there is limited evidence to gest either that it is cost-effective or even that it works at all. Implementation has been tedious, requiring extensive documentation and producing many appeals.

Family Caps. Family caps on programs would prevent families from obtaining additional benefits if they have children while eligible for AFDC, or at least reduce the size of the increased benefits. Under current federal law, families receive benefits based on the number of children they have. The rationale behind family cap proposals is that working families do not automatically receive raises when they have children—why should welfare recipients? In fact, however, those who have children but are not receiving welfare may obtain additional federal benefits through the tax code and the earned income tax credit.

Four states (California, New Jersey, Virginia, and Wisconsin) have received waivers to experiment with family caps. Only New Jersey and Virginia are currently implementing this program. In 1992, legislatures in seventeen states, including California and Wisconsin, considered and rejected the family cap idea (although Governor Thompson of Wisconsin claims he has restored it through that state's unique item veto). One possible reason for the reluctance of states to enact the family cap is the difficulty of fairly enforcing it in practice. Women can become pregnant through no fault of their own, as a result of rape, incest, or contraceptive failure. It is not an appealing prospect to punish these women by imposing family caps. And how easy is it for the government to determine whether a child was born for one of these reasons? Furthermore, family caps are likely to increase the number of abortions—an unappealing prospect to many people.

Family Planning. Federal law currently forbids states to require individuals to obtain family planning services as a prerequisite to receiving AFDC. However, the federal Title X program offers, at no charge, family planning services to any person below the poverty line. Still, a few states (Mississippi, South Carolina, and Tennessee) considered but rejected proposals to provide bonuses to women who became sterilized while receiving AFDC. Although there is little support for policies that promote sterilization, there is also, unfortunately, little enthusiasm for making family planning services in general more accessible to welfare recipients or to individuals at risk of going on welfare. It appears that large percentages of women who end up on welfare did not receive family planning counseling (Levin-Epstein and Greenberg 1992).

The prospects for state welfare experiments are strong. At the national level, Democrats and Republicans agree that national welfare reform should provide states flexibility and encourage them to innovate. In early 1995, Republican congressional leaders called for the federal government to consolidate the funds for its welfare programs, turn these funds over to the states in the form of block grants, and give the states full responsibility for designing and administering welfare programs. Before one concludes that the Republicans had a mandate to do this, however, it is worth remembering that President Ronald Reagan called—futilely—for a similar transfer of funds and authority in his New Federalism program. During the summer of 1995, Congress continued to debate shifting more responsibility for welfare to the states.

PREVENTION

Thus far I have focused on the main state and federal health and welfare programs. These programs, almost by definition, provide care to the sick and cash to the poor, especially poor women with children. They do not, by and large, work to prevent individuals from becoming sick or from needing pubic assistance. Our health and welfare programs emphasize treatment rather than prevention.

There are good reasons for this. The most important ones involve time and resource pressures. Policy makers usually face the situation in which people need immediate assistance, and there is not enough money both to help them with their needs and to prevent others from requiring the same assistance later. We all know this feeling: the roof is leaking and the furnace needs maintenance, but this month we have only enough money to choose one. Naturally, we try to fix the roof first and let the furnace go until next month. Unfortunately, next month something else will need fixing. The dilemma is that something needs fixing every month.[6]

Yet the maxim is true: an once of prevention is worth a pound of cure. It is cheaper (and perhaps easier) to keep people off welfare than to get them off; it is cheaper and easier to stay well than to heal. Most observers, conservative and liberal alike, agree that well-designed health and welfare prevention programs can be more effective and cost less than treatment programs. As a matter of policy, however, federal and state governments typically spend far more on treatment than prevention. In the late 1980s, the federal Centers for Disease Control and Prevention estimated that our national investment in prevention is less than 5 percent of our spending on health care (CDC 1992).

The dilemma that favors treatment over prevention can be overcome in two ways. If a state is rich enough, it can afford to do both prevention and treatment. Paradoxically, the states that need most to emphasize prevention often have the worst current problems and are least able to afford to look toward the future. At any rate, the richer the state, the better able it is to afford prevention. In addition, if a state is unified and committed enough politically, it might decide to spend on prevention despite its pressing treatment needs. Unity and commitment are necessary: there are never enough resources, so spending on prevention dictates that some constituents in need of treatment will be ignored. Ignoring constituents is possible to the extent that policy makers concur that it must be done and stick to this concurrence.

The combination of unity and commitment is scarce in partisan politics. But even when both political parties are committed to prevention they may have strong differences about what real prevention is. Liberals (and Democrats) in general view prevention as a set of positive incentives offered by the government. To keep individuals healthy, programs must provide them education or services so that they will be willing and able to become physically strong and economically self-sufficient. Conservatives (and Republicans) usually reject this view, placing responsibility for physical and economic health more squarely on the individual citizens. Government, from the conservative perspective, mainly creates incentives for persons to become dependent and diseased by providing welfare and health benefits in the first place. Accordingly, government practices prevention best by ensuring that individuals bear the consequences of their own actions.

Nonetheless, it is worth considering three questions. Why do people become ill (and so in need of medical care)? Why do families become needy (and so in need of welfare)? What can states do to prevent illness and neediness? Although the answers to the first two questions no doubt involve social (and even meta-

6. An alternative version of this problem involves the Arkansas Traveller (not President Clinton). The Traveller, noting that the Hillbilly's roof was leaking badly, asked him why he did not fix it. "I can't," the Hillbilly replied; "it's raining." "Well," suggested the Traveller, "why do you not fix it when the sun is shining?" The Hillbilly scoffed: "It never leaks then!"

Table 11-4 Nine Leading Behavioral Factors Contributing to Deaths in the United States, 1990

Contributing factor	Number of deaths	Contributing factor	Number of deaths
Tobacco	400,000	Sexual behavior	30,000
Diet and activity	300,000	Motor vehicles	25,000
Alcohol	100,000	Illicit drugs	20,000
Microbial agents	90,000	Other (not behavioral)	1,088,000
Toxic agents	60,000	Total	2,148,000
Firearms	35,000		

SOURCE: McGinnis and Foege 1993, 2207–2212.

physical) elements, I will focus here on behavioral answers: people need medical treatment and welfare in part because of the way they behave. State efforts at prevention therefore might need to address these behaviors.

The major behavioral factors contributing to premature death (and excessive need for medical care) have now been identified (McGinnis and Foege 1993). These behavioral risk factors are largely responsible for about half of all premature deaths each year (Table 11-4). The big three—tobacco, diet, and alcohol—contribute to perhaps 40 percent of all deaths and 75 percent of premature deaths. The other major factors identified—microbial or toxic agents, firearms, sexual behavior, motor vehicles, and illicit drugs—account for the other 25 percent of premature deaths. (Microbial agents are counted to the extent that individuals die from treatable diseases because they did not seek or receive treatment.) Paradoxically, our public policies devote resources to controlling these risks in inverse proportion to the risks they cause to public health (Glantz 1994). Glantz is referring to the federal government, but state priorities do not appear to differ.

The major behavioral factors that lead to welfare dependency are also clear. Families are most likely to spend long periods on welfare when children are born out of wedlock to young women. At the end of the 1980s in the United States, 80 percent of the children living in female-headed families in which the mother was younger than twenty-one were poor; virtually all these families received public assistance. Unfortunately, our welfare policies spend much more on providing assistance to these families than on preventing the need for assistance in the first place.

The behavioral risks that damage public health or create the need for public assistance each have distinctive politics. None of these politics is simple or rational. All involve personal activities—smoking, eating, drinking, shooting, and sex—that raise strong emotions in the political arena. Because they involve highly personal behaviors of millions of individuals, they are difficult for governments to control or change. Still, state governments have made at least temporary public health progress on some of these issues. Smoking rates are falling, as is the frequency of drunk driving. Other behaviors have been less susceptible to change. The public's willingness to adopt healthier diets and sexual behaviors has not been firmly established. And America's tolerance for gun violence remains undiminished.

Tobacco

Tobacco use, especially cigarette smoking, is by far the largest threat to public health. Each year tobacco use is responsible for approximately 400,000 deaths from a wide variety of causes, such as cancer, cardiovascular disease, lung disease, birth problems, and burns (HHS 1989). Although the federal and most state governments have treated the tobacco industry gently, in recent years policy makers have taken an increasingly tough stance in regard to cigarette smoking.

There are several reasons for the shift toward tougher policies on tobacco use. First, the scientific evidence has become incontrovertible that smoking creates large health risks without producing any positive health benefits. Second, these health risks exist not just for the smokers themselves, but also for those who live or work with them, although some scientific debate still exists regarding the effects of "environmental tobacco smoke" (see Sullum 1994). Third, economic and social elites—who are also typically those with the most political resources—have become more hostile toward tobacco use because they themselves smoke less; for example, in 1990 almost 32 percent of those with less than a high school education or those with incomes of less than $10,000 were current smokers, whereas only about 18 percent of those with more than a high school education or those with incomes over $50,000 were smokers (U.S. Bureau of the Census 1994, 139). Fourth, blame for tobacco use has been clearly placed on the tobacco industry itself; often depicted as the merchant of death, the industry has continued to deny any link between smoking, addiction, and health problems. Fifth, programs discouraging tobacco use need not cost much (through regulation) and indeed can raise substantial sums (through taxes).

The tobacco industry and users are not without their own political resources, however. The industry's main resource is money. It spends far more to promote smoking than the government does to discourage it; for example, the tobacco industry spends millions every year on advertising, not including the advertising inherent in its sponsorship of sporting events (the Virginia Slims Tennis Tour, for example, or the Winston 500 automotive races) and other activities. Tobacco interests also contribute extensively to political campaigns to ensure that their voice is heard. The tobacco users' main political strength is in their numbers. Because more than a quarter of the American public continues to smoke, politicians who threaten this activity (especially through taxation) face repercussions at the next election. Still, despite the tobacco industry's millions of smokers and millions of dollars, political strength is moving rapidly toward those who want to raise the cost and difficulty of smoking cigarettes.

State governments have acted with increasing vigor and creativity to discourage smoking. Twenty-seven states have moderate to extensive restrictions on smoking in public places, while nineteen other states have at least modest restrictions: four states (Alabama, Georgia, Kentucky, and Mississippi) have none. Forty-four states restrict smoking on school property, and ten states have banned it altogether (Hendrick 1994). In 1993, Vermont became the first state to ban smoking in all restaurants, motels, and hotels ("Vermont" 1993). Many cities around the country had also already passed similar laws, and many restaurants have voluntarily prohibited smoking. For example, by 1993, thirty-nine towns and the city of Oakland in California had banned smoking in all offices and restaurants. Laws do not necessarily mean results, of course, because state enforcement of tobacco laws are notoriously lax, particularly regarding sales to minors (see, for example, CDC 1993; for an analysis of the effect of state regulations on state smoking rates, see Devlin 1993). Still, these laws do send a message concerning state priorities.

California has perhaps the most ambitious smoking-control program, stemming from Proposition 99, approved by the state's voters in 1988. This proposition raised cigarette taxes by twenty-five cents per pack and launched a high-profile television campaign (as well as education efforts by schools and doctors) financed by $80 million of the $780 million raised each year by the tax. California's smoking rate has fallen faster than the national average, dropping from 27 percent to 22 percent between 1987 and 1992 (Zamichow 1992).

The states are also going to court. Minnesota, the first state to restrict smoking in public places (in 1975), and Blue Shield, the state's largest health insurer, have filed a joint suit against the tobacco companies for "conspiracy, fraud, and restraint of trade" ("Obscuring the Market" 1994). Minnesota, moreover, is the eighth state to file a suit since March 1994. Among the other seven, Mississippi was the first state to seek restitution for state expenditures on illnesses linked to smoking. Although the tobacco companies are not known for losing lawsuits, each lawsuit represents, at least, an attempt to pressure the industry. Still, the obstacles to reducing the prevalence of smoking in the United States are large (Satcher 1994).

Diet and Activity

Diet and activity (D&A) contribute to another 300,000 premature deaths each year, according to McGinnis and Foege (1993). (Because of the complex relationship between diet, activity, and premature death, these researchers present the lower bound of their estimates. Their analysis suggests that between 309,000 and 582,000 deaths in 1990 could be linked to diet and activity.) The problem is not too little food and too much work, but just the opposite: Americans in general eat too much fatty food and exercise too little. Federal and state policy makers have done much less to reduce D&A than to reduce tobacco as a risk to public health, however.

The political dynamics of D&A make it exceptionally difficult for policy makers to take effective action to reduce these risks. As is true of smoking, the evidence for the harmful effects of excessive fatty foods and lack of exercise is strong, and elites are generally sympathetic to the need for healthier diets and more exercise. A moderate correlation exists between income, education, exercise, and weight. Those with more than twelve years of education are twice as likely as those with less than twelve years to exercise regularly [52 and 26 percent, respectively]; the gap is somewhat less for those with incomes above $50,000 and below $10,000. Similarly, those with higher educations and incomes are less likely to be overweight than those with less education or income (see U.S. Bureau of the Census 1994, 139).

Yet the rest of the antagonism associated with smoking vanishes. The risks D&A create do not directly influence the health of others, as smoking does, so no natural opposition to poor D&A exists from those practicing healthier D&A. The risks associated with D&A create few obvious villains. Unlike tobacco, virtually all foods can be part of a healthy diet, and no one food can be singled out as the culprit (there is no "smoking gun" in the food business). Nor is there an obvious (and cheap) way to regulate or tax foods or activity to induce better diets and more exercise. Even more than tobacco use, D&A is regarded as a purely personal activity that the government has no authority to regulate or tax. Of course, food is regulated in many ways (for example, for contaminants and truth-in-labeling), and sales taxes are often applied. But nowhere in the United States is food regulated or taxed on the basis of content. Moreover, purveyors of fatty, salty food spend opulently on advertisements, whereas advocates of healthy D&A spend next to nothing. The number of Americans who have inferior D&A dwarfs the number of smokers.

As a result, there is no political momentum for legislatures to restrict diets or mandate exercise. Any policy activity that occurs comes from public health officials (or, for example, nutritionists), who understand the importance of improved D&A. Lacking regulatory authority, these officials have chosen to pursue an educational strategy to reduce the risks of D&A to public health. The one best place for state and local governments to intervene in D&A is in the schools, through the school lunch and physical education programs.

Still, the news is not promising. More Americans are overweight and fewer exercise vigorously than ever. One in three adults is now more than twenty pounds heavier than his or her ideal weight (Knight 1994; for details on America's D&A, see U.S. National Center for Health Statistics 1990).

Alcohol

Alcohol misuse accounts for 100,000 premature deaths annually. These deaths can occur through alcohol's effect on the body (for example, cirrhosis of the liver or fetal alcohol syndrome) and, perhaps more important, on behavior. Perhaps half of all homicides, assaults, car and boat fatalities, drownings and fire fatalities, and the like can be attributed at least in part to alcohol consumption (see HHS 1990; McGinnis and Foege 1993).

There are old politics and new politics of alcohol. The (mainly religious) call for prohibition defines the old politics. The public health consequences or the costs and benefits of alcohol use did not enter into the debate; the debate was about whether drinking was a sin. These politics still prevail in many parts of the country. Although no states maintain prohibition, numerous dry counties dot the map (especially through the parts of the country known as the Bible Belt). It is no small irony that the Jack Daniels (a Tennessee bourbon) distillery is located in a dry county.

The new politics of alcohol are a hybrid of those for tobacco and D&A. One of the main differences is that there is no real elite opposition to alcohol; those with higher incomes and educations drink as much as (if not more than) those with lower socioeconomic status. Alcohol use, moreover, is not seen (either medically or socially) as inherently harmful. Large portions of the public drink moderately, and medical research suggests that this might, in some circumstances, even be healthful. The alcohol companies themselves urge their buyers to "know when to say when."

While virtually all tobacco use and almost no D&A issues are politically vulnerable, the new politics of alcohol divides thus sharply between personal use and public misuse. In some central cities where personal alcohol consumption is itself seen as a major public health problem, there appears to be growing support for additional restrictions on the availability of alcohol (see, for example, Schneider 1994). In most places, however, additional policies to restrict purely personal use by adults have little political support. In contrast, public misuse—especially drunk driving—is being vigorously attacked around the country. Groups such as Mothers against Drunk Driving (MADD) and its offshoots (for example, Students against Drunk Driving) have mobilized much political and social support for their goal.

The states have led the way in these attacks, although not always willingly. The major impetus to state action was the 1984 federal law that required states to enact a minimum drinking age of twenty-one by 1986 or lose a portion of their federal highway funds (O'Malley and Wagenaar 1991). In 1982, for example, only fourteen states prohibited the purchase of alcohol by those under the age of twenty-one; all fifty states prohibited it by 1988. In recent years, numerous states have toughened their drunk driving laws by lowering the legal limit of intoxication, increasing penalties for violators, and expanding enforcement. These policies, as well as changing social mores, have contributed to the substantial decrease in the rate of deaths, injuries, and accidents attributed to alcohol-influenced driving.

Firearms

Firearms are increasingly seen as a threat to public health, and for good reason: in 1990, they were responsible for 35,000 fatalities through homicides, suicides, and accidents. The toll taken on our society by guns is unique among wealthy nations (Fingerhut and Kleinman 1990). Unique, also, is the widespread belief that gun ownership is a constitutionally protected citizen's right.

The politics of firearms are extraordinarily divisive. No claim concerning the role of firearms in our society's violence goes unquestioned (for a summary of some of the controversies, see Witkin 1994). Support for stricter gun control is broad among elites and the public as a whole, but opposition to controls is intense among gun owners and suppliers. Supporters of gun control recite with horror the toll taken by intentional and accidental gunfire each year. Gun advocates, for their part, correctly note that most gun owners pose no threat to public health; the others, the advocates contend, will pose a threat whether controls exist or not. As a result of the divisiveness of the politics of firearms, at least at the national level, the public is subjected to embarrassing debates about banning "assault weapons," as if such bans either would protect the public health or pose a threat to constitutional rights.

The extent of firearm violence varies widely from state to state and over time. In general, the southern and western states have much higher levels of violence than states in the Northeast or Midwest. Florida, for example, had almost 400 firearm-related violent crimes per 100,000 residents in 1990; North Dakota had just 6; the state average was about 200 per 100,000 residents (U.S. Department of Justice 1991).

The states also have a wide variety of policies to regulate and control the purchase, carrying, or ownership of firearms, and many states have attempted to strengthen these laws in recent years. (For a state-by-state summary of laws and regulations concerning handguns, see U.S. Department of Justice 1992, 133.) Unfortunately, none of these policies apparently has had any effect on gun violence (Brien et al. 1994). The meaning of this, of course, is debated. Opponents of gun control argue that these results demonstrate that such control does not work to reduce violence. Supporters contend that, in a society that so resembles an arsenal, the modest measures imposed by the states could not work to reduce violence.

Sexual Behavior

Alas, one of life's greatest pleasures is one of its greatest problems. Unprotected sexual intercourse can kill, injure, and deprive—and not just by transmitting the virus that causes AIDS. While the human immunodeficiency virus (HIV), sexually transmitted, accounted for about 21,000 deaths in 1990, unprotected sexual intercourse also contributed to 5,000 excess infant deaths (from unintended pregnancies), 4,000 extra deaths from cervical cancer, and 1,600 deaths from hepatitis B infection. In addition, some 12 million persons become infected with a sexually transmitted disease each year. Moreover, more than half of all pregnancies are unintended (McGinnis and Foege 1992).

The onset of AIDS has created special challenges for certain states' public health systems. Although every state has persons with AIDS (PWAs) as residents,

AIDS is not spread uniformly across the country: California, Florida, and New York, which contain about 25 percent of the nation's citizens, accounted for almost 50 percent of its AIDS cases diagnosed through 1992 (U.S. Bureau of the Census 1994, 134). Moreover, a large proportion of these individuals eventually receive Medicaid. Nationally, in the late 1980s, an estimated 40 percent of PWAs received Medicaid, and the proportion in some states was much higher; for example, perhaps 70 percent of PWAs in New York obtained care from Medicaid (Roper and Winkenwerder 1988). Typically, PWAs become eligible for Medicaid if they lose their own private insurance, their jobs, or their personal resources; through their eligibility in SSI or AFDC; or through a state's "medically needy" category of Medicaid (Green and Arno 1990). The result is that much of the health care cost of AIDS is shifted to the public sector. States with large numbers of PWAs, in particular, have been under tremendous pressure to contain the costs they have imposed on the public (for a discussion of state spending on AIDS, see Colby and Baker 1988 and Peterson and Schubert 1994). A principal way states have tried to cope is to seek Medicaid waivers so that PWAs may receive home- or community-based long-term care (rather than more expensive hospitalization).

The politics of sex is characterized by the struggle between those who view sexual behavior as a moral issue—primarily religious conservatives—and those who consider it a policy issue only to the extent that sexual behavior threatens public health—liberals, libertarians, and public health professionals (Nice 1994). The attitudes and policy preferences of these groups are fundamentally different. The former group believes that government policy should encourage or enforce only "moral" sex (that is, monogamous relations within a heterosexual marriage). The latter group argues that sexual relations between consenting adults are acceptable to the extent that they do not cause unintended pregnancies or spread disease; as a result, this group favors education concerning "safe sex" as the appropriate policy. State policies toward sexual behavior have to a large extent mirrored these divisions within their populations; more conservative states use less sex education; more liberal states rely less on moral messages.

The politics of sex have been especially unhelpful in regard to welfare policy. Unprotected sexual intercourse, of course, is literally the beginning of the nonmarital births to teenagers that put the family at special risk of needing public assistance. But prevention policies that focus directly on altering sexual behavior to reduce the number of teen pregnancies seem doomed to failure. There is not a great deal of evidence that government efforts either to encourage abstinence or to promote contraceptive use will reduce the rate of teen pregnancy.

Instead, it is becoming increasingly apparent that youth who become pregnant (or who impregnate) have academic, economic, and emotional difficulties before the pregnancy occurs. Dropping out of school, living in poverty, and having little hope for the future help create the conditions that lead teenagers to become parents (Dryfoos 1990; Lawson and Rhode 1993). Research suggests that it

434 CHAPTER 11

may be important to address teenagers' social conditions as a way to prevent teen pregnancies. Rather than focusing on pregnancy prevention by itself, public policy may also need to improve the educational, economic, and emotional circumstances of adolescents most at risk. For a discussion of the use by some local programs of strategies to prevent adolescent pregnancies, see Brindis 1993. The best form of birth control, perhaps, is realistic hope for a better future if childbearing is delayed. Providing such realistic hope will not be an easy task for the states.

SUMMARY

Each year federal and state governments spend almost $300 billion providing health care and welfare to assist more than 30 million needy individuals in the United States. We should not underestimate the help this assistance provides. Without this assistance, for millions of Americans health would be worse and poverty would be meaner.

Most government spending on health and welfare for the poor is channeled through just four programs: Medicaid, AFDC, SSI, and GA. Contrary to the common wisdom, the greatest part of this welfare does not consist of giving cash to the poor; programs that provide cash assistance cost only about one-third as much as those that provide medical services.

Although Medicaid, AFDC, and SSI are federal programs, the states carry a heavy burden in financing and operating them, especially for Medicaid. During recent decades Medicaid benefit levels have grown, recipient rolls have expanded, and total expenditures have soared. AFDC rolls and expenditures have also grown—although real benefits have steadily declined—placing further strain on state budgets.

These trends have not affected all states equally. Tremendous variation exists among the states in welfare benefits, caseloads, and expenditures. State policy responses to their health and welfare problems have also varied as a result of the specific political, economic, and demographic conditions existing within each state. Still, all states face similar pressures: their constitutions forbid them from running deficits, while economic competition with their peers restrains their abilities to raise taxes as well as their interest in redistributing income.

The states are now struggling with ways to fix their health and welfare programs so that services are provided to those most in need without encouraging others to become dependent on governmental largesse. State governments are also striving to develop ways to deliver these services while controlling costs. As a result, the states may be entering a period of extraordinary policy innovation—assuming that the federal government will give them the flexibility to conduct their experiments.

We can hope that these policy experiments will go beyond assisting the sick and the poor to preventing sickness and poverty. The barriers to doing so are high, of course. It is difficult for states to focus on prevention when there are so many demands for treatment. It is difficult to change individuals' behavior so that they will become healthy and independent. Yet such prevention is essential. Healthy citizens are less likely to become dependent on government support. Prosperous citizens are likely to need fewer medical services from the government. The best way for states to control their health and welfare spending is for them to help create healthy and independent citizens.

REFERENCES

Bane, Mary Jo, and David T. Ellwood. 1994. *Welfare Realities: From Rhetoric to Reform.* Cambridge: Harvard University Press.

Barrilleaux, Charles J., and Mark E. Miller. 1988. "The Political Economy of State Medicaid Policy." *American Political Science Review* 82:1089–1107.

Brien, Peter, Minnie Chen, Todd Colquitt, Larry Cordisco, and Tom Vander Wal. 1994. "State Gun Control Legislation and Firearm Violence." Georgetown University, Graduate Public Policy Program.

Brindis, Claire. 1993. "Antecedents and Consequences: The Need for Diverse Strategies in Adolescent Pregnancy Prevention." In *The Politics of Pregnancy,* edited by Annette Lawson and Deborah L. Rhode. New Haven, Conn.: Yale University Press.

Buchanan, Robert J., Joseph C. Cappelleri, and Robert L. Ohsfeldt. 1991. "The Social Environment and Medicaid Expenditures: Factors Influencing the Level of State Medicaid Spending." *Public Administration Review* 51:67–73.

CDC (Centers for Disease Control and Prevention). 1992. "Estimated National Spending on Prevention—United States." *Morbidity and Mortality Weekly Report* 41, July 24, 529–531.

———. 1993. *Morbidity and Mortality Review,* February 26.

Colby, David C., and David G. Baker. 1988. "State Policy Responses to the AIDS Epidemic." *Publius* 18, no. 3:113–30.

Daniels, R. Steven. 1991. "Administrative Patterns and Constraints in General Assistance." Paper presented at the annual meeting of the American Political Science Association, Chicago, August 29–September 1.

Devlin, Marion. 1993. "The Impact of State Tobacco Regulations on State Smoking Rates." Georgetown University, Graduate Public Policy Program.

Dryfoos, Joy G. 1990. *Adolescents at Risk: Prevalence and Prevention.* New York: Oxford University Press.

Duncan, Greg J., Martha S. Hill, and Saul D. Hoffman. 1988. "Welfare Dependence within and across Generations." *Science,* January 29.

Elazar, Daniel J. 1970. "The States and the Political Setting." In *Policy Analysis in Political Science,* edited by Ira Sharkansky. Chicago: Markham.

———. 1972. *American Federalism: A View from the States.* 2d ed. New York: Thomas Y. Crowell.

Elliott, Barbara A. 1993. "State 'Laboratories' Test Health Care Reform Solutions." *Minnesota Medicine* 76 (February): 21–25.

Erikson, Robert S., Gerald C. Wright, and John R. McIver. 1993. *Statehouse Democracy: Public Opinion and Policy in the American States.* Cambridge: Cambridge University Press.

Fingerhut, L. A., and J. C. Kleinman. 1990. "International and Interstate Comparisons of Homicide among Young Males." *JAMA,* June 27, 2210–2211.

Fox, Edward J. 1994. "States as Policy Laboratories: Health Care Policy Making, 1990–1994." Paper presented at the annual meeting of the American Political Science Association. New York, September 1–4.

GAO (General Accounting Office). 1992. *Access to Health Care: States Respond to Growing Crisis.* Washington, D.C.: U.S. General Accounting Office.

Glantz, Stanton A. 1994. Letter in response to "Actual Causes of Death in the United States," by J. Michael McGinnis and William H. Foege. *JAMA,* March 2, 660.

Gottschalk, Peter. 1992. "The Intergenerational Transmission of Welfare Participation: Facts and Possible Causes." *Journal of Policy Analysis and Management* 11:254–272.

Gray, Virginia. 1994. "Federalism and Health Care." *PS: Political Science and Politics* 27, no. 2: 217–220.

Green, Jesse, and Peter S. Arno. 1990. "The 'Medicaidization' of AIDS: Trends in the Financing of HIV-Related Medical Care." *JAMA,* September 12, 1261–1266.

Grogan, Colleen M. 1994a. "Political-Economic Factors Influencing State Medicaid Policy." *Political Research Quarterly* 47:565–588.

———. 1994b. "The Politics of Interstate Health Policy Competition and Intergovernmental Health Financing." Paper presented at the annual meeting of the American Political Science Association. New York, September 1–4.

Hanson, Russell. 1984. "Medicaid and the Politics of Redistribution." *American Journal of Political Science* 28:313–339.

Hendrick, Bill. 1994. "Smoking under Siege." *Atlanta Constitution,* March 6.

Hrebenar, Ronald, and Clive Thomas. 1987. *Interest Group Politics in the American West.* Salt Lake City: University of Utah Press.

HHS (U.S. Department of Health and Human Services). 1989. *Reducing the Health Consequences of Smoking: 25 Years of Progress—A Report of the Surgeon General.* Washington, D.C.: U.S. Department of Health and Human Services.

———. 1990. *Seventh Special Report to the U.S. Congress on Alcohol and Health.* Washington, D.C.: National Institute on Alcohol Abuse and Alcoholism.

IHPR (Intergovernmental Health Policy Project). 1993. *Major Health Legislation in the States: '92.* Washington, D.C.: IHPR.

Kause, Mickey. 1994. "You Say You Want a Revolution." *Economist,* June 18, 21.

Knight, Jerry. 1994. "Now We're a Nation of Lite-Heavyweights." *Washington Post,* September 1.

Lawson, Annette, and Deborah L. Rhode, eds. 1993. *The Politics of Pregnancy: Adolescent Sexuality and Public Policy.* New Haven, Conn.: Yale University Press.

Levin-Epstein, Jodie, and Mark Greenberg. 1992. *The Rush to Reform: 1992 State AFDC Legislative and Waiver Actions.* Washington, D.C.: Center for Law and Social Policy.

Lewin, John C., and Peter A. Sybinsky. 1993. "Hawaii's Employer Mandate and Its Contribution to Universal Access." *JAMA,* May 19, 2538–2543.

McGinnis, J. Michael, and William H. Foege. 1993. "Actual Causes of Death in the United States." *JAMA,* November 10, 2207–2212.

Moon, Marilyn, and John Holahan. 1992. "Can States Take the Lead in Health Care Reform?" *JAMA,* September 23–30, 1588–1594.

Murray, Charles A. 1984. *Losing Ground: American Social Policy, 1950–1980.* New York: Basic Books.

Nice, David C. 1994. *Policy Innovation in State Government.* Ames: Iowa State University Press.

"Obscuring the Market." 1994. *Economist,* August 27, 22.

O'Malley, Patrick M., and Alexander Wagenaar. 1991. "Effects of Minimum Drinking Age Laws on Alcohol Use, Related Behaviors, and Traffic Crash Involvement by American Youth: 1976–1987." *Journal of Studies on Alcohol* 52, no. 5:478–491.

Parmet, Wendy E. 1993. "Regulation and Federalism: Legal Impediments to State Health Care Reform." *American Journal of Law and Medicine* 19, nos. 1 and 2:121–144.

Peterson, Paul, and Mark Rom. 1990. *Welfare Magnets.* Washington, D.C.: Brookings Institution.

Peterson, Steven A., and James N. Schubert. 1994. "Predicting State AIDS Policy Spending." Paper presented at the annual meeting of the American Political Science Association, New York, September 1–4.

Plotnick, Robert D., and Richard F. Winters. 1985. "A Politico-Economic Theory of Income Redistribution." *American Political Science Review* 79:458–473.

Rank, Mark. 1989. "Fertility among Women on Welfare: Incidence and Determinants." *American Sociological Review* 54, no. 2:296–304.

Reutzel, T. J. 1989. "Medicaid Eligibility, Benefits, and Provider Payment: State Preferences and Implications for National Goals." *Health Policy* 11:209–226.

Roper, William L., and William Winkenwerder. 1988. "Making Fair Decisions about Financing Care for Persons with AIDS." *Public Health Reports,* May/June, 305–308.

Satcher, David. 1994. "The Paradox of Tobacco Control." *JAMA,* February 23, 627–628.

Schneider, Alison. 1994. "Booze City." *Washingtonian,* September, 83–84, 129–30.

Schneider, Saundra K. 1993. "Examining the Relationship between Public Policies: AFDC and Medicaid." *Public Administration Review* 53, no. 4:368–380.

Sharkansky, Ira. 1969. "The Utility of Elazar's Political Culture: A Research Note." *Polity* 2:67.

Shi, Yuhang. 1994. "Inter-Welfare Competition: An Explanation of State AFDC Benefit Policies in the 1980s." Paper presented at the annual meeting of the American Political Science Association, New York, September 1–4.

Sullum, Jacob. 1994. "Just How Bad Is Secondhand Smoke?" *National Review,* May 16, 51.

Tweedie, Jack. 1994. "Resources Rather Than Needs: A State-Centered Model of Welfare Policymaking." *American Journal of Political Science* 38:651–672.

U.S. Bureau of the Census. 1994. *Statistical Abstract of the United States, 1994.* Washington, D.C.: U.S. Government Printing Office.

U.S. Department of Justice. Bureau of Justice Statistics. 1991. *Sourcebook of Criminal Justice Statistics.* Washington, D.C.: U.S. Government Printing Office.

———. 1992. *Sourcebook of Criminal Justice Statistics.* Washington, D.C.: U.S. Government Printing Office.

U.S. House of Representatives. Committee on Ways and Means. 1994. *The Green Book, 1994.* Washington, D.C.: U.S. Government Printing Office.

U.S. National Center for Health Statistics. 1990. *Health Promotion and Disease Prevention, United States, 1990.* Hyattsville, Md.: U.S. Department of Health and Human Services.

"Vermont Passes Sweeping No-Smoking Law." 1993. *New York Times,* 2 May 2, sec. 1. 1993, 44.

Witkin, Gordon. 1994. "Should You Own a Gun?" *U.S. News and World Report,* August 15.

Zamichow, Nora. 1992. "Anti-Smoking Effort Works, Study Finds." *Los Angeles Times,* January 15, sec. B.

SUGGESTED READINGS

DiIulio, John J., Jr., and Richard P. Nathan, eds. *Making Health Reform Work: The View from the States.* Washington, D.C.: Brookings Institution, 1994. Focuses primarily on the administrative concerns and challenges the states face as they and the federal government attempt to provide greater health care coverage while simultaneously controlling health care costs.

Intergovernmental Health Policy Project (IHPR). *Major Health Legislation in the States: '92.* Washington, D.C.: IHPR, 1993. Provides an exhaustive summary of state legislative activity on a wide variety of health care issues. Summaries are organized by issue and by state. This report is the latest in an annual series.

Levin-Epstein, Jodie, and Mark Greenberg. *The Rush to Reform: 1992 State AFDC Legislative and Waiver Actions.* Washington, D.C.: Center for Law and Social Policy (CLASP), 1992. This report also summarizes state efforts by state legislatures to reform their welfare systems. It analyzes proposals and laws and assesses their impact.

Peterson, Paul, and Mark Rom. *Welfare Magnets: A New Case for a National Standard.* Washington, D.C.: Brookings Institution, 1990. The authors describe the evolution of welfare policy, provide a case study of the politics of welfare policy in Wisconsin, conduct statistical analyses to explain the dynamics of welfare policy among the states, and offer proposals for reform.

U.S. House of Representatives. Committee on Ways and Means. *The Green Book, 1994.* Washington, D.C.: U.S. Government Printing Office, 1994. The *Green Book* is the invaluable source of descriptions of and data from federal social welfare programs. It is published annually.

CHAPTER 12

The Politics of Education

DAN A. LEWIS AND SHADD MARUNA

For those interested in state politics, there is something exhilarating about the chaotic churning around educational reform in the United States. Debate rages about what the problems are and how to fix them. Some, but not too many, say this is the best of times for education; others say that it is the worst and that the country must face up to the problems of its schools. Liberals and conservatives compete to define both the problems and the solutions for the educational system. The administrations of George Bush and Bill Clinton both developed federal strategies based on the notion of fundamental change. The public seems interested in the problems, but for the most part it shies away from solutions that involve spending tax dollars. Politicians at all levels, but especially the state, hear both the calls for change and the reservations of taxpayers.

The American states have historically played an important, if complicated, role in the development of public education in the United States. Today that role has been enhanced enormously. States are now the focus of much of the effort to improve American education, either through their own efforts or federal action. In this chapter we analyze that role since 1970 and discuss the new importance of state government in the reform of education and in the delivery and finance of primary, secondary, and higher educational services.

To understand the role of the states we must place that role in the overall context of domestic policy development and policy implementation. American social and educational policy is made in a complex and fragmented environment.

The constitutional relations between the various layers of government and the separation of powers at all levels of government create the legal and political divisions that make power sharing the very basis of collective action. Our democratic institutions and the cultural commitment to individualism limit the power of government and the faith we put in its operation. These factors combine with the regional variety of the country and its size to make educational policy variegated and complex.

It is on this stage that the education reform agenda has been played out since the 1960s. Beginning in the early 1980s, the issues of educational reform shifted temporarily away from the questions of equity and race that were dominant in the 1960s and 1970s to a renewed focus on excellence and international competition. The states and their governors assumed a primary position as this new approach gained momentum.

Some commentators say that the states are beginning to change the way children are educated, wresting the control of the enterprise from entrenched interests that seek to maintain the status quo. Most scholars look at the reform endeavor with a rather jaundiced eye, though, seeing more rhetoric than result. What is surprising in this literature is the lack of much empirical, comparative work on the states' educational activity and reform. It turns out that we know very little about the factors associated with different outcomes at the state level. In other words, we do not know how states can help Mary and Johnny to read better. While there is much normative work on what scholars and activists want to happen, there is not much work on what has happened and what political factors produced those outcomes (notwithstanding the occasional comparative case study). This means that, despite much anticipation about state-level educational improvement, we are at a preliminary stage in our knowledge about improving the learning process.

Yet, the lack of knowledge has rarely stopped legislators from making laws, and the momentum continues for state action to improve education. The states are legally responsible for the education of resident children. The 1990s have produced a whirlwind of activity in most states to improve that education. We will now turn to how that task is attempted.

GOVERNING EDUCATION

The education of young people in the United States is an enormous enterprise. In the fall of 1993, nearly 63.9 million students were enrolled in U.S. schools and colleges, and about 7.9 million individuals were employed as teachers, faculty members, and support staff (NCES 1993). In all, more than one in four Americans participate in formal education every year. Not surprisingly, education represents the largest single cost for both local and state governments and has become one of the central political issues of our time.

Public schooling is not mentioned in the U.S. Constitution. The Tenth

Amendment to the U.S. Constitution states: "The powers not delegated to the United States by the Constitution, nor prohibited by it to the States, are reserved to the States respectively, or to the people." This amendment, ratified in 1791 as part of the Bill of Rights, has been interpreted as effectively leaving the right to establish an educational system to the states.

The nineteenth century saw the development of state responsibility for education with much delegation to local communities. All fifty state constitutions authorize education as a public good and require compulsory school attendance of all young people. These often vaguely worded provisions usually guarantee a "thorough" or "efficient" system of public education for all the children in the state. States also have authority over the various tax systems that finance individual schools and provide the basic administrative structure of public schooling through local school boards.

Much of that power has been delegated to local school districts created by the state government. This basic fact has led to a set of complex interactions between the fifty state governments and the more than 15,000 school districts that exist in the United States. When the federal and state judiciaries are added to this mix, we can predict heightened conflict over who should decide educational matters.

The Federal Role

Education has been a state responsibility and a local function throughout the twentieth century. Yet, the federal government has played a carefully defined, peripheral role as well. Article I, Section 8, of the U.S. Constitution gives Congress the power to collect taxes in order to "provide for the common Defence and general Welfare of the United States." This has been interpreted as authorizing federal investment in education. Most federal legislative power over school governance has been in the form of requiring states to comply with specific conditions in order to receive federal funding. In particular, the federal government has concentrated on areas of national concern like equal access to schooling, special education, and special programs for disabled, non-English-speaking, and disadvantaged children.

Federal funding for public schools was nearly doubled in the 1960s with the implementation of the Elementary and Secondary Education Act and the Bilingual Education Act, but the federal role has still remained quite minimal. Federal funding of elementary and secondary education in the United States grew from 2.9 percent of school funding in 1950 to 9.8 percent in 1980 (NCES 1993). Then, federal grants declined steadily under the administrations of Ronald Reagan and George Bush, bringing the federal share back to only 6.2 percent in 1991.

Whereas many countries feature versions of a "national curriculum," the diversity and social divisions within the United States have always made local control of school content the more politically feasible strategy. The only time the federal government has significantly ventured into the governance of curriculum was the Sputnik-inspired National Defense Education Act of the late 1950s, when cold war rivalry permitted such a serious break with the ideal of local and regional control (James 1987). The Clinton administration's education plan, for example, though broad in scope, carefully focuses on national, quasi-governmental groups and voluntary national standards rather than on a direct federal mandate for a national curriculum (Fuhrman 1994b).

The federal government began to take a leading role in the movement to desegregate America's schools following the *Brown v. Board of Education* (347 U.S. 483 [1954]) decision. Individual states and school districts in both the North and the South challenged federal authorities on the issue. One notorious standoff involved the Chicago public school system in 1965. Calling Chicago "by far the best case in the North of de facto segregation," Francis Keppel, the U.S. commissioner of education, threatened to withhold federal aid to the Chicago public schools, jeopardizing almost $32 million, if efforts were not made to bring the schools within compliance with Title VI of the 1964 Civil Rights Act. Yet, when Chicago's infuriated mayor Richard J. Daley flexed his political muscles on the issue, the administration of Lyndon B. Johnson immediately backed off and instructed the Department of Health, Education, and Welfare (HEW) to offer the mayor a face-saving compromise. Keppel found himself relieved of his education post and made the "assistant secretary of HEW in charge of nothing," as he put it (Lemann 1992, 197).

The Chicago fiasco effectively caused federal education authorities to retreat from pursuing northern school desegregation issues directly for the next thirty years (Lewis and Nakagawa 1995). By the 1980s, there was no serious federal action on desegregation issues at all. During the Reagan presidency, neither the Education Department's Office for Civil Rights nor the Justice Department filed a single school desegregation suit, and no positive policy proposals supporting desegregation emerged from any branch of the federal government (Orfield 1993).

Somewhat ironically, however, Reagan did play a major part in the school reform movement of the 1980s. Reagan's initial interest in education was mainly to dismantle the federal education bureaucracy and decentralize the public system by supporting tuition vouchers for private schooling. In fact, he reduced federal support to education by nearly 10 percent (Augenblick, Gold, and McGuire 1990). Nonetheless, the unwavering commitment of Terrel Bell, the secretary of education, to an "excellence in education" campaign eventually moved the president into a more proactive posture. Reagan's endorsement of Bell's *A Nation at Risk: The Imperative for Educational Reform* (National Commission on Excellence in Education 1983) lent the publication popular credibility and brought immediate attention to the shortcomings of the nation's school system. Following Reagan, Presidents Bush and Clinton have similarly used the "bully pulpit" of the presidency to demand increased innovation and a commitment to quality among the nation's schools.

The Tug-of-War between Local and State Governments

The frequently clashing values of equity and autonomy take the form of an endless tug-of-war between state educational agencies and local school districts. Some policy makers seek more centralized control over schools in order to guarantee students comparable educational opportunities, whereas others argue for decentralization in order to encourage innovation at the local level. Timar and Kirp (1988, 75) call this division a conflict between "hyper-rationalists who believe that schools are infinitely manipulable" and "romantic decentralists" who believe the key to school improvement "lies in deregulation and local control of schools."

Each approach reflects competing views of politics and human nature. The first assumes that hierarchical control exists and that one level of government can dictate to another what it is to do. Commands are given and with the right mix of incentives they are executed. Get tougher and hold subordinates responsible and results will follow. Allow individual districts complete autonomy and some might flourish, but many will fail miserably. Proponents of local control, in contrast, assume that progress comes from freeing individuals and institutions to pursue their own goals and interests. Institutions have better chances of achieving their formal goals unburdened by state regulation.

Federal policy makers also move back and forth between these two perspectives, sometimes even combining them (see the section "Systemic Reform" below) in the hopes of coming up with an approach that will be practical and advance educational practice. The forces of centralization were very strong in the early 1980s, pushing through a variety of state reforms that mandated more schooling and more academic classes for many states. Later in the decade, notions of decentralization and site-based management came into vogue. Timar and Kirp (1988) argue that only a balance between these ideals of state accountability and local authority can effectively bring about the type of results sought by policy makers. Achieving something like this middle ground, in fact, has become the reigning paradigm among education reformers and academics.

The State's Role

Despite "hortatory preambles, vague constitutional articles, terse statutes [and] a feeble administrative apparatus," the earliest system of common schools was clearly governed exclusively through "local control" (James 1987). Individual schools were financed almost entirely through local property taxes and granted nearly complete autonomy. Therefore, schools developed highly unevenly across the states with few checks for preventing corruption or poor performance.

State regulation of schools, beginning in the 1920s in most states, first took the shape of sporadically enforced minimum standards for staff qualifications and facilities. Since that time, state governments have gradually taken a more assertive role in coordinating education in order to promote equity between school districts and provide higher-quality services to overburdened districts. Fuhrman and Elmore (1990, 84) write, "[S]tate policy steadily escalated, with each new policy focus adding to rather than replacing previous laws, regulations and structures." By the mid-1980s, state regulation rose to unprecedented levels.

The post–World War II reigning myth that the public school system could be managed by neutral, objective administrators was widely abandoned following the sometimes violent conflicts surrounding school desegregation. In the 1960s, education became highly politicized. Governors and state legislators, who once shied away from mingling in school affairs, now frequently make statewide reform agendas the central part of their campaign strategies. Kirst (1987, 161) writes, "Now state government officials create education policies, and local groups react to them. Educators lost control of the state agenda quite a while ago." In fact, the Texas Supreme Court in its 1989 decision in *Edgewood v. Kirby* (777 S.W.2d 391, 397) decided that local control of the schools had become a relic of the past:

> Most of the incidents in the education process are determined and controlled by state statute and/or State Board of Education rule, including such matters as curriculum, course content, textbooks, hours of instruction, pupil-teacher ratios, training of teachers, administrators and board members, teacher testing, and review of personnel decisions and policies. (Quoted in Wise and Gendler 1989, 16)

The reasons that states assumed such power over schools range from increased judicial activism, the growing power of social movements demanding change, increasing education costs, and a recognized need for more efficient use of school resources. Some federal initiatives, like Title V and VI of the Elementary and Secondary Education Act, have also helped to broaden the role of individual states because state education departments are widely charged with enforcing these national laws. Some observers suggest that states have merely filled the void left when the Reagan administration scaled back federal education programs in the 1980s (Clark and Astuto 1986).

Proponents of centralization view this more coordinated control of schools as a means of overcoming the fragmentation, inequities, and inefficiency of the traditionally decentralized system of public education. Citing the multiple failures of urban school districts in particular, those hoping to reform education frequently rely on state-level policies in order to make schools more accountable to accepted standards of performance. Furthermore, Hochschild (1984) and others have called for continued centralization of control in order to combat rampant school segregation by race and social class.

On the surface, this growth in top-down governance would appear to reduce the freedom and control of individual schools and districts. Frymier (1987, 9) says such creeping centralization "neuters" educators. Kagan (1986, 64) calls it "regulatory unreasonableness." Nonetheless, Fuhrman and Elmore (1990, 89) caution that critics should not "mistake volume for significance" when assessing a state's control over the education system. Many new state reforms and regulations are merely symbolic in nature and do little to shift the balance of authority away from schools and local school districts. Enforcing severe sanctions for noncompliance with state standards can be costly and politically dangerous, so compliance is generally achieved more through bargaining and negotiation than top-down decree. In fact, research by Tyree (1993) and Fuhrman and Elmore (1990) indicates that even successful state activism has done little to reduce local control and may have even increased local initiative. Fuhrman (1994b, 83) writes, "State reforms appear to have exerted a multiplier rather than a depressive effect on local policies." In particular, researchers point to several state policies specifically designed to promote decentralization and site-based management.

Local Control

Every state except Hawaii has a long tradition of local control of the school system in the form of school districts and local school boards. The striking differences in content and quality that exist between even neighboring school districts in America are the result of this uniquely American system of local control. States continue to delegate considerable regulatory authority to these districts, governed by boards of lay citizens, although states have assumed a more centralized role since the 1970s.

School districts are quite separate from municipalities, even when their borders are the same. Whether elected or appointed, local school boards are essentially state agencies (Russo 1992). School board members hold office by virtue of legislative enactment, and the state has the authority to increase or diminish their powers. Although boards hold executive, legislative, and judicial power over the schools in their district, they are ultimately responsible to the state, and the only authority they hold is vested in them by the legislature. To facilitate increased coordination, in fact, the number of school districts across the country has been substantially consolidated, from 119,000 in 1938 to only about 15,000 today (NCES 1993).

Moreover, the role and influence of the local school board seems to be giving way to increased "building-level" decision making that gives individual school administrations control over much of the school board's former domain. Odden (1992) calls this a move toward education systems that are "focused at the top" and "loose at the bottom." These initiatives empower educators and principals but substantially neglect the district school board. In Chicago, for instance, the legitimacy of the district school board has been called into question because independent local school councils, made up of parents, teachers, and student representatives, now perform most of the functions once reserved for the district. Finn (1992), arguing that traditional district school boards have become dysfunctional and superfluous, even calls for the abolition of these "middle managers" in favor of a completely site-based system of control.

Behind the Classroom Door

State governments have assumed an unprecedented role in the finance and regulation of America's schools, yet they are still intrinsically limited in what they can accomplish once the classroom door closes. This interplay between policy, administration, and the actual practice of education can be both complicated and rather frustrating for observers.

Analysts like Weatherly and Lipsky (1977) suggest that "street-level bureaucrats"—in this case, individual teachers—rather than federal or state authorities, make the key decisions in implementing education policies. It is hard to describe, much less analyze, what these teachers do or how they do it. As Hanushek (1981, 20) says, "Our understanding of what makes for effective performance in schools is astonishingly primitive." Patterns of teaching and their correlates are even harder to know. Teachers can fill out surveys about what they do and students can be tested on what they know, but how those two phenomena are related is difficult to assess.

Therefore, despite the growing role of states in the governance of education, many observers suggest that local control of schools, in some aspects at least, is absolutely inevitable. Researchers have shown that the actual effect of state policies on the daily practice in the classroom is weak and inconsistent at best (Cuban 1990). Moreover, very little systematic evidence links state policies with improved educational outcomes (Berger and Toma 1994; Hanushek 1986).

In sum, states may play a large role in financing and governing education, but individual teachers and school administrators are still far more important to educational outcome than state policies. Reformers on the state level have only a limited range of policy options, and it seems highly difficult to affect the poorly understood aspects of "good teaching" with top-down mandates.

THE STATE POLICY-MAKING PROCESS

The education policy landscape has become increasingly crowded with groups competing to set the agenda. Policy initiatives can originate from the grass-roots agendas of individual schools or districts, from academic researchers, from teachers' lobbies, from the business community, or from top-down reform efforts of state leaders. Firestone (1989, 23) calls this education policy-making structure an "ecology of games," in order to emphasize the "messiness and discontinuities" of the multifaceted process.

Regional Diversity

Every state has its own constitutional language describing the purposes and goals of its educational system, as well as its own system and structure for implementation. State policy makers also work under the constraints of regional variations in political cultures and traditions that affect the character of school governance. A state's political culture has a traceable history and distinct continuities

Table 12-1   Order of Importance of Policy Actors in Selected States

	Six-state ranking	Arizona	West Virginia	California	Wisconsin	Pennsylvania	Illinois
Individual legislators	1	1	3	2	4*	1	3
State legislature as a whole	2	2	5*	1	6*	4	3
Chief state school officer	3	4	2	7*	1	3	12*
Education interest groups	4	9*	8*	3	5	6	4
Teachers' organizations	5	12*	6	4	2	7	1†
Governor and staff	6	13*	9	6	3	2†	5
Legislative staff	7	7	11*	5	9	5	6
State board of education	8	3†	4†	16*	—	9	14*
Others	9	10	7	8	13*	18*	7
School board association	10	6†	15*	11	7	11	8
Administrators' association	11	15*	12	9	8	8	13
Courts	12	11	1†	10	14	12	11
Federal policy mandates	13	8†	10	13	11	10	9
Noneducational groups	14	5†	13	12	10	13	10
Lay groups	15	14	16	15	12	14	15
Education research groups	16	16	14	17	15	15	17
State referenda	17	18	18	14	17	17	16
Education materials producers	18	17	17	18	16	16	18

SOURCE: Mitchell, Marshall, and Wirt 1986, 351.
NOTE: Dash indicates that none exists.
*Much lower than average.
†Much higher than average.

over time. Still, these cultures are malleable enough to change as states are confronted with new challenges from the larger environment. Changes in resources, demographic shifts, national movements, lessons from other states, accidents, and unexpected catastrophes all lead to such political evolution. This counterpoint between continuity and change is difficult to understand and predict, although in retrospect, stories can be told about why things happened.

Several scholars have tackled the complicated question of the social and cultural base of state educational politics. Marshall, Mitchell, and Wirt (1989) have looked carefully at the variations in the problem-solving techniques that develop in states as a function of the power of interest groups and government officials. They conclude that interest groups relate to each other depending on both the skills of those in the groups and, more important, the distinct systems of meaning and political cultures that have developed in the states over time. In other words, state policy makers bring to the table various "assumptive worlds" or subjective understandings of what is appropriate in the prevailing political and cultural ethos of the state. For instance, Marshall, Mitchell, and Wirt (1989, 376) found that in West Virginia, labor associations such as the School Service Personnel Association have to adjust their style of bargaining in order to survive the state's political traditions. Unlike other states, West Virginia's personnel association has taken an anti-collective-bargaining position and affiliates itself instead with key education lobbies.

From a series of interviews with policy makers and insiders, these researchers attempt to identify and describe the key influences on the formulation of state education policy. Marshall, Mitchell, and Wirt (1989) found considerable variation among states concerning which groups and individuals were allowed special control of the process (see Table 12-1).

Although the state court system is rated as one of the least influential policy actors in five of the six states in the survey, the courts play a leading role in West Virginia (Table 12-1). Similarly, while the chief state school officer (CSSO) fills an important role in most of these states, in Illinois the position is rated quite low in influence. These differences are rooted in personalities, local histories, traditions, and politics and can change over time.

Major Policy Actors

No longer the exclusive domain of powerful school lobbies, education reform and policy initiatives are now the product of many different institutions competing for resources and cooperating in efforts to achieve values such as equality, efficiency, and excellence.

State Legislatures. State legislatures have emerged as the supreme policy makers in American education (James 1987). In fact, Marshall, Mitchell, and Wirt (1989) found that individual legislators who specialize in education issues and lead various reform committees with the legislature are ranked as the most influential policy entrepreneurs by most of the states in their sample (see Table 12-1). These elected officials delegate their responsibility for actual governance and administration of schools to various bodies, but they have been the primary impetus for changes in education policy since the early 1970s.

Governors. With the assistance of more specialized staffs, as well as the National Governors' Association and the Education Commission of the States, many state governors began to take the lead in educational policy making in the early 1980s. Governors traditionally have had little interest in educational matters beyond fiscal concerns. Yet, governors like Tennessee's Lamar Alexander and Arkansas's Bill Clinton gained national prominence by taking activist roles during their respective states' reform periods in the 1980s. Moreover, the National Governors' Association report *A Time for Results* (1986) urged policy makers to focus their attention on school-based change rather than increasing state regulation. This document played nearly as influential a role in initiating the second wave of education reform as *A Nation at Risk* did in the first.

Governors, however, seem to deal more in imagery than specifics in regard to educational issues. Mazzoni (1993, 364) says that governors rarely act as innovators in the policy arena; instead, they "pick up, package and promote options formulated by others." Moreover, since governors are the most likely to be held directly accountable for the condition of a state's schools by voters, they inevitably favor reforms that can show clear and immediate effects, especially in election years. For this reason, James (1987, 198) suggests that governors are "drawn irresistibly to bold and unrefined ideals" and are likely to abandon their demands for immediate reform if the political landscape suddenly shifts.

Chief State School Officers. Marshall, Mitchell, and Wirt (1989) found that the CSSO was actually ranked as being more influential than governors in the design and implementation of reform in most states. In Wisconsin, in fact, the CSSO was rated as the most important single player in the policy process. Still, the role and importance of the CSSO varies considerably from state to state, as indicated in Table 12-1. In some states the CSSO is appointed by the governor and merely acts as the executive officer's spokesperson. In others, the State Board of Education selects the chief. In still other states, such as California, the CSSO runs for elective office.

Education Departments. State departments of education and state education bureaucracies have the function of implementing and administering state policies. Departments of education primarily play a regulatory role, ensuring that schools comply with state and federal law and assisting them in meeting state standards, but some departments have also begun providing incentives (money or services) for improvements in student outcomes as well (Lusi 1994). Traditionally, these highly structured and hierarchical education departments perform the routine, administrative work of licensing teachers, performing site visits, regulating building codes and accreditation requirements, and compiling educational statistics and school evaluations. For this reason, they were not included among the primary shapers of state education policy in the survey represented in Table 12-1.

Still, these once "mostly innocuous and invisible" agencies have tripled in size since the 1960s as a result of substantial federal aid (Murphy 1980, 2). Today, departments of education are actively involved in establishing curriculum standards, selecting texts, and appropriating funding for individual schools. Lusi (1994) argues that these departments are having to be fundamentally reinvented in order to help implement systemic or coherent reform efforts on the state level.

State Boards of Education. State boards of education, almost always appointed by the governor, tend to be rather minor players in the policy process. Although the board is charged with the general supervision of education for the state, chief state school officers tend to be more visibly influential in this regard. Marshall, Mitchell, and Wirt (1989, 22) write, "[N]o doubt it is an honor to be appointed, but it certainly does not signify high influence." State boards of education do have considerable power in a few states, such as Arizona and West Virginia, however, and are sometimes charged with the important task of selecting the state's chief school officer. Wisconsin is the only state that does not have such a board.

Teachers' Unions. Teachers' unions play an important role in state educational politics. Both the National Education Association and the American Federation of Teachers have considerable political power at the state level. The National Education Association has political action committees in many states and its members are organized to influence legislators and appointed officials. Albert Shanker, president of the American Federation of Teachers has played a key part in the national reform debate since the mid-1970s. He identified the need for educational reform in the early 1980s and challenged union members to think beyond the industrial union approach in formulating a perspective on reform. The adversarial approach to union management relations and the emphasis on work rules and bread-and-butter issues of pay and seniority have led to an attitude that ranges from cautious to hostile toward reform efforts in many communities.

Like traditional labor unions, teachers' unions work to secure the most favorable work conditions for their members. These conditions include not only pay scales but class sizes, length of workdays and school terms, curriculum content, and certification requirements—all of which have been debated in state legislatures. The power of these unions is evidenced not only by their strength in lobbying for favorable reforms but by their ability to influence the practice of education. Strikes by public school teachers increased from 25 in the years between 1960 and 1965 to more than 1,000 between 1975 and 1980 (Toch 1991).

Other Interest Groups. Formal and informal networks of experts and citizens' groups also are influential in pushing for changes in laws concerning educational practices. Such lobbying organizations as school board associations, civic and community groups, and parent organizations frequently have agendas for state policy. Although often hidden from the spotlight, these groups can exert considerable pressure on policy makers.

Business groups are also credited with inspiring many of the excellence-in-education reforms of the early 1980s as well. Linking higher educational standards with increased productivity, business leaders like H. Ross Perot in Texas have played instrumental roles in both encouraging and developing various reform efforts. Prior to his bid for the presidency, Perot chaired a school reform development committee and hired his own staff of lobbyists to promote the legislation. Similarly, powerhouse business lobbying groups have turned their focus and considerable influence to school politics and have helped shape important legislation. The Minnesota Business Partnership helped draft the Minnesota Plan, for example, which became the basis for the public school choice program in that state (Mazzoni 1993).

Finally, independent issue constituencies and "policy entrepreneurs" have emerged in the years since the 1950s to act as full-time advocates for various policy alternatives (Kingdon 1984). These groups generate policy innovations and lobby legislatures to support their strategies on issues like school choice or increased performance standards. Frequently these agencies are supported by business or labor interests as well.

State Courts. The state judiciary also plays an active, if reluctant, role in state education policy. Beyond the landmark school desegregation decision in *Brown v. Board of Education,* the U.S. Supreme Court has fairly consistently stressed the need for local control and maintained that education matters should be left to the states (Combs 1984). State court systems therefore have assumed a large role in nearly every aspect of the educational process.

State courts generally do not interfere with decisions made by a school board or educational administrators unless the action is deemed an abuse of power (Russo 1992). Still, courts now hold the final authority on such issues as the constitutional rights of students, which would have been considered strictly private matters for individual schools until the mid-1950s. Beckham (1993) identifies nearly fifty important state judicial decisions made between July 1992 and July 1993 alone, including the legality of dress codes, locker searches, loitering policies, teacher competency tests, graduation prayers, special education placements, and recitation of the "Pledge of Allegiance."

Still, the most obvious and dramatic role of the state court system since 1970 has been in determining the legality of school financing schemes, school desegregation policies, and school district consolidation plans. The state court system has intervened in these politically charged and difficult issues in part because legislators have been unwilling to risk the public disapproval that accompanies such divisive problems without at least the threat of court action.

In many states the courts have in fact taken the lead in educational policy. The Kentucky court system went as far as to declare the entire educational system for the state unconstitutional. The court essentially required the state to redesign its entire school system by enacting comprehensive educational and financial reforms. An Alabama ruling has already followed this remarkable precedent, which dramatically raises the stakes for education litigation and perhaps signifies an impending wave of judicial activism to spur failing systems of education.

Universities. University departments of education play a considerable role in determining the credentials for state educators and shaping the nature of teacher education. Also, university-level researchers, backed by both government support and foundation grants, have assumed considerable influence in the design and implementation of school governance systems. From the Reagan era to the Clinton administration, education scholars have been recruited to fill high-ranking positions atop the federal bureaucracies. For instance, before being named under secretary of education for the Clinton administration, Marshall S. Smith had been one of the key academic theorists behind the concept of school effectiveness and systemic reform.

EDUCATIONAL FINANCE

Education accounts for the single largest cost in most state and local budgets. For 1992–1993, expenditures were estimated at more than $375 billion for all public schools and colleges (NCES 1993). Generally this money comes from a combination of local taxes and state and federal grants-in-aid, but the balance between these sources has shifted considerably over the years. Local tax revenues consist almost entirely of property taxes except in states like Louisiana, where local sales taxes are common. The composition of state tax revenues was described in Chapter 9. Increasingly, states are also earmarking for the schools funds generated through state lotteries.

Fiscal Responsibilities of States

During World War I, 83 percent of school financing was provided by local districts, and state governments provided only about 17 percent (Wong 1989). In the 1970s and early 1980s, however, state governments began to assume the primary responsibility for educational funding in an unprecedented shift away from this local autonomy (see Figure 12-1). The state share of total educational funding increased from 41 percent in 1968 to about 50 percent in 1986, whereas local contributions to school expenses fell from 50 percent in the late 1960s to about 43 percent by the mid-1980s (Wong 1989).

Elementary and secondary education expenses now consume nearly a quarter of the average state budget, and postsecondary schools account for another 12 percent (Farrell 1988). Finance and governance of education have not gone hand-in-hand, however. As Fuhrman and Elmore (1990, 89) write, "[C]ontrol does not necessarily follow the dollar." States began assuming primary responsibility for educational finance nearly a decade before the increased regulation and centralization of the 1980s.

Figure 12-1   Sources of Revenue for Public Elementary and Secondary Schools

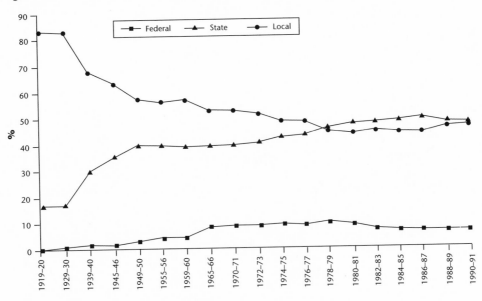

SOURCE: Adapted from National Center for Education Statistics 1993, 151.

Several explanations are possible for this shift. For instance, states have a broader revenue base than individual localities and have been better able to absorb the growing costs of education. Additionally, a widespread revolt by taxpayers led to legislation like Proposition 13 in California, Measure 5 in Oregon, and Proposition 2 1/2 in Massachusetts. These efforts put restrictions on property tax increases and strongly limit the ability of local districts to maintain fiscal control of their schools. Still, the most important factor has been the movement to equalize school expenditures across various school districts.

State Diversity

Wong (1989) points out that even though on the aggregate level states are assuming most of the burden of school funding, considerable interstate differences persist. Firestone, Fuhrman, and Kirst (1991, 242) found that "the local property tax is still alive and well" in many states. Although schools in Hawaii are funded almost entirely at the state level, some states, such as Oregon and Virginia, provided less than a third of school funding, and in New Hampshire, state funds accounted for less than a tenth (see Table 12-2). Moreover, while state spending in Minnesota and California rose by nearly 69 percent between 1983 and 1987 (Toch 1991), in twenty states the state share in education spending actually dropped (Firestone, Fuhrman, and Kirst 1991).

Table 12-2 States with the Highest Percentages of Local and State School Funding, 1990–1991

State and funding source	Local	State	Federal	Private
Locally funded schools				
New Hampshire	86.8	7.8	2.8	2.5
Oregon	65.6	25.4	6.1	2.9
Michigan	65.2	26.8	5.8	2.3
Vermont	61.1	32.1	4.9	1.9
Virginia	59.7	33.2	5.4	1.7
Illinois	59.0	31.7	6.6	2.6
South Dakota	58.3	27.5	11.3	2.8
New Jersey	57.0	37.8	4.0	1.2
Maryland	56.2	37.4	4.7	1.8
Connecticut	55.8	41.2	2.9	0
State funded schools				
Hawaii	0.5	89.9	7.8	1.8
New Mexico	12.5	72.7	12.2	2.5
Washington	19.0	72.1	5.7	3.2
Alaska	18.3	68.5	11.3	1.9
Delaware	24.4	68.5	7.1	0.1
Kentucky	21.4	66.9	9.5	2.1
West Virginia	24.0	66.6	7.8	1.6
North Carolina	24.5	66.1	6.6	2.8
California	25.6	66.0	7.2	1.2
Idaho	28.2	61.7	7.8	2.2
U.S. average	44.1	47.3	6.2	2.5

SOURCE: Adapted from National Center for Education Statistics 1993, 152.

Wong (1989) identified several factors associated with whether state governments experienced a shift from "parity to dominance" in the responsibility of education financing. Those states that did not experience a substantial shift in education funding responsibility, he said, frequently had no legal suits brought against the state system, were not subject to pressure to lower property taxes, had restrictions on state taxation, and often contained a large population of African-American students. Several of the states in his study, such as Michigan, however, have since experienced major shifts away from reliance on local taxes.

Wealth Disparity

Like school governance, the issue of financing America's schools has been characterized by the conflict between the ideals of local control and equal opportunity. In virtually every state, there is a wide range between school districts in taxable wealth and tax rates. Some school districts have far lower expenditures per pupil than others within the same state (see Table 12-3). Even when these poorer school districts tax themselves at higher rates than other districts, frequently they are able to spend only a third as much per student as areas with higher property values (Darling-Hammond 1994). Wealth disparity between districts is further exacerbated by the imbalance in the distribution of commercial, industrial, utility, public, tax-free, and residential property as well as an uneven distribution of school-aged children.

Critics claim that this uneven distribution of educational funding magnifies social inequalities by leaving the children who have the fewest educational resources at home with the fewest resources in their schools. Many studies have in-

Table 12-3 The Range of Annual School Funding per Pupil, 1990 (in 1990 dollars)

State and rank	Poorest districts	Richest districts	Gap
Largest Gaps			
Alaska	6,115	19,155	13,040
Massachusetts (secondary)	4,595	11,653	7,118
New York	5,439	11,725	6,286
Illinois (secondary)	3,796	9,484	5,688
Maine (elementary)	2,664	6,640	3,976
Illinois (elementary)	2,665	6,240	3,575
Montana (elementary)	2,720	5,593	2,873
Arizona (elementary)	2,419	5,014	2,595
Smallest Gaps			
Hawaii	4,288	4,288	0
West Virginia	3,160	4,023	863
Kentucky	2,509	3,520	1,011
Alabama	2,674	3,741	1,067
Iowa	3,593	4,700	1,107
Georgia	3,000	4,322	1,322
California	3,669	5,079	1,410
South Carolina	3,369	4,852	1,483

SOURCE: Adapted from Walters 1993, 750.

dicated that uneven school financing has a racial element as well. For instance, Berne and Stiefel (1992) found that in New York, districts with greater proportions of minority students had larger class sizes, less qualified and less experienced teachers, and fewer state and local expenditures per student than other districts.

First Wave "Equity" Reforms

During the early 1970s a wave of school reforms addressed these disparities. Coons, Clune, and Sugarman (1970) were among the first educational researchers to push for the principle of "fiscal neutrality" in public schooling. Appealing to the notion of equity in education, salient at least since *Brown v. Board of Education* (1954), they argue that the quality of public education should be a function, not of the wealth of a child's parents or neighbors, but of the state as a whole.

This notion of equalizing educational expenditures across districts within a state guided several court cases in the early 1970s. After losing lawsuits in Illinois (1968) and Virginia (1969), proponents of fiscal neutrality won a resounding victory in California. In *Serrano v. Priest* (5 Cal.3d 584, 585 [1971]), the California Supreme Court ruled by a six-to-one margin that the state's system of financing its schools "invidiously discriminates against the poor" and therefore violated the equal protection provisions of the state constitution. In the case, commonly called *Serrano I*, a group of parents from the Baldwin Park district of Los Angeles brought a class action suit against the state, charging that children in the neighboring Beverly Hills district were receiving far better educational services. Despite paying a tax rate that was less than half that of Baldwin Park, Beverly Hills residents were able to spend twice as much per student as the residents of Baldwin Park.

Following the court's decision, California underwent the first of several school financing reform plans in an effort to correct these disparities. Other state legislatures followed California's lead and pushed through reforms without court orders. In fact, in 1973 alone, thirteen states changed the way schools were financed in hopes of creating more equity across districts (Wong 1989).

Still, that same year, the U.S. Supreme Court strongly challenged the *Serrano I* precedent with its critical five-to-four decision in *San Antonio Independent School District v. Rodriguez* (411 U.S. 1 [1973]). In the case, Justice Lewis F. Powell, Jr., wrote that education is not "a fundamental interest" protected under the Constitution and that differences in per pupil expenditures cannot be shown to be directly related to the quality of education a district offers. State supreme courts in other states—for example, Arizona (1973), Idaho (1975), and Ohio (1979)—followed suit. Citing *Rodriguez,* these courts supported the need for local control and suggested that the proper arena for educational matters is the state legislature.

Table 12-4 Timing of Finance Reforms

State	Weak reform	Strong reform*	State	Weak reform	Strong reform*
Iowa	1972		Maine	1978	
Colorado	1973		Washington		1978
Florida	1973		West Virginia		1979
Illinois	1973–80		Arizona	1980	
Kansas	1973	1976	Arkansas		1983
Minnesota	1973		Wyoming		1983
Wisconsin	1973		Texas	1984	1989
New Mexico	1974		Massachusetts	1985	
Ohio	1975–82		New Hampshire	1985	
Virginia	1975		Rhode Island	1985	
Utah		mid-1970s	Georgia	1986	
New Jersey		1976, 1990	South Dakota	1986	
California	1977	1978	Oklahoma	1987	
Missouri	1977		Vermont	1987	
South Carolina	1977		Louisiana	1988	
Tennessee	1977		Kentucky		1989
Connecticut		1978	Montana		1989
Idaho	1978		Michigan		1993

SOURCE: Downes and Shah 1994, 22, table 1.
*Court-ordered reform.

While one might have assumed that this decision would have marked the end of the surge in school financing reform, the issue showed remarkable resiliency. In fact, only one month after the *Rodriguez* verdict, the New Jersey Supreme Court found that the state's system of financing its public schools should be invalidated for failing to meet constitutional requirements (*Robinson v. Cahill,* 62 N.J. 473 [1973]). The *Robinson* plaintiffs used the same argument concerning wealth disparity that was employed in *Serrano I,* but they focused on the specific language about education found in the New Jersey Constitution. Every state constitution includes an education clause, and usually there is some mention of a "thorough and efficient" or "equitable" system of schooling. Following *Robinson* and their defeat in *Rodriguez,* reformers generally concentrated on this state constitutional language rather than making appeals to the Fourteenth Amendment.

Roughly a third of the lawsuits of the 1970s concerning the financing of schools were successful in leading to equalization legislation, including those in Connecticut (1975), Washington (1977), Wyoming (1980), West Virginia (1982), and Arkansas (1983). Yet, even the threat of such a suit led many states to act independently in this regard. In all, about half of the states enacted school financing reform measures between 1971 and 1983 (see Table 12-4). Court-ordered reforms (the "Strong reform" in Table 12-4) tend to limit local discretion and result in considerable reductions in the magnitude of interdistrict spending disparities. "Weak reforms," however, are generally legislative reforms that tend to preserve substantial local discretion and result in smaller reductions in interdistrict disparities (Downes and Shah 1994).

Second Wave Reforms

During the 1980s, momentum toward achieving equitable financing was considerably overshadowed by the so-called excellence movement. Although states continued to tinker with their funding schemes, finance litigation all but disappeared. Still, the issue reemerged in the 1990s with considerable success for reformers.

Augenblick, Gold, and McGuire (1990) offer two general reasons for this resurgence of litigation and legislation concerning finance reform. First of all, the conditions to which finance systems must be sensitive, such as land values, student enrollments, and population demographics, have changed considerably since the 1970s, when many of the funding schemes were created. Second, the decade of attention to school quality and excellence in education raised the important question of how these reforms were to be paid for. Moreover, many observers suggest that the reforms of the 1970s did not adequately accomplish what they set out to do. Many state reforms were merely temporary or partial solutions, in which legislatures targeted a little money for poorer districts but failed to alter the fundamental design of their states' financing schemes. In fact, despite the number of reforms, funding inequalities between school districts did not substantially change between 1970 and the mid-1980s (Odden 1992).

In the past six years, courts in Massachusetts, Montana, New Jersey, and Texas have ruled those states' systems of school financing unconstitutional, and litigation is pending in dozens of other states. Even in states in which reformers seemed to win decisive victories in the 1970s, the equity of school-funding schemes continues to be a major issue. In fact, nearly every new legislative reform plan is sent back to the courts for protracted rounds of litigation. Although most state courts have tended to uphold existing school financing systems (Darling-Hammond 1994), recent court decisions have signaled possible new directions for innovation in finance reform.

Texas. Nowhere has the battle over finance reform been so contentious and protracted as in Texas. For twenty-five years, legal challenges against the Texas school system have flooded state and federal courts; yet achieving a legislative solution that appeals to voters in the aggressively antitax state has been nearly impossible. After losing their bid for finance reform in the landmark Supreme Court case *San Antonio v. Rodriguez,* parents from the Edgewood School District filed a second lawsuit, this time through the Texas state court system, in 1984. By a ruling of nine to zero, the Texas Supreme Court ordered the state to design a more equitable funding system for the state's schools (*Edgewood v. Kirby,* 1989).

Yet, the battle has far from ended with the *Edgewood* ruling. The first proposal offered by the legislature would have raised the funding levels for all school districts but would not have significantly reduced the disparities between districts. The court deemed this plan unacceptable (Rocha and Webking 1992). A second plan that would have redistributed $400 million to poorer districts was successfully derailed by representatives from wealthy districts on the grounds that the reform represented an illegal statewide property tax. Under the latest compromise, adopted in 1993, the wealthiest districts will have to limit their taxable property to $280,000 per student and the excess will go to poorer districts.

New Jersey. New Jersey has also experienced numerous school financing reform plans since the *Robinson v. Cahill* decision in 1973. Representatives from disadvantaged districts took the state to court a second time in the 1980s, alleging that the state's reforms have not done enough to help these predominantly minority areas. The state supreme court agreed and ordered the state to enact additional finance reform. This landmark decision (*Abbott v. Burke,* 575 A.2d 359, 400 [1990]) was unique in that it focused not on statewide disparities but rather on twenty-eight specific, disadvantaged urban districts, and the state's educational system was found unconstitutional only for those districts.

Two weeks after the decision, the Quality Education Act was passed by New Jersey's Democrat-controlled legislature, making a substantial amount of compensatory aid to poorer districts a constitutional requirement. The accompanying tax increase led to a tremendous popular backlash, however, and Republican majorities were elected to both houses of the state legislature in 1991. The new legislature amended the original reform bill in order to spread targeted spending throughout the state, not solely to urban areas, and reduced the total amount of redistribution.

Michigan. In some states, finance reform has not been quite so contentious. Michigan and Nebraska, in fact, have moved independently to reform funding distributions in recent years with innovations that might signal a new direction for legislative efforts. In 1993, with widespread fiscal disparity and several poorer school districts facing the real possibility of bankruptcy, Michigan's legislature and governor implemented one of the most radical reforms of the new wave. The state repealed roughly $6.9 billion in local property taxes without designating an alternative source of funding. This essentially denied to the state's school system what had been its primary funding source for the last 100 years and the source of over two-thirds of its budget the year before. The shock of losing most of the school system's budget was intended to force the state to design a more equitable method of funding schools than using local property taxes. Michigan citizens responded by overwhelmingly voting in support of a 2 percent sales tax increase and a tripling of cigarette taxes to fund the schools.

Under the plan, every school in the state will operate with a budget of between $4,200 and $6,500 per student in 1994 dollars (Pierce 1994). The Michigan strategy also includes reforms dealing with a core curriculum for the state and an extension of the school day. States like Wisconsin are already moving in a similar direction.

Kentucky and Alabama. Finally, large disparities in educational funding and quality exist between entire states as well as local districts, and state courts are beginning to see this as similarly unfair to the children of these poorer states. For instance, while some states, such as Alaska, Connecticut, and New Jersey, all spent more than $7,500 per student in 1992, Alabama, Idaho, Mississippi, and Utah spent less than half that amount that year (NCES 1993).

In Kentucky, the courts declared the entire educational system in the state unconstitutional for failing to meet the constitutional requirement of providing a "thorough and efficient" school system. The court even required the legislature to enact comprehensive educational reform in addition to new finance measures. Relying on the latest research and policy analysis, the court ordered the state to set achievement standards, complete with fiscal incentives and sanctions, increase teacher training, and create new compensatory programs for disadvantaged students. The incredibly ambitious, five-year strategy eventually enacted required much higher spending per pupil across the state but preserved local control in the form of increased site-based management.

In Alabama, where student achievement is among the lowest in the nation, a circuit court judge, Eugene Reese, similarly ruled in 1993 that schools need to be made more "adequate" as well as more equitable. The ruling provides specific criteria necessary for meeting the state's constitutional requirement for a quality education. This includes achieving educational outputs comparable to national and international standards.

The two decisions symbolize a possible new direction for finance reform litigation. It may be that courts will now, when warranted, order states not only to level the playing field for schools but to raise the entire floor and bring all schools within certain standards of excellence.

Achieving Equity

Achieving equity in school financing is anything but easy. Often, these equity reforms lead to some aggregate increase in education spending for the state but little equity. With education in direct competition with the increasingly expensive health care and corrections expenses, raising school spending across the board can be difficult without proposing politically unpopular tax hikes like those in New Jersey. Moreover, "Robin Hood" strategies that involve the redistribution of tax revenues from wealthy districts to poorer districts, can raise the ire of voters from the wealthier districts, who feel that their children are being unnecessarily punished by the reforms. In Kansas, voters from wealthy districts have fought reforms both at the ballot box and through the state court system, and every state legislature is wary of the type of backlash that followed the New Jersey reform. Still, many states have tried to put explicit spending caps on wealthier districts and sold the measure as "property-tax relief," rather than a redistributional scheme.

Furthermore, equity in education is not simply translated into the reality of fair school district funding across a state. Wise (1967, 133) cautions:

In the first place, price levels differ from one part of a state to another; this variation implies that equivalent services cost more in some parts of a state than in other parts. Second, sparsity and density of population generate diseconomies in the operation of schools. Third, the needs of different students vary, thus creating complications.

Other salient equity concerns frequently overlooked by reformers include the distribution of funds among individual schools within a district, among subject areas of the curriculum, among tracks and categories of students, and among levels of schooling (Darling-Hammond 1994).

Odden (1992) points out another problem of definition. If financial inequity is defined as variation in the tax base of local districts, this would lead to the enactment of a guaranteed tax base. Yet, when the problem is seen as differences in spending per pupil, the remedy is to mandate equal spending across all school districts. Although states differ in their interpretation, Odden observes that most are leaning toward the equal per pupil expenditures and away from equal access to property tax bases.

Finally, in many arguments for equity, school quality is casually used as a synonym for dollar expenditures. Yet, the relation between school spending and student output has been called into question at least since the highly influential report *Equality of Educational Opportunity* (HEW 1966). In the report, Coleman and his associates suggested that schools "bring little influence to bear on a child's achievement that is independent of his background and social context" (HEW 1966, 72). More recently, Hanushek (1981; 1986, 1162) surveyed nearly 150 studies of the effects of school financing and similarly found "no strong or systematic relationship between school expenditures and student performance." Hanushek (1986) accepts that teachers and schools "differ dramatically" in their effectiveness, but he argues that these differences have more to do with autonomy and innovation than school funding. The question for those interested in equity is what money for education actually buys. Studies seem to show that increases in spending do not necessarily correspond to increases in student achievement (Odden and Picus 1992).

To this line of argument, Coons, Clune, and Sugarman (1970, 30) reply, "If money is inadequate to improve education, the residents of poor districts should at least have equal opportunity to be disappointed by its failure." In addition, Card and Krueger (1992) have uncovered something of a paradox in this field. Their research suggests that even though student performance, as measured by test scores, does not clearly correlate with the amount of money spent per student, other positive correlations can be found. For instance, adult males who were educated in schools with lower pupil-teacher ratios and higher teacher salaries have a higher monetary "return to education" than other males. In other words, their post–high school earnings are higher than those of similar individuals educated in less affluent schools. This measure may be both more reliable and more valuable than test scores as a measure of the importance and efficiency of school funding. Moreover, a demonstrably strong link between expenditures and achievement is probably not necessary to justify finance reform. The goal of most court decisions and state reforms after all is not to guarantee improved outcomes but, rather, to provide an equal opportunity for educational success.

The Future for School Financing

Because more than half of the fifty states are currently involved in litigation in regard to school financing schemes, it seems clear that the issue will continue to dominate state politics in the 1990s. In fact, probably as long as the educational system is composed of semiautonomous local centers of control, concern that the distribution of educational funds is inequitable will linger. Verstegen (1990, 222) argues that "given the persistence of rich schools and poor schools . . . it may only be that states will cease to invidiously discriminate by wealth inside their borders when the federal government provides incentives, sanctions, or mandates that call for equal opportunity in the states." Indeed, there have been Senate subcommittee hearings on this possible course of action, but the financial and political costs of such a move are probably too high for such measures to be taken seriously.

Increasingly, it is likely that the future of litigation concerning school financing will center on outcomes as well as inputs (Odden 1992). Disparities in student achievement and in the way in which schools use tax dollars are beginning to be seen as more important criteria for judging the constitutionality of school systems than mere dollar expenditures. Many states are considering the use of fiscal incentives for raising student performance as well. Moreover, finance reform that is tied into a package of education reforms, like curriculum standards or choice proposals, are more likely to win the support of business and community groups.

REFORMING EDUCATION

The alarming national report *A Nation at Risk* (1983) and its warning of a "rising tide of mediocrity" in the nation's schools, inspired and legitimized an unprecedented wave of state reforms geared toward raising standards for students. Between 1984 and 1986, especially, education was the dominant issue in many state legislatures nationwide. Special sessions of state legislatures were called specifically to address reform issues—for example, in Arkansas and Florida in 1983 and Tennessee in 1984 (Toch 1991).

Critics warn that frequently such a rediscovery of educational shortcomings involves a type of collective amnesia, whereby recycled versions of earlier panaceas return as solutions to timeless problems of student discipline and apathy (Clark 1993). Still, reformers' concerns were substantiated by a growing body of research that showed that as spending on schools was increasing, student performance was on a downward slide. For instance, from 1963 to 1980, scores on the Scholastic Aptitude Test (SAT) steadily dropped from an average of 478 to 424 on the verbal section and 502 to 466 on the math (Murnane 1985).

Furthermore, when reports tied educational outcomes to the nation's economic competitiveness, state action seemed all the more critical. In *Making the Grade,* the Twentieth Century Fund (1983, 4) warns, "The skills that were once possessed by only a few must now be held by the many if the United States is to remain competitive in an advancing technological world." The pro-business stance of the Reagan administration combined with the weakened position of the United States in the world economy opened the door for a reform posture that was opposed to federal spending but in favor of improvement in educational outcomes. In fact, many of these reforms were endorsed by social conservatives as well as traditional progressives. Reagan's New Federalism approach de-emphasized the role of the federal government and emphasized volunteer activities, state actions, and a strengthening of standards.

While the costs of most popular reforms were low, states still pumped vast amounts of new revenue into these efforts. Fortunately, many of the more sweeping reforms coincided with periods of considerable economic expansion in many states. Although not all of the activist states benefited from this financial growth (Firestone, Fuhrman, and Kirst 1991), a strong correlation between a state's economic expansion and its education reform efforts does exist. Toch (1991, 37) writes: "The reform movement was lucky. Had the nation's economy not rebounded as dramatically as it did from the 1981–82 recession, leaving 37 states with budget surpluses and only 3 with deficits, there would have been much less money available to pay for education reforms."

The Excellence-in-Education Reforms

The initial reforms, originating in the first wave of the 1980s reform period, concentrated on raising standards and requirements in an effort to achieve educational excellence. The movement was highly regulatory in nature, consisting mostly of mandates, laws, and state prescriptions to be enforced through various mechanisms. Sometimes, fiscal incentives were used to encourage districts to increase standards for teachers and students on a voluntary basis. Other reforms focused on the need to create mechanisms to monitor student progress and performance better.

Student-Focused Reforms. The most popular educational reform in the excellence movement was raising graduation requirements. Forty-five states modified high school graduation requirements in the 1980s, usually requiring more credits in science and mathematics (Fuhrman 1994a). This was a low-cost, manageable reform with clear results (students did take more core course work) and therefore greatly appealed to legislators and governors eager to show their commitment to excellence. In many states, however, most school districts already met or surpassed state requirements in their graduation policies, so the state law did nothing to improve these programs (Firestone, Fuhrman, and Kirst 1991).

Led by the reform movement in Florida, many states have also moved toward new assessment techniques that measure the progress of students in multiple academic fields. Often these assessments take the form of "minimum competency tests," which assess whether students are qualified for graduation or promotion. These tests also sometimes help to link funding to measurable improvement in educational output. Other popular reforms include No Pass, No Play, which places restrictions on extracurricular activities, and statewide attendance policies. States have also experimented with comprehensive reform programs like Robert Slavin's Success for All and James Comer's School Development Program and have mandated additional classes for advanced students and students with special needs.

Many recommendations prompted by the excellence movement, especially those that would have proved rather expensive, were not widely implemented, however. For instance, suggestions for increasing the school year to 200 or more days were considered by thirty-seven states in the mid-1980s. Yet, only nine actually lengthened school terms, and no state lengthened the year beyond 180 days (Firestone, Fuhrman, and Kirst 1991). Costly recommendations to lengthen the school day, provide public preschooling, and establish state homework policies also were largely ignored.

Educator-Focused Reforms. States have even entered the once purely local domain of teacher compensation, which makes up over 70 percent of a typical school budget (Hanushek 1986). Prior to 1980, only a few, predominantly southern states got involved in teacher salaries, but during the 1980s, Darling-Hammond and Berry (1988, v) found, nearly every state enacted legislation to improve teacher compensation: "In all, over 1,000 pieces of legislation regarding teachers have been developed over the course of the decade, and a substantial fraction have been implemented." Some of these strategies include raising teachers' salaries across the board, raising the base pay for full-time faculty, and creating performance-based incentives, such as career ladders and merit pay programs. The career ladder program allows qualified educators to move through a progression of jobs, with increases in pay and responsibility.

Still, as the data in Table 12-5 make clear, states have moved at different rates in raising teacher salaries. While the average teacher salary in Connecticut grew by more than $3,000 between 1989 and 1991, salaries dropped in South Dakota and Mississippi during this time. Generally, as can be seen in Table 12-5, the salary increases of the first wave of education reform simply brought teacher salaries back to the level of twenty years earlier in most states.

Also, the first wave of the reform movement included often contradictory reforms in the area of teacher certification requirements. Some states increased subject-specific credentials and added teacher competency and certification testing. Similarly, many states required certain teachers to obtain advanced degrees or generally tightened entrance requirements for state teacher education programs. In contrast, other states purposely opened up alternative routes to teacher certification in an effort to attract increased numbers of applicants who were graduates of programs outside of the traditional education programs. Thus,

Table 12-5 Highest and Lowest Average Annual Salaries of Teachers in Public Elementary and Secondary Schools, 1992–1993 (in constant 1992–1993 dollars)

	1969–70	1979–80	1989–90	1992–93
Highest paid				
Connecticut	34,946	29,795	45,416	48,850
Alaska	39,843	49,954	48,438	46,373
New York	38,998	36,372	43,692	44,600
New Jersey	34,447	31,506	40,045	43,997
Michigan	37,073	36,066	41,612	43,331
Pennsylvania	33,421	30,320	37,421	41,580
California	38,918	33,083	42,651	41,400
Massachusetts	33,067	31,674	38,963	39,245
Maryland	35,402	32,234	40,767	39,141
Illinois	36,104	32,313	36,810	38,576
Lowest paid				
South Dakota	24,159	22,669	23,909	24,125
Mississippi	21,876	21,755	27,267	24,369
North Dakota	25,264	24,349	25,835	25,211
Oklahoma	25,966	24,063	25,895	26,051
Louisiana	26,517	25,262	27,276	26,074
New Mexico	29,414	27,331	27,788	26,355
Utah	28,841	27,371	26,587	26,997
Idaho	25,966	24,988	26,783	27,156
Alabama	25,724	23,977	27,869	27,490
Arkansas	23,796	22,580	25,089	27,598
U.S. average	32,546	29,319	35,235	35,334

SOURCE: Adapted from National Center for Education Statistics 1993, 85.

while some states decided to make it easier to become a teacher, others sought to make it more difficult, although both hoped for similar results.

The Restructuring Movement

The first wave of school reform lasted approximately from 1982 to 1986, when several critics began pronouncing the incremental reforms ineffective. For instance, Chubb and Moe (1986) argue that any reform that leaves the basic structure of the public education bureaucracy intact, as these reforms did, will "tend to be assimilated and neutralized." Thus, beginning in the late 1980s, this regulatory phase has been increasingly replaced by a movement that seeks to change the fundamental structure of the educational system by encouraging bottom-up improvements at the school site. More centralized excellence-in-education reforms, although no longer as faddish, continue to be enacted in some states, alongside decentralization efforts.

This second wave of reforms emphasizes "learning for understanding," teaching higher-order thinking, and improving the depth, rather than the quantity, of student course work. In regard to policy, this restructuring mostly translates into seed money to encourage local experimentation and a shift toward school site autonomy, shared decision making, school choice programs, and the profession-alization of teaching. In essence, while outcome goals are increasingly being set from the state, individual schools are being given fuller responsibility for admin-istering the reforms (Lewis 1993).

School site autonomy means providing schools with more decision-making authority through reallocating budgeting, curriculum, and personnel decisions from district offices to individual schools. Seven of the eight largest urban school districts in the United States, as well as, for example, the states of California, Florida, and Minnesota, are implementing various versions of decentralized, site-based management. Based on research on effective schools, these programs are intended to increase school productivity, accountability, and student perfor-mance.

Closely related to site-based management is the concept of teacher profession-alism. The Carnegie Task Force on Teaching as a Profession (1986, 55) and other groups urge that bureaucratic authority be replaced by "schools in which author-ity is grounded in the professional roles of teachers." Generally, this means giving teachers a clearer role in the making of policy and the administration of the schools in which they teach. In Pennsylvania, for instance, teacher participation in staff development programs is mandated by the state.

Parents, too, are being given more power in the schools during this wave of re-forms. Several states have made intentional efforts to enfranchise parents through school-parent councils like those implemented in Georgia (Firestone, Fuhrman, and Kirst 1991). A dozen states even implemented reforms that would give voters the opportunity to remove school administrators and school board members of low-achieving school systems (Toch 1991). In this movement toward local control, parents, educators, and community members are seen as agents of change with a common interest in the operation of schools that is somehow dif-ferent from that of other groups who have controlled education in the past (Lewis and Nakagawa 1995).

School Choice

The final link in this notion of decentralization is school choice and the em-powerment of parents as consumers. Nearly a dozen states have experimented with public school choice plans. These plans, while varying widely in content, all attempt to give parents an expanded choice (throughout either the state or a dis-trict) in regard to where their children attend school.

There are literally dozens of different approaches to expanding the number of options that are open to students and their parents when it comes to selecting the schools they wish to attend. Some of these options are the direct result of de-segregation litigation and are attempts to reduce racial isolation by offering stu-dents schooling in buildings that are in neighborhoods outside their own. Some involve magnet schools, or district-wide programs developed to attract and retain quality students in the public school system and promote voluntary racial integration by offering specialized curriculum to qualified students. Some involve interdistrict plans, while others are intradistrict. Most try to balance concerns about equity with attempts to improve quality.

All depend on serious implementation efforts and able personnel to administer the programs if they are to succeed. Implementing school choice programs is a problem that confronts many school boards and superintendents as districts expand the options they wish to offer students. To understand how well any program is implemented and what its effects are, one must look at the interaction between the people administering the plan and those who are supposed to change their behavior and choose to go to a new school (Lewis 1990).

These school choice plans have captured the imagination of many state legislatures and governors. Minnesota, led by Gov. Rudy Perpich (1976–1979 and 1983–1991) and powerful business lobbies, has been a pioneer in this effort and has experienced considerable success. During the 1992–1993 school year, more than 100,000 of Minnesota's 786,000 students took advantage of the state's choice program and attended a different school from the one they attended the previous year, and polls show that about 75 percent of Minnesota residents support the choice program (Nathan and Ysseldyke 1994). Besides open enrollment, Minnesota's choice package also features a Postsecondary Enrollment Options program, which provides tax funds to enable eleventh and twelfth graders to attend classes at colleges or universities, and a Second Chance program, which allows school dropouts to transfer to new schools.

Minnesota also implemented a program of charter schools in 1991. Charter schools are largely autonomous public schools that draw students from throughout a school district. Groups of interested teachers, parents, or community members can open these schools by signing a contract or charter with the local school board or state agency agreeing to follow various guidelines and quality standards. Like magnet schools, charter schools are intended to promote innovation and reinvigorate public school systems losing students to private schools. A dozen other states have already followed Minnesota's lead and have begun experimenting with charter school programs.

Private School Choice

Including private and parochial schools in these choice strategies is a quite different and much more controversial issue, although several states have experimented with such plans. Wisconsin, for instance, enacted a voucher program for a set number of low-income and minority students in Milwaukee that allowed parents and students to choose between public and private schools. Proponents of private school choice would like to see private school tuition vouchers offered across entire states, allowing students at all socioeconomic levels to attend private schools for reduced or no tuition.

Research by Chubb and Moe (1986, 1990) has been used extensively in support of this cause. Chubb and Moe show how centralized, bureaucratic authority over schooling reflects the needs and desires of the bureaucracy and politicians rather than those of students, parents, and educators. Public schools, they suggest, are "captives of democratic politics" and "subordinates in a hierarchic system of control," thus making institutional goals "heterogeneous, unclear and undemanding" (1986, 28). They write:

> The fundamental causes of poor academic performance are not to be found in the schools, but rather in the institutions by which the schools have traditionally been governed. Reformers fail by automatically relying on these institutions to solve the problem—when the institutions are the problem.
>
> The key to better schools, therefore, is institutional reform. What we propose is a new system of public education that eliminates most political and bureaucratic control over the schools and relies instead on indirect control through markets and parental choice. These new institutions naturally function to promote and nurture the kinds of effective schools that reformers have wanted all along (1990, 5).

The attack on the bureaucracies and the dispersal of authority and control are the hallmarks of choice plans. Nonetheless, critics contend that in the name of community and family, reforms have been introduced that remove equity and racial fairness from the policy agenda. Privatization and the blurring of boundaries between the state and parochial education are the result (Lewis 1990, 1993). Bureaucratic power is seen as the problem, and family choice is the solution. It is believed that if schooling is left to the professionals insulated in their bureaucracies, then it will surely fail (Bastian et al. 1986; LaNoue and Smith 1973).

The community and family are often contrasted favorably with the "heartless" institutions and bureaucracies. But the family and community can be stand-ins for race and class in the allocation environment. If we leave education to the family and community, pathology, discrimination, and personal income may dictate who gets ahead and who stays behind. Reliance on the community and family is the policy mechanism to replace the status quo, for education and economic power will dictate who gets what. Under a system of choice, wealthy communities and interested parents still have an advantage over poor communities and uneducated parents; indeed, their advantage may be increased by the shift of authority outside the bureaucracy.

School choice may be about shifting parent power and redistributing educational values. It is also about the basic nature of how the state regulates the poor, while improving the lives of the middle class. It is about creating new markets for private industry with the state serving as the provider of capital, and it is about legitimizing that social control function in the name of democratic values. Choice of schools as an institutional reform plays on the economic metaphor in policy making and may increase polarization of our society.

Systemic Reform

In the most recent wave of reform, the states are being asked by the federal government to create curricular frameworks that outline the goals and techniques for achieving high standards in different subjects. These state efforts are to be driven by national guidelines that give the country as a whole ways to achieve overall goals. The Clinton education policy, represented in Goals 2000, centers on "systemic reform." This would be a coordinated effort to raise standards and educational achievement uniformly across the country and overcome the fragmentation of the current education system. California began implementing curriculum standards similar to those put forth in Goals 2000 as far back as the mid-1980s, and even states traditionally strong on local control, such as Minnesota, New Jersey, and Vermont, have enacted versions of this "coherent" reform in recent years (Fuhrman 1994b).

According to the proponents of this national standards movement, existing policies, despite their rhetoric about excellence, drive curricula toward mediocrity because of their fragmentary and occasionally contradictory nature. A systemic national education policy would hold all students to a common high set of standards and encourage educators of students who are at risk of failing and disadvantaged students to create more ambitious instruction in order to meet the standards (Fuhrman 1994b). Furthermore, all states receiving federal assistance would have to establish assessment, professional development, and curriculum standards consistent with the unifying aims of the Goals 2000 plan, thus further improving the coherence among federal and state efforts. Finally, new achievement-based state assessments will augment and eventually replace standardized basic skills tests that primarily measure low-level abilities. The result will push teachers and schools toward improving educational outcomes.

Criticism of the proposals for systemic reform is just beginning to emerge. Clune (1993) argues that national curriculum standards may impede the process of matching curricula to diverse student needs and that high-stakes national examinations will lead to a highly prescriptive curriculum of "teaching to the test." He writes, "Low-income schools and students do not need a curriculum that is identical to a curriculum somewhere else in the state or country; they need a curriculum that is well adapted to produce dramatic gains in learning for their particular students" (1993, 237). Clune also warns that implementation of such systemic reforms under the current system of school governance would be nearly impossible. Schools in the United States, he suggests, can probably achieve a common curriculum "in name only."

Fuhrman (1994b, 89) counters such fears by insisting, "[W]e already have an informal national curriculum—a basic skills national curriculum." The proposed national standards are designed specifically to replace the emphasis teachers place on preparing students for standardized tests that measure only basic skills. Moreover, its proponents are quick to point out, systemic reform policy would encourage local experimentation by providing support and flexibility for innovative local programs. The Clinton administration is trying to combine national leadership with state responsibility to improve educational outcomes. History would suggest that the combination is not viable.

The Success of Reforms

Studies have shown that most of the 1980s reforms have been successful in achieving their desired immediate effects (Fuhrman and Elmore 1990). Odden (1991) found that local response to top-down initiatives was "swift, positive and in several instances enthusiastic." For example, students in states with increased graduation requirements are in fact taking more academic courses (Clune, White, and Patterson 1989). Still, little is yet known about whether these additional courses affect learning or improve educational outcomes (Cuban 1990), and our knowledge about the comparative success of these efforts is rudimentary at best.

Reports by the states on their own schools tend to magnify successes, and since many of these efforts are relatively new and not very well funded, it is difficult to assess systematically their impact on the classroom. School districts and individual schools have a great deal of autonomy in developing teaching and learning strategies, and while compliance can be achieved superficially, it is difficult to ascertain how deep that compliance runs. Courses can have their titles changed and administrators can write reports that attest to compliance, but those claims are of dubious strength.

These hierarchical approaches to improving learning have met with mixed results in regard to measurable improvements in learning. For instance, comparative studies have failed to show significant correlation between improvement in student test scores and the teacher's experience or education (Murnane 1985). Neither specific college training in education nor obtaining a master's degree seems to correlate with the ability to improve student outputs (Hanushek 1981, 1986). Furthermore, Hanushek (1986) reviewed nearly 150 studies of educational outcome and could not find any evidence that indicated that smaller class sizes were correlated with positive student outcomes.

Following the first round of reforms, students did show some improvement in basic skills, measured by standardized tests, but this success was short-lived. SAT scores increased by sixteen points between 1980 and 1985 but declined by ten points again between 1987 and 1991 (Fuhrman 1994a). Toch (1991) attributes this lack of consistent improvement to the movement's failure to address the critical issue of alienation and apathy among students and educators. Other research suggests that, to be effective, state policies must be sensitive to local conditions and appealing to educators.

Besides ineffectiveness, critics also fear that school reforms will have unintended consequences. Possible examples include an increase in dropout rates following increased graduation standards and an increase in "teaching to the test" pedagogy in response to high-stakes examinations (Murnane 1985). Berger and

Toma (1994) illustrate how in one instance excellence-in-education reforms seem to have actually led to lower student achievement. Using SAT scores as a measure of student performance and holding student background characteristics constant, they found that students in states that required a master's degree for teacher certification actually performed worse than students in states without the reform.

HIGHER EDUCATION

McGuinness (1988, 11) calls state coordination of higher education "the most complex, difficult balancing act in state government." Colleges and universities, approximately half of which are publicly operated and governed, are historically decentralized and notorious for their aloofness and outright opposition to outside intervention. Newman (1987, 1) writes, "It is not unusual to hear, within the university walls, the argument that the state has no proper role with regard to the university beyond providing adequate funding." Yet, seeking a balance between autonomy and accountability in higher education, state governments have assumed increasingly centralized control over the higher-educational realm, even in sensitive areas such as admissions policy and curriculum requirements. In fact, Newman suggests, "It is no longer simple to describe where the state ends and the university begins" (1987, 12).

Governance of Higher Education

In 1950 only sixteen states featured strong, centralized coordinating boards to oversee college and university policy decisions; this number had more than doubled twenty years later (Berdahl 1975). Today, all states assign some degree of responsibility for coordinating the state's higher-education system to one or several governing bodies. These boards, usually called a board of trustees or board of regents, are charged with some level of planning, policy making, fiscal, and management functions for a state's postsecondary institutions. They are designed to coordinate the program selection among schools to serve better the needs of the state. For the most part these state agencies regulate public institutions, not private ones. Zumeta (1992) makes the case, however, that states will need to pay increasing attention to private and independent universities in order to maintain the quality of state higher education.

The emergence of state boards has made the higher-education system appear more like other parts of state government—dealing with a governing board is easier for governors and legislators than working directly with individual university presidents (Newman 1987). Therefore, it is no coincidence that the 1970s and early 1980s also first saw increasingly sophisticated governors, legislators, and their staffs become directly involved in higher-education policy development. Additionally, boards give the university system a clearer mission and buffer campuses from inappropriate intrusion from the state by improving the communication procedures between legislatures and campuses (Newman 1987).

In general, states feature one of the following types of intermediate agencies between the legislature and its public campuses: a consolidated governing board, a coordinating board, or a planning agency (Skolnick and Jones 1992). Although variations exist, these groupings describe differences in the formal authority of the board.

Usually a *governing board* has authority over most if not all state colleges and universities. The members usually appoint and evaluate campus presidents and have the authority to intervene in the governance and budget decisions of individual campuses, including the establishment of admission standards, tuition costs, and campus organizational structures (Hines 1988). A *coordinating board,* in contrast, merely acts as a liaison between campus governing bodies and the state legislature. Whereas many governing boards function as advocates for the colleges and universities they govern, coordinating boards more often reflect the interests of the state government. Both typically have the authority to review and recommend the appropriation of funds, approve degree programs and formulate a master plan for the state's higher-education system (Millett 1984). Finally, *planning agencies*—found in Delaware, Michigan, Nebraska, and Vermont—have more limited authority. Colleges governed by planning agencies have the most autonomy because state education policy tends to be determined predominantly by individual university presidents.

Many individual colleges and universities also feature a board of trustees, charged with selecting the college's president, managing the school's budget, evaluating staff and assessing legal matters, and enhancing the school image (Hines 1988). These trustees are usually appointed by the governor, but the board of trustees for the University of Illinois and a handful of other schools are popularly elected in statewide elections.

The Increasing State Role

Several explanations exist for the increasing centralization of control over colleges and universities. Higher education has grown rapidly in America since World War II, making policy decisions increasingly complex. Today, higher education frequently represents the greatest item of discretionary spending in a state's budget (Zusman 1986).

The G.I. Bill, enacted at the end of World War II, allowed millions of veterans to attend college. The bill created considerable growth in the size and scope of the postsecondary education system in the late 1940s and 1950s. The expansion of community colleges, federal financial aid, and student loans during the 1960s and 1970s further contributed to the burgeoning size of higher education. Enrollment grew by 41 percent between 1970 and 1980 and another 20 percent between 1980 and 1992 (NCES 1993). In one striking example, the University of California system grew from 41,925 students and a $135 million annual budget in 1957 to 150,065 students and a $4.2 billion budget only thirty years later (Newman 1987). Today, college enrollment in the United States has risen to a record level of more than 14 million and is expected to grow to nearly 15.5 million by fall 2000 (NCES 1993).

Furthermore, state legislatures are increasingly concerned about the link between higher education and state economic growth. A study conducted for the Joint Economic Committee of the U.S. Congress found, "[i]n an extraordinary number of cases, a university played a major role in the history of the companies that have chosen to relocate" (Newman 1987, 4).

Reformers in the 1950s and 1960s also argued that a strong centralized coordinating board would be more effective and equitable than a patchwork of autonomous units in planning and developing higher-education policy (Hearn and Griswold 1994). "Left totally to its own," Newman (1987, 8) writes, "the university will evolve toward self-interest rather than public interest." State boards seek to improve the coordination of courses offered by two-year and four-year universities and prevent so-called "turf wars" between campuses, vying for the role atop the state pyramid as the research university.

Finally, some federal legislation also inspired more centralized state oversight. Congress even provided funds to assist states in establishing coordinating boards and stipulated the character these boards should take (Skolnick and Jones 1992).

Criticism of this creeping centralization has been widespread among university scholars and administrators concerned about a loss of autonomy (Millett 1984; Mingle 1983). Critics suggest that the most damaging state intrusion occurs in the affairs of nonresearch institutions and community colleges (Hines 1988). Although it is difficult to prove systematically, Newman (1987) even suggests that an inverse relation probably exists between state intervention in the affairs of a university and that university's perceived quality. As a result, several states, like Colorado in 1981, have moved to "deregulate" their system of higher education and transfer the responsibility for financial management back to the individual university boards.

Reforming Higher Education

The surge of reform initiatives in primary and secondary education has caused many states to consider similar changes in the postsecondary education system. Some of the most important state higher-education reforms, in fact, have been directly related to improving state elementary schools and high schools. For example, in order to improve the caliber of their teachers, several states raised the graduation requirements for college students majoring in education. Other higher-education reform proposals, such as raising admission standards and creating outcome assessment programs for college students, nicely mirror reforms in state high school programs. In many ways, these developments in higher education, therefore, have emerged somewhat in tandem with primary and secondary school reforms. Despite considerable differences in structure, the two systems are intimately connected. The fate of one level, in fact, has immediate and obvious consequences on the other.

The main focus of postsecondary reforms has been on better defining the mission of the university system and linking that to the goals and needs of the state. For instance, many reformers perceive that state resources are being wasted on duplicative and repetitious programs at neighboring campuses. They therefore advocate increased "distinctiveness" and "mission differentiation" among college programs (Hines 1988).

Furthermore, many reformers have called for increased attention to the problem of insufficient minority enrollment and completion rates in state four-year colleges. After a rapid increase in access to higher education in the late 1960s and early 1970s, minority participation in colleges and universities has suffered a puzzling and dramatic stagnation and even decline (Carter and Wilson 1992). In 1990, whereas 32.5 percent of all white 18- to 24-year-olds were enrolled in college, only 25.4 percent of all African Americans and 15.8 percent of all Latinos in this age group were similarly enrolled (Carter and Wilson 1992).

Stabilizing and reducing tuition costs have been another area of concern. Between 1982–1983 and 1992–1993, the cost of a public university education rose by nearly 83 percent, substantially surpassing the rise in the consumer price index of 45 percent for that same period (NCES 1993). In order to promote equal opportunity and competition within the schools, California and other states have passed legislation to keep these costs to a minimum for applicants from within the state.

Governors and legislators usually instigate these reforms, as they do other school reforms, but state coordinating boards are also emerging as key players in negotiating and designing statewide postsecondary policy. Hearn and Griswold (1994) try to account for the variation across states in the amount of postsecondary reform by determining specific characteristics common to activist and nonactivist states. Among other factors, they found that states with considerable postsecondary reform, such as Iowa and Texas, often have more centralized and powerful governing boards than less activist states, such as Mississippi and New Mexico.

In general, higher education has not embraced the reform agenda nearly as readily or completely as the primary and secondary education systems (Hines 1988). Despite increasing centralization, colleges and universities expect and demand far more autonomy from state interference. While states are developing more elaborate oversight mechanisms to increase accountability, colleges and universities are not likely to give up this considerable independence.

CONCLUSION: THE POLITICS OF EDUCATION

The delivery of educational services depends on the coordination of activities between many organizations. Teachers are hired, textbooks are purchased, students show up for class, and something called learning happens more than occasionally. School boards are elected, taxes are collected, and proms are chaperoned. These activities require many people working together.

State politics play a role in all of this, but most of that role is removed from the day-to-day business of schooling. It affects that business, but at a considerable distance. Of course from a political perspective, governors and legislators are usually more intent on giving the appearance of movement and reform than they are on worrying about the eventual effect of the changes they make. Given the need to show movement within an electoral time frame, the eventual effects of reforms pale in political significance. The real world of state politics has to do primarily with the distribution of resources and symbols. Educating young people is the business of schools and teachers. It is the task of future scholars to tie these two levels together into a meaningful synthesis.

The politics of education, that is, the process through which resources are distributed to learning institutions and the students who attend them, must be understood if we are to make this effort intelligently and effectively. There have been politics around public education since the states began taxing their citizens to pay for schooling. Those politics have been about money, authority, and content: who pays for the education, who controls the education, and finally, what gets taught.

Until recently, this political discourse has been dominated by school district personnel, local politicians, state politicians, and state bureaucrats, although public-spirited reformers occasionally got into the fray. Since 1980, however, several new and powerful actors have been added to the mix, and the salience of the issues we have just adumbrated has risen for the public. Many of the new faces active in the state capitols challenge the conventional models that political scientists use to explain state politics. For example, the demand for privatization and more choice in schooling has become a highly contentious issue in many states, and in most states litigation about it has occurred. Yet, the conventional institutional actors of a generation ago—superintendents, school boards, teachers' unions, and federal officials—do not dominate these struggles. Rather, national think tanks, advocacy groups, and business organizations define much of this agenda, and much of the agenda is played out at the state level. Similarly, the push for higher academic standards, more accountability, and improved outcomes also originates from groups outside the traditional policy actors.

In the terrain of state education politics, the mix of political forces and actors varies, as does their relative strength. But the power to make things happen has shifted to a set of actors that either did not exist until the mid-1970s or was relatively uninvolved and quiescent. Governors are taking political chances and committing themselves to reform agendas that were unheard of just a short time ago. National policy entrepreneurs are shaping state debates with concerted efforts to make a political impact. National movements to cut state spending shape the debate about financing.

Political scientists are challenged by these changes to think about state educational politics in new ways. Old frameworks and ways of conceptualizing political behavior are inadequate to the task of understanding what is happening in education. New frameworks are needed to account for the power of these new actors and to explain how decisions are being made about the distribution of resources. Furthermore, while the federal government and the school district were once thought to be the sites of political activity in past decades, today the state is primarily where these issues will play themselves out. Therefore, in order to understand the profound and exciting changes taking place in schools across the country, one must understand the push and pull of competing interests on the state level.

REFERENCES

Augenblick, John, Steven D. Gold, and Kent McGuire. 1990. *Education Finance in the 1990's.* Washington, D.C.: Education Commission of the States.

Bastian, Ann, Norm Fruchter, Marilyn Gittell, Colin Greer, and Kenneth Haskins. 1986. *Choosing Equality: The Case for Democratic Schooling.* Philadelphia: Temple University Press.

Beckham, Joseph C. 1993. *School Officials and the Courts: Update 1993.* Arlington, Va.: Educational Research Service.

Berdahl, Robert O. 1975. "Problems in Evaluating Statewide Boards." In *Evaluating Statewide Boards,* edited by Robert O. Berdahl. Washington, D.C.: American Council on Education.

Berger, Mark C., and Eugenia F. Toma. 1994. "Variations in State Education Policies and Effects on Student Performance." *Journal of Policy Analysis and Management* 13:477–491.

Berne, Robert, and Leanna Stiefel. 1992. *The Relationship between School Resources and Racial/Ethnic Status of Students in New York State Public Schools.* New York: New York State Education Department.

Card, David, and Alan B. Krueger. 1992. "Does School Quality Matter? Returns to Education and the Characteristics of Public Schools in the United States." *Journal of Political Economy* 100:1–40.

Carnegie Task Force on Teaching as a Profession. 1986. *A Nation Prepared: Teachers for the 21st Century.* New York: Carnegie Forum on Education and the Economy.

Carter, Deborah, and Reginald Wilson. 1992. *Minorities in Higher Education: Tenth Annual Status Report.* Washington, D.C.: American Council on Education.

Chubb, John E., and Terry M. Moe. 1986. "No School Is an Island: Politics, Markets, and Education." *Brookings Review* 4, no.4:21–28.

———. 1990. *Politics, Markets, and American Schools.* Washington, D.C.: Brookings Institution.

Clark, David L., and Terry A. Astuto. 1986. *The Significance and Performance of Changes in the Federal Educational Policy 1980–88.* Bloomington, Ind.: Policy Studies Center of the University Council for Educational Administration.

Clark, Shirley M. 1993. "Higher Education and School Reform." *Review of Higher Education* 17:1–20.

Clune, William H. 1993. "The Best Path to Systemic Educational Policy: Standard/Centralized or Differentiated/Decentralized?" *Educational Evaluation and Policy Analysis* 15:233–254.

Clune, William H., Paula White, and Janice Patterson. 1989. *The Implementation and Effects of High School Graduation Requirements.* Princeton, N.J.: Rutgers University, Center for Policy Research in Education.

Combs, Michael W. 1984. "The Federal Judiciary and Northern School Desegregation: Judicial Management in Perspective." *Journal of Law and Education* 13:345–399.

Coons, John E., William H. Clune, and Stephen D. Sugarman. 1970. *Private Wealth and Public Education.* Cambridge: Harvard University Press.

Cuban, Larry. 1990. "Reforming Again, Again, and Again." *Educational Researcher* 19, no. 1:3–13.

Darling-Hammond, Linda. 1994. "Inequality and Access to Knowledge." In *The Handbook of Multicultural Education,* edited by James A. Banks. New York: Macmillan.

Darling-Hammond, Linda, and Barnett Berry. 1988. *The Evolution of Teacher Policy.* Santa Monica, Calif.: RAND Corporation.

Downes, Thomas A., and Shah, Mona P. 1994. "The Effect of School Finance Reforms on the

Level and Growth of Per Pupil Expenditures." Paper presented at the annual meeting of the Association for Public Policy Analysis and Management, Chicago, October 27–29.

Farrell, Kenneth A. 1988. *State Expenditure Report, 1988.* Washington, D.C.: National Association of State Budget Officers.

Finn, Chester E. 1992. "Reinventing Local Control." In *School Boards: Changing Local Control,* edited by Patricia F. First and Herbert J. Walberg. Berkeley, Calif.: McCutchan Publishing.

Firestone, William A. 1989. "Education Policy as an Ecology of Games." *Educational Researcher* 18, no. 7:18–24.

Firestone, William A., Susan H. Fuhrman, and Michael W. Kirst. 1991. "State Educational Reform since 1983: Appraisal and the Future." *Educational Policy* 5, no. 3:233–250.

Frymier, Jack R. 1987. "Bureaucracy and the Neutering of Teachers." *Phi Delta Kappan* 69:9–14.

Fuhrman, Susan H. 1994a. "Legislatures and Education Policy." In *The Governance of Curriculum,* edited by Richard F. Elmore and Susan H. Fuhrman. Alexandria, Va.: Association for Supervision and Curriculum Development.

———. 1994b. "Intergovernment Relations in Education in the 1990's." *Publius* 24, no. 3:83–98.

Fuhrman, Susan H., and Richard F. Elmore. 1990. "Understanding Local Control in the Wake of State Education Reform." *Educational Evaluation and Policy Analysis* 12:82–96.

Hanushek, Eric A. 1981. "Throwing Money at Schools." *Journal of Policy Analysis and Management* 1, no. 1:19–41.

———. 1986. "The Economics of Schooling: Production and Efficiency in Public Schools." *Journal of Economic Literature* 24:1141–1177.

Hearn, James C., and Carolyn P. Griswold. 1994. "State-Level Centralization and Policy Innovation in U.S. Postsecondary Education." *Educational Evaluation and Policy Analysis* 16:161–190.

HEW (U.S. Department of Health, Education, and Welfare). Office of Education. 1966. *Equality of Educational Opportunity,* by James S. Coleman, Ernest Q. Campbell, Carol J. Hobson, James McPartland, Alexander M. Mood, Frederic D. Weinfeld, and Robert L. Yonk. Washington, D.C.: U.S. Government Printing Office.

Hines, Edward R. 1988. *Higher Education and State Governments.* ASHE-ERIC Higher Education Report No. 5. Washington, D.C.: Association for the Study of Higher Education.

Hochschild, Jennifer. 1984. *The New American Dilemma.* New Haven, Conn.: Yale University Press.

James, Thomas. 1987. "State Authority and the Politics of Educational Change." *Review of Research in Education* 17:169–224.

Kagan, Robert A. 1986. "Regulating Business, Regulating Schools: The Problem of Regulatory Unreasonableness." In *School Days, Rule Days: The Legalization and Regulation of Education,* edited by David L. Kirp and Donald N. Jensen. Philadelphia: Falmer Press.

Kingdon, John W. 1984. *Agendas, Alternatives, and Public Policies.* Boston: Little, Brown.

Kirst, Michael W. 1987. "The Crash of the First Wave." *Bacharach* 85:20–29.

LaNoue, George R., and Smith, Bruce L. 1973. *The Politics of School Decentralization.* Lexington, Mass.: Lexington Books.

Lemann, Nicholas. 1992. *The Promised Land.* New York: Vintage Books.

Lewis, Dan A. 1990. "Implementing Choice." In *Choice and Control in American Education,* edited by William H. Clune and John F. Witte. New York: Falmer Press.

———. 1993. "Deinstitutionalization and School Decentralization: Making the Same Mistake Twice." In *Decentralization and School Improvement,* edited by Jane Hannaway and Martin Conroy. San Francisco: Jossey-Bass.

Lewis, Dan A., and Nakagawa, Kathryn. 1995. *Race and Educational Reform in the American Metropolis.* Albany: State University of New York Press.

Lusi, Susan F. 1994. "Systemic School Reform: The Challenges Faced by State Departments of Education." In *The Governance of Curriculum,* edited by Richard F. Elmore and Susan H. Fuhrman. Alexandria, Va.: Association for Supervision and Curriculum Development.

McGuinness, Aims C. 1988. *State Postsecondary Education Structures Handbook.* Denver, Colo.: Education Commission of the States.

Marshall, Catherine, Douglas Mitchell, and Frederick Wirt. 1989. *Culture and Education Policy in the American States.* New York: Falmer Press.

Mazzoni, Tim L. 1993. "The Changing Politics of State Education Policy Making: A 20-Year Minnesota Perspective." *Educational Evaluation and Policy Analysis* 15:357–379.

Millett, John D. 1984. *Conflict in Higher Education: State Government Coordination versus Institutional Independence.* San Francisco: Jossey-Bass.

Mingle, James R., ed. 1983. *Management Flexibility and State Regulation in Higher Education.* Atlanta, Ga.: Southern Regional Education Board.

Mitchell, Douglas, Catherine Marshall, and Frederick Wirt. 1986. "The Context of State-Level Policy Formation." *Educational Evaluation and Policy Analysis* 8:347–378.

Murnane, Richard J. 1985. "An Economist's Look at Federal and State Education Policies." In *American Domestic Priorities: An Economic Appraisal,* edited by John M. Quigley and Daniel L. Rubinfeld. Berkeley: University of California Press.

Murphy, Jerome T., ed. 1980. *State Leadership in Education: On Being a Chief State School Officer.* Washington, D.C.: George Washington University, Institute for Educational Leadership.

Nathan, Joe, and James Ysseldyke. 1994. "What Minnesota Has Learned about School Choice." *Phi Delta Kappan* 75, no. 9:682–688.

NCES (National Center for Education Statistics). 1993. *Digest of Education Statistics.* Washington, D.C.: Office of Educational Research and Improvement.

National Commission on Excellence in Education. 1983. *A Nation at Risk: The Imperative for Educational Reform.* Washington, D.C.: National Commission on Excellence in Education.

National Governors' Association. 1986. *Time for Results: The Governors' 1991 Report on Education.* Washington, D.C.: National Governors' Association.

Newman, Frank. 1987. *Choosing Quality: Reducing Conflict between the State and the University.* Denver, Colo.: Education Commission of the States.

Odden, Allan R. 1992. "School Finance and Education Reform: An Overview." In *Rethinking School Finance,* edited by Allan R. Odden. San Francisco: Jossey-Bass.

———, ed. 1991. *Education Policy Implementation.* Albany: State University of New York Press.

Odden, Allan R., and Larry O. Picus, eds. 1992. *School Finance: A Policy Perspective.* New York: McGraw-Hill.

Orfield, Gary. 1993. *The Growth of Segregation in American Schools: Changing Patterns of Separation and Poverty since 1968.* Alexandria, Va.: National School Boards Association, Council of Urban Boards of Education.

Pierce, Neal R. 1994. "How a Bit of Brinksmanship Paid Off." *National Journal,* April 9, 851.

Rocha, Gregory G., and Webking, Robert H. 1992. *Politics and Public Education: Edgewood v. Kirby and the Reform of Public School Financing in Texas.* Minneapolis, Minn.: West Publishing.

Russo, Charles J. 1992. "The Legal Status of School Boards in the Intergovernmental System." In *School Boards: Changing Local Control,* edited by Patricia F. First and Herbert J. Walberg. Berkeley, Calif.: McCutchan Publishing.

Skolnick, Michael L., and Glen A. Jones. 1992. "A Comparative Analysis of Arrangements for State Coordination of Higher Education in Canada and the United States." *Journal of Higher Education* 63, no. 2:121–142.

Timar, Thomas B., and David L. Kirp. 1988. "State Efforts to Reform Schools: Treading between a Regulatory Swamp and an English Garden." *Educational Evaluation and Policy Analysis* 10:75–88.

Toch, Thomas. 1991. *In the Name of Excellence.* New York: Oxford University Press.

Twentieth Century Fund. 1983. *Making the Grade.* New York: Twentieth Century Fund.

Tyree, Alexander K. 1993. "Examining the Evidence: Have States Reduced Local Control of Curriculum?" *Educational Evaluation and Policy Analysis* 15:34–50.

Verstegen, Deborah. 1990. "Invidiousness and Inviolability in Public Education Finance." *Education Administration Quarterly* 26, no. 3:205–234.

Walters, Jonathan. 1993. "School Funding." *CQ Researcher* 3:747–762.

Weatherly, Richard, and Michael Lipsky. 1977. "Street-Level Bureaucrats and Institutional Innovations: Implementing Special Education Reform." *Harvard Educational Review* 47:171–197.

Wise, Arthur. 1967. *Rich Schools, Poor Schools: The Promise of Equal Educational Opportunities.* Chicago: University of Chicago Press.

Wise, Arthur, and Tamar Gendler. 1989. "Rich Schools, Poor Schools: The Persistence of Unequal Education." *College Board Review* 151:12–18.

Wong, Kenneth. 1989. "Fiscal Support for Education in American States: The 'Parity-to-Dominance' View Examined." *American Journal of Education* 97:329–357.

Zumeta, William. 1992. "State Policies and Private Higher Education." *Journal of Higher Education* 63, no. 4:364–417.

Zusman, Ami. 1986. "Legislature and University Conflict: The Case of California." *Review of Higher Education* 9:397–418.

SUGGESTED READINGS

Chubb, John E., and Terry M. Moe. *Politics, Markets, and American Schools.* Washington, D.C.: Brookings Institution, 1990. Chubb and Moe provide an evocative analysis of the effects of institutions on school effectiveness. They recommend a new system of education based on parent-student choice and school competition.

Elmore, Richard F., and Fuhrman, Susan H., eds. *The Governance of Curriculum.* Alexandria, Va.: Association for Supervision and Curriculum Development, 1994. This collection provides a broad overview of the politics of curriculum reform and policy development. It includes thorough discussions of the interaction between policy actors on the district, state, and federal levels.

Marshall, Catherine, Douglas Mitchell, and Frederick Wirt. *Culture and Education Policy in the American States.* New York: Falmer Press, 1989. This important analysis focuses on the ways in which values affect state education policy. Drawing from data collected on six states, the researchers provide a cultural framework for studying state policy and describe the differences between states in terms of these varying cultural influences and regional values.

Smith, Marshall S., and O'Day, Jennifer A., eds. *Politics of Education Association Yearbook.* Vol. 4. New York: Falmer Press, 1990. This collection offers a groundbreaking analysis on how to improve education in the United States. Smith and O'Day's work focuses on setting national standards in curriculum content and creating incentives for school districts and states to meet these standards.

Wirt, Frederick W., and Michael W. Kirst. *Schools in Conflict: The Politics of Education.* Berkeley, Calif.: McCutchan Publishing, 1992, 3d ed. Wirt and Kirst offer a valuable approach to the politics of education. They analyze public education as a political system and provide valuable insight into the political behavior of individuals within this system and the ways in which institutions function.

CHAPTER 13

 *Economic Regulation and Environmental Protection*

BRUCE A. WILLIAMS

Government regulation has long been the whipping boy of American politics. While the scope of regulatory policy dramatically increased in the 1960s and early 1970s in areas like consumer protection, environmental protection, and workplace safety, by the late 1970s both Democratic and Republican politicians made cutting "unnecessary" and "wasteful" regulations a priority. The general condemnation of government regulation originated with the claim by conservative academics and politicians that government interference in the economy was imposing a significant drain on productivity and was a prime cause of economic decline. During the administrations of Ronald Reagan and George Bush, efforts were made to cut back severely on regulations by subjecting them to the most stringent cost-benefit review possible.

This focus on the wastefulness of regulation has come to be shared by most liberal politicians as well, who, despite their support for the general goals of regulation, concede that in many instances it has been largely unsuccessful. Vice President Albert Gore's National Performance Review, issued in September 1993, thus noted, "Many federal regulations impose too many constraints on individuals and businesses (such as by unnecessarily using command-and-control structures that tell regulated parties precisely what to do) while still failing to accomplish the goals for which they were imposed" (Office of the Vice President 1993, 3). Public opinion polling finds that "while Americans dislike regulations as a general matter, when asked about specific programs, such as for health and safety, they respond favorably" (Office of the Vice President 1993, 7). So, although there is support for individual regulations, overall, the general reputation of government regulation has fallen on hard times. It is no longer seen as a guardian of the "public interest" but, instead, as an inefficient drag on the economy to be avoided whenever possible and pared back at all times.

In this chapter, I examine the ways in which regulatory policy affects and is affected by state governments. Focusing especially on economic regulation and environmental protection, I attempt to clarify the concept of regulation, especially economic regulation; dispel some myths about its history and operation; and examine the reasons for the persistent attacks on it. The discussion of regulation is guided by three themes.

First, I emphasize the inevitability of government interference in the private market economy. Although some politicians and scholars hark back to a golden age when the private market was allowed to operate unhindered by the actions of government, in fact, such a laissez-faire age never existed. Throughout American history, the question has never been whether government will intervene in the market; rather, it has always been what specific policies will be pursued and which levels of government will be responsible for them. Less federal activity in this policy area means greater policy-making responsibilities for states and localities. For example, the failure of the federal government to enact new regulations in an area like health care, as happened in 1994, does not mean that the health care system is made free from government interference. Rather, it means that the burden falls on state governments to manage the health care system.

The second theme involves the significance of federalism in understanding the different options facing regulators at different levels of government. Federalism imposes two types of limits on the regulatory process: constitutional and structural. The U.S. Constitution reserves for the federal government the right to regulate interstate commerce. Since the courts have interpreted interstate commerce quite broadly, states have very limited ability to regulate the flow of capital across their borders. This constitutional restriction on state activity means that, even though the states have had more responsibility for making regulatory policies since the late 1970s, state policy makers are quite limited in the types of policies they can enact.

Legal limitations combine with features of a capitalist economy to constrain further the options open to states. In a capitalist economy, the private businesses that ultimately control investment decisions are free to shift their resources between states. State policy makers must therefore compete with one another to attract the investment upon which their economic well-being depends (see Chapter 14). To the extent that the demand by states exceeds the supply of factories, retail stores, high-technology research centers, and so forth, the terms of this competition are defined by the business interests that states try to attract.[1] Un-

---

1. This dynamic is much less a factor at the federal level because the ability to shift investment between countries is far more constrained than the ability to shift between states. That is, the exit costs of moving between states are far lower than the exit costs of moving between countries. Pas-

Table 13-1 Developmental, Allocational, and Redistributive Public Policies

	Policy arenas		
	Developmental	Allocational	Redistributive
Characteristics	Policies that increase resources available to government by expanding the tax base.	Policies that distribute public services funded out of existing revenues without affecting the state or local economy.	Policies that shift income from one group to another. Especially policies that benefit those who pay proportionately less in taxes at the expense of those who pay proportionately more.
Examples	Economic Development (for example, tax credits, enterprise zones, venture capital programs).	Police and fire protection.	Welfare policy and many types of economic and social regulation (for example, air pollution controls, hazardous waste regulation).

SOURCE: Adapted from Peterson 1981.

derstanding the limits on state policy makers in this regard is essential for analyzing regulatory policies in the states.

Of particular importance here is the argument developed by Peterson (1981), which emphasizes the significant policy-making differences between federal, state, and local governments.[2] Peterson builds his theory around three public policy arenas: developmental, allocational, redistributive (see Table 13-1). Developmental policies "strengthen the local economy, enhance the local tax base, and generate additional resources that can be used for the community's welfare." Redistributive policies "help the needy and unfortunate and . . . provide reasonably equal access to public services." Allocational policies fall between developmental and redistributive policies: they consist of "marginal expenditures for services [that] have neither much of a positive nor much of a negative effect on the local economy" (Peterson 1981, 41, 43, 44).

Peterson argues that states and localities tend to pursue developmental policies and avoid redistributive policies. The former are in what he defines as the general interests of the community: increasing the tax base—without increasing tax rates—provides more resources for improving the state or community. Redistributive policies are avoided because they tend to provide services for those who pay proportionately less in taxes by taking from those who pay proportionately more. Such policies provide an incentive for the latter to leave the state and relocate in an area where they will receive a higher level of services for their taxes. A central consideration for states is that relatively low exit costs make such

sage of the North American Free Trade Agreement (NAFTA) with its encouragement of industry flight beyond national borders changes this calculus somewhat. It is just such a complication, of course, that led to the skepticism with which environmentalists treated NAFTA.

2. Peterson focuses primarily on city politics, but he notes that his arguments also apply in large measure to the dynamics of state policy making. Indeed, he tests his theory on state expenditure data. And in Peterson, Rabe, and Wong (1987) he tests this approach on state implementation of federal policy initiatives.

movement a real possibility. An exodus of those who pay proportionately more in taxes would work against the overriding goal of economic development.

Peterson concludes that state and local governments are thus limited in their ability to pursue redistributive policies: they are locked into interjurisdictional competition to attract industry and middle-class households that might bolster their tax bases. State and local policy makers attempt to blunt redistributive demands made by disadvantaged groups either by responding symbolically (for example, by passing, but not enforcing, legislation) or by redirecting the allocation of existing revenues (that is, by transforming redistributive demands into allocative demands). Economic and environmental regulation, because they inevitably alter market-based distributions, has the effect of redistributing income. Understanding the developmental and redistributive aspects of regulatory policies is important to an analysis of state actions.

The third theme of the chapter, following from the second, is that the impact of shifting regulatory policy-making responsibilities between levels of government is not neutral. Rather, such shifts systematically and predictably present advantages and disadvantages to various groups in society. Reducing federal responsibility and increasing the state role in various types of regulatory activities, depending on the specific characteristics of that regulation and the states within which they are promulgated, changes the formulation and implementation of these policies. In particular, the redistributive aspects of many regulatory policies make them difficult for states to enforce effectively.

GOVERNMENT REGULATION

A general discussion of regulatory policy is first necessary in order to set the discussion of state economic regulation policies within the broader context of the overall themes of this chapter: the inevitability of government interference in the private market; the importance of federalism; and the effect of changes in the level of government responsible for various economic policies.

Regulation, in the most general sense, involves the authoritative bounding of behavior by government. In this sense, most of the activities of all levels of government might be called regulation. When, for example, a law requires motor vehicles to stop at a red light, it regulates the behavior of drivers. When the law requires that all drivers have a license, it further regulates them.

The government regulation of behavior imposes different sets of costs and benefits on different groups of individuals. The general public can easily see, calculate, and share one set of costs: the costs of enforcing regulation. In the examples, government must pay for traffic lights and traffic police, as well as for a bureau of motor vehicles. The public, as we know, must pay—through taxes—for government. A second set of costs falls on those whose behavior is directly affected by the regulations. These costs are more difficult to calculate than the first, and because they are not as self-evident as a tax bill, they are less visible than the first set. If I am hurrying to an important business meeting, waiting at a traffic light costs me valuable time. If the traffic light's delay causes me to be late, it may cost me a valuable sale.

Regulations are adopted on the assumption that their benefits will outweigh their costs. Indeed, the explicit or implicit justification for most regulation is that its benefits—usually defined in terms of an overriding public interest—justify the imposition of costs on specific groups or on the entire population. Benefits, however, are usually difficult to calculate. The benefits of safe street intersections are obvious and significant. Determining an optimal level of even obvious benefits is often quite difficult. Where, for example, do we place traffic lights? How many should we buy? If we place lights at every intersection, travel will be very safe but quite slow: increasing benefits usually increases costs. The question then becomes, how many traffic lights are we willing to pay for and how much convenience are we willing to subject ourselves to in exchange for how many avoided accidents? Determining an optimal answer to this question is complicated by the fact that one's response will depend on whether one is a motorist in a hurry, a pedestrian trying to cross the street, a harried politician attempting to minimize local taxes, or the owner of a company that manufactures traffic lights. What this example illustrates is that even in the case of regulations that are clearly in the interest of almost the entire public (imagine intersections without traffic lights!), individuals' and groups' costs and benefits vary quite dramatically. Regulation becomes a difficult political issue to the extent that, with little regard to collective costs or benefits, people attempt to influence the decisions of government in order either to raise their individual benefits or to lower their individual costs.

Economic Regulation and Environmental Protection

Most of the regulations imposed by government are, like traffic laws, noncontroversial. This chapter deals, however, with more controversial regulation: the regulation of economic activity and environmental protection.

At first glance, it might seem that regulation of the private market by government is unnecessary. One of the supposed advantages of a private market economy is that the behavior of individuals pursuing their own self-interest is aggregated through the invisible hand of the market into a social good. The prices determined by the free and competitive interaction of supply and demand most efficiently allocate the resources of a society. Thus, the public interest is seemingly served by the private market, without the heavy hand of government interference.

Economists have long realized, however, that the market often fails to aggregate individual greed into a social good. They suggest that even in a private market society, government interference is justified in such instances of *market failure.*

There are three general conditions under which markets fail. First, markets fail when there are significant *externalities* involved in transactions. Externalities are significant costs or benefits from a transaction falling on individuals who are not involved in the buying or selling of the goods produced. Because they are not involved in the transaction, the costs or benefits to such individuals are ignored in the exchange of goods and services. For example, the production of industrial goods is often accompanied by environmental pollution. Many of the costs of this pollution fall on those who live near the polluting factory, however, and are not included in the price of the good. The commodity is thus produced and sold for less than it actually costs—its selling price does not include the cost of pollution borne by the affected public. Hence, the good—along with the pollution that accompanies its production—is underpriced and overproduced. Since it imposes costs on consumers that are not determined by the costs of production, monopoly is considered an example of a market failure involving significant externalities.

Market failures that produce significant externalities cannot be readily solved by the market itself. The competition between producers to produce goods at the lowest possible price prevents even civic-minded producers from raising the cost of their goods to cover the cost of pollution controls. In a truly competitive market, such well-meaning entrepreneurs would quickly be driven out of business by their less-public-minded competitors. In such a case, government is justified in interfering in the market in order to ensure that the externalities are somehow accurately reflected in the price of the good. In the example, government might require that all producers install pollution control equipment; this would force all producers to include the costs of their pollution in the price of the good.

The second kind of market failure is in the market's inability to provide public goods. Public goods are those goods and services that, when provided, are not divisible: that is, those who do not pay for the goods cannot practically be excluded from their consumption. National defense is the classic case of a public good. If the state of Iowa were to stop paying its share of the cost of national defense, it would be impractical to exclude that state from enjoying the benefits of the defense protection provided for the rest of the states. Since individuals cannot be excluded from consuming a public good once it is provided, they have every incentive to avoid paying for it—becoming what economists call "free riders." Since individuals will seek to avoid paying for public goods, such goods are unlikely to be provided in the private market. To the extent that specific public goods are deemed necessary or desirable (for example, defense or parks), government must intervene in the private market either to produce the goods themselves or to create incentives for their production by the private sector.

The third kind of market failure occurs when consumers cannot obtain accurate information about the quality of a product. In these cases, individual consumers will be either unable or unlikely to acquire the information needed to make informed choices in the market. Thus, government may justifiably intervene to ensure that their choices will not result in disaster: for example, it requires that all foodstuffs be demonstrated to be safe for human consumption.

Lack of accurate information leads to poor or even dangerous decisions in the marketplace.

There are three categories of this type of market failure: individuals are often unaware of the risks associated with their jobs; individuals are often unable to make informed choices about the competencies of professionals that they might hire (for example, doctors); individuals are sometimes unable to judge the safety of products that they might purchase, such as electrical appliances or processed foods. Government intervention in the private market is justifiable to ensure safety, competence, and quality of products.

We can distinguish between two broad kinds of regulation that address market failures. Economic regulation addresses natural monopoly; social regulation deals with "the externalities and impacts of economic activity" (Vogel 1981, 238). In areas like environmental protection, health care reform, occupational safety, and consumer protection, these externalities and impacts often include "quality of life" issues that are difficult to define, requiring regulators to "affect the economy in nonmarket dimensions" (Litan and Nordhaus 1983, 10).

For example, price closely captures the full value of an airline ticket, train ride, or kilowatt hour of electricity: the challenge for economic regulation is to attach accurate price tags to such commodities when markets fail to do so. In contrast, price is less appropriate for capturing the full value of a healthy environment or avoiding cancer. Although their value certainly has a component that is captured by money, they are not traded on the market, and estimating their price becomes a political rather than an economic determination. Social regulation, then, raises fundamental questions about the relation between technological progress, capitalism, and democracy.

Thus, various conditions exist that seem to mandate the government regulation of economic activity: sometimes, markets fail to produce socially beneficial outcomes. Indeed, there are many who reject the market as an allocator of society's scarce resources because of its overemphasis on the production of material goods (Schumacher 1973). The conditions under which most economists would concede that government regulation is necessary, however, are frequently not the same conditions under which government regulation is enacted and implemented: the rationale for and the reality of economic regulation can be quite disparate. Political factors, rather than economic logic, often govern policy making.

Since the 1950s, studies of the creation and activities of regulatory agencies have revealed that regulation is not always guided by a consideration of market failure and the public interest. Rather, government regulation often serves the interests of those groups that are being regulated. This suggests that, in many instances, regulation has actually become a service that industry "purchases" from government in order to obtain government subsidies, control the entry of new competitors into the market, limit the use of substitute products, and fix prices that ensure desired profit levels (Stigler 1975). Thus, market failure may establish the preconditions for "government failure" (Weisbrod, Handler, and Komesar

1977). Indeed, most of the classic scholarly work on regulation focuses on the *capture* of regulatory agencies by the groups that they are charged with regulating (Bernstein 1955; Huntington 1952)—that is, rather than speaking in the interest of the public, regulatory agencies serve the narrow interests of the regulated. Thus, one reason for current discontent with economic regulation is the contention that we have it where we don't need it, and need it where we don't have it. Such arguments have fueled deregulation efforts in fields like transportation and communications (Derthick and Quirk 1985).

A second reason for the discontent with regulation centers on the way its costs and benefits are distributed across organized interests even when government action is successfully remedying market failures: many environmental protection measures serve as examples. In such cases, those adversely affected by regulation, such as industrial polluters, attempt to alter regulations in order to reduce the costs they must bear. Even when the purpose of the regulation is being achieved—for example, when pollution is effectively reduced—it still generates opposition from those who must bear the costs.

Costs, Benefits, and Controversy

This discontent with regulation has resulted in an explosion of interest in the actual effect of government regulations. If they are not remedying market failure, then what are they doing? If they are remedying market failure, then why is there so much opposition to regulation? Attempts to answer these questions have fueled the controversy surrounding economic and social regulation.

Increasingly, scholarly attention has turned to an analysis of the costs and benefits of regulation. Actual government expenditures for regulation—the costs of paying the salaries of regulators and their staffs, publicizing regulations, holding hearings, and the like—are minimal in comparison with, for example, the amount of money spent to build roads or schools. Furthermore, many types of state regulatory activity may actually result in a net profit: professional licensing, for example, generates income through the fees that are paid for examinations and licensing.

The costs and benefits of regulation, however, do not end with government expenditures. Rather, the costs and benefits of regulation reverberate throughout the economy. For example, regulations promulgated by the Environmental Protection Agency (EPA) to control smokestack emissions require the industries generating air pollution to purchase and install expensive pollution control equipment. If the regulations are successfully implemented, the air will be cleaner and many people will benefit. The obvious question then becomes, Do the benefits of regulation outweigh the costs?

The focus on costs and benefits of regulation has led to the unpleasant recognition that difficult trade-offs must be made between economic growth and social goals such as safe jobs and clean air. These trade-offs have become even more difficult to face in times of high inflation, unemployment, and slow economic growth. If, for example, we decide that a safe workplace is a desirable social goal, we pass regulations that require employers to spend money to make factories safer. In turn, this results in higher production costs and prices, which presumably slow economic growth. Increasingly, such difficult choices must be faced. How much are we willing to spend to save the lives of workers in dangerous jobs? How much productivity are we willing to forgo in order to preserve clean air and water? How much risk are we willing to endure for cheap energy? Moreover, there is moral resistance to attaching any price tag to such items that lie outside "the domain of dollars" (Okun 1976, 137). Hence, the very act of establishing a "price" for human life or clean water in regulatory calculations remains controversial. The political theorist Robert E. Goodin (1982) flatly states that even attempting to reduce such values to dollar equivalents degrades them and lessens the possibility of enlightened public policy. He nicely illustrates the inability of price to capture fully such values when he notes that, no matter what the price established for contracting lung cancer, losing one's eyesight, and so on, no one would freely choose to accept the money in exchange for the loss. Market transactions are simply unable to compensate individuals fully for such catastrophic losses.

Because decisions about regulation involve implicit or explicit answers to such questions, regulation generates controversy. That controversy is further fueled by the fact that preferences about such trade-offs are not randomly distributed throughout the population. Rather, persons' preferences depend on whether they stand to gain or lose from a particular policy decision. In addition, the people who reap the benefits are usually not the same people who bear the costs. Workers in a chemical company are likely to value a safe workplace, even at the cost of increased prices; in contrast, the owners and customers of the company are likely to prefer a lesser degree of safety and its attendant lower prices or greater profits.

A final reason for the controversy surrounding regulation is that underlying this controversy is the conflict between an economic system presumably built on the unfettered use of private property and a government philosophy that limits the free use of that property for the sake of the public interest. The implications of regulation for the relation between unrestrained property rights and the public interest were clearly understood in 1877 by the Supreme Court in *Munn v. Illinois* (94 U.S. 113): "Property does become clothed with a public interest when used in a manner to make it of public consequence, and affect the community at large. When, therefore, one devotes his property to a use in which the public has an interest, he, in effect, grants to the public an interest in that use, and must submit to be controlled by the public for the common good" (quoted in Shepherd and Wilcox 1979, 228).

The public interest, however, is not readily and objectively defined. Understandably, its invocation in constraint of private property is controversial. For example, many northern industrial states have seen movements to pass bills limiting the ability of companies to move their plants to other states or out of the country. Is the public interest best served by maintaining jobs in the state, or by allowing owners the freedom to exercise control over private property? Do the benefits of such regulations outweigh and justify the costs imposed on owners, as well as the costs that might flow from interfering in the private market? Clearly, no objectively correct definition of the public interest can be found for this case. A person's definition will likely be determined by whether he or she is a factory worker in Youngstown, Ohio, or a stockholder in United States Steel.

Trends in State Regulation: The Myth of Laissez Faire

Most popular and scholarly attention has focused on the federal government's activities, but states were actively involved in regulating market relations, often in minute detail, long before the federal government became involved. As noted at the beginning of the chapter, the myth of a laissez-faire era is sustainable only if we ignore the role of states. State regulations, in fact, created many precedents for later activities by federal regulatory officers. It is certainly true that federal regulation was largely nonexistent prior to the creation of the Interstate Commerce Commission in 1887. In the states, however, the regulation of commerce had been attempted before the commission was established. As in other areas of early federal regulation, actions by the states—in this case, Illinois, Iowa, Minnesota, and Wisconsin—paved the way for federal action. Throughout the post–Civil War period, states were also increasingly active in the regulation of banks and the rapidly growing insurance industry (discussed later in this chapter).

As the American economy became national in scope, the federal government became an increasingly important source of regulatory authority. Still, it tended to supplement—rather than supplant—the states' regulatory efforts. Clearly, states have historically maintained an enduring involvement in a great deal of regulatory activity. Emmette Redford (1965, 151–153) distinguishes between four different types of state regulatory power.

1. *Areas of Authority Mandated to the States by the Constitution or Left to the States as a Result of Congressional Inaction.* States maintain, for example, the jurisdiction to define the rights of property owners, as well as the jurisdiction to limit those rights and to regulate the ways in which property can be transmitted, such as by establishing procedures for transferring title to real estate and laws governing the rights of citizens of foreign countries to own property. States also regulate relations between employer and employees through the workers' compensation system and laws governing the ability of unions to establish closed shops. They regulate the provision of some collective goods, such as public services like road construction and maintenance, school construction and staffing, and recreational facilities. States have always regulated the activities of businesses, labor relations, and trades and professions that are intrastate in nature. Of course, such regulations often do affect interstate or even foreign commerce. For example, states are free to pass right-to-work laws, prohibiting union shops. Of the twenty states in which right-to-work laws are in effect, eleven are in the

South. Such laws have effectively hindered union organizers. The absence of extensive unionization has tended to keep wages and production costs down in these states, thereby providing incentives for the flight of many industries from the North to the South—and affecting interstate commerce.

2. *Regulatory Authority Delegated to States by the Federal Government.* Included here are areas of policy under federal authority that Congress has specifically delegated to the states; many regulatory activities are of this type. Insurance regulation, for instance, was returned to the states in 1949 under the McCarran-Ferguson Act. This legislation was a response to federal court rulings that the insurance industry was involved in interstate commerce and hence the province of federal and not state regulation. After intense lobbying by the insurance industry, Congress decided to delegate its regulatory authority to the states (discussed below). The licensing of hydroelectric projects and the rates they charge are controlled by the states, unless the state chooses not to create a commission for this purpose. Price maintenance agreements authorized by states have been exempted from federal antitrust statutes. Similarly, states may exercise jurisdiction in labor disputes when the National Labor Relations Board does not assert its authority. Where a state commission for the regulation of public utilities' securities exists, the federal government stands aside. Moreover, in several regulatory acts of Congress (for example, the Occupational Safety and Health Act and the Resource Conservation and Recovery Act, discussed below), the states may opt to enforce provisions themselves.

3. *Areas of Parallel Activity Where Both States and the Federal Government Exercise Authority.* Both levels of government maintain regulatory agencies that oversee utility rate levels and structures, banking practices, securities transactions, railroad rates and services, labor relations, and some areas of consumer protection.

4. *Areas of Cooperation between the States and the Federal Government.* Most congressional regulatory legislation attempts to establish cooperative relations between state and federal agencies, even when the federal government is the source of regulatory legislation; in such cases federal agencies are usually highly dependent on the activities of state officials. Provisions for such cooperation are found in regulations affecting environmental protection, some areas of consumer protection, occupational safety and health, communications, power, and natural gas, among others. As discussed later, such major pieces of federal environmental legislation as the Clean Air and Clean Water acts, the Resource Conservation and Recovery Act, and the Superfund all depended heavily on the implementation abilities of state environmental agencies. Similarly, joint state and federal inspections are mandated under the federal Coal Mine Inspection Act of 1952; soil conservation districts have been established by the states as part of national soil conservation programs; and unemployment insurance programs are established by the states but are jointly administered by both levels of government and must conform to federal standards.

For three reasons, state regulatory activity is likely to become increasingly important in the future. First, there is intense competition between states to attract investment (see Chapter 14). To the extent that businesses attend to the costs of regulation, states are likely to compete with one another for industries by lowering such costs. In order to attract businesses, states can be expected to reduce their regulatory burdens, even at the expense of the benefits of such regulation to the general population. Indeed, the lack of regulatory activity in many southern states has already been used as a means to attract businesses. The outcome of such competition will, along with economic development policies, determine the economic health of many states and, in some cases, both the physical and economic health of their citizens.

Second, the Reagan and Bush administrations reduced—or attempted to reduce—federal regulatory activities. This retreat at the federal level presents states with important decisions about whether or not to assume full responsibility for the regulation of areas such as air and water pollution control, consumer protection, and occupational health and safety. In short, the focus of many political battles over regulation has shifted from the federal to the state level.

Third, the responsibility and costs for enforcing many regulations passed by Congress fall on the states in the form of unfunded mandates. Unfunded mandates are the reason that the old theme song of state and local officials "Give Me Money!"—a favorite throughout the lean years of the Reagan and Bush administrations—has finally given way to a new tune, "Leave Me Alone" (Stanfield 1994, 726). Consider the revisions made in 1994 to the 1974 Safe Drinking Water Act. The act, in order to regulate the safety of America's drinking water, requires local governments to build state-of-the-art water treatment facilities and to monitor drinking water for a wide variety of contaminants. Given the widespread concern of most Americans with drinking water safety, the goals of the act had wide public support. In the twenty years between the act's passage and its revisions in 1994, however, much had changed in the dynamics of federalism. Concern about rising federal deficits made it increasingly difficult for Congress to provide the money for localities to carry out its mandates. Yet, public support for environmental protection remained strong. The result was that the cost burden of complying with federally mandated standards fell on state and local governments. This brought howls of protest from organizations representing local governments. Consequently, revision of the Clean Water Act became a highly charged and controversial topic as conservatives in Congress, already opposed to stringent federal environmental standards, joined forces with state and local officials who opposed additional federal burdens without additional federal funds to pay for them.

It is difficult to predict the shape of future regulatory activity in the states. First, the relative power of interest groups affected by regulations in the states (see Chapter 4) is quite different from the balance of interest group power at the federal level. Thus, our experience with federal regulation during the past century is of little use in the prediction of specific policy outcomes at the state level. Second, the balance of interest group power differs from one state to another: thus, knowledge of regulatory practices in Idaho is of little use in predicting Alabama's actions.

Despite the fact that we cannot predict the future of state regulation, past research and writing on regulatory activity identifies the factors that determine the outcome of a state's regulatory decision making: political perceptions of the regulation's costs and benefits (in particular, perceptions of its redistributive implications); the degree to which those affected by the regulation are mobilized and powerful; the ability of affected parties to manipulate multiple decision-making arenas; and the limited ability of states to enforce regulations with redistributive effects. In listing these four factors as the determinants of regulatory decision making, I am not arguing that the activities of elected politicians like legislators or governors are unimportant. Rather, I am suggesting that the kinds of political pressures that can be brought to bear on these actors in regard to regulatory decision making are usually determined by these four systemic factors.

First, because regulation always involves the government imposition of costs and benefits on various segments of the population, the distribution of these must be identified. Any interference by government inevitably alters the status quo of the market, bettering the condition of some actors and worsening the condition of others. If affected segments of the population recognize the costs or benefits of the regulation to them, they will pressure the government to recognize their interests in making regulatory decisions. Thus, the "proper" calculation of regulation's costs and benefits becomes a highly political issue. How many dollars' worth of smokestack-scrubbing equipment should be considered the equivalent of a single asthma attack brought on by air pollution? Furthermore, many types of costs and benefits are inherently difficult to measure: for example, what is the actual benefit of a given reduction in air pollution? Combined, these two factors make it difficult—if not impossible—to render an "objective" cost-benefit measurement in most cases.

Second, because regulation bestows costs and benefits on groups, regulatory decision making is usually determined by the interplay of interest groups. As Bernstein (1955, 18) notes, "[R]egulation is largely a product of the clash of organized private economic interests seeking to utilize governmental powers for the enhancement of private interests." The attention accorded a particular group's costs and benefits is usually a function of the group's political clout in relation to other interested and active groups. As Olson (1965) has observed, however, different kinds of individuals have widely different potentials for organizing into formal interest groups. In regulation, it is frequently the case that large numbers of unorganized individuals are each only slightly affected by the actions of government: for example, a consumer of a regulated product is usually only marginally affected by regulation's effect on the price of that product—even though, the total costs to all individuals may amount to a huge sum. Since the cost imposed on each individual is small, no one individual has an incentive to spend the resources in time and money required to organize all of those similarly affected into a formal interest group. Even if such "latent groups" (as Olson calls them) manage to organize around a particular regulatory issue, they are unlikely to stay organized for very long. The size of the benefit that will accrue to each individual member is, quite simply, too small to induce people to bear the cost of organization for very long.

In contrast, when regulations impose large costs on a small number of individuals, such "privileged groups" (as Olson [1965] calls them) tend to form strong and well-maintained organizations to represent their interests. It is for this reason that, in the long run, interest groups representing business interests are better organized and more powerful than those representing consumers. For example, consider the individual businesses in a regulated industry such as insurance. Because each insurance company has such a high stake in the outcome of regulatory decision making, all of the affected companies are willing to invest their resources in organizing to pursue their interests in the regulatory process.

Once organized, different groups have vastly different levels of resources that can be translated into political influence. The outcome of regulatory politics is determined by the actual resources brought to bear by organized groups, rather than by any neutral government calculation of the public interest (Bernstein 1955, 17–18; Fainsod, Gordon, and Palamountain 1959, 253). Thus, the outcome of regulatory politics will change as the balance of power among competing groups changes. In certain areas, past regulation may have been as predictable as it is portrayed by those who speak of the capture of regulatory agencies. But currently, at the state level, regulation is a dynamic area of public policy making.

A third determinant of the outcome of state regulatory decision making is the diversity of regulatory arenas provided by our federal system of government. Business corporations can choose the state in which their headquarters will be located and thereby select the state that will be their primary regulator. In some cases, an industry can seek to be subject to federal regulation rather than a plethora of individual states' regulations.

Finally, it must be kept in mind that states are much more limited than the federal government in their ability to implement regulatory policies with redistributive implications. As they become the sole regulatory force in these areas, their competition for industry will simultaneously pressure them to reduce the economic impact of their regulatory structure. Because economic regulation is designed to interfere in the private market allocation of resources, its effect is always to redistribute from one group to another. Recall the argument put forth by Peterson (1981) that states and localities are severely limited in their ability to pursue redistributive policies. That is, when the groups standing to lose income as a result of economic regulations are above-average taxpayers (for example, corporations forced to bear the burden of environmental regulations), states may be caught between the desire to protect the environment and the fear that such taxpayers will move to a state with less stringent regulations. Thus, stringent state regulation can conflict with the overriding state goal of economic development.

There are two ways that those adversely affected by state policies can try to escape the costs of regulation (Williams and Matheny 1995, chap. 4). One way is to make a geographic move within the same level of government. So, for instance, businesses often move, or threaten to move, from one city to another or one state to another. We call this horizontal exit. Another way is to shift the level of government that has authority over regulatory decisions. So, for instance, the insurance industry, unhappy with the prospect of coming under the regulatory authority of the federal government, supported passage of the McCarran-Ferguson Act, which delegated regulatory authority to the states. We call this vertical exit.

The effect of federalism on regulation, as characterized by the ideas of both horizontal and vertical exit, is illustrated by controversies in the regulation of savings and loan institutions (S&Ls). Such thrift institutions had the option of operating under either federal or state charters; they could shift their charters from one level of government to another ("Many Harried S&Ls" 1981, 1). In the 1970s and 1980s, state-chartered S&Ls claimed that state regulators were overly sensitive to the wishes of consumer groups and that they artificially depressed the interest rates on home mortgages. In order to escape such restrictions, many S&Ls threatened to shift to the federal charter system. Given the pro-business climate and the corresponding weakness of consumer groups in Washington, these S&Ls believed that federal regulators would grant them greater latitude to set adjustable interest rates; such rates, the bankers argued, were necessary to ensure adequate levels of profit. When a financial institution shifts its charter to the federal system, however, the state loses more than the power to regulate: it also loses substantial tax revenues. The mere threat of such a shift has created tremendous pressures for the states to align their regulations with federal standards.

The pressures on state regulators, however, resulted from more than intergovernmental competition for regulatory powers and revenues. Interstate competition for these resources is always fierce. Several pioneering states—notably, Texas and Virginia—attracted banks to their state systems by eliminating many restrictions on home mortgage interest rates. The inability or unwillingness of states to regulate these institutions effectively resulted in the S&L crisis of the 1980s, when thrifts across the country collapsed under the weight of bad investments and outright fraud (Sherrill 1990).

A FRAMEWORK FOR STUDYING STATE REGULATORY POLICY AND POLITICS

Scholarly work on regulatory politics has increasingly incorporated the four determining factors in state regulatory decision making discussed above. In a synthesizing work, Wilson (1980) argues that regulatory politics is best understood through an analysis of regulation's perceived costs and benefits. Costs and benefits may be either concentrated on a specific group or more widely dispersed

Table 13-2 Categories of Regulatory Policy

	Perceived benefits of regulation	
	Diffuse	Concentrated
Perceived costs of regulation		
Diffuse	Majoritarian politics: social security	Client politics: insurance regulation
Concentrated	Entrepreneurial politics: environmental protection, hazardous waste regulation	Interest group struggle: health care reform, medical malpractice regulation

SOURCE: Adapted from Wilson 1980.

throughout the entire population. Taxes on income, for example, are costs of regulation that are widely distributed. The benefits of price supports for a particular farm crop—tobacco, for example—are concentrated. Although many people may be affected by the higher prices that can result from such supports, they are affected only slightly, whereas a small group of people are deeply affected by the structure of such supports—the farmers themselves. Because the concentration or dispersion of costs and benefits affects the probability of interest groups forming to represent those affected, this concentration or dispersion will determine the type of politics that surrounds each type of regulation.

Based on an analysis of the dispersion of costs and benefits, Wilson identifies four major types of regulatory politics (Table 13-2).

When both costs and benefits are widely dispersed, regulatory politics will be majoritarian. The passage in 1935 of federal Social Security legislation is a prime example of majoritarian politics. All—or at least all of those covered under the act—expected to gain something: the provision of Social Security benefits upon retirement, disability, or death. All expected to pay some sort of cost: Social Security taxes, regularly deducted from paychecks. Because costs and benefits were so widely dispersed, no strong and long-lived interest groups formed around the issue. The possible benefits or losses to individuals were not sufficiently great to persuade them to mobilize for political action.

Because of the problem of mobilizing such majorities of the whole, and the general absence of interest group agitation concerning such issues, instances of majoritarian politics are relatively rare in state regulatory politics. The examples Wilson uses—Social Security, wartime drafts, the Sherman Antitrust Act—are all federal issues.

In client politics, the benefits of a policy affect a concentrated group, and the costs are dispersed throughout the population. In such cases, the former group has much motivation to organize and pressure the political system to provide the benefit. Since the costs of the policy are widely distributed and most likely inconsequential for any one individual, opposition groups have little incentive to form. Price subsidies are a prime example of this type of regulation: when they are granted, subsidized producers profit quite handsomely. In large part, the cost of the subsidy is found in higher prices for the subsidized product: each individual consumer, however, may pay only a few cents more than the unsubsidized good would have cost. Thus, the cost of such a subsidy is a matter of indifference to those who pay but is of great importance to those receiving the subsidy. Hence, those who pay will be unlikely to spend the time and money necessary to stop the subsidy. Client politics fit well with the classic capture model of regulation: where government regulation originally was intended to serve the public interest, it ends up serving the interests of the small organized group. In the states, it is well illustrated by certain aspects of insurance regulation.

When both the costs and benefits of regulation are narrowly concentrated in their effect on particular groups, Wilson (1980) suggests that interest group struggle will dominate the politics of the issue. Some categories of actors will clearly be dramatically affected by the regulation; this realization precipitates their mobilization; mobilization leads to active and competitive lobbying efforts. In such cases, the policy that is eventually adopted is likely a function of the ability of such groups to gain organizational strength and of the relative strength of the competing groups. Recent conflicts arising in regard to the regulation of certain types of insurance (for example, medical malpractice and liability), provide excellent examples of this type of regulatory policy.

Finally, regulations may provide widely dispersed benefits while imposing concentrated costs on a particular group. Attempts to regulate pollution provide the best example of such policy. Such regulations are passed when political entrepreneurs can mobilize latent groups and can act as the "vicarious representatives of groups not part of the legislative process" (Wilson 1980, 370). The benefits (cleaner air) affect anyone who lives in the area in which pollution is reduced. At the same time, the costs of cleaner air are borne by the industries that must pay for pollution control devices—unless, of course, they can manage to pass these costs on to consumers in the form of increased prices. As Wilson notes, the emergence of entrepreneurial policies is difficult to explain. "Since the incentive to organize is strong for opponents of the policy but weak for the beneficiaries, and since the political system provides many points at which opposition can be registered, it may seem astonishing that regulatory legislation of this sort is ever passed" (Wilson 1980, 370). This seeming puzzle is explained by the ability of political entrepreneurs, such as the consumer advocate Ralph Nader, to use a crisis or scandal as the means for mobilizing public opinion. Their ringing denunciations of some offensive condition put the offending group on the defensive and render elected officials unwilling to ally themselves with the denounced party. Hence, governors and state legislators will often support regulations that impose heavy costs on concentrated interests. Indeed, many politicians have seized upon such issues and used them to generate media attention and to build constituencies for election to public office.

While elected officials will often support the passage of stringent entrepreneurial regulations, enforcement of such legislation is usually difficult. Although entrepreneurs may manage to mobilize a public outcry on specific issues, such mobilization is apt to be transitory. For example, the groups organized to protect consumers' rights formed a powerful political coalition at both the state and federal level during the early 1970s, but the coalition then drastically declined in size and power (Nadel 1975). In contrast, the groups organized to protect the interests of those who bear the concentrated costs of consumer protection regulation— that is, the industrial and retail trade associations—tended to maintain their organization and power. Thus, although entrepreneurial regulation has frequently been passed in the states, the enforcement of such legislation has fallen far short of the laws' goals after the public outcry and media attention have faded away. As the groups that pressed for its passage dwindled in strength and as entrepreneurs moved on to other issues, only the concentrated interests remained organized and active. Under their relentless pressure, enforcement weakened. This process is even more severe at the state level, where the threat of exit is a powerful club in the hands of industries unwilling to bear the costs of regulation.

Thus, an analysis of regulatory politics must include more than the relative power of competing groups at a given moment in time: it must also include the relative staying power of those groups. Coalitions operating on behalf of large latent interests are notoriously unstable and transitory. In the long run, they can succeed only by institutionalizing regulatory procedures that will protect the interests of their members even after the organized groups have faded away. In order to illustrate the utility of the preceding analysis for understanding regulatory policy, I now turn to an examination of specific state regulatory policies that fall within each cell of our typology.

CLIENT POLITICS IN THE STATES: STABILITY AND CHANGE IN GOVERNMENT REGULATION

The "traditional" areas of state regulation are a logical starting point for a discussion of the different types of state regulatory politics and policies. Such regulation generally falls into the client politics cell of Wilson's typology (Table 13-2). Thus, in this section, I focus on policies like those involved in the licensing of professions, the regulation of the insurance and banking industries, and various forms of economic promotions and subsidies designed to improve the position of a state's industries. While some benefits of this type of regulation are enjoyed by the general public (for example, protection from incompetent doctors or lawyers), most affect a concentrated group, such as a particular industry (for example, banking) or profession (as in the licensing of pharmacists). Such benefits can come in the form of direct subsidies, limited market entry for rivals and substitute products, or direct price fixing to ensure a profit. The costs fall on the general public in the form of higher prices, limited competition, lack of alternative producers, and, of course, higher taxes to pay for the maintenance of the government's regulatory apparatus. Weidenbaum (1977, 163) has the following to say:

The requirement for licensing of certain professions is a popular means of limiting the number of those engaged in a particular trade. Every state has at least 10 licensing boards, and some have as many as 40. Occupations requiring licenses range from television repairs to midwives. New Hampshire licenses lightning rod sales people and Hawaii licenses its tattoo artists. A majority of states have laws forbidding the advertising of the prices of prescription drugs, eyeglasses, or hearing aids. As a result, in Texas, where price advertising is allowed, single-vision eyeglasses sell for $20; in California, where a price blackout exists, the same glasses cost $60.

Well-organized groups can readily obtain beneficial regulation. Although professional licensing is one of the oldest forms of regulation (the average state licenses thirty-seven occupations) and despite many states' attempts to limit the number of licensed occupations, the number of groups requesting—and receiving—this type of regulation is actually on the increase (Roederer 1980, 480–481). Opposition to such regulation is unlikely to be felt by legislators and regulators, because each individual usually bears only a small portion of the overall cost and thus has no incentive to organize against it.

State regulation of the insurance industry provides excellent examples of the dynamics of client politics and the ways in which a changing balance of interest group power can sometimes alter the basic structure of state regulation. The 6,000 companies that make up the insurance industry constitute one of the most economically significant industries regulated by the states (Warren 1992). State agencies oversee the financial soundness of companies, the fairness of the industry's trade practices, and the rates charged for insurance. Life insurance companies have assets of more than $200 billion. The investment of these assets provides one-quarter of all nonfarm mortgages, one-third of all farm mortgages, and 70 percent of all outside capital borrowed by American industry (Orren 1974, 15). Like the banking industry, life insurance has been regulated since the early nineteenth century. Initially, state governments attempted to control the use of the enormous resources of the insurance companies. Strict regulation of company investments was a common feature of early state control over the industry. By such regulations state governments sought to ensure that the profits generated by state-chartered insurance companies would remain within the state.

The insurance companies eventually rebelled at states' interference with what they regarded as a private area of corporate activity. Organizing into powerful trade associations (for example, the Chamber of Life Insurance, created in 1866), the industry pressed, as early as the 1860s, for federal regulation of the industry. In the opinion of trade association organizers, the federal government was more likely than state governments to be sympathetic to and easily influenced by the insurance industry. Although this threat of vertical exit failed to change the industry's regulatory arena, it did manage to establish the practice of exploiting the system of federalism. This strategy is based on the idea that states would prefer to moderate their regulations than lose the tax revenue and state jobs created by state regulation. Thus, the industry has been astute at taking advantage of the peculiarities of regulation in a federal system.

The industry's strategy of threatening to move the locus of regulatory authority was endangered in 1944 when the Supreme Court ruled that insurance was, in fact, interstate commerce and therefore subject to federal regulation. If allowed to stand, such a ruling would have made it impossible for the insurance industry to continue to take advantage of the system of federalism. This seeming setback for the industry, however, was reversed in 1949 by congressional action in the McCarran-Ferguson Act. This act—strongly supported by the industry—returned the regulatory authority to the states. As the political scientist Karen Orren (1974, 35) points out, the situation has provided a good deal of political leverage for the industry:

> [The] fact that the seat of regulation has continuously been in the states has afforded vital strategic opportunities for preventing the enactment of laws obnoxious to the insurance industry. The simple existence of a federal alternative creates an immediate vulnerability of state officials to the strictures and demands of the industry—in this case a vulnerability enhanced by the long history of constitutional uncertainty and the present probationary status of state regulation.

As long as regulation remains at the state level, insurance companies are able to prevent the passage of onerous legislation in a particular state by threatening to move. Indeed, companies have done more than simply threaten to move from a state. Twenty-nine insurance companies left Texas after regulations were passed that restricted their freedom of investment. After the passage of reforms in Wisconsin, twenty-three companies left (Orren 1974, 36); combined, they held almost half of the life insurance in these states. Such interstate mobility also pressures states to adopt the favorable regulations passed in other states: if they don't, they risk corporate moves to more permissive states.

According to Orren, despite early attempts by states to control the life insurance industry, the industry and its representatives have used the threat of mobility to hinder effective regulation and to capture the regulatory process. In such a regulator-regulated relationship, the much-vaunted benefits of regulation disappear. A study by the General Accounting Office (GAO) analyzes the costs and benefits of state regulation of the insurance industry (GAO 1979). Investigations by the GAO concluded that regulations make very little difference in the behavior of insurance companies. The report stated that "the type of regulatory laws does not appear to be related to the aggregate cost of insurance" (GAO 1979, 79). The reason is simple: the regulated industry has captured the regulatory agencies, despite the formal imposition of "regulation in the public interest," so the industry is indistinguishable from its unregulated equivalents in other states. The regulators' capture was comprehensive. Only two of the seventeen states in which the GAO did extensive fieldwork (Massachusetts and Texas) actually did their own independent analyses to determine if industry requests for rate increases are justified. In the other fifteen states that were examined, requests for increases were routinely approved—solely on the basis of the insurance companies' own analyses (U.S. Senate 1980, 13–14).

Not only do captured state regulatory agencies fail to guard against unjustifiable rate hikes, they similarly fail in fulfilling other aspects of their mandates. For example, one of the traditional rationales for industrial regulation is to compensate for consumer ignorance. Despite this, the GAO concluded, "Most state insurance departments do not actively attempt to correct the problems of consumers' lack of information" (GAO 1979, 95). They found that state departments generally do not act to protect consumers from arbitrary termination or denial of insurance, nor do they assist in comparison shopping, nor do they effectively analyze and act on consumer complaints about insurance companies.

Little was done in response to the 1979 GAO report, however, and the issue of lax regulation surfaced again in the 1990s, following the failure of several large companies (Quint 1994; Warren 1992). As in the past, one response to lax state regulation was the threat of federal regulatory preemption. Legislation introduced by Rep. John D. Dingell (D-Mich.) called for the federal government to assume regulatory authority, but strong industry opposition led to its defeat. In response to the threat of federal takeover and the consequent loss of regulatory autonomy for the states and industry, the National Association of Insurance Commissioners developed a set of model laws that states would have to adopt to receive accreditation for their regulatory structure. While supposedly a way to ensure more effective regulation, there is much question about the model laws' effectiveness and purpose. The Center for Insurance Research accuses the commissioners of doing very little in their model laws actually to improve the practices of insurance companies (Quint 1994, D1). Indeed, fifteen states remain unaccredited, including Connecticut and New Jersey, the homes of several of the nation's largest insurance companies. New York, long recognized as the leader in effective regulation was stripped of its accreditation in 1993. According to a new GAO study, the National Association of Commissioners has used inconsistent standards for its accreditation process, and there remain large questions about whether this approach can work to regulate the industry effectively.

On the basis of the available evidence, we must conclude that state regulation—at least in many of the "traditional" regulatory arenas—is remarkably ineffective. In the words of the acting deputy insurance commissioner of Texas, who resigned because of the state's inability to discipline the industry in an effective manner: "We do not regulate the insurance companies, the companies regulate us" (quoted in Hayes 1989, 25).

Overall, then, we find that state regulation of the traditional regulatory arenas is remarkably ineffective and seemingly as expensive as federal regulation would be. The expense and apparent shortcomings raise two significant questions. First, why isn't state regulation more responsive to the interests of consumers? Second, given the shortcomings of state regulation, why has federal regulation failed to take its place? Both questions may be answered by examining the dynamics of state regulatory policy making in regard to the insurance industry.

The absence of change in the regulation of insurance and the generally pro-industry outcomes of regulatory politics are explained by the intimate relationship between the regulators and the regulated that is at the heart of client politics. First, many individuals move back and forth between jobs in the insurance industry and the office of the insurance commissioner. This "revolving door" is a classic attribute of the captured regulatory agency. Although such an exchange of personnel is not necessarily pernicious, individuals who have worked (or plan to work) for the insurance industry are likely to learn the insurance business from a pro-industry perspective and take that perspective to their positions in the regulatory agency. Second, the insurance commissioner's office, because of a generally small budget and staff, must rely on the insurance industry itself for the information necessary to its regulatory decisions. Third, the insurance industry is a potent lobbying force in most state legislatures and a source of large campaign contributions. In addition to its economic clout, its influence is undoubtedly strengthened by the large number of legislators whose backgrounds are in insurance. In fact, as discussed in Chapter 4, the insurance industry was ranked seventh in strength among forty interests at the state level. This is up six ranks since 1990. Fourth, the avowedly technical nature of many regulatory decisions affecting insurance regulation makes participation in decision making extremely difficult for anyone not familiar with the industry. Hence, those with insurance backgrounds tend to dominate the process. Fifth, while the industry is a well-organized lobbying force, no organized opposition usually exists. When such organized opposition does emerge, insurance regulation can change quite dramatically.

If insurance regulation is truly captured, all the state's citizens may consequently pay higher insurance rates, lack necessary information about policies, and be subject to inaccurate actuarial decisions. However, these costs are not readily calculable by the consumer and are not strikingly large for the average person. Hence, while the aggregate costs may be extremely large, individuals have little incentive to spend the requisite time and money to organize insurance consumers. Furthermore, even if such an organization were founded, it would be unlikely to have the resources of the interest groups representing the insurance industry.

Client politics are not, however, always stable. The relationship between captured regulator and captor regulatee may be changed if the costs imposed on the general population increase to the point where organizations representing their diffuse interests are formed or if some specific event such as a political scandal focuses public attention on the costs of regulation.

This is exactly what happened to automobile insurance in California and New Jersey during the 1980s. Dramatically escalating rates for automobile insurance increased the costs to consumers to the point that client politics gave way to entrepreneurial regulatory activity. Consumer groups did form, and the costs of insurance were so substantial that public consciousness reached a high-enough level to pass a ballot initiative forcing a substantial rollback of automobile insurance rates. This occurred despite expensive efforts by the insurance industry to discredit consumer efforts and confuse the issue by placing many of their own initiatives on the ballot in November 1988. However, as would have been predicted from the analysis of entrepreneurial regulatory politics below, the long-run effect of this consumer victory is in doubt: insurance companies have both challenged the initiative in court and exercised the threat of exit by refusing to write or renew policies in other states that adopt such laws. After several years, there is evidence that California may, nevertheless, be able to succeed in controlling costs because of its large market and the consequently high exit costs for insurance companies ("Write-off" 1992). However, as long as the locus of regulatory authority is the states, the available options for smaller states are much more limited. This episode illustrates how difficult and rare it is to break out of the hold of client politics when the costs of regulation are imposed on a large latent group.

A far more serious challenge to the client politics of insurance regulation results from emerging conflicts between other powerful interest groups—especially those representing the legal and medical professions—involving the reform of health care, in general, and the costs of medical malpractice insurance, in particular.

INTEREST GROUP STRUGGLE: MEDICAL MALPRACTICE INSURANCE

When regulation bestows costs and benefits on concentrated and organized groups with conflicting interests, the dynamics of policy making differ from those of client politics. Since the interests of both kinds of groups are similarly affected by the decisions made by regulatory agencies, both kinds of groups can be expected to pressure legislators, governors, and regulators. Consequently, in contrast to client politics, no single interest group is likely to capture the state agency. Moreover, because such groups tend to remain mobilized around issues directly and continuously affecting them, the pattern of policy making in such areas is one of persistent group struggle. Such ongoing and routinized conflict also contrasts sharply with the long periods of stable capture—broken only occasionally by an outburst of entrepreneurial activity—that are typical of client politics.

The analysis of regulatory politics involving interest groups is more complicated at the state than at the federal level. As in all regulatory politics, the outcome of regulatory decision making reflects the relative strength of the competing groups. Unlike the case of client politics, however, the potential for organizing competing groups affected by regulation is fairly equal. Thus, interstate differences in the relative power of the groups determine the outcome of regulatory decision making.

To illustrate the interest group style of regulatory politics, I discuss debates about state regulation of medical malpractice insurance. This regulatory arena pits against each other powerful interest groups representing the medical profession, the legal profession, and the insurance industry.

While the failure of Congress to enact sweeping national health care reform in 1994 was the focus of most media and popular attention, it is important to remember that this simply meant that the states would remain major players in such reform. As would be expected, given the diversity of interest group strength among the major players in this arena, states have adopted a wide variety of programs and "virtually every state has looked at some type of reform in the early 1990s" (Buerger 1994, 568). For example, although insurance companies have run vigorous campaigns against such regulations, nineteen states have adopted community-rating systems that require insurance companies to offer uniform premiums to all citizens.

Although none of the health care reforms debated in Washington addresses the issue specifically, malpractice laws are an important reason for the rising costs of health care. Indeed, while most health care reform proposals aim to control costs by regulating the supply of and demand for health care services, "[t]his ignores the body of medical malpractice law that will exist no matter how supply and demand are structured, and could result in more malpractice litigation as doctors will be forced to be cost-conscious in their treatments" (Frankel 1994, 1297).

During the 1980s, increasing jury awards for malpractice suits, dramatically escalating premiums for medical malpractice insurance, and the refusal of insurance companies to write policies in several states, gave rise to what has been called a crisis in this line of insurance. In 1984, for example, one of every five jury awards for malpractice litigation exceeded $1 million ("Malpractice Mess" 1986; however, if we exclude such large awards, the average award had not much changed since 1976, hovering at about $200,000). These increased costs have been passed on to doctors in the form of increased premiums for malpractice insurance.[3] In Florida, a state where the crisis was regarded as most severe, premium rates for medical malpractice insurance soared between 1983 and 1987. In Dade and Broward counties, the most urbanized areas of the state, premiums for obstetricians went from $27,073 in 1983 to $130,817 in 1987 (Blair and Makar 1988). In 1986, premiums were raised 38 percent for doctors in Georgia ("Malpractice Mess" 1986).

My purpose in choosing this issue is to contrast the ways in which this insurance crisis differs from both the normal client politics of insurance regulation and the entrepreneurial politics of attempts to lower rates for auto insurance. Unlike the latter two cases, in which the costs of regulation fall on a diffuse latent group of difficult-to-organize consumers, here, the potential costs and benefits of

---

3. Interestingly, one of the reasons costs have been passed on so rapidly is that, as a result of legislative efforts on the part of the insurance industry, state regulation of price increases has declined.

regulation fall on highly organized and powerful interests. In fact, as Chapter 4 reveals, these interests are among the most powerful at the state level: doctors (rated sixth), represented by the American Medical Association; lawyers (rated fourth), represented by bar associations; health care organizations, such as hospitals (rated ninth); and the insurance industry (rated seventh). The difference in the distribution of costs and benefits results in a very different style of state regulatory politics. Because interest groups are organized and sustained, regulation of malpractice insurance rates has become a visible and active arena of legislative action. The response to rapidly increased auto insurance rates was an isolated ballot initiative in California, but the crisis in medical malpractice insurance has moved to the legislative agenda in many states: "[M]edical malpractice emerged as the most visible and probably most serious area of concern with the tort and insurance systems (Blair and Makar 1988, 427).

When powerful interest groups bear the concentrated costs and benefits of regulation, it is to be expected that such issues will conform to the dynamics of pluralist politics. They will be placed on the legislative agenda, and outcomes will be a function of the relative power of the groups involved. Furthermore, because the balance of interest group power is likely to remain relatively constant, policy will be much more stable than when regulatory issues conform to the dynamics of entrepreneurial politics (as in the case of the ballot initiatives concerning auto insurance rates in California, in which the potential for dramatic policy change is present).

It is important to emphasize that there is no objectively correct explanation for, or solution to, the crisis of medical malpractice insurance. While serving the public interest is often piously invoked as the goal of regulatory legislation, this is a difficult standard to define and of little use to regulators. The absence of such a standard makes policy making in this area a fully political exercise. The three organized interests involved offer differing and plausible explanations for the changes in malpractice insurance.

Both the legal and medical professions, in addition to blaming each other, criticize the insurance industry. Angoff (1988), a lawyer, argues that increased premiums are the result of collusion on the part of the insurance industry. He argues that, since the early 1980s, insurance companies have drastically cut premiums below actuarily sound levels. This has been done in order to generate liquid assets that can be invested by insurance companies for high returns. Such premium cutting is done, Angoff suggests, because insurance companies know that, through the collusive practices allowed under the McCarran-Ferguson Act, they will be able to raise rates above actuarily sound levels at some future date. This allows them to make up whatever shortfalls may result from periods of declining premiums. The net result is that McCarran-Ferguson's antitrust exemptions (while limited in scope) serve to guarantee the profits of the industry and also lead to extreme swings in insurance premiums. The solution is repeal or modification of the McCarran-Ferguson Act along with stricter regulation of premium rates.

The insurance industry denies that collusion or the McCarran-Ferguson Act has played any role in the crisis in medical malpractice. Clarke et al. (1987), for example, show that this line of insurance has behaved quite differently from almost any other line of property-casualty insurance: the increase in payouts because of increasing jury awards and the resulting increases in premiums have been constant since the 1970s and do not vary with any swings in the business cycle. Clarke et al. (1987, 383–384) also show that, despite dramatic increases in premiums, profits on this line of insurance have not risen. Hassan (1991, 74), in a study for Blue Cross–Blue Shield, found that "from 1978 through 1986 . . . medical malpractice insurance ranked medium in underwriting profitability compared with other lines of insurance, and during 1985–86 it was the least profitable insurance business." Finally, both Clarke et al. and Hassan argue that the low barriers to entry in the insurance industry make it unlikely that any sort of collusive pricing could long be effective (see also Blair and Makar 1988; Lefkin 1988).

Instead, the insurance industry has argued that the true problems are increased litigation and dramatically escalating jury awards. The solution is tort reform: the industry supports state laws that specify awards for certain kinds of injuries and cap awards for pain and suffering. To this end, in 1986, the Insurance Information Institute spent $6.5 million on a television, newspaper, and magazine advertising campaign aimed at replacing the notion of an insurance crisis with the idea of a lawsuit crisis (Angoff 1988). Along the same line, another insurance trade association ran an advertisement in the *Washington Post* under the banner headline "There's a Price to Be Paid for Excessive Liability Awards in Our Courts. Guess Who's Going to Pay It?" In part the answer was:

> The word "tort" means any civil wrong. And once our tort laws protected anyone injured by the negligence of another. But over the years courts have eroded the definition of negligence to the point that it's almost meaningless. The result is a landslide of litigation that costs society billions but adds nothing to our gross national product. And as the tort system recycles its enormous costs among all of us, they'll show up in the prices we pay for products, in medical bills and insurance premiums, in taxes and inflation. We may see a day when doctors can't afford to treat the sick, municipalities won't be able to provide needed services and manufacturers won't be able to make critical products. ("There's a Price" 1985, A16)

Unsurprisingly, the medical profession has agreed with this assessment of the causes of the rise in malpractice premiums, and the American Medical Association has pushed for reforms of the tort system; equally as unsurprising, these reforms have been rejected by the American Bar Association ("Malpractice Mess" 1986, 74). To complete the picture, both the insurance industry and the legal profession have blamed the rise in premiums on the medical profession, which, they say, has been unwilling to regulate itself by imposing more effective procedures for rooting out the small percentage of incompetent physicians ("Malpractice Mess" 1986, 74).

This issue has been fought out in the legislatures of several states with varying results. Responding to pressure from the insurance industry and the medical profession, Colorado, Florida, and Washington enacted extensive tort reform in 1986. These states capped noneconomic damages and otherwise dramatically limited the ability of plaintiffs to collect damages. Still, despite such reforms, premiums did not decline in these states (Angoff 1988). Indeed, after reforms were enacted, the Hartford Insurance Company announced that it would no longer issue medical malpractice policies in Colorado.[4]

In 1986, West Virginia, responding to a coalition of interest groups, enacted legislation that both reformed the tort system (by capping damage awards) and increased regulatory oversight of insurance premiums (by requiring disclosure of certain types of financial information by insurance companies and prohibiting midterm cancellation of policies). Reaction to this reform is instructive in evaluating the relative power of the contending interest groups. Unlike California in the case of automobile insurance regulation, West Virginia is not so large a market that companies cannot exercise the horizontal exit option. Three carriers of malpractice insurance announced that, because of the weakness of tort reform and severity of the new regulations, they would cancel all policies in the state the day before the new law was to go into effect. Responding to this threat of exit, the state legislature came back into session and both strengthened tort reform and lessened the amount of financial disclosure required.[5]

Based on our identification of the costs and benefits of regulation as the critical determinant of state policy, we would expect that regulatory reform would be dependent on the balance of interest group power in each state. We would also expect that attention to this issue would be more sustained and incremental than is the case with the entrepreneurial politics of automobile rate reform. By 1988 fourteen states had adopted some form of damage cap on malpractice suits (Javitt and Lu 1992). However, only two states, Florida and Virginia, went further by adopting no-fault medical compensation systems, although similar systems have been proposed in the legislatures of New York and Utah (Jost 1994).

As the West Virginia case illustrates, the insurance industry has an advantage not held by the medical and legal professions—a credible threat of exit. It is much easier for a national insurance industry to refuse to write policies in a specific state than it is for doctors or lawyers to pick up their practices and move to another state. This gives the industry the same sort of advantage when dealing with state policy makers as seen in the case of state efforts to attract industrial development in Chapter 14. In both cases, state governments must provide a favorable climate for businesses that can choose to locate in any of several states.

4. Angoff (1988, 398n. 10) further supports the case for collusion on the part of insurance companies when he notes that extensive reforms in municipal liability laws during the late 1970s in Iowa, New Mexico, and Pennsylvania failed to reduce premiums for governments in these states.
5. Interestingly enough, West Virginia sued to prevent such a boycott and the courts ruled that McCarran-Ferguson did not protect such behaviors and that, therefore, collusive attempts to withdraw from a state were violations of the Sherman Antitrust Act (Angoff 1988, 402–403). Nevertheless, the threat of exit was still credible enough to force modification of the reform legislation.

CONCENTRATED COSTS AND DIFFUSE BENEFITS:
ENVIRONMENTAL PROTECTION

Environmental protection is a type of regulatory policy that bestows benefits on a diffuse group and imposes costs on a concentrated interest. Because it theoretically benefits the whole society, this type of regulation has often been called *social regulation*. The areas of regulation that fall within this category are among the most controversial regulatory policies of federal and state governments: land-use management, in which government attempts to control the use and development of public and private lands; consumer protection, in which costs are imposed on businesses in order to benefit the unwary consumer (including regulation of automobile insurance rates); and environmental protection, in which frequently considerable costs are imposed on polluting industries in order to benefit those who might be affected by such pollution. These areas are especially controversial when, as is often the case, costs are imposed on concentrated interests in the present for the benefit of future generations. Needless to say, organized interest groups representing those who must pay now are generally better represented than latent interest groups composed of those who are not yet born.

Since 1970, major pieces of environmental protection regulation have been passed at the federal level. The federal attention to environmental regulation was brought about, in large part, by organizations representing the interests of previously unorganized or poorly organized latent groups. This first wave of the environmental movement emerged in the late 1960s and early 1970s, its appearance highlighted by Earth Day 1970 and formalized by the organization of new public interest groups, primarily at the federal level, dedicated to protecting our natural resources. The movement was not an isolated phenomenon but, rather, was part of a much broader questioning by many citizens about the worth of technological progress and the ability of established political institutions to represent the public interest (Harris and Milkis 1989). Environmental groups such as the Natural Resources Defense Council and the Environmental Defense Fund pressed for strong, new federal laws and regulations. Many states had established agencies to deal with resource management in the 1950s, but they paid little attention to environmental protection until the passage of federal legislation like the Clean Air Act and Clean Water Act in the 1970s (Switzer 1994, 67–68). This legislation relied on states to implement federal regulations and provided much of the money that funded the creation of state environmental protection agencies. At least initially, federal attempts to impose redistributive regulatory policies were backed up by federal budgetary commitments.

However, this initial commitment did not last. Over the entire course of the development of environmental regulation, federal commitments—either to funding or to attempts to overcome the fragmentation of state efforts—have been only sporadic and often ineffective (Rabe 1986). Indeed, as state environmental agencies grew in their ability and competence, so too did business resistance to state environmental regulation. Exercising what we have called vertical exit, "[t]hey turned to the federal government for regulatory relief and federal preemption of state authority" (Switzer 1994, 67). This strategy of regulatory relief was particularly effective during the Reagan administration, when arguments about getting government off the backs of the people found an especially receptive ear in Washington.

Richard Harris and Sydney Milkis discuss a specific case of the granting of regulatory relief in the area of environmental protection. Despite general support for reducing federal regulatory control and increasing state autonomy, the Reagan administration reversed its position when the state of Washington pressed for more stringent enforcement standards in the cleanup of the Department of Energy's nuclear facility in Hanford:

> One cannot help noting the impressive irony of these administrative actions in a presidency fully dedicated to reducing the role of the central government. The heavy-handed intervention of the Department of Justice in the RCRA [Resource Conservation and Recovery Act] negotiations over the Hanford site . . . seems to abandon a strong commitment to federalism. At a minimum it shows that the concerns of a state received relatively short shrift when they conflict with conservative principles. It is difficult to see how, in the abstract, this situation differs from a Democratic administration intervening in state affairs to impose some liberal principle such as affirmative action. (Harris and Milkis 1989, 317)

The locus of authority over environmental protection has alternated between state and federal levels. In addition, the relative strength of contending groups has also changed at these two levels of government. According to the political scientist Helen Ingram (1978), the federal government was often assumed to be more sensitive to the demands of organized latent interests than state governments. State governments, many scholars argue, are beholden to industrial interest groups in a way that makes adequate land-use, consumer, or environmental regulations impossible. In consequence, first wave environmental groups initially concentrated their efforts at the federal level; through legislation at this level, they forced the reluctant states to act on their behalf—as, for example, in the implementation of the federal Clean Air and Clean Water acts and their more recent amendments.

Reflecting, however, growing disenchantment with the federal government, whose commitment to the effective implementation of environmental regulations was waning, a second wave of environmentalism developed in the late 1970s. The paradigmatic group was the Love Canal Homeowners Association, but an array of other local groups also formed early on, notably FACE (For a Clean Environment), organized to fight against contaminated groundwater in Woburn, Massachusetts, and the citizens of Times Beach, Missouri, who protested against dioxin. The focus of these groups was, of necessity, state and local governments (Tesh and Williams 1994).

The case examined here, hazardous waste regulation, well illustrates the dynamics of social regulation in a federal system. In particular, it highlights the difficulties faced by state policy makers as they attempt to balance environmental group pressures against the redistributive effects of regulation. For many states with the worst hazardous waste problems, state officials respond to environmental groups with vigorous laws, but underfunding of programs leads to lax enforcement. In addition, states tend to blunt the redistributive impacts of regulation by shifting the fiscal burden of legislation away from the regulated industry and onto the state treasury: thus, they tend to transform redistributive policies into allocative ones.

Most industrial processes result in the production of large amounts of waste. When hazardous waste first became defined as an environmental problem, the Environmental Protection Agency estimated that 344 million metric tons were produced each year (Raloff 1979). A hazardous waste, according to Congress, is any waste that "may cause an increase in death, serious irreversible illness or incapacitating ailments, or pose a substantial present or potential hazard to human health or the environment when improperly treated, stored, transported, disposed of, or otherwise managed" (quoted in Raloff 1979, 348). Most research reveals that little effort is made to dispose safely of the many highly toxic waste substances—one ounce of the chemical dioxin in a reservoir could kill millions of people. Although only dramatic cases like Love Canal make headlines, the problem of the safe disposal of hazardous wastes is widespread.

The potential health hazards posed by the leaching out of wastes from unsound disposal sites are difficult to overemphasize. Once these substances enter underground water supplies, no existing technology can clean that water. Moreover, 80 percent of American municipal water supplies—serving 30 percent of the entire population—depend entirely on groundwater pumped from wells, and this groundwater is becoming increasingly polluted as a result of the unsafe disposal of hazardous wastes (Brown 1980, 99–101).

State regulation of hazardous waste disposal is guided by the 1976 Resource Conservation and Recovery Act (RCRA). The act required the EPA to establish criteria for treatment, disposal, and storage facilities, and to create a system for tracking hazardous wastes from their manufacture to their disposal sites. Like many other pieces of regulatory legislation at both the state and the federal level, RCRA was written in a vague and general manner; therefore, EPA personnel found it difficult to delegate the responsibility for its implementation. In fact, the actual rules for implementing RCRA were not finished until May 1980, four years after the passage of the act. During this period, as the federal government struggled to write the rules, state regulators waited for the federal government to provide guidelines for actions. This lag provided an opportunity for many companies to dispose of their wastes before the implementation of stringent new rules. As finally written, the regulations govern 501 specific wastes, waste processes, and waste sources—or approximately 40 million of the 57 million metric tons of hazardous wastes produced each year ("CMA Says States Can Handle Chemical Waste" 1980).

While the federal government has been passing and trying to implement comprehensive legislation, state governments have also been attempting to deal with the problem of hazardous wastes. Indeed, RCRA is a good example of the trend in social regulation, beginning during the administration of Jimmy Carter and accelerating during the Reagan and Bush years, to devolve authority to the states. RCRA's Subtitle C recognizes that the states are the appropriate level for developing specific plans for dealing with waste disposal. It allows the EPA to authorize a state to operate a hazardous waste program in lieu of federal operation if the program meets standards established by the EPA. Forty-two states administer their own hazardous waste programs.

Although most states have assumed the responsibility for administering RCRA, the redistributive implications of such activities pose serious obstacles to effective state implementation. Producers of hazardous wastes seek to minimize their costs by disposing of such wastes in the least expensive manner. Often, this is accomplished unsafely, posing long-run health threats to the community at large. Because the purpose of regulation is to force such producers to dispose of their wastes safely, regulations, presumably, lead producers to factor into their production costs the "true" expense of safe disposal. Furthermore, the purpose of programs such as the Superfund (formally, the Comprehensive Environmental Response, Compensation, and Liability Act), which deal with the cleanup of abandoned and leaking hazardous waste sites, is to force those responsible for the sites to pay for cleanup, either by locating and charging the actual firms that abandoned the sites, or by taxing the chemical and petroleum industries in order to pay for cleanup when responsible firms cannot be located. These regulations have the effect of raising producers' costs, and thus the prices that consumers must pay for their products. This increase in costs to producers and consumers is imposed in order to raise the income of the community at large (in the form of lowered health care costs, increased property values, and so forth); thus, one effect of such regulation is the redistribution of income from producers and consumers to the general public. To the extent that the industries that bear the costs of regulation are well organized and significant to a state's economy, states may have a difficult time enforcing hazardous waste regulation.

According to quantitative analyses by Williams and Matheny (1984, 1995), states respond to these cross-pressures in an interesting fashion. Where the problems of hazardous waste disposal are severe, states tend to pass more stringent regulations. However, neither the severity of the problem nor the stringency of the laws increases the regulatory burden on the industries that produce the wastes. Rather, funding for the proper disposal and regulation of hazardous wastes is drawn from the state treasury, where this policy area competes with other issues for a share of the state budget.

> When state environmental groups are strong, more state resources flow to the enforcement of hazardous waste regulations. However, these group pressures do not translate into increased spending by private industry: such increases would consti-

tute the sort of redistributive policy that state policy-makers are constrained to avoid. Indeed, the more significant polluting industries are to a state's economy, the less industry spends on pollution abatement. This follows from the pressure on state and local government to foster economic development: the more important an industry is to a state's economy, the less the state is able to impose increased costs on that industry because of fear that these costs might lead that industry to migrate. For these reasons, the most significant determinant of state effort is the size of the state budget, rather than the severity of the problem, quality of the laws, or any other factor. (Williams and Matheny 1995, 148)

The dynamics of regulation in three states with serious hazardous waste problems, New Jersey, Ohio, and Florida, illustrate the specific ways in which the pressures indicated by quantitative analysis play themselves out in concrete cases.[6]

New Jersey

In its initial hazardous waste regulations, New Jersey seemed to overcome the problems of state enforcement of redistributive regulations. As the issue developed, however, the state's policies demonstrated the pressures at the state level that tend to shift regulatory policy from the redistributive to the allocational arenas. By the 1990s, a diversifying economic base and general economic growth allowed New Jersey to find the funds for more extensive regulatory enforcement.

New Jersey was one of the first states to enact and fund hazardous waste regulations, acting before the passage of significant federal legislation. In 1975 the state enacted a funding mechanism for the cleanup of waste sites. Based on a tax imposed on the petroleum and chemical industries in the state, New Jersey's "spill fund" served as the model for the Superfund. Undoubtedly, its innovation resulted from a combination of the presence of well-organized environmental groups and a highly visible hazardous waste problem. Initially, policy dynamics were consistent with Wilson's (1980) description of entrepreneurial regulatory politics: when New Jersey sites began to attract public attention (for example, by exploding), existing groups were ready to exploit public concern in order to gain passage of regulations with decidedly redistributive effects.

Despite early state action, interviews conducted with state officials and environmental group leaders indicated that during the early 1980s, little of the spill-fund moneys were used to clean up waste sites. Reasons for this failure are suggested by the structural analysis of regulation. The spill-fund tax on the chemical industry raises approximately $5 million per year; if the fund is exhausted, an accelerator in the law doubles the tax. Thus, industry lobbied hard against exhausting the fund and activating the accelerator. Furthermore, several large petroleum companies either closed down their refineries in the state (for example, Hess) or diverted new investment to other states (for example, Exxon).

6. These case studies are based on research that I and Albert R. Matheny conducted. See Williams and Matheny 1995, chaps. 4 and 5.

In response, the legislature authorized the state to float $100 million in general obligation bonds to pay for the cleanup of hazardous waste sites. These bonds, to be retired out of general state revenues, would effectively socialize the costs of cleanup by transforming state expenditures from the redistributive to the allocational arena.

By decade's end, however, the situation had changed. Diversification of the state's economy removed its heavy dependence on the older industries. The state's image as an ecological disaster area, fueled by the dramatic stories we described above, turned effective regulation into an economic development issue, since it would be difficult to attract cleaner industries and their middle-class employees unless the state got tough on toxics. Thus, funding increases for hazardous waste regulation began to come from increased taxes on polluting industries (in a redistributive fashion) as well as from a growing tax base (in an allocational fashion). Political and economic forces in the state had produced a large, durable majority supporting tough legislation and the funds for implementation. By the end of the 1980s, the new, bipartisan acceptability of redistributive funding in New Jersey was illustrated by Gov. Thomas Kean's outspoken support for new taxes on polluters—surprising for a prominent Republican.

The New Jersey experience highlights the constellation of forces required to overcome the structural limitations on state action: a severe and well-publicized problem, the specter of public scandal, and a strong and diversified economy. However, as Peterson (1981) suggests, such actions appear to threaten the economic development of the state and, over the long run, will give way to funding mechanisms that are more allocative.

Ohio

Economic downturn in Ohio made it difficult for the legislature to impose additional costs on already troubled industries. Instead, the state funds its hazardous waste program through a tax on such wastes brought to secured landfills. Interviews with state officials indicated problems with such a funding plan. First, taxing disposal at approved landfill sites increases the costs of safe disposal and creates an incentive for generators to dump their wastes in cheaper but unsafe ways. Given substantial monitoring problems, it is difficult for the state to control such illegal disposal. Second, since the Ohio Environmental Protection Agency relies on funds from landfill operations, several respondents suggested that the agency might be reluctant to crack down on the operators of landfills for safety violations lest agency revenues be reduced. While most concurred on the problems with this funding mechanism, our legislative respondents agreed that Ohio's economic problems made it politically impossible to tax the generators. As they saw it, the only alternative was to increase hazardous waste funding out of already strained general revenues.

Florida

Florida did not seriously address the hazardous waste issue until the early 1980s. Revelations that the state had one of the most serious hazardous waste problems in the nation placed the issue at the top of the 1983 legislative agenda. The result was passage of an omnibus Water Quality Assurance Act (WQAA): it provided for great increases in the resources granted to Florida's Department of Environmental Regulation (DER) for the monitoring of hazardous waste disposal; furthermore, it added several millions of dollars to the state's trust fund for matching federal Superfund moneys. The debate over funding for this increase was particularly interesting. The proposal made by the Florida House of Representatives was to increase the tax on chemicals and petroleum to pay for the new program. Such a formula would have placed the funding burden squarely and redistributively on polluting industries. However, this method of funding had been discarded by the time the legislation was passed. Instead, funding for the new programs was derived from a reallocation of extant state funds (for example, speeded-up collection of state sales taxes, transfer of interest payments from other environmental trust funds). Thus, while the new legislation represents a truly significant change in the state's laws, the impact of the new policy was altered from redistributive to allocational.

By 1989, the DER's budget for implementing the provisions of the RCRA alone totaled $3 million, which supported a staff of about 300 employees statewide. These seemingly dramatic increases in staff and funding were spread thinly across the state, and grumbling about water quality enforcement, both within and outside the DER, continued. Turnover at the DER had always been a problem, but during the 1980s, it became critical. Salaries in the DER were much lower than in comparable environmental agencies in neighboring states. For that matter, county and city environmental officials in Florida often earned more money than comparable DER personnel. In 1986, a DER study committee found that the turnover rate between mid-1983 and mid-1985, precisely coinciding with the early implementation of the RCRA, the Superfund, and the WQAA, reached nearly 40 percent among agency specialists. In 1985 alone, the engineering staff of the DER recorded a 16 percent turnover rate. In Palm Beach County, a part of the densely populated and industrialized southeastern region of the state, the entire enforcement section of the DER district office resigned in 1986. At the local level, county officials whom I interviewed were consistently frustrated with the lack of direction from the DER. They complained that, because of staff turnover, the DER spent a great deal of time and resources training new local-level employees rather than enforcing the law.

This sort of policy making left the WQAA short of its potential in the regulation of hazardous wastes, and thus it remained largely symbolic. Like Superfund activities at the federal level, state efforts were consumed in preliminary actions, rather than completed cleanups. Throughout the decade, the Florida legislature consistently repelled attempts to open new sources of revenue, either in the form of general taxation or more targeted levies. The state continued to rely on "creative financing," leaving effective enforcement of the WQAA in jeopardy.

Hazardous Waste Regulation in the States

These case studies illustrate some of the limitations inherent in solving hazardous waste problems at the state level. All three states tended to transform potentially redistributive hazardous waste regulation into allocational policies. Only in New Jersey did a changing and growing economy allow the state to impose substantial redistributive costs on polluting industries. Even then, as such regulation becomes an allocational issue its funding is not likely to increase in relation to the severity of the problem. Thus, while publicity about the issue led to strict state regulations, in the style of entrepreneurial politics described by Wilson (1980), their long-run enforcement is much more problematic as public attention shifts to other pressing issues.

Hazardous waste management is a particularly appropriate issue with which to close this chapter. The stakes of safely regulating such wastes are exceedingly high: indeed, in the case of groundwater pollution, they may involve basic questions of a region's ability to sustain life. Responsibility for such regulatory enforcement has increasingly fallen on the states as the federal government withdraws from direct or indirect involvement in it. However, several of the themes I have been stressing in this chapter place severe limits on the ability of states to pick up where the federal government has left off. In particular, increased competition for investment, coupled with the mobility of capital, may make it difficult for states to impose costs on the industries that are the source of the problem. Furthermore, the balance of costs and benefits produces a balance of interest group power that makes long-term, sustained attention to the problem unlikely.

CONCLUSION

Although the locus of policy making has often shifted between levels of government, political interference in the economy has been an important feature of American political life since the founding of the Republic. However, policy making is only partially guided by the traditional economic rationale for government regulation. Policy makers are also guided and constrained by the political logic that governs economic policy making.

Although specific regulatory policies differ considerably from one state to the next, three factors that seem to determine variation in the content of these policies have been identified. First, regulatory policy is a function of the ability of the individuals affected by regulation to organize. The propensity of individuals to organize—to become an interest group—is determined by their perceptions of the magnitude of the costs and benefits bestowed on them by regulation. In turn, the configuration of the interest groups that mobilize around an issue determines the resultant style of regulatory politics: interest group struggle, regulatory capture, or entrepreneurial crusading.

Second, both the enactment and the implementation of regulations are affected by the political power of organized groups and by their ability to stay organized. Considerable interstate variation exists in both the political clout and the staying power of interest groups. Regulatory politics in a particular area may shift between styles as the perceived costs or benefits of regulation change and as groups wax and wane in strength.

Third, the redistributive implications of regulatory policies constrain the ability of state regulators to enforce those policies. To the extent that the trend continues of delegating regulatory authority to the states, enforcement will be compromised, especially in the most economically hard-pressed states.

Fourth, and finally, the balance of regulatory responsibility between state and federal governments has important implications for the kinds of policies we are likely to see. As the federal role declines, interstate variability in policy will increase. Of course, this variation will be a partial function of the constellation of political and economic forces in specific states. However, the outcomes of state policies are constrained, in ways that federal policy is not, by the structural reality of the increased interstate competition for economic growth. Thus, states are limited by the need to foster developmental policies and avoid redistributive policies. The balance between these two imperatives at the state level will increasingly determine the economic and physical well-being of most Americans.

REFERENCES

Angoff, Jay. 1988. "Insurance against Competition: How the McCarran-Ferguson Act Raises Prices and Profits in the Property-Casualty Insurance Industry." *Yale Journal on Regulation* 5:397–416.
Berman, Daniel. 1978. *Death on the Job.* New York: Monthly Review Press.
Bernstein, Marver H. 1955. *Regulating Business by Independent Commission.* Princeton, N.J.: Princeton University Press.
Blair, Roger D., and Scott D. Makar. 1988. "The Structure of Florida's Medical Malpractice Insurance Market: If It Ain't Broke, Don't Fix It." *Yale Journal on Regulation* 5:427–454.
Brown, Michael. 1980. *Laying Waste: The Poisoning of America by Toxic Chemicals.* New York: Pantheon Books.
Buerger, Elizabeth. 1994. "State-Health-Care Reform Initiatives." *Book of the States, 1994–95.* Lexington, Ky.: Council of State Governments.
Clarke, Richard C., Frederick Warren-Boulton, David D. Smith, and Marilyn J. Simon. 1987. "Sources of the Crisis in Liability Insurance: An Economic Analysis." *Yale Journal on Regulation* 5:367–396.
"CMA Says States Can Handle Chemical Wastes." 1980. *Chemical and Engineering News* 58:7.
Derthick, Martha, and Paul J. Quirk. 1985. *The Politics of Deregulation.* Washington, D.C.: Brookings Institution.
Fainsod, Merle, Lincoln Gordon, and Joseph C. Palamountain, Jr. 1959. *Government and the American Economy.* New York: W. W. Norton.
Frankel, Jonathan J. 1994. "Medical Malpractice Law and Health Care Cost Containment: Lessons for Reformers from the Clash of Cultures." *Yale Law Journal* 103:1297–1331.
GAO (General Accounting Office). 1979. *Issues and Needed Improvements in State Regulation of the Insurance Business.* Washington, D.C.: U.S. Government Printing Office.

Goodin, Robert E. 1982. *Political Theory and Public Policy.* Chicago: University of Chicago Press.

Harris, Richard A., and Sidney M. Milkis. 1989. *The Politics of Regulatory Change.* New York: Oxford University Press.

Hassan, Mahmud. 1991. "How Profitable Is Medical Malpractice Insurance?" *Inquiry* 28:74.

Hayes, Thomas C. 1989. "Texas Insurance Regulator Quits, Calling System Lax." *New York Times,* January 17.

Huntington, Samuel P. 1952. "The Marasmus of the ICC: The Commission, the Railroads, and the Public Interest." *Yale Law Journal* 61:467–509.

Ingram, Helen. 1978. "Future Policy Directions: Challenges for the States." *American Behavioral Scientist* 22:311–320.

Javitt, Gail, and Elaine Lu. 1992. "Capping the Crisis: Medical Malpractice and Tort Reform." *Law, Medicine, and Health Care* 20:258–261.

Jost, Kenneth. 1994. "Fault-free Malpractice: Two More States Propose Testing the Waters in a Controversial Approach to Medical Injury Claims." *ABA Journal* 80:46.

Lefkin, Peter A. 1988. "Shattering Some Myths on the Insurance Liability Crisis: A Comment on the Article by Clarke, Warren-Boulton, Smith, and Simon." *Yale Journal on Regulation* 5:417–426.

Litan, Robert E., and William D. Nordhaus. 1983. *Reforming Federal Regulation.* New Haven: Yale University Press.

"The Malpractice Mess." 1986. *Newsweek,* February 17.

"Many Harried S&L's, Irked by States' Rules, Seek Federal Charters." 1981. *Wall Street Journal,* August 13.

Nadel, Mark V. 1975. "Consumerism: A Coalition in Flux." *Policy Studies Journal* 4:31–35.

Office of the Vice President. 1993. *Accompanying Report of the National Performance Review.* Washington, D.C.: Government Printing Office.

Okun, Arthur. 1976. *Equality vs. Efficiency: The Big Tradeoff.* Washington, D.C.: Brookings Institution.

Olson, Mancur. 1965. *The Logic of Collective Action.* Cambridge: Harvard University Press.

Orren, Karen. 1974. *Corporate Power and Social Change: The Politics of the Life Insurance Industry.* Baltimore, Md.: Johns Hopkins University Press.

Peterson, Paul E. 1981. *City Limits.* Chicago: University of Chicago Press.

Peterson, Paul E., Barry G. Rabe, and Kenneth K. Wong. 1987. *When Federalism Works.* Washington, D.C.: Brookings Institution.

Quint, Michael. 1994. "A Battle over Regulating Insurers." *New York Times,* July 29.

Rabe, Barry. 1986. *Fragmentation and Integration in State Environmental Management.* Washington, D.C.: Conservation Foundation.

Raloff, Janet. 1979. "Abandoned Dumps: A Chemical Legacy." *Science News,* May, 348–351.

Redford, Emmette S. 1965. *American Government and the Economy.* New York: Macmillan.

Roederer, Doug. 1980. "State Regulation of Occupations and Professions." *The Book of the States, 1980–81.* Lexington, Ky.: Council of State Governments.

Schumacher, E. F. 1973. *Small Is Beautiful.* New York: Harper and Row.

Shepherd, William G., and Clair Wilcox. 1979. *Public Policies toward Business.* Homewood, Ill.: Richard D. Irwin.

Sherrill, Robert. 1990. "The Looting Decade." *Nation,* October 27.

Stanfield, Rochelle L. 1994. "Thanks a Lot for Nothing, Washington." *National Journal,* March 26.

Stigler, George. 1975. *The Citizen and the State.* Chicago: University of Chicago Press.

Switzer, Jacqueline Vaughn. 1994. *Environmental Politics.* New York: St. Martin's Press.

Tesh, Sylvia, and Bruce A. Williams. 1994. "Science, Identity Politics, and Environmental Racism." Paper presented at the annual meeting of the American Political Science Association, New York, September 1.

"There's a Price to Be Paid for Excessive Liability Awards." 1985. *Washington Post,* December 17.

U.S. Senate. Committee of the Judiciary. 1980. *Hearings before the Subcommittee on Antitrust, Monopoly and Business Rights on State Insurance Regulation.* 97th Cong.

Vogel, David. 1981. "The 'New' Social Regulation in Historical and Comparative Perspective." In *Regulation in Perspective,* edited by Thomas K. McCraw. Cambridge: Harvard University Press.

Warren, William T. 1992. "Wrestling over Insurance Regulation." *State Legislatures* 18:35–39.

Weidenbaum, Murray L. 1977. *Business, Government, and the Public.* Englewood Cliffs, N.J.: Prentice-Hall.

Weisbrod, Burton A., Joel F. Handler, and Neil K. Komesar. 1977. *Public Interest Law: An Economic and Institutional Analysis.* Berkeley: University of California Press.

Williams, Bruce A., and Albert R. Matheny. 1984. "Testing Theories of Social Regulation: Hazardous Waste Regulation in the American States." *Journal of Politics* 46:428–458.

———. 1995. *Democracy, Dialogue, and Social Regulation: The Contested Languages of Environmental Disputes.* New Haven: Yale University Press.

Wilson, James Q. 1980. "The Politics of Regulation." In *The Politics of Regulation,* edited by James Q. Wilson. New York: Basic Books.

"Write-off: Insurance in California." 1992. *Economist,* July 11, 76.

SUGGESTED READINGS

Hartz, Louis. *Economic Policy and Democratic Thought: Pennsylvania, 1776–1860.* Cambridge: Harvard University Press, 1948. The classic study of the relation between the development of capitalism and democratic government in the early republic.

Orren, Karen. *Corporate Power and Social Change: The Politics of the Life Insurance Industry.* Baltimore, Md.: Johns Hopkins University Press, 1974. Orren provides an excellent history of the development of the insurance industry in America. More important, she also analyzes the connection between the industry's economic power and its political clout, especially with respect to attempts at government regulation.

Rabe, Barry. *Fragmentation and Integration in State Environmental Management.* Washington, D.C.: Conservation Foundation, 1986. An excellent overview of the development of state environmental regulation with a particular emphasis on state attempts to develop more coherent approaches to the interaction between different types of pollution.

Szasz, Andrew. *Ecopopulism: Toxic Waste and the Movement for Environmental Justice.* Minneapolis: University of Minnesota Press, 1994. This book explores the ways in which the shift of focus in the environmental movement to the state and local level has helped to radicalize and reinvigorate this movement. The author is especially strong on demonstrating the connection between local environmental activism and broader issues of political participation and democracy.

Williams, Bruce A., and Albert R. Matheny. *Democracy, Dialogue, and Social Regulation: The Contested Languages of Environmental Disputes.* New Haven, Conn.: Yale University Press. The authors examine the dynamics of environmental disputes, primarily at the state and local levels, and the competing languages used by citizens, policy makers, experts, and interest groups as they struggle over public policy. They also analyze the ways in which issues of race and gender affect the ability of various groups to influence environmental policy.

CHAPTER 14

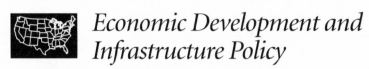

Economic Development and Infrastructure Policy

SUSAN E. CLARKE AND
MARTIN R. SAIZ

The efforts of state and local governments to attract jobs and industry have been characterized as "a blood sport" (Barrett and Schwartz 1992), a "new war between the states" (Guskind 1993), and even the equivalent of an "arms race" (Hanson 1993). These descriptions seem apt when states act as adversaries, as several did in 1992 by making and countering each other's offers of cash gifts, cheap loans, low taxes, and free land to lure a United Airlines maintenance center and its 6,300 jobs within their boundaries. The "winner" was Indiana, whose capital city, Indianapolis, agreed to give the airline $300 million in grants, loans, and tax abatements with the help of the state government.

Yet, there is much more to state economic development policy in the 1990s than this classic "smokestack chasing" approach in which states compete for firms. Consider Osborne's description (1988, 56) of Pennsylvania's Ben Franklin Partnership program:

> If an entrepreneur needs inexpensive start-up space, Pennsylvania has 30 incubators—more than any other state. If he or she needs technical assistance, each center

Gary L. Gaile, Department of Geography, University of Colorado at Boulder, was Co-Principal Investigator on the Economic Development Administration grant (no. 99-07-13709) that partially supported this research. We are grateful for his guidance in our analyses here and his assistance in preparing the state policy maps. At the Center for Public Policy Research, University of Colorado at Boulder, Mara Sidney and Caroline Tolbert provided able and timely research assistance while Luzie Mason patiently solved all our file transfer, e-mail, and basic coordination problems. We appreciate Virginia Gray's succinct and persuasive editorial comments on an earlier version of this chapter.

offers several options. If research is the problem, challenge and seed grants are available or the local Ben Franklin staff can help the firm apply for a federal grant. If capital is the problem, both seed and traditional venture capital funds are available. If the company needs loans rather than equity, the staff can refer it to local banks who specialize in its area, or to the right state or regional loan fund. If an older company needs new technology to survive, teams of experts are available to help.

The sheer diversity and complexity of recent state economic development strategies and the emergent global marketplace in which states must compete prompt us to rethink our assumptions about this policy arena. Four dimensions merit special attention in this chapter: (a) the significance of federalism and globalization in shaping state economic development options; (b) the changing definitions of the problems that emphasize investment in the infrastructure, locational incentives, and entrepreneurial "solutions" to state economic development issues; (c) apparent shifts in orientation of state policy from conventional cost-reduction, smokestack chasing strategies to more entrepreneurial policy approaches; and (d) the enduring debate on the effectiveness of state economic development policies in influencing state growth and development. These policy contexts signal realignments in the politics of making state economic development policy in the coming decade.

FEDERALISM, GLOBALIZATION, AND STATE ECONOMIC DEVELOPMENT POLICY

In contrast to national economic policy concerns with aggregate economic growth, the objective of the creators of state economic development policy is to promote investment in a particular location. It is hoped that the incentive provided by the state will stimulate new private investment that would otherwise not be made in that location but for the inducement. Theoretically, a modest stimulus on the part of the state government can be of consequence to a local economy if the new private expenditure sets in motion a multiplier effect, creating new jobs or retaining existing ones, diversifying the local economy, and ultimately increasing the income and well-being of the populace.

Most scholars have emphasized the constraints on making state economic development policy imposed by the decentralized federal context. Because of the limited fiscal capacities of state governments and the relatively low levels of aid given to them by the national government, one of the most significant constraints is interstate competition for private investment that brings jobs and tax revenues to the state. The incentives to compete with other states remain in place in the 1990s; if anything, the restrictions they impose on state policy choices are even more harsh in light of federal cuts in state programs in the last decade. But globalization trends are emerging as perhaps equally important influences on state economic development policy. Thus, the traditional emphasis on the effects of interstate competition on state policy choices must be complemented by attention to the changing global economic context.

Federalism and State Policy Choices

American states are relatively free from direct oversight from a central government, but they are fiscally dependent on the health of their own economy. The fiscal features of American federalism include limited state authority and heavy reliance on inelastic tax revenues that are less responsive to economic growth. Given these economic and political constraints, many analyses of state economic development policies reflect the themes articulated by Peterson in *City Limits* (1981). Peterson's policy model centers on how economic forces drive the policy choices of state and local governments in a decentralized American federal structure. Peterson assumes that people and businesses act to maximize their self-interests, thus he claims that business and residents are attracted to places with the most favorable ratio of taxes paid to services received. Certain development policies promise to enhance that ratio. In Peterson's view, states have a unitary, or common, interest in development policies that create economic activity to employ residents, generate tax revenues, and enhance attractive locations for capital and households. So it is in the interest of a polity to enact such development policies because the results will be enjoyed by all citizens; correspondingly, it is in the states' interest to avoid policies that direct services and benefits to those paying fewer taxes because they will distort this ratio. By this logic, states enact development policies to enhance a state's economic position because each state is in competition with other states for private investment that will contribute to the tax base. They do so under the implicit threat that residents and firms will leave for other communities if they perceive that the benefit-tax ratio is no longer favorable.

The challenges to Peterson have been directed not so much at the logic of the model but at his interpretation of the political dynamics resulting from these limits. Peterson's emphasis on the structural constraints imposed by the political and economic systems and the unitary interests in development replaces a model of decision making rooted in conflict and bargaining with one of consensual development politics based on expertise. This model implies that whoever is in power must respond to these structural imperatives and seek to maximize state economic competitiveness—that is, a Republican governor will make many of the same choices as a Democratic governor. Other implications center on the policy dynamics created when states seek to maximize their economic position in a web of interjurisdictional and global competition. Both states and localities, for example, face a classic "prisoners' dilemma" situation in which they must make strategic policy choices without knowing how others will act (Brace 1993; King 1990). When states offer incentives to retain and attract companies by lowering production costs in relation to other states, they do so under conditions of uncertainty. As in the United Airlines case, governments compete with other states for private investments but are uncertain of the deals being offered by other states as well as the needs of the firms. This puts every state government in the "prisoner" position of having to act without sufficient information about the bids of other states. Consequently, they often promise more than is wise or necessary to secure the deal. Because most state governments pursue this strategy and few dare disengage from the competition, their economies end up weaker than they would be otherwise: they may promise more than needed to gain the investment with no guarantee that the benefits will outweigh the costs.

In addition, firms enjoy a decided advantage in making decisions about where to locate because they know what their real costs and needs are. State incentives ratchet up because only the firm knows what it really needs, and states do not want to make a bid that is too low to attract the firm or to be competitive with other states (Jones and Bachelor 1986). As a result, businesses can play states off each other to get the best deal; state and local governments take part in this bidding war because there are political advantages to winning the investment competition with other states (Wolman 1988). This competitive environment of bidding up incentives across states sometimes resembles the spiral of decisions in an arms race (Hanson 1993; Peretz 1986). More than thirty-five states, for example, competed in 1993 to be the site for Mercedes-Benz's new sports-utility vehicle plant. With Mercedes-Benz in the "auctioneer's" seat, states presented custom-tailored incentive packages to entice the German firm to bring an estimated 1,500 jobs to their state. Alabama's $300 million winning package included tax breaks, promises to buy the vehicles for the state fleet, payments to workers while in training, commitments to develop the new site, and construction of a welcome center for visitors to the plant, as well as more traditional infrastructure development. The estimated price tag of $200,000 per job dwarfs Tennessee's $26,000 per job costs in winning the famous thirty-state bidding war over the Saturn automotive plant in the 1980s and Kentucky's $50,000 per job costs in bringing a Toyota plant to the state (Mahtesian 1994).

Periodically, governors weary of diverting public resources to subsidize private investors and attempt to establish truces in these bidding wars. In August 1993 the National Governors' Association adopted voluntary guidelines on tax breaks and subsidies aimed at winding down the "wars between the states" over private investment (Wyatt 1994). But this latest truce is likely to be as unstable and short-lived as its predecessors. With few incentives for cooperation, governors continuously sacrifice collaborative strategies to respond to pressures for competing in a globalized economy.

Globalization and State Policy Choices

The emergent global economy challenges conventional assumptions about state development processes. It is clear that economic growth and development processes at the state level now must be considered in the context of larger trends, that growth no longer can be captured within politically bounded and relatively closed economies, that investment flows and decision makers are international rather than local or national, and that the very nature of economic competition and productivity is changing. The most salient features of globalization include the greater mobility of capital, a new international division of labor with many production jobs moving outside the United States, the elimination of national trade barriers, new information and transportation technologies, and global competition driven by innovation rather than factor costs—for example, the costs of land, labor, and capital (Reich 1991). These features alter the investment priorities of firms and the policy options of states.

National and state policy makers, however, have very different perceptions of the effects of these globalization trends. When one region prospers while another languishes, most national policy makers interpret the result as short-term, or "frictional," unemployment and the price of an open economy and global competitiveness. From a national perspective, what is important is the ability of the economic system as a whole to absorb workers displaced from traditional manufacturing into new jobs that allow a decent standard of living.

From the perspective of state government officials, however, globalization can have a much more direct impact. Economic decline such as that experienced in much of the industrial Midwest and Northeast is devastating to local communities. When the major employer in New Castle, Pennsylvania, left town in the late 1970s, shifting its production of truck springs overseas and taking away nearly 2,000 jobs, the local economy went into a tailspin (Stokes 1994). In parts of the community, 43 percent of the residents descended to below the poverty line, and the city's property and sales tax revenues fell so sharply the city had to cut basic services, including police and fire forces. When major manufacturing firms shut down to relocate where production costs are lower, it often means the loss of a whole complex of businesses associated with the base enterprise, as it did in New Castle. At worst, the entire commercial network collapses because the service and ancillary industries were extensions of the manufacturing enterprise and depended on it. The resulting social problems begin with temporary unemployment and income loss but often expand to include long-term, or "structural," unemployment that can destroy the wealth and health of the community's families.

State policy makers are faced with the need to make their communities competitive in a global arena, where increasingly mobile capital and new telecommunications technologies may make locations appear interchangeable to firms. Furthermore, the traditional interjurisdictional competition for investment takes on a new dimension when the costs of production are lower at sites outside the United States; all states become losers in this new game. Even regional economic recovery does not necessarily solve these problems. In the recent resurgence of the old manufacturing states in the midwestern Rust Belt area, neither the number of new jobs nor their wage rates match those lost during the earlier decline. Faced with the pressures of international competition, regional recovery creates "islands of success" (Stokes 1994) but leaves behind communities and workers not able to find a niche in the global marketplace. In the absence of a national industrial policy, states have been compelled to craft their own responses to the diverse effects of globalization trends.

CHANGING PROBLEM DEFINITIONS:
ECONOMIC DEVELOPMENT AS A POLICY PROBLEM

Almost any policy initiative can be justified in terms of its economic development potential. When public school officials argue for a new bond issue, they often point out that improvements to the educational system will help local employers find more productive employees. Likewise, efforts to reduce air pollution or even programs designed to fight crime are justified by assertions that resolving these community problems will attract new business and create jobs. This reasoning has broad political appeal, but it makes economic development policy seem vague and overly inclusive. It may be true that solving community problems will enhance economic conditions, but an analysis of economic development policy requires a more precise definition.

To this end, we define economic development policy as those policies intended to encourage new business investment in specific locations in the hopes of developing the local economy both by producing jobs and enhancing and diversifying the local tax base (Eisinger 1988, 4).[1] This definition allows us to consider the full range of problem definitions states use to diagnose their development needs and identify appropriate solutions, from infrastructure programs to efforts to affect firms' locational decisions to more process-oriented strategies to encourage indigenous growth.

States as Economic Policy Activists

The American states are not neophytes in the practice of economic development. Since the first days of the Republic, they have been involved in promoting economic growth. The current array of economic development policies is only the latest stage in a continuing, albeit wavering, process of state intervention in economic activities. Prior to 1800 most of the U.S. population lived and worked on small, self-sufficient farms. Commercial farming was insignificant because the cost of transporting crops was overwhelming. For example, the overland journey between Boston and New York took more than a week; between Philadelphia and Pittsburgh, more than twenty days (Fainsod, Gordon, and Palamountain 1959, 54). The cost of transporting a ton of goods thirty miles overland was roughly equivalent to transporting them three thousand miles overseas from Boston to London (Takaki 1990, 75). A community's share of trade was determined by the efficient movement of raw materials and finished products. Thus, communities located on waterways had the greatest commercial potential. States supported commercial development by building infrastructures (roads, bridges, and so forth) to facilitate the movement of foodstuffs and raw materials to the coasts and then to other eastern cities or overseas. As competi-

---

1. We are adopting Eisinger's definition verbatim except for the word *direct*. This allows us to consider business climates as an explicit strategy; Eisinger discusses business climates as a key component of supply-side, or what we are calling locational, orientations.

tion developed between seaports the states rushed to build canals. Cumberland (1971) estimates that the public investment in canal building was $432 million, of which $300 million was paid by the states and $125 million by local governments. The federal government contributed only $7 million (North, Anderson, and Hill 1983).

Shortly after the turn of the century, the U.S. economy grew quickly and entered an era economic historians call the Market Revolution. Within two generations, the American economy changed from a simple agrarian-commercial pattern to a complex industrial economy characterized by interregional specialization. By 1860 the Northeast, West (Illinois, Indiana, and Ohio), and South were economically integrated. Both the Northeast and the South depended on the West for the production of foodstuffs. The Southeast specialized in cotton production and supplied the textile factories in the Northeast. The South and the West purchased manufactured goods from the East (North 1966). The Market Revolution was spurred in large part by technological improvements that enabled, then led to demands for, an integrated transportation system, setting in motion the forces leading to what George Rogers Taylor (1977) called the transportation revolution. After the railroads, came highways with automobiles, then air transportation, all of which improved the movement of goods and information and further stimulated state economic growth.

The economic role of the states did not end with financing harbors and canals. The states contributed 48 million of the 179 million acres allocated to railroads for development of rail systems (North, Anderson, and Hill 1983). By the end of the nineteenth century, giant corporations began to emerge. Monopoly practices by the railroad, manufacturing, oil, and banking industries triggered a wave of industrial reform movements. The mass distribution of food products gave rise to demands for protection against contamination or adulteration. The states acted to resolve these problems before the national government stepped in. But these state acts proved ineffective; they were eventually supplanted by uniform federal legislation that could more effectively control problems that extended beyond state boundaries. Eventually, the federal regulation of interstate commerce contributed to an enormous expansion in national government functions and radically altered the pattern of federalism by shifting power to the center. The centralization of responsibility for business and transportation regulation did not mean that the states completely gave up their role in the economic development process. In fact, national politicians at the time were disinclined to usurp state power (Fainsod, Gordon, and Palamountain 1959).

Formal state economic development responsibilities, however, have a sporadic history. State economic development policy as an activity separate from transportation policy became a formal function of state government in Alabama, Florida, Maine, and North Carolina in the 1920s. In other states, economic development planning was adopted as an aspect of participation in the New Deal economic recovery programs in the 1930s and 1940s or as a way to coordinate industrial production in World War II. But except for a few in the South, all states had phased out their economic development agencies by the 1950s (Eisinger 1988).

Only within the last two decades has economic development policy resurfaced as a major concern among the states' governors (Herzik 1983). Prior to the 1980s, Herzik described economic development as a "cyclical" policy—one that grows in concern, peaks, and then steadily declines (Beyle 1990, 231). But since the mid-1970s the issue of economic development has been a perennial state issue. Throughout the 1980s, state governors ranked economic development with education, highways, corrections, welfare, and health care as enduring state policy issues. Today, every state recognizes economic development as an integral part of state government (Clarke 1986; Vaughn, Pollard, and Dyer 1984).

Variations in State Problem Definitions

Each state, however, varies in how they define their economic development problems and thus they differ in the bundles of policy solutions they construct. These competing problem definitions and ideas are as much a part of state politics as political institutions and practices: the seemingly technical matter of defining and diagnosing economic problems influences who has access to the public agenda and what types of public solutions are considered as well as what sorts of political dynamics ensue (Portz 1993; Rochefort and Cobb 1994, 4). In this arena, these problem definitions vary according to the economic growth models policy makers use when they attribute state development problems to particular causes to be corrected. In Rochefort and Cobb's terms (1994, 16), these notions of causality allow policy makers to construct an "edifice of understanding" about state economic development that pinpoints what causes development problems, what the appropriate solutions might be, and what the consequences of policy failure or nonaction would be.

Policy making for state economic development is especially intriguing in the 1990s because of the competing problem definitions. The historical predominance of state smokestack-chasing strategies reflected a model of economic growth that emphasized the importance of factor costs—basically, the costs of land, labor, and capital—in production processes. Given this causal logic, states, under the threat of the loss of investment to competing states if incentives proved insufficient, worked to promote policies that would reduce those costs (Ambrosius and Welch 1988). In the wake of globalization trends, however, a different economic model is emerging. State development problems, as diagnosed by this new model, stem not from high relative factor costs but from high transaction costs—the "costs of doing business"—and inflexible environments that are not receptive to new and innovative technologies and business activities. State officials persuaded by this new perspective are experimenting with more entrepreneurial policies to address these concerns; such approaches emphasize flexibility, risk taking, market structuring, and facilitative policies on the part of state government to encourage innovation and to minimize barriers to growth processes (Clarke and Gaile 1989).

This activist state role can take many forms. The Minnesota Partnership Initial Product Assessment Program, for example, helps businesses and individuals develop new products by granting them up to $9,500 to evaluate, test, or build a prototype of a new product or production process and by seeking support from investors. More than seventeen states have gone further and established state venture capital programs that use public funds to provide high-risk equity capital for investment in small new businesses. The Ben Franklin Seed Venture Capital Fund in Pennsylvania drew on $4.5 million in state funds to help start up five privately managed venture capital firms (Eisinger 1993). From the globalization perspective, the costs of policy failure are not loss of investment to another locale but relegation to a global backwater while wealth is generated by new centers of innovation. In this "politics of ideas," state entrepreneurial strategies have become ideas in good currency (Derthick and Quirk 1985). That is, they are congruent with economic theories of globalization processes, and they are politically feasible in that they appeal to both liberals and conservatives.

As Lindblom (1977) points out, governments cannot command business to invest, they must induce investment. The variety of incentives states offer for business investment is impressive. For example, the *Book of the States* for 1986–1987 listed fifty-nine different kinds of programs offered by the states, ranging from industrial revenue bonds to customized job training to regulatory policies such as right-to-work laws (CSG 1986). All states have at least one loan or grant program available to eligible businesses, but states also subsidize firms indirectly through tax breaks or by providing the infrastructure needed to support a new or expanded enterprise. Although there are many different ways to classify these different state economic development policies (see, for example, Gray and Lowery 1990; Hanson and Berkman 1991; Leicht and Jenkins 1994; Sternberg 1987), we discuss these various strategies in terms of their infrastructure *investment* objectives and their business *promotional* objectives; the latter include incentives aimed at influencing locational decisions or entrepreneurial growth processes.[2]

2. Our state program data are drawn from *The Directory of Incentives for Business Investment and Development in the United States* for 1983, 1986, 1991 (*Directory of Incentives,* various years). The directory presents the state programs in a narrative format that includes a description of the incentive, its terms, conditions, and eligibility criteria. The program information is self-reported by the states in a standardized format. A review of the directory confirms that identical program tools do not necessarily share the same policy orientation. For example, the offer of financial assistance either as a loan or grant says little by itself about whether the policies are used in an entrepreneurial or a locational manner, or to provide infrastructure. This means that a simple classification of programs that, for example, labels all direct loans as entrepreneurial policies will be ambiguous as to whether the program contains the properties of that orientation. Classification based on the core attributes of the policy programs allows a more fine-grained consideration of the tools and orientations.

ALTERNATIVE ORIENTATIONS FOR ECONOMIC DEVELOPMENT POLICY

We discuss three major policy strategies: infrastructure strategies, locational incentives, and entrepreneurial strategies. Briefly, strategies for infrastructure emphasize the construction and maintenance of physical infrastructure such as roads and highways to encourage and support development. Locational incentives seek to reduce the costs of production factors in relation to other locations in order to attract businesses that wish to relocate or expand. Entrepreneurial strategies emphasize facilitating growth processes rather than influencing particular firms in their choice of location. Each of these policy paths implies distinctive strategies that reflect different understandings of the logic underlying economic development processes. In addition, policy makers must also be pragmatists and seek orientations that accord with the dispositions of state voters (Beaumont and Hovey, 1985; Erikson, Wright, and McIver 1993). While these investment and promotional strategies do not entail mutually exclusive choices, each state nevertheless has a distinctive economic development policy profile. We compare these state policy profiles by developing a standardized index of policy attributes for each of the three policy orientations: the infrastructure investment approach, the locational incentive approach, and the entrepreneurial approach.[3]

The Infrastructure Development Approach

Although traditional infrastructure strategies center on the provision of seemingly prosaic fixed assets such as highways, sewers, and waste treatment plants, there is a sense of crisis surrounding infrastructure policy, and the very term itself is subject to debate. Perry (1994a) traces the evolving taxonomy from a focus on internal improvements in the early nineteenth century to the concern with public works projects in the Great Depression era to the more inclusive and systemic view of infrastructure systems in the 1980s. In contrast to a specific focus on bridges or roads, the term *infrastructure* now signifies a concern with both the technological systems of physical facilities and the roles, particularly the economic role, these assets play in future growth and development. This link between infrastructure and development became prominent in the 1970s, when economic development needs displaced historical concerns with health, safety,

3. To construct our indexes, we coded the program descriptions from the 1983, 1986, and 1991 editions of the *Directory of Incentives for Business Investment and Development in the United States* (*Directory of Incentives,* various years). In all, we coded 465 program descriptions from the 1983 directory, 591 program descriptions from the 1986 directory, and 788 program descriptions from the 1991 directory. We gave the programs one point for each attribute identified and then divided the number of attributes found by the number of programs the state offers. Thus, our standardized index scores are simply the ratio of attributes to programs for each state for the infrastructure, locational, and entrepreneurial incentive approaches. For example, we found thirty-one locational attributes among Illinois's ten economic development programs in 1983; accordingly, their locational economic development policy score is 31/10, or 3.10.

and environmental needs as the primary justification for infrastructure investment (Felbinger 1994). In the continued absence of national infrastructure policy initiatives, however, there is a concern that there will be continued underinvestment in public capital infrastructure, with potentially negative effects on national and subnational policies.

Federalism and Infrastructure Investment. In the early 1980s, Choate and Walter's report (1981) on public capital infrastructure, *America in Ruins: Beyond the Public Works Pork Barrel,* galvanized public attention. Choate and Walter argued that local economic development was hampered by obsolete and deteriorating public facilities. Their diagnosis of a national infrastructure crisis demanded a national policy response. Federal participation in infrastructure provision, however, has been erratic and reluctant. The national government has perceived most public works projects as affecting limited geographic jurisdictions and has, thus, been averse to taxing or borrowing for such purposes (GAO 1993). This aversion has been overcome when infrastructure issues have been framed as national in scope, as in the 1956 National Highway Act for provision of interstate highways for defense purposes or the Water Pollution Control Act of 1972 to ensure water quality. With these nationally supported systems in place, the federal role is shrinking again.

The federal government's responsibilities in financing and regulating development of the infrastructure are now in question. Federal capital spending for the nation's infrastructure peaked in the 1960s. Since 1970 there has been a retrenchment of funding support and a precipitous decline in federal support for state and local infrastructure—a loss in constant dollars of more than 60 percent in federal grants-in-aid between 1970 and 1990. This left state and local governments in a dilemma—their existing infrastructure was deteriorating, and they needed to invest in new facilities to retain their economic competitiveness. State and local governments now account for 90 percent of all public works spending, with a growing share (43 percent) of those expenditures by special purpose governments such as public authorities and special districts (Leigland 1994). By the mid-1980s, federal efforts were characterized as an ad hoc federal infrastructure strategy that emphasized aid for transportation programs; trust fund financing rather than grants-in-aid; and support for research, management, training, technical assistance, and demonstration projects (Man and Bell 1993, 19).

Despite numerous proposals for new funding and new institutional arrangements to invigorate state infrastructure investment, there has been little resolution of the national policy gridlock (Nathan 1992; NCPWI 1988; U.S. Advisory Commission 1993; U.S. Congress 1984, 1990). One exception to this stalemate was the passage of the Intermodal Surface Transportation Efficiency Act of 1991 (IS-TEA), authorizing expenditures of $155 billion over six years for addressing "mobility needs" through intermodal transit—highways, mass transit, and safety and research programs—as well as nonroadway enhancements such as greenways, bike paths, and historic preservation (U.S. Department of Transportation 1993).

It gives the states a prominent and flexible policy role in exchange for providing 20 percent of transportation funding while the federal government pays the remaining 80 percent; ISTEA, however, promises to transform the historical federal-state transportation partnership by requiring states to share planning for new transportation projects with metropolitan planning organizations (MPOs) (Kincaid 1992). While this does not remove political considerations from determining infrastructure priorities—the bane of traditional state highway politics—it shifts them to a metropolitan and regional scale. This restores urban and suburban constituencies to the same playing field, making allocation of funds under the "use it or lose it" provisions of the legislation contingent on their cooperation (Peirce 1994a).

State Infrastructure Policy Agendas. In this national policy vacuum, states have had to forge their own path. They have done so sustained by the belief that infrastructure investment is linked to positive changes in productivity and economic growth. Infrastructure investment is the traditional state investment and development tool and a good gauge of state involvement in economic development. This was especially so in the early part of the nineteenth century, when states and cities introduced diverse debt-financing mechanisms in support of aggressive public works policies. The dire consequences of many of these speculative financing gambits, however, led most states to limit the debt-financing powers of both state and local governments. This created a later need for circumventing these debt limits through establishment of special authorities that allowed public works to be financed through "the back door" (Perry 1994b); it also made states more dependent on federal financing for large-scale public works.

Whether by default or design, since the mid-1980s infrastructure policies have become increasingly decentralized. States are forced to rethink their infrastructure roles and priorities. At the state and local level, this is rarely a debate on whether infrastructure investment and maintenance are necessary; rather, the central issues are how to provide and pay for them. Even where the national government pays significant infrastructure construction costs, as in the highways programs, states and localities are responsible for the continued maintenance of these facilities. This stewardship is expensive, and it is tempting to defer maintenance; indeed, until recently the perverse incentives of federal capital grants for replacement and renewal activities encouraged delays on maintenance until deteriorating structures became eligible for federal funds that provided 80 percent of the restoration costs (Perry 1994a). The 1991 federal highway law created a National Highway System to channel money to states for maintenance and improvement of highways that receive the greatest use. The law devolves significant authority to state transportation officials (rather than congressional committees) to decide when, where, and how much to spend, and Washington puts aside at least 30 percent of all federal highway dollars for these improvement projects (Rapp 1994a).

Historically, most of these state public works activities have been supported by taxes and bond financing, but the financing has become increasingly complex. Two financing trends center on the use of state revolving funds, as introduced by federal capitalization of revolving funds for water pollution control facilities (the 1987 Clean Water Act) and the development of public-private partnerships to attract private capital to infrastructure provision (Lemov 1994). The revolving fund mechanism allows states to act as brokers, encouraging investment in local water pollution control projects by using loans of public money to attract private funds. California is providing a number of prototypes of public-private partnerships to construct transportation infrastructure. The state Department of Transportation, for example, entered into franchise agreements with private investors in order to construct transportation facilities that otherwise faced political stalemates. One project involved construction of four toll lanes on the median strip of state route 91, which links Orange County and Riverside County; the private partners provided most of the financing, which is to be repaid by tolls.

To gain a more precise sense of state infrastructure policy agendas, we examined state programs that offered incentives either to communities or private companies to develop infrastructure. In 1983, no state offered an infrastructure assistance program, but by 1991, fifteen states did and some now have more than one program. The Gund Foundation, for example, worked with the state of Ohio to draw up a comprehensive infrastructure development plan for Cleveland, carried out by the Build Up Greater Cleveland public-private partnership (Licate 1994). We also considered incentives targeted to the transportation sector more generally. The number of transportation sector incentives offered by the states—such as the tax preferences given to the trucking, railroad, and shipping industries—have remained relatively stable throughout the 1980s. Currently, twenty-eight states offer such incentives. On the basis of these attributes—infrastructure incentives and targeted transportation incentives—we create an infrastructure index by summing attributes across programs. (See footnote 3 on p. 525.)

Our index of state infrastructure programs (Table 14-1) measures the commitment of states to infrastructure policies in relation to their overall economic development policy effort. The higher the score, the higher the states' commitment to infrastructure. An examination of infrastructure index scores shows that despite the increase in the number of infrastructure-related programs, the magnitude of the index scores remains about the same over time. This is because the number of programs highlighting transportation or infrastructure incentives adopted by the states is low in relation to the total number of incentives the state offers.

Infrastructure for the Future State Economy. Recent information technology changes are likely to reshape state infrastructure agendas by the end of the century. Technological changes provide new ways of communicating and producing, but they also transform social and political dynamics in unanticipated ways. The political impacts of technological changes are not automatic, nor will they occur in the same way in every state. Rather, into the next century state infrastructure

Table 14-1 Infrastructure Economic Development Policy Indexes

State	Infrastructure index			State	Infrastructure index		
	1983	*1986*	*1991*		*1983*	*1986*	*1991*
Alabama	0.00	0.00	0.08	Montana	0.13	0.05	0.05
Alaska	0.00	0.00	0.00	Nebraska	0.00	0.00	0.00
Arizona	0.00	0.00	0.00	Nevada	0.00	0.00	0.00
Arkansas	0.00	0.00	0.00	New Hampshire	0.29	0.14	0.40
California	0.22	0.20	0.25	New Jersey	0.27	0.13	0.14
Colorado	0.11	0.14	0.08	New Mexico	0.00	0.00	0.11
Connecticut	0.00	0.00	0.00	New York	0.06	0.06	0.08
Delaware	0.00	0.00	0.00	North Carolina	0.00	0.00	0.00
Florida	0.00	0.00	0.11	North Dakota	0.00	0.00	0.00
Georgia	0.00	0.00	0.00	Ohio	0.00	0.00	0.00
Hawaii	0.08	0.07	0.07	Oklahoma	0.00	0.00	0.00
Idaho	0.00	0.00	0.00	Oregon	0.43	0.33	0.27
Illinois	0.00	0.00	0.08	Pennsylvania	0.17	0.23	0.27
Indiana	0.19	0.15	0.16	Rhode Island	0.10	0.07	0.08
Iowa	0.00	0.00	0.00	South Carolina	0.13	0.09	0.06
Kansas	0.00	0.00	0.08	South Dakota	0.00	0.00	0.00
Kentucky	0.20	0.33	0.27	Tennessee	0.30	0.33	0.40
Louisiana	0.00	0.00	0.00	Texas	0.40	0.40	0.08
Maine	0.00	0.00	0.00	Utah	0.33	0.25	0.11
Maryland	0.00	0.00	0.00	Vermont	0.33	0.00	0.00
Massachusetts	0.00	0.00	0.00	Virginia	0.00	0.00	0.05
Michigan	0.07	0.06	0.13	Washington	0.20	0.20	0.20
Minnesota	0.15	0.06	0.10	West Virginia	0.00	0.00	0.00
Mississippi	0.00	0.00	0.08	Wisconsin	0.14	0.11	0.07
Missouri	0.00	0.17	0.13	Wyoming	0.00	0.00	0.00

SOURCES: Computed from program descriptions in *Directory of Incentives*, various years.

politics are likely to reflect the changing nature of global competition, persistent tensions in intergovernmental relations, the continual question of public finance (Perry 1994a), as well as the particular social and economic conditions in each state. The effects of these contextual changes are already evident in struggles to define information infrastructure policy, or policy for the information highway.

As in the broader infrastructure debate, the concept of an information highway is elusive. Most definitions emphasize the connecting of technologies through networks that can carry voice, video, data, and imaging. The channels, or "pipes," carrying these different forms of information must be connected with each other and eventually linked into local area networks and wide-area networks. In 1994, state and local officials ranked network integration as the most important emerging information technology (Richter 1994a, 78). The value of an integrated information technology stems both from its contribution to the information-intensive work of state government operations and from its facilitation of service delivery to citizens, such as verification of unemployment benefits or renewal of drivers' licenses at kiosk terminals. This spreading information web depends on the provision of a statewide fiber-optic grid that facilitates high-speed communication; linking these state and regional networks to national networks still awaits national legislation, although citizens with Internet access can already link to various national and international networks.

Federalism and globalization are important influences on the infrastructure highway as well. The analogy of the "information highway" with the federal interstate highway system is somewhat imperfect. In contrast to the interstate highway program, the fiber-optic networks supporting the information highway are funded by private sector capital, so many governance issues arise (Richter 1994b). What level or type of technological access, for example, would constitute the "universal service" provided for in earlier communication regulations and how would this be achieved? The proposal by the administration of President Bill Clinton for a nationwide communication network, the National Information Infrastructure (NII), calls on the private telecommunications industry to construct this information highway (Information Infrastructure Task Force 1993) and seeks to preempt state regulation of telecommunication rates and services that discourages new entrants in the telecommunications market.

These federal preemptions of state regulatory powers trouble many state officials, particularly if they are interpreted to restrict the rights of states to build or promote their own telecommunications networks (Richter 1994b, 72). In the absence of national policy on the information infrastructure, many states moved ahead to develop innovative information infrastructures. Iowa, for example, is financing and building its own fiber-optic network to ensure universal service and maintain public control; in addition to plans for public access, Iowa hopes to lease the use of its information superhighway to private firms. North Carolina, in contrast, formed a public-private partnership with twenty-eight state telephone firms in 1993 to develop a statewide information highway. In return for the commitment to be an early and large user of the computer network, the state government hopes to induce private companies to wire more than 3,000 public institutions to the statewide interactive system (Fulton and Newman 1993; Rapp 1994b, 84). Rewiring the state is part of North Carolina's economic development strategy: officials anticipate that the existence of a statewide information highway will attract businesses to North Carolina because they will not have to build their own private networks (Richter 1994b, 68). They also anticipate that the network will add nearly $3 billion to the state economy and 44,000 jobs between 1994 and 2003 (Richter 1994b, 68).

The demand for these new kinds of infrastructure, in which information is a critical economic resource and distance is overcome by communication technology, will change the politics of scale in state politics. These issues of scale ask which level of government should pay for these new infrastructures, whether existing jurisdictional arrangements are sufficient, and whether new financing tools are needed. In many ways the implications parallel the political effects of sewer developments in the nineteenth century. To be economical, sewer extensions transcended existing political jurisdictions and required new financing arrangements to amass sufficient capital. This led to unanticipated governance and financing issues that demanded innovative responses. Similarly, the emergence of statewide information highways as development strategies will require state governments to address issues of access, popular control, public financing, and jurisdictional boundaries (Schwartz 1990).

The Locational Incentive Approach

Locational economic development policies aim at improving a community's ability to compete with other locations for industry, jobs, and economic growth.[4] This policy orientation is grounded in economic location theory, which suggests that, other things being equal, firms will seek those locations where the combined costs of land, labor, capital, energy, and transportation are minimal (Weber 1984). Thus, the state seeking a competitive advantage over other states must create an advantageous price structure for "production factors," thereby creating a comparative locational advantage. The goal of the policy orientation is to create an attractive investment site for new branches, start-up businesses, and relocating firms.

Common tools used in making locational policy include low-interest financing, frequently offered in the form of industrial revenue bonds, tax credits, abatements, deferments and exemptions, subsidized industrial job training, and assistance with site selection and preparation (Fosler 1988). The beneficiaries need not be American firms: between 1978 and 1992, states and cities gave away more than $1 billion in incentives to foreign automobile firms (Atkinson 1993). The rubric of locational economic development policy also includes the notion of creating a "positive business climate" and the image of a pro-business atmosphere. A "positive business climate" is a vague concept, but the associated policies often include low taxes and regulatory policies designed to keep production costs low, such as right-to-work laws and relaxed environmental legislation (Plaut and Pluta 1983). Flaunting its new automotive muscles, Kentucky's promotional advertisements urge investors to "park it here" and promise policies featuring "low financing," "rebates," and "low finance." Overall, the defining characteristic of locational policies is the effort to produce lower costs for business in relation to the costs in other states. Thus, locational economic development policies imply an acceptance of prevailing economic forces; other than attempting to lower costs within the state, the economic role of state governments remains subordinate to private sector decisions (Eisinger 1988; Fosler 1988).[5]

4. State economic development policy efforts continue to expand. As reported by the *Directory of Incentives* (various years), between 1983 and 1986 the number of economic development programs rose from 465 to 591, a 27 percent increase in three years. The number of programs increased again from 591 in 1986 to 788 in 1991, an increase of 33 percent. Between 1983 and 1991 the states increased the number of economic development programs by 41 percent; only two states, Idaho and Ohio, reduced the total number of their incentive programs.

5. Our indexes appear to be reliable measures of the different policy measures. A factor analysis confirms that the attributes loaded onto three underlying factors correspond to the three economic

Attributes of Locational Policy Orientations. We assess the degree to which states pursue a locational economic development approach by measuring the extent to which their policies include four key attributes reflecting aspects of the locational orientation. First, we distinguish programs whose primary purpose is to reduce capital costs to business. Such programs are quite common and include direct grants, loans, and loan guarantees. Second, we isolate policies that rely on subsidies to entice businesses indirectly—specifically through tax incentives. Third, we single out polices granting subsidies to any firm meeting general criteria, such as providing a minimum number of jobs, in contrast to policies targeting specific areas or economic sectors. And fourth, we characterize locational policies as administratively passive in that they require little initiative on the part of a government agency to implement in contrast to programs requiring a more activist stance, such as those targeting high technology or small business start-ups (Hansen 1989a).

Changes in Locational Orientations. The locational policy index measures the degree to which state governments have adopted policies with locational attributes in relation to the state's overall economic development policy effort. Thus, states with the higher index scores (as shown in Table 14-2) reveal greater commitments to a locational policy orientation than the other states. In 1983, states with the strongest locational policy orientations were Arizona, Nevada, South Dakota, Utah, and Wyoming. All but Nevada maintained this relative emphasis on locational strategies through 1991; in 1991, New Hampshire, South Carolina, and Tennessee also emerged as giving priority to locational strategies. The states with the highest average locational policy index scores for the three time periods (1983, 1986, and 1991) include Alabama, Arizona, Idaho, New Hampshire, South Carolina, South Dakota, Tennessee, Utah, Washington, and Wyoming. Figure 14-1, together with Table 14-2, suggests that there is no obvious regional pattern to these locational policy orientations, although less densely populated, less urbanized states and southern states with historical usage of locational policies are prominent adopters.

Although these particular states increased their locational policy orientations, most states do not seem to be pursuing locational approaches as much as in the past. The average value of the locational indexes dropped 8.1 percent between 1983 and 1986 and 9.6 percent between 1986 and 1991, despite increases in the total number of state economic development programs. This indicates that the number of programs with locational attributes adopted by a state declined in relation to the total number of programs the state offers. Only ten states increased their locational index score between 1983 and 1986, while index scores in thirty-

---

development approaches and that the pattern became more distinctive over time. Cronbach's alphas were all over 0.75. Our entrepreneurial index compares positively with other empirical measures of state economic development policy: Gray and Lowery's (1990) state industrial policy measure (0.48 in 1983, 0.54 in 1986) and Berman and Martin's (1992) measures of state economic development policy (0.24 in 1983, 0.23 in 1986, and 0.35 in 1991).

Figure 14-1 Locational Policy Index, 1991

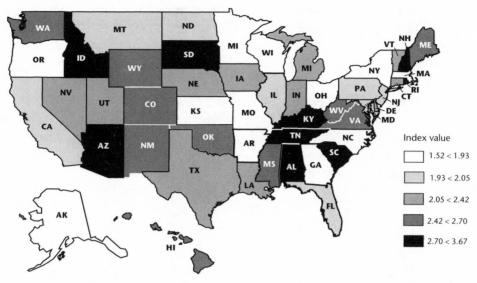

SOURCE: Calculated by the authors.

Table 14-2 Locational Economic Development Policy Indexes

State	Locational index			State	Locational index		
	1983	1986	1991		1983	1986	1991
Alabama	3.10	3.00	2.77	Montana	2.88	1.95	1.95
Alaska	2.75	3.25	1.93	Nebraska	2.63	2.50	2.36
Arizona	3.50	3.67	3.67	Nevada	3.50	1.92	2.25
Arkansas	3.10	2.78	1.75	New Hampshire	3.14	3.14	3.60
California	2.22	2.10	2.00	New Jersey	2.55	2.38	2.05
Colorado	2.89	3.14	2.50	New Mexico	2.60	3.00	2.67
Connecticut	2.43	2.35	2.10	New York	2.75	2.22	1.65
Delaware	2.20	2.88	2.31	North Carolina	3.40	1.89	1.90
Florida	2.73	2.70	1.95	North Dakota	2.09	2.33	2.00
Georgia	2.50	1.64	1.65	Ohio	2.50	1.93	1.92
Hawaii	2.92	2.50	2.43	Oklahoma	2.86	2.89	2.70
Idaho	3.13	3.14	3.14	Oregon	2.43	1.89	1.73
Illinois	3.10	2.56	2.00	Pennsylvania	2.42	1.68	1.95
Indiana	2.56	2.15	2.26	Rhode Island	3.00	2.50	2.85
Iowa	2.30	2.67	2.06	South Carolina	2.88	2.73	2.89
Kansas	2.63	2.45	1.92	South Dakota	3.75	3.00	2.75
Kentucky	2.50	2.67	2.73	Tennessee	2.90	3.22	3.30
Louisiana	2.50	2.53	2.21	Texas	2.20	2.60	2.42
Maine	2.62	2.50	2.62	Utah	3.67	3.75	2.11
Maryland	2.36	2.21	2.00	Vermont	2.75	2.42	2.29
Massachusetts	2.46	2.43	2.05	Virginia	2.63	2.43	2.50
Michigan	2.86	2.39	2.21	Washington	3.40	3.40	2.50
Minnesota	2.23	2.18	1.52	West Virginia	2.75	2.40	2.53
Mississippi	2.75	2.72	2.46	Wisconsin	2.57	2.11	1.87
Missouri	2.37	1.75	1.80	Wyoming	3.75	2.83	2.50

SOURCES: Computed from program descriptions in *Directory of Incentives*, various years.

four states declined (six states stayed about the same). This trend was even more pronounced between 1986 and 1991. Looking at the changes in locational index scores, only a few states are placing greater emphasis on locational economic development policy orientation. New state programs are more likely to include entrepreneurial attributes.

Entrepreneurial Economic Development Policy Approaches

According to Eisinger (1988, 230), entrepreneurial states shift the aims of their economic development incentives from affecting locational decisions to fostering "those indigenous capacities to serve new or expanding demands by providing resources that permit direct penetration or capture of a particular market or that permit a risky but potentially productive undertaking that would not have gone forward without government support." Thus, entrepreneurial policies are grounded in a theoretical model of economic development processes that emphasizes the wealth-generating capacities of innovative activities as the engine of economic growth.

These policies are recent additions to the states' economic development policy arsenal, most having been adopted during and after the recession of the early 1980s (Clarke and Gaile 1992; Gray and Lowery 1990; Leicht and Jenkins 1994). This entrepreneurial approach generates new roles for state governments, particularly a more central role in efforts to create jobs and facilitate growth processes (Osborne 1988, 249). Although the assumption that economic development processes are driven primarily by private sector decisions is not challenged, states, it is thought, can support those processes by creating new institutions and public-private partnerships. These new organizations, generally outside the electoral arena and staffed by development professionals, provide a means of coordinating public and private investment decisions. They often also furnish means for overcoming the historic restrictions on debt capacity still in place in many states; these public-private organizations often have independent financing authority and can leverage private-sector investments with public funds in ways not available to state agencies. This public development financing capability is critical, since many entrepreneurial strategies rely on taking greater and longer-term risks with public funds; for example, quasi-public state organizations may supply "seed" money to stimulate new business formation or to fund the research needed to bring technological innovations to the commercial market. These state organizational innovations allow state governments to be more flexible and versatile than bureaucratic structures permit; advocates claim they permit the state to anticipate, specialize, experiment, evaluate, and adjust to changing economic forces (Fosler 1988, 4). In contrast to the more typical short-term, incremental nature of state public policy, these approaches demand some effort in state economic development planning (Goldstein and Bergman 1986, 274–275). As of 1990 at least twenty-eight states had written or were writing a

Table 14-3   Entrepreneurial Economic Development Policy Indexes

State	Entrepreneurial index 1983	1986	1991	State	Entrepreneurial index 1983	1986	1991
Alabama	0.60	0.60	0.92	Montana	0.88	1.74	1.80
Alaska	1.25	1.50	1.93	Nebraska	0.63	1.00	1.45
Arizona	0.00	0.00	0.00	Nevada	0.00	1.17	1.50
Arkansas	0.70	0.89	2.38	New Hampshire	0.86	0.86	0.40
California	1.00	1.00	1.17	New Jersey	1.27	1.31	2.14
Colorado	0.33	0.43	0.92	New Mexico	1.00	0.60	0.67
Connecticut	1.57	1.41	1.65	New York	1.19	1.72	2.51
Delaware	1.00	0.88	1.54	North Carolina	0.60	2.67	2.50
Florida	1.27	1.30	1.95	North Dakota	1.55	1.58	2.00
Georgia	1.00	2.21	2.29	Ohio	1.94	1.93	1.92
Hawaii	0.58	0.86	1.14	Oklahoma	0.71	0.78	0.80
Idaho	0.63	0.43	0.43	Oregon	1.57	2.11	2.27
Illinois	0.80	1.11	1.69	Pennsylvania	1.42	2.36	2.36
Indiana	1.00	1.25	1.42	Rhode Island	0.60	1.21	1.00
Iowa	0.80	1.08	1.50	South Carolina	0.63	1.00	1.00
Kansas	0.88	0.91	1.79	South Dakota	0.25	0.60	0.75
Kentucky	1.40	1.33	1.18	Tennessee	0.90	0.56	0.50
Louisiana	1.00	1.13	1.37	Texas	1.00	1.00	0.92
Maine	1.31	1.43	1.31	Utah	0.67	0.25	1.56
Maryland	1.64	1.68	1.67	Vermont	1.33	1.50	1.71
Massachusetts	1.85	1.93	2.29	Virginia	1.25	1.43	1.30
Michigan	1.07	1.56	1.71	Washington	0.40	0.60	1.20
Minnesota	1.38	1.35	2.57	West Virginia	1.00	1.33	1.35
Mississippi	0.58	0.94	1.15	Wisconsin	1.43	1.67	1.73
Missouri	1.32	2.00	2.17	Wyoming	0.00	1.00	1.00

SOURCES: Computed from program descriptions in *Directory of Incentives*, various years.

long-term economic development strategy (NCSL 1991), an increase from the seventeen states in 1986 reported by Eisinger (1988, 27).

Attributes of Entrepreneurial Economic Development Orientations. Four core attributes of entrepreneurial economic development programs distinguish them from more conventional locational economic development approaches. Each attribute constitutes a single dimension of the more complex policy orientation. First, following Bowman (1987), we distinguish state efforts to create an environment in which innovative firms can flourish by increasing a firm's capacity to take advantage of, or adjust to, new production processes. Second, we single out programs that fund high-technology firms, new business development, research and development, and community development corporations (Bowman 1987, 11). Third, we catalog efforts to create market opportunities, such as state-chartered local development corporations, in which an attempt is made to control the spatial relations of firms to markets and promote the economies of juxtaposition and agglomeration (Sternberg 1987, 159). These public-private partnerships increase a firm's opportunities by leveraging private capital with public, thereby increasing the pool of local investment funds. Fourth, we identify more interventionist strategies, such as venture capital programs, that challenge prevailing economic forces (Hansen 1989a). In Table 14-3, we display the index of state entrepreneurial policy approaches based on these attributes.

Changes in Entrepreneurial Orientations. The index score reflects the degree to which state governments adopted policies with entrepreneurial attributes in relation to their overall economic development policy effort. The higher the value, the greater the state reliance on this approach. A clear trend can be seen in Table 14-3 toward adoption of state policies with more entrepreneurial attributes. Thirty-three states increased their index scores between 1983 and 1986, for an average increase of 22 percent. The increases were greatest between 1986 and 1991: the average index increased by 34 percent, and thirty-nine states showed greater use of entrepreneurial approaches. The spread of this state policy orientation between 1983 and 1991 can be seen in Figure 14-2 and Table 14-3. In contrast to some state policy diffusion patterns, this pattern of adoption shows no contiguity or distinctive regional bias.

Georgia, North Carolina, and Pennsylvania more than doubled their scores between 1983 and 1986, while Arkansas, Colorado, Utah, and Washington more than doubled their scores between 1986 and 1991. In the mid-1990s, Georgia, Massachusetts, Minnesota, New York, Oregon, and Pennsylvania place greatest emphasis on entrepreneurial approaches. These states ranked high in the early indexes and maintained their positions by consistently adding programs with entrepreneurial attributes.

As is graphically confirmed in Figure 14-2, states are moving in the direction of entrepreneurial economic development orientations. Osborne (1988) charac-

Figure 14-2 Entrepreneurial Policy Index, 1991

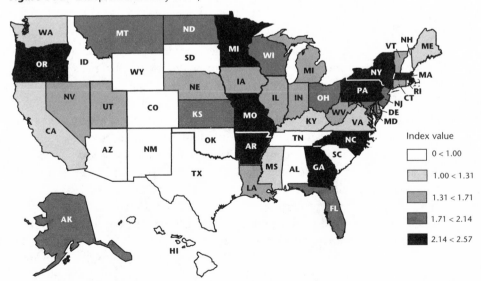

SOURCE: Calculated by the authors.

terizes this change as "paradigmatic," reflecting a new way of linking ideas that promises a better understanding of events and a more coherent worldview. A paradigmatic policy change would mean that the worldview of economic development policy makers is moving away from infrastructure and locational orientations to the logic of more entrepreneurial policy approaches. But in line with Eisinger's contention (1988) that states will maintain a mix of traditional and entrepreneurial economic development policies, our measures indicate that states continue to combine approaches. Some states, such as New York, Oregon, and Pennsylvania, have taken a leadership position in adoption of entrepreneurial economic development strategies; other states, such as California, Indiana, Iowa, and Michigan, consistently fall in the middle range of both indexes for any given year.

This apparent balancing act is not surprising when we consider the political context of policy adoption. Although states increasingly are adopting new approaches with entrepreneurial attributes, these new policies are an overlay on previously adopted development programs characterized by locational attributes. Given the difficulty of terminating programs with influential beneficiaries, the shift toward entrepreneurial orientations is likely to appear slow, partial, and uneven. Some analysts would argue that it could even be reversed as state governments contend with revenue needs in the face of antitax sentiments and declining federal and state aid (Brace 1993). Kentucky's Saturn deal, Alabama's Mercedes-Benz package, Indiana's United Airlines coup, and other such negotiations of megadeals could signal the return of smokestack-chasing strategies (Guskind 1993; Mahtesian 1994), A careful state-by-state analysis of the full array of state development policies, however, indicates that even states caught up in these bidding wars continue to lay the groundwork for more entrepreneurial approaches. While we can confirm a general movement of the states toward an entrepreneurial orientation, it is not yet clear that the shift constitutes a new policy paradigm. It does, however, exemplify a maturation of policy thinking (Hanson 1993) as state policy makers rethink the changing context of development issues.

Explaining the Adoption of Entrepreneurial Economic Development Policies. While rising levels of state economic development activism can be interpreted in terms of the incentives embedded in decentralized federalism structures, the reasons why states favor one orientation rather than another are less clear. The logic of competitive federalism may be sufficient for explaining policy activism involving conventional cost-reduction strategies, in which states seek to retain and attract investment by lowering production costs in relation to those in other states. But the incentives for entrepreneurial use of state authority to shape market structures, to create public-private partnerships, or to pursue strategies involving higher-risk and longer-term investments with public funds are less obvious. The growing reliance on entrepreneurial orientations suggests that state officials may be reframing their definitions of economic development problems in terms of the global rather than federal context.

Several analysts (Eisinger 1988; Fosler 1988; Lampe 1988; Osborne 1988) interpret these new state roles and entrepreneurial approaches as responses to a globalizing economy. But the theoretical links between global economic change and particular state policy responses are weak. Entrepreneurial policies are not simply rational, technical responses to new economic conditions. Changing economic conditions and a competitive federal context do provide constraints and opportunities for state decision makers, but these conditions are interpreted and mediated by political actors such as voters, interest groups, political parties, and public officials themselves. This underscores the political nature of state economic development policy making, a dimension confirmed by empirical analyses of the conditions associated with state adoption of entrepreneurial policy orientations.

In trying to sort out this puzzle of state policy choice, Gray and Lowery (1990) find that states with more structured and integrated political relationships are more likely to pursue entrepreneurial policy options, or what they refer to as industrial policy activism. While they show that economic conditions are important to the rise of economic activism, Gray and Lowery contend that these integrative institutions structure the resolution of economic and social issues between interests in ways that allow coordinated and cooperative action on development issues. Similarly, Berman and Martin (1992) find that political institutional features, such as the level of interparty competition and well-developed interest groups, and changing economic conditions are important factors in the adoption of entrepreneurial strategies. It also appears that state political culture shapes the types of strategies states select; states with moralistic political cultures are more likely to rely on entrepreneurial strategies, although traditionalistic states are now less wedded to locational approaches (Boeckelman 1991; Hanson 1991; and see Chapter 1 of this volume).

Analyses of economic and political conditions associated with our measures of state entrepreneurial development policies support and amplify these arguments (Saiz 1991).[6] In addition to confirming the importance of state economic change, our findings support Eisinger's argument (1988) that the indirect effects of economic decline on the ability of state governments to provide goods and services to its citizenry are an additional impetus to policy change. As Eisinger suggests, global competition may be the basic reason that states adopt entrepreneurial economic development policies, but it is declining state revenues that trigger the shift. Although we also uncover a relationship between well-established interest groups, interparty competition, and entrepreneurial policy choices, our analyses detect a significant and robust relationship between entrepre-

6. In empirical analyses of the determinants of entrepreneurial policies (Clarke and Gaile 1992; Saiz 1991), we test for the effects of deindustrialization, fiscal stress, socioeconomic environment, state political culture, interparty competition, state public opinion liberalism, policy liberalism, interest groups, gubernatorial turnover, the formal power of the governor, general state partisanship, and policy innovation.

neurial policy adoption and the role of the states' governors. Gubernatorial turnover is an important factor in explaining early adoption of these polices, and the formal powers of the governors are associated with policy adoptions throughout the 1980s. In our analyses, states adopting more entrepreneurial policies were states where gubernatorial turnover occurred because of interparty competition rather than constitutional requirements. This competition encourages the advocacy of new ideas that fit the ideological and partisan preferences in the state electorate (Erikson, Wright, and McIver 1993). Even though it is uncertain whether particular economic development approaches will work, the potential political payoffs of announcing new strategies outweigh the risks. If the programs work, or if development simply happens anyway, governors can take credit for the success—but only if new policies are on the table.

Diffusion of Locational and Entrepreneurial Policy Orientations

Competition among the states also spreads policies across the states as they imitate their neighbors or other states with reputations for policy innovation (Eyestone 1977). The states are often criticized for offering, matching, and raising development incentives to businesses in the hope of attracting jobs and increasing their tax bases (Goodman 1979; Grady 1987; Peretz 1986). Even though the statistical support for the effectiveness of these incentives is weak, many state policy makers believe these incentives can make a difference at the regional level because variations in transportation, energy, and labor costs are likely to be narrow. The result is a general belief that incentives offered by other states have to be matched (Grady 1987), although this is most often the case for incentives that lower the costs of labor rather than capital (Hanson 1993).

The arms-race model (Peretz 1986) of interstate competition for investment implies that the adoption and diffusion of any particular economic development policy are primarily reactions to adoption by competing states. It appears, however, that this model approximates the diffusion patterns for locational policies but not for the diffusion of entrepreneurial orientations. We tested the arms-race logic to see if state policy scores change in response to the policies adopted in surrounding states. For each state, we derived a predicted 1991 policy index by assuming that state policy makers would try to move toward the 1986 scores of their near neighbors. We find that a near neighbor's past locational scores do have some power to explain a state's recent locational scores. But entrepreneurial policy scores do not change in this same pattern: a near neighbor's past entrepreneurial scores do not help predict whether a state will adopt more entrepreneurial strategies (Saiz 1991). Again, this indicates that federalism shapes the diffusion of one type of development policies—those locational policies that are directly designed for interstate competition—but is less salient in the diffusion of entrepreneurial policies.

THE POLICY EFFECTIVENESS DEBATE

Do state economic development policies make a difference? Evaluating whether these policies bring about net increases in employment, tax revenues, and long-term growth is a complex task. Given the political context and the uncertainty involved, policy makers are tempted, in the words of Rubin (1988), to "shoot anything that flies; claim anything that falls." Needless to say, this temptation complicates evaluations. Another problem, as we have demonstrated above, is that states combine several economic development approaches in making policy. Some approaches may be more effective than others, but the combined effect obscures the contribution of any particular policy. In addition, measures of policy effectiveness become normative questions. Should we simply count the number of new jobs, or should we evaluate their quality? What if few new jobs were added, but the incentives kept jobs in the state that would have left but for the incentives? Should we expect policies to lower the unemployment rate or raise the state's per capita income? Is it good policy if employment growth in Ohio comes at the expense of employment loss in Michigan?

Many studies have examined the effect of basic tax structures on economic growth (for example, Dye 1980). Despite the rhetoric of the tax revolt, the evidence seems to be that lower state taxes have little to do with higher rates of economic growth, although Brace (1993) claims that higher per capita taxation is negatively related to growth in his study (for reviews, see Ledebur and Hamilton 1986; Litvak and Daniels 1983; Wasylenko 1981, 1984). Other elements, such as proximity to markets, labor supplies, transportation, and utility costs, tend to be more important cost factors than taxes (Schmenner 1982). This does not mean that taxes are unimportant to businesses. At the metropolitan level, taxes may have more influence on location decisions because the larger cost differences that exist between major economic regions are not relevant (Peretz 1986; Wasylenko 1984). International competition may revive the salience of tax differences as firms move beyond national borders to scan the globe seeking the best combination of services and taxes for their investment.

Not surprisingly, when businesses are asked about incentives, they claim they make a difference, although businesses vary in the types of incentives they prefer (Glaser and Yeager 1992). Early studies of the effectiveness of state locational incentives emphasized their inefficient use of public capital (Bridges 1965), but recent studies are more ambivalent (Peirce 1994b). McHone (1984) finds that local communities that offer industrial bond programs, tax abatements, and accelerated depreciation are somewhat better off economically than their metropolitan counterparts. Kale (1984) reports a negative relationship between industrial development incentives and employment growth in the 1960s and early 1970s but a positive link in the later 1970s. Yet, Hansen (1984) finds that incentives are negatively related to employment growth but positively related to business formation rates. Similarly, Brace's study of economic development policy activism in four states (1993) reveals a negative relation between high policy usage and income growth. Nevertheless, Bartik (1991) concludes that these incentives can have positive effects on long-term business growth and labor market conditions, including prospects for African Americans and less-educated workers. His arguments are open to challenge (Accordino 1994) but have prompted a reconsideration of the potential effects of state incentives.

Studies of entrepreneurial policy approaches are more limited, but the results, while tentative, are more optimistic. Eisinger's research (1988) shows that entrepreneurial policies do stimulate new investment and create jobs. Lowery and Gray assess the impact of state industrial policy activism on gross state product measures; their initial analyses (1992) reveal positive but not robust effects on state growth, leading them to argue that state economic conditions would have been worse but for the policies. In measuring impacts over a longer time period (1982–1989), they find there is little long-term economic benefit from such policies (Lowery and Gray 1995). Hansen (1984, 1989a) also finds limited effects from more activist, targeted policies. Oregon, a leader in entrepreneurial approaches, devised a benchmark strategy for measuring its policy effectiveness. Since the policy goals center on improving the standard of living, rather than more narrow job creation goals, the state identified benchmarks, or standards to be achieved, for a wide range of economic and social goals—from economic diversification to babies born to drug-free mothers—that would reflect true state development (Mattoon 1993). Establishing benchmarks to measure program performance on a regular basis, and tying performance to budget decisions as in Oregon, is a basic but still uncommon evaluation tool (Livengood 1993). Only two states—Illinois and Indiana—have formal cost-benefit guidelines for evaluation of economic development options (Peirce 1994b).

THE NEW POLITICS OF STATE ECONOMIC DEVELOPMENT POLICIES

Our discussion of this changing policy arena brings out several reasons to reconsider assumptions about state economic development politics in a global era. Although states are as concerned with economic development as deductive models predict, their approaches to development are taking on new and distinctive features. While decentralized federal structures continue to limit state policy options and offer incentives for interjurisdictional competition, globalization trends alter these locational calculations. As a result, a vibrant "politics of ideas" is in play across state governments. To many state officials, globalization trends render locational approaches irrelevant; instead, the changing nature of global competition prompts attention to state incentives that support innovation and growth processes. There is some initial evidence of an emergent "paradigm shift" in state economic development policy orientations: a definite move toward more entrepreneurial approaches and less emphasis on firm-specific or locational incentives, even though many states seek to balance these approaches. These economic transformations affect infrastructure policy as well. States are increasingly responsible for infrastructure investments in an era in which technological changes have radically altered the costs of production as well as the costs of overcoming distance. In contrast to the segmented infrastructure programs of the past, these new policies emphasize integration of infrastructure systems and competition rather than regulation. The recent ISTEA legislation exemplifies this perspective as do several information infrastructure systems that have been initiated by states.

While the decentralized federal structure historically encouraged arms-race-type bidding wars and the homogenization of state development policies, globalization forces may make state governments more important economic actors and encourage more differentiated policies (Jessop 1993). As firms seek the best locational fit for their needs, states and regions have become the arena for global competition. This paradoxical turn of events means that the context for the decisions of state officials is now broader than state or national boundaries. These changing politics of scale are exemplified by the formalization of regional markets such as those created by the North American Free Trade Agreement. In this global marketplace, firms compete through technology and export capacity; the issue is whether states can adjust to this turbulent environment and capture these new sources and forms of growth and wealth.

In addition to the economic logic implicit in both federalism and globalization, the political logic merits further attention. Models of state development policy centered on assumptions about federalism slight the political changes associated with globalization. For many American communities, globalization brings increasing inequalities and social polarization between those benefiting from these economic changes and the many with less certain futures. Even though these deteriorating social conditions serve as potential grounds for political action within the states (Goetz 1993), the logic of interstate competition suggests that policies that redistribute benefits to those paying little or no taxes are not in a state's interest. Indeed, there is even concern that state responses may create welfare magnets (Peterson and Rom 1990) and discourage future private investment. But Hwang and Gray (1991) find that redistributive policies are more prevalent at the state level than anticipated. They reason that political conditions—such as coherent party structures and interparty competition—allow the mobilization of constituencies and articulation of challenges with a narrow focus on economic development at the expense of other social and environmental concerns. This corresponds to the empirical analyses reported here: both political organizations bringing together diverse constituencies and political leadership play a critical role in producing ideas in good currency and reorienting state economic development policy. In short, the state context is more politicized and the organization of state politics is more amenable to political negotiation in regard to economic development issues than previously assumed.

The political terrain, however, bears little resemblance to the assumptions underlying more deductive models. These models assume that policy choices stem from the self-interest of officials predominantly concerned with their own reelection chances and tax-based budgets. But the third wave of economic development strategies, following earlier locational and entrepreneurial initiatives, features new organizational approaches to carrying out development policies (Atkinson 1993; Clarke and Gaile 1992; Goldstein and Bergman 1986; Ross and Friedman 1990). Increasingly, state development politics are characterized by nonelected public and private actors as well as organizations and partnership arrangements that cannot be labeled as belonging to either the public or private sector (Andre 1994; Gray and Lowery 1990; Hansen 1989b; Horan 1991). This trend includes the growing prominence of foundations and nonprofit organizations, as well as the privatization of some state economic development functions. For example, the Economic Development Corporation of Utah, a statewide, nonprofit, public-private organization formed in 1987, provides a privately run business development marketing program in tandem with the state's Department of Community and Economic Development. Similar privatization initiatives are under way in other states, including Arizona, Florida, Kentucky, Minnesota, and Wisconsin. In each instance, the objective is to find new institutional and organizational arrangements with sufficient scope, responsiveness, and flexibility to provide the foundation for economic development. Yet few of these new arrangements address the need for representing the voices of those often adversely affected by globalization trends (Cable, Feiock, and Kim 1993; Clarke and Gaile 1992).

In the 1990s, state economic development policy is being reconfigured by shifting federal and global policy contexts. In responding to these new conditions, state policy makers are reconsidering the problem definitions that have guided policy making in the past: the determinants of growth are less clear in a global context and the very meanings of location, distance, and competition are undergoing a transformation. The resultant new politics of ideas at the state level is prompting a shift in policy orientations, new economic roles for state governments, and a realignment of the political dynamics of making state economic development policy.

REFERENCES

Accordino, John J. 1994. "Evaluating Economic Development Strategies." *Economic Development Quarterly* 8:218–229.

Ambrosius, Margery, and Susan Welch. 1988. "State Legislators' Perceptions of Business and Labor Interests." *Legislative Studies Quarterly* 13:199–209.

André, Rae. 1994. "A National Study of Economic Development Organizations at the State Level: The Key Organizations, Their Industrial Constituencies, and Their Networks." *Economic Development Quarterly* 8:292–301.

Atkinson, Robert D. 1993. "The Next Wave in Economic Development." *Commentary* 17:12–18.

Barrett, Todd, and John Schwartz. 1992. "Can You Top This?" *Newsweek*, February 17.

Bartik, Timothy J. 1991. *Who Benefits from State and Local Economic Development Policies?* Kalamazoo, Mich.: W. E. Upjohn Institute for Employment Research.

Beaumont, Enid, and Harold Hovey. 1985. "State, Local, and Federal Economic Development Policies: New Federal Patterns, Chaos, or What?" *Public Administration Review* 45 (March/April): 327–332.

Berman, David R., and Lawrence L. Martin. 1992. "The New Approach to Economic Development: An Analysis of Innovativeness in the States." *Policy Studies Journal* 20:10–21.

Beyle, Thad L. 1990. "Governors." In *Politics in the American States,* 5th ed., edited by Virginia Gray, Herbert Jacob, and Robert Albritton. Glenview, Ill.: Scott, Foresman/Little, Brown.

Boeckelman, Keith. 1991. "Political Culture and State Development Policy." *Publius* 21, no. 2:49–61.

Bowman, Ann O'M. 1987. "Tools and Targets: The Mechanics of City Economic Development." A Research Report of the National League of Cities. Washington, D.C.: National League of Cities.

Brace, Paul. 1993. *State Government and Economic Performance.* Baltimore, Md.: Johns Hopkins University Press.

Bridges, Benjamin. 1965. "State and Local Inducements for Industry, Part II." *National Tax Journal* 18, no. 1:1–14.

Cable, Gregory, Richard C. Feiock, and Jae-On Kim. 1993. "The Consequences of Institutionalized Access for Economic Development Policy Making in U.S. Cities." *Economic Development Quarterly* 7:91–97.

Choate, Patrick, and Susan Walter. 1981. *America in Ruins: Beyond the Public Works Pork Barrel.* Washington, D.C.: Council of State Planning Agencies.

Clarke, Marianne K. 1986. *Revitalizing State Economies.* Washington, D.C.: National Governors' Association.

Clarke, Susan E., and Gary L. Gaile. 1989. "Moving towards Entrepreneurial Economic Development Strategies: Opportunities and Barriers." *Policy Studies Journal* 17:574–598.

———.1992. "The Next Wave: Local Economic Development Strategies in the Post-Federal Era." *Economic Development Quarterly* 6:187–198.

CSG (Council of State Governments). 1986. *The Book of the States, 1986–87.* Lexington, Ky.: Council of State Governments.

Cumberland, John H. 1971. *Regional Development Experiences and Prospects in the United States of America.* The Hague: Mouton.

Derthick, Martha, and Paul J. Quirk 1985. *The Politics of Deregulation.* Washington, D.C.: Brookings Institution.

Directory of Incentives for Business Investment and Development in the United States. Various years. Washington, D.C.: Urban Institute.

Dye, Thomas R. 1980. "Taxing, Spending, and Economic Growth in the States." *Journal of Politics* 42:1085–1087.

Eisinger, Peter. 1988. *The Rise of the Entrepreneurial State: State and Local Economic Development Policy in the United States.* Madison: University of Wisconsin Press.

———. 1993. "State Venture Capitalism, State Politics, and the World of High-Risk Investment." *Economic Development Quarterly* 7:131–139.

Erikson, Robert S., Gerald C. Wright, and John P. McIver. 1993. *Statehouse Democracy.* Cambridge: Cambridge University Press.

Eyestone, Robert. 1977. "Confusion, Diffusion, and Innovation." *American Political Science Review* 71:441–447.

Fainsod, Merle, Lincoln Gordon, and Joseph C. Palamountain, Jr. 1959. *Government and the American Economy.* New York: W. W. Norton.

Felbinger, Claire F. 1994. "Conditions of Confusion and Conflict: Rethinking the Infrastructure-Economic Development Linkage." In *Building the Public City,* edited by David C. Perry. Urban Affairs Annual Review 43. Newbury Park, Calif.: Sage Publications.

Fosler, R. Scott, ed. 1988. *The New Economic Role of American States.* New York: Oxford University Press.

Fulton, William, and Morris Newman. 1993. "Who Will Wire America?" *Governing,* October, 28–30.

GAO (U.S. General Accounting Office). 1993. *Federal Budget: Choosing Public Investment Programs.* Washington, D.C.: U.S. Government Printing Office.

Glaser, Mark A., and Samuel J. Yeager. 1992. "Business Priorities and the Relative Importance of

State and Local Economic Development Incentives." *International Journal of Public Adminis-tration* 15:1527–1551.

Goetz, Edward. 1993. *Shelter Burden.* Philadelphia: Temple University Press.

Goldstein, Harvey A., and Edward M. Bergman. 1986. "Institutional Arrangements for State and Local Industrial Policy." *Journal of the American Planning Association* 52 (Summer): 265–276.

Goodman, Robert. 1979. *The Last Entrepreneurs: America's Regional Wars for Jobs and Dollars.* New York: Simon and Schuster.

Grady, Dennis O. 1987. "State Economic Development Incentives: Why Do States Compete?" *State and Local Government Review* 19:86–94.

Gray, Virginia, and David Lowery. 1990. "The Corporatist Foundations of State Industrial Policy." *Social Science Quarterly* 71:3–23.

Guskind, Robert. 1993. "The New Civil War" *National Journal,* April 3, 817–821.

Hansen, Susan B. 1984. "The Effects of State Industrial Policies on Economic Growth." Paper pre-sented at the annual meeting of the American Political Science Association, Washington, D.C., September 2.

———. 1989a. "Targeting in Economic Development: Comparative State Perspectives." *Publius* 19, no. 2:47–62.

———. 1989b. "Industrial Policy and Corporatism in the American States." *Governance* 2, no. 2:172–197.

Hanson, Russell L. 1991. "Political Cultural Variations in State Economic Development Policy." *Publius* 21, no. 2:63–81.

———. 1993. "Bidding for Business: A Second War between the States?" *Economic Development Quarterly* 7:183–198.

Hanson, Russell L., and Michael B. Berkman. 1991. "Gauging the Rainmakers: Toward a Meteorol-ogy of State Legislative Climates." *Economic Development Quarterly* 5:213–228.

Herzik, Eric. 1983. "The Governors and Issues: A Typology of Concerns." *State Government* 51:58–62.

Horan, Cynthia. 1991. "Beyond Governing Coalitions: Analyzing Urban Regimes in the 1990s." *Journal of Urban Affairs* 13:119–136.

Hwang, Sung-Don, and Virginia Gray. 1991. "External Limits and Internal Determinants of State Public Policy." *Western Political Quarterly* 44 (June): 277–298.

Information Infrastructure Task Force. 1993. *The National Information Infrastructure: Agenda for Action.* Washington, D.C.: Executive Office of the President.

Jessop, Bob. 1993. "Towards a Schumpeterian Workfare State? Preliminary Remarks on Post-Fordist Political Economy." *Studies in Political Economy* 40 (Spring): 7–39.

Jones, Bryan, and Lynn Bachelor. 1986. *The Sustaining Hand.* Lawrence: University Press of Kansas.

Kale, Steven. 1984. "U.S. Industrial Development Incentives and Manufacturing Growth during the 1970s." *Growth and Change* 15, no. 1:26–34.

Kincaid, John. 1992. "Developments in Federal-State Relations, 1990–91." *The Book of the States, 1992–93.* Lexington, Ky.: Council of State Governments.

King, Desmond S. 1990. "Economic Activity and the Challenge to Local Government." In *Chal-lenges to Local Government,* edited by Desmond S. King and Jon Pierre. London: Sage Publica-tions.

Lampe, David. 1988. *The Massachusetts Miracle: High Technology and Economic Revitalization.* Cambridge: MIT Press.

Ledebur, Larry, and Walton Hamilton. 1986. *Tax Concessions in State and Local Economic Develop-ment.* Washington, D.C.: Aslan Press.

Leicht, Kevin T., and J. Craig Jenkins. 1994. "Three Strategies of State Economic Development: Entrepreneurial, Industrial Recruitment, and Deregulation Policies in the American States." *Economic Development Quarterly* 8:256–269.

Leigland, James. 1994. "Public Infrastructure and Special Purpose Governments: Who Pays and How?" In *Building the Public City: Politics, Governance, and Finance of Public Infrastructure,* edited by David C. Perry. Urban Affairs Annual Review 43. Newbury Park, Calif.: Sage Publi-cations.

Lemov, Penelope. 1994. "Public Works and the Art of Creative Financing." *Governing,* September, 56–57.

Licate, Jack. 1994. "Cities Can Take Back Their Infrastructure." *Governing,* July, 68–71.

Lindblom, Charles E. 1977. *Politics and Markets.* New York: Basic Books.

Livengood, Rebecca. 1993. "Evaluating the Impact of Economic Development Programs." *Commentary* 17, no. 2:10–17.

Litvak, Lawrence, and Belden Daniels. 1983. "Innovations in Development Finance." In *Financing State and Local Economic Development,* edited by M. Barker. Durham, N.C.: Duke University Press.

Lowery, David, and Virginia Gray. 1992. "Holding Back the Tide of Bad Economic Times: The Compensatory Impact of State Industrial Policy." *Social Science Quarterly* 73:483–495.

———. 1995. "The Compensatory Impact of State Industrial Policy: An Empirical Assessment of Mid-Term Effects." *Social Science Quarterly* 76:438–446.

McHone, Warren W. 1984. "State Industrial Development Incentives and Employment Growth in Multi-State SMSA's." *Growth and Change* 15, no. 4:8–15.

Mahtesian, Charles. 1994. "Romancing the Smokestack." *Governing,* November, 36–40.

Man, Joyce Y., and Michael E. Bell. 1993. "Federal Infrastructure Grants-in-Aid: An Ad Hoc Infrastructure Strategy." *Public Budgeting and Finance* 13:9–22.

Mattoon, Richard H. 1993. "Economic Development Policy in the 1990s—Are State Economic Development Agencies Ready?" *Economic Perspectives* 17:11–23.

Nathan, Richard P. 1992. "Needed: A Marshall Plan for Ourselves." *Economic Development Quarterly* 6:347–355.

NCPWI (National Council for Public Works Improvement). 1988. *Fragile Foundations.* Washington, D.C.: U.S. Government Printing Office.

NCSL (National Conference of State Legislatures). 1991. "1989 State Economic Development Survey Results." Report. Denver, Colo.

North, Douglass C. 1966. *The Economic Growth of the United States, 1790 to 1860.* Englewood Cliffs, N.J.: Prentice-Hall.

North, Douglas C., Terry Anderson, and Peter Hill. 1983. *Growth and Welfare in the American Past.* Englewood Cliffs, N.J.: Prentice-Hall.

Osborne, David. 1988. *Laboratories of Democracy.* Boston: Harvard Business School Press.

Peirce, Neal R. 1994a. "California's Walloping Wake-up Call." *National Journal,* February 12, 382.

———. 1994b. "The When, How, and Why of Wooing." *National Journal,* February 26, 488.

Peretz, Paul. 1986. "The Market for Incentives: Where Angels Fear to Tread." *Policy Studies Journal* 5:624–633.

Perry, David C. 1994a. "Introduction: Building the Public City." In *Building the Public City: Politics, Governance, and Finance of Public Infrastructure,* edited by David C. Perry. Urban Affairs Annual Review 43. Newbury Park, Calif.: Sage Publications.

———. 1994b. "Building the City through the Backdoor: The Politics of Debt, Law, and Public Infrastructure." In *Building the Public City: Politics, Governance, and Finance of Public Infrastructure,* edited by David C. Perry. Urban Affairs Annual Review 43. Newbury Park, Calif.: Sage Publications.

Peterson, Paul E. 1981. *City Limits.* Chicago: University of Chicago Press.

Peterson, Paul E., and Mark C. Rom. 1990. *Welfare Magnets: A Case for a National Standard.* Washington, D.C.: Brookings Institution.

Plaut, Thomas, and Joseph Pluta. 1983. "Business Climate Taxes and Expenditures, and State Industrial Growth in the United States." *Southern Economic Journal* 50 (September): 99–119.

Portz, John. 1993. "State Economic Development Programs: The Trials and Tribulations of Implementation." *Economic Development Quarterly* 7:160–171.

Rapp, David. 1994a. "Route 66 Gets a Federal Fix." *Governing,* March, 100.

———. 1994b. "The Digital Democrats." *Governing,* June, 84.

Reich, Robert. 1991. *The Work of Nations.* New York: Alfred A. Knopf.

Richter, M. J. 1994a. "A Guide to Emerging Technologies." *Governing,* May, 65–80.

———. 1994b. "Let the States Help Pave the Information Superhighway." *Governing,* November, 72.

Rochefort, David A., and Roger W. Cobb. 1994. "Problem Definition: An Emerging Perspective." In *The Politics of Problem Definition,* edited by David A. Rochefort and Roger W. Cobb. Lawrence: University Press of Kansas.

Ross, Doug, and Robert E. Friedman. 1990. "The Emerging Third Wave: New Economic Development Strategies in the 90s." *Entrepreneurial Economy Review* 9 (December): 3–10.

Rubin, Herbert J. 1988. "Shoot Anything That Flies; Claim Anything That Falls: Conversations with Economic Development Practitioners." *Economic Development Quarterly* 2:236–251.

Saiz, Martin. 1991. "Determinants of Economic Development Policy Innovation among the U.S. States." Ph.D. diss., University of Colorado at Boulder.

Schmenner, Roger. 1982. *Making Business Location Decisions.* Englewood Cliffs, N.J.: Prentice-Hall.

Schwartz, Gail Garfield. 1990."Telecommunications and Economic Development Policy." *Economic Development Quarterly* 4:83–91.

Sternberg, Ernest. 1987. "A Practitioner's Classification of Economic Development Policy Instruments, with Some Inspiration from Political Economy." *Economic Development Quarterly* 1:149–161.

Stokes, Bruce. 1994. "Out of the Rubble." *National Journal,* October 15, 2398–2403.

Takaki, Ronald. 1990. *Iron Cages.* New York: Oxford University Press.

Taylor, George R. 1977. *The Transportation Revolution, 1815–1860.* New York: M. E. Sharpe.

U.S. Advisory Commission on Intergovernmental Relations. 1993. *High Performance Public Works: A New Federal Infrastructure Investment Strategy for America.* Washington, D.C.: U.S. Government Printing Office.

U.S. Congress. 1984. National Infrastructure Advisory Committee. *Hard Choices: A Report on the Increasing Gap between America's Infrastructure Needs and Our Ability to Pay for Them.* Prepared for the Subcommittee on Economic Goals and Intergovernmental Policy of the Joint Economic Committee. 98th Cong., 2d sess. Committee print.

U.S. Congress. 1990. Office of Technology Assessment. *Rebuilding the Foundations: Public Works Technologies, Management, and Financing.* Washington, D.C.: U.S. Government Printing Office.

U.S. Department of Transportation. Federal Highway Administration. 1993. *Intermodal Surface Transportation Efficiency Act of 1991: Selected Fact Sheets.* Washington, D.C.: U.S. Government Printing Office.

Vaughn, Roger, Robert Pollard, and Barbara Dyer. 1984. *The Wealth of States: Policies for a Dynamic Economy.* Washington, D.C.: Council of State Planning Agencies.

Walker, Jack L. 1969. "The Diffusion of Innovations among the American States." *American Political Science Review* 63:880–899.

Wasylenko, M. 1981. "The Location of Firms: The Role of Taxes and Fiscal Incentives." In *Urban Government Finance: Emerging Trends,* edited by Roy Bahl. Beverly Hills, Calif.: Sage Publications.

———. 1984. "Disamenities, Local Taxation, and the Intra-Metropolitan Location of Households and Firms." In *Research in Urban Economics,* edited by Robert Ebel. Greenwich, Conn.: JAI Press.

Weber, Melvin. 1984. *Industrial Location.* Beverly Hills, Calif.: Sage Publications.

Wolman, Harold. 1988. "Local Economic Development Policy: What Explains the Divergence between Policy Analysis and Political Behavior?" *Journal of Urban Affairs* 6:19–28.

Wyatt, Cathleen Magennis. 1994. "Zero-Sum Games." *State Government News,* April, 28–32.

SUGGESTED READINGS

Bartik, Timothy J. *Who Benefits from State and Local Economic Development Policies?* Kalamazoo, Mich.: W. E. Upjohn Institute for Employment Research, 1991. Bartik asks three questions: whether state and local development policies affect growth, whether local growth helps the unemployed and low-income families, and whether interjurisdictional competition is a zero-sum game or actually helps the economy? He presents a cogent argument that development incentives may raise business activities as well as help disadvantaged workers.

Brace, Paul. *State Government and Economic Performance.* Baltimore: Johns Hopkins University Press, 1993. Brace examines the "mystery of state political economy" and finds that despite previous evidence, state governments can influence their economies. Using both case studies and rigorous quantitative analyses, he emphasizes the importance of national economic conditions in determining the success of particular state economic development strategies. He shows that state governments willing and able to invest in their economies are in a better position to endure national hard times.

Eisinger, Peter. *The Rise of the Entrepreneurial State: State and Local Economic Development Policy in the United States.* Madison: University of Wisconsin Press, 1988. Eisinger develops an analytical framework for comparing "supply-side" state policies designed to reduce the costs of land, labor, capital, and taxes with "demand-side" entrepreneurial strategies aimed at facilitating growth processes through the active intervention of state governments. He traces the evolution of these approaches and surveys evidence for the effectiveness of specific strategies in contributing to growth.

Fosler, R. Scott, ed. *The New Economic Role of American States.* New York: Oxford University Press, 1988. Fosler collects case studies of state policy orientations in Arizona, California, Indiana, Massachusetts, Michigan, Minnesota, and Tennessee. Each study addresses the extent to which the state pursues an activist entrepreneurial strategy and addresses labor and capital issues. The case studies include critical analyses of policy effectiveness and emphasize the role of public-private partnerships.

Hwang, Sung-Don, and Virginia Gray. "External Limits and Internal Determinants of State Public Policy." *Western Political Quarterly* 44 (1991): 277–298. In one of the few empirical tests of Paul E. Peterson's model at the state level, the authors find that development policies are significant but that redistributive policies are more prevalent than anticipated. They attribute this to state political conditions that potentially allow mobilization and articulation of challenges to narrow economic goals.

CHAPTER 15

The Politics of Family Policy

SUSAN WELCH, SUE THOMAS, AND
MARGERY M. AMBROSIUS

State legislation regulating family formation is as old as the Republic. Setting up conditions for marriage, ensuring that newborns are duly registered, and regulating divorce and child support are state actions that long preceded contemporary interest in "family policy." Even today, family law is dominated by state action, although the federal government has, in this arena as in others, increased its regulatory and financial scope.

Despite government oversight of a myriad of family concerns, political scientists have traditionally been disinterested in family policy, content to relegate the topic to the preserve of sociologists, demographers, and anthropologists. Recently, however, interest has grown, paralleling and reflecting the concern of public policy makers.

THE CHANGING FAMILY

Several factors explain the increased attention to family policy.[1] Families have changed for numerous reasons. The transformation of women's roles has led to a later age of marriage and parenthood and a greater participation in the work force, even after the birth of children.

Other shifts in societal norms have produced transformations of the family

---

1. Much of the discussion here and in the following section is drawn from Aldous and Dumon (1990) and Moen and Schorr (1987).

too. Divorce is at a high level, and more children are born into families without fathers. Teenage pregnancy is higher than in any other industrial nation in the world. More than half of all children can expect to live in a single-parent household sometime during their childhood. Consequently, poverty rates for children have increased. Twenty percent of American children are poor, most living in families with one or no wage earner.

Families consisting of partners of the same sex and those who are of the opposite sex but unmarried are increasing too, giving further evidence of changing norms. Life spans have become longer, leading to more elderly couples and more elderly people living alone.

It is hard to find a common thread in these changes except that families are becoming more diverse and their functions are shrinking. At frequent intervals, journalists trumpet that fewer than one-quarter of all American families are "traditional" families of husband, nonworking wife, and minor children. Single-parent families, elderly couples with grown children, couples without children, and unmarried couples, all are part of what we define as families. As families become more diverse, expectations of family obligations are also becoming more disparate. Sociologists and demographers appear to agree on the trends, but they disagree on their implications and the extent to which we should be concerned about the changing family (see, for example, Cowen 1993; Levitan, Belous, and Gallo 1988; Popenoe 1993; Stacey 1993). Many fear that the family is in danger, and that "widespread family breakdown is bound to have a pervasive and debilitating impact not only on the quality of life but on the vitality of the body politic as well" (Levitan, Belous, and Gallo 1988). And there is relatively little agreement about the stance government should take in supporting families.

The weakened traditional family ties, as measured by the increased number of single-parent families, and the concomitant impact on the economic and sometimes emotional well-being of children, have led many people to argue that the federal government, and the states, should have policies to try to assist families, especially children. Support for family policies comes from diverse sources and for different reasons. For example, liberals and women's rights advocates support policies to ease the burden of working parents through parental leave, flextime, shared jobs, and subsidized day care. Conservatives favor reforming welfare to encourage families to stay together and tax breaks to encourage women to stay at home with their children. Both liberals and conservatives favor policies to mandate that fathers support their children.

DEFINING FAMILY POLICY

The variety of these policies raises the question: what exactly is *family policy*? This common term has many different meanings. Some define it as all legislation that affects the family (Bane 1980, 156; Steiner 1980), but that definition would include most social and economic legislation, even if the word *family* is not mentioned (Aldous and Dumon 1990). After all, minimum wage laws affect the family. So do housing, welfare, health, and most labor policies. Other definitions focus more specifically on policies affecting children (Aldous and Dumon 1980, 255; Lynn 1980).

Still others believe that family policy is that focusing on a "widely agreed-on set of objectives for families" (Moen and Schorr 1987, 795). And many observers implicitly define family policy as something that is directed toward poor families or other specific kinds of families (Aldous and Dumon 1980).

The problems with these definitions are obvious. There are few "widely agreed-on" objectives for families. Some argue, for example, that family policy should be directed toward restoring the two-parent family; others disagree. Some believe that family policy should be targeted toward providing income security for families; others believe this is not the job of government. Nor do most observers believe that family policy is something focused only on poor families, problem families, or other specific types of families.

In this discussion, we will take a broader view of family policy, defining it, as did Aldous and Dumon (1990), as policy specifically directed toward family well-being. We focus on several aspects of family policy: regulations of marriage and divorce, family planning, abortion, and helping parents balance work and child rearing through parental leave and day care regulation.

THE ROLE OF THE STATES IN FAMILY POLICY

States have been making family policy since the nation began. Traditionally, state family policy was regulatory in nature, setting conditions for marriage, divorce, adoption, abortions, and removal of children from parental homes; defining spousal and children's rights in inheritance; and overseeing other such matters. Much of what states do is still of that nature.

Since about 1940, and especially since the mid-1970s, states have become much more active in promoting child welfare, protecting women in violent relationships, and aiding poor families. Some of this activism still comes in the form of regulation, such as enforcing standards for child care facilities, whereas other policies are distributive, providing services for families. Several states have given family policy a priority. For example, Connecticut declared 1987 "The Year of the Family," and Mario Cuomo, then governor of New York, announced that 1988–1997 would be the "Decade of the Child." Other states, such as California, Illinois, and Massachusetts, set up special task forces or committees to study how the state could better preserve families (Wisensale 1990).

We are concerned here with the many family policies states have implemented. We are interested both in common trends and in the ways that states diverge in their adoption of policies designed to help the family. In explaining differences among states, we look at the impact of diverse political cultures (Elazar 1984) as well as diverse socioeconomic conditions in the states. Zimmerman (1992) has explored the several influences of political culture on family policies. For example, she shows that people from states with individualistic political cultures are less likely than others to agree that government shares with families responsibility for meeting the needs of children and the elderly and that government should allocate more money for these needs (Zimmerman 1992, 69; see Chapter 1 of this volume). Her case studies of Minnesota, Nevada, and South Carolina also illustrate that Minnesota, the most moralistic state by some definitions, had the most family policies, while Nevada, a prototypic individualistic state had the least (Zimmerman 1992, chap. 5).

REGULATING MARRIAGE AND DIVORCE

Marriage

State regulations of marriage are mostly unexceptional and not very interesting, except perhaps to young couples below the minimum age requirement who want to elope. Rates of marriage have not changed much since the 1920s, averaging about ten marriages per 1,000 people, although the rates were somewhat lower in the 1940s and 1960s and higher in the 1950s (see U.S. Bureau of the Census 1994, table 90). The one highly controversial issue surrounding the regulation of marriage is the status of same-sex partners.

Divorce

Whereas marriage rates and marriage laws have changed little, divorce rates have skyrocketed during the past century, and divorce laws have changed dramatically since the mid-1960s. Obtaining a divorce has traditionally been difficult in Western society. Until the last century, the Christian idea that marriage is a permanent bond made divorce a rare occurrence. Even in the early part of this century, the grounds for divorce were narrow and the social consequences of divorce often devastating. Couples could divorce only when one of the spouses was proved to be unwilling or unable to uphold his or her part of the marriage because of antisocial behaviors, such as desertion, cruelty, adultery, and drunkenness. Only in a few states was it possible to divorce even after a prolonged separation that indicated the marriage was dead (Jacob 1988; Marvell 1989). Moreover, spouses filing for divorce had to be without blame; they could not be guilty of any acts that might have led their partners to engage in cruelty, desert the family, or commit another of the justifiable grounds for divorce.

Beginning in the 1960s, state legislatures began writing new types of laws making divorce relatively easy. The legislation, labeled "no fault," permitted divorce when the couple could show "irretrievable breakdown" of the marriage. No longer did one partner have to prove that the other committed some act of cruelty, desertion, or worse. These legal changes both reflected and shaped more relaxed societal views toward divorce.

By 1985, when South Dakota adopted some no-fault grounds, all states had no-fault divorce statutes. This striking change was part of a movement throughout the Western world that resulted in liberalized divorce laws. Nineteen states had only no-fault statutes; the rest retained some fault statutes alongside the no-fault grounds (Glendon 1987). No-fault grounds include such criteria as incompatibility, irreconcilable differences, and irretrievable breakdown of the marriage.

The Impact of No-Fault Statutes on Divorce Rates. At the time no-fault laws were passed, some argued that these laws would make divorce easier and thus more frequent, by removing legal barriers that forced couples who wanted to divorce into untruthful accusations of wrongdoing. Other observers argued that the new laws were likely to have little effect on divorce rates, because the laws were so frequently subverted. Previous divorce laws were flouted; parties to divorces under the old rules committed perjury and colluded with each other to make their case for divorce (Jacob 1988).

Overall divorce rates in the United States have increased tenfold in the last 100 years. Much of this increase long preceded no-fault divorce, as rates crept up from 0.4 per 1,000 population in 1880 to 1.6 in 1920 to 2.5 in 1950. In the era of no-fault divorce, these rates doubled to 5.2 in 1980 but have declined since (Bystydzienski 1993).

Most social scientists who have examined divorce rates before and after the adoption of no-fault laws have found that these laws have had little effect on the rates of divorce. (Jacob 1988; Wright and Stetson 1978; for a summary, see Marvell 1989). These findings support the argument that the no-fault laws brought laws in line with common widespread practice. However, Marvell (1989), using a sophisticated analysis, found that the implementation of no-fault rules clearly increased the divorce rate in eight states: California, Delaware, Florida, New Jersey, North Carolina, Pennsylvania, Rhode Island, and South Carolina. In seven other states, the changes may have slightly increased the divorce rate: Alabama, Connecticut, New Hampshire, Vermont, Virginia, West Virginia, and Wisconsin. In the remaining states Marvell found little effect. He summarized these findings by noting that the laws seemed to affect the rate of divorce more in the eastern states. However, he could not explain why this should be so. The variation in available grounds for divorce in states did not provide any explanation. One possible explanation might be that the northeastern states have large populations of Catholics, whose church had been most opposed to divorce; individuals may not have wanted to lie to the civil authority and flout the authority of the church at the same time. Similarly, many southeastern states have large populations of fundamentalist Protestants, whose religious training also is very much opposed to divorce.

Alimony and Property Division. In a pathbreaking analysis, Weitzman (1985) argued that the replacement of fault divorce with no-fault standards has dramatically worsened the lives of divorced women. In particular, she argues that women are, on average, financially worse off under no-fault laws than they were under the traditional divorce laws. She asserts that no-fault laws improved men's economic condition because no-fault standards meant that men who left the marriage were not obligated to pay alimony. Thus she contends that no-fault divorce widens the income gap between men and women.

Weitzman's book has been influential in the debate about divorce and women's status in the 1980s and 1990s (see also Peters 1986). Her conclusion that after divorce women are financially worse off and men financially better off has been replicated in other studies, although other scholars suggest that her estimates of the magnitude of those effects are exaggerated. Some of her analyses of the particular effects of no-fault divorce are flawed in that they contrast the actual situation during the era of no-fault laws with an idealized vision of divorce in the era before them. It is divorce, not just no-fault divorce, that widens the economic gender gap. As Singer (1989, 1106) points out, only a minority of women received alimony under the old laws (from 6 to 15 percent in her historical sampling). In Weitzman's data from California, the proportion of divorcing women receiving alimony dropped only from 19 percent to 16.5 percent. Singer (1989, 1107) also shows that the proportion of women married more than nine years who were awarded alimony actually increased in the no-fault era and the proportion of homemakers married more than nine years who received alimony increased substantially.

Still, other research (Welch and Price-Bonham 1983) does show that alimony awards decreased slightly after no-fault standards were added. However, there appears to be no recent research that examines the effect in the longer term.

Women have benefited from new legislation governing the division of property in divorce settlements. Most states now allot women half of all marital property, and federal law gives them claim to half of their husband's vested pension funds. Such laws have particularly aided middle-class women, who, with their husbands, are likely to have accumulated significant property during the marriage (Jacob 1988, 1989).

Child Custody. In most divorces, the parents agree on who is to have custody of the children, but in about 10 percent of divorces involving children, litigation is necessary to solve the custody issue (Buehler 1989). Some reformers believed that no-fault divorce would lead to more diversity in child custody arrangements. Husbands might win custody more frequently, if they were not charged with being the guilty party in a divorce. This does not seem to be the case, however. A study of child custody settlements over time, before and after the switch to no-fault divorce, showed the patterns of awarding custody unchanged. Women won custody about 90 percent of the time under the fault system and about 90 percent in the first years under the no-fault rules (McEvoy 1978).

Nevertheless, some changes in child custody policies have occurred. As more women have entered the work force and more men become involved in their parenting role, legal doctrine has shifted from the presumption that the mother's preference should be honored to the assumption that custody should be for "the best interests of the child" (Buehler 1989; Glendon 1987). Evidence from the late 1980s shows a slight increase in custody awards to fathers (Buehler 1989). Joint custody agreements, in which both parents share physical custody, have increased. Whereas joint custody provisions were nearly unheard of until the mid-1960s, most states now have such provisions (Jacob 1988).[2] Some women's groups have opposed this trend toward joint custody, fearing that it would give men an excuse to argue for less child support (Polikoff 1983), although some evidence suggests that joint custody arrangements seem to improve compliance with child support orders (Seltzer 1991).

Gay and lesbian rights issues have entered into the debate on child custody. States handle this issue in diverse ways. Eleven states have laws indicating that sexual orientation is irrelevant to child custody, and in California, Indiana, Massachusetts, Michigan, New Mexico, Ohio, and Washington, the appellate courts have ruled that the sexual orientation of a parent by itself cannot be grounds for denying custody. In contrast, the courts in eleven other states, including Arkansas, Kentucky, Nevada, and Virginia, have assumed that lesbians and gays are unfit for custody (see Achtenberg and Moulding 1994, 1–11).

Child Support. Half the children now born in the United States will be part of a single-parent household at some time in their lives. Some are born to single mothers; others experience the divorce of their parents. In 1993, 29 percent of all children were currently living with only one parent or neither parent; of those 29 percent, about 30 percent were living with mothers who had never married; about the same percentage lived with divorced mothers; and the rest were divided between those living with their mothers separated from husbands, those living with fathers (about 10 percent), those living with widowed mothers, and those living with neither parent (about 10 percent; U.S. Bureau of the Census 1994, table 80).

Children in single-parent families have much higher probabilities of living in poverty and much lower family incomes than children in two-parent families. About 57 percent of young children living with single parents live in poverty, compared with only 13 percent of children living in two-parent families (U.S. Bureau of the Census 1994, table 729).

Inadequate or absent child support is a major contributor to this situation. When parents divorce, the custodial parent is usually entitled to some amount of child support. However, perhaps one-fifth of divorced women with children are not awarded support at all (Teachman 1990). A significant portion of noncustodial divorced parents do not meet their child support commitments (although Peters, Argys, Maccoby, and Mnookin (1993) argue that in some cases couples modify their child support agreements from time to time without necessarily reporting back to the courts). Thus, many of those awarded child support do not receive it. Census figures for 1993 indicate that only slightly more than half of di-

2. States not having joint custody statutes include Arkansas, Delaware, Hawaii, Maine, North Dakota, Washington, and Wyoming.

vorced women with children received child support in that year (U.S. Bureau of the Census 1994, table 605).

Unwed mothers are also entitled to child support, but they have a much lower probability of receiving it than do divorced mothers. In a recent year, only about 14 percent received it (U.S. Bureau of the Census 1994, table 605).

One recent study in Colorado showed that women with child support orders received only half what they were due; the average woman was owed $12,000 in support (Pearson, Thoennes, and Anhalt 1992; see also Pearson, Thoennes, and Tjaden 1989). Sometimes nonpayment is part of a complicated pattern of difficulties between the divorced couple, where withdrawal of support is countered by withdrawal of visiting privileges with the child, and an endless cycle of hostility begins. In other cases, the absent parent withdraws support because he becomes less emotionally involved with the children, perhaps because he has formed a new family (Bartfeld and Meyer 1994). In still other cases, the absent parent cannot afford to meet the payments.

Inadequate child support, whether from deliquency in payments or lack of ability to pay, plays a major part in explaining the high levels of poverty among single-parent families and the prevalence of female-headed families who participate in the Aid to Families with Dependent Children (AFDC) program (Meyer 1993; Veum 1992). Child support seems crucial to helping single mothers enter the labor market. Female-headed families are only about one-sixth of all families, but they make up about one-half the families under the poverty line (see Teachman 1990).

Some changes are being made in the awarding of child support and its collection, but the laws have changed faster than the willingness of states to implement them. Traditionally, state laws required support and left it to local courts to decide whether and how much support should be paid. Local judges had wide discretion to set the amount of support. In only a few jurisdictions were formal guidelines or formulas used to set child support.

Enforcement of these awards was lax, although absent fathers were sometimes jailed for failing to pay support. Inequities in levels of support abounded, but generally awards were too low to keep children out of poverty and often were far lower than the absent father could have afforded (see Garfinkel 1994; Garfinkel, Oellerich, and Robins 1991).

Increased concern over children in poverty and escalating costs of supporting families on welfare led the federal government and the states to change this traditional system. In 1974, legislation created a federal Office of Child Support Enforcement and required all states to establish such offices. Federal funding supported three-fourths of the amount states spent on child-support enforcement. At first, priority was given to AFDC cases, but in 1980, all cases were put on an equal footing.

The federal government moved further in 1984 when it required states to adopt child support guidelines or formulas that could be used by judges to determine child support levels (Goldfarb 1989). Four years later, federal legislation made the guidelines the presumptive child support level (Garfinkel 1994). Judges can deviate from the guidelines only with a written justification. Moreover, states are required to withhold child support obligations from wages.

Federal legislation also mandated states to increase their efforts to establish paternity and trace absent fathers by requiring their social security numbers before issuing birth certificates to their children, and requiring all parties in a contested paternity case to take genetic tests (largely paid for by the federal government). In 1992, states located 3,700,000 absent parents, established 517,000 paternities, and established nearly 900,000 support obligations (U.S. Bureau of the Census 1994, table 606). Each of these activities had grown substantially since the early 1980s.

Although states have established support guidelines, and judges are using the guidelines, enforcement remains lax. Despite federal and state legislation and the intentions of many people to crack down on "deadbeat dads," states do not have information and other systems to withhold support payments from wages or to establish paternity in all cases that need attention. Federal requirements are far from being completely met. Spending to create these systems is not a high priority of many state legislatures, where the representatives of those who pay child support is considerably greater than those who receive it. While awarding and collecting child support are hardly panaceas for the high rate of children living in poverty, state efforts toward increased enforcement would clearly contribute to an amelioration of poverty in many families.

FAMILY PLANNING POLICY

No family policy is more controversial than that concerning family planning. The conflict is visible not only in the heated public debate and activism concerning adult access to abortion but also in the political battles related to minors' access to both birth control and abortion.

The reasons behind the heightened and sustained controversy over family planning policy, particularly abortion, are numerous. First, religious beliefs clash on several issues related to family planning. For example, traditional Catholics believe that the purpose of sex is for procreation, thus making illegitimate the use of artificial birth control devices. Catholics and fundamentalist Christians, among others, believe that human life begins at conception and that abortion is therefore murder. Many other religious groups disagree heatedly with both these assumptions.

Different conceptions of family values also provide fuel to debates about family planning. Allowing minors access to abortion services stands in direct contradiction to the maintenance of parental control over children.

Political issues are almost as starkly defined. Pro-choice forces focus on whether government has any right whatsoever to intrude on the decisions a woman makes about her body. Pro-life forces argue that the issue is not that clear-cut. Two lives are at stake, they assert, and the pregnant woman's control over her own body is not the only issue.

Abortion is also one of the primary symbolic issues separating feminists from antifeminists, and advocates of gender equality from advocates of traditional women's roles. If women have the sole right to make the decision to terminate their pregnancy, their other choices in life are more plentiful. They are less dependent on their husbands. Their freedom to move between traditionally male and female worlds increases. Traditionalists believe that the abandonment of a woman's unique role is not just problematic for individual women, and not just important to the issue of abortion, but has implications that go to the very fabric of society, affecting marriage, child rearing, the nature of families, and the social and economic composition of the work force.

Birth Control

Although access to birth control is often taken for granted in the United States, such nonchalance about the topic was not always possible. Prior to the 1870s, a variety of birth control methods was widely used, although doing so was often controversial (Gray 1979; Sapiro 1994). In fact, it was common for birth control to be linked with notions of obscenity.

Just beyond the middle of the nineteenth century, a political and social movement that focused on purity and moral rectitude aimed to place birth control advocacy, availability, and use directly into obscenity law. In 1873, in a matter of a mere month, the antiobscenity and anticontraception crusader Anthony Comstock of Pennsylvania successfully lobbied the U.S. Congress and saw passed (with no opposition and only fifteen minutes of debate) the Act for the Suppression of Trade in and Circulation of Obscene Literature and Articles of Immoral Use (Stetson 1991b, 72). The Comstock Law prohibited the use of the U.S. mails for distribution of "obscene" materials, specifically labeling as obscene "the dissemination of any pornography, abortion devices, and any drug, medicine, article or thing designed, adapted, or intended for preventing conception" (McGlen and O'Connor 1994). Within twenty-five years, about half of the states across the nation passed "Little Comstock laws." Consequently, it became almost impossible for women legally to obtain information about contraception or, for that matter, abortion (Gray 1979; Sapiro 1994; Stetson 1991b).

Political activists, such as Margaret Sanger, advocated removal of private reproductive matters from the realm of criminal activity whether in state or federal law. As public sentiment grew less repressive, advocates like Sanger found ways around the dissemination of some types of information. The judicial system gave them their real successes in challenging the laws. In the 1930s, several federal court decisions held that contraceptives were no longer considered obscene, and federal prosecutions for the sale of contraceptives ended (Stetson 1991b, 74). State courts subsequently made similar decisions with respect to the Little Comstock

Table 15-1 Minors' Access to Birth Control and Abortion

Contraceptive services	Abortion*	
Minor may consent	Parental consent not needed	Parental consent needed, no bypass
Alaska	Connecticut	Alaska
Arkansas	Florida	Arizona
California	Hawaii	California
Colorado	Iowa	Colorado
Delaware	Maine	Delaware
Florida	New Hampshire	Idaho
Georgia	New Jersey	Illinois
Hawaii	New York	Kentucky
Idaho	North Carolina	Montana
Illinois	Oklahoma	Nevada
Kansas	Oregon	New Mexico
Kentucky	Texas	South Dakota
Maine	Vermont	
Maryland	Virginia	
Mississippi	Washington	
Montana		
New Mexico		
New York		
North Carolina		
Oklahoma		
Oregon		
Tennessee		
Virginia		
Wyoming		

SOURCES: Compiled from data in Donovan 1992, 57; NARAL Foundation / NARAL 1993, 72.
NOTE: The age of majority in all states is eighteen, except Alabama, Nebraska, and Wyoming, where it is nineteen, and Mississippi, where it is twenty-one. *Contraceptive services* refers to birth control devices and medications.
*States not listed have parental consent law with provisions for bypass.

laws. Then, in 1965, the U.S. Supreme Court in *Griswold v. Connecticut* (381 U.S. 479) held that a Connecticut law prohibiting contraceptive use by married persons was unconstitutional. The majority opinion noted that inherent in the Bill of Rights was the right to privacy (see Garrow 1994). In 1972, in *Eisenstadt v. Baird* (405 U.S. 438), the Court held that the right to have a child was a private decision regardless of marital status and that contraceptives could not be denied to adults on that basis. In what was by then a largely symbolic move, Congress finally repealed the Comstock Law in 1971 (Davidson, Ginsburg, and Kay 1974; Dionisopoulos and Ducat 1976; Gray 1979; Sapiro 1994; Stetson 1991b).

Today, neither federal nor state laws attempt to regulate birth control decisions for adults, whether married or unmarried. Choice and ability to pay regulate access to a variety of available devices. Ability to pay is less of an obstacle than it might otherwise be because Medicaid programs assist the indigent, and family planning clinics offer prescriptions and medical services at reduced rates (Stetson 1991b).

The access of minors to birth control information and devices still engenders controversy. It has been the rule rather than the exception in state law for minors to be disallowed medical treatment unless a parent has consented. Certain exceptions, such as medical emergencies, have been allowed, however. Birth control has not traditionally been one of the few exceptions to parental consent. It was not until 1977, when the U.S. Supreme Court, in *Carey v. Population Services International* 431 U.S. 678 (1977), held that minors too have a constitutional right to privacy, which includes the right to obtain contraceptives. Subsequent to *Carey,* some states passed laws that allowed "mature" minors (those demonstrating the mental acuity and maturity to understand the type of treatment and its potential consequences) to seek medical treatment without parental consent. Other states have laws that allow minors to get medical treatment related to sexual activity, among other conditions (Donovan 1992; Melton, Koocher, and Saks 1983; Stetson 1991b).

Table 15-1 gives a complete picture of minors' status across the states. All but four states define a minor as someone under eighteen; Alabama, Nebraska, and Wyoming define minors as under nineteen; Mississippi adheres to twenty-one as the age of majority. As shown, twenty-four states have laws that allow minors to obtain contraceptive services without parental consent or notification. The others have no law at all pertaining to this issue (Donovan 1992).

Of course, allowing minors access not only to birth control but also to information about sexuality remains highly controversial for all the religious and political reasons suggested earlier. Battles are being fought continuously about whether and at what ages minors ought to be given information, and numerous local school board and state legislative races have highlighted these issues. The topic may in fact heat up even more as the incidence of HIV infection and AIDS increases.

Abortion

The Early Era. Not unlike the situation with contraceptive access, abortion was not generally legally prohibited in the United States up through the late 1820s. Prior to that time, the United States followed English common law, which held that abortion was not a criminal act if performed before quickening (the time when the movement of the fetus could be felt in the mother's womb). In fact, according to Sapiro (1994, 368–369), in 1821 Connecticut passed the first U.S. law on abortion, and it followed common law precepts (Sapiro 1994; Luker 1984; Stetson 1991b). Furthermore, as far back as 1809, the Supreme Court of Massachusetts dismissed an indictment for abortion because the prosecution had not reliably proved that the woman was "quick with child" (Luker 1984, 15).

From 1828, when New York passed a law criminalizing abortion for unquickened fetuses, a movement grew to outlaw abortion. The American Medical Association passed a resolution in the late 1850s that condemned abortion and urged state legislatures to pass laws prohibiting it (Luker 1984; Sapiro 1994). One view is that the AMA was concerned about the danger to women of improper abortions; another interpretation is that the AMA was more concerned about professionalizing their occupation and monopolizing services. The Roman Catholic church was among those in the forefront of the movement to criminalize abortion (Luker 1984, 15; Stetson 1991b); until the 1860s, church law had ignored early abortions, but after that time, the church condemned all abortions. By 1900, every state in the nation had passed legislation prohibiting abortion throughout pregnancy unless necessary to save the life of the mother. Penalties were imposed, usually on doctors, but in some states, on women themselves (Luker 1984; Stetson 1991b).

The Modern Era. In the 1960s, in part influenced by the civil rights movement and the feminist movement, political activists began advocating state legalization of abortion. They cited the vast number of illegal abortions that risked the health and lives of women and the right of women to control their procreation choices. With a model state law developed by the American Law Institute, several states— for example, California, Colorado, Hawaii, New York, and North Carolina—liberalized their abortion laws to allow the procedure when a women's life or health were endangered or when the pregnancy was the result of rape or incest. A 1970 New York law went the farthest and allowed abortion for any reason during the first six months of pregnancy (Luker 1984; Mezey 1992; Sapiro 1994; Stetson 1991b).

Activists were pressing state legislatures in many places to follow the lead of New York and others when the issue was addressed at the national level. These actions culminated in the 1973 U.S. Supreme Court case, *Roe v. Wade* (410 U.S. 113). The Court struck down a Texas law that prohibited abortion and held that a women's right to privacy (as established in *Griswold*), included the right to end a pregnancy. The Court, however, did not make this an absolute right. Rather, it held that in the first trimester (three months) of a pregnancy, the decision was solely up to a woman and her doctor. In the second trimester, states were allowed to regulate abortion to protect maternal health. In the third trimester, the states, said the Court, had an interest in potential life and, at the point of fetal viability could prohibit abortion altogether (Davidson, Ginsburg, and Kay 1974; Dionisopoulos and Ducat 1976; Luker 1984; Mezey 1992; Sapiro 1994; Stetson 1991b).

Since the *Roe* decision, state legislatures across the nation have challenged it by passing laws that seek to limit its scope. In fact, reports Mezey (1992, 22), within two years, sixty-two laws were passed in thirty-two states to regulate consent requirements, record keeping and reporting, the location where abortions could be performed and who could perform them, funding, advertising, and fetal protection, and to allow those whose conscience forbade them to participate not to be required to do so. A great many of these laws were immediately challenged by women's organizations; subsequent court decisions made clear that most of the regulations were inconsistent with the holding in *Roe*. Only funding laws and laws related to parental notification and consent were ultimately upheld (Dionisopoulos and Ducat 1976; Mezey 1992; Melton, Koocher, and Saks 1983; Sapiro 1994; Stetson 1991b).[3]

Although the abortion policy arena is changeable, as of December 1994, most states had adopted laws requiring parental consent or notification (thirty-five states) and informed consent (thirty-one states). Smaller numbers had mandatory waiting periods of at least twenty-four hours (thirteen states), requirements to exclude coverage for abortion from health insurance (ten states), and prohibitions against the use of public facilities to perform abortions (five states) (NARAL Foundation/NARAL 1994).

In contrast to those states that seek to restrict abortion, four states (Connecticut, Maryland, Nevada, and Washington) have passed legislation, referenda, or initiatives to affirm explicitly the right to abortion (Alan Guttmacher Institute 1993). Twelve states allow state funds for abortions for indigent women (Alaska, California, Connecticut, Hawaii, Massachusetts, New Jersey, New York, North Carolina, Oregon, Vermont, Washington, and West Virginia). Eleven states have laws to protect clinic workers and women seeking abortions (NARAL Foundation/NARAL 1993).

Meier and McFarlane (1993) investigated the correlates of state laws prohibiting or allowing state funding of abortions. They note wide variations in state practices. For example, "In 1990, New York funded 10.24 abortions per 1000 women aged 15–44, but Wisconsin funded only .005" (Meier and McFarlane 1993, 251). These authors found that state policies on public funding of abortions can be attributed to the activity of citizen action on either side of the issue. The Catholic population and the membership of the National Abortion Rights Action League (NARAL), for example, were two such groupings. Partisan forces in each state were also important determinants of whether or not a state funded abortions.

The states' role in abortion policy has been accentuated as a result of two recent U.S. Supreme Court cases. First, in 1989, in *Webster v. Reproductive Heath Services* (492 U.S. 490), the Court upheld a Missouri law that, among other things, required tests of fetal viability before abortions were performed, banned public funds to counsel women to have abortions if their lives were not in danger, and prohibited use of public facilities and public employees to perform abortions unless the woman's life was at issue. The Court did not explicitly overturn *Roe*, but it allowed these state restrictions on abortion decisions. The Court left open the question of what other restrictions could be legislated (Goggin 1993; Mezey 1992; Sapiro 1994; Stetson 1991b). The restrictions that would be al-

3. *Consent* refers to the necessity of having the express permission of one or both parents for the minor girl to obtain an abortion, whereas *notification* refers simply to informing one or both parents that the procedure is about to take place. Most states that have such laws require the permission or notification of only one parent, but some states require permission or notification of both. Many pro-choice activists argue that notification is interchangeable with consent because of the parent's considerable ability to prevent the procedure (Melton, Koocher, and Saks 1983; Mezey 1992; Stetson 1991b).

Table 15-2 Post-*Roe* Policies

Challengers	Codifiers	Acquiescers	Supporters
Idaho	Arizona	Alabama	Alaska
Illinois	California	Arkansas	Colorado
Indiana	Florida	Delaware	Connecticut
Kentucky	Georgia	Iowa	Hawaii
Louisiana	Maine	Maryland	Kansas
Massachusetts	Montana	Michigan	New Hampshire
Minnesota	Ohio	Mississippi	Oregon
Missouri	Oklahoma	New Jersey	Vermont
Nebraska	South Dakota	New Mexico	Washington
Nevada	Virginia	New York	
North Dakota	Wisconsin	North Carolina	
Pennsylvania	Wyoming	South Carolina	
Rhode Island		Texas	
Tennessee		West Virginia	
Utah			

SOURCE: Halva-Neubauer 1990.

lowed was addressed in part in 1992 in *Planned Parenthood of Southeastern Pennsylvania v. Casey* (112 S.Ct. 2791). Here the Court ruled that while women still retained the right to choose abortion, it was no longer a fundamental right. Abortion could be restricted as long as the nature of those restrictions did not constitute an undue burden, defined as "a substantial obstacle in the path of a woman seeking abortion." The precise operational definition of the phrase is not yet clear; however, the spousal consent requirement in the Pennsylvania law was deemed an undue burden. Nevertheless, the Court allowed parental consent for minors and a twenty-four-hour waiting period (Donovan 1992; Goggin 1993; Sapiro 1994).

The *Casey* ruling, of course, opens the door to the states to impose regulations similar to Pennsylvania's, as well as others not specifically mentioned in that statute. Since the decision, state legislators have introduced dozens of bills. Such was also the case after the *Webster* decision in 1989, which was followed by the introduction of forty state legislative bills within a few months. In many states there were calls for special sessions to deal with the abortion issue (Goggin 1993, 2–3).

Since states have been routinely involved with either pro-choice or pro-life legislation, those patterns are likely to continue. A study by Halva-Neubauer (1990) describes four categories of state action from 1973 to 1989 (see Table 15-2). These include supporters of *Roe* (nine states), challengers (fifteen states), codifiers (twelve states that have been willing to pass restrictions upheld as constitutional), and acquiescers (fourteen states that have ignored the issue for the most part or passed limited restrictions).

Naturally, past state legislative action on abortion is not the only influence on whether or not states may seek to restrict abortion in the future. Public opinion

Table 15-3   Distribution of State Public Opinion on Abortion, 1990

Pro-life*	Even[†]	Majority pro-choice[‡]	Landslide pro-choice[§]	Consensus pro-choice[ǁ]
Kentucky	Alabama	Indiana	Arizona	California
South Dakota	Arkansas	Iowa	Colorado	Connecticut
	Nebraska	Montana	Delaware	Maine
	West Virginia	New Mexico	Florida	Oregon
		North Carolina	Georgia	Vermont
		Oklahoma	Hawaii	
		Pennsylvania	Illinois	
		South Carolina	Kansas	
		Tennessee	Maryland	
		Wisconsin	Massachusetts	
		Wyoming	Michigan	
			Minnesota	
			Nevada	
			New Hampshire	
			New Jersey	
			New York	
			Ohio	
			Rhode Island	
			Texas	

SOURCE: Cohen and Barrilleaux 1993, 206. Reprinted by permission.
NOTE: Data are unavailable for the states that are not listed.
*Predominately pro-life, more than a 5 percent margin in the pro-choice direction.
[†]Pro-choice, pro-life proportions within 5 percent.
[‡]5 to 15 percent pro-choice majority.
[§]16 to 35 percent pro-choice majority.
[ǁ]More than 35 percent pro-choice majority.

in the state, political and socioeconomic factors, the work of interest groups, and the views of current legislators will have an impact.

Strickland and Whicker (1992) provide insight into the ways in which political and socioeconomic conditions contribute to abortion policies. These researchers studied the effect on state abortion restrictions of such political variables as liberalism and partisanship and such socioeconomic factors as religion, ethnicity, and income. Socioeconomic factors were more important than political factors in predicting abortion policy during all three periods they examined, pre-*Roe,* pre-*Webster,* and post-*Webster.* Only in the post-*Webster* era were political factors also related to abortion restrictiveness.

Public opinion is another key element in assessing the future of abortion restrictions in the states (Goggin and Wlezien 1993). Generally, public opinion since *Roe* continues to reflect a pro-choice stance. Cohen and Barrilleaux (1993) have arrayed the states according to the distribution of public opinion based on a 1990 *Washington Post* exit poll. As shown in Table 15-3, public opinion in two states was predominantly pro-life, and in another four states it was evenly split. In all other states, a majority was pro-choice, including a landslide pro-choice position in nineteen states.

Of course, public opinion is not the only factor that affects policy. Cohen and Barrilleaux find that when there is no clear majority on one side, interest groups may prevail. Even when opinion is overwhelmingly on one side, interest groups on the other side win about half the time. They conclude, "Only when opinion is nearly consensual will public opinion consistently defeat organized interests" (Cohen and Barrilleaux 1993, 214). (For information about the effect of abortion on state electoral races, see Dodson and Burnbauer 1990; Goggin 1993.)

The demographic makeup of state legislatures also has an effect on the types of abortion policies that are likely to pass in the future.[4] As we discuss later in the chapter, a greater proportion of women in state legislatures generally leads to less restrictive action on this issue (Berkman and O'Connor 1993; Witt and Moncrief 1993). The religious affiliation and party composition of state legislators are also strongly correlated with voting behavior (Witt and Moncrief 1993).

Minors' Access. Minors' access to abortion continues to be a highly charged political and social issue. As soon as the Court decided *Roe v. Wade,* state legislatures across the nation began passing parental consent and parental notification laws.

Legal challenges to state consent and notification laws began soon after their passage and, starting in 1976, the U.S. Supreme Court began deciding these cases. In that year, in *Planned Parenthood of Central Missouri v. Danforth* (428 U.S. 52) the Court ruled that states cannot give parents absolute veto power over daughters' decisions to have an abortion. In other cases, the Court further refined the scope of parental involvement, allowing states to require a minor to get consent of one or both parents if there is an alternative provided to girls who feel they cannot inform their parents.[5] This alternative usually consists of a judicial bypass, which means that a minor may go before a judge for a ruling on whether or not she is mature enough to make her own decision. If the girl is found too immature, the judge can also order an abortion for her if it is considered to be in her best interest. In another set of cases, the Court ruled that a state may require a doctor to notify one or both parents of abortion plans (Davidson, Ginsburg and Kay 1974; Melton, Koocher, and Saks 1983; Mezey 1992; Sapiro 1994; Stetson 1991b).

As indicated above, thirty-five states have laws to prevent a minor from obtaining an abortion without parental consent or notice. Three of those states have physician bypass laws and twenty-three have judicial bypass laws. Two states require pre-abortion counseling in which the benefit of parental consultation must be discussed.

---

4. Not surprisingly, political culture is also modestly related to the presence of restrictive abortion policies. The moralistic states, largely those of the northern plains, Northwest, and New England, have the fewest restrictions on abortion. In a multivariate equation with a dependent variable measuring the permissiveness-strictness of abortion controls, controlling for median family income, proportion of single-parent families, and proportion of families on AFDC, the only variable with a significant relationship was the moralistic political culture variable (b [unstandardized regression coefficient] = 0.86, SE = 0.40).

5. *Bellotti v. Baird* (443 U.S. 622 [1979]), *City of Akron v. Akron Center for Reproductive Health* (462 U.S. 416 [1983]), and *Planned Parenthood Association of Kansas City, Missouri, Inc. v. Ashcroft* (462 U.S. 476 [1983]).

Public Policy and Abortion Rates. The link between abortion policy at the state level and incidence of abortion appears minimal. The most recent data available suggest that the approximately 1.5 million abortions in 1992 were the lowest total since 1979, although the fluctuations from year to year are fairly small (U.S. Bureau of the Census 1994, table 113). Since 1980, the abortion rates (per woman of child-bearing age) have decreased in all but seven states. Since 1988, however, the rates have increased in fourteen states.

There are vast differences among the states in the ratio of abortions to women of child-bearing age, ranging from 4 per 1,000 in Wyoming and 7 in South Dakota and Idaho to 46 per 1,000 in Hawaii and New York. Almost one-third of all abortions take place in California, New York, and Texas, although Texas is not among the states with the highest ratio of abortions to women of child-bearing age. New York, with 46.2 per 1,000 women, has the highest rate of all the states.

One might expect that rates of abortion and changes in rates of abortion are related to restrictive abortion policies we have discussed. However, a study by Hansen (1993, 223) suggests that legal restrictions did not produce declines in abortion rates in the 1980s. Our own analysis indicates that abortion rates in 1992 are highly related to those of 1980, suggesting that recent restrictions had little effect.[6] Moreover, states with moralistic political cultures have the least restrictive abortion policies. Yet, moralistic states have significantly lower abortion rates than do other cultures (see Table 15-4). Not only did moralistic states have the lowest abortion rate in 1992, they have also decreased their abortion rate the most.

Table 15-4   Abortion Rates and Political Culture

Culture	1992	1980	% change 1980–1992
Moralistic	17.9	23.2	-23
Traditionalistic	19.8	22.7	-13
Individualistic	24.5	26.3	- 7
Eta*	.27	.17	.35

SOURCE: Calculated by the authors.
NOTE: The rates are per 1,000 women aged fifteen to forty-four.
*Eta is a measure of association for ordinal variables that captures curvilinearity; a zero value indicates no relationship and a one indicates a perfect relationship.

6. Our analysis, with abortion rates as the dependent variable, and states as the unit of analysis, yielded the following unstandardized regression coefficients for 1992 (SE in parentheses; $R^2 = 0.87$): number of abortions, 1980: b = 0.90 (0.09); moralistic political culture: b = -3.31 (1.62); traditionalistic political culture: b = -0.28 (1.57); median family income: b = 0.30 (0.14); proportion single-parent families: b = -0.15 (0.32); percentage of families in AFDC program: b = 0.32 (0.39); restrictive abortion policies: b = -0.58 (0.58); restrictive abortion policies for minors: b = 0.12 (0.72). Measurement of restrictive policies was an additive scale with one point for each type of restrictive policy. Using the standard rule of thumb of b/SE > 1.64 in a one-tailed test, only number of abortions in 1980, moralistic political culture, and median family income would be considered statistically significant if this were a sample.

In 1980, abortion rates in the moralistic states were slightly higher than in the traditionalistic and slightly lower than in the individualistic states. Rates in the moralistic states fell by 23 percent between 1980 and 1992, even though they have the least restrictive laws. Rates in the individualistic states fell by only 7 percent, even though their post-1980 laws are much more restrictive.

We speculate that these changes are mostly a result of decreased access to abortion services. The number of abortion providers dropped 8 percent between 1988 and 1992, and the incidence of clinic violence increased (Alan Guttmacher Institute 1994). Anecdotal evidence indicates that much of the decrease in providers has occurred in the more rural states. These states are disproportionately included in the moralistic category (Idaho, Iowa, Maine, Montana, New Hampshire, North Dakota, South Dakota, Vermont, and Wisconsin are nine of the seventeen moralistic states). Most of the individualistic states, in contrast, have large cities where access is easier (notable exceptions are Alaska, West Virginia, and Wyoming). Thus, although their laws are more restrictive, women can cope with the laws because providers are available.

Hansen's analysis (1993) also suggested that neither funding cutbacks nor violence directed at clinics produced any declines in abortion rates in the 1980s. Whether that noneffect is continuing is difficult to say. In a letter to supporters on August 2, 1994, Helen Neuborne, the executive director of the Legal Defense and Education Fund of the National Organization for Women (NOW), reported that "[s]ince 1977 there have been over 600 clinic blockades, as well as 300 bomb threats. Nearly 200 arson, bombings, and fire-bombing [attacks] against abortion providers have been attempted or completed. Abortion providers have reported receiving 178 threats." In the same letter, Neuborne stated that the murder of Dr. David Gunn in Pensacola, Florida, at the beginning of this decade spurred the U.S. Congress to pass the Freedom of Access to Clinic Entrances Act, signed by President Clinton in 1994. Some states have also passed legislation to protect clinic workers.

Legislation is, of course, not always an effective deterrent. More murders of abortion providers and abortion clinic staff occurred in August 1994 and again in January 1995. Given this atmosphere, it is no surprise that providers of abortion services have decreased.

Thus, the risk of intimidation and violence, sometimes fatal, may affect both the number of providers of abortion and the number of procedures done. The issue may no longer be primarily whether the state or federal legislatures or courts allow abortion or whether the public continues to support its availability; instead, it may be the level of risk patients and providers are willing to take and the immediacy with which the RU-486 drug becomes available as an alternative to surgical abortion. The stakes are rising.

CHILD CARE AND CHILD PROTECTION

Government assistance to help families with child care and to prevent child abuse is not nearly as publicly controversial as abortion, yet disputes about the extent of government involvement have placed the United States at the bottom of the industrial world in the help it gives families. Indeed, as Representative Patricia Schroeder (D-Colo.) once remarked, "There's no capital city in the world that talks more about family and does less" (quoted in Roemer 1988, 188).

Still, states are increasingly active in a variety of child protection and child care activities. For example, one author estimated that between 1987 and 1990, forty-seven states strengthened their child abuse and neglect laws, forty-one fortified their child support enforcement bills, and seventeen passed laws designed to preserve and protect families, including laws regulating foster care (Wisensale 1991). We examine three types of policies: parental leave, day care regulation, and child abuse prevention.

Family Leave

Family leave policies are those guaranteeing employees a minimum benefit that would entitle them to keep their jobs even if they had to take a few days, weeks, or possibly months off to care for a new child, disabled parent, or other family member. The impetus for these laws was the massive numbers of women who have entered the labor market. By 1993, 82 percent of women aged thirty-five through forty-four and 75 percent of those aged twenty-five through thirty-four were in the labor force (U.S. Bureau of the Census 1994, table 624). Many of these women have primary responsibility for the care of their children and for elderly relatives. More than half of all mothers with children under one year of age work outside the home (Lenhoff and Becker 1989), and 60 percent of all mothers with children under six are in the labor force (U.S. Bureau of the Census 1994, table 626). Nevertheless, our society "continues to operate as if mothers stay home to care for their children" (Lenhoff and Becker 1989, 405). If a family member quits work or leaves a full-time job to work part time in order to meet a home crisis, the economic well-being of the family is often sacrificed, and the family's stability shattered.

The History of Family Leave Policy. Family leave policy grew out of earlier policies on maternity protection and pregnancy leave. Each of these issues, in turn, challenged policy makers to redefine the link between motherhood and work. Some early feminists considered work to be harmful to women. Sweatshops and factories with poor ventilation, noxious fumes, and inadequate or too much heat were difficult for everyone, but reformers thought these conditions were particularly hard on women and their ability to bear children. Thus, the reform movement of the 1890s advocated protective labor legislation for women (see Stetson 1991a). Legislatures passed and the Supreme Court upheld, in *Muller v. Oregon* (208 U.S. 412 [1908]), state policies barring women entirely from positions considered dangerous (which often happened to be higher-paying jobs); dismissing women when they married, presumably because they were then entering their child-bearing years and because they no longer needed to work to support themselves; and limiting their benefits and their hours of work (Gelb and Palley 1982, 156).[7]

Others, including feminist groups such as the National Woman's Party, believed that motherhood was not incompatible with work and that workers who were pregnant had rights, including the right of prenatal and postnatal leave (Stetson 1991a, 409). Rhode Island, in 1942, became the first state to incorporate into law the idea of pregnancy as a covered disability. But other states excluded pregnancy from coverage, as they noted the cost to Rhode Island's employers for this provision. This exclusion garnered support from the federal Equal Opportunity Commission, which in the 1960s told employers that it was not a violation of civil rights to exclude pregnancy benefits because pregnancy was a disability unique to women (Kamerman, Kahn, and Kingston 1983, 39–40). The Supreme Court continued to rule that failure to include pregnancy under temporary disability benefits was not sex discrimination, although the justices also ruled that mandatory maternity leave and deprivation of seniority protection after a childbirth leave were discriminatory.[8]

The status quo changed in 1978. That year, prompted by support from unions, feminist groups, and civil rights groups, and recognition that more than 40 percent of the work force was made up of women (Gelb and Palley 1982, 157), Congress passed, and President Jimmy Carter signed, the Pregnancy Discrimination Act. Pregnancy was now defined as a temporary disability, and employers were obligated to provide the same fringe benefits for pregnancy and childbirth as for other medical disabilities (Gelb and Palley 1987). By 1982, 89 percent of employees with medical insurance had some form of maternity benefits, as opposed to only 57 percent in 1977 (Kamerman 1991). However, this federal law did not require employers to provide any disability benefits at all, and only five states (California, Hawaii, New Jersey, New York, and Rhode Island) had acted to do so (Kamerman 1991; Stetson, 1991a, 413).

Current Family Leave Policies. The entrance of mothers of small children into the work force was dramatic during the 1980s. In 1977, the year before the Pregnancy Discrimination Act was passed, 32 percent of mothers of children one year old or less were in the work force; by 1988, 52 percent were (Kamerman 1991). Yet, the supply of child care facilities had not grown proportionally to this striking social change. Thus, demand increased for the federal government and the states to do more to help the working mother. One of those demands was that states

---

7. Much of this discussion is drawn from Stetson 1991b.

8. See *Geduldig v. Aiello* (417 U.S. 484 [1974]), *General Electric v. Gilbert* (429 U.S. 125 [1976]), *Cleveland Board of Education v. La Fleur* (414 U.S. 632 [1973]), and *Nashville Gas Co. v. Satty* (434 U.S. 136 [1977]).

Table 15-5 Family Leave Provisions

States with laws covering private and public employers	States with laws covering only public employers
Colorado	Alaska
California	Delaware
Colorado	Florida
Connnecticut	Georgia
Hawaii	Illinois
Iowa	Maryland
Kansas	Missouri
Kentucky	North Dakota
Louisiana	Oklahoma
Maine	South Carolina
Massachusetts	Texas
Minnesota	Virginia
Montana	West Virginia
New Hampshire	
New Jersey	
New York	
Oregon	
Rhode Island	
Tennessee	
Vermont	
Washington	
Wisconsin	

SOURCE: DiMona and Herndon, 1994, 136–140.
NOTE: States not listed have no legislation.

should guarantee that working women could take maternity leaves without risking their jobs.

Montana, in 1972, was the first state to adopt a maternity leave act. This act made it unlawful to terminate a woman's employment or to refuse to grant a reasonable leave of absence because of pregnancy. This maternal leave policy went much further than previous legislation because it mandated protection for pregnant employees and recognized women's maternal as well as employee role.

After Montana had done so, many other states adopted maternal or parental leave policies. By 1995, two-thirds of the states had such policies (see Table 15-5). Family leaves potentially benefit most families, not just low-income families (see Kean 1988). However, many employees are not able to take advantage of these leaves. Family leave guarantees only leave; employers are not obligated to provide any pay, and most do not. Thus, family leave policy will likely affect middle- and upper-income workers much more than lower-income ones, and two-earner families more than single-parent households.

The issue of who should be covered has at least two important dimensions. One is whether the state should mandate parental leave only for its own agencies or whether it should mandate it for all employers. Only twenty-one states cover both private and state employees (Table 15-5). In twelve other states, only state employees are covered (Makuen 1988).

Another issue of coverage is whether the act should apply to men and women, or only women. The original proposals focused on maternity leave, but many argued that men too need to be allowed leave when a child is born. Gradually, maternal leaves became defined as parental leaves.

What circumstances other than the birth of a child should entitle employees to these rights? Early versions of these bills covered only care for a newborn, but later policies extended this coverage to adoption, to care of elderly parents, sick children who were not newborns, spouses, and other family members. Currently, most state parental leave laws include both childbirth and adoption, but there are exceptions (DiMona and Herndon 1994). The statutes of Iowa, Montana, New Hampshire, and Tennessee mention only pregnancy, whereas that of Kentucky mentions only adoption. Many states (such as California, Connecticut, Maine, Maryland, New Jersey, North Dakota, Oregon, Rhode Island, South Carolina, Texas, Vermont, and Wisconsin) provide leave for a family member other than a child or dependent.

How long a leave should employees be allowed with a job guaranteed to be waiting for them on their return? Some states, such as Colorado, provide only the vague definition of "reasonable period." Some guarantee as little as four weeks (Hawaii), others as long as one year (California, for its state employees). The length specified in most laws is between six and sixteen weeks, the latter being the most common.

Although not all states have adopted their own parental leave laws, employees throughout the nation are now covered if they work for firms having more than fifty employees. Despite the opposition of many business organizations, such as the U.S. Chamber of Commerce and the National Federation of Independent Businesses ("Clinton Signs" 1993), federal parental leave legislation was passed by Congress and signed by President Clinton in 1993.

The federal law requires employers of fifty or more workers to allow employees to take up to twelve weeks of unpaid leave during any twelve-month period for the birth or adoption of a child, serious illness in the family, or the employee's own health. In addition to the unpaid leave provision, the bill also prohibits the loss of employment benefits during the leave and requires the employer to maintain health care benefits for employees on leave. These criteria obviously were the result of substantial compromises. For example, the larger the minimum number of employees in firms to be covered, the less opposition from small business interests but the fewer workers who would be covered. The threshold of fifty workers covers only 60 percent of all employees and applies to only 5 percent of employers (Lenhoff and Becker 1991). In contrast, a threshold of fifteen employees would cover 71 percent of employees and would apply to 82 percent of all firms.

Still, employees in firms covered by the federal bill have broader coverage than under many state laws; for example, the twelve weeks exceed the guarantee in all but nine states, and the federal guarantee of leave in the event of serious illness in the family or for the employee's own health is found in only a minority of states.

Some state legislation, however, covers firms smaller than those included in the federal mandate.

The presence and scope of family leave laws, like abortion laws, do reflect cultural and economic differences among the states. We would expect states with moralistic political cultures to be more active in promoting ways to reconcile women's maternal and work roles, and we would expect states where financial resources are more plentiful also to be more supportive of parental leave laws. After all, some short-term cost is borne by businesses when employees go on leave. As expected, family leave laws are significantly more likely to be found in states with moralistic political cultures and those of higher incomes.[9] For example, fully 69 percent of moralistic states have parental leave laws covering both private and public employers. Only 40 percent of individualistic states and a mere 21 percent of traditionalistic states have such laws.

Day Care

States and localities have long been involved in regulating certain kinds of day care, specifically in licensing, inspecting, and setting minimum standards for child care facilities. But regulatory activities in child care are increasing. Wisensale (1990) estimated that in 1987 alone, thirty-three states passed 124 bills relating to child care and early education.[10]

The massive increase of women in the work force has also stimulated calls for better child care services. Family leave policies are targeted to special conditions: the birth of a child or a severe illness. They are not designed to help parents cope with the routine but essential day-to-day care of young children. The day care services that do exist are generally filled to capacity and have long waiting lists (Lewin 1989).

Increasing Accessibility. Some recent state and federal legislation has attempted to increase access to high-quality day care services. For example, in the late 1980s, seven states adopted policies encouraging employers to support child care. Oregon and Rhode Island, for example, created employer tax credits for child care assistance. Six states passed policies improving day care availability for low-income families, and four others did so for children with special needs.

The federal government has also stepped into the child care policy arena. In 1990, Congress passed and the president approved the ABC bill, the Act for Better Child Care Services. Although the act sounds broad in its impact, it is largely

9. In a regression where the general scope of the family leave law is the dependent variable (no law = 0, law covering only state workers = 1, and law covering all types of employees = 2), the moralistic cultural variable was significantly related (b = 0.57, SE = 0.32) as was median state income (b = 0.05, SE = 0.02). The proportion of single-parent families in the state and the dummy variable measuring traditional political culture were unrelated. Overall, the R2 was 0.19; the adjusted R2 was 0.12.

10. This section relies heavily on Wisensale 1990; Gormley 1990, 1991a, and 1991b; and Gormley and Peters 1992.

aimed at low-income families. It gives tax credits to low-income families to help pay for child care, and it gives grants to the states to help provide child care.

Who Is Regulated? There are many types of day care facilities, but the two basic regulatory categories are day care homes, where children are cared for by an individual, and group day care centers. The latter may be run by a business for profit; by a business as a service for its own employees; or by a church, university, or other type of nonprofit organization. All states regulate group day care centers, and all states but Louisiana regulate family day care facilities.

However, regulatory coverage is far from complete. Twelve states, for example, exempt church-run day care centers from all or most regulations. In those states, this removes about one-third of all group day care centers from serious regulatory activity (cited in Gormley and Peters 1992). Some states exempt other sorts of day care facilities as well, such as summer day camps or day care centers run by colleges and universities.

Some day care facilities are exempt because they serve only a few children. For example, thirty-six states exempt family day care homes serving three or fewer children from mandatory regulation and inspections (Adams 1990).

States typically require less of family day care homes than group day care centers. Gormley (1990) points out that group day care centers would typically be required to have sprinkler systems, family homes only fire extinguishers; group centers might be required to have safe surfaces for jungle gyms, family homes only a fenced backyard; group homes would need general liability insurance, family homes only access to a car in case of emergencies.

What Is Regulated? Day care facilities are increasingly heavily regulated. States and localities regulate the physical facilities of the day care centers, the program personnel, and the health status of the children. The average number of pages of state regulations for family day care homes is about seventeen, those for group day care centers about thirty. Each page typically contains more than one regulation, so centers are covered by dozens. Connecticut's nineteen-page handbook includes 133 regulations (Gormley 1990).

Among the many regulations, some for health and safety, Gormley identifies at least three kinds of important *program* regulations. States regulate child-to-staff ratios, maximum group sizes, and the amount of training required of staff. Having many staff members in relation to the number of children, serving relatively few children, and having highly trained staff all contribute to the quality of care offered (Vandell, Henderson, and Wilson 1988). Gormley and Peters (1992) found that states in the Northeast and Midwest have much stricter child-to-staff ratios than do states in the South and West. Fewer differences are apparent in the size of group allowed.

Training requirements vary widely among the states. Nearly half require little or no training or experience, but more than one-third require a high school diploma or some college training (Gormley and Peters 1992, 388). Compared to day care workers in other nations, those in the United States tend to be very low paid, reflecting the lack of qualifications needed (Gormley and Peters 1992). It is not surprising, perhaps, that annual turnover of personnel in group day care facilities is 40 percent (Gormley 1990).

Gormley's study of the impact of regulations shows that some regulations decrease the availability of day care facilities (1991b). In particular, requiring lower child-staff ratios depresses the number and increases the cost of group day care facilities, while strict inspection diminishes the numbers of family day care facilities. Other regulations, however, such as training requirements, do not limit access and have many positive features. Training requirements, for example, although they are found in only a minority of states, appear to improve the quality of the program and are not opposed by most day care operators (Gormley 1990, 1991b).

Enforcing Regulations. In contrast to the large number of regulations that day care providers must follow, the number of officials available to inspect facilities to ensure that the regulations are being followed is small. Thus, many regulations are simply not enforced (Gormley 1990).

The primary regulators are state human service agencies, which license and inspect day care facilities. Local governments and other state agencies are usually involved, however. For example, building inspections are sometimes the jurisdiction of local or state building inspection departments; health inspections are sometimes done by local, county, or state health agencies. Local governments usually have jurisdiction over the zoning regulations that determine where day care facilities may be placed.

The Future. Few political scientists have analyzed day care policies. One notable exception, William Gormley, argues that states need to modify their stance toward regulating child care services. On the one hand, he believes they need to lighten the hand of regulation, especially for family day care centers, making it less onerous on a family to provide day care services. For example, he proposes that states ensure that family day care services can locate in single-family neighborhoods, and he urges localities and states to use a rule of reason in the kinds of physical changes that home day care providers must make to their houses. He also urges states to look carefully at the impact of some kinds of regulations, especially the child-staff ratio, on limiting access and driving up costs. On the other hand, he believes that states should not exempt large classes of day care providers from regulation. He believes that care provided by churches and universities should be subject to state regulation just as much as that provided by nonprofit and for-profit agencies.

With some modifications of their approach, and without substantial subsidies, then, states may be able to increase the access to, and lower the cost of, quality day care services. While this will not solve the day care problem for those parents whose minimum wage jobs allow almost nothing for day care, these reforms have the potential to provide access to a substantially greater number of parents.

Child Abuse

Reports of child abuse and neglect have grown rapidly. Fully 400,000 abused and neglected children are living in foster homes and residential institutions (Farrow 1991), but this is only a fraction of the estimated 2.5 million to 3 million children abused or neglected each year (McCurdy and Daro 1994). Experts disagree about whether abuse and neglect are increasing or whether increases in reported numbers reflect increased attention to the problem, better reporting standards, or changing standards of appropriateness in how children should be treated (Straus and Gelles 1990, chap. 7). Reports indicate that about half the cases of child abuse concern neglect, another 30 percent physical abuse, 11 percent sexual abuse, and 11 percent other forms of abuse, including emotional (McCurdy and Daro 1994).

We do not have an exact estimate of the extent of child abuse even now. A recent study indicated that although federal legislation of 1974 (the Child Abuse Prevention and Treatment Act) mandated uniform operating standards for the identification and management of child abuse cases, in practice these uniform standards do not exist. States vary in how they count instances of abuse (by family, by incident, or by number of children affected), how they classify different types of abuse, who should handle abuse cases (police or child protective services), and other dimensions of processing abuse cases (Berger 1992; McCurdy and Daro 1994; Wells 1988).

State and local agencies dealing with child abuse are extremely fragmented. Police services, child welfare agencies, schools, mental health agencies, and other agencies all play a role. Abusive families often have other problems, which contribute to abuse problems, such as drug or alcohol abuse or poverty and unemployment (Daro and Cohn 1988). Many are single-parent families.

New state initiatives are focusing on prevention of abuse by trying to provide services for families beset by multiple problems. Home visiting services are being implemented in most states to help new parents learn parenting skills and are especially directed to at-risk families. Currently, some states are experimenting with "family preservation services," designed to help families with multiple problems that could lead to removal of children from their homes. Washington's Homebuilders program offers intensive services. The program provides a family with one worker for an average of ten to fifteen hours per week, to be available twenty-four hours a day every day, but for a short term. Detroit's Family First program focuses on families with substance abuse and helps parents to seek treatment. Iowa, Kentucky, Missouri, New Mexico, and Tennessee are also developing these intensive family services (Farrow 1991). The Federal Family Preservation and Support Services Program of 1993 provided increased funding for such services, although even before this legislation, most states had increased funding for child protective services.

These preventive measures do not deal with those children already abused.

Two generations ago, most states closed their orphanages, believing that foster care would serve the welfare of children better than large institutions. Foster care, however, has brought with it its own problems, in particular, finding families who are willing and capable of being good foster parents. The number of foster parents has declined dramatically in the past decade, while the number of children needing such families has increased.

The possibility of opening new orphanages has recently been introduced into the debate about welfare reform. Most experts agree that large institutional orphanages would not improve the lives of many abused youth, although smaller group homes might be an improvement for many. The costs of establishing appropriate group homes, however, would probably dwarf any savings from taking such children off the welfare rolls. Whatever the outcome of the orphanage debate, states must confront the breakdown of the foster care system.

GAY AND LESBIAN ISSUES IN FAMILY POLICY

The emerging issue of family rights for gays and lesbians is so controversial that many do not acknowledge that these issues are related to family policy at all. Because the notion of family policy often evokes nostalgic images of popular idealized circumstances of a mother, father, two children, and the family dog, no issue is more highly charged than the recent political movement to extend family status to gay and lesbian couples and their children.

The religious and political symbolism surrounding other family issues such as abortion policy extends to the legal protection for gay and lesbian families. From some religious points of view, especially the view of the Catholic church and many fundamentalist Protestant groups, sexual relations between persons of the same sex, and therefore claims to family status based on such relationships, is against the word of God and not to be sanctioned in civil law. Other religious groups take a more neutral stand on homosexuality, arguing that biblical interpretation is at best ambiguous on this issue and that the views of only a subset of religious bodies should not be written into law.

In the political arena, advocates of gay and lesbian rights have squared off against conservative politicians and activists about a variety of issues (DaVanzo and Rahman 1993, 351). The modern gay rights movement stems from the 1969 riots set off by a police raid of the Stonewall Inn, a gay bar in New York City. Since then, there has been an active state and federal movement to secure civil liberties for gays and lesbians (Cohan 1982).

Proponents of gay rights argue that constructed as well as biological families are capable of contributing to society, including caring for children, and that one's sexual orientation should have nothing to do with one's legal rights. Conservatives suggest that constructed families send the wrong messages to society about what is proper and moral, and that legal encouragement of alternative lifestyles threatens the perpetuation of traditional family structures. According to this point of view, the frequency and consequences of the breakdown of families are the result of the breakdown of moral values sustaining the traditional family. Only restoration of traditional family values will rescue society from a downward spiral.

Consensual Sex

Adult consensual sex is one family-related issue affecting gays and lesbians.[11] Sodomy is currently illegal for all citizens in fourteen states: Alabama, Arizona, Florida, Georgia, Idaho, Louisiana, Minnesota, Mississippi, North Carolina, Oklahoma, Rhode Island, South Carolina, Utah, and Virginia. Sodomy is illegal only for same-sex couples in Arkansas, Kansas, Kentucky, Maryland, Missouri, Montana, Tennessee, and Texas (Greenberg 1993). These laws were legitimized in a 1986 U.S. Supreme Court case, *Bowers v. Hardwick* (478 U.S. 186), in which the majority held that "the constitutional right to privacy does not extend to 'homosexual sodomy'" (Melton 1989, 933).

Marriage and Partnerships

Other family issues also impinge on the rights heterosexual couples can take for granted. These include the legal right to marry or register as domestic partners; the extension of employment benefits, such as health insurance to one's family; family leave; the ability of married couples as well as single people to adopt children and serve as foster parents; transfer of property to a family member after death; bereavement leave; guardianship; and in the case of a divorcing couple, the issue of custody and visitation of children. No states currently provide to homosexuals each of these protections or rights enjoyed by heterosexuals. A few states, however, provide nontraditional families the ability to register their status. California was the first state that allowed nontraditional families to register as nonprofit associations. Since that time, similar laws have been passed in Michigan, New Jersey, Oregon, Virginia, West Virginia, and Wisconsin. According to Achtenberg and Moulding (1994, 1–13), however, "organizers of the drive see this registration as a purely symbolic act conferring no [direct] legal benefits, but an act that is important in establishing the right to bereavement leave, family membership rates, and hospital visitation rights that are restricted to 'family' members."

The Hawaii Supreme Court was the first to rule on an issue related to gay marriage. In 1993, in *Baehr v. Lewin* (852 P.2d 44 [Haw.]) the Court held that the Hawaii law that defines marriage as a union between heterosexual couples only is a sex-based classification and deserves heightened scrutiny under the law (Achtenberg and Moulding 1994).

Other cases do not address directly the issue of marriage but concern preroga-

11. We do not discuss more general civil liberties protection for homosexuals. Eight states currently include sexual orientation in their protected classes in civil rights laws. Such laws afford protection in employment, housing, public accommodation, and access to state services (Greenberg 1993). In addition, dozens of cities have civil rights ordinances that include sexual orientation.

tives normally thought to be those of a marriage partner or other family member. In 1989 the New York Court of Appeals held in *Braschi v. Stahl Associates Co.* (74 N.Y.2d 201) that a gay man's partner could take over his rent-controlled apartment. The court noted that the partner of the deceased was indeed a family member (Slavin 1991) after being given a host of evidence, including confirmation that the relationship was of long duration and that the community had recognized the couple as partners (Achtenberg and Moulding 1994). Additionally, in 1991 the Minnesota Court of Appeals allowed one lesbian, Karen Thompson, to be named the legal guardian of her severely disabled partner, Sharon Kowalski. This came after the disabled person's parents fought for years to prevent this occurrence and to obtain guardianship for themselves. The case received a great deal of national attention and is looked to by the homosexual community as having broad significance concerning legal acknowledgment of partner status (Achtenberg and Moulding 1994).

Adoption and Foster Care

Earlier, we discussed state policies concerning granting homosexuals child custody in divorce cases. Adoption and foster care are also issues of growing importance to lesbian and gay couples. Whether one adopts privately or through a public agency, the state is involved. Social workers are assigned in both types of cases. Currently, no state has a law that affirms the right of homosexuals to adopt, and only New Hampshire has a law that prohibits homosexuals from adopting a child. In Arizona, a bisexual male was denied the right to adopt a child by an appellate court because the part of his sexual conduct considered homosexual was illegal under Arizona law (Achtenberg and Moulding 1994).

With respect to foster care, California, New Jersey, New Mexico, New York, and Vermont have laws that prohibit discrimination based on sexual orientation (among other things). Massachusetts, however, has a policy "disfavoring" homosexual foster care (Achtenberg and Moulding).

The family law status of homosexuals is, as we have illustrated, a patchwork of legislation and court decisions pertaining to domestic partnerships (and the attendant ramifications of that status for job-related benefits and child care). Hence, the legal rights, status, and protection of private relationships of gays and lesbians are, at this point, highly dependent on the state and city in which they live.

Public Opinion and Political Elites

One of the reasons that homosexuals have more protection in their employment and housing status than in their partnerships and child custody status and have been more successful in winning protection at local rather than state levels may have to do with public opinion on such matters. According to Gibson and Tedin (1988, 587), nearly three-quarters of Americans in a 1985 national survey indicated that they believed homosexual relationships were always wrong. Still, four years later, "a Gallup Poll indicated that by a 47 to 36 margin (with the remainder undecided), Americans prefer legalization of homosexual relations between consenting adults" (quoted in Horowitz 1991, 180). These public opinion polls suggest that while most Americans do not wish to endorse homosexuality, they also do not want to see gays and lesbians discriminated against. Given the fine line of tolerance toward homosexuals it may be too early to expect state laws to extend to gays and lesbians the family rights and benefits that currently accrue to heterosexual couples. However, given the variation in attitudes across the country, it is not surprising to find some communities extending some protection to homosexual activities.

Gibson and Tedin (1988) explored the "origins of political intolerance of homosexuals" using a survey of registered voters in Houston, Texas. They found that intolerance is highly related to lower levels of education and psychological inflexibility. Furthermore, after determining the policy position of public officials and noting recent city actions related to homosexual rights, these authors concluded that a majority of local elected officials were supportive of civil liberties protection for homosexuals. These public officials were able to "block demands from the majority for political repression" (Gibson and Tedin 1988, 602).

The Future

Since about 1970 there has been increasing support for providing homosexuals with civil rights protection afforded to other groups in society. The AIDS epidemic, the public acknowledgment of gay or lesbian status by sports heroes and movie stars, and the increased attention to the presence of homosexuals in American society have no doubt contributed to this support. Although family law is still largely silent or even opposed to expanding definitions of the family to include homosexual unions, the trends are toward increased legal acceptance. Because public opinion is generally unsupportive of such action and because the religious and moral overtones of this debate are strong, however, we do not anticipate quick state action on these issues.

MAKING FAMILY POLICY

Scholars who contemplate the future of family policy across the fifty states are interested in the kinds of changes in the policy-making environment that might affect policy generally and family policy in particular. Several recent studies of the composition of state legislatures suggest that the sort of representatives who inhabit governmental bodies makes a difference to the policy bottom line (Tatalovich and Schier 1993; Witt and Moncrief 1993). Thomas (1991, 1994) and Welch and Thomas (1991), for example, suggest that the increased presence of women in state legislatures affects the types of policy decisions that are made. In particular, women, more than men, in state legislative life have an affinity for and promote legislation dealing with issues of women, children, and families. Men are more likely to promote business and economic issues.[12] How do we know this? Several indicators, all pointing in the same direction, offer evidence.

First, more women (57 percent) than men (33 percent) believed that representing women in the constituency was a very important part of their job. Second, women state legislators were more proud than men of the passage of bills concerning women, children, and families. Conversely, there was a difference in feelings of pride in accomplishments related to business issues. Male state representatives, much more than women, cited these areas as sources of pride. Perhaps most important, women's lists of priority bills contain more legislation pertaining to children (topics such as child care, family leave, and early childhood education) than the lists of men. With respect to women's issues (such as domestic violence, sexual harassment, and child support enforcement), female state legislators were apt to make them a priority. Another way to illuminate this trend is a composite indicator of all women's, children's, and family issues. By this measure, 42 percent of women had on their list of priority bills at least one dealing with issues of women, children, and families, whereas only 16 percent of men had such a bill.

Bill introduction without passage is no more than symbolic. Hence, it is important to compare the success rates of bills. The ratio of passage to introduction of women's, children's, and family issues is higher for women state legislators than men (27.1 percent for women compared with 11.1 percent for men). Similar if not more dramatic patterns are evident with respect to obtaining gubernatorial signature. Women legislators' average ratio of introduction to signature of these types of bills is 25.6, whereas that of men is only 8.0.

Thomas (1991, 1994) and Thomas and Welch (1991) also found that women state legislators in states with higher proportions of female membership tend to introduce more priority legislation dealing with women, children, and families than the men in their states and are more successful in the passage of these bills. Additionally, the proportion of women in a state legislature can affect the overall passage of family policy. In these studies, the states with either a very high proportion of women or a formal women's legislative caucus were the ones in which the highest level of legislation dealing with these issues was introduced and passed.[13]

Additional work measuring the effect of women on state legislative politics re-

---

12. These findings are from the Welch and Thomas study (1991) of women and men in state legislatures in these twelve states: Arizona, California, Georgia, Illinois, Iowa, Mississippi, Nebraska, North Carolina, Pennsylvania, South Dakota, Vermont, and Washington.

13. The legislatures were divided into three categories of proportionality. Mississippi and Pennsylvania make up the low category because they had less than 10 percent female representation. In the middle category are states whose legislatures include from 10 to 20 percent women; some of the states in this category are California, Georgia, Illinois, Iowa, Nebraska, North Carolina, and South Dakota. Finally, Arizona, Vermont, and Washington constitute the high category, with legislatures of at least 30 percent women.

lated to families reinforces and extends these findings. First, researchers at the Center for the American Woman and Politics at Rutgers University found that women state legislators were more likely than men to have worked on bills dealing with women's issues (Dodson and Carroll 1991; see also Dodson 1991; Kathlene, Clarke, and Fox 1991; Saint-Germain 1989). There were also differences in the single most important legislative priorities of women and men. About three times as many women as men had a top priority bill dealing with women and families. Also, women in statehouses, more often than men, listed, as top priorities, bills dealing with health and welfare issues. Finally, women legislators in this study, like the ones in the research done by Thomas and Welch (1991), were just as successful as the men in getting their top priority bills passed (Dodson and Carroll 1991).

Carroll and Taylor (1989) suggest that the types of committees on which women state legislators sit also have an impact on the kind of legislation that relates to family policy. Women are significantly more likely than men to be assigned to a health and welfare committee. Women are also less likely than men to sit on committees dealing with business and private economic concerns. This pattern is replicated in committee chair assignments. Women are more likely than men to chair health and welfare committees and less likely to chair business committees.

Research related directly to the issue of abortion also supports the proposition that the composition of legislatures matters in regard to policy outcomes. First, Hansen (1993) explored various correlates of state restrictions on access to abortion. She finds that religion, the proportion of hospital providers, and a history of policy liberalism or previous restrictions are all associated with recent state policies. More to the point here, she concludes that all else being equal, the states with the least restrictive abortion laws tend to have a higher percentage of women in the state legislatures.

Berkman and O'Connor (1993) examine the effect of women legislators on abortion bills across all fifty states and find that once there is a certain percentage of women in a legislature, they have a discernible effect on the making of policy on parental notification issues. Further, the presence of women on committees in which legislative decisions on abortion are made is key. Women tend to work on committees that allow them to block pro-life legislation, and this is especially true in states with low proportions of female legislators and states most likely to entertain pro-life policies. Thus, women are strategic players of the political game and work at all stages of the legislative process to achieve their policy ends.

Taken together, these studies suggest that as new groups join public life, policy outcomes will be affected. Of course, personal characteristics of legislators are not the only factors exerting influence on policy making in the states. Public opinion, the activity of interest groups, court decisions, the actions of the executive, and the endeavors of federal and local governments are all critical. All else being equal, however, broadening the range of individuals in state government does make a difference.

CONCLUSION

Government has always been involved in making family policy, but this activity has greatly increased since the mid-1960s. Traditionally, state governments dominated family policy, through their regulation of marriage, divorce, and certain kinds of relations between parents and children. Although the federal government provided some benefits to widows and orphans after the Civil War, it had little role in family policy until the New Deal. Then, federal policies were aimed at low-income families, through the Aid to Families with Dependent Children program.

The flood of women into the work force and the increasing poverty level of America's children have prompted considerably more family policy activity. The federal government's activity is largely directed to low-income families, although the family and medical leave act is a significant exception. States are engaged in a wide variety of activities designed to aid families, and especially children, at all income levels.

Action, however, lags far behind the pro-family rhetoric so prominent in both federal and state political discourse. States do little to provide incentives for marriage or disincentives for divorce. Despite a decade of "getting tough" on fathers who do not pay child support, collection rates are pathetically low, and states are reluctant to make enforcement a priority. Working parents in the United States have far fewer child care services available than do those in most other industrial nations, and they have far fewer services that make it easier to combine the roles of bread-winning and parenting. Abused and neglected children pose a different challenge, and politicians and social welfare experts wrestle with the dilemmas of when to remove children from their homes. And many families must struggle to meet even their basic needs for food, clothing, shelter, and medical care (see Edelman 1980).

There are important reasons for the failure of America's family policies. One is the lack of consensus about the appropriate role of government in aiding families. Not everyone agrees that government should support day care or garnish wages to enforce child support payments, let alone promote family planning efforts, protect the right to abortion, or help same-sex couples obtain rights offered to married partners. People disagree strongly about the conditions under which it is appropriate to remove children from their parents to protect their health and safety. Family issues do not just have to do with the size and scope of government, about which compromise is difficult; family issues have to do with religion and morality, about which compromise is sometimes nearly impossible.

Another impediment to a comprehensive family policy is federalism. As in almost every other policy arena, our federal system has created a set of family laws and services that are byzantine in their complexity. National, state, and local courts, legislatures, and executives all play a role in family policy. These overlapping jurisdictions, coupled with the fact that many people do not want government to play a role at all, sometimes make for large gaps in the family safety net that are slow to be filled.

States are at the nexus of these issues. And they are beginning to move beyond their traditional roles in regulating families and child welfare. In many states, more comprehensive services are springing up that seek to tie together families, schools, and communities to provide increased support to families, especially those at risk. Minnesota's Early Childhood and Family Education Program, Connecticut's family resource centers, Maryland's family support programs, and Kentucky's family resource and youth service center, for example, all illustrate the attempts of states to bring together schools and social services to provide more comprehensive assistance to families. Given that the deterioration in family ties bodes poorly for community and societal ties, the challenge to the states in their key role is awesome indeed.

REFERENCES

Achtenberg, Roberta, and Karen B. Moulding, eds. 1994. *Sexual Orientation and the Law.* San Francisco: National Lawyers Guild Lesbian, Gay, Bisexual Rights Committee.

Adams, Gina. 1990. *Who Knows How Safe? The Status of State Efforts to Ensure Quality Child Care.* Washington, D.C.: Children's Defense Fund.

Alan Guttmacher Institute. 1993. "The States and Abortion Policy." *Issues in Brief,* January.

———. 1994. *News,* June 16.

Aldous, Joan, and Wilfried Dumon. 1980. *The Policies and Programs of Family Policy: United States and European Perspective.* Notre Dame, Ind.: Center for the Study of Man, University of Notre Dame, and Leuvan Press.

———. 1990. "Family Policy in the 1980s: Controversy and Consensus." *Journal of Marriage and the Family* 52:1136–1151.

Bane, Mary Jane. "Toward a Description and Evaluation of United States Family Policy." In *The Policies and Programs of Family Policy: United States and European Perspective,* edited by Joan Aldous and Wilfried Dumon. Notre Dame, Ind.: Center for the Study of Man, University of Notre Dame, and Leuvan Press.

Bartfield, Judi, and Daniel R. Meyer. 1994. "Are There Really Deadbeat Dads? The Relationship between Ability to Pay, Enforcement, and Compliance in Nonmarital Child Support Cases." *Social Service Review* 68:219–235.

Berger, Brigitte. 1992. "On the Limits of the Welfare State: The Case of Foster Care." In *The American Family and the State,* edited by Joseph Peden and Fred Glake. San Francisco, Calif.: Pacific Research Institute for Public Policy.

Berkman, Michael B., and Robert E. O'Connor. 1993. "Do Women Legislators Matter? Female Legislators and State Abortion Policy." *American Politics Quarterly* 21:102–124.

Boles, Janet K. 1991. "Advancing the Women's Agenda within Local Legislatures: The Role of Female Elected Officials." In *Gender and Policymaking: Studies of Women in Office,* edited by Debra L. Dodson. New Brunswick, N.J.: Center for the American Woman and Politics.

Buehler, Cheryl. 1989. "Influential Factors and Equity Issues in Divorce Settlements." *Family Relations* 38 (January): 76–82.

Bystydzienski, Jill. 1993. "Marriage and Family in the United States and Canada: A Comparison." *American Review of Canadian Studies* 23:565–582.

Carroll, Susan J., and Ella Taylor. 1989. "Gender Differences in Policy Priorities of U.S. State Legislators." Paper presented at the annual meeting of the American Political Science Association, Atlanta, Ga., August 31–September 3.

"Clinton Signs Family Leave Act." 1993. *Congressional Quarterly Almanac.* Washington, D.C.: Congressional Quarterly.

Cohan, A. S. 1982. "Obstacles to Equality: Government Responses to the Gay Rights Movement in the United States." *Political Studies* 30 (March): 59–76.

Cohen, Jeffrey E., and Charles Barrilleaux. 1993. "Public Opinion, Interest Groups, and Public Policy Making: Abortion Policy in the American States." In *Understanding the New Politics of Abortion,* edited by Malcolm L. Goggin. Newbury Park, Calif.: Sage Publications.

Cowan, Philip. 1993. "The Sky Is Falling, but Popenoe's Analysis Won't Help Us Do Anything about It." *Journal of Marriage and the Family* 55:548–552.

Daro, Deborah, and Anne Cohn. 1988. "Child Maltreatment Evaluation Efforts." In *Coping with Family Violence,* edited by Gerald T. Hotaling, David Finkelhor, John T. Kirkpatrick, and Murray Straus. Newbury Park, Calif.: Sage Publications.

DaVanzo, Julie, and M. Omar Rahman. 1993. "American Families: Trends and Correlates." *Population Index* 59 (Fall): 350–386.

Davidson, Kenneth M., Ruth B. Ginsburg, and Herma H. Kay. 1974. *Sex-Based Discrimination: Text, Cases, and Materials.* St. Paul, Minn.: West Publishing.

DiMona, Lisa, and Constance Herndon, eds. 1994. *1995 Information Please Women's Sourcebook: Resources and Information to Use Everyday.* Boston: Houghton Mifflin.

Dionisopoulos, P. Allan, and Craig R. Ducat. 1976. *The Right to Privacy: Essays and Cases.* St. Paul, Minn.: West Publishing.

Dodson, Debra L., ed. 1991. *Gender and Policymaking: Studies of Women in Office.* New Brunswick, N.J.: Center for the American Woman and Politics.

Dodson, Debra L., and Lauren D. Burnbauer. 1990. *Election 1989: The Abortion Issue in New Jersey and Virginia.* New Brunswick, N.J.: Center for the American Woman and Politics.

Dodson, Debra L., and Susan J. Carroll. 1991. *Reshaping the Agenda: Women in State Legislatures.* New Brunswick, N.J.: Center for the American Woman and Politics.

Donovan, Patricia. 1992. *Our Daughters' Decisions: The Conflict in State Law on Abortion and Other Issues.* New York: Alan Guttmacher Institute.

Edelman, Marian Wright. 1980. *Families in Peril: An Agenda for Social Change.* Cambridge: Harvard University Press.

Elazar, Daniel. 1984. *American Federalism: A View from the States.* New York: Harper and Row.

Farrow, Frank. 1991. "Services to Families: The View from the States." *Families in Society: The Journal of Contemporary Human Services* 72 (May): 268–276.

Garfinkel, Irwin. 1994. "The Child Support Revolution." *American Economic Review* 84 (May): 81–85.

Garfinkel, Irwin, Donald Oellerich, and Philip K. Robins. 1991. "Child Support Guidelines." *Journal of Family Issues* 12:404–429.

Garrow, David. 1994. *Liberty and Sexuality: The Right to Privacy and the Making of Roe v. Wade.* New York: Macmillan.

Gelb, Joyce, and Marian Lief Palley. 1982. *Women and Public Policies.* Princeton, N.J.: Princeton University Press.

———. 1987. *Women and Public Policies.* Rev. ed. Princeton, N.J.: Princeton University Press.

Gibson, James L., and Kent L. Tedin. 1988. "The Etiology of Intolerance of Homosexual Politics." *Social Science Quarterly* 69: 587–604.

Glass, Becky. 1990. "Child Support Enforcement: An Implementation Analysis." *Social Service Review* 64:542–558.

Glendon, Mary Ann. 1987. *Abortion and Divorce in Western Law.* Cambridge: Harvard University Press.

Goggin, Malcolm L., ed. 1993. *Understanding the New Politics of Abortion.* Newbury Park, Calif.: Sage Publications.

Goggin, Malcolm L., and Christopher Wlezien. 1993. "Abortion Opinion and Policy in the American States." In *Understanding the New Politics of Abortion,* edited by Malcolm L. Goggin. Newbury Park, Calif.: Sage Publications.

Goldfarb, Sally. 1989. "Working with Child Support Guidelines." *Trial* 25 (April): 43–47.

Gormley, William T., Jr. 1990. "Regulating Mr. Rogers' Neighborhood: The Dilemmas of Day Care Regulation." *Brookings Review* 8, no. 4:21–28.

———. 1991a. "Day Care in a Federal System." *Social Service Review* 65:582–596.

————. 1991b. "State Regulations and the Availability of Child-Care Services." *Journal of Policy Analysis and Management* 10:78–95.

Gormley, William T., and B. Guy Peters. 1992. "National Styles of Regulation: Child Care in Three Countries." *Policy Sciences* 25:318–399.

Gray, Madeline. 1979. *Margaret Sanger: A Biography of the Champion of Birth Control.* New York: Richard Marek.

Greenberg, Pam. 1993. "Gay Rights or Special Rights?" *NCSL Legislative Brief* 1 (August).

Halva-Neubauer, Glen A. 1990. "Abortion Policy in the Post-*Webster* Age." *Publius* 20: 32.

Hansen, Susan B. 1993. "Differences in Public Policies toward Abortion: Electoral and Policy Context." In *Understanding the New Politics of Abortion,* edited by Malcolm L. Goggin. Newbury Park, Calif.: Sage Publications.

Hertzke, Alan, and Mary Scribner. 1989. "The Politics of Federal Day Care: The Nexus of Family, Church, and the Positive State." Paper presented at the annual meeting of the American Political Science Association, Atlanta, Ga., August 31–September 3.

Horowitz, Carl F. 1991. "Homosexuality's Legal Revolution." *Freeman,* May, 173–181.

Jacob, Herbert. 1988. *Silent Revolution: The Transformation of Divorce Law in the United States.* Chicago: University of Chicago Press.

————. 1989. "Another Look at No-Fault Divorce and the Post-Divorce Finances of Women." *Law and Society Review* 23:95.

Kamerman, Sheila B. 1991. "Parental Leave and Infant Care: U.S. and International Trends and Issues, 1978–1988." In *Parental Leave and Child Care,* edited by Janet Shibley Hyde and Marilyn J. Essex. Philadelphia: Temple University Press.

Kamerman, Sheila B., Alfred J. Kahn, and Paul W. Kingston. 1983. *Maternity Policies and Working Women.* New York: Columbia University Press.

Kathlene, Lyn, Susan E. Clarke, and Barbara A. Fox. 1991. "Ways Women Politicians Are Making a Difference." In *Gender and Policymaking: Studies of Women in Office,* edited by Debra L. Dodson. New Brunswick, N.J.: Center for the American Woman and Politics.

Kean, Thomas. 1988. "The State's Role in the Implementation of Infant Care Leave." In *The Parental Leave Crisis: Toward a National Policy,* edited by Edward F. Zigler and Meryl Frank. New Haven: Yale University Press.

Lenhoff, Donna, and Sylvia M. Becker. 1989. "Family and Medical Leave Legislation in the States: Toward a Comprehensive Approach." *Harvard Journal of Legislation* 26:402–451.

Levitan, Sol, R. S. Belous, and F. Gallo. 1988. *What's Happening to the American Family.* Rev. ed. Baltimore: Johns Hopkins University Press.

Lewin, Tamar. 1989. "Small Tots, Big Biz." *New York Times Magazine,* January 29.

Luker, Kristin. 1984. *Abortion and the Politics of Motherhood.* Berkeley: University of California Press.

Lynn, L. E. 1980. "Fiscal and Organizational Constraints on United States Family Policy." In *The Policies and Programs of Family Policy: United States and European Perspective,* edited by Joan Aldous and Wilfried Dumon. Notre Dame, Ind.: Center for the Study of Man, University of Notre Dame, and Leuvan Press.

McCulloch, Kenneth J. 1990. "State Family Leave Laws and the Legal Questions They Raise." *Employment Relations Today.* (Summer): 103–109.

McCurdy, Karen, and Debarah Daro. 1994. *Current Trends in Child Abuse Reporting and Fatalities.* Chicago: National Center on Child Abuse Prevention.

McEvoy, Lawrence T. 1978. "The Impact of No-Fault Divorce: The Missouri Experience." *State Government* 5 (Spring): 95–105.

McGlen, Nancy E., and Karen O'Connor. 1994. *Women, Politics, and American Society.* Englewood Cliffs, N.J.: Prentice Hall.

Makuen, Kathleen. 1988. "Public Servants, Private Parents: Parental Leave Policies in the Public Sector." In *The Parental Leave Crisis: Toward a National Policy,* edited by Edward F. Zigler and Meryl Frank. New Haven: Yale University Press.

Marvell, Thomas B. 1989. "Divorce Rates and the Fault Requirement." *Law and Society Review* 23:543–567.

Meier, Kenneth J., and Deborah R. McFarlane. 1993. "Abortion Politics and Abortion Funding Policy." In *Understanding the New Politics of Abortion,* edited by Malcolm L. Goggin. Newbury Park, Calif.: Sage Publications.

Melton, Gary B. 1989. "Public Policy and Private Prejudice." *American Psychologist* 44: 933–940.

Melton, Gary B., Gerald P. Koocher, and Michael J. Saks, eds. 1983. *Children's Competence to Consent.* New York: Plenum Press.

Meyer, Daniel. 1993. "Child Support and Welfare Dynamics: Evidence from Wisconsin." *Demography* 30:45–62.

Mezey, Susan Gluck. 1992. *In Pursuit of Equality: Women, Public Policy, and the Federal Courts.* New York: St. Martin's Press.

Moen, Phyllis, and Alvin L. Schorr. 1987. "Families and Social Policy." In *Handbook of Marriage and the Family,* edited by M. Sussman and S. Steinmetz. New York: Plenum Press.

The NARAL Foundation/NARAL. 1993. *Who Decides? A State-by-State Review of Abortion Rights.* 4th ed. N.p.

Pearson, Jessica, Nancy Thoennes, and Jean Anhalt. 1992. "Child Support in the United States: The Experience in Colorado." *International Journal of Law and the Family* 6:321–337.

Pearson, Jessica, Nancy Thoennes, and Patricia Tjaden. 1989. "Legislating Adequacy: The Impact of Child Support Guidelines." *Law and Society Review* 23:569–590.

Peters, Elizabeth. 1986. "Marriage and Divorce: Informational Constraints and Private Contracts." *American Economic Review* 76 (June): 437–454.

Peters, H. Elizabeth, Laura M. Argys, Eleanor E. Maccoby, and Robert Mnookin. 1993. "Enforcing Divorce Settlements: Evidence from Child Support Compliance and Award Modifications." *Demography* 30:719–735.

Polikoff, Nancy. 1983. "Gender and Child Custody Determination." In *Families, Politics, and Public Policy,* edited by Irene Diamond. New York: Longman.

Popenoe, David. 1993. "American Family Decline, 1960–1990: A Review and Appraisal." *Journal of Marriage and the Family* 55:527–543.

Roemer, Julie. 1988. "Democrats Lining Up behind 'Family' Banner." *Congressional Quarterly Weekly Report,* January 30.

Saint-Germain, Michelle A. 1989. "Does Their Difference Make a Difference? The Impact of Women on Public Policy in the Arizona Legislature." *Social Science Quarterly* 70:956–968.

Sapiro, Virginia. 1994. *Women in American Society: An Introduction to Women's Studies.* 3d ed. Mountain View, Calif.: Mayfield.

Seltzer, Judith. 1991. "Legal Custody Arrangements and Children's Economic Welfare." *American Journal of Sociology* 96:895–929.

Singer, Jana. 1989. "Divorce Reform and Gender Justice." *North Carolina Law Review* 67:1103–1121.

Slavin, Edward A. 1991. "What Makes a Marriage Legal?" *Human Rights* 18 (Spring): 16–19.

Stacey, Judith. 1993. "Good Riddance to 'The Family.'" *Journal of Marriage and the Family* 55:545–547.

Steiner, Gilbert Y. 1980. "Looking for Family Policy—Big Tickets on Moral Judgments." In *The Policies and Programs of Family Policy: United States and European Perspective,* edited by Joan Aldous and Wilfried Dumon. Notre Dame, Ind.: Center for the Study of Man, University of Notre Dame, and Leuvan Press.

Stetson, Dorothy McBride. 1991a. "The Political History of Parental Leave Policy." In *Parental Leave and Child Care,* edited by Janet Shibley Hyde and Marilyn J. Essex. Philadelphia: Temple University Press.

————. 1991b. *Women's Rights in the U.S.A.: Policy Debates and Gender Roles.* Belmont, Calif.: Brooks/Cole.

Straus, Murray, and Richard Gelles. 1990. *Physical Violence in American Families.* New Brunswick, N.J.: Transaction Books.

Strickland, Ruth Ann, and Marcia Lynn Whicker. 1992. "Political and Socioeconomic Indicators of State Restrictiveness toward Abortion." *Policy Studies Journal* 20:598–617.

Tatalovich, Raymond, and David Schier. 1993. "The Persistence of Ideological Cleavage in Voting on Abortion Legislation in the House of Representatives, 1973–1988." In *Understanding the New Politics of Abortion,* edited by Malcolm L. Goggin. Newbury Park, Calif.: Sage Publications.

Teachman, Jay D. 1990. "Socioeconomic Resources of Parents and Award of Child Support in the United States: Some Exploratory Models." *Journal of Marriage and the Family* 52:689–699.

Thomas, Sue. 1991. "The Impact of Women on State Legislative Policies." *Journal of Politics* 53:958–976.

————. 1994. *How Women Legislate.* New York: Oxford University Press.

Thomas, Sue, and Susan Welch. 1991. "The Impact of Gender on Activities and Priorities of State Legislators." *Western Political Quarterly* 44:445–456.

U.S. Bureau of the Census. 1994. *Statistical Abstract of the United States, 1994.* Washington D.C.: U.S. Government Printing Office.

Vandell, Deborah, V. Kay Henderson, and Kathy Shores Wilson. 1988. "A Longitudinal Study of Children with Day-Care Experiments of Varying Quality." *Child Development* 59:1286–1292.

Veum, Jonathan. 1992. "Interrelation of Child Support, Visitation, and Hours of Work." *Monthly Labor Review* 115, no. 6:40–47.

Weitzman, Lenore. 1985. *The Divorce Revolution: The Unexpected Social and Economic Consequences for Women and Children in America.* New York: Free Press.

Welch, Charles E., III, and Sharon Price-Bonham. 1983. "A Decade of No-fault Divorce Revisited: California, Georgia, and Washington." *Journal of Marriage and the Family* 45:411–418.

Welch, Susan, and Sue Thomas. 1991. "Do Women in Public Office Make a Difference?" In *Gender and Policymaking Studies of Women in Office,* edited by Debra L. Dodson. New Brunswick, N.J.: Center for the American Woman and Politics.

Wells, Susan. 1988. "Factors Influencing the Response of Child Protective Service Workers to Reports of Abuse and Neglect." In *Coping with Family Violence,* edited by Gerald T. Hotaling, David Finkelhor, John T. Kirkpatrick, and Murray Straus. Newbury Park, Calif.: Sage Publications.

Wisensale, Steven K. 1990. "Approaches to Family Policy in State Government: A Report on Five States." *Family Relations* 39 (April): 136–140.

———. 1991. "State Initiatives in Family Policy." In *The Reconstruction of Family Policy,* edited by Elaine Anderson and Richard Hula. New York: Greenwood Press.

Witt, Stephanie L., and Gary Moncrief. 1993. "Religion and Roll-Call Voting in Idaho: The 1990 Abortion Controversy." In *Understanding the New Politics of Abortion,* edited by Malcolm L. Goggin. Newbury Park, Calif.: Sage Publications.

Wright, Gerald, and Dorothy Stetson. 1978. "The Impact of No-Fault Divorce Law Reform on Divorce in American States." *Journal of Marriage and the Family* 45:411.

Zimmerman, Shirley. 1992. *Family Policies and Family Well-Being: The Role of Political Culture.* Newbury Park, Calif.: Sage Publications.

SUGGESTED READINGS

Aldous, Joan, and Wilfried Dumon. "Family Policy in the 1980s: Controversy and Consensus." *Journal of Marriage and the Family* 52 (November 1992):1136–1151. Provides a review of the state of the family and family policies at the beginning of the 1990s.

Garrow, David. *Liberty and Sexuality: The Right to Privacy and the Making of* Roe v. Wade. New York: Macmillan, 1994. An engaging but encyclopedic account of the history, personalities, and issues leading up to the Supreme Court's landmark abortion rights decision.

Glendon, Mary Ann. *Abortion and Divorce in Western Law.* Cambridge: Harvard University Press, 1987. Compares U.S. abortion and divorce policies with those of several western European nations.

Jacob, Herbert. *Silent Revolution: The Transformation of Divorce Law in the United States.* Chicago: University of Chicago Press, 1988. Analyzes the dynamics of the dramatic change in divorce law in the United States from the 1960s through the 1980s.

Zimmerman, Shirley. *Family Policies and Family Well-Being: The Role of Political Culture.* Newbury Park, Calif.: Sage Publications, 1992. Examines the family policies of the states, with a specific look at Nevada, Minnesota, and South Carolina.

Epilogue

We end this book at a particularly exciting time in the history of American federalism. The Republican party seized control of the U.S. Congress in January 1995, and they vowed to vote on the various provisions in their Contract with America in the first hundred days of rule. Many of the elements of the "contract" concerned the downsizing and reshaping of government and have dramatic implications for state governments: balancing the federal budget in the context of other promises made would reduce grants-in-aid to states by about 30 percent (Rosenbaum 1995, A8). But the commitment to end the so-called unfunded mandates sweetened the deal; these are federal laws that require states to provide certain services without allocating money to pay for them. Also the Republicans in both Houses voted to replace the Aid to Families with Dependent Children (AFDC) program with block grants, although even the governors disagreed among themselves about how much flexibility states should have in spending federal welfare dollars.

The congressional debate about a smaller government provoked a reexamination of the meaning of federalism, a debate that had last been heard in the early days of the Ronald Reagan administration. This time it seems clear that regardless of the fate of individual items in the contract, more devolution will take place; that is, federal responsibilities will move down to the states. The states, in turn, will have the choice of continuing the programs or terminating them. Thus, the real choices about the size of government will be made in fifty state capitals, not in the nation's capital.

588

Nobody can predict with certainty the final outcome in the states, but for guidance we can look at what the states did the last time they were presented with this dilemma, namely, when the Reagan administration sought to cut back social spending in the early 1980s. In that era state and local governments responded to devolution by increasing their own support for programs axed at the federal level, thereby undercutting Reagan's goal of social policy retrenchment. As the scholars Nathan and Doolittle (1987, 362) put it, Reagan's "stamp appears to have been canceled—not fully, but partially—by state government policies and actions." Will history repeat itself? Or will the public's dissatisfaction with government preclude a similar response?

While we cannot gaze into our crystal ball and answer this question here, we have given readers the analytic tools to begin to sketch out a response. We have emphasized the differences among states in social, economic, political, and institutional characteristics and how these differences affect states' policy choices. We have stressed the modernization in state government institutions that has occurred since the 1960s and the policy innovations that states have offered. At the same time, we have discussed the pressure on states to reduce budgets and to hold down taxes. All of these factors will affect how states respond to the challenges posed by the federal government in the 1990s.

State government institutions have modernized and improved themselves substantially since the mid-1960s. State legislatures have become so professional and careerist that the citizens of twenty states have decided to impose term limits on their legislators to return them to amateur status. Governors head state bureaucracies that are more professional; indeed, their executive branches have led the "reinventing and privatizing government" movement in many parts of the country. State courts similarly have modernized and streamlined their structures; state judges have struck out on their own in many areas of the law, including school finance reform, tort liability, and privacy rights. The conduct of state politics has improved: many states have instituted public financing of elections and have sought to improve the ethical standards of lobbying. These reforms are not uniform across the states, but the improvement among states as a whole is undeniable.

These efforts at modernization in state governments have been accompanied by substantial efforts in policy innovation. As detailed in Chapter 11, some states have enacted comprehensive health care reforms and other states have tried "workfare, not welfare," to the extent allowed by current federal law. Many states have acted as entrepreneurs in attracting new industries and retaining old ones, using new economic development strategies. They have improved business infrastructure, from building bridges to funding the new "information highways." In the field of education, states have initiated numerous reforms to achieve excellence and equity among schools.

Such innovations may start in one state and diffuse to other states as their leaders hear about the idea. Or sometimes, ideas are tried out at the state level and are then picked up by federal officials. Several notions currently being considered in Washington have their origins in the states. For example, the line-item veto proposed in the Contract with America would be a radical change in Washington but has been used in most states for years. Similarly, states have experience in balancing their budgets and in separating operating expenses from capital expenses, ideas that are being floated in the nation's capital. And many states have already successfully privatized some of the functions of government.

Certainly there are plenty of difficult problems left for states to resolve. One is the continuing expenditure pressure on the budget, derived primarily from explosive growth in spending on corrections, health care, and elementary and secondary education. The growth of expenditures in these areas derives from demographic trends, which show increases in immigration, poverty, homelessness, family disruption, and the aging population, all of which make the provision of social services more expensive. The devolution of programs from the national government to the states will only intensify the challenge.

The other question mark for states is the impact of interstate competitive pressures upon them. As emphasized throughout the book, there is pressure on a state to lower its taxes to "fit in" with its neighbors, to lower its welfare or health benefits so as not to be a magnet for the poor, and to relax its pollution regulations so as to retain certain industries. Two important reasons for past political pressure to adopt programs at the federal level has been to provide national uniformity and to make it possible to adopt policies that benefit the nation as a whole even though they may penalize particular regions. Air pollution control is one of many examples; pollution is often produced in certain areas and then drifts with the wind to others. In addition, interest groups who can marshal their strength at the national level seek federal programs because they cannot be equally successful in each of the fifty states; that is true of groups favoring protection of the rights of minorities, advocates of programs for children, and supporters of programs for the elderly.

As devolution proceeds, more functions will be handed over to the states, and there will be a greater possibility that competitive rivalries will not only reduce state activity but jeopardize people's access to government programs and protections simply on the basis of where they happen to live. In many ways, the devolution is a return to nineteenth century government practices but in a society with twenty-first century social and economic conditions. These developments promise to revive old political conflicts and bring their heat to state capitals. The outcome is impossible to predict.

REFERENCES

Nathan, Richard P., Fred C. Doolittle, and Associates. 1987. *Reagan and the States.* Princeton, N.J.: Princeton University Press.

Rosenbaum, David E. 1995. "Budget Amendment May Be Short of Enough States for Ratification." *New York Times,* January 23.

Name Index

Subject Index